Green type indicates global example

ECONOMICS IN ACTION

1: Got a Penny? ■ When Economists Agree ■ The Model that Ate the Economy ■ Rich Nation, Poor Nation

2: Beating the Traffic ■ Only Creatures Small and Pampered ■ The Rice Run of 2008

3: Giffen Goods ■ Estimating Elasticities ■ Responding to Your Tuition Bill ■ Will China Save the U.S. Farming Sector?

4: A Matter of Life and Death

5: Hunger and Price Controls in Venezuela ■ Price Floors and School Lunches ■ The Clams of the Jersey Shore ■ Who Pays the FICA?

6: Skill and Comparative Advantage ■ Beefing Up Exports

7: The Cost of a Life ■ "The Jingle Mail Blues" ■ Buying Your Way Out of Temptation

8: The Mythical Man-Month ■ Don't Put Out The Welcome Mat ■ There's No Business Like Snow Business

9: What's a Standardized Product? ■ Prices Are Up . . . but So Are Costs ■ Baling In, Bailing Out

10: Shocked by the High Price of Electricity ■ Chained by Your Cable ■ Sales, Factory Outlets, and Ghost Cities

11: Bitter Chocolate? ■ Prisoners of the Arms Race ■ The Price Wars of Christmas ■ The Housing Bust and the Demise of the 6% Commission ■ Any Color, So Long as It's Black

12: Talking, Texting, and Driving ■ Cap and Trade ■ Voting as a Public Good ■ Long-Term Trends in Income Inequality in the United States

13: The Factor Distribution of Income in the United States ■ Help Wanted! ■ The Overworked American?

14: How Big Is That Jackpot, Anyway?

BUSINESS CASES

1: Efficiency, Opportunity Cost, and the Logic of Lean Production

2: The Chicago Board of Trade

3: The Airline Industry: Fly Less, Charge More

4: StubHub Shows Up the Boss

5: Medallion Financial: Cruising Right Along

6: Li & Fung: From Guangzhou to You

7: Citi Puts Card Holders "inControl"

8: Kiva Systems' Robots versus Humans: The Challenge of Holiday Order Fulfillment

9: TheFind Finds the Cheapest Price

10: Newly Emerging Markets: A Diamond Monopolist's Best Friend

11: Virgin Atlantic Blows the Whistle…or Blows It?

12: A Tale of Two Research Clusters

13: Alta Gracia: Can Fair Trade Work?

THIRD EDITION

MICROECONOMICS IN MODULES

Paul Krugman • Robin Wells

Princeton University

WORTH PUBLISHERS

A Macmillan Higher Education Company

Vice President, Editorial and Production: Catherine Woods
Publisher: Charles Linsmeier
Executive Development Editor: Sharon Balbos
Associate Development Editor: Mary Walsh
Editorial Assistant: Fay Kelly
Marketing Manager: Thomas Digiano
Marketing Assistant: Tess Sanders
Senior Media Editor: Marie McHale
Director of Market Research and Development: Steven Rigolosi
Director of Digital and Print Production: Tracey Kuehn
Associate Managing Editor: Lisa Kinne
Project Editor: Liz Geller
Art Director: Babs Reingold
Cover Designers: Lyndall Culbertson and Babs Reingold
Interior Layout: Paul Lacy
Interior Design: Charles Yuen
Photo Editor: Cecilia Varas
Photo Researcher: Elyse Rieder
Production Manager: Barbara Anne Seixas
Supplements Production Manager: Stacey Alexander
Supplements Project Editor: Edgar Bonilla
Composition and Illustration: TSI Graphics
Printing and Binding: RR Donnelley

ISBN-13: 978-1-4641-3904-8
ISBN-10: 1-4641-3904-0

Library of Congress Control Number: 2013953528

Printed in the United States of America

First printing

Worth Publishers
41 Madison Avenue
New York, NY 10010
www.worthpublishers.com

Photo Credits

Front cover *Glass rectangles:* xlaoke ma/E+/Getty Images. *Abstract grid pattern:* Ralf Hiemisch/Getty Images. *Group of friends carrying shopping bags on city street:* Monkey Business Images/Shutterstock. *Loading dock*: Glow Images/Superstock. *Silhouettes of passengers in airport:* Exactostock/Superstock. *Cotton field:* © Fábio Salles/Dreamstime.com. *Girl writing on graph:* iStockphoto/Thinkstock. *Airplane being assembled:* © Edward Rozzo/Corbis. Fish: iStockphoto. *Veterinarian doctor:* iStockphoto/Thinkstock. **p. viii** *Young woman and young man in TV store:* iStockphoto. *Cotton boll:* iStockphoto/Thinkstock. **p. ix** *Vaccination:* iStockphoto/Thinkstock. *Used books:* Thinkstock. **p. x** *Yellow cab:* iStockphoto. *Container ship:* © Juice Images/Alamy. **p. xi** *Portrait of young woman:* Ashley Hildreth. *Wheat field:* Vaclav Volrab/Shutterstock. **p. xii** *Strawberry pickers:* Thinkstock. *Model with enormous diamond ring:* Icogenic/Getty Images. **p. xiii** *Office corridor:* Pressmaster/Shutterstock. *No fishing sign:* iStockphoto/Thinkstock. **p. xiv** *Students on graduation day:* Exactostock/Superstock. **p. xv** *Female café owner:* © Tetra Images/Alamy. **p. xxxii** *Portrait:* Rubberball/Superstock. *Young woman and young man in TV store:* iStockphoto. *Young woman writing on glass graph:* iStockphoto/Thinkstock. *Boeing plane:* UPI/Alan Marts/Boeing/Landov. *Chinese package:* Kees Metselaar/Alamy. **p. 1** *Wright Brothers:* Landov Photos. **p. 34** *Portrait:* iStockphoto. *Jeans-clad legs:* Thinkstock. *Cotton field:* Casadphoto/Dreamstime.com. *Crowd carrying things through floodwater:* AP Photo/Khalid Tanveer. **p. 35** *Cotton boll:* iStockphoto/Thinkstock. **p. 70** *Red-capped bottles:* iStockphoto/Thinkstock. *Open house:* © Monkey Business Images/Dreamstime.com. *Hot dogs:* Msheldrake/Dreamstime.com. **p. 71** *Vaccination:* iStockphoto/Thinkstock. **p. 100** *Portrait:* Malyugin/Shutterstock. *Two people in textbook store:* Peter Huoppi. *Outdoor produce market:* iStockphoto/Thinkstock. **p. 101** *Used books:* Thinkstock. **p. 126** *Portrait:* © Simon Stanmore/Blend Images/Corbis. *Fire escapes:* Thinkstock/Photodisc. *Man hailing cab:* Alamy Images. *Uncle Sam* image courtesy of Library of Congress. **p. 127** *Yellow cab:* iStockphoto. **p. 164** *Portrait:* © Sherrie Nickol/Citizen Stock/Corbis. *Ford Mustang:* Scott Olsen/Getty Images. *Repairman:* Susana Gonzalez/Bloomberg via Getty Images. *Container ship dock:* Glow Images/Superstock. **p. 165** *Container ship:* © Juice Images/Alamy. **p. 190** *Portrait:* Tim Roberts/Getty Images. *Highway direction signs:* Vividpixel/Dreamstime. *3-D brain map:* Thinkstock. *Man eating hamburgers:* craftvision/Getty Images. **p. 191** *Portrait of a young woman:* Ashley Hildreth. **p. 228** *Portrait:* Thinkstock. *Harvesters:* Terrance Klassen/AgePhotostock. *Strawberry pickers:* Ilene MacDonald/Alamy. *Cookie packagers:* iStockphoto. **p. 229** *Wheat field:* Vaclav Volrab/Shutterstock. **p. 258** *Portrait:* Luis Alvarez/Getty Images. *Coca Cola: Tomatillos and tomatoes:* iStockphoto. **p. 259** *Strawberries:* Thinkstock. **p. 300** *Portrait:* © Ocean/Corbis. *Loose diamonds:* iStockphoto. *Seated woman with bills:* Sacks/Getty Images. *Airport lounge:* Exactostock/Superstock. **p. 301** *Model with enormous diamond ring:* Icogenic/Getty Images. **p. 328** *Portrait:* gulfimages/Alamy. *Office conference:* Martin Barraud/Getty Images. *Chess game:* Photosindia/Getty Images. *Mobil sign:* AP Photo/Steven Senne. *Exxon sign:* Tim Sloan/AFP/Getty Images/Newscom. *Mall:* iStockphoto. *Mall advertisements:* Andrew Moore/Gallery Stock. **p. 329** *Office corridor:* Pressmaster/Shutterstock. **p. 370** *Portrait:* © Image Source. *Smokestacks:* iStockphoto/Thinkstock. *Oil spill cleanup workers:* © AccentAlaska.com/Alamy. *Steamroller:* Telekhovskyi/Shutterstock. **p. 371** *No fishing sign:* iStockphoto/Thinkstock. **p. 422** *Portrait:* © Martin Palombini/Corbis. Fallow field: iStockphoto/Thinkstock. *Large imaging machine:* iStockphoto/Thinkstock. *Two young men:* iStockphoto/Thinkstock. *People of different professions in hardhats:* Kurhan/Shutterstock. *Office workers at desks with computers and telephones:* AAGIA/Getty Images. **p. 423** *Students on graduation day:* Exactostock/Superstock. **p. 452** *Portrait:* © Paul Burns/Corbis. *Robot worker:* Beth Hail/Bloomberg via Getty Images. *Human worker:* iStockphoto. *Line at bank teller:* Thinkstock. *Lemons:* iStockphoto. **p. 453** *Female café owner:* Tetra Images/Alamy.

ABOUT THE AUTHORS

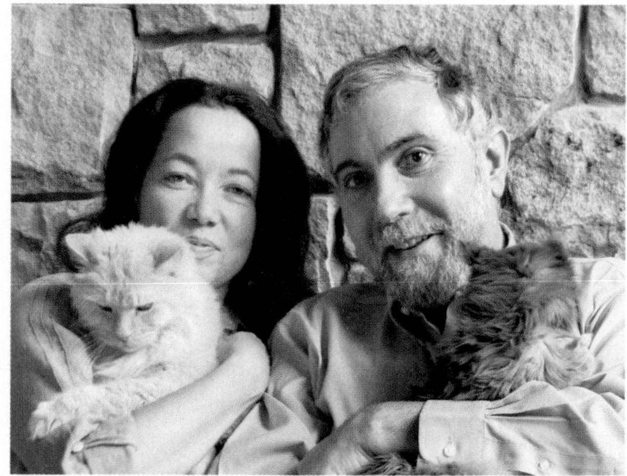

Paul Krugman, recipient of the 2008 Nobel Memorial Prize in Economic Sciences, is Professor of Economics at Princeton University, where he regularly teaches the principles course. He received his BA from Yale and his PhD from MIT. Prior to his current position, he taught at Yale, Stanford, and MIT. He also spent a year on the staff of the Council of Economic Advisers in 1982–1983. His research is mainly in the area of international trade, where he is one of the founders of the "new trade theory," which focuses on increasing returns and imperfect competition. He also works in international finance, with a concentration in currency crises. In 1991, Krugman received the American Economic Association's John Bates Clark medal. In addition to his teaching and academic research, Krugman writes extensively for nontechnical audiences. He is a regular op-ed columnist for the *New York Times*. His latest trade books, both best sellers, include *End This Depression Now!,* a look at the recent global financial crisis and recovery, and *The Return of Depression Economics and the Crisis of 2008,* a history of recent economic troubles and their implications for economic policy. His earlier books, *The Conscience of a Liberal, Peddling Prosperity,* and *The Age of Diminished Expectations,* have become modern classics.

Robin Wells was a Lecturer and Researcher in Economics at Princeton University. She received her BA from the University of Chicago and her PhD from the University of California at Berkeley; she then did postdoctoral work at MIT. She has taught at the University of Michigan, the University of Southampton (United Kingdom), Stanford, and MIT. The subject of her teaching and research is the theory of organizations and incentives.

To beginning students everywhere,
which we all were at one time.

BRIEF CONTENTS

CONTENTS

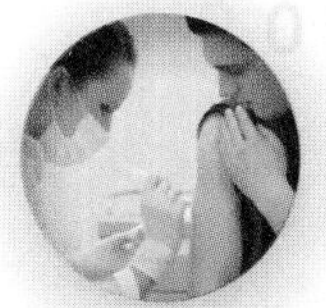

Section 5

Section 6

Section 7
Economics and Decision Making 191

Section 8
Production and Costs 229

Section 9
Market Structure and Perfect Competition 259

Section 10
Monopoly 301

Section 11
Imperfect Competition 329

Section 12
Market Failure and the Role of Government 371

PREFACE

"The ability to simplify means to eliminate the unnecessary so that the necessary may speak."

—*Hans Hofmann*

An Innovative Modular Format

For a long while, we have been hearing from instructors who wanted to use the Krugman/Wells text in their principles course, but needed a less comprehensive version: a book that was shorter overall, with less meaty chapters, and with a focus on the essential principles of economics and less in the way of theory and analytics. We've responded to these requests, and you are holding the result in your hands.

***Microeconomics in Modules* is a streamlined textbook that incorporates an innovative format geared toward how students learn today.** Instead of tackling 24 chapters of about 25 to 40 pages each, students encounter 6- to 10-page *modules* designed to be read in a single sitting. What exactly is a module? We think users and reviewers have come up with the best definition. They consistently describe modules as "short, digestible chunks" of text that students actually read. We should also add that shorter does not mean taking shortcuts. Although each module is a short, easy-to-manage reading assignment, each is also informative and thorough, with adequate rigor.

This text includes carefully crafted pedagogy that works within the modular format to enhance the student learning experience. The modular format offers a unique opportunity for structured learning and assessment. Each module concentrates on a specific topic using a learning-objectives approach and then concludes with three types of self-assessment questions: "Check Your Understanding" and multiple-choice questions that allow students to test their comprehension of module content, followed by critical-thinking questions that encourage reflection and analysis. Answers to these questions appear at the end of the book, so students can actually see how well they've mastered concepts.

There is additional opportunity for assessment at the end of each section (a section is a grouping of modules): thoughtful problems that test related concepts across all of the modules in a section, encouraging students to make connections among ideas as well apply and practice what they've learned.

We've also refined the modular structure in this edition to offer even greater flexibility. We've added six new sections to help unpack some of the more module-heavy sections. The result is more focused sections with fewer modules in each. Important topics like elasticity, efficiency, government policy, and monopoly are contained within their own sections, making it easier for instructors to assign the topics they want to teach without having to break chapters apart, which can undermine narrative flow and diminish comprehension. We've also added two sections covering completely new topics, which we'll get to shortly. And, we hope that because sections (and the modules within them) are brief, instructors may be able to find the time to cover some of the more compelling and interesting material that too often gets cut from the course because of time constraints.

The Science Behind Modules

We see it for ourselves, we have heard it from reviewers, and the research confirms it: students are reading less, for shorter periods of time, and they continue to struggle with comprehension. So, when we began thinking about the idea of developing a more streamlined principles text, we also thought a lot about the best way to format it.

The modular format, which is popular in other disciplines, appealed to us. It was in keeping with the findings of cognitive psychologists who have demonstrated that comprehension is best attained when material is "chunked" into smaller reading assignments, reinforced with frequent questioning (the "testing effect"), and incentivized by a sense of accomplishment earned from completing discrete reading tasks. These findings are at the heart of the modular format of this text and its pedagogy.

Comments from users seem to confirm the benefits of this new way of presenting economic concepts. Each user reported an almost identical story: students were actually completing their reading assignments, something that was rare when traditional textbook chapters were assigned. Their feeling was that students were also taking advantage of the end-of-module self-assessment questions. Overall, they found students coming to lectures better prepared. And, each of these users couldn't imagine returning to a textbook with a more traditional format.

This result makes intuitive sense. Why wouldn't students prefer to read short modules instead of long chapters? Of course it would enrich the learning experience if students could check their comprehension more frequently, at the end of short modules. **For a more up-close look at the text's format and feature set, see the walk through on pages xx–xxiii.**

About the Revision

We've made several changes in this edition to keep it current and relevant, while retaining the narrative approach. There are a few new modules, a new feature, and many updates.

New Modules

A new section (with two new modules) on decision making and behavioral economics We devote an entire new section to this important topic: Section 7, "Economics and Decision Making." It includes two new modules. The first new module is on the types of decisions made by individuals and firms, as well as the process of making decisions that leads to the best possible economic outcomes. The second new module, on behavioral economics, looks at types of irrational decision making. We've also moved our module on utility maximization into this section to round out the coverage.

This section was added because many instructors are now covering the groundbreaking perspective on irrational decision making in their principles courses. Originating in the research of Amos Tversky and Nobel laureate Daniel Kahneman, and further developed by a new generation of economists, this is a topic area that gets students excited about economics because it's so true to life and relevant. In fact, in the opening story for the section, we tell the story of an actual student who was faced with a big, life-defining decision after graduating from college.

We firmly believe that by learning how people make persistently irrational choices, students gain a deeper understanding of what constitutes rational economic decision making.

Four new modules—on taxes, international trade, and the welfare state New Module 15, "Taxes," has allowed us to devote a separate module to this topic and expand our coverage to include more detail on tax rates and revenues.

New Section 6, "International Trade," includes two new fully integrated and up-to-date modules: Module 16, "Gains from Trade," and Module 17, "Supply, Demand, and International Trade."

New Module 39, "The Economics of the Welfare State," addresses a timely topic that is very much in the news and of particular importance to us. This module includes completely new, current coverage of health care policy as well as a fully updated discussion of poverty, inequality, and welfare state programs.

New Feature: Business Case Studies

Now, more than ever, students need a strong understanding of economic principles and their applications to business decisions. To meet this need, virtually every section now concludes with a real-world business case that illustrates how the economic principles just covered play out in the world of entrepreneurs and bottom lines.

The cases are wide-ranging and provide insight into business decision making at American and global companies, both large and small. They include an examination of how lean production techniques at Boeing and Toyota increased efficiency at both companies and led to a worldwide manufacturing revolution. (Section 1: "Efficiency, Opportunity Cost, and the Logic of Lean Production at Boeing"). There is a look at how producers evaluate costs to make hiring decisions (Section 8: "Kiva Systems' Robots versus Humans: The Challenge of Holiday Order Fulfillment"). A very timely case, and one of our personal favorites, is the story of the incredibly successful "supply chain manager," Li & Fung, which has made billions because of their comparative advantage in getting the clothes we wear into stores (Section 6: "Li & Fung: From Guangzhou to You").

Each case concludes with "Questions for Thought" that help students engage more deeply with economic concepts by seeing them applied in actual business situations. A list of the new Business Cases appears on the inside front cover.

Extensive Updates

This edition includes 20 new "Economics in Actions" (formerly called "In Real Life"). Virtually every module includes at least one "Economics in Action" feature. Many of our section-opening stories have been updated, and three of them are new to this edition. In addition, we have updated examples, data, and applications throughout.

It is important to us to emphasize currency and to use stories from real life and the news. This makes every revision a work-intensive endeavor, but we believe that being current drives student interest.

A Closer Look at the Table of Contents and Feature Set

The annotated table of contents that follows shows how the modular format works and explains the focus of each section. Although the sections are grouped into building blocks in which conceptual material learned at one stage is built upon and then integrated into the next stage, the coverage is also flexible enough to allow instructors to organize content to best meet their needs.

Following the table of contents is a visual tour of our feature set that clarifies how well the content of this text is supplemented by real-world examples and ample opportunity for practice and review (pages xx–xxiii).

Annotated Table of Contents . . . A Closer Look at Content and Format

The text contains 14 sections with two to five modules in each.

An introduction to basic economic principles that will help students develop an understanding of economic modeling and the nature of markets.

Individual modules are devoted to each component of the supply and demand model so students can master the model incrementally.

Introduces the various elasticity measures, including income and substitution effects and price, cross-price, and income elasticity of demand.

Introduces students to market efficiency, the ways markets fail, the role of prices as signals, and property rights.

This newly subdivided section focuses on market interventions, price and quantity controls, and inefficiency. It also includes a **New Module** devoted to taxes.

NEW TO THIS EDITION This new section on trade offers integraged early coverage for those instructors who wish to expand on the earlier treatment of comparative advantage in Module 4.

NEW TO THIS EDITION This new section includes two **New Modules:** one on rational choice and another on behavioral economics. The section concludes with coverage of utility maximization.

Develops the production function and various cost measures of the firm, including coverage of the differences between average cost and marginal cost.

Explains the output decision of the perfectly competitive firm, its entry/exit decision, the industry supply curve, and long-run outcomes.

A thorough treatment of monopoly, including coverage of price discrimination and the welfare effects of monopoly.

These manageable modules offer coverage on game theory, monopolistic competition, and product differentiation.

The section focuses on externalities and solutions to them. Also examined: positive externalities and public goods. The section concludes with a **New Module** on applications within the welfare state.

Covers the efficiency wage model of the labor market, market power, and a discussion of income distribution.

These additional topics appear for those instructors who typically cover them. The modules are easily integrated into earlier discussions. There is a **New Module** on the time value of money.

A review of graphing and math skills for use as a helpful refresher on economic literacy.

Tools for Learning . . . Getting the Most from This Book

Each section consists of interrelated modules with a consistent set of features and pedagogy. Each module is self-contained giving students discrete reading assignments to complete. Instructors have the freedom to assign only those modules that are important to their course.

The SECTION-OPENING OUTLINE offers a quick opening preview of the modules in each section.

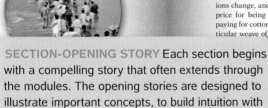

SECTION-OPENING STORY Each section begins with a compelling story that often extends through the modules. The opening stories are designed to illustrate important concepts, to build intuition with realistic examples, and then to encourage students to read on and learn more.

MODULE

5 Demand

Thinkstock

WHAT YOU WILL LEARN

1. What a competitive market is and how it is described by the supply and demand model
2. What the demand curve is
3. The difference between movements along the demand curve and changes in demand
4. The factors that shift the demand curve

Each module begins with WHAT YOU WILL LEARN, a numbered list of learning objectives in an easy-to-review format that alerts students to critical concepts in the pages ahead.

Supply and Demand: A Model of a Competitive Market

Cotton sellers and cotton buyers constitute a *market*—a group of producers and consumers who exchange a good or service for payment. In this section, we'll focus on a particular type of market known as a *competitive market*. Roughly, a **competitive market** is a market in which there are many buyers and sellers of the same good or service. More precisely, the key feature of a competitive market is that no individual's actions have a noticeable effect on the price at which the good or service is sold. It's important to understand, however, that this is not an accurate description of every market.

For example, it's not an accurate description of the market for cola beverages. That's because in the market for cola beverages, Coca-Cola and Pepsi account for such a large proportion of total sales that they are able to influence the price at which cola beverages are bought and sold. But it *is* an accurate description of the market for cotton. The global marketplace for cotton is so huge that even a jeans maker as large as Levi Strauss & Co. accounts for only a tiny fraction of transactions, making it unable to influence the price at which cotton is bought and sold.

It's a little hard to explain why competitive markets are different from other markets until we've seen how a competitive market works. For now, let's just say that it's ...ets. When taking an exam, it's ...r questions. In this book, we're ...etitive markets. ...l described by the **supply and** ...itive, the supply and demand

A competitive market is a market in which there are many bu... ers of the same good or ... of whom can influence th... which the good or servic...

The supply and deman... a model of how a compet... works.

KEY TERMS Every key term is defined in the text and then again in the margin, making it easier for students to study and review important vocabulary.

There are f...
- The dema...
- The supp...
- The set o... cause the...
- The mark... quantity...
- The way ... shifts

To explain ... in turn. In thi...

The De...

How many p... around the w... answer this q... around the w... make a pair c... question, bec... cotton—cons...

When the ... higher price ... switching con... linen. In gene... want to buy, c... people want ... purchase.

So the ans... to buy?" depe... price will be, ... would want tc... *schedule*. This ... elements of th...

The Dema...

A **demand sc**... want to buy at... demand schec... world demanc...

According ... will want to p... is $1.25 a pou... $0.75 a pound... price, the few... the price rises... willing to buy...

The graph ... (For a refresh... vertical axis s... quantity of cc... tries in the ta... curve is a gra... the relationsh...

ECONOMICS IN ACTION WORLD VIEW

GLOBAL STAMPS identify features that are global in focus.

BEATING THE TRAFFIC

All big cities have traffic problems, and many local authorities try to discourage driving in the crowded city center. If we think of an auto trip to the city center as a good that people consume, we can use the economics of demand to analyze anti-traffic policies.

One common strategy is to reduce the demand for auto trips by lowering the prices of substitutes. Many metropolitan areas subsidize bus and rail service, hoping to lure commuters out of their cars. An alternative is to raise the price of complements: several major U.S. cities impose high taxes on commercial parking garages and impose short time limits on parking meters, both to raise revenue and to discourage people from driving into the city.

A few major cities—including Singapore, London, Oslo, Stockholm, and Milan—have been willing to adopt a direct and politically controversial approach: reducing congestion by raising the price of driving. Under "congestion pricing" (or "congestion charging" in the United Kingdom), a charge is imposed on cars entering the city center during business hours. Drivers buy passes, which are then debited electronically as they drive by monitoring stations. Compliance is monitored with automatic cameras that photograph license plates.

The current daily cost of driving in London ranges from £8 to £10 (about $13 to $16). And drivers who don't pay and are caught pay a fine of £120 (about $195) for each transgression.

Not surprisingly, studies have shown that after the implementation of congestion pricing, traffic does indeed decrease. In the 1990s, London had some of the worst traffic in Europe. The introduction of its congestion charge in 2003 immediately reduced traffic in the London city center by about 15%, with overall traffic falling by 21% between 2002 and 2006. And there was increased use of substitutes, such as public transportation, bicycles, motorbikes, and ride-sharing.

In the United States, the U.S. Department of Transportation has implemented pilot programs to study congestion pricing. The programs were so successful that conges-

Citie... raisi...

ECONOMICS IN ACTION This feature, which appears in virtually every module, provides a compelling real-life application of major concepts covered in the module. Students experience an immediate payoff when they can apply concepts they've just read about to real phenomena.

Each module concludes with a unique set of **REVIEW QUESTIONS**.

5 Review

Solutions appear at the back of the book.

Check Your Understanding

1. Explain whether each of the following events represents (i) a *change in demand* (a *shift of* the demand curve) or (ii) a *change in the quantity demanded* (a *movement* ...e).
...that customers are willing to pay ...on rainy days.
..., a long-distance telephone ...ered reduced rates on weekends, ...d calling increased sharply.
c. People buy more long-stem roses the week of Valentine's Day, even though the prices are higher than at other times during the year.
d. A sharp rise in the price of gasoline leads many commuters to join carpools in order to reduce their gasoline purchases.

CHECK YOUR UNDERSTANDING review questions allow students to immediately test their understanding of a module. By checking their answers with those found in the back of the book, students will know when they need to reread the module before moving on.

SECTION 2 SUPPLY AND DEMAND

Multiple-Choice Questions

1. Which of the following would increase demand for a normal good? A decrease in
   a. price.
   b. income.
   ...price of a substitute.
   ...umer taste for a good.
   ...price of a complement.
...ase in the price of butter would most likely ...se the demand for
   ...garine.
   ...ls.
   c. jelly.
   d. milk.
   e. syrup.
3. If an increase in income leads to a decrease in demand, the good is
   a. a complement.
   b. a substitute.
   c. inferior.
   d. abnormal.
   e. normal.
4. Which of the following will occur if consumers expect the price of a good to fall in the coming months?
   a. The quantity demanded will rise today.
   b. The quantity demanded will remain the same today.
   c. Demand will increase today.
   d. Demand will decrease today.
   e. No change will occur today.
5. Which of the following will increase the demand for disposable diapers?
   a. a new "baby boom"
   b. concern over the environmental effect of landfills
   c. a decrease in the price of cloth diapers
   d. a move toward earlier potty training of children
   e. a decrease in the price of disposable diapers

MULTIPLE-CHOICE QUESTIONS offer students additional opportunity to practice what they've learned.

Critical-Thinking Question

...correctly labeled graph showing the demand for ...On your graph, illustrate what happens to the de... ...or apples if a new report from the Surgeon General ...at an apple a day really *does* keep the doctor away.

CRITICAL-THINKING QUESTIONS offer students an opportunity to think more deeply about content in the module.

PITFALLS

DEMAND VERSUS QUANTITY DEMANDED

? Consider how the term *demand* is used in the following sentence. Why is the sentence incorrect?

If the price of the good goes up then people will buy less and this will lead to a fall in demand which shifts the demand curve to the left.

> THIS STATEMENT MISTAKES A CHANGE IN QUANTITY DEMANDED FOR A CHANGE IN DEMAND. WHEN DOING ECONOMIC ANALYSIS, IT IS IMPORTANT TO MAKE THE DISTINCTION BETWEEN CHANGES IN *DEMAND*, WHICH MEAN SHIFTS OF THE DEMAND CURVE, AND CHANGES IN *QUANTITY DEMANDED*. When economists say "an increase in demand," they mean a rightward shift of the demand curve, and when they say "a decrease in demand," they mean a leftward shift of the demand curve—that is, when they're being careful. In or... ...st people, including professional econ... ...ord *demand* casually. For example, an ...ay "the demand for air travel has dou... ...fifteen years, partly because of falling ...or she really means that the *quantity de...* ...led. The key point to remember is that ...causes a *movement along the demand* ...ift of the demand curve.

...Figure 5.3 for an illustration of a movement ...ve versus a shift of the demand curve. For an ...rence, see pages 38–40.

NEW The **PITFALLS** feature, appearing at the end of select modules, helps students come to a better understanding of commonly misunderstood concepts, using a question-and-answer format.

Solutions to all module-review questions can be found at the back of the book.

BUSINESS CASE: The Chicago Board of Trade

Around the world, commodities are bought and sold on "exchanges," markets organized in a specific location, where buyers and sellers meet to trade. But it wasn't always like this.

The first modern commodity exchange was the Chicago Board of Trade, founded in 1848. At the time, the United States was already a major wheat producer. And St. Louis, not Chicago, was the leading city of the American West and the dominant location for wheat trading. But the St. Louis wheat market suffered from a major flaw: there was no central marketplace, no specific location where everyone met to buy and sell wheat. Instead, sellers would sell their grain from various warehouses or from stacked sacks of grain on the river levee. Buyers would wander around town, looking for the best price.

In Chicago, however, sellers had a better idea. The Chicago Board of Trade, an association of the city's leading grain dealers, created a much more efficient method for trading wheat. There, traders gathered in one place—the "pit"—where they called out offers to sell and accepted offers to buy. The Board guaranteed that these contracts would be fulfilled, removing the need for the wheat to be physically in place when a trade was agreed upon.

This system meant that buyers could very quickly find sellers and vice-versa, reducing the cost of doing business. It also ensured that everyone could see the latest price, leading the price to rise or fall quickly in response to market conditions. For example, news of bad weather in a wheat-growing area hundreds of miles away would send the price in the Chicago pit soaring in a matter of minutes.

The Chicago Board of Trade went on to become the world's most important trading center for wheat and many other agricultural commodities, a distinction it retains to this day. And the Board's rise helped the rise of Chicago, too. The city, as Carl Sandburg put it in his famous poem, "Chicago," became:

CHICAGO BOARD OF TRAD

Jim West

NEW BUSINESS CASES appear at the end of virtually every section, applying key economic principles to real-life business situations in both American and international companies. Each case concludes with critical-thinking questions.

Questions for Thought

1. In Module 6 we mention how prices can vary in a tourist trap. Which market, St. Louis or Chicago, was more likely to behave like a tourist trap? Explain.
2. What was the advantage to buyers from buying their wheat in the Chicago pit instead ...e advantage to sellers?
...ned from this case, explain why the online auction site eBay ...as it been so successful as a marketplace for second-hand ... composed of various flea markets and dealers?

SECTION 2 REVIEW

Summary

Demand

1. The **supply and demand model** illustrates how a **competitive market,** one with many buyers and sellers of the same product, works.
2. The **demand schedule** shows the **quantity demanded** at each price and is represented graphically by a **demand curve.** The **law of demand** says that demand curves slope downward, meaning that as price decreases, the quantity demanded increases.
3. A **movement along the demand curve** occurs when the price changes and causes a change in the quantity demanded. When economists talk of **changes in demand,** they mean shifts of the demand curve—a change in the quantity demanded at any given price. An increase in demand causes a rightward shift of the demand curve. A decrease in demand causes a leftward shift.
4. There are five main factors that shift the demand curve:
   - A change in the prices of related goods, such as **substitutes** or **complements**
   - A change in income: when income rises, the demand for **normal goods** increases and the demand for **inferior goods** decreases
   - A change in tastes
   - A change in expectations
   - A change in the number of consumers

Supply and Equilibrium

5. The **supply schedule** shows the **quantity supplied** at each price and is represented graphically by a **supply curve.** Supply curves usually slope upward.
6. A **movement along the supply curve** occurs when the price changes and causes a change in the quantity supplied. When economists talk of **changes in supply,** they mean shifts of the supply curve—a change in the quantity supplied at any given price. An increase in supply causes a rightward shift of the supply curve. A decrease in supply causes a lef...
7. There are five main factors tha...
   - A change in **input** prices
   - A change in the prices of rel...
   - A change in technology
   - A change in expectations
   - A change in the number of p...
8. The supply and demand mode... ple that the price in a market n... **price,** or **market-clearing pr...** the quantity demanded is equ... plied. This quantity is the **equil...** the price is above its market-clearing level, there is a **surplus** that pushes the price down. When the price is below its market-clearing level, there is a **shortage** that ...

Cha...
9. ...
10. ...

Key Terms

Competitive market, p. 36
Supply and demand model, p. 36
Demand schedule, p. 37
Quantity demanded, p. 37
Demand curve, p. 37
Movement along the demand curve, p. 39
Substitutes, p. 41
Complements, p. 41
Normal good, p. 42
Inferior good, p. 42
Supp...
Supp...
Law...
Char...
Mov... cur...

END-OF-SECTION REVIEW AND PROBLEMS In addition to the opportunities for review at the end of every module, each section ends with a brief but complete summary of concepts, a list of key terms, and a comprehensive problem set that includes concepts from across all of the modules in the section.

Problems

1. A survey indicated that chocolate ice cream is America's favorite ice-cream flavor. For each of the following, indicate the possible effects on the demand and/or supply, equilibrium price, and equilibrium quantity of chocolate ice cream.
   a. A severe drought in the Midwest causes dairy farmers to reduce the number of milk-producing cows in their herds by a third. These dairy farmers supply cream that is used to manufacture chocolate ice cream.
   b. A new report by the American Medical Association reveals that chocolate does, in fact, have significant health benefits.
   c. The discovery of cheaper synthetic vanilla flavoring lowers the price of vanilla ice cream.
   d. New technology for mixing and freezing ice cream lowers manufacturers' costs of producing chocolate ice cream.
2. In a supply and demand diagram, draw the change in demand for hamburgers in your hometown due to the following events. In each case show the effect on equilibrium price and quantity.

   a. the market for newspapers in your town
      Case 1: The salaries of journalists go up.
      Case 2: There is a big news event in your town, which is reported in the newspapers, and residents want to learn more about it.
   b. the market for St. Louis Rams cotton T-shirts
      Case 1: The Rams win the championship.
      Case 2: The price of cotton increases.
   c. the market for bagels
      Case 1: People realize how fattening bagels are.
      Case 2: People have less time to make themselves a cooked breakfast.
5. Find the flaws in reasoning in the following statements, paying particular attention to the distinction between changes in and movements along the supply and demand curves. Draw a diagram to illustrate what actually happens in each situation.
   a. "A technological innovation that lowers the cost of producing a good might seem at first to result in a reduc...

Supplements and Media

Worth Publishers is pleased to offer an enhanced and completely revised supplements and media package to accompany this textbook. The package has been crafted to help instructors teach their principles course and to give students the tools to develop their skills in economics.

For Instructors

Instructor's Resource Manual with Solutions Manual

The Instructor's Resource Manual, revised by Nora Underwood, University of Central Florida, is a resource meant to provide materials and tips to enhance the classroom experience.

The Instructor's Resource Manual provides the following:

- Module objectives
- Module outlines
- Teaching tips and ideas that include:
  - Hints on how to create student interest
  - Tips on presenting the material in class
- Discussion of the examples used in the text, including points to emphasize with your students
- Activities that can be conducted in or out of the classroom
- Hints for dealing with common misunderstandings that are typical among students
- Web resources (includes tips for using EconPortal)
- Solutions manual with detailed solutions to all of the end-of-section problems from the textbook

The files for the Instructor's Resource Manual will be available for download by adopting instructors.

Test Bank

The Test Bank, coordinated by Doris Bennett, Jacksonville State University, provides a wide range of questions appropriate for assessing your students' comprehension, interpretation, analysis, and synthesis skills. The Test Bank offers multiple-choice, true/false, and short-answer questions designed for comprehensive coverage of the text concepts. Questions have been checked for continuity with the text content, overall usability, and accuracy.

The Test Bank features include the following:

- To aid instructors in building tests, each question has been categorized according to its general *degree of difficulty.* The three levels are: *easy, moderate,* and *difficult.*
  - *Easy* questions require students to recognize concepts and definitions. These are questions that can be answered by direct reference to the textbook.
  - *Moderate* questions require some analysis on the student's part.
  - *Difficult* questions usually require more detailed analysis by the student.
- Each question has also been categorized according to a *skill descriptor.* These include: *Fact-Based, Definitional, Concept-Based, Critical Thinking,* and *Analytical Thinking.*
  - *Fact-Based* questions require students to identify facts presented in the text.
  - *Definitional* questions require students to define an economic term or concept.
  - *Concept-Based* questions require a straightforward knowledge of basic concepts.
  - *Critical Thinking* questions require the student to apply a concept to a particular situation.
  - *Analytical Thinking* questions require another level of analysis to answer the question. Students must be able to apply a concept and use this knowledge for further analysis of a situation or scenario.
- To further aid instructors in building tests, each question is conveniently cross-referenced to the appropriate topic heading in the textbook. Questions are presented in the order in which concepts are presented in the text.
- The Test Bank includes questions with tables that students must analyze to solve for numerical answers. It also contains questions based on the graphs that appear in the book. These questions ask students to use the graphical models developed in the textbook and to interpret the information presented in the graph. Selected questions are paired with scenarios to reinforce comprehension.

The Diploma Computerized Test Bank and software is available in CD-ROM format for both Windows and Macintosh users. With this program, instructors can easily create and print tests and write and edit questions. Tests can be printed in a wide range of formats. The software's unique synthesis of flexible word-processing and database features creates a program that is extremely intuitive and capable.

Lecture PowerPoint Presentation

Created by Tori Knight, Carson-Newman University, these PowerPoint presentation slides are designed to assist with lecture preparation and presentations. The slides are organized by topic and contain graphs, data tables, and bulleted lists of key concepts suitable for lecture presentation. Key figures from the text are replicated and animated to demonstrate how they build. These slides can be customized to suit your individual needs by adding your own data, questions, and lecture notes.

Dynamic PowerPoint Presentations

This dynamic set of slides, designed by Solina Lindahl, CalPoly San Luis Obispo, is available as an alternative to the traditional lecture outline slides. The slides are brief, interactive, and visually interesting to keep students' attention in class. The slides utilize additional graphics and animations to demonstrate key concepts. The slides include additional (and interesting) real-world examples. The slides include hyperlinks to other relevant outside sources to illustrate real world examples and key concepts (including links to videos!). The slides also include opportunities to incorporate active learning in your classroom.

For Students

Study Guide

Prepared by Elizabeth Sawyer-Kelly, University of Wisconsin–Madison, the Study Guide reinforces the topics and key concepts covered in the text. For each module, the Study Guide is organized as follows:

Before You Read the Module

- Summary: an opening paragraph that provides a brief overview of the module.
- Objectives: a numbered list outlining and describing the material that the student should have learned in the module. These objectives can be easily used as a study tool for students.
- Key Terms: a list of boldface key terms with their definitions—including room for note-taking.

After You Read the Module

- Tips: numbered list of learning tips with graphical analysis.
- Worked Problems: A set of worked-out problems that take the student step-by-step through a particular problem/exercise.
- Problems and Exercises: a set of comprehensive problems.

Before You Take the Test

- Module Review Questions: a set of multiple-choice questions that focus on the key concepts students should grasp after reading the module. These questions are designed for student exam preparation.

Answer Key

- Answers to Problems and Exercises: detailed solutions to the Problems and Exercises in the Study Guide.
- Answers to Module Review Questions: solutions to the multiple-choice questions in the Study Guide—along with thorough explanations.

Online Offerings

www.saplinglearning.com

Sapling Learning provides the most effective interactive homework and instruction that improves student-learning outcomes for the problem-solving disciplines.

Sapling Learning offers an enjoyable teaching and effective learning experience that is distinctive in three important ways:

- **Ease of Use:** Sapling Learning's easy-to-use interface keeps students engaged in problem-solving, not struggling with the software.
- **Targeted Instructional Content:** Sapling Learning increases student engagement and comprehension by delivering immediate feedback and targeted instructional content.
- **Unsurpassed Service and Support:** Sapling Learning makes teaching more enjoyable by providing a dedicated Masters- or PhD-level colleague to service instructors' unique needs throughout the course, including content customization.

CoursePacks

Plug our content into your course management system. Registered instructors can download cartridges with no hassle, no strings attached. For more information, go to http://worthpublishers.com/catalog/Other/Coursepack.

Further Resources Offered

CourseSmart eTextbooks

http://www.coursesmart.com/ourproducts

CourseSmart textbooks offer the complete book in PDF format. Students can save money, up to 60% off the price of print textbooks. With the CourseSmart textbook, students have the ability to take notes, highlight, print pages, and more. A great alternative to renting print textbooks!

Worth Noting

Worth Noting keeps you connected to your textbook authors in real time. Whether they were just on CNBC or published in the *New York Times*, this is the place to find out about it. Visit Worth Noting at http://blogs.worthpublishers.com/econblog/.

i>clicker

Developed by a team of University of Illinois physicists, i>clicker is the most flexible and reliable classroom response system available. It is the only solution created *for* educators, *by* educators—with continuous product improvements made through direct classroom testing and faculty feedback. You'll love i>clicker, no matter your level of technical expertise, because the focus is on *your* teaching, *not the technology*. To learn more about packaging i>clicker with this textbook, please contact your local sales rep or visit www.iclicker.com.

Dismal Scientist

A high-powered business database and analysis service comes to the classroom! Dismal Scientist offers real-time monitoring of the global economy, produced locally by economists and professionals at Economy.com's London, Sydney, and West Chester offices. Dismal Scientist is *free* when packaged with the Krugman/Wells textbook. Please contact your local sales rep for more information or go to www.economy.com.

ECONPORTAL IS NOW LAUNCHPAD

Because Technology Should Never Get in the Way

LaunchPad

http://www.worthpublishers.com/launchpad

LaunchPad is an online homework, e-Book, and teaching and learning system that can be used as a stand-alone course management system or integrated into many campus course management systems such as Blackboard, Canvas, Desire2Learn, and others. And now, drawing on what we've learned from thousands of instructors and hundreds of thousands of students over the past several years, we are proud to introduce a new generation of Macmillan's Portals—***LaunchPad***.

LaunchPad features include:

- **LaunchPad Units** that provide the ability to build a course in minutes. LaunchPad offers selected resources compiled into ready-to-use teaching units, complete with problem sets, activities, e-Book sections, and state-of-the-art online homework and testing. Instructors can quickly set up their course using precreated LaunchPad units. They can also enhance LaunchPad units or create their own original assignments, adding selections from our extensive resource library of questions and activities, and their own materials as well.
- **LearningCurve:** A popular student resource, LearningCurve is an adaptive quizzing engine that automatically adjusts questions to the student's mastery level. With LearningCurve activities, each student follows a unique path to understanding the material. The more questions a student answers correctly, the more difficult the questions become. Each question is written specifically for the text and is linked to the relevant e-Book section. LearningCurve also provides a personal study plan for students as well as complete metrics for instructors. Proven to raise student performance, LearningCurve serves as an ideal formative assessment and learning tool. For detailed information, visit http://learningcurveworks.com.

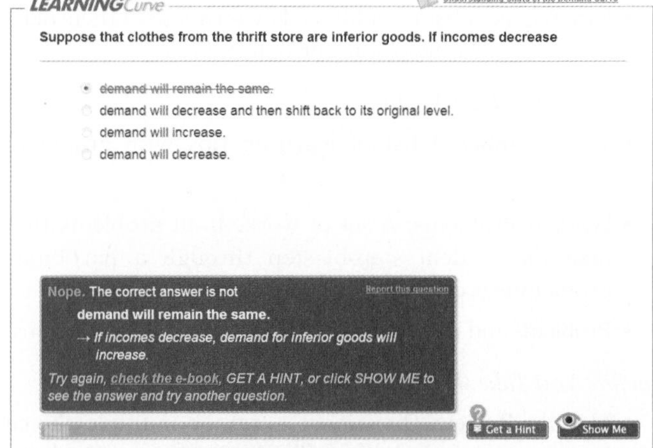

- **Clear, consistent interface:** LaunchPad integrates and unifies a consistent series of resources— LaunchPad units, the e-Book, media, assessment tools, instructor materials, and other content—to a degree unmatched by other online learning systems.
- **Robust, interactive e-Book:** The e-Book offers powerful study tools for students and easily customizable features for instructors. Our simple note-taking tool allows instructors to post notes, hyperlinks, content and more with a few simple clicks. Students can also take their own notes and can view all notes within each module to allow for easy study and review. Students can also highlight, access a glossary, and enlarge images within the text.

- **Powerful online quizzing and homework:** In addition to the LaunchPad units, instructors can create their own assignments using their own questions or drawing on quiz items within EconPortal, including:
  - **The complete test bank** for the textbook for use in creating exams, quizzes, or homework problems. Instructors can use built-in filters and settings to ensure the right questions are chosen and displayed to their preferences.
  - **The end-of-section problem sets** are carefully edited and available in a self-graded format—perfect for in-class quizzes and homework assignments.
  - **Electronically gradable graphing problems** using a robust graphing engine. Students will be asked to draw their response to a question, and the software will automatically grade that response. Graphing questions are tagged to appropriate textbook sections and range in difficulty level and skill.

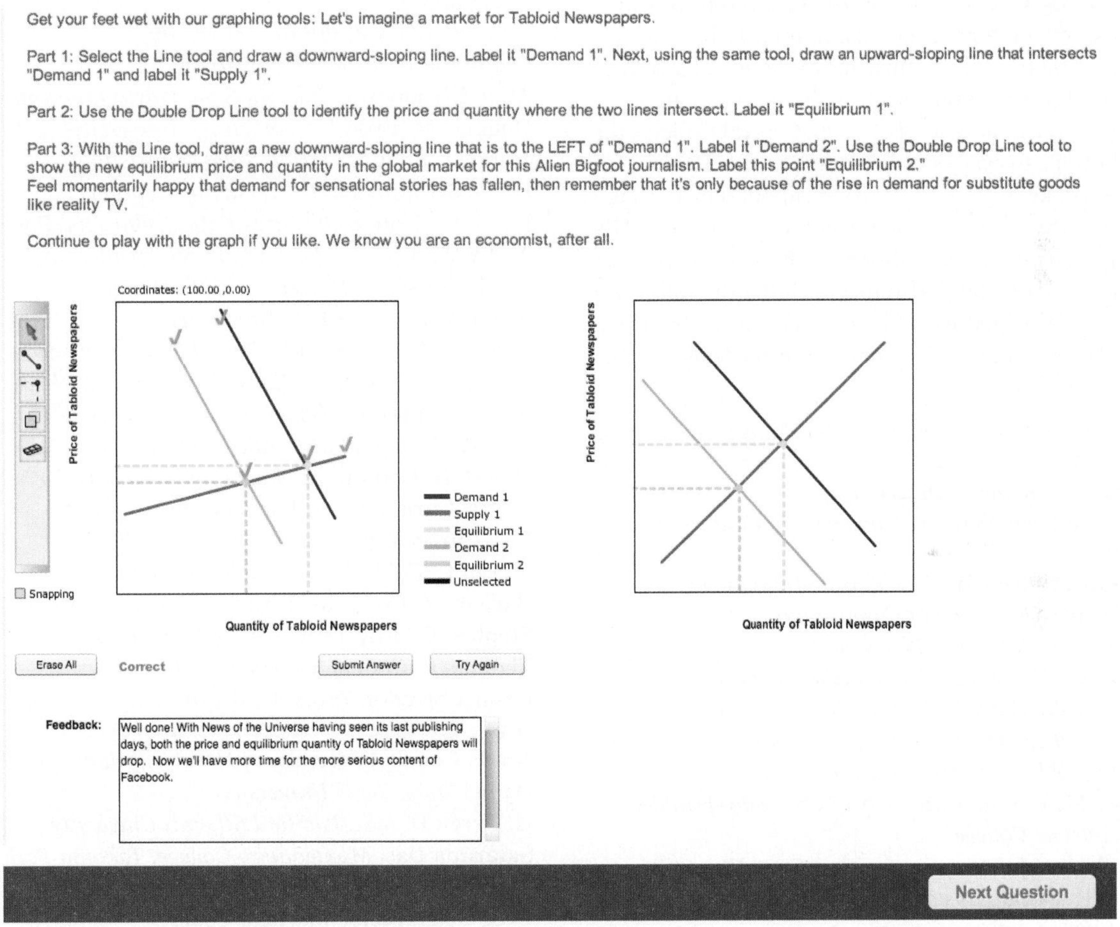

Get your feet wet with our graphing tools: Let's imagine a market for Tabloid Newspapers.

Part 1: Select the Line tool and draw a downward-sloping line. Label it "Demand 1". Next, using the same tool, draw an upward-sloping line that intersects "Demand 1" and label it "Supply 1".

Part 2: Use the Double Drop Line tool to identify the price and quantity where the two lines intersect. Label it "Equilibrium 1".

Part 3: With the Line tool, draw a new downward-sloping line that is to the LEFT of "Demand 1". Label it "Demand 2". Use the Double Drop Line tool to show the new equilibrium price and quantity in the global market for this Alien Bigfoot journalism. Label this point "Equilibrium 2."
Feel momentarily happy that demand for sensational stories has fallen, then remember that it's only because of the rise in demand for substitute goods like reality TV.

Continue to play with the graph if you like. We know you are an economist, after all.

Coordinates: (100.00 ,0.00)

Price of Tabloid Newspapers

Demand 1
Supply 1
Equilibrium 1
Demand 2
Equilibrium 2
Unselected

Snapping

Quantity of Tabloid Newspapers

Price of Tabloid Newspapers

Quantity of Tabloid Newspapers

Erase All Correct Submit Answer Try Again

Feedback: Well done! With News of the Universe having seen its last publishing days, both the price and equilibrium quantity of Tabloid Newspapers will drop. Now we'll have more time for the more serious content of Facebook.

Next Question

ACKNOWLEDGMENTS

Our deep appreciation and heartfelt thanks go out to Margaret Ray, University of Mary Washington, and David Anderson, Centre College, for their hard work on the previous edition of this text. Their efforts and innovations, inspired by many years of working with students in the classroom, provided us with a foundation for the modular approach that we have extended and built upon in this third edition. Thank you, Margaret and Dave, for doing such an exceptional job.

We must also thank Brian Peterson, Central College, for his contributions to every single module in this edition. He helped us to make important decisions about how to shape the content in this revision: what to cut, keep, and add. His efforts helped us create an edition of the book with even broader appeal. We would also like to thank the following instructors who helped us with the revision of this third edition of the modular textbook. Your enthusiasm for this project has been infectious.

Giuliana Campanelli Andreopoulos, *William Paterson University*
Becca Arnold, *San Diego Mesa College*
Margaret apRoberts-Warren, *University of California–Santa Cruz*
Robert Baden, *University of California–Santa Cruz*
Bryce Casavant, *University of Connecticut*
Dixie Dalton, *College of the Low Country*
Julie Gonzalez, *University of California–Santa Cruz*
Janet Koscianski, *Shippensburg University*
Sang Lee, *Southeastern Louisiana University*
Bill McLean, *Oklahoma State University*
Christopher McMahan, *University of Colorado–Boulder*
Joan Nix, *Queens College*
Dimitrios Pachis, *Eastern Connecticut State University*
Matthew S. Rutledge, *Boston College*
Robert Schlack, *Carthage College*
Fahlino Sjuib, *Framingham State University*
Bryan Snyder, *Bentley University*
Cheryl Wachenheim, *North Dakota State University*

We are indebted to the following reviewers, focus group participants, and other consultants for their suggestions and advice on earlier editions of this book.

Miki Brunyer Anderson, *Pikes Peak Community College*
Myra L. Moore, *University of Georgia*
Elizabeth Sawyer-Kelly, *University of Wisconsin, Madison*
Carlos Aguilar, *El Paso Community College*
Terence Alexander, *Iowa State University*
Morris Altman, *University of Saskatchewan*
Farhad Ameen, *State University of New York, Westchester Community College*
Christopher P. Ball, *Quinnipiac University*
Sue Bartlett, *University of South Florida*
Scott Beaulier, *Mercer University*
David Bernotas, *University of Georgia*
Marc Bilodeau, *Indiana University and Purdue University, Indianapolis*
Kelly Blanchard, *Purdue University*
Emily Blank, *Howard University*
Anne Bresnock, *California State Polytechnic University*
Douglas M. Brown, *Georgetown University*
Joseph Calhoun, *Florida State University*
Douglas Campbell, *University of Memphis*
Kevin Carlson, *University of Massachusetts, Boston*
Andrew J. Cassey, *Washington State University*
Shirley Cassing, *University of Pittsburgh*
Sewin Chan, *New York University*
Mitchell M. Charkiewicz, *Central Connecticut State University*
Joni S. Charles, *Texas State University, San Marcos*
Adhip Chaudhuri, *Georgetown University*
Eric P. Chiang, *Florida Atlantic University*
Hayley H. Chouinard, *Washington State University*
Kenny Christianson, *Binghamton University*
Lisa Citron, *Cascadia Community College*
Steven L. Cobb, *University of North Texas*
Barbara Z. Connolly, *Westchester Community College*
Stephen Conroy, *University of San Diego*
Thomas E. Cooper, *Georgetown University*
Cesar Corredor, *Texas A&M University and University of Texas, Tyler*
Jim F. Couch, *University of Northern Alabama*
Daniel Daly, *Regis University*
H. Evren Damar, *Pacific Lutheran University*
Satarupa Das, *Montgomery College, Takoma Park*
Antony Davies, *Duquesne University*
Greg Delemeester, *Marietta College*
Patrick Dolenc, *Keene State College*
Christine Doyle-Burke, *Framingham State College*
Ding Du, *South Dakota State University*
Jerry Dunn, *Southwestern Oklahoma State University*
Robert R. Dunn, *Washington and Jefferson College*
Ann Eike, *University of Kentucky*
Tisha L. N. Emerson, *Baylor University*
Hadi Salehi Esfahani, *University of Illinois*
William Feipel, *Illinois Central College*
Rudy Fichtenbaum, *Wright State University*
David W. Findlay, *Colby College*
Mary Flannery, *University of California, Santa Cruz*
Robert Francis, *Shoreline Community College*
Shelby Frost, *Georgia State University*
Frank Gallant, *George Fox University*
Robert Gazzale, *Williams College*

Seth Gitter, *Towson University*
Robert Godby, *University of Wyoming*
Michael Goode, *Central Piedmont Community College*
Douglas E. Goodman, *University of Puget Sound*
Marvin Gordon, *University of Illinois at Chicago*
Kathryn Graddy, *Brandeis University*
Mike Green, *College of Southern Maryland*
Yoseph Gutema, *Howard Community College*
Alan Day Haight, *State University of New York, Cortland*
Mehdi Haririan, *Bloomsburg University*
Clyde A. Haulman, *College of William and Mary*
Richard R. Hawkins, *University of West Florida*
Michael Heslop, *Northern Virginia Community College, Annandale*
Mickey A. Hepner, *University of Central Oklahoma*
Michael Hilmer, *San Diego State University*
Tia Hilmer, *San Diego State University*
Jane Himarios, *University of Texas, Arlington*
Jim Holcomb, *University of Texas, El Paso*
Don Holley, *Boise State University*
Alexander Holmes, *University of Oklahoma*
Julie Holzner, *Los Angeles City College*
Robert N. Horn, *James Madison University*
Steven Husted, *University of Pittsburgh*
John O. Ifediora, *University of Wisconsin, Platteville*
Hiro Ito, *Portland State University*
Mike Javanmard, *Rio Hondo Community College*
Robert T. Jerome, *James Madison University*
Shirley Johnson-Lans, *Vassar College*
David Kalist, *Shippensburg University*
Lillian Kamal, *Northwestern University*
Roger T. Kaufman, *Smith College*
Herb Kessel, *St. Michael's College*
Rehim Kiliç, *Georgia Institute of Technology*
Grace Kim, *University of Michigan, Dearborn*
Michael Kimmitt, *University of Hawaii, Manoa*
Robert Kling, *Colorado State University*
Sherrie Kossoudji, *University of Michigan*
Andrew Kozak, *St. Mary's College of Maryland*
Charles Kroncke, *College of Mount Saint Joseph*
Reuben Kyle, *Middle Tennessee State University (retired)*
Katherine Lande-Schmeiser, *University of Minnesota, Twin Cities*
David Lehr, *Longwood College*
Mary Jane Lenon, *Providence College*
Mary H. Lesser, *Iona College*
Solina Lindahl, *California Polytechnic State University, San Luis Obispo*
Haiyong Liu, *East Carolina University*
Jane S. Lopus, *California State University, East Bay*
María José Luengo-Prado, *Northeastern University*
Rotua Lumbantobing, *North Carolina State University*
Ed Lyell, *Adams State College*
Mireille Makambira, *Montgomery College, Rockville*
John Marangos, *Colorado State University*
Ralph D. May, *Southwestern Oklahoma State University*
Wayne McCaffery, *University of Wisconsin, Madison*
Dennis McCornac, *Anne Arundel Community College*
Bill McLean, *Oklahoma State University*
Larry McRae, *Appalachian State University*
Mary Ruth J. McRae, *Appalachian State University*
Ellen E. Meade, *American University*
Meghan Millea, *Mississippi State University*
Norman C. Miller, *Miami University (of Ohio)*
Khan A. Mohabbat, *Northern Illinois University*
Myra L. Moore, *University of Georgia*
Jay Morris, *Champlain College in Burlington*
Akira Motomura, *Stonehill College*
Kevin J. Murphy, *Oakland University*
Robert Murphy, *Boston College*
Ranganath Murthy, *Bucknell University*
Anthony Myatt, *University of New Brunswick, Canada*
Randy A. Nelson, *Colby College*
Charles Newton, *Houston Community College*
Daniel X. Nguyen, *Purdue University*
Dmitri Nizovtsev, *Washburn University*
Thomas A. Odegaard, *Baylor University*
Constantin Oglobin, *Georgia Southern University*
Charles C. Okeke, *College of Southern Nevada*
Terry Olson, *Truman State University*
Una Okonkwo Osili, *Indiana University and Purdue University, Indianapolis*
Chris Osuanah, *J. Sargeant Reynolds Community College, Downtown*
Maxwell Oteng, *University of California, Davis*
P. Marcelo Oviedo, *Iowa State University*
Jeff Owen, *Gustavus Adolphus College*
James Palmieri, *Simpson College*
Walter G. Park, *American University*
Elliott Parker, *University of Nevada, Reno*
Michael Perelman, *California State University, Chico*
Nathan Perry, *Utah State University*
Dean Peterson, *Seattle University*
Ken Peterson, *Furman University*
Paul Pieper, *University of Illinois at Chicago*
Dennis L. Placone, *Clemson University*
Michael Polcen, *Northern Virginia Community College*
Raymond A. Polchow, *Zane State College*
Linnea Polgreen, *University of Iowa*
Michael A. Quinn, *Bentley University*
Eileen Rabach, *Santa Monica College*
Matthew Rafferty, *Quinnipiac University*
Jaishankar Raman, *Valparaiso University*
Margaret Ray, *Mary Washington College*
Helen Roberts, *University of Illinois, Chicago*
Jeffrey Rubin, *Rutgers University, New Brunswick*
Rose M. Rubin, *University of Memphis*
Lynda Rush, *California State Polytechnic University, Pomona*
Michael Ryan, *Western Michigan University*
Sara Saderion, *Houston Community College*
Djavad Salehi-Isfahani, *Virginia Tech*
Elizabeth Sawyer-Kelly, *University of Wisconsin, Madison*
Jesse A. Schwartz, *Kennesaw State University*
Chad Settle, *University of Tulsa*

Steve Shapiro, *University of North Florida*
Robert L. Shoffner III, *Central Piedmont Community College*
Joseph Sicilian, *University of Kansas*
Judy Smrha, *Baker University*
John Solow, *University of Iowa*
John Somers, *Portland Community College*
Stephen Stageberg, *University of Mary Washington*
Monty Stanford, *DeVry University*
Rebecca Stein, *University of Pennsylvania*
William K. Tabb, *Queens College, City University of New York (retired)*
Sarinda Taengnoi, *University of Wisconsin, Oshkosh*
Henry Terrell, *University of Maryland*
Rebecca Achée Thornton, *University of Houston*
Michael Toma, *Armstrong Atlantic State University*
Brian Trinque, *University of Texas, Austin*
Boone A. Turchi, *University of North Carolina, Chapel Hill*
Nora Underwood, *University of Central Florida*
J. S. Uppal, *State University of New York, Albany*
John Vahaly, *University of Louisville*
Jose J. Vazquez-Cognet, *University of Illinois at Urbana-Champaign*
Daniel Vazzana, *Georgetown College*
Roger H. von Haefen, *North Carolina State University*
Andreas Waldkirch, *Colby College*
Christopher Waller, *University of Notre Dame*
Gregory Wassall, *Northeastern University*
Robert Whaples, *Wake Forest University*
Thomas White, *Assumption College*
Jennifer P. Wissink, *Cornell University*
Mark Witte, *Northwestern University*
Kristen M. Wolfe, *St. Johns River Community College*
Larry Wolfenbarger, *Macon State College*
Louise B. Wolitz, *University of Texas, Austin*
Gavin Wright, *Stanford University*
Bill Yang, *Georgia Southern University*
Jason Zimmerman, *South Dakota State University*

In the past, we always trusted Andreas Bentz and his indefatigable eye for detail while we focused on big-picture issues in the sections. We count ourselves extremely fortunate that Michael Reksulak, Georgia Southern University, stepped in when Andreas was unavailable to devote as much time to this project as in the past. Andreas was a helpful advisor during early stages of the revision. Michael turned out to be more than capable of providing expert-level guidance in the later stages of manuscript development and in the page-proof stage, when tending to accuracy and details is paramount. Michael's efforts as accuracy coordinator were supported by the invaluable contributions of accuracy checkers Dixie Dalton, Southside Virginia Community College, Matthew S. Rutledge, Boston College, and Sang Lee, Southeastern Louisiana University. In addition, we thank Becca Arnold, San Diego Mesa College, Janet Koscianski, Shippensburg University, and Cheryl Wachenheim, North Dakota State University, for their contributions to the accuracy of this text. Many thanks to Solina Lindahl, California Polytechnic State University, who provided expert guidance on the media program associated with the textbook.

We must also thank the many people at Worth Publishers for their contributions. Elizabeth Widdicombe, president, and Catherine Woods, senior vice president, for their role in planning for this revision. Charles Linsmeier, publisher, ably oversaw the revision and contributed throughout. A special thanks to Craig Bleyer, our original publisher and now national sales manager, who put so much effort into making all of our textbooks a success. To Scott Guile, associate director of marketing, and once our long-time marketing manager, who recognized a need for a more streamlined Krugman/Wells text and whose enthusiasm for the modular format helped to bring an innovative approach to fruition.

Once again, we have an incredible production and design team, people whose hard work, creativity, patience, and dedication continue to amaze us. Once again, you have outdone yourselves. Thank you all: Tracey Kuehn, Lisa Kinne, Liz Geller, for producing this book; Babs Reingold, Lyndall Culbertson, Chuck Yuen, and Paul Lacy for their beautiful interior design, layout, and cover; Deborah Heimann for her thoughtful copyedit; Barbara Seixas, who worked her magic, as always, despite the vagaries of the project schedule; Cecilia Varas and Elyse Rieder who have worked with us through numerous editions to get the photos just right; Stacey Alexander and Edgar Bonilla for coordinating all the supplemental materials; Mary Walsh, associate editor, who wore many hats during this revision, each of them equally well; and Fay Kelly, editorial assistant, who did a fine job preparing the manuscript and art program for production.

Many thanks to Marie McHale for devising and coordinating the impressive collection of media and supplements that accompany our book. With each edition you've shown how far we've come in supporting instructors who choose to adopt our textbook. Thanks to the incredible team of writers and coordinators who worked with Marie on the supplements and media package; we are forever grateful for your tireless efforts.

Thanks to Tom Digiano, marketing manager, who picked up where Scott Guile left off, and to the many members of the sales force, some who have been with us from the beginning, on your tireless efforts in promoting our book to a wider audience.

And most of all, special thanks to Sharon Balbos, executive development editor on each of our editions. Much of the success of this book is owed to Sharon's dedication and professionalism; in this edition, perhaps more so than most. Sharon, we're not sure we deserved an editor as good as you, but we're sure that everyone involved as well as our adopters and their students have been made better off by your presence.

Paul Krugman

Robin Wells

MICROECONOMICS
IN MODULES

Module 1: The Study of Economics
Module 2: Models and the Circular Flow
Module 3: The Production Possibility Frontier Model
Module 4: Comparative Advantage and Trade

SECTION 1

Basic Economic Concepts

THINKING LIKE AN ECONOMIST

All economic analysis is based on a set of common principles that apply to many different issues. Some of these principles involve *individual choice*—for economics is, first of all, about the choices that individuals make. Do you save your money and take the bus or do you buy a car? Do you keep your old smart phone or upgrade to a new one?

But in a market economy we make decisions in an environment shaped by the decisions of others—through *economic interaction*. Even the simplest decisions—like what to have for breakfast—are shaped by the decisions of thousands of other people, from the banana grower in Costa Rica who decided to grow the fruit we eat to the farmer in Iowa who provided the corn in our cornflakes.

To arrive at their theories about markets, economists use models, simplified representations of economic reality that allow for an understanding of a variety of economic issues. How helpful are models in the study of economics? To answer this question, let's consider the experience of the Wright brothers.

In 1901, Wilbur and Orville Wright built a device that would change the world. It was not the airplane—their successful flight at Kitty Hawk (pictured above) would come two years later. What made the Wright brothers true visionaries was their wind tunnel, an apparatus that let them experiment with many different designs for wings and control surfaces. These experiments gave them the knowledge that would make heavier-than-air flight possible.

A miniature airplane sitting motionless in a wind tunnel isn't the same thing as an actual aircraft in flight. But it is a very useful *model* of a flying plane. Needless to say, testing an airplane design in a wind tunnel is cheaper and safer than building a full-scale version and hoping it will fly. More generally, models play a crucial role in almost all scientific research—economics very much included. In fact, you could say that economic theory consists mainly of a collection of models.

In this section, we'll introduce you to the study of economics, including the role of individual choice. We'll look at how economists think and, in particular, how they use models in their work. We will then consider two economic models that are crucially important in their own right and also illustrate why such models are so useful.

MODULE 1 The Study of Economics

iStockphoto

WHAT YOU WILL LEARN

1. How scarcity and choice are central to the study of economics
2. The importance of opportunity cost in individual choice and decision making
3. The difference between positive economics and normative economics
4. When economists agree and why they sometimes disagree
5. What makes macroeconomics different from microeconomics

Individual Choice: The Core of Economics

Economics is the study of scarcity and choice. Every economic issue involves, at its most basic level, **individual choice**—decisions by individuals about what to do and what *not* to do. In fact, you might say that it isn't economics if it isn't about choice.

Step into a big store such as Walmart or Target. There are thousands of different products available, and it is extremely unlikely that you—or anyone else—could afford to buy everything you might want to have. And anyway, there's only so much space in your home. Given the limitations on your budget and your living space, you must choose which products to buy and which to leave on the shelf.

The fact that those products are on the shelf in the first place involves choice—the store manager chose to put them there, and the manufacturers of the products chose to produce them. The **economy** is a system that coordinates choices about production with choices about consumption, and distributes goods and services to the people who want them. The United States has a **market economy,** in which production and consumption are the result of decentralized decisions by many firms and individuals. There is no central authority telling people what to produce or where to ship it. Each individual producer makes what he or she thinks will be most profitable, and each consumer buys what he or she chooses.

All economic activities involve individual choice. Let's take a closer look at what this means for the study of economics.

Economics is the study of scarcity and choice.

Individual choice is decisions by individuals about what to do, which necessarily involve decisions about what not to do.

An **economy** is a system for coordinating a society's productive and consumptive activities.

In a **market economy,** the decisions of individual producers and consumers largely determine what, how, and for whom to produce, with little government involvement in the decisions.

Resources Are Scarce

You can't always get what you want. Almost everyone would like to have a beautiful house in a great location (and help with the housecleaning), two or three luxury cars, and frequent vacations in fancy hotels. But even in a rich country like the United States, not many families can afford all of that. So they must make choices—whether to go to Disney World this year or buy a better car, whether to make do with a small backyard or accept a longer commute in order to live where land is cheaper.

Limited income isn't the only thing that keeps people from having everything they want. Time is also in limited supply: there are only 24 hours in a day. And because the time we have is limited, choosing to spend time on one activity also means choosing not to spend time on a different activity—spending time studying for an exam means forgoing a night at the movies. Indeed, many people feel so limited by the number of hours in the day that they are willing to trade money for time. For example, convenience stores usually charge higher prices than larger supermarkets. But they fulfill a valuable role by catering to customers who would rather pay more than spend the time traveling farther to a supermarket where they might also have to wait in longer lines.

Why do individuals have to make choices? The ultimate reason is that *resources are scarce.* A **resource** is anything that can be used to produce something else. The economy's resources, sometimes called *factors of production,* can be classified into four categories: **land** (including timber, water, minerals, and all other resources that come from nature), **labor** (the effort of workers), **physical capital** (machinery, buildings, tools, and all other manufactured goods used to make other goods and services), and **human capital** (the educational achievements and skills of the labor force, which enhance its productivity).

A resource is **scarce** when there is not enough of it available to satisfy the various ways a society wants to use it. For example, there are limited supplies of oil and coal, which currently provide most of the energy used to produce and deliver everything we buy. And in a growing world economy with a rapidly increasing human population, even clean air and water have become scarce resources.

Just as individuals must make choices, the scarcity of resources means that society as a whole must make choices. One way for a society to make choices is simply to allow them to emerge as the result of many individual choices. For example, there are only so many hours in a week, and Americans must decide how to spend their time. How many hours will they spend going to supermarkets to get lower prices rather than saving time by shopping at convenience stores? The answer is the sum of individual decisions: each of the millions of individuals in the economy makes his or her own choice about where to shop, and society's choice is simply the sum of those individual decisions.

For various reasons, there are some decisions that a society decides are best not left to individual choice. For example, two of the authors live in an area that until recently was mainly farmland but is now being rapidly built up. Most local residents feel that the community would be a more pleasant place to live if some of the land were left undeveloped. But no individual has an incentive to keep his or her land as open space, rather than sell it to a developer. So a trend has emerged in many communities across the United States of local governments purchasing undeveloped land and preserving it as open space. Decisions about how to use scarce resources are often best left to individuals but sometimes should be made at a higher, community-wide, level.

A **resource** is anything that can be used to produce something else.

Land refers to all resources that come from nature, such as minerals, timber, and petroleum.

Labor is the effort of workers.

Physical capital refers to manufactured goods used to make other goods and services.

Human capital refers to the educational achievements and skills of the labor force, which enhance its productivity.

A **scarce** resource is not available in sufficient quantities to satisfy all the various ways a society wants to use it.

The real cost of an item is its **opportunity cost:** what you must give up in order to get it.

Opportunity Cost: The Real Cost of Something Is What You Must Give Up to Get It

It is the last term before you graduate, and your class schedule allows you to take only one elective. There are two, however, that you would really like to take: Intro to Computer Graphics and History of Jazz.

Suppose you decide to take the History of Jazz course. What's the cost of that decision? It is the fact that you can't take the computer graphics class, your next best alternative choice. Economists call that kind of cost—what you must give up in order to get an item you want—the **opportunity cost** of that item. So the opportunity cost of taking the History of Jazz class is the benefit you would have derived from the Intro to Computer Graphics class.

.shock/Dreamstime

AP Photo/Paul Sakuma, FILE

Mark Zuckerberg understood the concept of opportunity cost.

The concept of opportunity cost is crucial to understanding individual choice because, in the end, all costs are opportunity costs. That's because every choice you make means forgoing some other alternative. Sometimes critics claim that economists are concerned only with costs and benefits that can be measured in dollars and cents. But that is not true. Much economic analysis involves cases like our elective course example, where it costs no extra tuition to take one elective course—that is, there is no direct monetary cost. Nonetheless, the elective you choose has an opportunity cost—the other desirable elective course that you must forgo because your limited time permits taking only one. More specifically, the opportunity cost of a choice is what you forgo by not choosing your next best alternative.

You might think that opportunity cost is an add-on—that is, something *additional* to the monetary cost of an item. Suppose that an elective class costs additional tuition of $750; now there is a monetary cost to taking History of Jazz. Is the opportunity cost of taking that course something separate from that monetary cost?

Well, consider two cases. First, suppose that taking Intro to Computer Graphics also costs $750. In this case, you would have to spend that $750 no matter which class you take. So what you give up to take the History of Jazz class is still the computer graphics class, period—you would have to spend that $750 either way. But suppose there isn't any fee for the computer graphics class. In that case, what you give up to take the jazz class is the benefit from the computer graphics class *plus* the benefit you could have gained from spending the $750 on other things.

Either way, the real cost of taking your preferred class is what you must give up to get it. As you expand the set of decisions that underlie each choice—whether to take an elective or not, whether to finish this term or not, whether to drop out or not—you'll realize that all costs are ultimately opportunity costs.

Sometimes the money you have to pay for something is a good indication of its opportunity cost. But many times it is not. One very important example of how poorly monetary cost can indicate opportunity cost is the cost of attending college. Tuition and housing are major monetary expenses for most students; but even if these things were free, attending college would still be an expensive proposition because most college students, if they were not in college, would have a job. That is, by going to college, students *forgo* the income they could have earned if they had worked instead. This means that the opportunity cost of attending college is what you pay for tuition and housing plus the forgone income you would have earned in a job.

It's easy to see that the opportunity cost of going to college is especially high for people who could be earning a lot during what would otherwise have been their college years. That is why star athletes like LeBron James and entrepreneurs like Mark Zuckerberg, founder of Facebook, often skip or drop out of college.

ECONOMICS IN ACTION

GOT A PENNY?

At many cash registers there is a little basket full of pennies. People are encouraged to use the basket to round their purchases up or down. If an item costs $5.02, you give the cashier $5.00 and take two pennies from the basket to give to the cashier. If an item costs $4.99, you pay $5.00 and the cashier throws a penny into the basket. It makes everyone's life a bit easier. Of course, it would be easier still if we just abolished the penny, a step that some economists have urged.

But why do we have pennies in the first place? If it's too small a sum to worry about, why calculate prices that precisely?

The answer is that a penny wasn't always such a negligible sum: the purchasing power of a penny has been greatly reduced by *inflation,* a general rise in the prices of all goods and services over time. Forty years ago, a penny had more purchasing power than a nickel does today.

Why does this matter? Well, remember the saying "A penny saved is a penny earned"? Of course, there are other ways to earn money, so you must decide whether saving a penny is a productive use of your time. Could you earn more by devoting that time to other uses?

Almost seventy years ago, the average wage was about $1.20 an hour. A penny was equivalent to 30 seconds' worth of work, so it was worth saving a penny if doing so took less than 30 seconds. But wages have risen along with overall prices, so that the average worker is now paid more than $23 per hour. A penny is therefore equivalent to just a little under 2 seconds of work, so it's not worth the opportunity cost of the time it takes to worry about a penny more or less.

In short, the rising opportunity cost of time in terms of money has turned a penny from a useful coin into a nuisance.

Microeconomics is the study of how people make decisions and how those decisions interact.

Macroeconomics is concerned with the overall ups and downs in the economy.

Economic aggregates are economic measures that summarize data across many different markets.

Microeconomics versus Macroeconomics

We have presented economics as the study of choices and described how, at its most basic level, economics is about individual choice. The branch of economics concerned with how individuals make decisions and how these decisions interact is called **microeconomics.** Microeconomics focuses on choices made by individuals, households, or firms—the smaller parts that make up the economy as a whole.

Macroeconomics focuses on the bigger picture—the overall ups and downs of the economy. When you study macroeconomics, you learn how economists explain these fluctuations and how governments can use economic policy to minimize the damage they cause. Macroeconomics focuses on **economic aggregates**—economic measures such as the unemployment rate, the inflation rate, and gross domestic product—that summarize data across many different markets.

Table 1-1 lists some typical questions that involve economics. A microeconomic version of the question appears on the left, paired with a similar macroeconomic question on the right. By comparing the questions, you can begin to get a sense of the difference between microeconomics and macroeconomics.

As these questions illustrate, microeconomics focuses on how individuals and firms make decisions, and the consequences of those decisions. For example, a school will use microeconomics to determine how much it would cost to offer a new course, which includes the instructor's salary, the cost of class materials, and so on. By weighing the costs and benefits, the school can then decide whether or not to offer the course. Macroeconomics, in contrast, examines the *overall* behavior of the economy—how the actions of all of the individuals and firms in the economy interact to produce a particular economy-wide level of economic performance. For example, macroeconomics is concerned with the general level of prices in the economy and how high or low they are relative to prices last year, rather than with the price of a particular good or service.

TABLE 1-1

Microeconomic versus Macroeconomic Questions

Microeconomic Questions	Macroeconomic Questions
Should I go to business school or take a job right now?	How many people are employed in the economy as a whole this year?
What determines the salary offered by Citibank to Cherie Camajo, a new MBA?	What determines the overall salary levels paid to workers in a given year?
What determines the cost to a university or college of offering a new course?	What determines the overall level of prices in the economy as a whole?
What government policies should be adopted to make it easier for low-income students to attend college?	What government policies should be adopted to promote employment and growth in the economy as a whole?
What determines whether Citibank opens a new office in Shanghai?	What determines the overall trade in goods, services, and financial assets between the United States and the rest of the world?

Positive economics is the branch of economic analysis that describes the way the economy actually works.

Normative economics makes prescriptions about the way the economy should work.

Positive versus Normative Economics

Economic analysis, as we will see throughout this book, draws on a set of basic economic principles. But how are these principles applied? That depends on the purpose of the analysis. Economic analysis that is used to answer questions about the way the world works, questions that have definite right and wrong answers, is known as **positive economics.** In contrast, economic analysis that involves saying how the world *should* work is known as **normative economics.**

Imagine that you are an economic adviser to the governor of your state and the governor is considering a change to the toll charged along the state turnpike. Below are three questions the governor might ask you.

1. How much revenue will the tolls yield next year?
2. How much would that revenue increase if the toll were raised from $1.00 to $1.50?
3. Should the toll be raised, bearing in mind that a toll increase would likely reduce traffic and air pollution near the road but impose some financial hardship on frequent commuters?

There is a big difference between the first two questions and the third one. The first two are questions about facts. Your forecast of next year's toll revenue without any increase will be proved right or wrong when the numbers actually come in. Your estimate of the impact of a change in the toll is a little harder to check—the increase in revenue depends on other factors besides the toll, and it may be hard to disentangle the causes of any change in revenue. Still, in principle there is only one right answer.

istockphoto

Should the toll be raised?

But the question of whether or not tolls should be raised may not have a "right" answer—two people who agree on the effects of a higher toll could still disagree about whether raising the toll is a good idea. For example, someone who lives near the turnpike but doesn't commute on it will care a lot about noise and air pollution but not so much about commuting costs. A regular commuter who doesn't live near the turnpike will have the opposite priorities.

This example highlights a key distinction between the two roles of economic analysis and presents another way to think about the distinction between positive and normative analysis: positive economics is about description, and normative economics is about prescription. Positive economics occupies most of the time and effort of the economics profession.

Looking back at the three questions the governor might ask, it is worth noting a subtle but important difference between questions 1 and 2. Question 1 asks for a simple prediction about next year's revenue—a forecast. Question 2 is a "what if" question, asking how revenue would change if the toll were to change. Economists are often called upon to answer both types of questions. Economic *models*, which provide simplified representations of reality such as graphs or equations, are especially useful for answering "what if" questions.

The answers to such questions often serve as a guide to policy, but they are still predictions, not prescriptions. That is, they tell you what will happen if a policy is changed, but they don't tell you whether or not that result is good. Suppose that your economic model tells you that the governor's proposed increase in highway tolls will raise property values in communities near the road but will tax or inconvenience people who currently use the turnpike to get to work. Does that information make this proposed toll increase a good idea or a bad one? It depends on whom you ask. As we've just seen, someone who is very concerned with the communities near the road will support the increase, but someone who is very concerned with the welfare of drivers will feel differently. That's a value judgment—it's not a question of positive economic analysis.

Still, economists often do engage in normative economics and give policy advice. How can they do this when there may be no "right" answer? One answer is that economists are also citizens, and we all have our opinions. But economic analysis can often be used to show that some policies are clearly better than others, regardless of individual opinions.

Suppose that policies A and B achieve the same goal, but policy A makes everyone better off than policy B—or at least makes some people better off without making other people worse off. Then A is clearly more efficient than B. That's not a value judgment: we're talking about how best to achieve a goal, not about the goal itself.

For example, two different policies have been used to help low-income families obtain housing: rent control, which limits the rents landlords are allowed to charge, and rent subsidies, which provide families with additional money with which to pay rent. Almost all economists agree that subsidies are the more efficient policy. (In a later module we'll see why this is so.) And so the great majority of economists, whatever their personal politics, favor subsidies over rent control.

When policies can be clearly ranked in this way, then economists generally agree. But it is no secret that economists sometimes disagree.

When and Why Economists Disagree

Economists have a reputation for arguing with each other. Where does this reputation come from?

One important answer is that media coverage tends to exaggerate the real differences in views among economists. If nearly all economists agree on an issue—for example, the proposition that rent controls lead to housing shortages—reporters and editors are likely to conclude that there is no story worth covering, and so the professional consensus tends to go unreported. But when there is some issue on which prominent economists take opposing sides—for example, whether cutting taxes right now would help the economy—that does make a good news story. So you hear much more about the areas of disagreement among economists than you do about the many areas of agreement.

It is also worth remembering that economics is, unavoidably, often tied up in politics. On a number of issues, powerful interest groups know what opinions they want to hear. Therefore, they have an incentive to find and promote economists who profess those opinions, which gives these economists a prominence and visibility out of proportion to their support among their colleagues.

Although the appearance of disagreement among economists exceeds the reality, it remains true that economists often *do* disagree about important things. For example, some highly respected economists argue vehemently that the U.S. government should replace the income tax with a *value-added tax* (a national sales tax, which is the main source of government revenue in many European countries). Other equally respected economists disagree. What are the sources of this difference of opinion?

One important source of differences is in values: as in any diverse group of individuals, reasonable people can differ. In comparison to an income tax, a value-added tax typically falls more heavily on people with low incomes. So an economist who values a society with more social and income equality will likely oppose a value-added tax. An economist with different values will be less likely to oppose it.

A second important source of differences arises from the way economists conduct economic analysis. Economists base their conclusions on models formed by making simplifying assumptions about reality. Two economists can legitimately disagree about which simplifications are appropriate—and therefore arrive at different conclusions.

ECONOMICS ▶ IN ACTION

WHEN ECONOMISTS AGREE

"If all the economists in the world were laid end to end, they still couldn't reach a conclusion." So goes one popular economist joke. But do economists really disagree that much?

Not according to a classic survey of members of the American Economic Association, reported in the May 1992 issue of the *American Economic Review.* The authors asked respondents to agree or disagree with a number of statements about the economy; what they found was a high level of agreement among professional economists on many of the statements. At the top of the list, with more than 90% of the economists agreeing, were the statements "Tariffs and import quotas usually reduce general economic welfare" and "A ceiling on rents reduces the quantity and quality of housing available." What's striking about these two statements is that many noneconomists disagree: tariffs and import quotas to keep out foreign-produced goods are favored by many voters, and proposals to do away with rent control in cities like New York and San Francisco have met fierce political opposition.

So is the stereotype of quarreling economists a myth? Not entirely. Economists do disagree quite a lot on some issues, especially in macroeconomics, but there is a large area of common ground.

Suppose that the U.S. government was considering a value-added tax. Economist A may rely on a simplification of reality that focuses on the administrative costs of tax systems—that is, the costs of monitoring compliance, processing tax forms, collecting the tax, and so on. This economist might then point to the well-known high costs of administering a value-added tax and argue against the change. But economist B may think that the right way to approach the question is to ignore the administrative costs and focus on how the proposed law would change individual savings behavior. This economist might point to studies suggesting that value-added taxes promote higher consumer saving, a desirable result. Because the economists have made different simplifying assumptions, they find themselves on different sides of the issue.

Most such disputes are eventually resolved by the accumulation of evidence that shows which of the various simplifying assumptions made by economists does a better job of fitting the facts. However, in economics, as in any science, it can take a long time before research settles important disputes—decades, in some cases. And since the economy is always changing in ways that make old approaches invalid or raise new policy questions, there are always new issues on which economists disagree. The policy maker must then decide which economist to believe.

MODULE 1 Review

Solutions appear at the back of the book.

Check Your Understanding

1. What are the four categories of resources? Give an example of a resource from each category.
2. What type of resource is each of the following?
   a. time spent flipping hamburgers at a restaurant
   b. a bulldozer
   c. a river
3. You make $45,000 per year at your current job with Whiz Kids Consultants. You are considering a job offer from Brainiacs, Inc., which would pay you $50,000 per year. Which of the following are elements of the opportunity cost of accepting the new job at Brainiacs, Inc.? Answer yes or no, and explain your answer.
   a. the increased time spent commuting to your new job
   b. the $45,000 salary from your old job
   c. the more spacious office at your new job

4. Identify each of the following statements as positive or normative, and explain your answer.

   a. Society should take measures to prevent people from engaging in dangerous personal behavior.

   b. People who engage in dangerous personal behavior impose higher costs on society through higher medical costs.

Multiple-Choice Questions

1. Which of the following is an example of a resource?

   I. petroleum
   II. a factory
   III. a cheeseburger dinner

   a. I only
   b. II only
   c. III only
   d. I and II only
   e. I, II, and III

2. Which of the following situations represent(s) resource scarcity?

   I. Rapidly growing economies experience increasing levels of water pollution.
   II. There is a finite amount of petroleum in the physical environment.
   III. Cassette tapes are no longer being produced.

   a. I only
   b. II only
   c. III only
   d. I and II only
   e. I, II, and III

3. Suppose that you prefer reading a book you already own to watching TV and that you prefer watching TV to listening to music. If these are your only three choices, what is the opportunity cost of reading?

   a. watching TV and listening to music
   b. watching TV
   c. listening to music
   d. sleeping
   e. the price of the book

4. Which of the following statements is/are normative?

   I. The price of gasoline is rising.
   II. The price of gasoline is too high.
   III. Gas prices are expected to fall in the near future.

   a. I only
   b. II only
   c. III only
   d. I and III only
   e. I, II, and III

5. Which of the following questions is studied in microeconomics?

   a. Should I go to college or get a job after I graduate?
   b. What government policies should be adopted to promote employment in the economy?
   c. How many people are employed in the economy this year?
   d. Has the overall level of prices in the economy increased or decreased this year?
   e. What determines the overall salary levels paid to workers in a given year?

Critical-Thinking Question

In what type of economic analysis do questions have a “right” or “wrong” answer? In what type of economic analysis do questions not necessarily have a “right” answer? On what type of economic analysis do economists tend to disagree most frequently? Why might economists disagree? Explain.

MODULE 2 Models and the Circular Flow

istockphoto/Thinkstock

WHAT YOU WILL LEARN

1. Why models are an important tool in the study of economics
2. How to interpret the circular-flow diagram of the economy
3. How individual decisions affect the larger economy

In the section opener, you saw how the Wright brothers' experimenting with a miniature airplane in a wind tunnel—a simplified representation of the real thing—served as a very useful model of a flying plane. In this module, we will look at why models are so useful to economists. We'll also examine one important simplified representation of economic reality—the circular-flow diagram.

Models Take Flight in Economics

A **model** is any simplified version of reality that is used to better understand real-world situations. But how do we create a simplified representation of an economic situation?

One possibility—an economist's equivalent of a wind tunnel—is to find or create a real but simplified economy. For example, economists interested in the economic role of money have studied the system of exchange that developed in World War II prison camps, in which cigarettes became a universally accepted form of payment, even among prisoners who didn't smoke.

Another possibility is to simulate the workings of the economy on a computer. For example, when changes in tax law are proposed, government officials use *tax models*—large mathematical computer programs—to assess how the proposed changes would affect different groups of people.

Models are important because their simplicity allows economists to focus on the effects of only one change at a time. That is, they allow us to hold everything else constant and to study how one change affects the overall economic outcome. So when building economic models, an important assumption is the **other things equal assumption,** which means that all other relevant factors remain unchanged. Sometimes the Latin phrase *ceteris paribus,* which means "other things equal," is used.

A **model** is a simplified representation used to better understand a real-world situation.

The **other things equal assumption** means that all other relevant factors remain unchanged. This is also known as the *ceteris paribus* assumption.

But it isn't always possible to find or create a small-scale version of the whole economy, and a computer program is only as good as the data it uses. (Programmers have a saying: garbage in, garbage out.) For many purposes, the most effective form of economic modeling is the construction of "thought experiments": simplified, hypothetical versions of real-world situations.

As you will see throughout this book, economists' models are often in the form of a graph. In Module 3 we will look at graphs of the *production possibility frontier,* a model that helps economists think about the choices made in every economy. In Module 4 we turn to *comparative advantage,* a model that clarifies the principle of gains from trade—trade both between individuals and between countries. Models can also be represented in diagrams. In this module we will use the circular-flow diagram to better understand the workings of the economy.

ECONOMICS ▶ IN ACTION

THE MODEL THAT ATE THE ECONOMY

A model is just a model, right? So how much damage can it do? Economists probably would have answered that question differently before the financial meltdown of 2008–2009 than after it. It turns out that a *bad* economic model played a significant role in the origins of the crisis.

"The model that ate the economy" originated in finance theory, the branch of economics that seeks to understand what assets like stocks and bonds are worth. Financial theorists often devise complex mathematical models to help investment companies decide what assets to buy and sell and at what price.

Finance theory has become increasingly important as Wall Street (a district in New York City where nearly all major investment companies have their headquarters) has shifted from trading simple assets like stocks and bonds to more complex assets—notably, mortgage-backed securities (or MBSs for short). An MBS is an asset that entitles its owner to a stream of earnings based on the payments made by thousands of people on their home loans. Investors wanted to know how risky these complex assets were. That is, how likely was it that an investor would lose money on an MBS?

Although we won't go into the details, estimating the likelihood of losing money on an MBS is a complicated problem. It involves calculating the probability that a significant number of the thousands of homeowners backing your security will stop paying their mortgages. Until that probability could be calculated, investors didn't want to buy MBSs.

In 2000, a Wall Street financial theorist announced that he had solved the problem by devising a simple model for estimating the risk of buying an MBS. Financial traders loved the model, as it opened up a huge and extraordinarily profitable market for them. Using this simple model, Wall Street was able to create and sell billions of MBSs, generating billions in profits for itself.

Or investors *thought* they had calculated the risk of losing money on an MBS. Some financial experts warned from the sidelines that the estimates of risk calculated by this simple model were just plain wrong. They said that in the search for simplicity, the model underestimated the likelihood that many homeowners would stop paying their mortgages at the same time, leaving MBS investors in danger of incurring huge losses.

Billions of dollars worth of MBSs were sold to investors both in the United States and abroad. In 2008–2009, the problems critics warned about exploded in catastrophic fashion. Over the previous decade, American home prices had risen too high, and mortgages had been extended to many who were unable to pay. As home prices fell, millions of homeowners didn't pay their mortgages. With losses mounting for MBS investors, it became all too clear that the model had indeed underestimated the risks. When investors and financial institutions around the world realized the extent of their losses, the worldwide economy ground to an abrupt halt.

Nikada/iStockphoto

The **circular-flow diagram** represents the transactions in an economy by flows around a circle.

A **household** is a person or a group of people who share income.

A **firm** is an organization that produces goods and services for sale.

Product markets are where goods and services are bought and sold.

Factor markets are where resources, especially capital and labor, are bought and sold.

The Circular-Flow Diagram

The U.S. economy is a vastly complex entity, with more than 155 million workers employed by more than 27 million companies, producing millions of different goods and services. Yet you can learn some very important things about the economy by considering the simple graphic shown in Figure 2-1. This **circular-flow diagram** is a simplified representation of the way money, goods and services, and factors of production flow through the economy. The yellow arrows show how goods, services, labor, and raw materials flow in one direction, and the bluish–green arrows show how the money that pays for these things flows in the opposite direction. The underlying principle is that the flow of money into each market or sector is equal to the flow of money coming out of that market or sector.

This simple model illustrates an economy that contains only two types of participants: households and firms. A **household** consists of either an individual or a group of people (typically a family) who share their income. A **firm** is an organization or business that produces goods or services for sale—and that employs members of households.

As shown in Figure 2-1, there are two kinds of markets in this simple economy. On the left side are markets for goods and services, also known as **product markets,** in which households buy the goods and services they want from firms. This produces a flow of goods and services to households and a return flow of money to firms.

On the right side are **factor markets** in which firms buy the resources they need to produce goods and services. Recall from the preceding module that the factors of production are land, labor, physical capital, and human capital.

The best known factor market is the *labor market,* in which workers are paid for their time and effort. Besides labor, we can think of households as owning the other factors of production as well, and selling them to firms. For example, when a corporation pays dividends to its stockholders, who are members of households, it is in effect paying them for the use of the machines and buildings that belong to those investors.

FIGURE 2-1 The Circular-Flow Diagram

This diagram represents the flows of money and of goods and services in the economy. In the markets for goods and services, households purchase goods and services from firms, generating a flow of money to the firms and a flow of goods and services to the households. The money flows back to households as firms purchase factors of production from the households in factor markets.

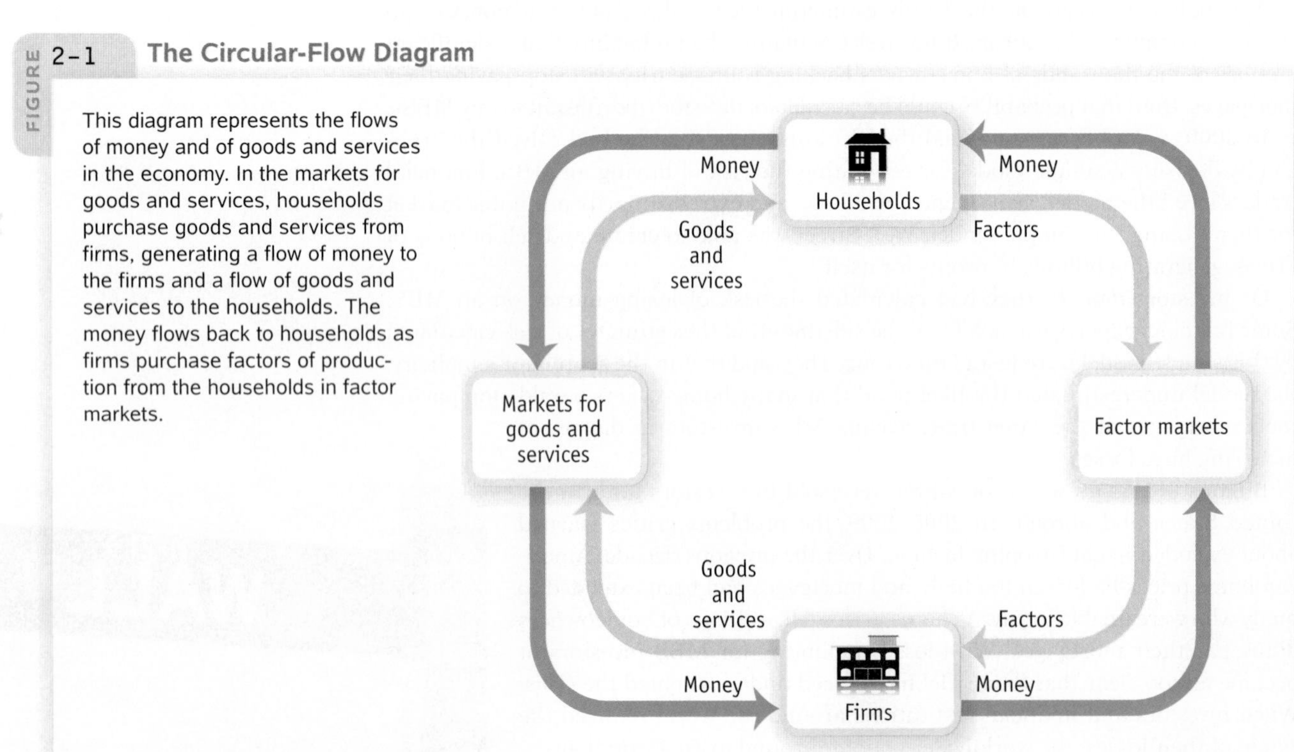

In the interest of simplicity, the circular-flow diagram in Figure 2-1 does not include a number of real-world complications. A few examples:

- In the real world, the distinction between firms and households isn't always that clear-cut. Consider a small, family-run business—a farm, a shop, a small hotel. Is this a firm or a household? A more complete picture would include a separate box for family businesses.
- A more complete picture would include the flows of goods, services, and money within the business sector.
- A more complete picture would include the sale of goods by firms to other firms; for example, steel companies sell mainly to other companies such as auto manufacturers, not to households.
- The diagram doesn't show the government, which takes money out of the circular flow in the form of taxes and injects it back into the flow as spending.

Figure 2-1, in other words, is by no means a complete picture of the economy's participants and the flows that take place among them. But despite its simplicity, the circular-flow diagram is a useful guide to how the economy works and how the participants are interconnected. Next we'll take a closer look at the relationship between individual decision making and broader economic outcomes.

One Person's Spending Is Another Person's Income

The circular-flow diagram shows that what goes around comes around. The circularity of spending magnifies the importance of individual and firm behavior at every level. And it helps to explain why reduced spending by one segment of the economy can lead to problems for almost everyone in the economy.

Consider Wichita, Kansas, known as the "Air Capital of the World" because so many airplanes are made there. In 2010, even as the economy recovered from the recession of 2007–2009, several corporations that had been buying a lot of airplanes decided to cut back on their purchases. These cuts bruised the Wichita economy, and spending dropped off at the city's retail stores. A similar problem occurred at the national level in 2001 and 2008, when cuts in business investment spending fueled a sharp downfall in retail sales.

But why should cuts in spending on airplanes by businesses mean empty stores in the shopping malls? After all, malls are places where families, not businesses, go to shop. The answer is that lower business spending led to lower incomes throughout the economy, because people who had been making those airplanes lost their jobs or were forced to take pay cuts. Between 2008 and 2010, Wichita's aviation industry lost about 13,000 jobs. As incomes evaporated in the aviation industry, so did spending by consumers who worked in the aviation industry. And then incomes and spending in industries supported by aviation workers—retail sales, day care, home construction, and so on—fell, and the domino effect of falling consumption and falling incomes continued.

This story illustrates a general principle: *One person's spending is another person's income.* In a market economy, people make a living selling things—including their labor—to other people. If some group in the economy decides, for whatever reason, to spend more, the income of other groups will rise. If some group decides to spend less, the income of other groups will fall.

© INSADCO Photography/Alamy

If one group in the economy spends more, the income of other groups will rise.

istockphoto/thinkstock

If one group spends less, the income of other groups will fall.

Because one person's spending is another person's income, a chain reaction of changes in spending behavior occurs. Spending cuts lead to reduced family incomes; families respond by reducing consumer spending, which leads to reductions in hiring by firms, and another round of income cuts; and so on.

Through these repercussions, individual and firm decisions send ripple effects throughout the economy. Keep in mind that behavior on the micro level can have macro consequences.

MODULE 2 Review

Solutions appear at the back of the book.

Check Your Understanding

1. Use the circular-flow diagram to explain how an increase in the amount of money spent by households results in an increase in the number of jobs in the economy.

2. Oil companies are investing heavily in projects that will extract oil from the "oil sands" of Canada. Near these projects, in Edmonton, Alberta, restaurants and other consumer businesses are booming. Explain why on the basis of a principle you learned about in this module.

Multiple-Choice Questions

1. The other things equal assumption allows economists to
   a. avoid making assumptions about reality.
   b. focus on the effects of only one change at a time.
   c. oversimplify.
   d. allow nothing to change in their model.
   e. reflect all aspects of the real world in their model.

2. Which of the following is true? The simple circular-flow diagram
   I. includes only the product markets.
   II. includes only the factor markets.
   III. is a simplified representation of the macroeconomy.
   a. I only
   b. II only
   c. III only
   d. I and III only
   e. none of the above

3. A firm is necessarily
   a. an employer of lawyers or accountants.
   b. a service provider.
   c. an organization.
   d. a corporation or business.
   e. a manufacturer of goods.

4. In the United States, we can think of the factors of production as being owned by
   a. firms.
   b. the government.
   c. factor markets.
   d. households.
   e. economists.

5. Economists are drawn to models by their
   a. good looks.
   b. realism.
   c. high level of detail.
   d. snap-on parts.
   e. simplicity.

Critical-Thinking Question

The inhabitants of the fictional economy of Atlantis use money in the form of cowry shells. Draw a circular-flow diagram showing households and firms. Firms produce potatoes and fish, and households buy potatoes and fish. Households also provide the land and labor to firms. Identify where, within the flows of cowry shells, goods and services, or resources, each of the following impacts would occur. Describe how this impact spreads around the circle.

a. A devastating hurricane floods many of the potato fields.

b. A productive fishing season yields an especially large number of fish.

c. The inhabitants of Atlantis discover the music of singer Beyoncé and spend several days a month at dancing festivals.

The Production Possibility Frontier Model

UPI/Alan Marts/Boeing/Landov

WHAT YOU WILL LEARN

1. The importance of trade-offs in economic analysis
2. What the production possibility frontier model tells us about efficiency, opportunity cost, and economic growth
3. The two sources of economic growth—increases in the availability of resources and improvements in technology

On December 15, 2009, Boeing's newest jet, the 787 Dreamliner, took its first three-hour test flight. It was a historic moment: the Dreamliner was the result of an aerodynamic revolution—a superefficient airplane designed to cut airline operating costs and the first to use superlight composite materials. The jet underwent over 15,000 hours of wind tunnel tests that resulted in subtle design changes to improve its performance. Boeing engineers owe an enormous debt to the Wright brothers' wind tunnel, which they used to model actual aircraft in flight. It made modern airplanes, including the Dreamliner, possible.

A good economic model can be a tremendous aid to understanding. In this module, we look at the *production possibility frontier,* a model that helps economists think about the *trade-offs* every economy faces. The production possibility frontier helps us understand three important aspects of the real economy: efficiency, opportunity cost, and economic growth.

Trade-offs: The Production Possibility Frontier

One of the important principles of economics we introduced in Module 1 was that resources are scarce. As a result, any economy—whether it contains one person or millions of people—faces trade-offs. You make a **trade-off** when you give up something in order to have something else. No matter how lightweight the Boeing Dreamliner is, and no matter how efficient Boeing's assembly line, producing Dreamliners means using resources that therefore can't be used to produce something else.

To think about the trade-offs necessary in any economy, economists often use the **production possibility frontier** model. The idea behind this model is to improve our

You make a **trade-off** when you give up something in order to have something else.

The **production possibility frontier (PPF)** illustrates the trade-offs facing an economy that produces only two goods. It shows the maximum quantity of one good that can be produced for each possible quantity of the other good produced.

understanding of trade-offs by considering a simplified economy that produces only two goods. This simplification enables us to show the trade-offs graphically.

Suppose, for a moment, that the United States was a one-company economy, with Boeing its sole employer and aircraft its only product. But there would still be a choice of what kinds of aircraft to produce—say, Dreamliners versus small commuter jets.

Figure 3-1 shows a hypothetical production possibility curve representing the trade-off this one-company economy would face. The curve—the dark-blue line in the diagram—shows the maximum quantity of small jets that Boeing can produce per year *given* the quantity of Dreamliners it produces per year, and vice versa. That is, it answers questions of the form, "What is the maximum quantity of small jets that Boeing can produce in a year if it also produces Dreamliners that year?"

There is a crucial distinction between points *inside* or *on* the production possibility curve (the shaded area) and *outside* the curve. If a production point lies inside or on the curve—like point *C*, at which Boeing produces 20 small jets and 9 Dreamliners in a year—it is feasible. After all, the curve tells us that if Boeing produces 20 small jets, it could also produce a maximum of 15 Dreamliners that year, so it could certainly make 9 Dreamliners. However, a production point that lies outside the curve—such as the hypothetical production point *D*, where Boeing produces 40 small jets and 30 Dreamliners—isn't feasible.

In Figure 3-1 the production possibility curve intersects the horizontal axis at 40 small jets. This means that if Boeing dedicated all its production capacity to making only small jets, it could produce 40 small jets per year. The production possibility curve intersects the vertical axis at 30 Dreamliners. This means that if Boeing dedicated all its production capacity to making Dreamliners, it could produce a maximum of 30 Dreamliners per year.

The figure also shows less extreme trade-offs. For example, if Boeing's managers decide to make 20 small jets this year, they can produce at most 15 Dreamliners; this production choice is illustrated by point *A*. And if Boeing's managers decide to produce 28 small jets, they can make at most 9 Dreamliners, as shown by point *B*.

Thinking in terms of a production possibility frontier simplifies the complexities of reality. The real-world U.S. economy produces millions of different goods. Even Boeing produces more than two different types of planes. Yet it's important to realize that even in its simplicity, this stripped-down model gives us important insights about the real world.

By simplifying reality, the production possibility frontier helps us understand some aspects of the real economy better than we could without the model: efficiency, opportunity cost, and economic growth.

FIGURE 3-1 **The Production Possibility Frontier**

The production possibility frontier illustrates the trade-offs Boeing faces in producing Dreamliners and small jets. It shows the maximum quantity of one good that can be produced given the quantity of the other good produced. Here, the maximum quantity of Dreamliners manufactured per year depends on the quantity of small jets manufactured that year, and vice versa. Boeing's feasible production is shown by the area *inside* or *on* the curve. Production at point *C* is feasible but not efficient. Points *A* and *B* are feasible and efficient in production, but point *D* is not feasible.

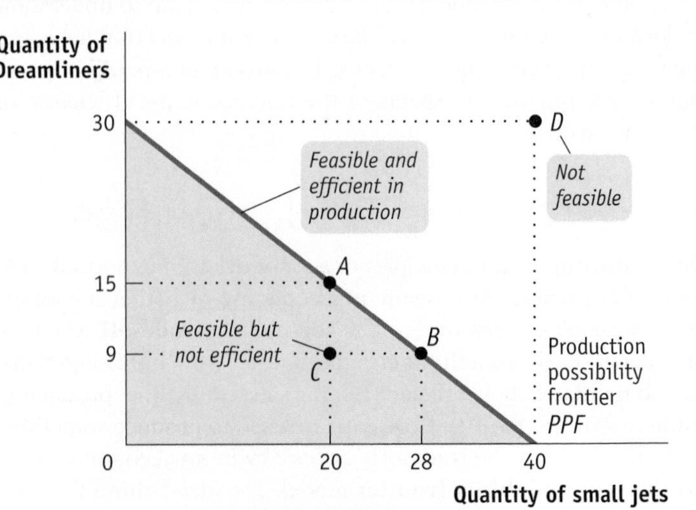

Efficiency

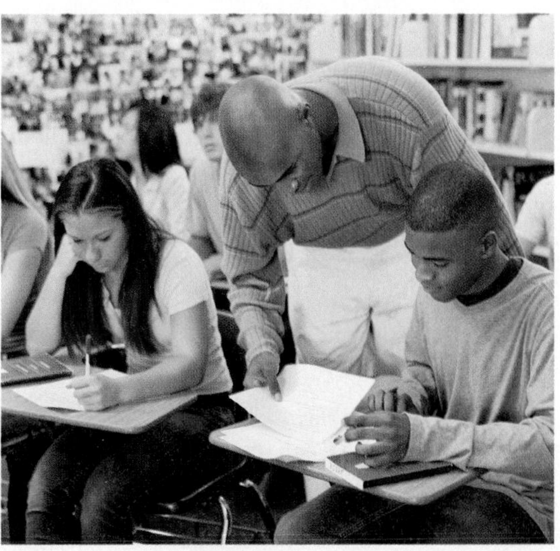
Alamy RF

Crowded classrooms reflect inefficiency if switching to a larger space would make some students better off without making anyone worse off.

The production possibility frontier is useful for illustrating the general economic concept of efficiency. An economy is **efficient** if there are no missed opportunities—meaning that there is no way to make some people better off without making other people worse off. For example, suppose a course you are taking meets in a lecture hall or classroom that is too small for the number of students—some may be forced to sit on the floor or stand—despite the fact that a larger space nearby is empty during the same period. Economists would say that this is an *inefficient* use of resources because there is a way to make some people better off without making anyone worse off—after all, the larger space is empty. The school is not using its resources efficiently.

When an economy is using all of its resources efficiently, the only way one person can be made better off is by rearranging the use of resources in such a way that the change makes someone else worse off. So in our classroom example, if all larger classrooms or lecture halls were already fully occupied, we could say that the school was run in an efficient way; your classmates could be made better off only by making people in the larger classroom worse off—by moving them to the room that is too small.

Returning to our Boeing example, as long as Boeing operates on its production possibility curve, its production is efficient. At point *A,* 15 Dreamliners are the maximum quantity feasible given that Boeing has also committed to producing 20 small jets; at point *B,* 9 Dreamliners are the maximum number that can be made given the choice to produce 28 small jets; and so on.

But suppose for some reason that Boeing was operating at point *C,* making 20 small jets and 9 Dreamliners. In this case, it would not be operating efficiently and would therefore be *inefficient:* it could be producing more of both planes.

Another example of inefficiency in production occurs when people in an economy are involuntarily unemployed: they want to work but are unable to find jobs. When that happens, the economy is not efficient in production because it could produce more output if those people were employed. The production possibility frontier shows the amount that can *possibly* be produced if all resources are fully employed. In other words, changes in unemployment move the economy closer to, or further away from, the PPF. But the curve itself is determined by what would be possible if there were full employment in the economy. Greater unemployment is represented by points farther below the PPF—the economy is not reaching its possibilities if it is not using all of its resources. Lower unemployment is represented by points closer to the PPF—as unemployment decreases, the economy moves closer to reaching its possibilities.

Although the production possibility frontier helps clarify what it means for an economy to be efficient in production, it's important to understand that efficiency in production is only *part* of what's required for the economy as a whole to be efficient. Efficiency also requires that the economy allocate its resources so that consumers are as well off as possible. If an economy does this, we say that it is *efficient in allocation*.

To see why efficiency in allocation is as important as efficiency in production, notice that points *A* and *B* in Figure 3-1 both represent situations in which the economy is efficient in production, because in each case it can't produce more of one good without producing less of the other. But these two situations may not be equally desirable. It may be more desirable to have more small jets and fewer Dreamliners than at point *A;* such as 28 small jets and 9 Dreamliners, corresponding to point *B.* In this case, point *A* is inefficient from the point of view of the economy as a whole: it is possible to move from point *A* to point *B,* and have some be made better off without making anyone else worse off.

This example shows that efficiency for the economy as a whole requires *both* efficiency in production and efficiency in allocation. To be efficient, an economy must produce as much of each good as it can, given the production of other goods, and it must also produce the mix of goods that people want to consume.

An economy is **efficient** if there is no way to make anyone better off without making anyone else worse off.

Opportunity Cost

The production possibility frontier is also useful as a reminder that the true cost of any good isn't the money it costs to buy, but what must be given up in order to get that good—the *opportunity cost.* If, for example, Boeing decides to change its production from point *A* to point *B*, it will produce 8 more small jets but 6 fewer Dreamliners. So the opportunity cost of 8 small jets is 6 Dreamliners—the 6 Dreamliners that can't be produced if Boeing produces 8 more small jets. This means that each small jet has an opportunity cost of 6/8 = 3/4 of a Dreamliner.

If Boeing decides to produce more small jets, the opportunity cost is the Dreamliners it must forego producing.

Is the opportunity cost of an extra small jet in terms of Dreamliners always the same, no matter how many small jets and Dreamliners are currently produced? In the example illustrated by Figure 3-1, the answer is yes. If Boeing increases its production of small jets from 28 to 40, the number of Dreamliners it produces falls from 9 to zero. So Boeing's opportunity cost per additional small jet is 9/12 = 3/4 of a Dreamliner, the same as it was when Boeing went from 20 small jets produced to 28. The fact that the opportunity cost is always the same number—3/4 in this case—is just one possible assumption we could make in this case. Anytime we make the assumption that the opportunity cost of an additional unit of a good doesn't change regardless of the output mix, the production possibilities curve is drawn as a straight line, as it is in Figure 3-1.

Moreover, as you might have already guessed, the slope of a straight-line production possibility curve is equal to the opportunity cost—specifically, the opportunity cost for the good measured on the horizontal axis in terms of the good measured on the vertical axis. In Figure 3-1, the production possibility curve has a *constant slope* of −3/4, implying that Boeing faces a *constant opportunity cost* for 1 small jet equal to 3/4 of a Dreamliner. (A review of how to calculate the slope of a straight line is found in Appendix A at the back of the book.) This is the simplest case, but the production possibility frontier model can also be used to examine situations in which opportunity costs change as the mix of output changes.

Figure 3-2 illustrates a different assumption, a case in which Boeing faces *increasing opportunity cost*. Here, the more small jets it produces, the more costly it is to

FIGURE 3-2 **Increasing Opportunity Cost**

The bowed-out shape of the production possibility frontier reflects increasing opportunity cost. In this example, to produce the first 20 small jets, Boeing must give up producing 5 Dreamliners. But to produce an additional 20 small jets, Boeing must give up manufacturing 25 more Dreamliners.

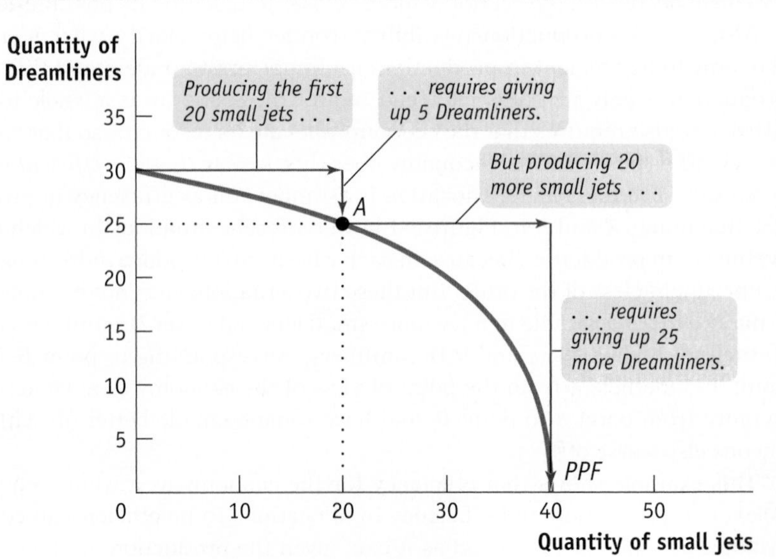

produce yet another small jet in terms of reduced production of a Dreamliner. For example, to go from producing zero small jets to producing 20, Boeing has to give up producing 5 Dreamliners. That is, the opportunity cost of those 20 small jets is 5 Dreamliners. But to increase its production of small jets to 40—that is, to produce an additional 20 small jets—it must produce 25 fewer Dreamliners, a much higher opportunity cost. And the same holds true in reverse: the more Dreamliners Boeing produces, the more costly it is to produce yet another Dreamliner in terms of reduced production of small jets. As you can see in Figure 3-2, when opportunity costs are increasing rather than constant, the production possibility curve is bowed outward rather than a straight line.

Although it's often useful to work with the simple assumption that the production possibility curve is a straight line, economists believe that in reality, opportunity costs are typically increasing. When only a small amount of a good is produced, the opportunity cost of producing that good is relatively low because the economy needs to use only those resources that are especially well suited for its production. For example, if an economy grows only a small amount of corn, that corn can be grown in places where the soil and climate are perfect for growing corn but less suitable for growing anything else, such as wheat.

So growing that corn involves giving up only a small amount of potential wheat output. Once the economy grows a lot of corn, however, land that is well suited for wheat but isn't so great for corn must be used to produce corn anyway. As a result, the additional corn production involves sacrificing considerably more wheat production. In other words, as more of a good is produced, its opportunity cost typically rises because well-suited inputs are used up and less adaptable inputs must be used instead.

Economic Growth

Finally, the production possibility frontier helps us understand what it means to talk about *economic growth,* which economists describe as creating *a sustained rise in aggregate output.* Economic growth is one of the fundamental features of the economy. But are we really justified in saying that the economy has grown over time? After all, although the U.S. economy produces more of many things than it did a century ago, it produces less of other things—for example, horse-drawn carriages. In other words, production of many goods is actually down. So how can we say for sure that the economy as a whole has grown?

The answer, illustrated in Figure 3-3, is that economic growth means an *expansion of the economy's production possibilities:* the economy *can* produce more of everything. In it, we assume again that our economy is only made up of Boeing, and therefore, our economy only produces two goods, Dreamliners and small jets. For example, if Boeing's production is initially at point *A* (20 small jets and 25 Dreamliners) economic growth means that Boeing could move to point *E* (25 small jets and 30 Dreamliners). Point *E* lies outside the original curve, so in the production possibility frontier model, growth is shown as an outward shift of the curve.

What can lead the production possibility curve to shift outward? There are basically

FIGURE 3-3 Economic Growth

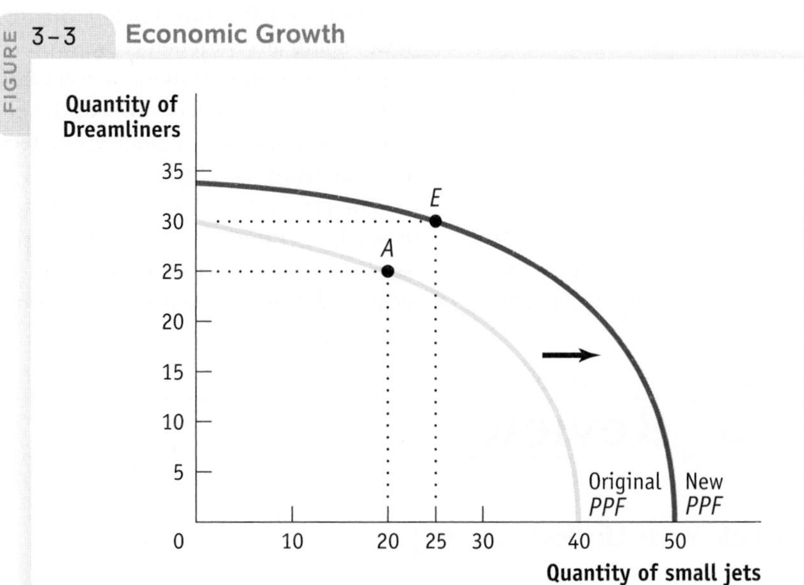

Economic growth results in an *outward shift* of the production possibility curve because production possibilities are expanded. The economy can now produce more of everything. For example, if production is initially at point *A* (25 Dreamliners and 20 small jets), economic growth means that the economy could move to point *E* (30 Dreamliners and 25 small jets).

iStockphoto

Comstock/Thinkstock

iStockphoto/Thinkstock

iStockphoto/Thinkstock

The four factors of production: land, labor, physical capital, and human capital.

two sources of economic growth. One is an increase in the economy's **factors of production,** the resources used to produce goods and services. Broadly speaking, the main factors of production are the resources land, labor, physical capital, and human capital. As you learned in Module 1, land is a resource supplied by nature; labor is the economy's pool of workers; physical capital refers to created resources such as machines and buildings; and human capital refers to the educational achievements and skills of the labor force, which enhance its productivity.

To see how adding to an economy's factors of production leads to economic growth, suppose that Boeing builds another construction hangar that allows it to increase the number of planes—small jets or Dreamliners or both—it can produce in a year. The new construction hangar is a factor of production, a resource Boeing can use to increase its yearly output. We can't say how many more planes of each type Boeing will produce; that's a management decision that will depend on, among other things, customer demand. But we can say that Boeing's production possibility curve has shifted outward because it can now produce more small jets without reducing the number of Dreamliners it makes, or it can make more Dreamliners without reducing the number of small jets produced.

The other source of economic growth is progress in **technology,** the technical means for the production of goods and services. Composite materials had been used in some parts of aircraft before the Boeing Dreamliner was developed. But Boeing engineers realized that there were large additional advantages to building a whole plane out of composites. The plane would be lighter, stronger, and have better aerodynamics than a plane built in the traditional way. It would therefore have longer range, be able to carry more people, and use less fuel, in addition to being able to maintain higher cabin pressure. So in a real sense Boeing's innovation—a whole plane built out of composites—was a way to do more with any given amount of resources, pushing out the production possibility curve.

But even if, for some reason, Boeing chooses to produce either fewer Dreamliners or fewer small jets than before, we would still say that this economy has grown, because it *could* have produced more of everything. At the same time, if an economy's production possibility curve shifts inward, the economy has become smaller. This could happen if the economy loses resources or technology (for example, if it experiences war or a natural disaster).

Factors of production are resources used to produce goods and services.

Technology is the technical means for producing goods and services.

The production possibility frontier is a very simplified model of an economy. Yet it teaches us important lessons about real-world economies. It gives us our first clear sense of what constitutes economic efficiency, it illustrates the concept of opportunity cost, and it makes clear what economic growth is all about.

MODULE 3 Review

Solutions appear at the back of the book.

Check Your Understanding

1. True or false? Explain your answer.
   a. An increase in the amount of resources available to Boeing for use in producing Dreamliners and small jets does not change its production possibility curve.
   b. A technological change that allows Boeing to build more small jets for any amount of Dreamliners built results in a change in its production possibility curve.
   c. The production possibility frontier is useful because it illustrates how much of one good an economy must give up to get more of another good regardless of whether resources are being used efficiently.

Multiple-Choice Questions

Refer to the accompanying graph to answer the following questions.

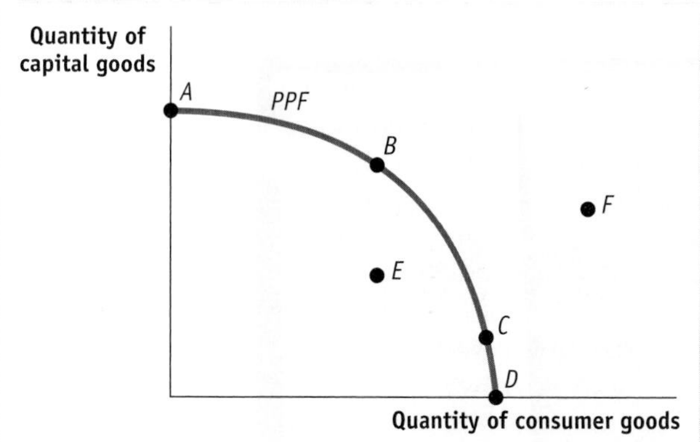

1. Which point(s) on the graph represent efficiency in production?
   a. *B* and *C*
   b. *A* and *D*
   c. *A, B, C,* and *D*
   d. *A, B, C, D,* and *E*
   e. *A, B, C, D, E,* and *F*

2. For this economy, an increase in the quantity of capital goods produced without a corresponding decrease in the quantity of consumer goods produced
   a. cannot happen because there is always an opportunity cost.
   b. is represented by a movement from point *E* to point *A*.
   c. is represented by a movement from point *C* to point *B*.
   d. is represented by a movement from point *E* to point *B*.
   e. is only possible with an increase in resources or technology.

3. An increase in unemployment could be represented by a movement from point
   a. *D* to point *C*.
   b. *B* to point *A*.
   c. *C* to point *F*.
   d. *B* to point *E*.
   e. *E* to point *B*.

4. Which of the following might allow this economy to move from point *B* to point *F*?
   a. more workers
   b. discovery of new resources
   c. building new factories
   d. technological advances
   e. all of the above

5. This production possibility curve shows the trade-off between consumer goods and capital goods. Since capital goods are a resource, an increase in the production of capital goods today will increase the economy's production possibilities in the future. Therefore, all other things being equal, producing at which point today will result in the largest outward shift of the PPF in the future?
   a. *A*
   b. *B*
   c. *C*
   d. *D*
   e. *E*

Critical-Thinking Questions

Assume that an economy can choose between producing food and producing shelter at a constant opportunity cost. Graph a correctly labeled production possibility curve for the economy. On your graph:

1. Use the letter *E* to label one of the points that is efficient in production.
2. Use the letter *U* to label one of the points at which there might be unemployment.
3. Use the letter *I* to label one of the points that is not feasible.

2. For Country A, the opportunity cost of a bushel of wheat is
   - a. ½ units of textiles
   - b. ⅔ units of textiles
   - c. 1⅓ units of textiles
   - d. 1½ units of textiles
   - e. 2 units of textiles

3. Use the graph to determine which country has a comparative advantage in producing each good.

	Comparative advantage in wheat production	*Comparative advantage in textile production*
a.	Country A	Country B
b.	Country A	Country A
c.	Country B	Country A
d.	Country B	Country B
e.	Country A	Neither Country

4. If the two countries specialize and trade, which of the choices below describes the countries' imports?

	Import Wheat	*Import Textiles*
a.	Country A	Country A
b.	Country A	Country B
c.	Country B	Country B
d.	Country B	Country A
e.	Neither Country	Country B

5. What is the highest price Country B is willing to pay to buy wheat from Country A?
   - a. ½ unit of textiles
   - b. ⅔ unit of textiles
   - c. 1 unit of textiles
   - d. 1½ units of textiles
   - e. 2 units of textiles

Critical-Thinking Questions

Refer to the table below to answer the following questions. These two countries are producing textiles and wheat using equal amounts of resources.

	Weekly output per worker	
	Country A	Country B
Bushels of Wheat	15	10
Units of Textiles	60	60

1. What is the opportunity cost of producing a bushel of wheat for each country?
2. Which country has the absolute advantage in wheat production?
3. Which country has the comparative advantage in textile production? Explain.

PITFALLS

? Back in the 1980s, when the U.S. economy seemed to be lagging behind that of Japan, one often heard commentators warn that if we didn't improve our productivity, we would soon have no comparative advantage in anything. What is wrong with this statement?

> IT IS INACCURATE; THOSE COMMENTATORS MISUNDERSTOOD COMPARATIVE ADVANTAGE. It happens all the time. Students, pundits, and politicians confuse *comparative* advantage with *absolute* advantage. What the commentators meant was that we would have no *absolute* advantage in anything—that there might come a time when the Japanese were able to produce more goods in an absolute sense than we were. (It didn't turn out that way, but that's another story.) And they had the idea that in that case we would no longer be able to benefit from trade with Japan.

A country has an absolute advantage in producing a good or service if the country can produce more output per worker than other countries. Likewise, an individual has an absolute advantage in producing a good or service if he or she is better at producing it than other people. Having an absolute advantage is not the same thing as having a comparative advantage.

Just as Brazil, in our example, is able to benefit from trade with the United States (and vice versa) despite the fact that the United States may be able to produce absolutely more goods than Brazil, in the real world, nations will still gain from trade even if they are less productive in all industries than the countries with whom they trade.

Review the section "Comparative Advantage and International Trade, in Reality" on page 27, and Figure 4-2 on page 25, to learn more.

BUSINESS CASE: Efficiency, Opportunity Cost, and the Logic of Lean Production

WORLD VIEW

Corbis/Photolibrary

In the summer and fall of 2010, workers were rearranging the furniture in Boeing's final assembly plant in Everett, Washington, in preparation for the production of the Boeing 767. It was a difficult and time-consuming process, however, because the items of "furniture"—Boeing's assembly equipment—weighed on the order of 200 tons each. It was a necessary part of setting up a production system based on "lean manufacturing," also called "just-in-time" production. Lean manufacturing, pioneered by Toyota Motors of Japan, is based on the practice of having parts arrive on the factory floor just as they are needed for production. This reduces the amount of parts Boeing holds in inventory as well as the amount of the factory floor needed for production—in this case, reducing the square footage required for manufacture of the 767 by 40%.

Boeing had adopted lean manufacturing in 1999 in the manufacture of the 737, the most popular commercial airplane. By 2005, after constant refinement, Boeing had achieved a 50% reduction in the time it takes to produce a plane and a nearly 60% reduction in parts inventory. An important feature is a continuously moving assembly line, moving products from one assembly team to the next at a steady pace and eliminating the need for workers to wander across the factory floor from task to task or in search of tools and parts.

Toyota's lean production techniques have been the most widely adopted of all manufacturing techniques and have revolutionized manufacturing worldwide. In simple terms, lean production is focused on organization and communication. Workers and parts are organized so as to ensure a smooth and consistent workflow that minimizes wasted effort and materials. Lean production is also designed to be highly responsive to changes in the desired mix of output—for example, quickly producing more sedans and fewer minivans according to changes in customers' demands.

Toyota's lean production methods were so successful that they transformed the global auto industry and severely threatened once-dominant American automakers. Until the 1980s, the "Big Three"—Chrysler, Ford, and General Motors—dominated the American auto industry, with virtually no foreign-made cars sold in the United States. In the 1980s, however, Toyotas became increasingly popular in the United States due to their high quality and relatively low price—so popular that the Big Three eventually prevailed upon the U.S. government to protect them by restricting the sale of Japanese autos in the United States. Over time, Toyota responded by building assembly plants in the United States, bringing along its lean production techniques, which then spread throughout American manufacturing.

Questions for Thought

1. What is the opportunity cost associated with having a worker wander across the factory floor from task to task or in search of tools and parts?
2. How does lean manufacturing improve the economy's efficiency in allocation?
3. How will the shift in location of Toyota's production from Japan to the United States alter the pattern of comparative advantage in automaking between the two countries?

SECTION 1 REVIEW

Summary

The Study of Economics

1. Everyone has to make choices about what to do and what *not* to do. **Individual choice** is the basis of **economics**—if it doesn't involve choice, it isn't economics. The **economy** is a system that coordinates choices about production and consumption. In a **market economy,** these choices are made by many firms and individuals.
2. The reason choices must be made is that **resources**—anything that can be used to produce something else—are **scarce.** The four categories of resources are **land, labor, physical capital,** and **human capital.** Individuals are limited in their choices by money and time; economies are limited by their supplies of resources.
3. Because you must choose among limited alternatives, the true cost of anything is what you must give up to get it—all costs are **opportunity costs.**
4. Economists use economic models for both **positive economics,** which describes how the economy works, and for **normative economics,** which prescribes how the economy *should* work. Positive economics often involves making forecasts. Economics can determine correct answers for positive questions, but typically not for normative questions, which involve value judgments. Exceptions occur when policies designed to achieve a certain prescription can be clearly ranked in terms of efficiency.
5. There are two main reasons economists disagree. One, they may disagree about which simplifications to make in a model. Two, economists may disagree—like everyone else—about values.
6. **Microeconomics** is the branch of economics that studies how people make decisions and how those decisions interact. **Macroeconomics** is concerned with the overall ups and downs of the economy, and focuses on **economic aggregates** such as the unemployment rate and gross domestic product, that summarize data across many different markets.

Models and the Circular Flow

7. Almost all economics is based on **models,** "thought experiments" or simplified versions of reality, many of which use analytical tools such as mathematics and graphs. An important assumption in economic models is the **other things equal (*ceteris paribus*) assumption,** which allows analysis of the effect of change in one factor by holding all other relevant factors unchanged.
8. In the simplest economies, people trade goods and services for one another rather than trade them for money, as in a modern economy. The **circular-flow diagram** represents transactions within the economy as flows of goods, services, and money between **households** and **firms.** These transactions occur in **markets for goods and services** and **factor markets,** markets for **factors of production**—land, labor, physical capital, and human capital. It is useful in understanding how spending, production, employment, income, and growth are related in the economy.

The Production Possibility Frontier

9. One important economic model is the **production possibility frontier,** which illustrates the **trade-offs** facing an economy that produces only two goods. The PPF illustrates three elements: opportunity cost (showing how much less of one good must be produced if more of the other good is produced), **efficiency** (an economy is efficient in production if it produces on the production possibility curve and efficient in allocation if it produces the mix of goods and services that people want to consume), and economic growth (an outward shift of the production possibility curve).
10. There are two basic sources of growth in the production possibility frontier model: an increase in resources and improved **technology.**

Comparative Advantage and Trade

11. There are **gains from trade:** by engaging in the **trade** of goods and services with one another, the members of an economy can all be made better off. Underlying gains from trade are the advantages of **specialization,** of having individuals engage in the tasks they are comparatively good at.
12. **Comparative advantage** explains the source of gains from trade between individuals and countries. Everyone has a comparative advantage in something—some good or service in which that person has a lower opportunity cost than everyone else. But it is often confused with **absolute advantage,** an ability to produce more of a particular good or service than anyone else. This confusion leads some to erroneously conclude that there are no gains from trade between people or countries.

Key Terms

Economics, p. 2
Individual choice, p. 2
Economy, p. 2
Market economy, p. 2
Resource, p. 3
Land, p. 3
Labor, p. 3
Physical capital, p. 3
Human capital, p. 3
Scarce, p. 3
Opportunity cost, p. 3
Microeconomics, p. 5
Macroeconomics, p. 5
Economic aggregates, p. 5
Positive economics, p. 6
Normative economics, p. 6
Model, p. 10
Other things equal assumption, p. 10
Circular-flow diagram, p. 12
Household, p. 12
Firm, p. 12
Product markets, p. 12
Factor markets, p. 12
Trade-off, p. 15
Production possibility frontier (PPF), p. 15
Efficient, p. 17
Factors of production, p. 20
Technology, p. 20
Trade, p. 22
Gains from trade, p. 22
Specialization, p. 22
Comparative advantage, p. 25
Absolute advantage, p. 26

Problems

1. Imagine a firm that manufactures textiles (pants and shirts). List the four categories of resources, and for each category, give an example of a specific resource that the firm might use to manufacture textiles.

2. Describe some of the opportunity costs of the following choices.

a. Attend college instead of taking a job.

b. Watch a movie instead of studying for an exam.

c. Ride the bus instead of driving your car.

3. Use the concept of opportunity cost to explain the following situations.

a. More people choose to get graduate degrees when the job market is poor.

b. More people choose to do their own home repairs when the economy is slow and hourly wages are down.

c. There are more parks in suburban areas than in urban areas.

d. Convenience stores, which have higher prices than supermarkets, cater to busy people.

4. A representative of the U.S. clothing industry recently made this statement: "Workers in Asia often work in sweatshop conditions earning only pennies an hour. American workers are more productive and, as a result, earn higher wages. In order to preserve the dignity of the American workplace, the government should enact legislation banning imports of low-wage Asian clothing."

a. Which parts of this quotation are positive statements? Which parts are normative statements?

b. Is the policy that is being advocated consistent with the statement about the wages and productivities of American and Asian workers?

c. Would such a policy make some Americans better off without making any other Americans worse off? That is, would this policy be efficient from the viewpoint of all Americans?

d. Would low-wage Asian workers benefit from or be hurt by such a policy?

5. Are the following statements true or false? Explain your answers.

a. "When people must pay higher taxes on their wage earnings, it reduces their incentive to work" is a positive statement.

b. "We should lower taxes to encourage more work" is a positive statement.

c. Economics cannot always be used to determine what society ought to do.

d. "The system of public education in this country generates greater benefits to society than the cost of running the system" is a normative statement.

e. All disagreements among economists are generated by the media.

6. Evaluate this statement: "It is easier to build an economic model that accurately reflects events that have already occurred than to build an economic model to forecast future events." Do you think that this is true or not? Why? What does this imply about the difficulties of building good economic models?

7. An economist might say that colleges and universities "produce" education, using faculty members and students as inputs. According to this line of reasoning, education is then "consumed" by households.

a. Construct a circular-flow diagram to represent the sector of the economy devoted to college education: colleges and universities represent firms, and households both consume education and provide faculty and students to universities. What are the relevant markets in this diagram? What is being bought and sold in each direction?

b. Now suppose that the government decided to subsidize 50% of all college students' tuition. How would this affect the circular-flow diagram that you created in part a?

8. Suppose Atlantis is a small, isolated island in the South Atlantic. The inhabitants grow potatoes and catch fish. The accompanying table shows the maximum annual output combinations of potatoes and fish that can be produced. Obviously, given their limited resources and available technology, as they use more of their resources for potato production, there are fewer resources available for catching fish.

Maximum annual output options	Quantity of potatoes (pounds)	Quantity of fish (pounds)
A	1,000	0
B	800	300
C	600	500
D	400	600
E	200	650
F	0	675

a. Draw a production possibility curve with potatoes on the horizontal axis and fish on the vertical axis, and illustrate these options, showing points *A–F.*

b. Can Atlantis produce 500 pounds of fish and 800 pounds of potatoes? Explain. Where would this point lie relative to the production possibility curve?

c. What is the opportunity cost of increasing the annual output of potatoes from 600 to 800 pounds?

d. What is the opportunity cost of increasing the annual output of potatoes from 200 to 400 pounds?

e. Explain why the answers to parts c and d are not the same. What does this imply about the slope of the production possibility curve?

9. Two important industries on the island of Bermuda are fishing and tourism. According to data from the World Resources Institute and the Bermuda Department of Statistics, in the year 2009 the 306 registered fishermen in Bermuda caught 387 metric tons of marine fish. And the 2,719 people employed by hotels produced 554,400 hotel stays (measured by the number of visitor arrivals). Suppose that this production point is efficient in production. Assume also that the opportunity cost of one additional metric ton of fish is 2,000 hotel stays and that this opportunity cost is constant (the opportunity cost does not change).

a. If all 306 registered fishermen were to be employed by hotels (in addition to the 2,719 people already working in hotels), how many hotel stays could Bermuda produce?

b. If all 2,719 hotel employees were to become fishermen (in addition to the 306 fishermen already working in the fishing industry), how many metric tons of fish could Bermuda produce?

c. Draw a production possibility curve for Bermuda, with fish on the horizontal axis and hotel stays on the vertical axis, and label Bermuda's actual production point for the year 2009.

10. In the ancient country of Roma, only two goods, spaghetti and meatballs, are produced. There are two tribes in Roma, the Tivoli and the Frivoli. By themselves, the Tivoli each month can produce either 30 pounds of spaghetti and no meatballs, or 50 pounds of meatballs and no spaghetti, or any combination in between. The Frivoli, by themselves, each month can produce 40 pounds of spaghetti and no meatballs, or 30 pounds of meatballs and no spaghetti, or any combination in between.

a. Assume that all production possibility curves are straight lines. Draw one diagram showing the monthly production possibility curve for the Tivoli and another showing the monthly production possibility curve for the Frivoli.

b. Which tribe has the comparative advantage in spaghetti production? In meatball production?

In A.D. 100, the Frivoli discovered a new technique for making meatballs that doubled the quantity of meatballs they could produce each month.

c. Draw the new monthly production possibility curve for the Frivoli.

d. After the innovation, which tribe had an absolute advantage in producing meatballs? In producing spaghetti? Which had the comparative advantage in meatball production? In spaghetti production?

11. In recent years, the United States used 124 million acres of land for wheat or corn farming. Of those 124 million acres, farmers used 50 million acres to grow 2.158 billion bushels of wheat, and 74 million acres of land to grow 11.807 billion bushels of corn. Suppose that U.S. wheat and corn farming is efficient in production. At that production point, the opportunity cost of producing one additional bushel of wheat is 1.7 fewer bushels of corn. However, farmers have increasing opportunity costs, so additional bushels of wheat have an opportunity cost greater than 1.7 bushels of corn. For each of the production points described below, decide whether that production point is (i) feasible and efficient in production, (ii) feasible but not efficient in production, (iii) not feasible, or (iv) uncertain as to whether or not it is feasible.

a. From their original production point, farmers use 40 million acres of land to produce 1.8 billion bushels of wheat, and they use 60 million acres of land to produce 9 billion bushels of corn. The remaining 24 million acres are left unused.

b. From their original production point, farmers transfer 40 million acres of land from corn to wheat production. They now produce 3.158 billion bushels of wheat and 10.107 billion bushels of corn.

c. From their original production point, farmers reduce their production of wheat to 2 billion bushels and increase their production of corn to 12.044 billion bushels. Along the production possibility curve, the opportunity cost of going from 11.807 billion bushels of corn to 12.044 billion bushels of corn is 0.666 bushel of wheat per bushel of corn.

12. The Hatfield family lives on the east side of the Hatatoochie River, and the McCoy family lives on the west side. Each family's diet consists of fried chicken and corn-on-the-cob, and each is self-sufficient, raising their own chickens and growing their own corn. Explain the conditions under which each of the following statements would be true.

    a. The two families are made better off when the Hatfields specialize in raising chickens, the McCoys specialize in growing corn, and the two families trade.

    b. The two families are made better off when the McCoys specialize in raising chickens, the Hatfields specialize in growing corn, and the two families trade.

13. According to the U.S. Census Bureau, back in July 2006 the United States exported aircraft worth $1 billion to China and imported aircraft worth only $19,000 from China. During the same month, however, the United States imported $83 million worth of men's trousers, slacks, and jeans from China but exported only $8,000 worth of trousers, slacks, and jeans to China. Using what you have learned about how trade is determined by comparative advantage, answer the following questions.

    a. Which country has the comparative advantage in aircraft production? In production of trousers, slacks, and jeans?

    b. Can you determine which country has the absolute advantage in aircraft production? In production of trousers, slacks, and jeans?

14. Peter Pundit, an economics reporter, states that the European Union (EU) is increasing its productivity very rapidly in all industries. He claims that this productivity advance is so rapid that output from the EU in these industries will soon exceed that of the United States and, as a result, the United States will no longer benefit from trade with the EU.

    a. Do you think Peter Pundit is correct or not? If not, what do you think is the source of his mistake?

    b. If the EU and the United States continue to trade, what do you think will characterize the goods that the EU exports to the United States and the goods that the United States exports to the EU?

Supply and Demand

BLUE JEAN BLUES

If you bought a pair of blue jeans in 2011, you may have been shocked at the price. Or maybe not: fashions change, and maybe you thought you were paying the price for being fashionable. But you weren't—you were paying for cotton. Jeans are made of denim, which is a particular weave of cotton, and by December 2010, the price of a pound of cotton had hit a 140-year high, the highest cotton price since records began in 1870.

And why were cotton prices so high?

On one side, demand for clothing of all kinds was surging. In 2008–2009, as the world struggled with the effects of a financial crisis, nervous consumers cut back on clothing purchases. But by 2010, with the worst apparently over, buyers were back in force. On the supply side, Pakistan, the world's fourth-largest cotton producer, was hit by devastating floods that put one-fifth of the country underwater and virtually destroyed its cotton crop.

Fearing that consumers had limited tolerance for large increases in the price of cotton clothing, apparel makers began scrambling to find ways to reduce costs. They adopted changes like smaller buttons, cheaper linings, and—yes—polyester, doubting that consumers would be willing to pay more for cotton goods. In fact, some experts on the cotton market warned that the sky-high prices of cotton in 2010–2011 might lead to a permanent shift in tastes, with consumers becoming more willing to wear synthetics even when cotton prices came down.

At the same time, it was not all bad news for everyone connected with the cotton trade. In the United States, cotton producers had not been hit by bad weather and were relishing the higher prices. American farmers responded to sky-high cotton prices by sharply increasing the acreage devoted to the crop. None of this was enough, however, to produce immediate price relief.

Wait a minute: how, exactly, does flooding in Pakistan translate into higher jeans prices and more polyester in your T-shirts? It's a matter of supply and demand—but what does that mean? Many people use "supply and demand" as a sort of catchphrase to mean "the laws of the marketplace at work." To economists, however, the concept of supply and demand has a precise meaning: it is a *model of how a market behaves*.

In this section, we lay out the pieces that make up the *supply and demand model*, put them together, and show how this model can be used to understand how many—but not all—markets behave.

MODULE 5 Demand

Thinkstock

WHAT YOU WILL LEARN

1. What a competitive market is and how it is described by the supply and demand model
2. What the demand curve is
3. The difference between movements along the demand curve and changes in demand
4. The factors that shift the demand curve

Supply and Demand: A Model of a Competitive Market

Cotton sellers and cotton buyers constitute a *market*—a group of producers and consumers who exchange a good or service for payment. In this section, we'll focus on a particular type of market known as a *competitive market*. Roughly, a **competitive market** is a market in which there are many buyers and sellers of the same good or service. More precisely, the key feature of a competitive market is that no individual's actions have a noticeable effect on the price at which the good or service is sold. It's important to understand, however, that this is not an accurate description of every market.

For example, it's not an accurate description of the market for cola beverages. That's because in the market for cola beverages, Coca-Cola and Pepsi account for such a large proportion of total sales that they are able to influence the price at which cola beverages are bought and sold. But it *is* an accurate description of the market for cotton. The global marketplace for cotton is so huge that even a jeans maker as large as Levi Strauss & Co. accounts for only a tiny fraction of transactions, making it unable to influence the price at which cotton is bought and sold.

It's a little hard to explain why competitive markets are different from other markets until we've seen how a competitive market works. For now, let's just say that it's easier to model competitive markets than other markets. When taking an exam, it's always a good strategy to begin by answering the easier questions. In this book, we're going to do the same thing. So we will start with competitive markets.

When a market is competitive, its behavior is well described by the **supply and demand model.** Because many markets *are* competitive, the supply and demand model is a very useful one indeed.

A **competitive market** is a market in which there are many buyers and sellers of the same good or service, none of whom can influence the price at which the good or service is sold.

The **supply and demand model** is a model of how a competitive market works.

There are five key elements in this model:

- The *demand curve*
- The *supply curve*
- The set of factors that cause the demand curve to shift and the set of factors that cause the supply curve to shift
- The *market equilibrium,* which includes the *equilibrium price* and *equilibrium quantity*
- The way the market equilibrium changes when the supply curve or demand curve shifts

To explain the supply and demand model, we will examine each of these elements in turn. In this module we begin with demand.

The Demand Curve

How many pounds of cotton, packaged in the form of blue jeans, do consumers around the world want to buy in a given year? You might at first think that we can answer this question by looking at the total number of pairs of blue jeans purchased around the world each day, multiply that number by the amount of cotton it takes to make a pair of jeans, and then multiply by 365. But that's not enough to answer the question, because how many pairs of jeans—in other words, how many pounds of cotton—consumers want to buy depends on the price of a pound of cotton.

When the price of cotton rises, as it did in 2010, some people will respond to the higher price of cotton clothing by buying fewer cotton garments or, perhaps, by switching completely to garments made from other materials, such as synthetics or linen. In general, the quantity of cotton clothing, or of any good or service that people want to buy, depends on the price. The higher the price, the less of the good or service people want to purchase; alternatively, the lower the price, the more they want to purchase.

So the answer to the question "How many pounds of cotton do consumers want to buy?" depends on the price of a pound of cotton. If you don't yet know what the price will be, you can start by making a table of how many pounds of cotton people would want to buy at a number of different prices. Such a table is known as a *demand schedule*. This, in turn, can be used to draw a *demand curve*, which is one of the key elements of the supply and demand model.

The Demand Schedule and the Demand Curve

A **demand schedule** is a table showing how much of a good or service consumers will want to buy at different prices. On the right side of Figure 5-1, we show a hypothetical demand schedule for cotton. It's hypothetical in that it doesn't use actual data on the world demand for cotton and it assumes that all cotton is of equal quality.

According to the table, if a pound of cotton costs $1, consumers around the world will want to purchase 10 billion pounds of cotton over the course of a year. If the price is $1.25 a pound, they will want to buy only 8.9 billion pounds; if the price is only $0.75 a pound, they will want to buy 11.5 billion pounds; and so on. So, the higher the price, the fewer pounds of cotton consumers will want to purchase. In other words, as the price rises, the **quantity demanded** of cotton—the actual amount consumers are willing to buy at some specific price—falls.

The graph in Figure 5-1 is a visual representation of the information in the table. (For a refresher on graphs in economics, see Appendix A at the back of the book.) The vertical axis shows the price of a pound of cotton and the horizontal axis shows the quantity of cotton in pounds. Each point on the graph corresponds to one of the entries in the table. The curve that connects these points is a **demand curve.** A demand curve is a graphical representation of the demand schedule, another way of showing the relationship between the quantity demanded and the price.

A **demand schedule** shows how much of a good or service consumers will want to buy at different prices.

The **quantity demanded** is the actual amount of a good or service consumers are willing to buy at some specific price.

A **demand curve** is a graphical representation of the demand schedule. It shows the relationship between quantity demanded and price.

FIGURE 5-1 The Demand Schedule and the Demand Curve

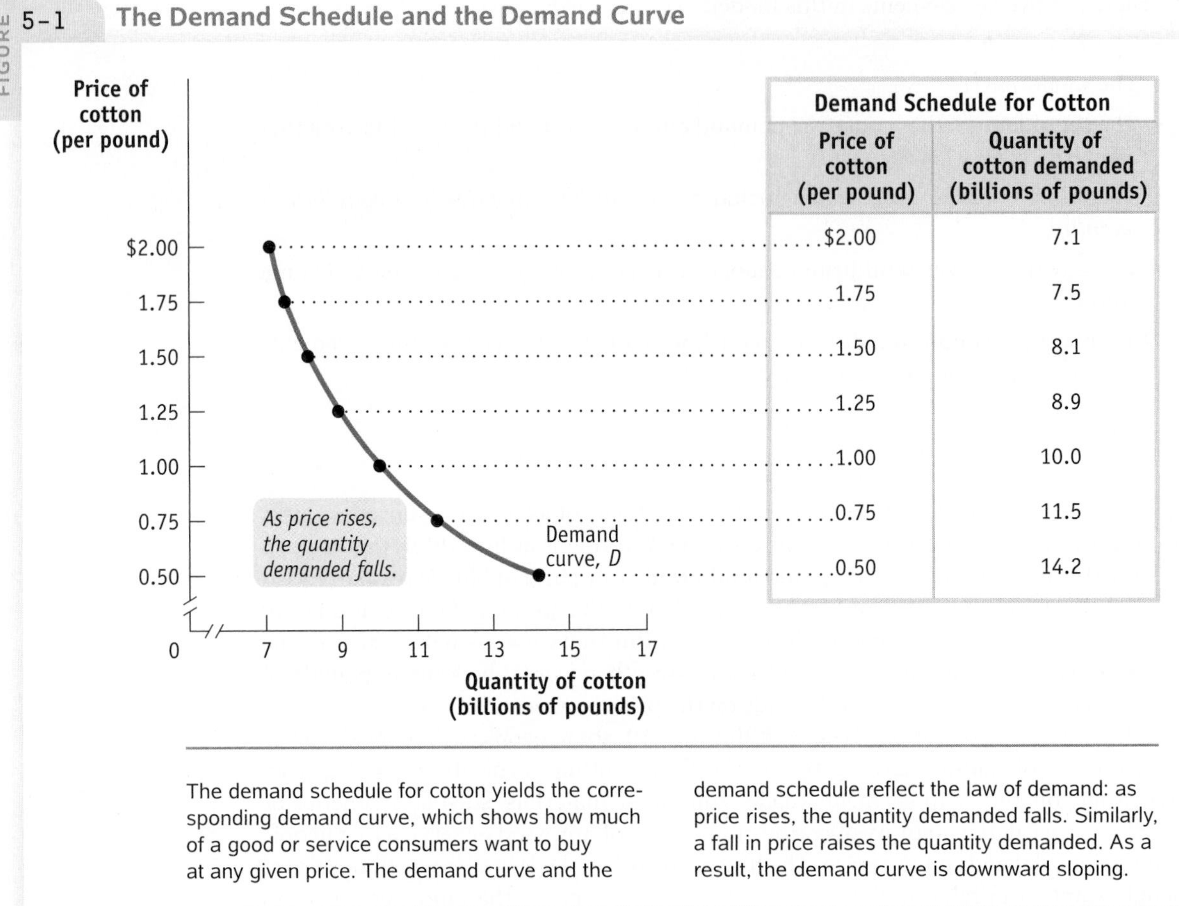

Demand Schedule for Cotton	
Price of cotton (per pound)	Quantity of cotton demanded (billions of pounds)
$2.00	7.1
1.75	7.5
1.50	8.1
1.25	8.9
1.00	10.0
0.75	11.5
0.50	14.2

The demand schedule for cotton yields the corresponding demand curve, which shows how much of a good or service consumers want to buy at any given price. The demand curve and the demand schedule reflect the law of demand: as price rises, the quantity demanded falls. Similarly, a fall in price raises the quantity demanded. As a result, the demand curve is downward sloping.

The **law of demand** says that a higher price for a good or service, all other things being equal, leads people to demand a smaller quantity of that good or service.

Note that the demand curve shown in Figure 5-1 slopes downward. This reflects the general proposition that a higher price reduces the quantity demanded. For example, jeans-makers know that they will sell fewer pairs when the price of a pair of jeans is higher, reflecting a $2 price for a pound of cotton, compared to the number they will sell when the price of a pair is lower, reflecting a price of only $1 for a pound of cotton. In the real world, demand curves almost always *do* slope downward. (The exceptions are so rare that for practical purposes we can ignore them.) Generally, the proposition that a higher price for a good, all other things equal, leads people to demand a smaller quantity of that good is so reliable that economists are willing to call it a "law"—the **law of demand.**

Higher prices for jeans will reduce the quantity demanded.

Image Source/Alamy

Shifts of the Demand Curve

Even though cotton prices in 2010 were higher than they had been in 2007, total world consumption of cotton was higher in 2010. How can we reconcile this fact with the law of demand, which says that a higher price reduces the quantity demanded, all other things being equal?

The answer lies in the crucial phrase all other things being equal. In this case, all other things weren't equal: the world had changed between 2007 and 2010, in ways that increased the quantity of cotton demanded at any given price. For one thing, the world's population, and therefore the number of potential cotton clothing wearers, increased. In addition, the growing popularity of cotton clothing, as well as higher incomes in countries like China that allowed people to buy more clothing than before, led to an increase in the quantity of cotton demanded at any given price. Figure 5-2 illustrates this

FIGURE 5-2 An Increase in Demand

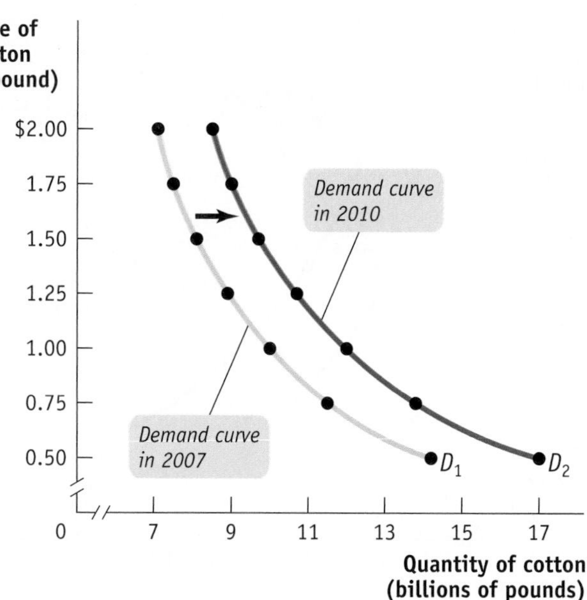

Demand Schedules for Cotton		
Price of cotton (per pound)	Quantity of cotton demanded (billions of pounds) in 2007	in 2010
$2.00	7.1	8.5
1.75	7.5	9.0
1.50	8.1	9.7
1.25	8.9	10.7
1.00	10.0	12.0
0.75	11.5	13.8
0.50	14.2	17.0

An increase in the population is one factor that generates an increase in demand—a rise in the quantity demanded at any given price. This is represented by the two demand schedules—one showing demand in 2007, before the rise in population, the other showing demand in 2010, after the rise in population—and their corresponding demand curves. The increase in demand shifts the demand curve to the right.

phenomenon using the demand schedule and demand curve for cotton. (As before, the numbers in Figure 5-2 are hypothetical.)

The table in Figure 5-2 shows two demand schedules. The first is the demand schedule for 2007, the same as shown in Figure 5-1. The second is the demand schedule for 2010. It differs from the 2007 demand schedule due to factors such as a larger population and the increased popularity of cotton clothing, factors that led to an increase in the quantity of cotton demanded at any given price. So at each price the 2010 schedule shows a larger quantity demanded than the 2007 schedule. For example, the quantity of cotton consumers wanted to buy at a price of $1 per pound increased from 10 billion to 12 billion pounds per year, the quantity demanded at $1.25 per pound went from 8.9 billion to 10.7 billion, and so on.

What is clear from this example is that the changes that occurred between 2007 and 2010 generated a *new* demand schedule, one in which the quantity demanded was greater at any given price than in the original demand schedule. The two curves in Figure 5-2 show the same information graphically. As you can see, the demand schedule for 2010 corresponds to a new demand curve, D_2, that is to the right of the demand schedule for 2007, D_1. This **change in demand** shows the increase in the quantity demanded at any given price, represented by the shift in position of the original demand curve D_1 to its new location at D_2.

It's crucial to make the distinction between such changes in demand and **movements along the demand curve,** changes in the quantity demanded of a good that result from a change in that good's price. Figure 5-3 illustrates the difference.

The movement from point *A* to point *B* is a movement along the demand curve: the quantity demanded rises due to a fall in price as you move down D_1. Here, a fall in the price of cotton from $1.50 to $1 per pound generates a rise in the quantity demanded from 8.1 billion to 10 billion pounds per year. But the quantity demanded can also rise when the price is unchanged if there is an *increase in demand*—a rightward shift

A **change in demand** is a shift of the demand curve, which changes the quantity demanded at any given price.

A **movement along the demand curve** is a change in the quantity demanded of a good that is the result of a change in that good's price.

FIGURE 5-3 **Movement Along the Demand Curve versus Shift of the Demand Curve**

The rise in quantity demanded when going from point *A* to point *B* reflects a movement along the demand curve: it is the result of a fall in the price of the good. The rise in quantity demanded when going from point *A* to point *C* reflects a shift of the demand curve: it is the result of a rise in the quantity demanded at any given price.

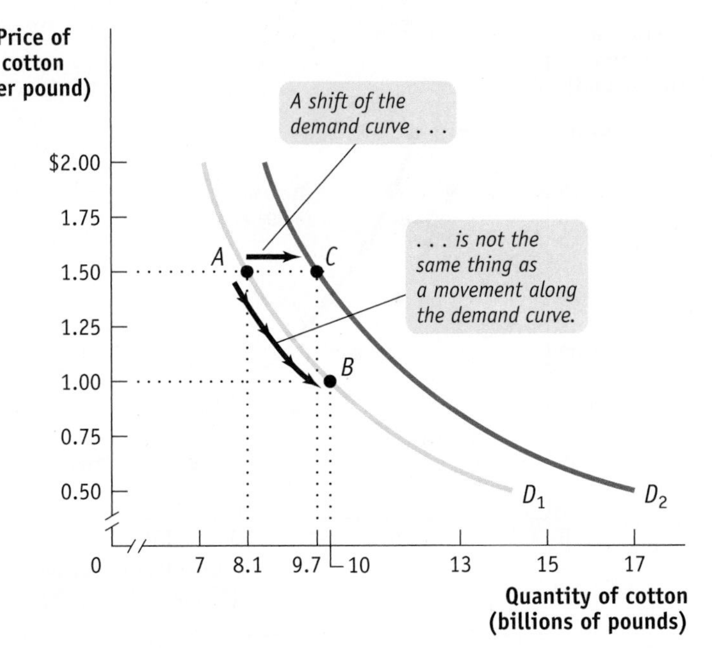

of the demand curve. This is illustrated in Figure 5-3 by the shift of the demand curve from D_1 to D_2. Holding the price constant at $1.50 a pound, the quantity demanded rises from 8.1 billion pounds at point *A* on D_1 to 9.7 billion pounds at point *C* on D_2.

When economists talk about a "change in demand," saying for example "the demand for *X* increased" or "the demand for *Y* decreased," they mean that the demand curve for *X* or *Y* shifted—*not* that the quantity demanded rose or fell because of a change in the price.

Understanding Shifts of the Demand Curve

Figure 5-4 illustrates the two basic ways in which demand curves can shift. When economists talk about an "increase in demand," they mean a *rightward* shift of the demand curve: at any given price, consumers demand a larger quantity of the good or service than before. This is shown by the rightward shift of the original demand curve D_1 to D_2. And when economists talk about a "decrease in demand," they mean a *leftward* shift of the demand curve: at any given price, consumers demand a smaller quantity of the good or service than before. This is shown by the leftward shift of the original demand curve D_1 to D_3.

What caused the demand curve for cotton to shift? We have already mentioned two reasons: changes in population and a change in the popularity of cotton clothing. If you think about it, you can come up with other things that would be likely to shift the demand curve for cotton. For example, suppose that the price of polyester rises. This will induce some people who previously bought polyester clothing to buy cotton clothing instead, increasing the demand for cotton.

Economists believe that there are five principal factors that shift the demand curve for a good or service:

- Changes in the prices of related goods or services
- Changes in income
- Changes in tastes
- Changes in expectations
- Changes in the number of consumers

FIGURE 5-4 Shifts of the Demand Curve

Any event that increases demand shifts the demand curve to the right, reflecting a rise in the quantity demanded at any given price. Any event that decreases demand shifts the demand curve to the left, reflecting a fall in the quantity demanded at any given price.

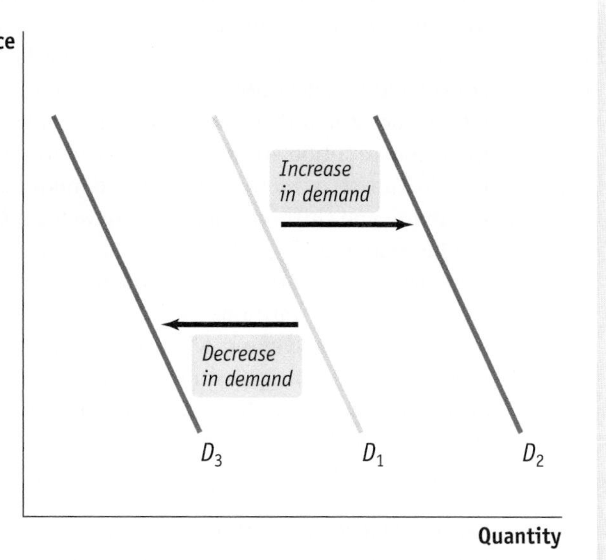

Although this is not an exhaustive list, it contains the five most important factors that can shift demand curves. So when we say that the quantity of a good or service demanded falls as its price rises, all other things being equal, we are in fact stating that the factors that shift demand are remaining unchanged. Let's now explore, in more detail, how those factors shift the demand curve.

Two goods are **substitutes** if a rise in the price of one of the goods leads to an increase in the demand for the other good.

Two goods are **complements** if a rise in the price of one good leads to a decrease in the demand for the other good.

CHANGES IN THE PRICES OF RELATED GOODS OR SERVICES While there's nothing quite like a comfortable pair of all-cotton blue jeans, for some purposes khakis—generally made from polyester blends—aren't a bad alternative. Khakis are what economists call a *substitute* for jeans. A pair of goods are **substitutes** if a rise in the price of one good (jeans) makes consumers more willing to buy the other good (khakis). Substitutes are usually goods that in some way serve a similar function: concerts and theater plays, muffins and doughnuts, train rides and air flights. A rise in the price of the alternative good induces some consumers to purchase the original good *instead* of it, shifting demand for the original good to the right.

But sometimes a rise in the price of one good makes consumers *less* willing to buy another good. Such pairs of goods are known as **complements.** Complements are usually goods that in some sense are consumed together: computers and software, cappuccinos and croissants, cars and gasoline. Because consumers like to consume a good and its complement together, a change in the price of one of the goods will affect the demand for its complement. In particular, when the price of one good rises, the demand for its complement decreases, shifting the demand curve for the complement to the left. So, for example, when the price of gasoline rises, the demand for gas-guzzling cars falls.

CHANGES IN INCOME When individuals have more income, they are normally more likely to purchase a good at any given price. For example, if a family's income rises, it is more likely to take that long-anticipated summer trip to Disney World—and therefore also more likely to buy plane tickets. So a rise in consumer incomes will cause the demand curves for most goods to shift to the right.

Thinkstock

When a rise in income increases the demand for a good—the normal case—it is a **normal good.**

When a rise in income decreases the demand for a good, it is an **inferior good.**

Why do we say "most goods," not "all goods"? Most goods are **normal goods**—the demand for them increases when consumer income rises. However, the demand for some products falls when income rises. Goods for which demand decreases when income rises are known as **inferior goods.** Usually an inferior good is one that is considered less desirable than more expensive alternatives—such as a bus ride versus a taxi ride. When they can afford to, people stop buying an inferior good and switch their consumption to the preferred, more expensive alternative. So when a good is inferior, a rise in income shifts the demand curve to the left. And, not surprisingly, a fall in income shifts the demand curve for inferior goods to the right.

One example of the distinction between normal and inferior goods that has drawn considerable attention in the business press is the difference between so-called casual-dining restaurants such as Applebee's or Olive Garden and fast-food chains such as McDonald's and KFC. When their incomes rise, Americans tend to eat out more at casual-dining restaurants. However, some of this increased dining out comes at the expense of fast-food venues—to some extent, people visit McDonald's less once they can afford to move upscale. So casual dining is a normal good, while fast-food appears to be an inferior good.

CHANGES IN TASTES Why do people want what they want? Fortunately, we don't need to answer that question—we just need to acknowledge that people have certain preferences, or tastes, that determine what they choose to consume and that these tastes can change. Economists usually lump together changes in demand due to fads, beliefs, cultural shifts, and so on under the heading of changes in *tastes* or *preferences.*

For example, once upon a time men wore hats. Up until around World War II, a respectable man wasn't fully dressed unless he wore a dignified hat along with his suit. But the returning GIs adopted a more informal style, perhaps due to the rigors of the war. And President Eisenhower, who had been supreme commander of Allied Forces before becoming president, often went hatless. After World War II, it was clear that the demand curve for hats had shifted leftward, reflecting a decrease in the demand for hats.

Economists have relatively little to say about the forces that influence consumers' tastes. (Marketers and advertisers, however, have plenty to say about them!) However, a *change* in tastes has a predictable impact on demand. When tastes change in favor of a good, more people want to buy it at any given price, so the demand curve shifts to the right. When tastes change against a good, fewer people want to buy it at any given price, so the demand curve shifts to the left.

istockphoto/thinkstock

As tastes change, styles come and go.

CHANGES IN EXPECTATIONS When consumers have some choice about when to make a purchase, current demand for a good is often affected by expectations about its future price. For example, savvy shoppers often wait for seasonal sales—say, buying next year's holiday gifts during the post-holiday markdowns. In this case, expectations of a future drop in price lead to a decrease in demand today. Alternatively, expectations of a future rise in price are likely to cause an increase in demand today. For example, as cotton prices began to rise in 2010, many textile mills began purchasing more cotton and stockpiling it in anticipation of further price increases.

Expected changes in future income can also lead to changes in demand: if you expect your income to rise in the future, you will typically borrow today and increase your demand for certain goods; if you expect your income to fall in the future, you are more likely to save today and reduce your demand for some goods.

CHANGES IN THE NUMBER OF CONSUMERS As we've already noted, one of the reasons for rising cotton demand between 2007 and 2010 was a growing world population.

Because of population growth, overall demand for cotton would have risen even if the demand of each individual wearer of cotton clothing had remained unchanged.

An **individual demand curve** illustrates the relationship between quantity demanded and price for an individual consumer.

Let's introduce a new concept: the **individual demand curve,** which shows the relationship between quantity demanded and price for an individual consumer. For example, suppose that Darla is a consumer of cotton blue jeans; also suppose that all pairs of jeans are the same, so they sell for the same price. Panel (a) of Figure 5-5 shows how many pairs of jeans she will buy per year at any given price. Then D_{Darla} is Darla's individual demand curve.

The *market demand curve* shows how the combined quantity demanded by all consumers depends on the market price of that good. (Most of the time, when economists refer to the demand curve, they mean the market demand curve.) The market demand curve is the *horizontal sum* of the individual demand curves of all consumers in that market.

FIGURE 5-5 Individual Demand Curves and the Market Demand Curve

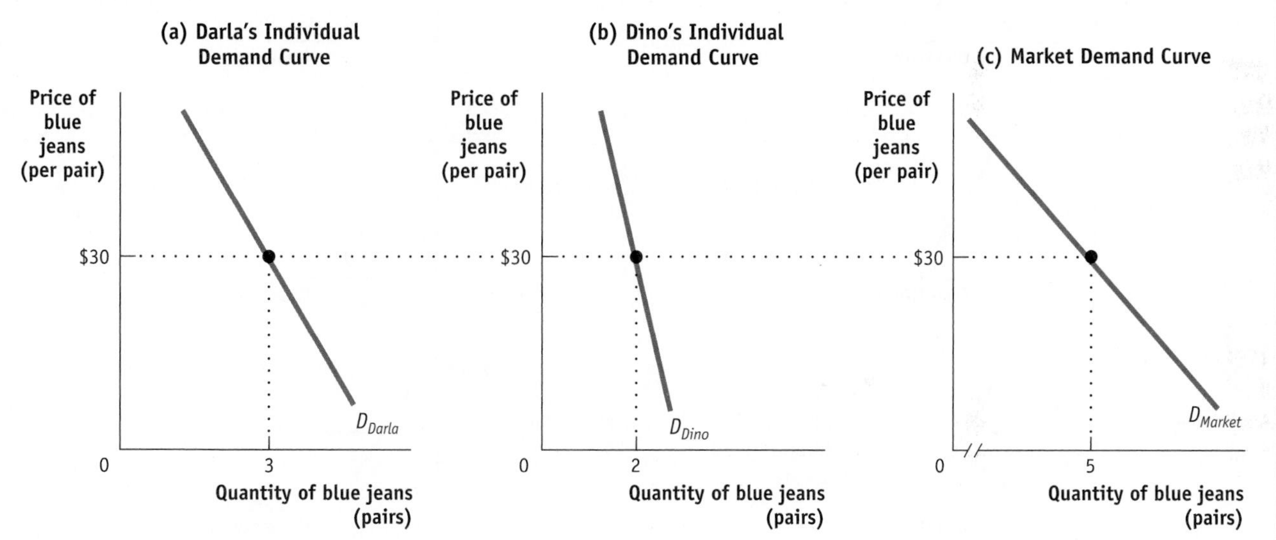

Darla and Dino are the only two consumers of blue jeans in the market. Panel (a) shows Darla's individual demand curve: the number of pairs of blue jeans she will buy per year at any given price. Panel (b) shows Dino's individual demand curve. Given that Darla and Dino are the only two consumers, the *market demand curve,* which shows the quantity of blue jeans demanded by all consumers at any given price, is shown in panel (c). The market demand curve is the *horizontal sum* of the individual demand curves of all consumers. In this case, at any given price, the quantity demanded by the market is the sum of the quantities demanded by Darla and Dino.

To see what we mean by the term *horizontal sum,* assume for a moment that there are only two consumers of blue jeans, Darla and Dino. Dino's individual demand curve, D_{Dino}, is shown in panel (b). Panel (c) shows the market demand curve. At any given price, the quantity demanded by the market is the sum of the quantities demanded by Darla and Dino. For example, at a price of $30 per pair, Darla demands 3 pairs of jeans per year and Dino demands 2 pairs per year. So the quantity demanded by the market is 5 pairs per year.

Clearly, the quantity demanded by the market at any given price is larger with Dino present than it would be if Darla were the only consumer. The quantity demanded at any given price would be even larger if we added a third consumer, then a fourth, and so on. So an increase in the number of consumers leads to an increase in demand.

For a review of the factors that shift demand, see Table 5-1.

TABLE 5-1

Factors That Shift Demand

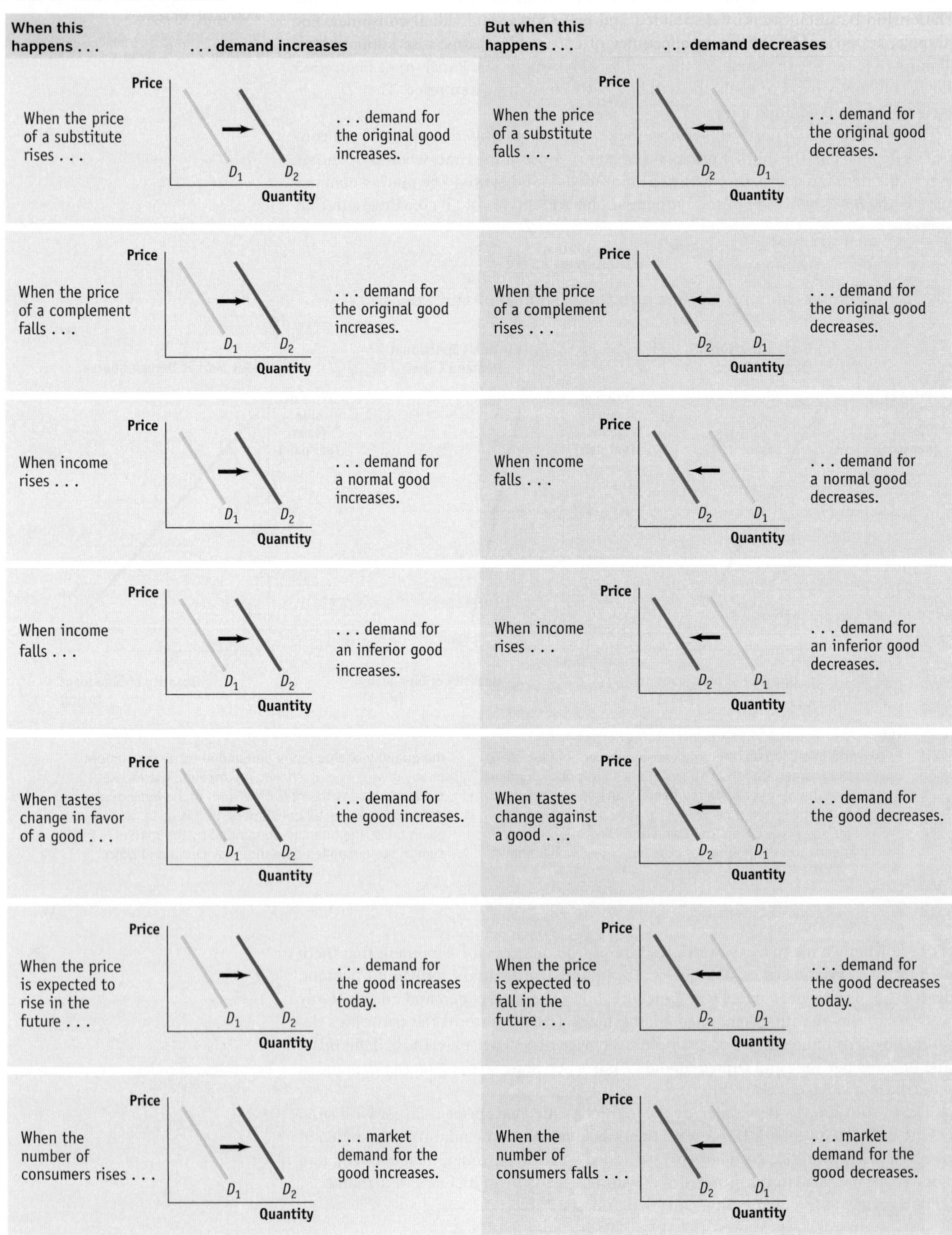

When this happens . . .	. . . demand increases	But when this happens . . .	. . . demand decreases
When the price of a substitute rises . . .	. . . demand for the original good increases.	When the price of a substitute falls . . .	. . . demand for the original good decreases.
When the price of a complement falls . . .	. . . demand for the original good increases.	When the price of a complement rises . . .	. . . demand for the original good decreases.
When income rises . . .	. . . demand for a normal good increases.	When income falls . . .	. . . demand for a normal good decreases.
When income falls . . .	. . . demand for an inferior good increases.	When income rises . . .	. . . demand for an inferior good decreases.
When tastes change in favor of a good . . .	. . . demand for the good increases.	When tastes change against a good . . .	. . . demand for the good decreases.
When the price is expected to rise in the future . . .	. . . demand for the good increases today.	When the price is expected to fall in the future . . .	. . . demand for the good decreases today.
When the number of consumers rises . . .	. . . market demand for the good increases.	When the number of consumers falls . . .	. . . market demand for the good decreases.

ECONOMICS IN ACTION

WORLD VIEW

BEATING THE TRAFFIC

All big cities have traffic problems, and many local authorities try to discourage driving in the crowded city center. If we think of an auto trip to the city center as a good that people consume, we can use the economics of demand to analyze anti-traffic policies.

One common strategy is to reduce the demand for auto trips by lowering the prices of substitutes. Many metropolitan areas subsidize bus and rail service, hoping to lure commuters out of their cars. An alternative is to raise the price of complements: several major U.S. cities impose high taxes on commercial parking garages and impose short time limits on parking meters, both to raise revenue and to discourage people from driving into the city.

A few major cities—including Singapore, London, Oslo, Stockholm, and Milan—have been willing to adopt a direct and politically controversial approach: reducing congestion by raising the price of driving. Under "congestion pricing" (or "congestion charging" in the United Kingdom), a charge is imposed on cars entering the city center during business hours. Drivers buy passes, which are then debited electronically as they drive by monitoring stations. Compliance is monitored with automatic cameras that photograph license plates.

Congestion
charging
zone
C
Mon - Fri
7am - 6.30 pm
2½ miles

Global Warming Images/Alamy

Cities can reduce traffic congestion by raising the price of driving.

The current daily cost of driving in London ranges from £8 to £10 (about $13 to $16). And drivers who don't pay and are caught pay a fine of £120 (about $195) for each transgression.

Not surprisingly, studies have shown that after the implementation of congestion pricing, traffic does indeed decrease. In the 1990s, London had some of the worst traffic in Europe. The introduction of its congestion charge in 2003 immediately reduced traffic in the London city center by about 15%, with overall traffic falling by 21% between 2002 and 2006. And there was increased use of substitutes, such as public transportation, bicycles, motorbikes, and ride-sharing.

In the United States, the U.S. Department of Transportation has implemented pilot programs to study congestion pricing. The programs were so successful that congestion pricing has become policy in some states. Other states, taking suggestions from traffic experts, are trying variable congestion prices, raising prices during peak commuting hours. So even though congestion pricing has been controversial, it appears to be gaining acceptance.

MODULE 5 Review

Solutions appear at the back of the book.

Check Your Understanding

1. Explain whether each of the following events represents (i) a *change in demand* (a *shift of* the demand curve) or (ii) a *change in the quantity demanded* (a *movement along* the demand curve).
   a. A store owner finds that customers are willing to pay more for umbrellas on rainy days.
   b. When XYZ Telecom, a long-distance telephone service provider, offered reduced rates on weekends, its volume of weekend calling increased sharply.
   c. People buy more long-stem roses the week of Valentine's Day, even though the prices are higher than at other times during the year.
   d. A sharp rise in the price of gasoline leads many commuters to join carpools in order to reduce their gasoline purchases.

FIGURE 6-1 The Supply Schedule and the Supply Curve

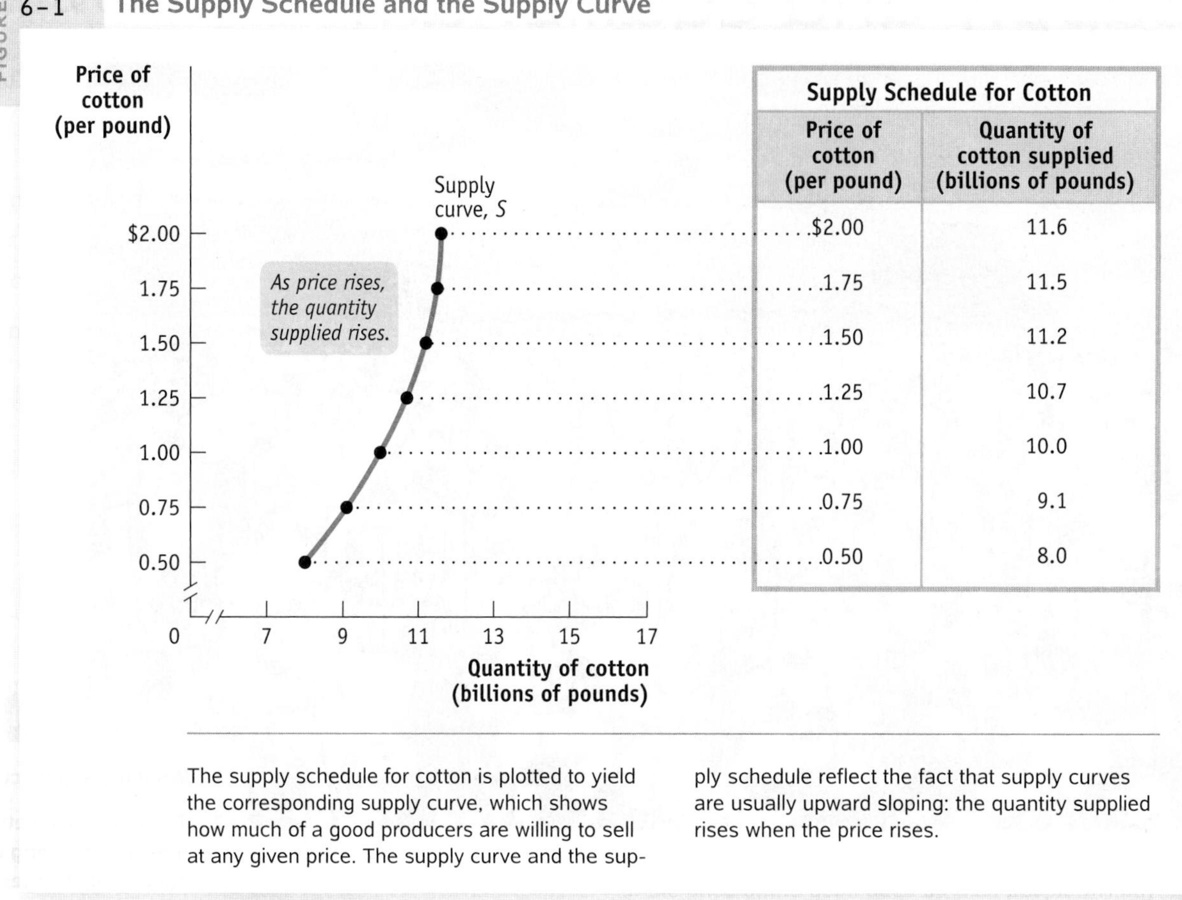

Supply Schedule for Cotton	
Price of cotton (per pound)	Quantity of cotton supplied (billions of pounds)
$2.00	11.6
1.75	11.5
1.50	11.2
1.25	10.7
1.00	10.0
0.75	9.1
0.50	8.0

The supply schedule for cotton is plotted to yield the corresponding supply curve, which shows how much of a good producers are willing to sell at any given price. The supply curve and the supply schedule reflect the fact that supply curves are usually upward sloping: the quantity supplied rises when the price rises.

is the normal situation for a supply curve, reflecting the general proposition that a higher price leads to a higher quantity supplied. Some economists refer to this relationship as the **law of supply.**

The **law of supply** is the general proposition that, all else constant, a higher price leads to higher quantity supplied, and a lower price leads to lower quantity supplied.

A **change in supply** is a shift of the supply curve, which changes the quantity supplied at any given price.

A **movement along the supply curve** is a change in the quantity supplied of a good arising from a change in the good's price.

Shifts of the Supply Curve

Until recently, cotton remained relatively cheap for several decades. One reason is that the amount of land cultivated for cotton expanded by more than 35% from 1945 to 2007. However, the major factor accounting for cotton's relative cheapness was advances in the production technology, with output per acre more than quadrupling from 1945 to 2007. Figure 6-2 illustrates these events in terms of the supply schedule and the supply curve for cotton.

The table in Figure 6-2 shows two supply schedules. The schedule before improved cotton-growing technology was adopted is the same one as in Figure 6-1. The second schedule shows the supply of cotton *after* the improved technology was adopted. Just as a change in demand schedules leads to a shift of the demand curve, a change in supply schedules leads to a shift of the supply curve—a **change in supply.** This is shown in Figure 6-2 by the shift of the supply curve before the adoption of new cotton-growing technology, S_1, to its new position after the adoption of new cotton-growing technology, S_2. Notice that S_2 lies to the right of S_1, a reflection of the fact that quantity supplied rises at any given price.

As in the analysis of demand, it's crucial to draw a distinction between such shifts of the supply curve and **movements along the supply curve**—changes in the quantity supplied arising from a change in price. We can see this difference in Figure 6-3. The movement from point A to point B is a movement along the supply curve: the quantity supplied rises along S_1 due to a rise in price. Here, a rise in price from $1 to

FIGURE 6-2 **An Increase in Supply**

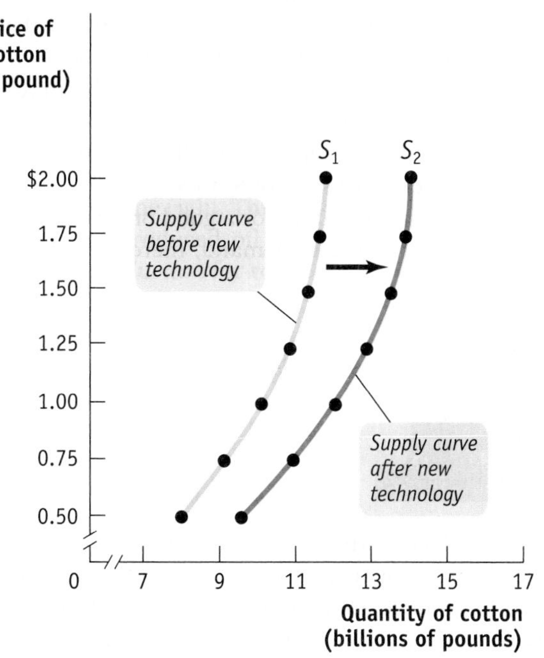

Supply Schedules for Cotton

Price of cotton (per pound)	Quantity of cotton supplied (billions of pounds)	
	Before new technology	After new technology
$2.00	11.6	13.9
1.75	11.5	13.8
1.50	11.2	13.4
1.25	10.7	12.8
1.00	10.0	12.0
0.75	9.1	10.9
0.50	8.0	9.6

The adoption of improved cotton-growing technology generated an increase in supply—a rise in the quantity supplied at any given price. This event is represented by the two supply schedules—one showing supply before the new technology was adopted, the other showing supply after the new technology was adopted—and their corresponding supply curves. The increase in supply shifts the supply curve to the right.

$1.50 leads to a rise in the quantity supplied from 10 billion to 11.2 billion pounds of cotton. But the quantity supplied can also rise when the price is unchanged if there is an increase in supply—a rightward shift of the supply curve. This is shown by the rightward shift of the supply curve from S_1 to S_2. Holding the price constant at $1, the quantity supplied rises from 10 billion pounds at point *A* on S_1 to 12 billion pounds at point *C* on S_2.

FIGURE 6-3 **Movement Along the Supply Curve versus Shift of the Supply Curve**

The increase in quantity supplied when going from point *A* to point *B* reflects a movement along the supply curve: it is the result of a rise in the price of the good. The increase in quantity supplied when going from point *A* to point *C* reflects a shift of the supply curve: it is the result of an increase in the quantity supplied at any given price.

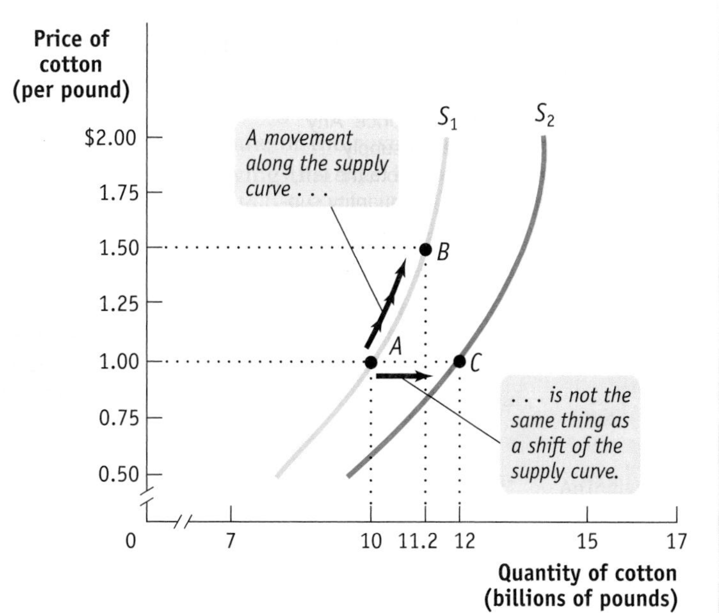

that Mr. Silva is a Brazilian cotton farmer and that panel (a) of Figure 6-5 shows how many pounds of cotton he will supply per year at any given price. Then S_{Silva} is his individual supply curve.

The *market supply curve* shows how the combined total quantity supplied by all individual producers in the market depends on the market price of that good. Just as the market demand curve is the horizontal sum of the individual demand curves of all consumers, the market supply curve is the horizontal sum of the individual supply curves of all producers. Assume for a moment that there are only two producers of cotton, Mr. Silva and Mr. Liu, a Chinese cotton farmer. Mr. Liu's individual supply curve is shown in panel (b). Panel (c) shows the market supply curve. At any given price, the quantity supplied to the market is the sum of the quantities supplied by Mr. Silva and Mr. Liu. For example, at a price of $2 per pound, Mr. Silva supplies 3,000 pounds of cotton per year and Mr. Liu supplies 2,000 pounds per year, making the quantity supplied to the market 5,000 pounds.

FIGURE 6-5 The Individual Supply Curve and the Market Supply Curve

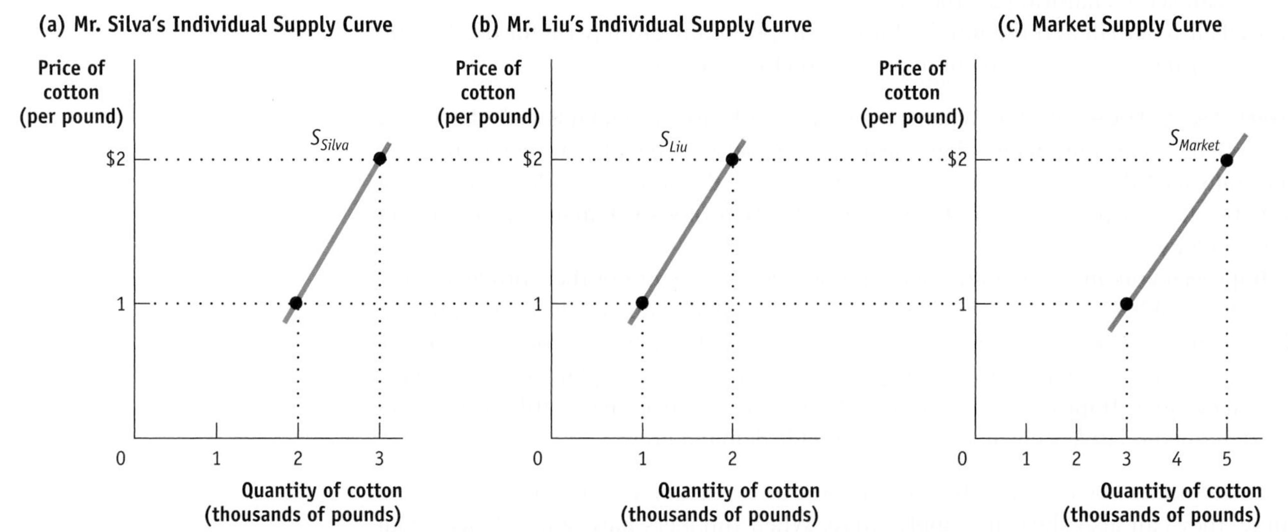

Panel (a) shows the individual supply curve for Mr. Silva, S_{Silva}, the quantity of cotton he will sell at any given price. Panel (b) shows the individual supply curve for Mr. Liu, S_{Liu}. The market supply curve, which shows the quantity of cotton supplied by all producers at any given price, is shown in panel (c). The market supply curve is the horizontal sum of the individual supply curves of all producers.

Clearly, the quantity supplied to the market at any given price is larger with Mr. Liu present than it would be if Mr. Silva were the only supplier. The quantity supplied at a given price would be even larger if we added a third producer, then a fourth, and so on. So an increase in the number of producers leads to an increase in supply and a rightward shift of the supply curve.

For a review of the factors that shift supply, see Table 6-1.

TABLE 6-1

Factors That Shift Supply

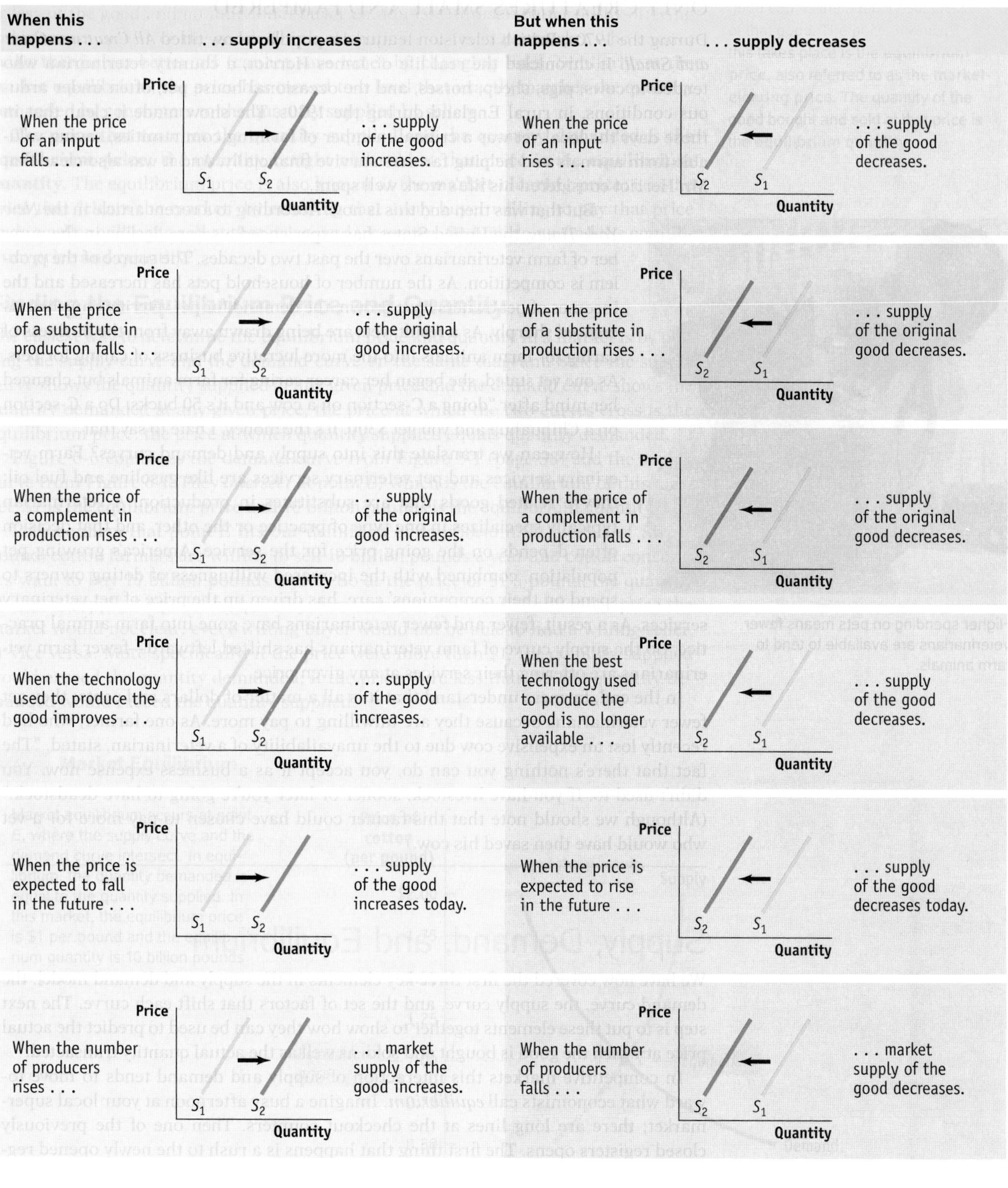

When this happens . . .	. . . supply increases	But when this happens . . .	. . . supply decreases
When the price of an input falls . . .	. . . supply of the good increases.	When the price of an input rises . . .	. . . supply of the good decreases.
When the price of a substitute in production falls . . .	. . . supply of the original good increases.	When the price of a substitute in production rises . . .	. . . supply of the original good decreases.
When the price of a complement in production rises . . .	. . . supply of the original good increases.	When the price of a complement in production falls . . .	. . . supply of the original good decreases.
When the technology used to produce the good improves . . .	. . . supply of the good increases.	When the best technology used to produce the good is no longer available . . .	. . . supply of the good decreases.
When the price is expected to fall in the future . . .	. . . supply of the good increases today.	When the price is expected to rise in the future . . .	. . . supply of the good decreases today.
When the number of producers rises . . .	. . . market supply of the good increases.	When the number of producers falls . . .	. . . market supply of the good decreases.

MODULE

7 Changes in Equilibrium

AP Photo/Khalid Tanveer

WHAT YOU WILL LEARN

1. How equilibrium price and quantity are affected when there is a change in either supply or demand
2. How equilibrium price and quantity are affected when there is a simultaneous change in both supply and demand

Changes in Supply and Demand

The 2010 floods in Pakistan came as a surprise, but the subsequent increase in the price of cotton was no surprise at all. Suddenly there was a fall in supply: the quantity of cotton available at any given price fell. Predictably, a fall in supply raises the equilibrium price.

The flooding in Pakistan is an example of an event that shifted the supply curve for a good without having much effect on the demand curve. There are many such events. There are also events that shift the demand curve without shifting the supply curve. For example, a medical report that chocolate is good for you increases the demand for chocolate but does not affect the supply. Events often shift either the supply curve or the demand curve, but not both; it is therefore useful to ask what happens in each case.

We have seen that when a curve shifts, the equilibrium price and quantity change. We will now concentrate on exactly how the shift of a curve alters the equilibrium price and quantity.

What Happens When the Demand Curve Shifts

Cotton and polyester are substitutes: if the price of polyester rises, the demand for cotton will increase, and if the price of polyester falls, the demand for cotton will decrease. But how does the price of polyester affect the *market equilibrium* for cotton?

Figure 7-1 shows the effect of a rise in the price of polyester on the market for cotton. The rise in the price of polyester increases the demand for cotton. Point E_1 shows the equilibrium corresponding to the original demand curve, with P_1 the equilibrium price and Q_1 the equilibrium quantity bought and sold.

An increase in demand is indicated by a *rightward* shift of the demand curve from D_1 to D_2. At the original market price P_1, this market is no longer in equilibrium: a shortage occurs because the quantity demanded exceeds the quantity supplied. So the

FIGURE 7-1 Equilibrium and Shifts of the Demand Curve

The original equilibrium in the market for cotton is at E_1, at the intersection of the supply curve and the original demand curve, D_1. A rise in the price of polyester, a substitute, shifts the demand curve for cotton products rightward to D_2. A shortage exists at the original price, P_1, causing both the price and quantity supplied to rise, a movement along the supply curve. A new equilibrium is reached at E_2, with a higher equilibrium price, P_2, and a higher equilibrium quantity, Q_2. When demand for a good or service increases, the equilibrium price and the equilibrium quantity of the good or service both rise.

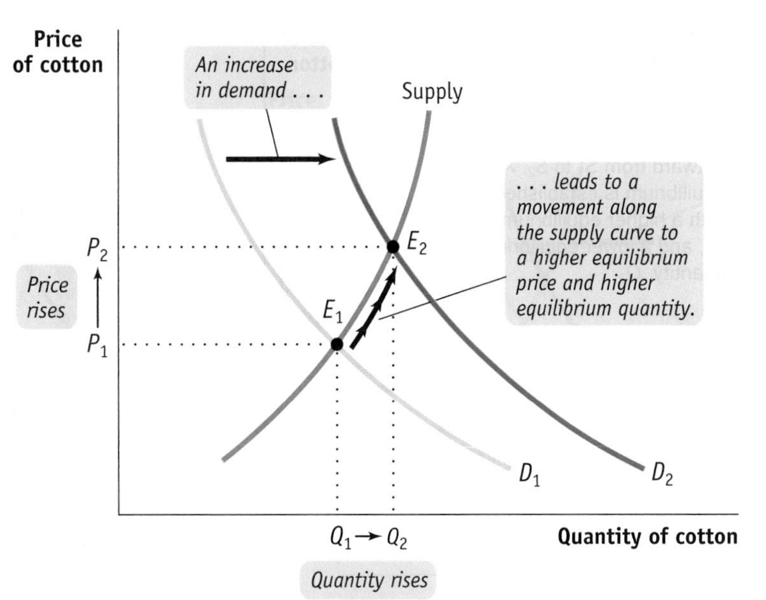

price of cotton rises and generates an increase in the quantity supplied, an upward *movement along the supply curve.* A new equilibrium is established at point E_2, with a higher equilibrium price, P_2, and higher equilibrium quantity, Q_2. This sequence of events reflects a general principle: *When demand for a good or service increases, the equilibrium price and the equilibrium quantity of the good or service both rise.*

What would happen in the reverse case, a fall in the price of polyester? A fall in the price of polyester reduces the demand for cotton, shifting the demand curve to the *left.* At the original price, a surplus occurs as quantity supplied exceeds quantity demanded. The price falls and leads to a decrease in the quantity supplied, resulting in a lower equilibrium price and a lower equilibrium quantity. This illustrates another general principle: *When demand for a good or service decreases, the equilibrium price and the equilibrium quantity of the good or service both fall.*

To summarize how a market responds to a change in demand: *An increase in demand leads to a rise in both the equilibrium price and the equilibrium quantity. A decrease in demand leads to a fall in both the equilibrium price and the equilibrium quantity.*

A fall in the price of polyester reduces the demand for cotton, shifting the demand curve to the left.

What Happens When the Supply Curve Shifts

In the real world, it is a bit easier to predict changes in supply than changes in demand. Physical factors that affect supply, like the availability of inputs, are easier to get a handle on than the fickle tastes that affect demand. Still, with supply as with demand, what we can best predict are the *effects* of shifts of the supply curve.

As we mentioned in this chapter's opening story, devastating floods in Pakistan sharply reduced the supply of cotton in 2010. Figure 7-2 shows how this shift affected the market equilibrium. The original equilibrium is at E_1, the point of intersection of the original supply curve, S_1, and the demand curve, with an equilibrium price P_1 and equilibrium quantity Q_1. As a result of the bad weather, supply falls and S_1 shifts *leftward* to S_2. At the original price P_1, a shortage of cotton now exists and the market is no longer in equilibrium. The shortage causes a rise in price and a fall in quantity demanded, an upward movement along the demand curve. The new equilibrium is at E_2, with an equilibrium price P_2 and an equilibrium quantity Q_2. In the new equilibrium,

ECONOMICS IN ACTION

THE RICE RUN OF 2008

In April 2008, the price of rice exported from Thailand—a global benchmark for the price of rice traded in international markets—reached $950 per ton, up from $360 per ton at the beginning of 2008. Within hours, prices for rice at major rice-trading exchanges around the world were breaking record levels. The factors that lay behind the surge in rice prices were both demand-related and supply-related: growing incomes in China and India, traditionally large consumers of rice; drought in Australia; and pest infestation in Vietnam. But it was hoarding by farmers, panic buying by consumers, and an export ban by India, one of the largest exporters of rice, that explained the breathtaking speed of the rise in price.

In much of Asia, governments are major buyers of rice. They buy rice from their rice farmers, who are paid a government-set price, and then sell it to the poor at subsidized prices (prices lower than the market equilibrium price). In the past, the government-set price was better than anything farmers could get in the private market.

Now, even farmers in rural areas of Asia have access to the Internet and can see the price quotes on global rice exchanges. And as rice prices rose in response to changes in demand and supply, farmers grew dissatisfied with the government price and instead hoarded their rice in the belief that they would eventually get higher prices. This was a self-fulfilling belief, as the hoarding shifted the supply curve leftward and raised the price of rice even further.

At the same time, India, one of the largest growers of rice, banned Indian exports of rice in order to protect its domestic consumers, causing yet another leftward shift of the supply curve and pushing the price of rice even higher.

As shown in Figure 7-4, the effects even spilled over to the United States, which had not suffered any fall in its rice production. American rice consumers grew alarmed when large retailers limited some bulk rice purchases in response to the turmoil in the global rice market.

Fearful of paying even higher prices in the future, panic buying set in. As one woman who was in the process of buying 30 pounds of rice said, "We don't even eat that much rice. But I read about it in the newspaper and decided to buy some." In San Francisco, some Asian markets reported runs on rice. And, predictably, this led to even higher prices as panic buying shifted the demand curve rightward, further feeding the buying frenzy. As one market owner said, "People are afraid. We tell them, 'There's no shortage yet' but it was crazy in here."

FIGURE 7-4 Rising Rice Prices in the United States, 2003–2011

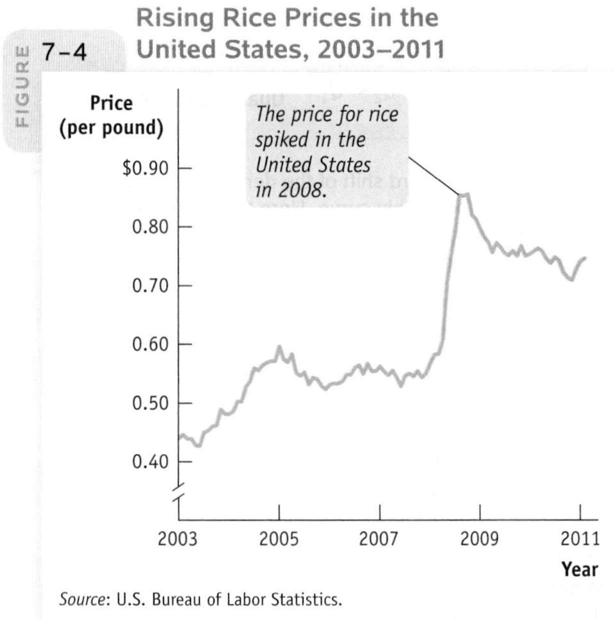

Source: U.S. Bureau of Labor Statistics.

MODULE 7 Review

Solutions appear at the back of the book.

Check Your Understanding

1. For each of the following examples, explain how the indicated change affects supply or demand for the good in question and how the shift you describe affects equilibrium price and quantity.
   a. As the price of gasoline fell in the United States during the 1990s, more people bought large cars.
   b. As technological innovation has lowered the cost of recycling used paper, fresh paper made from recycled stock is used more frequently.
   c. When a local cable company offers cheaper pay-per-view films, local movie theaters have more unfilled seats.

2. Periodically, a computer chip maker like Intel introduces a new chip that is faster than the previous one. In response, demand for computers using the earlier chip decreases as customers put off purchases in anticipation of machines containing the new chip. Simultaneously, computer makers increase their production of computers containing the earlier chip in order to clear out their stocks of those chips.

   Draw two diagrams of the market for computers containing the earlier chip: (a) one in which the equilibrium quantity falls in response to these events and (b) one in which the equilibrium quantity rises. What happens to the equilibrium price in each diagram?

Multiple-Choice Questions

1. Which of the following describes what will happen in the market for tomatoes if a salmonella outbreak is attributed to tainted tomatoes?
   a. Supply will increase and price will increase.
   b. Supply will increase and price will decrease.
   c. Demand will decrease and price will increase.
   d. Demand will decrease and price will decrease.
   e. Supply and demand will both increase.

2. Which of the following will lead to an increase in the equilibrium price of product "X"? A(n)
   a. increase in consumer incomes if product "X" is an inferior good
   b. increase in the price of machinery used to produce product "X"
   c. technological advance in the production of good "X"
   d. decrease in the price of good "Y" (a substitute for good "X")
   e. expectation by consumers that the price of good "X" is going to fall

3. The equilibrium price will rise, but equilibrium quantity may increase, decrease, or stay the same if
   a. demand increases and supply decreases.
   b. demand increases and supply increases.
   c. demand decreases and supply increases.
   d. demand decreases and supply decreases.
   e. demand increases and supply does not change.

4. An increase in the number of buyers and a technological advance will cause
   a. demand to increase and supply to increase.
   b. demand to increase and supply to decrease.
   c. demand to decrease and supply to increase.
   d. demand to decrease and supply to decrease.
   e. no change in demand and an increase in supply.

5. Which of the following is certainly true if demand and supply increase at the same time?
   a. The equilibrium price will increase.
   b. The equilibrium price will decrease.
   c. The equilibrium quantity will increase.
   d. The equilibrium quantity will decrease.
   e. The equilibrium quantity may increase, decrease, or stay the same.

Critical-Thinking Question

Draw a correctly labeled graph showing the market for cotton in equilibrium. On your graph, show the effect of an increase in the supply of cotton on equilibrium price and equilibrium quantity in the market for cotton.

Problems

1. A survey indicated that chocolate ice cream is America's favorite ice-cream flavor. For each of the following, indicate the possible effects on the demand and/or supply, equilibrium price, and equilibrium quantity of chocolate ice cream.

   a. A severe drought in the Midwest causes dairy farmers to reduce the number of milk-producing cows in their herds by a third. These dairy farmers supply cream that is used to manufacture chocolate ice cream.

   b. A new report by the American Medical Association reveals that chocolate does, in fact, have significant health benefits.

   c. The discovery of cheaper synthetic vanilla flavoring lowers the price of vanilla ice cream.

   d. New technology for mixing and freezing ice cream lowers manufacturers' costs of producing chocolate ice cream.

2. In a supply and demand diagram, draw the change in demand for hamburgers in your hometown due to the following events. In each case show the effect on equilibrium price and quantity.

   a. The price of tacos increases.

   b. All hamburger sellers raise the price of their french fries.

   c. Income falls in town. Assume that hamburgers are a normal good for most people.

   d. Income falls in town. Assume that hamburgers are an inferior good for most people.

   e. Hot dog stands cut the price of hot dogs.

3. The market for many goods changes in predictable ways according to the time of year, in response to events such as holidays, vacation times, seasonal changes in production, and so on. Using supply and demand, explain the change in price in each of the following cases. Note that supply and demand may shift simultaneously.

   a. Lobster prices usually fall during the summer peak harvest season, despite the fact that people like to eat lobster during the summer months more than during any other time of year.

   b. The price of a Christmas tree is lower after Christmas than before and fewer trees are sold.

   c. The price of a round-trip ticket to Paris on Air France falls by more than $200 after the end of school vacation in September. This happens despite the fact that generally worsening weather increases the cost of operating flights to Paris, and Air France therefore reduces the number of flights to Paris at any given price.

4. Show in a diagram the effect on the demand curve, the supply curve, the equilibrium price, and the equilibrium quantity of each of the following events on the designated market.

   a. the market for newspapers in your town

      Case 1: The salaries of journalists go up.

      Case 2: There is a big news event in your town, which is reported in the newspapers, and residents want to learn more about it.

   b. the market for St. Louis Rams cotton T-shirts

      Case 1: The Rams win the championship.

      Case 2: The price of cotton increases.

   c. the market for bagels

      Case 1: People realize how fattening bagels are.

      Case 2: People have less time to make themselves a cooked breakfast.

5. Find the flaws in reasoning in the following statements, paying particular attention to the distinction between changes in and movements along the supply and demand curves. Draw a diagram to illustrate what actually happens in each situation.

   a. "A technological innovation that lowers the cost of producing a good might seem at first to result in a reduction in the price of the good to consumers. But a fall in price will increase demand for the good, and higher demand will send the price up again. It is not certain, therefore, that an innovation will really reduce price in the end."

   b. "A study shows that eating a clove of garlic a day can help prevent heart disease, causing many consumers to demand more garlic. This increase in demand results in a rise in the price of garlic. Consumers, seeing that the price of garlic has gone up, reduce their demand for garlic. This causes the demand for garlic to decrease and the price of garlic to fall. Therefore, the ultimate effect of the study on the price of garlic is uncertain."

6. In *Rolling Stone* magazine, several fans and rock stars, including Pearl Jam, were bemoaning the high price of concert tickets. One superstar argued, "It just isn't worth $75 to see me play. No one should have to pay that much to go to a concert." Assume this star sold out arenas around the country at an average ticket price of $75.

   a. How would you evaluate the argument that ticket prices are too high?

   b. Suppose that due to this star's protests, ticket prices were lowered to $50. In what sense is this price too low? Draw a diagram using supply and demand curves to support your argument.

   c. Suppose Pearl Jam really wanted to bring down ticket prices. Since the band controls the supply of its services, what do you recommend they do? Explain using a supply and demand diagram.

d. Suppose the band's next CD was a total dud. Do you think they would still have to worry about ticket prices being too high? Why or why not? Draw a supply and demand diagram to support your argument.

e. Suppose the group announced their next tour was going to be their last. What effect would this likely have on the demand for and price of tickets? Illustrate with a supply and demand diagram.

7. After several years of decline, the market for handmade acoustic guitars is making a comeback. These guitars, which are normal goods, are usually made in small workshops employing relatively few highly skilled luthiers. Assess the impact on the equilibrium price and quantity of handmade acoustic guitars as a result of each of the following events. In your answers, indicate which curve(s) shift(s) and in which direction.

    a. Environmentalists succeed in having the use of Brazilian rosewood banned in the United States, forcing luthiers to seek out alternative, more costly woods.

    b. A foreign producer reengineers the guitar-making process and floods the market with identical guitars.

    c. Music featuring handmade acoustic guitars makes a comeback as audiences tire of heavy metal and grunge music.

    d. The country goes into a deep recession and the income of the average American falls sharply.

8. Will Shakespeare is a struggling playwright in sixteenth-century London. As the price he receives for writing a play increases, he is willing to write more plays. For the following situations, use a diagram to illustrate how each event affects the equilibrium price and quantity in the market for Shakespeare's plays.

    a. The playwright Christopher Marlowe, Shakespeare's chief rival, is killed in a bar brawl.

    b. The bubonic plague, a deadly infectious disease, breaks out in London.

    c. To celebrate the defeat of the Spanish Armada, Queen Elizabeth declares several weeks of festivities, which involves commissioning new plays.

9. The small town of Middling experiences a sudden doubling of the birth rate. After three years, the birth rate returns to normal. Use a diagram to illustrate the effect of these events on the following:

    a. the market for an hour of babysitting services in Middling today

    b. the market for an hour of babysitting services 14 years into the future, after the birth rate has returned to normal, by which time children born today are old enough to work as babysitters

    c. the market for an hour of babysitting services 30 years into the future, when children born today are likely to be having children of their own

10. Use a diagram to illustrate how each of the following events affects the equilibrium price and quantity of pizza.

    a. The price of mozzarella cheese rises.

    b. The health hazards of hamburgers are widely publicized.

    c. The price of tomato sauce falls.

    d. The incomes of consumers rise and pizza is an inferior good.

    e. Consumers expect the price of pizza to fall next week.

11. Although he was a prolific artist, Pablo Picasso painted only 1,000 canvases during his "Blue Period." Picasso is now dead, and all of his Blue Period works are currently on display in museums and private galleries throughout Europe and the United States.

    a. Draw a supply curve for Picasso Blue Period works. Why is this supply curve different from ones you have seen?

    b. Given the supply curve from part a, the price of a Picasso Blue Period work will be entirely dependent on what factor(s)? Draw a diagram showing how the equilibrium price of such a work is determined.

    c. Suppose that rich art collectors decide that it is essential to acquire Picasso Blue Period art for their collections. Show the impact of this on the market for these paintings.

FOR
RENT

SECTION 3

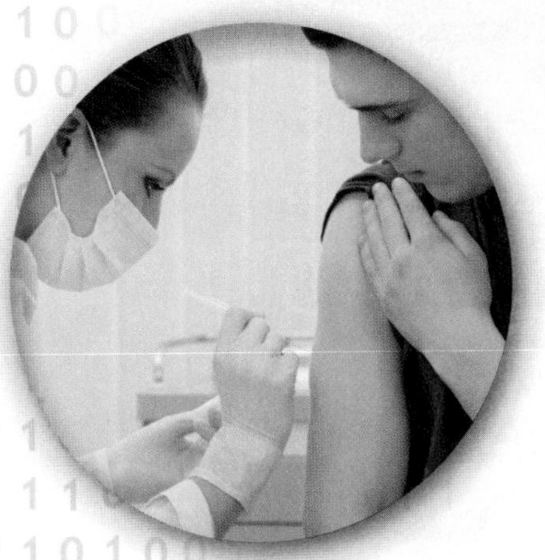

Elasticity and the Law of Demand

MORE PRECIOUS THAN A FLU SHOT

If you've ever had a real case of the flu, you know just how unpleasant an experience it is. And it can be worse than unpleasant: every year the flu kills around 36,000 Americans and sends another 200,000 to the hospital.

So, it was no surprise that panic was the only word to describe the situation at hospitals, clinics, and nursing homes across America in October 2004. Early that month, Chiron Corporation, one of only two suppliers of flu vaccine for the entire U.S. market, announced that contamination problems would force the closure of its manufacturing plant.

With that closure, the U.S. supply of vaccine for the 2004–2005 flu season was suddenly cut in half, from 100 million to 50 million doses. Because making flu vaccine is a costly and time-consuming process, no more doses could be made to replace Chiron's lost output. And since every country jealously guards its supply of flu vaccine for its own citizens, none could be obtained from other countries.

Victims of the flu are most commonly children, senior citizens, or those with compromised immune systems. In a normal flu season, this part of the population, along with health care workers, are immunized first. But the flu vaccine shortfall of 2004 upended those plans. As news of it spread, there was a rush to get the shots. People lined up in the middle of the night at the few locations that had somehow obtained the vaccine and were offering it at a reasonable price: the crowds included seniors with oxygen tanks, parents with sleeping children, and others in wheelchairs.

Meanwhile, some pharmaceutical distributors—the companies that obtain vaccine from manufacturers and then distribute it to hospitals and pharmacies—detected a profit-making opportunity in the frenzy. One company, Med-Stat, which normally charged $8.50 for a dose, began charging $90, more than 10 times the normal price. A survey of pharmacists found that price-gouging was fairly widespread.

Although most people refused or were unable to pay such a high price for the vaccine, many others undoubtedly did. Med-Stat judged, correctly, that consumers of the vaccine were relatively *unresponsive* to price; that is, the large increase in the price of the vaccine left the quantity demanded by consumers relatively unchanged.

Clearly, the demand for flu vaccine is unusual in this respect. For many, getting vaccinated meant the difference between life and death. Let's consider a very different and less urgent scenario. Suppose, for example, that the supply of a particular type of breakfast cereal was halved due to manufacturing problems. It would be extremely unlikely, if not impossible, to find a consumer willing to pay 10 times the original price for a box of this particular cereal. In other words, consumers of breakfast cereal are much more responsive to price than consumers of flu vaccine. But how do we define *responsiveness?* Economists measure consumers' responsiveness to price with a particular number, called the *price elasticity of demand.*

In this section we take a closer look at the supply and demand model developed early in this book and present several economic concepts used to evaluate market results. We will see how the price elasticity of demand is calculated and why it is the best measure of how the quantity demanded responds to changes in price. We will then discover that the price elasticity of demand is only one of a family of related concepts, including the *income elasticity of demand* and the *price elasticity of supply.*

MODULE 8

Income Effects, Substitution Effects, and Elasticity

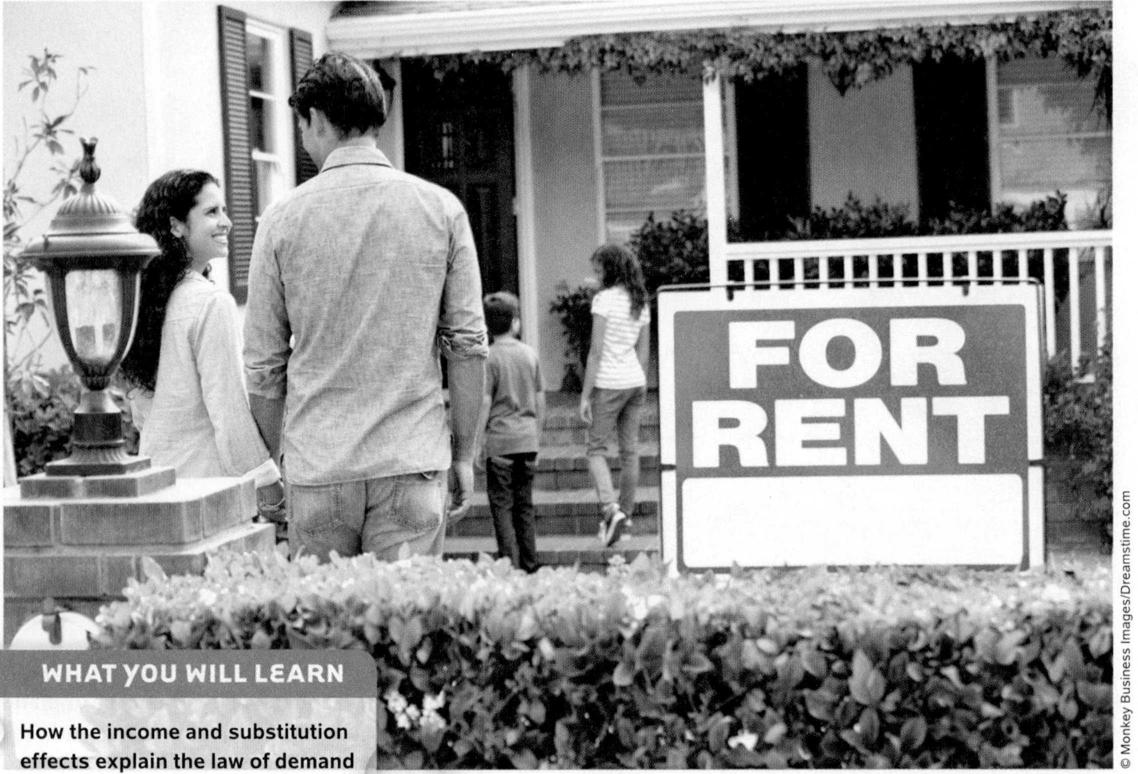

© Monkey Business Images/Dreamstime.com

WHAT YOU WILL LEARN

1. How the income and substitution effects explain the law of demand
2. The definition of elasticity, a measure of responsiveness to changes in prices or incomes
3. The importance of the price elasticity of demand, which measures the responsiveness of the quantity demanded to changes in price
4. How to calculate the price elasticity of demand

Explaining the Law of Demand

We introduced the demand curve and the law of demand in the previous section on supply and demand. To this point, we have accepted that the demand curve has a negative slope. And we have drawn demand curves that are somewhere in the middle between flat and steep (with a negative slope). In this module, we present more detail about why demand curves slope downward and what the slope of the demand curve tells us. We begin with the *income* and *substitution effects,* which explain why the demand curve has a negative slope.

The Substitution Effect

When the price of a good increases, an individual will normally consume less of that good and more of other goods. Correspondingly, when the price of a good decreases, an individual will normally consume more of that good and less of other goods. This explains why the individual demand curve, which relates an individual's consumption of a good to the price of that good, normally slopes downward—that is, it obeys the law of demand.

An alternative way to think about why demand curves slope downward is to focus on opportunity costs. For simplicity, let's suppose there are only two goods between which to choose. When the price of one good decreases, an individual doesn't have to give up as many units of the other good in order to buy one more unit of the first good. That makes it attractive to buy more of the good whose price has gone down. Conversely, when the price of one good increases, one must give up more units of the other good to buy one more unit of the first good, so consuming that good becomes less attractive and the consumer buys fewer.

The change in the quantity demanded as the good that has become relatively cheaper is substituted for the good that has become relatively more expensive is known as the **substitution effect.** When a good absorbs only a small share of the typical consumer's income, as with pillow cases and swim goggles, the substitution effect is essentially the sole explanation of why the market demand curve slopes downward. There are, however, some goods, like food and housing, that account for a substantial share of many consumers' incomes. In such cases another effect, called the *income effect,* also comes into play.

The **substitution effect** of a change in the price of a good is the change in the quantity of that good demanded as the consumer substitutes the good that has become relatively cheaper for some other good that has become relatively more expensive.

The **income effect** of a change in the price of a good is the change in the quantity of that good demanded that results from a change in the consumer's purchasing power when the price of the good changes.

The Income Effect

Consider the case of a family that spends half of its income on rental housing. Now suppose that the price of housing increases everywhere. This will have a substitution effect on the family's demand: other things equal, the family will have an incentive to consume less housing—say, by moving to a smaller apartment—and more of other goods. But the family will also, in a real sense, be made poorer by that higher housing price—its income will buy less housing than before.

When income is adjusted to reflect its true purchasing power, it is called *real income,* in contrast to *money income* or *nominal income,* which has not been adjusted. And this reduction in a consumer's real income will have an additional effect, beyond the substitution effect, on the family's consumption choices, including its consumption of housing. The **income effect** is the change in the quantity of a good demanded that results from a change in the overall purchasing power of the consumer's income due to a change in the price of that good.

It's possible to give more precise definitions of the substitution effect and the income effect of a price change, but for most purposes, there are only two things you need to know about the distinction between these two effects.

1. For the majority of goods and services, the income effect is not important and has no significant effect on individual consumption. Thus, most market demand curves slope downward solely because of the substitution effect—end of story.
2. When it matters at all, the income effect usually reinforces the substitution effect. That is, when the price of a good that absorbs a substantial share of income rises, consumers of that good become a bit poorer because their purchasing power falls. And the vast majority of goods are *normal* goods, goods for which demand decreases when income falls. So this effective reduction in income leads to a reduction in the quantity demanded and reinforces the substitution effect.

However, in the case of an *inferior* good, a good for which demand increases when income falls, the income and substitution effects work in opposite directions. Although the substitution effect decreases the quantity of any good demanded as its price increases, the income effect of a price increase for an inferior good is an *increase* in the quantity demanded. This makes sense because the price increase lowers the real income of the consumer, and as real income falls, the demand for an inferior good increases.

If a good were so inferior that the income effect exceeded the substitution effect, a price increase would lead to an increase in the quantity demanded. There is controversy over whether such goods, known as "Giffen goods," exist at all. (See the following Economics in Action for more on "Giffen goods"). If they do, they are very rare. You can generally assume that the income effect for an inferior good is smaller than the substitution effect, and so a price increase will still lead to a decrease in the quantity demanded.

ECONOMICS IN ACTION WORLD VIEW

GIFFEN GOODS

Two hundred years ago, when Ireland was under British rule and desperately poor, it was claimed that the Irish would eat *more* potatoes when the price of potatoes went up. That is, some observers claimed that Ireland's demand curve for potatoes sloped upward, not downward.

Can this happen? In theory, yes. If Irish demand for potatoes actually sloped upward, it would have been a real-life case of a "Giffen good," named after a nineteenth-century statistician who thought (probably wrongly) that he saw an upward-sloping demand curve in some data he was studying.

Here's the story. Suppose that there is some good that absorbs a large share of consumers' budgets and that this good is also *inferior*—people demand less of it when their income rises. The classic supposed example was, as you might guess, potatoes in Ireland, back when potatoes were an inferior good—they were what poor people ate—and when the Irish were very poor.

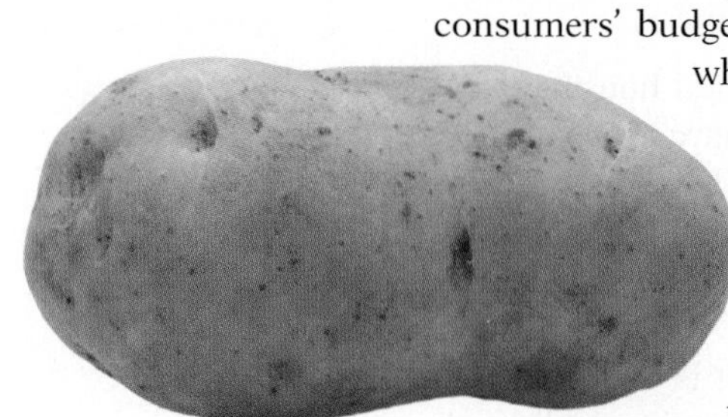

iStockphoto/Thinkstock

Now suppose that the price of potatoes increases. This would, *other things being equal,* cause people to substitute other goods for potatoes. But other things are not equal: given the higher price of potatoes, people are poorer. And this *increases* the demand for potatoes, because potatoes are an inferior good.

If this income effect outweighs the substitution effect, a rise in the price of potatoes would increase the quantity demanded; the law of demand would not hold.

In a way the point of this story—which has never been validated in any real situation, nineteenth-century Ireland included—is how unlikely such an event is. The law of demand really is a law, with few exceptions.

Defining and Measuring Elasticity

Most graphs in economics depict relationships between two variables: the value of one determining variable (the *independent variable*) directly influences the value of the other (the *dependent variable*). If two variables are negatively related and the independent variable increases, the dependent variable will respond by decreasing. (For a review of graphing variables, see Appendix A on graphs in economics, at the back of the book.) But often the important question is not whether the variables are negatively or positively related, but how responsive the dependent variable is to changes in the independent variable (that is, ***by how much*** will the dependent variable change?). If price increases, we know that quantity demanded will decrease (that is the *law of demand*). The question in this context is *by how much* will quantity demanded decrease if price goes up?

Economists use the concept of *elasticity* to measure the responsiveness of one variable to changes in another. For example, *price elasticity of demand* measures the responsiveness of quantity demanded to changes in price—something a firm considering changing its price would certainly want to know! Elasticity can be used to measure responsiveness using any two related variables. We will start by looking at the price elasticity of demand and then move on to other examples of elasticities commonly used by economists.

Think back to the opening story of the 2004 flu shot panic. In order for Flunomics, a hypothetical flu vaccine distributor, to know whether it could raise its revenue by significantly raising the price of its flu vaccine during the 2004 flu vaccine panic, it would have to know whether the price increase would decrease the quantity demanded by a lot or a little. That is, it would have to know the price elasticity of demand for flu vaccinations.

Calculating the Price Elasticity of Demand

Figure 8-1 shows a hypothetical demand curve for flu vaccinations. At a price of \$20 per vaccination, consumers would demand 10 million vaccinations per year (point *A*); at a price of \$21, the quantity demanded would fall to 9.9 million vaccinations per year (point *B*).

Figure 8-1, then, tells us the change in the quantity demanded for a particular change in the price. But how can we turn this into a measure of price responsiveness? The answer is to calculate the price elasticity of demand. The **price elasticity of demand** compares the *percent change in quantity demanded* to the *percent change in price* as we move along the demand curve. As we'll see later, the reason economists use percent changes is to get a measure that doesn't depend on the units in which a good is measured (say, a child-size dose versus an adult-size dose of vaccine). But before we get to that, let's look at how elasticity is calculated.

FIGURE 8-1 The Demand for Vaccinations

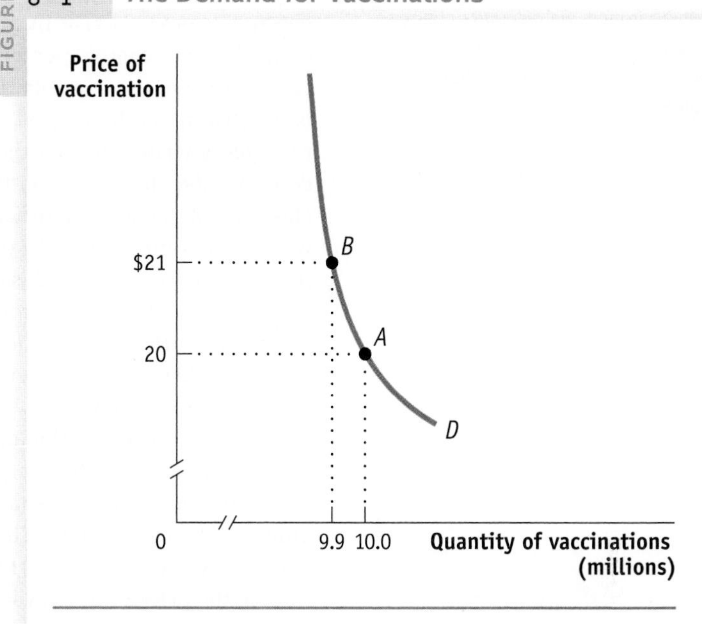

At a price of \$20 per vaccination, the quantity of vaccinations demanded is 10 million per year (point *A*). When price rises to \$21 per vaccination, the quantity demanded falls to 9.9 million vaccinations per year (point *B*).

To calculate the price elasticity of demand, we first calculate the *percent change in the quantity demanded* and the corresponding *percent change in the price* as we move along the demand curve. These are defined as follows:

$$\textbf{(8-1)} \quad \text{\% change in quantity demanded} = \frac{\text{Change in quantity demanded}}{\text{Initial quantity demanded}} \times 100$$

and

$$\textbf{(8-2)} \quad \text{\% change in price} = \frac{\text{Change in price}}{\text{Initial price}} \times 100$$

In Figure 8-1, we see that when the price rises from \$20 to \$21, the quantity demanded falls from 10 million to 9.9 million vaccinations, yielding a change in the quantity demanded of 0.1 million vaccinations. So the percent change in the quantity demanded is

$$\text{\% change in quantity demanded} = \frac{-0.1 \text{ million vaccinations}}{10 \text{ million vaccinations}} \times 100 = -1\%$$

The initial price is \$20 and the change in the price is \$1, so the percent change in the price is

$$\text{\% change in price} = \frac{\$1}{\$20} \times 100 = 5\%$$

To calculate the price elasticity of demand, we find the ratio of the percent change in the quantity demanded to the percent change in the price:

$$\textbf{(8-3)} \quad \text{Price elasticity of demand} = \frac{\text{\% change in quantity demanded}}{\text{\% change in price}}$$

In Figure 8-1, the price elasticity of demand is therefore

$$\text{Price elasticity of demand} = \frac{1\%}{5\%} = 0.2$$

The **price elasticity of demand** is the ratio of the percent change in the quantity demanded to the percent change in the price as we move along the demand curve.

Notice that the minus sign has been dropped from this equation. Why have we done this?

The **midpoint method** is a technique for calculating the percent change. In this approach, we calculate changes in a variable compared with the average, or midpoint, of the initial and final values.

The *law of demand* says that demand curves slope downward, so price and quantity demanded always move in opposite directions. In other words, a positive percent change in price (a rise in price) leads to a negative percent change in the quantity demanded; a negative percent change in price (a fall in price) leads to a positive percent change in the quantity demanded. This means that the price elasticity of demand is, in strictly mathematical terms, a negative number. However, it is inconvenient to repeatedly write a minus sign. So when economists talk about the price elasticity of demand, they usually drop the minus sign and report the *absolute value* of the price elasticity of demand. In other words, the absolute value of a negative number appears without the minus sign. In this case, for example, economists would usually say "the price elasticity of demand is 0.2," taking it for granted that you understand they mean *minus* 0.2. We follow this convention here.

The larger the price elasticity of demand, the more responsive the quantity demanded is to the price. When the price elasticity of demand is large—when consumers change their quantity demanded by a large percentage compared to the percent change in the price—economists say that demand is highly elastic.

As we'll see shortly, a price elasticity of 0.2 indicates a small response of quantity demanded to price. That is, the quantity demanded will fall by a relatively small amount when price rises. This is what economists call *inelastic* demand. And inelastic demand was exactly what Flunomics needed for its strategy to increase revenue by raising the price of its flu vaccines.

An Alternative Way to Calculate Elasticities: The Midpoint Method

We've seen that price elasticity of demand compares the *percent change in quantity demanded* with the *percent change in price.* When we look at some other elasticities, which we will do shortly, we'll see why it is important to focus on percent changes. But at this point we need to discuss a technical issue that arises when you calculate percent changes in variables and how economists deal with it.

The best way to understand the issue is with a real example. Suppose you were trying to estimate the price elasticity of demand for gasoline by comparing gasoline prices and consumption in different countries. Because of high taxes, gasoline usually costs about three times as much per gallon in Europe as it does in the United States. So what is the percent difference between American and European gas prices?

Well, it depends on which way you measure it. Because the price of gasoline in Europe is approximately three times higher than in the United States, it is 200 percent higher. Because the price of gasoline in the United States is one-third as high as in Europe, it is 66.7 percent lower.

© Dan Van Den Broeke/Dreamstime.com

This is a nuisance: we'd like to have a percent measure of the difference in prices that doesn't depend on which way you measure it. A good way to avoid computing different elasticities for rising and falling prices is to use the *midpoint method* (sometimes called the *arc method*).

The **midpoint method** replaces the usual definition of the percent change in a variable, *X*, with a slightly different definition:

$$\textbf{(8-4)} \quad \%\text{ change in } X = \frac{\text{Change in } X}{\text{Average value of } X} \times 100$$

where the average value of *X* is defined as

$$\text{Average value of } X = \frac{\text{Starting value of } X + \text{Final value of } X}{2}$$

When calculating the price elasticity of demand using the midpoint method, both the percent change in the price and the percent change in the quantity demanded are found using average values in this way. To see how this method works, suppose you have the following data for some good:

	Price	Quantity demanded
Situation A	$0.90	1,100
Situation B	$1.10	900

To calculate the percent change in quantity going from situation A to situation B, we compare the change in the quantity demanded—a fall of 200 units—with the *average* of the quantity demanded in the two situations. So we calculate

$$\% \text{ change in quantity demanded} = \frac{-200}{(1{,}100 + 900)/2} \times 100 = \frac{-200}{1{,}000} \times 100 = -20\%$$

In the same way, we calculate the percent change in price as

$$\% \text{ change in price} = \frac{\$0.20}{(\$0.90 + \$1.10)/2} \times 100 = \frac{\$0.20}{\$1.00} \times 100 = 20\%$$

So in this case we would calculate the price elasticity of demand to be

$$\text{Price elasticity of demand} = \frac{\% \text{ change in quantity demanded}}{\% \text{ change in price}} = \frac{20\%}{20\%} = 1$$

again dropping the minus sign.

The important point is that we would get the same result, a price elasticity of demand of 1, whether we went up the demand curve from situation A to situation B or down from situation B to situation A.

ECONOMICS IN ACTION

ESTIMATING ELASTICITIES

You might think it's easy to estimate price elasticities of demand from real-world data: just compare percent changes in prices with percent changes in quantities demanded. Unfortunately, it's rarely that simple because changes in price aren't the only thing affecting changes in the quantity demanded: other factors—such as changes in income, changes in population, and changes in the prices of other goods—shift the demand curve, thereby changing the quantity demanded at any given price.

To estimate price elasticities of demand, economists must use careful statistical analysis to separate the influence of these different factors, holding other things equal.

The most comprehensive effort to estimate price elasticities of demand was a mammoth study by the economists Hendrik S. Houthakker and Lester D. Taylor. Some of their results are summarized in Table 8-1. These estimates show a wide range of price elasticities. There are some goods, like eggs, for which demand hardly responds at all to changes in the price; there are other goods, most notably foreign travel, for which the quantity demanded is very sensitive to the price.

Notice that Table 8-1 is divided into two parts: inelastic and elastic demand. We'll explain in the next module the significance of that division.

TABLE 8-1

Some Estimated Price Elasticities of Demand

Good	Price elasticity of demand
Inelastic demand	
Eggs	0.1
Beef	0.4
Stationery	0.5
Gasoline	0.5
Elastic demand	
Housing	1.2
Restaurant meals	2.3
Airline travel	2.4
Foreign travel	4.1

Source: Hendrick S. Houthakker and Lester D. Taylor, *Consumer Demand in the United States, 1929–1970* (Cambridge: Harvard University Press, 1970)

To arrive at a more general formula for price elasticity of demand, suppose that we have data for two points on a demand curve. At point 1 the quantity demanded and price are (Q_1, P_1); at point 2 they are (Q_2, P_2). Then the formula for calculating the price elasticity of demand is:

$$\textbf{(8-5)} \quad \text{Price elasticity of demand} = \frac{\dfrac{Q_2 - Q_1}{(Q_1 + Q_2)/2}}{\dfrac{P_2 - P_1}{(P_1 + P_2)/2}}$$

As before, when reporting a price elasticity of demand calculated by the midpoint method, we drop the minus sign and report the absolute value.

MODULE 8 Review

Solutions appear at the back of the book.

Check Your Understanding

1. In each of the following cases, state whether the income effect, the substitution effect, or both are significant. In which cases do they move in the same direction? In opposite directions? Why?
   a. Orange juice represents a small share of Clare's spending. She buys more lemonade and less orange juice when the price of orange juice goes up. She does not change her spending on other goods.
   b. Apartment rents have risen dramatically this year. Since rent absorbs a major part of her income, Delia moves to a smaller apartment. Assume that rental housing is a normal good.
   c. The cost of a semester-long meal ticket at the student cafeteria rises, representing a significant increase in living costs. As a result, many students have less money to spend on weekend meals at restaurants and eat in the cafeteria instead. Assume that cafeteria meals are an inferior good.
2. The price of strawberries falls from \$1.50 to \$1.00 per carton, and the quantity demanded goes from 100,000 to 200,000 cartons. Use the midpoint method to find the price elasticity of demand.
3. At the present level of consumption, 4,000 movie tickets, and at the current price, \$5 per ticket, the price elasticity of demand for movie tickets is 1. Using the midpoint method, calculate the percentage by which the owners of movie theaters must reduce the price in order to sell 5,000 tickets.
4. The price elasticity of demand for ice-cream sandwiches is 1.2 at the current price of \$0.50 per sandwich and the current consumption level of 100,000 sandwiches. Calculate the change in the quantity demanded when price rises by \$0.05. Use Equations 8-1 and 8-2 to calculate percent changes and Equation 8-3 to relate price elasticity of demand to the percent changes.

Multiple-Choice Questions

1. Which of the following statements is true?
   I. When a good absorbs only a small share of consumer spending, the income effect explains the demand curve's negative slope.
   II. A change in consumption brought about by a change in purchasing power describes the income effect.
   III. In the case of an inferior good, the income and substitution effects work in opposite directions.

   a. I only
   b. II only
   c. III only
   d. II and III only
   e. I, II, and III

2. The income effect is most likely to come into play for which of the following goods?
   a. water
   b. clothing
   c. housing
   d. transportation
   e. entertainment

3. If a decrease in price from $2 to $1 causes an increase in quantity demanded from 100 to 120, using the midpoint method, price elasticity of demand equals
   a. 0.17.
   b. 0.27.
   c. 0.40.
   d. 2.5.
   e. 3.72.

4. Which of the following is likely to have the highest price elasticity of demand?
   a. eggs
   b. beef
   c. housing
   d. gasoline
   e. foreign travel

5. If a 2% change in the price of a good leads to a 10% change in the quantity demanded of a good, what is the value of price elasticity of demand?
   a. 0.02
   b. 0.2
   c. 5
   d. 10
   e. 20

Critical-Thinking Questions

Assume the price of an inferior good increases.

1. In what direction will the substitution effect change the quantity demanded? Explain.
2. In what direction will the income effect change the quantity demanded? Explain.
3. Given that the demand curve for the good slopes downward, what is true of the relative sizes of the income and substitution effects for the inferior good? Explain.

9 Interpreting Price Elasticity of Demand

iStockphoto/Thinkstock

WHAT YOU WILL LEARN

1. **The difference between elastic and inelastic demand**
2. **The relationship between elasticity and total revenue**
3. **Changes in the price elasticity of demand along a demand curve**
4. **The factors that determine price elasticity of demand**

A Closer Look at the Price Elasticity of Demand

Med-Stat and other pharmaceutical distributors believed they could sharply drive up flu vaccine prices in the face of a shortage because the price elasticity of vaccine demand was low. But what does that mean? How low does a price elasticity have to be for us to classify it as low? How high does it have to be for us to consider it high? And what determines whether the price elasticity of demand is high or low, anyway? To answer these questions, we need to look more deeply at the price elasticity of demand.

How Elastic Is Elastic?

As a first step toward classifying price elasticities of demand, let's look at the extreme cases.

First, consider the demand for a good when people pay no attention to the price of, say, shoelaces. Suppose that consumers would buy 1 billion pairs of shoelaces per year regardless of the price. If that were true, the demand curve for shoelaces would look like the curve shown in panel (a) of Figure 9-1: it would be a vertical line at 1 billion pairs of shoelaces. Since the percent change in the quantity demanded is zero for *any* change in the price, the price elasticity of demand in this case is zero. The case of a zero price elasticity of demand is known as **perfectly inelastic** demand.

Demand is **perfectly inelastic** when the quantity demanded does not respond at all to changes in the price. When demand is perfectly inelastic, the demand curve is a vertical line.

The opposite extreme occurs when even a tiny rise in the price will cause the quantity demanded to drop to zero or even a tiny fall in the price will cause the quantity demanded to get extremely large.

Panel (b) of Figure 9-1 shows the case of pink tennis balls; we suppose that tennis players really don't care what color their balls are and that other colors, such as neon

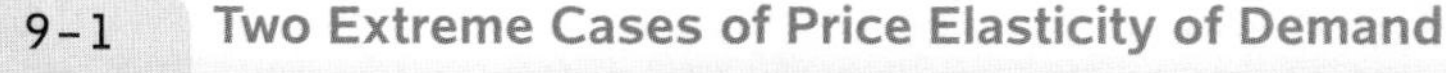

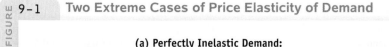

FIGURE 9-1 Two Extreme Cases of Price Elasticity of Demand

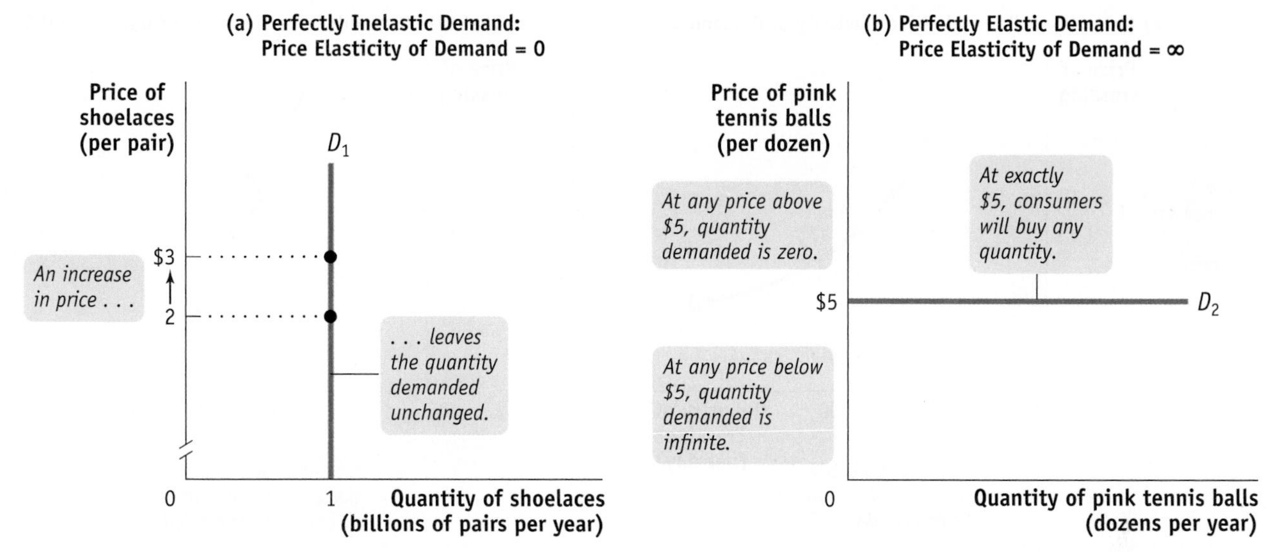

Panel (a) shows a perfectly inelastic demand curve, which is a vertical line. The quantity of shoelaces demanded is always 1 billion pairs, regardless of price. As a result, the price elasticity of demand is zero—the quantity demanded is unaffected by the price. Panel (b) shows a perfectly elastic demand curve, which is a horizontal line. At a price of $5, consumers will buy any quantity of pink tennis balls, but will buy none at a price above $5. If the price falls below $5, they will buy an extremely large number of pink tennis balls and none of any other color.

green and vivid yellow, are available at $5 per dozen balls. In this case, consumers will buy no pink balls if they cost more than $5 per dozen but will buy only pink balls if they cost less than $5. The demand curve will therefore be a horizontal line at a price of $5 per dozen balls. As you move back and forth along this line, there is a change in the quantity demanded but no change in the price. When you divide a number by zero, you get infinity, denoted by the symbol ∞. So a horizontal demand curve implies an infinite price elasticity of demand. When the price elasticity of demand is infinite, economists say that demand is **perfectly elastic.**

Demand is **perfectly elastic** when any price increase will cause the quantity demanded to drop to zero. When demand is perfectly elastic, the demand curve is a horizontal line.

Demand is **elastic** if the price elasticity of demand is greater than 1, **inelastic** if the price elasticity of demand is less than 1, and **unit-elastic** if the price elasticity of demand is exactly 1.

The price elasticity of demand for the vast majority of goods is somewhere between these two extreme cases. Economists use one main criterion for classifying these intermediate cases: they ask whether the price elasticity of demand is greater or less than 1. When the price elasticity of demand is greater than 1, economists say that demand is **elastic.** When the price elasticity of demand is less than 1, they say that demand is **inelastic.** The borderline case is **unit-elastic** demand, where the price elasticity of demand is—surprise—exactly 1.

To see why a price elasticity of demand equal to 1 is a useful dividing line, let's consider a hypothetical example: a toll bridge operated by the state highway department. Other things being equal, the number of drivers who use the bridge depends on the toll, the price the highway department charges for crossing the bridge: the higher the toll, the fewer the drivers who use the bridge.

©Rorem/Dreamstime.com

Knowing the price elasticity of demand allows the highway department to determine the drop in bridge use that would result from higher tolls.

Figure 9-2 shows three hypothetical demand curves—one in which demand is unit-elastic, one in which it is inelastic, and one in which it is elastic. In each case, point *A* shows the quantity demanded if the toll is $0.90 and point

FIGURE 9-2 Unit-Elastic Demand, Inelastic Demand, and Elastic Demand

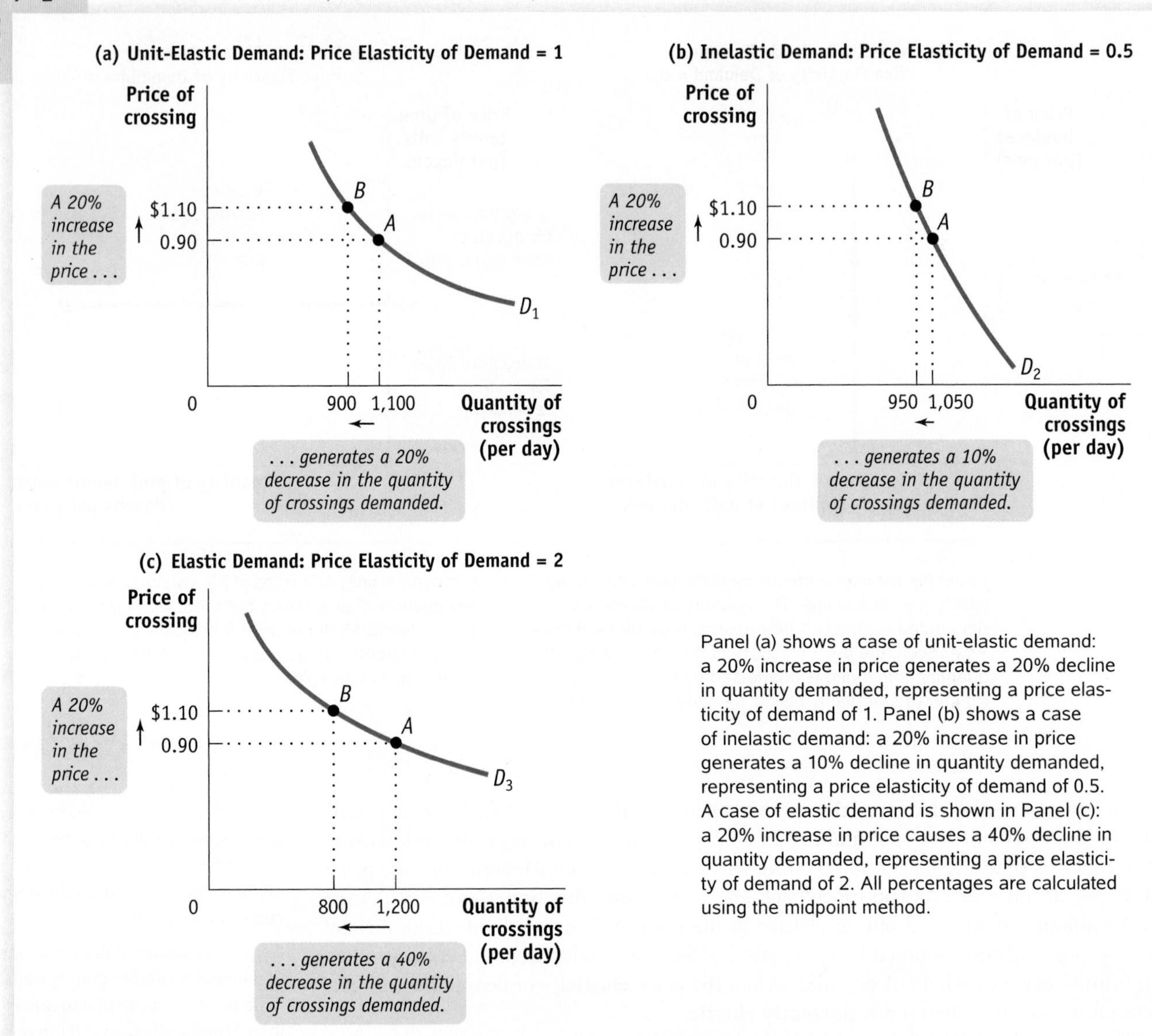

Panel (a) shows a case of unit-elastic demand: a 20% increase in price generates a 20% decline in quantity demanded, representing a price elasticity of demand of 1. Panel (b) shows a case of inelastic demand: a 20% increase in price generates a 10% decline in quantity demanded, representing a price elasticity of demand of 0.5. A case of elastic demand is shown in Panel (c): a 20% increase in price causes a 40% decline in quantity demanded, representing a price elasticity of demand of 2. All percentages are calculated using the midpoint method.

B shows the quantity demanded if the toll is $1.10. An increase in the toll from $0.90 to $1.10 is an increase of 20% if we use the midpoint method to calculate percent changes.

Panel (a) shows what happens when the toll is raised from $0.90 to $1.10 and the demand curve is unit-elastic. Here the 20% price rise leads to a fall in the quantity of cars using the bridge each day from 1,100 to 900, which is a 20% decline (again using the midpoint method). So the price elasticity of demand is 20%/20% = 1.

Panel (b) shows a case of inelastic demand when the toll is raised from $0.90 to $1.10. The same 20% price rise reduces the quantity demanded from 1,050 to 950. That's only a 10% decline, so in this case the price elasticity of demand is 10%/20% = 0.5.

Panel (c) shows a case of elastic demand when the toll is raised from $0.90 to $1.10. The 20% price increase causes the quantity demanded to fall from 1,200 to 800, a 40% decline, so the price elasticity of demand is 40%/20% = 2.

Why does it matter whether demand is unit-elastic, inelastic, or elastic? Because this classification predicts how changes in the price of a good will affect the *total revenue* earned by producers from the sale of that good. In many real-life situations, such as the one faced by Med-Stat, it is crucial to know how price changes affect total revenue. **Total revenue** is defined as the total value of sales of a good or service: the price multiplied by the quantity sold.

Total revenue is the total value of sales of a good or service. It is equal to the price multiplied by the quantity sold.

(9-1) Total revenue = Price × Quantity sold

Total revenue has a useful graphical representation that can help us understand why knowing the price elasticity of demand is crucial when we ask whether a price rise will increase or reduce total revenue. Panel (a) of Figure 9-3 shows the same demand curve as panel (a) of Figure 9-2. We see that 1,100 drivers will use the bridge if the toll is \$0.90. So the total revenue at a price of \$0.90 is \$0.90 × 1,100 = \$990. This value is equal to the area of the green rectangle, which is drawn with the bottom left corner at the point (0, 0) and the top right corner at (1,100, 0.90). In general, the total revenue at any given price is equal to the area of a rectangle whose height is the price and whose width is the quantity demanded at that price.

To get an idea of why total revenue is important, consider the following scenario. Suppose that the toll on the bridge is currently \$0.90 but that the highway department must raise extra money for road repairs. One way to do this is to raise the toll on the bridge. But this plan might backfire, since a higher toll will reduce the number of drivers who use the bridge. And if traffic on the bridge dropped a lot, a higher toll would actually reduce total revenue instead of increasing it. So it's important for the highway department to know how drivers will respond to a toll increase.

We can see graphically how the toll increase affects total bridge revenue by examining panel (b) of Figure 9-3. At a toll of \$0.90, total revenue is given by the sum of the areas *A* and *B*. After the toll is raised to \$1.10, total revenue is given by the sum of areas *B* and *C*. So when the toll is raised, revenue represented by area *A* is lost but revenue represented by area *C* is gained.

These two areas have important interpretations. Area *C* represents the revenue gain that comes from the additional \$0.20 paid by drivers who continue to use the bridge. That is, the 900 drivers who continue to use the bridge contribute an additional \$0.20 × 900 = \$180 per day to total revenue, represented by area *C*. But 200 drivers who would have used the bridge at a price of \$0.90 no longer do so, generating

FIGURE 9-3 Total Revenue

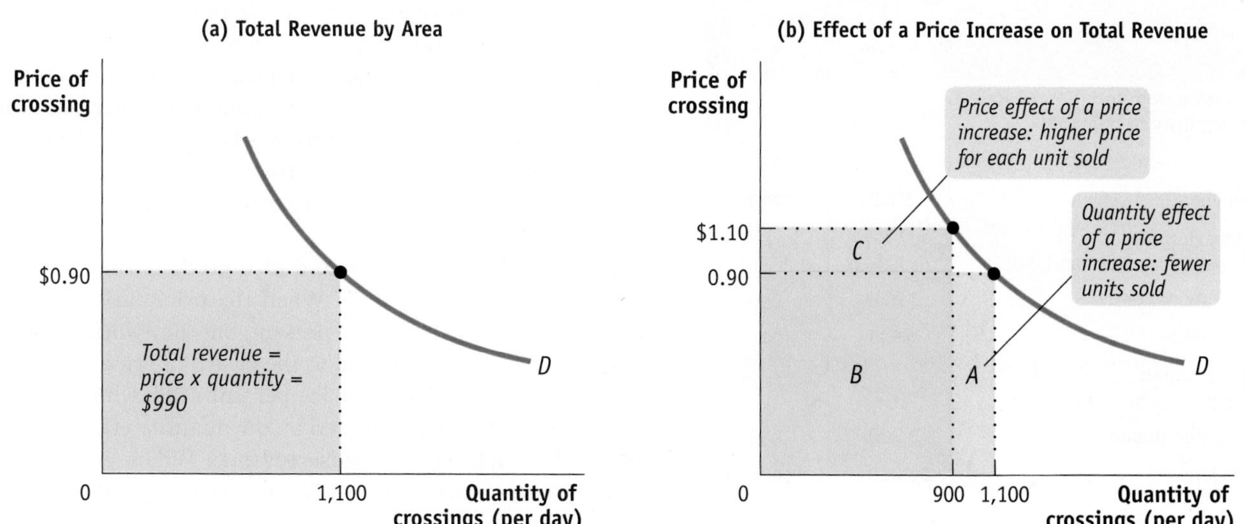

The green rectangle in panel (a) represents total revenue generated from 1,100 drivers who each pay a toll of \$0.90. Panel (b) shows how total revenue is affected when the price increases from \$0.90 to \$1.10. Due to the quantity effect, total revenue falls by area *A*. Due to the price effect, total revenue increases by area *C*. In general, the overall effect can go either way, depending on the price elasticity of demand.

a loss to total revenue of $0.90 × 200 = $180 per day, represented by area *A*. (In this particular example, because demand is unit-elastic between the two points—the same as in panel (a) of Figure 9-2—the rise in the toll has no effect on total revenue; areas *A* and *C* are the same size.)

Except in the rare case of a good with perfectly elastic or perfectly inelastic demand, when a seller raises the price of a good, two countervailing effects are present:

- *A price effect.* After a price increase, each unit sold sells at a higher price, which tends to raise revenue.
- *A quantity effect.* After a price increase, fewer units are sold, which tends to lower revenue.

But then, you may ask, what is the net ultimate effect on total revenue: does it go up or down? The answer is that, in general, the effect on total revenue can go either way—a price rise may either increase total revenue or lower it. If the price effect, which tends to raise total revenue, is the stronger of the two effects, then total revenue goes up. If the quantity effect, which tends to reduce total revenue, is the stronger, then total revenue goes down. And if the strengths of the two effects are exactly equal—as in our toll bridge example, where a $180 gain offsets a $180 loss—total revenue is unchanged by the price increase.

The price elasticity of demand tells us what happens to total revenue when price changes: its size determines which effect—the price effect or the quantity effect—is stronger. Specifically:

- If demand for a good is *unit-elastic* (the price elasticity of demand is 1), an increase in price does not change total revenue. In this case, the quantity effect is weaker than the price effect.
- If demand for a good is *inelastic* (the price elasticity of demand is less than 1), a higher price increases total revenue. In this case, the quantity effect is weaker than the price effect.
- If demand for a good is *elastic* (the price elasticity of demand is greater than 1), an increase in price reduces total revenue. In this case, the quantity effect is stronger than the price effect.

TABLE 9-1

Price Elasticity of Demand and Total Revenue

	Price of crossing = $0.90	Price of crossing = $1.10
Unit-elastic demand (price elasticity of demand = 1)		
Quantity demanded	1,100	900
Total revenue	$990	$990
Inelastic demand (price elasticity of demand = 0.5)		
Quantity demanded	1,050	950
Total revenue	$945	$1,045
Elastic demand (price elasticity of demand = 2)		
Quantity demanded	1,200	800
Total revenue	$1,080	$880

Table 9-1 shows how the effect of a price increase on total revenue depends on the price elasticity of demand, using the same data as in Figure 9-2. An increase in the price from $0.90 to $1.10 leaves total revenue unchanged at $990 when demand is unit-elastic. When demand is inelastic, the quantity effect is dominated by the price effect; the same price increase leads to an increase in total revenue from $945 to $1,045. And when demand is elastic, the quantity effect dominates the price effect; the price increase leads to a decline in total revenue from $1,080 to $880.

The price elasticity of demand also predicts the effect of a *fall* in price on total revenue. When the price falls, the same two countervailing effects are present, but they work in the opposite directions as compared to the case of a price rise. There is the price effect of a lower price per unit sold, which tends to lower revenue. This is countered by the quantity effect of more units sold, which tends to raise revenue. Which effect dominates depends on the price elasticity. Here is a quick summary:

- When demand is *unit-elastic,* the two effects exactly balance each other out; so a fall in price has no effect on total revenue.
- When demand is *inelastic,* the quantity effect is dominated by the price effect; so a fall in price reduces total revenue.
- When demand is *elastic,* the quantity effect dominates the price effect; so a fall in price increases total revenue.

Price Elasticity Along the Demand Curve

Suppose an economist says that "the price elasticity of demand for coffee is 0.25." What he or she means is that *at the current price* the elasticity is 0.25. In the previous discussion of the toll bridge, what we were really describing was the elasticity *at a specific price.* Why this qualification? Because for the vast majority of demand curves, the price elasticity of demand at one point along the curve is different from the price elasticity of demand at other points along the same curve.

To see this, consider the table in Figure 9-4, which shows a hypothetical demand schedule. It also shows in the last column the total revenue generated at each price and quantity combination in the demand schedule. The upper panel of the graph in Figure 9-4 shows the corresponding demand curve. The lower panel illustrates the same data on total revenue: the height of a bar at each quantity demanded—which corresponds to a particular price—measures the total revenue generated at that price.

In Figure 9-4, you can see that when the price is low, raising the price increases total revenue: starting at a price of $1, raising the price to $2 increases total revenue from $9 to $16. This means that when the price is low, demand is inelastic. Moreover, you can see that demand is inelastic on the entire section of the demand curve from a price of $0 to a price of $5.

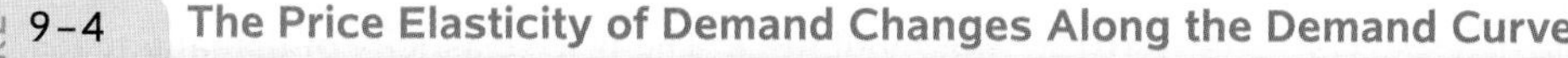

FIGURE 9-4 The Price Elasticity of Demand Changes Along the Demand Curve

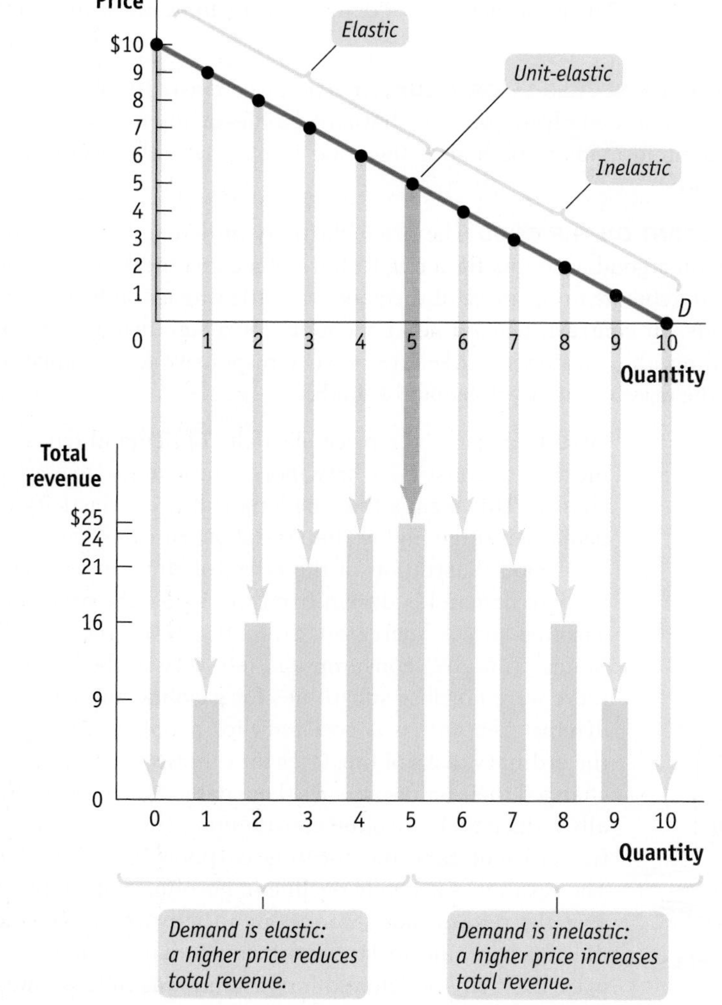

Demand Schedule and Total Revenue for a Linear Demand Curve

Price	Quantity demanded	Total revenue
$0	10	$0
1	9	9
2	8	16
3	7	21
4	6	24
5	5	25
6	4	24
7	3	21
8	2	16
9	1	9
10	0	0

The upper panel shows a demand curve corresponding to the demand schedule in the table. The lower panel shows how total revenue changes along that demand curve: at each price and quantity combination, the height of the bar represents the total revenue generated. You can see that at a low price, raising the price increases total revenue. So demand is inelastic at low prices. At a high price, however, a rise in price reduces total revenue. So demand is elastic at high prices.

When the price is high, however, raising it further reduces total revenue: starting at a price of $8, for example, raising the price to $9 reduces total revenue, from $16 to $9. This means that when the price is high, demand is elastic. Furthermore, you can see that demand is elastic over the section of the demand curve from a price of $5 to $10.

For the vast majority of goods, the price elasticity of demand changes along the demand curve. So whenever you measure a good's elasticity, you are really measuring it at a particular point or section of the good's demand curve.

What Factors Determine the Price Elasticity of Demand?

The flu vaccine shortfall of 2004–2005 allowed vaccine distributors to significantly raise their prices for two important reasons: there were no substitutes, and for many people the vaccine was a medical necessity.

People responded in various ways. Some paid the high prices, and some traveled to Canada and other countries to get vaccinated. Some simply did without (and over time often changed their habits to avoid catching the flu, such as eating out less often and avoiding mass transit). This experience illustrates the four main factors that determine elasticity: whether close substitutes are available, whether the good is a necessity or a luxury, the share of income a consumer spends on the good, and how much time has elapsed since the price change. We'll briefly examine each of these factors.

WHETHER CLOSE SUBSTITUTES ARE AVAILABLE The price elasticity of demand tends to be high if there are other goods that consumers regard as similar and would be willing to consume instead. The price elasticity of demand tends to be low if there are no close substitutes.

WHETHER THE GOOD IS A NECESSITY OR A LUXURY The price elasticity of demand tends to be low if a good is something you must have, like a life-saving medicine. The price elasticity of demand tends to be high if the good is a luxury—something you can easily live without.

SHARE OF INCOME SPENT ON THE GOOD The price elasticity of demand tends to be low when spending on a good accounts for a small share of a consumer's income. In that case, a significant change in the price of the good has little impact on how much the consumer spends. In contrast, when a good accounts for a significant share of a consumer's spending, the consumer is likely to be very responsive to a change in price. In this case, the price elasticity of demand is high.

TIME In general, the price elasticity of demand tends to increase as consumers have more time to adjust to a price change. This means that the long-run price elasticity of demand is often higher than the short-run elasticity.

A good illustration of the effect of time on the elasticity of demand is drawn from the 1970s, the first time gasoline prices increased dramatically in the United States. Initially, consumption fell very little because there were no close substitutes for gasoline and because driving their cars was necessary for people to carry out the ordinary tasks of life. Over time, however, Americans changed their habits in ways that enabled them to gradually reduce their gasoline consumption (by buying more fuel-efficient cars and forming carpools, for example). The result was a steady decline in gasoline consumption over the next decade, even though the price of gasoline did not continue to rise, confirming that the long-run price elasticity of demand for gasoline was indeed much larger than the short-run elasticity.

"Three hundred dollars' of regular."

ECONOMICS IN ACTION

RESPONDING TO YOUR TUITION BILL

College costs more than ever—and not just because of overall inflation. Tuition has been rising faster than the overall cost of living for years. But does rising tuition keep people from going to college? Two studies found that the answer depends on the type of college. Both studies assessed how responsive the decision to go to college is to a change in tuition.

A 1988 study found that a 3% increase in tuition led to an approximately 2% fall in the number of students enrolled at four-year institutions, giving a price elasticity of demand of 0.67 (2%/3%). In the case of two-year institutions, the study found a significantly higher response: a 3% increase in tuition led to a 2.7% fall in enrollments, giving a price elasticity of demand of 0.9. In other words, the enrollment decision for students at two-year colleges was significantly more responsive to price than for students at four-year colleges. The result: students at two-year colleges are more likely to forgo getting a degree because of tuition costs than students at four-year colleges.

Photodisc

How responsive are college enrollment rates to changes in tuition?

A 1999 study confirmed this pattern. In comparison to four-year colleges, it found that two-year college enrollment rates were significantly more responsive to changes in state financial aid (a decline in aid leading to a decline in enrollments), a predictable effect given these students' greater sensitivity to the cost of tuition. Another piece of evidence suggests that students at two-year colleges are more likely to be paying their own way and making a trade-off between attending college and working: the study found that enrollments at two-year colleges are much more responsive to changes in the unemployment rate (an increase in the unemployment rate leading to an increase in enrollments) than enrollments at four-year colleges. So is the cost of tuition a barrier to getting a college degree in the United States? Yes, but more so at two-year colleges than at four-year colleges.

Interestingly, the 1999 study found that for both two-year and four-year colleges, price sensitivity of demand had fallen somewhat since the 1988 study. One possible explanation is that because the value of a college education has risen considerably over time, fewer people forgo college, even if tuition goes up.

MODULE 9 Review

Solutions appear at the back of the book.

Check Your Understanding

1. For each case, choose the condition that characterizes demand: elastic demand, inelastic demand, or unit-elastic demand.
   a. Total revenue decreases when price increases.
   b. When price falls, the additional revenue generated by the increase in the quantity sold is exactly offset by the revenue lost from the fall in the price received per unit.
   c. Total revenue falls when output increases.
   d. Producers in an industry find they can increase their total revenues by working together to reduce industry output.
2. For the following goods, is demand elastic, inelastic, or unit-elastic? Explain. What is the shape of the demand curve?
   a. demand by a snake-bite victim for an antidote
   b. demand by students for blue pencils

Multiple-Choice Questions

1. A perfectly elastic demand curve is
   a. upward sloping.
   b. vertical.
   c. not a straight line.
   d. horizontal.
   e. downward sloping.

2. Which of the following would cause the demand for a good to be relatively inelastic?
   a. The good has a large number of close substitutes.
   b. Expenditures on the good represent a large share of consumer income.
   c. There is ample time to adjust to price changes.
   d. The good is a necessity.
   e. The price of the good is in the upper left section of a linear demand curve.

3. Which of the following is true if the price elasticity of demand for a good is zero?
   a. The slope of the demand curve is zero.
   b. The slope of the demand curve is one.
   c. The demand curve is vertical.
   d. The demand curve is horizontal.
   e. The price of the good is high.

4. Which of the following is correct for a price increase? When demand is __________, total revenue will __________.

	Demand	*Total Revenue*
a.	inelastic	decrease
b.	elastic	decrease
c.	unit-elastic	increase
d.	unit-elastic	decrease
e.	elastic	increase

5. Total revenue is maximized when demand is
   a. elastic.
   b. inelastic.
   c. unit-elastic.
   d. zero.
   e. infinite.

Critical-Thinking Questions

Draw a correctly labeled graph illustrating a demand curve that is a straight line and is neither perfectly elastic nor perfectly inelastic.

1. On your graph, indicate the half of the demand curve along which demand is elastic.
2. In the elastic range, how will an increase in price affect total revenue? Explain.

Other Elasticities

(left) Msheldrake/Dreamstime.com • (right) © Lauri Patterson/iStockphoto

WHAT YOU WILL LEARN

1. **How the cross-price elasticity of demand measures the responsiveness of demand for one good to changes in the price of another good**
2. **The meaning and importance of the income elasticity of demand, a measure of the responsiveness of demand to changes in income**
3. **The significance of the price elasticity of supply, which measures the responsiveness of the quantity supplied to changes in price**
4. **The factors that influence the size of these various elasticities**

Using Other Elasticities

We stated earlier that economists use the concept of *elasticity* to measure the responsiveness of one variable to changes in another. However, up to this point we have focused on the price elasticity of demand. Now that we have used elasticity to measure the responsiveness of quantity demanded to changes in price, we can go on to look at how elasticity is used to understand the relationship between other important variables in economics.

The quantity of a good demanded depends not only on the price of that good but also on other variables. In particular, demand curves shift because of changes in the prices of related goods and changes in consumers' incomes. It is often important to have a measure of these other effects, and the best measures are—you guessed it—elasticities. Specifically, we can best measure how the demand for a good is affected by prices of other goods using a measure called the *cross-price elasticity of demand,* and we can best measure how demand is affected by changes in income using the *income elasticity of demand.*

Finally, we can also use elasticity to measure supply responses. The *price elasticity of supply* measures the responsiveness of the quantity supplied to changes in price.

The Cross-Price Elasticity of Demand

The demand for a good is often affected by the prices of other, related goods—goods that are substitutes or complements. A change in the price of a related good shifts the demand curve of the original good, reflecting a change in the quantity demanded at any given price. The strength of such a "cross" effect on demand can be measured by the **cross-price elasticity of demand,** defined as the ratio of the percent change in the quantity demanded of one good to the percent change in the price of another.

The **cross-price elasticity of demand** between two goods measures the effect of the change in one good's price on the quantity demanded of the other good. It is equal to the percent change in the quantity demanded of one good divided by the percent change in the other good's price.

(10-1) Cross-price elasticity of demand between goods A and B

$$= \frac{\text{\% change in quantity of A demanded}}{\text{\% change in price of B}}$$

When two goods are substitutes, like hot dogs and hamburgers, the cross-price elasticity of demand is positive: a rise in the price of hot dogs increases the demand for hamburgers—that is, it causes a rightward shift of the demand curve for hamburgers. If the goods are close substitutes, the cross-price elasticity will be positive and large; if they are not close substitutes, the cross-price elasticity will be positive and small. So when the cross-price elasticity of demand is positive, its size is a measure of how closely substitutable the two goods are, with a higher number meaning the goods are closer substitutes.

When two goods are complements, like hot dogs and hot dog buns, the cross-price elasticity is negative: a rise in the price of hot dogs decreases the demand for hot dog buns—that is, it causes a leftward shift of the demand curve for hot dog buns. As with substitutes, the size of the cross-price elasticity of demand between two complements tells us how strongly complementary they are: if the cross-price elasticity is only slightly below zero, they are weak complements; if it is very negative, they are strong complements.

Note that in the case of the cross-price elasticity of demand, the sign (plus or minus) is very important: it tells us whether the two goods are complements or substitutes. So we cannot drop the minus sign as we did for the price elasticity of demand.

Our discussion of the cross-price elasticity of demand is a useful place to return to a point we made earlier: elasticity is a *unit-free* measure—that is, it doesn't depend on the units in which goods are measured.

To see the potential problem, suppose someone told you that "if the price of hot dog buns rises by $0.30, Americans will buy 10 million fewer hot dogs this year." If you've ever bought hot dog buns, you'll immediately wonder: is that a $0.30 increase in the price *per bun,* or is it a $0.30 increase in the price *per package* of buns? It makes a big difference what units we are talking about! However, if someone says that the cross-price elasticity of demand between buns and hot dogs is −0.3, it doesn't matter whether buns are sold individually or by the package. So elasticity is defined as a ratio of percent changes, which avoids confusion over units.

The Income Elasticity of Demand

The **income elasticity of demand** measures how changes in income affect the demand for a good. It indicates whether a good is normal or inferior and specifies how responsive demand for the good is to changes in income. Having learned the price and cross-price elasticity formulas, the income elasticity formula will look familiar:

(10-2) Income elasticity of demand $= \frac{\text{\% change in quantity demanded}}{\text{\% change in income}}$

Just as the cross-price elasticity of demand between two goods can be either positive or negative, depending on whether the goods are substitutes or complements, the income elasticity of demand for a good can also be either positive or negative. Recall that goods can be either *normal goods,* for which demand increases when income rises, or *inferior goods,* for which demand decreases when income rises. These definitions relate directly to the sign of the income elasticity of demand:

- When the income elasticity of demand is positive, the good is a normal good—that is, the quantity demanded at any given price increases as income increases.
- When the income elasticity of demand is negative, the good is an inferior good—that is, the quantity demanded at any given price decreases as income increases.

The **income elasticity of demand** is the percent change in the quantity of a good demanded when a consumer's income changes divided by the percent change in the consumer's income.

Economists often use estimates of the income elasticity of demand to predict which industries will grow most rapidly as the incomes of consumers grow over time. In doing this, they often find it useful to make a further distinction among normal goods, identifying which are *income-elastic* and which are *income-inelastic.*

The demand for a good is **income-elastic** if the income elasticity of demand for that good is greater than 1. When income rises, the demand for income-elastic goods rises *faster* than income. Luxury goods such as second homes and international travel tend to be income-elastic. The demand for a good is **income-inelastic** if the income elasticity of demand for that good is positive but less than 1. When income rises, the demand for income-inelastic goods rises, but more slowly than income. Necessities such as food and clothing tend to be income-inelastic.

The demand for a good is **income-elastic** if the income elasticity of demand for that good is greater than 1.

The demand for a good is **income-inelastic** if the income elasticity of demand for that good is positive but less than 1.

ECONOMICS IN ACTION — WORLD VIEW

WILL CHINA SAVE THE U.S. FARMING SECTOR?

In the days of the Founding Fathers, the great majority of Americans lived on farms. As recently as the 1940s, one American in six—or approximately 17%—still did. But in 2007, the official number was less than 1%. Why do so few people now live and work on farms in the United States? There are two main reasons, both involving elasticities.

First, the income elasticity of demand for food is much less than 1—it is income-inelastic. As consumers grow richer, other things being equal, spending on food rises less than income. As a result, as the U.S. economy has grown, the share of income it spends on food—and therefore the share of total U.S. income earned by farmers—has fallen.

Second, the demand for food is price-inelastic. This is important because technological advances in American agriculture have steadily raised yields over time and led to a long-term trend of lower U.S. food prices for most of the past century and a half. The combination of price inelasticity and falling prices led to falling total revenue for farmers. That's right: progress in farming has been good for American consumers but bad for American farmers.

The combination of these effects explains the long-term relative decline of farming in the United States. The low income elasticity of demand for food ensures that the income of farmers grows more slowly than the economy as a whole. And the combination of rapid technological progress in farming with price-inelastic demand for foodstuffs reinforces this effect, further reducing the growth of farm income.

Cultura Limited/SuperStock

Why do so few Americans live and work on farms?

That is, up until now. Starting in the mid-2000s, increased demand for foodstuffs from rapidly growing developing countries like China has pushed up the prices of agricultural products around the world. And American farmers have benefited, with U.S. farm net income rising 47% in 2011 alone. Eventually, as the growth in developing countries tapers off and agricultural innovation continues to progress, it's likely that the agricultural sector will resume its downward trend. But for now and for the foreseeable future, American farmers are enjoying the sector's revival.

The Price Elasticity of Supply

In the wake of the flu vaccine shortfall of 2004, attempts by vaccine distributors to drive up the price of vaccines would have been much less effective if a higher price had induced a large increase in the output of flu vaccines by flu vaccine manufacturers other than Chiron. In fact, if the rise in price had precipitated a significant increase in flu vaccine production, the price would have been pushed back down. But that didn't happen because, as we mentioned earlier, it would have been far too costly and technically difficult to produce more vaccine for the 2004–2005 flu season. (In reality, the production of flu vaccine is begun a year before it is to be distributed.)

The **price elasticity of supply** is a measure of the responsiveness of the quantity of a good supplied to the price of that good. It is the ratio of the percent change in the quantity supplied to the percent change in the price as we move along the supply curve.

There is **perfectly inelastic supply** when the price elasticity of supply is zero, so that changes in the price of the good have no effect on the quantity supplied. A perfectly inelastic supply curve is a vertical line.

There is **perfectly elastic supply** if the quantity supplied is zero below some price and infinite above that price. A perfectly elastic supply curve is a horizontal line.

This was another critical element in the ability of some flu vaccine distributors, like Med-Stat, to get significantly higher prices for their product: a low responsiveness in the quantity of output supplied to the higher price of flu vaccine by flu vaccine producers. To measure the response of producers to price changes, we need a measure parallel to the price elasticity of demand—the *price elasticity of supply*.

Measuring the Price Elasticity of Supply

The **price elasticity of supply** is defined the same way as the price elasticity of demand (although there is no minus sign to be eliminated here):

$$\textbf{(10-3)}\quad \text{Price elasticity of supply} = \frac{\%\text{ change in quantity supplied}}{\%\text{ change in price}}$$

The only difference is that now we consider movements along the supply curve rather than movements along the demand curve.

Suppose that the price of tomatoes rises by 10%. If the quantity of tomatoes supplied also increases by 10% in response, the price elasticity of supply of tomatoes is 1 (10%/10%) and supply is unit-elastic. If the quantity supplied increases by 5%, the price elasticity of supply is 0.5 and supply is inelastic; if the quantity supplied increases by 20%, the price elasticity of supply is 2 and supply is elastic.

As with the demand side, the extreme values of the price elasticity of supply have a simple graphical representation. Panel (a) of Figure 10-1 shows the supply of cell phone frequencies, the portion of the radio spectrum that is suitable for sending and receiving cell phone signals. Governments own the right to sell the use of this part of the radio spectrum to cell phone operators inside their borders. But governments can't increase or decrease the number of cell phone frequencies they have to offer—for technical reasons, the quantity of frequencies suitable for cell phone operation is fixed.

So the supply curve for cell phone frequencies is a vertical line, which we have assumed is set at the quantity of 100 frequencies. As you move up and down that curve, the change in the quantity supplied by the government is zero, whatever the change in price. So panel (a) illustrates a case of **perfectly inelastic supply,** meaning that the price elasticity of supply is zero.

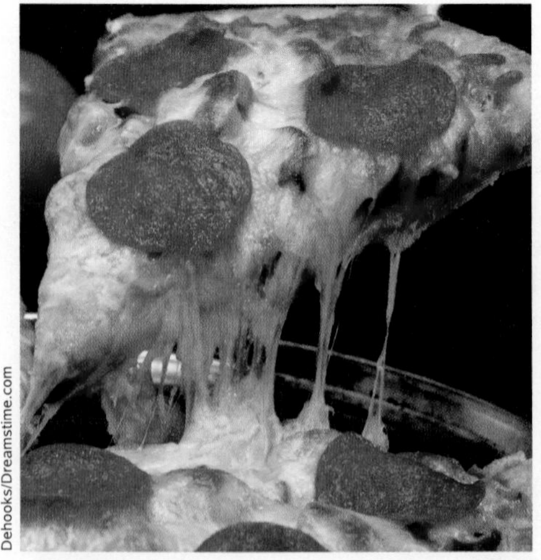

Dehooks/Dreamstime.com

The price elasticity of supply for pizza is very high because the inputs needed to make more of it are readily available.

Panel (b) shows the supply curve for pizza. We suppose that it costs $12 to produce a pizza, including all opportunity costs. At any price below $12, it would be unprofitable to produce pizza and all the pizza parlors would go out of business. At a price of $12 or more, there are many producers who could operate pizza parlors. The ingredients—flour, tomatoes, cheese—are plentiful. And if necessary, more tomatoes could be grown, more milk could be produced to make mozzarella cheese, and so on. So by allowing profits, any price above $12 would elicit the supply of an extremely large quantity of pizzas. The implied supply curve is therefore a horizontal line at $12.

Since even a tiny increase in the price would lead to an enormous increase in the quantity supplied, the price elasticity of supply would be virtually infinite. A horizontal supply curve such as this represents a case of **perfectly elastic supply.**

As our cell phone frequencies and pizza examples suggest, real-world instances of both perfectly inelastic and perfectly elastic supply are easier to find than their counterparts in demand.

What Factors Determine the Price Elasticity of Supply?

Our examples tell us the main determinant of the price elasticity of supply: the availability of inputs. In addition, as with the price elasticity of demand, time may also play a role in the price elasticity of supply. Here we briefly summarize the two factors.

THE AVAILABILITY OF INPUTS The price elasticity of supply tends to be large when inputs are readily available and can be shifted into and out of production at a relatively

FIGURE 10-1 Two Extreme Cases of Price Elasticity of Supply

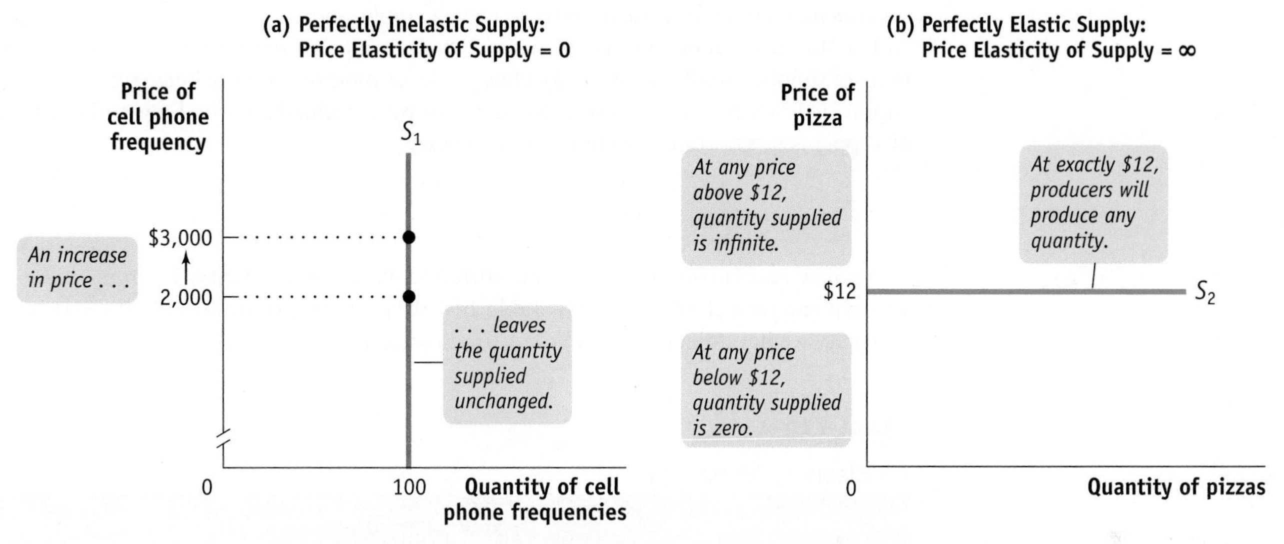

Panel (a) shows a perfectly inelastic supply curve, which is a vertical line. The price elasticity of supply is zero: the quantity supplied is always the same, regardless of price. Panel (b) shows a perfectly elastic supply curve, which is a horizontal line. At a price of $12, producers will supply any quantity, but they will supply none at a price below $12. If the price rises above $12, they will supply an extremely large quantity.

low cost. It tends to be small when inputs are available only in a more-or-less fixed quantity or can be shifted into and out of production only at a relatively high cost.

TIME The price elasticity of supply tends to grow larger as producers have more time to respond to a price change. This means that the long-run price elasticity of supply is often higher than the short-run elasticity. In the case of the flu vaccine shortfall, time was the crucial element because flu vaccine must be grown in cultures over many months.

The price elasticity of the supply of pizza is very high because the inputs needed to make more pizza are readily available. The price elasticity of cell phone frequencies is zero because an essential input—the radio spectrum—cannot be increased at all.

Many industries are like pizza and have large price elasticities of supply: they can be readily expanded because they don't require any special or unique resources. On the other hand, the price elasticity of supply is usually substantially less than perfectly elastic for goods that involve limited natural resources: minerals like gold or copper, agricultural products like coffee that flourish only on certain types of land, and renewable resources like ocean fish that can be exploited only up to a point without destroying the resource.

But given enough time, producers are often able to significantly change the amount they produce in response to a price change, even when production involves a limited natural resource. For example, consider again the effects of a surge in flu vaccine prices, but this time focus on the supply response. If the price were to rise to $90 per vaccination and stay there for a number of years, there would almost certainly be a substantial increase in flu vaccine production. Producers such as Chiron would eventually respond

iStockphoto

The price elasticity of supply is usually less than perfectly elastic for goods, such as ocean fish, that are limited natural resources.

by increasing the size of their manufacturing plants, hiring more lab technicians, and so on. But significantly enlarging the capacity of a biotech manufacturing lab takes several years, not weeks or months or even a single year.

For this reason, economists often make a distinction between the short-run elasticity of supply, usually referring to a few weeks or months, and the long-run elasticity of supply, usually referring to several years. In most industries, the long-run elasticity of supply is larger than the short-run elasticity.

An Elasticity Menagerie

We've just run through quite a few different types of elasticity. Keeping them all straight can be a challenge. So in Table 10-1 we provide a summary of all the types of elasticity we have discussed and their implications.

TABLE 10-1

An Elasticity Menagerie

Price elasticity of demand = $\frac{\text{\% change in quantity demanded}}{\text{\% change in price}}$ (dropping the minus sign)	
0	**Perfectly inelastic:** price has no effect on quantity demanded (vertical demand curve).
Between 0 and 1	**Inelastic:** a rise in price increases total revenue.
Exactly 1	**Unit-elastic:** changes in price have no effect on total revenue.
Greater than 1, less than ∞	**Elastic:** a rise in price reduces total revenue.
∞	**Perfectly elastic:** any rise in price causes quantity demanded to fall to 0. Any fall in price leads to an infinite quantity demanded (horizontal demand curve).
Cross-price elasticity of demand = $\frac{\text{\% change in quantity } \textit{of one good} \text{ demanded}}{\text{\% change in price } \textit{of another good}}$	
Negative	**Complements:** quantity demanded of one good falls when the price of another rises.
Positive	**Substitutes:** quantity demanded of one good rises when the price of another rises.
Income elasticity of demand = $\frac{\text{\% change in quantity demanded}}{\text{\% change in income}}$	
Negative	**Inferior good:** quantity demanded falls when income rises.
Positive, less than 1	**Normal good, income-inelastic:** quantity demanded rises when income rises, but not as rapidly as income.
Greater than 1	**Normal good, income-elastic:** quantity demanded rises when income rises, and more rapidly than income.
Price elasticity of supply = $\frac{\text{\% change in quantity supplied}}{\text{\% change in price}}$	
0	**Perfectly inelastic:** price has no effect on quantity supplied (vertical supply curve).
Greater than 0, less than ∞	ordinary upward-sloping supply curve.
∞	**Perfectly elastic:** any fall in price causes quantity supplied to fall to 0. Any rise in price elicits an infinite quantity supplied (horizontal supply curve).

MODULE 10 Review

Solutions appear at the back of the book.

Check Your Understanding

1. After Chelsea's income increased from $12,000 to $18,000 a year, her purchases of DVDs increased from 10 to 40 DVDs a year. Calculate Chelsea's income elasticity of demand for DVDs using the midpoint method.
2. As the price of margarine rises by 20%, a manufacturer of baked goods increases its quantity of butter demanded by 5%. Calculate the cross-price elasticity of demand between butter and margarine. Are butter and margarine substitutes or complements for this manufacturer?
3. Using the midpoint method, calculate the price elasticity of supply for web-design services when the price per hour rises from $100 to $150 and the number of hours supplied increases from 300,000 hours to 500,000. Is supply elastic, inelastic, or unit-elastic?

Multiple-Choice Questions

1. If the cross-price elasticity between two goods is negative, this means that the two goods are
   a. substitutes.
   b. complements.
   c. normal.
   d. inferior.
   e. luxuries.
2. If Kylie buys 200 units of good X when her income is $20,000 and 300 units of good X when her income increases to $25,000, her income elasticity of demand, using the midpoint method, is
   a. 0.06.
   b. 0.5.
   c. 1.65.
   d. 1.8.
   e. 2.00.
3. The income elasticity of demand for a normal good is
   a. zero.
   b. 1.
   c. infinite.
   d. positive.
   e. negative.
4. A perfectly elastic supply curve is
   a. positively sloped.
   b. negatively sloped.
   c. vertical.
   d. horizontal.
   e. U-shaped.
5. Which of the following leads to a more inelastic price elasticity of supply?
   I. the use of inputs that are easily obtained
   II. a high degree of substitutability between inputs
   III. a shorter time period in which to supply the good
   a. I only
   b. II only
   c. III only
   d. I and II only
   e. I, II, and III

Critical-Thinking Questions

Assume the price of corn rises by 20% and this causes suppliers to increase the quantity of corn supplied by 40%.

1. Calculate the price elasticity of supply.
2. In this case, is supply elastic or inelastic?
3. Draw a correctly labeled graph of a supply curve illustrating the most extreme case of the category of elasticity you found in part b (either perfectly elastic or perfectly inelastic supply).
4. What would likely be true of the availability of inputs for a firm with the supply curve you drew in part c? Explain.

BUSINESS CASE: The Airline Industry: Fly Less, Charge More

The recession that began in 2008 hit the airline industry very hard as both businesses and households cut back their travel plans. According to the International Air Transport Association, the industry lost $11 billion in 2008. However, by 2009, despite the fact that the economy was still extremely weak and airline traffic was still well below normal, the industry's profitability began to rebound. And by 2010, even in the midst of continued economic weakness, the airline industry's prospects had definitely recovered, with the industry achieving an $8.9 billion profit that year, with continued profitability in 2011 and 2012. As Gary Kelly, CEO of Southwest Airlines said, "The industry is in the best position—certainly in a decade—to post profitability."

Chris Sweda/Chicago Tribune/MCT via Getty Images

How did the airline industry achieve such a dramatic turnaround? Simple: fly less and charge more. In 2011, fares were 14% higher than they had been the previous year, and flights were more crowded than they had been in decades, with fewer than one in five seats empty on domestic flights.

In addition to cutting back on the number of flights—particularly money-losing ones—airlines implemented more extreme variations in ticket prices based on when a flight departed and when the ticket was purchased. For example, the cheapest day to fly is Wednesday, with Friday and Saturday the most expensive days to travel. The first flight of the morning (the one that requires you to get up at 4 A.M.) is cheaper than flights departing the rest of the day. And the cheapest time to buy a ticket is Tuesday at 3 P.M. Eastern Standard Time, with tickets purchased over the weekend carrying the highest prices.

And it doesn't stop there. As every beleaguered traveler knows, airlines have tacked on a wide variety of new fees and increased old ones—fees for food, for a blanket, for checked bags, for carry-on bags, for the right to board a flight first, for the right to choose your seat in advance, and so on. Airlines have also gotten more inventive in imposing fees that are hard for travelers to track in advance—such as claiming that fares have not risen during the holidays while imposing a "holiday surcharge." In 2011, airlines collected more than $22.6 billion from fees for checking baggage and changing tickets, up 66% from 2010.

But the question in the minds of industry analysts is whether airlines can manage to maintain their currently high levels of profitability. In the past, as travel demand picked up, airlines increased capacity—added seats—too quickly, leading to falling airfares. "The wild card is always capacity discipline," says William Swelbar, an airline industry researcher. "All it takes is one carrier to begin to add capacity aggressively, and then we follow and we undo all the good work that's been done."

Questions for Thought

1. How would you describe the price elasticity of demand for airline flights following the 2008 recession given the information in this case? Explain.
2. Using the concept of elasticity, explain why airlines would create such great variations in the price of a ticket depending on when it is purchased and the day and time the flight departs. Assume that some people are willing to spend time shopping for deals as well as fly at inconvenient times, but others are not.
3. Using the concept of elasticity, explain why airlines have imposed fees on things such as checked bags. Why might they try to hide or disguise fees?
4. Use an elasticity concept to explain under what conditions the airline industry will be able to maintain its high profitability in the future. Explain.

SECTION 3 REVIEW

Summary

Income Effects, Substitution Effects, and Elasticity

1. Changes in the price of a good affect the quantity consumed as a result of the **substitution effect,** and in some cases the **income effect.** Most goods absorb only a small share of a consumer's spending; for these goods, only the substitution effect—buying less of the good that has become relatively more expensive and more of the good that has become relatively cheaper—is significant. The income effect becomes substantial when there is a change in the price of a good that absorbs a large share of a consumer's spending, thereby significantly changing the purchasing power of the consumer's income.
2. Many economic questions depend on the size of consumer or producer responses to changes in prices or other variables. *Elasticity* is a general measure of responsiveness that can be used to answer such questions.
3. The **price elasticity of demand**—the percent change in the quantity demanded divided by the percent change in the price (dropping the minus sign)—is a measure of the responsiveness of the quantity demanded to changes in the price. In practical calculations, it is usually best to use the **midpoint method,** which calculates percent changes in prices and quantities based on the average of the initial and final values.

Interpreting Price Elasticity of Demand

4. Demand can fall anywhere in the range from **perfectly inelastic,** meaning the quantity demanded is unaffected by the price, to **perfectly elastic,** meaning there is a unique price at which consumers will buy as much or as little as they are offered. When demand is perfectly inelastic, the demand curve is a vertical line; when it is perfectly elastic, the demand curve is a horizontal line.
5. The price elasticity of demand is classified according to whether it is more or less than 1. If it is greater than 1, demand is **elastic;** if it is less than 1, demand is **inelastic;** if it is exactly 1, demand is **unit-elastic.** This classification determines how **total revenue,** the total value of sales, changes when the price changes. If demand is elastic, quantity demanded is relatively more responsive to changes in price, total revenue falls when the price increases and rises when the price decreases. If demand is inelastic, quantity demanded is relatively less responsive to changes in price, total revenue rises when the price increases and falls when the price decreases.
6. The price elasticity of demand depends on whether there are close substitutes for the good in question, whether the good is a necessity or a luxury, the share of income spent on the good, and the length of time that has elapsed since the price change.

Other Elasticities

7. The **cross-price elasticity of demand** measures the effect of a change in one good's price on the quantity of another good demanded. The cross-price elasticity of demand can be positive, in which case the goods are substitutes, or negative, in which case they are complements.
8. The **income elasticity of demand** is the percent change in the quantity of a good demanded when a consumer's income changes divided by the percent change in income. The income elasticity of demand indicates how intensely the demand for a good responds to changes in income. It can be negative; in that case the good is an inferior good. Goods with positive income elasticities of demand are normal goods. If the income elasticity is greater than 1, a good is **income-elastic;** if it is positive and less than 1, the good is **income-inelastic.**
9. The **price elasticity of supply** is the percent change in the quantity of a good supplied divided by the percent change in the price. If the quantity supplied does not change at all, we have an instance of **perfectly inelastic supply;** the supply curve is a vertical line. If the quantity supplied is zero below some price but infinite above that price, we have an instance of **perfectly elastic supply;** the supply curve is a horizontal line.
10. The price elasticity of supply depends on the availability of resources to expand production and on time. It is higher when inputs are available at relatively low cost and when more time has elapsed since the price change.

Key Terms

Substitution effect, p. 73
Income effect, p. 73
Price elasticity of demand, p. 75
Midpoint method, p. 76
Perfectly inelastic demand, p. 80
Perfectly elastic demand, p. 81
Elastic demand, p. 81
Inelastic demand, p. 81
Unit-elastic demand, p. 81
Total revenue, p. 83
Cross-price elasticity of demand, p. 89
Income elasticity of demand, p. 90
Income-elastic demand, p. 91
Income-inelastic demand, p. 91
Price elasticity of supply, p. 92
Perfectly inelastic supply, p. 92
Perfectly elastic supply, p. 92

MODULE 11

Consumer and Producer Surplus

Peter Huoppi

WHAT YOU WILL LEARN

1. The meaning of consumer surplus and its relationship to the demand curve
2. The meaning of producer surplus and its relationship to the supply curve

Consumer Surplus and the Demand Curve

First-year college students are often surprised by the prices of the textbooks required for their classes. The College Board estimates that in 2011–2012 students at four-year schools spent, on average, about $1,200 for books and supplies. But at the end of the semester, students might again be surprised to find out that they can sell back at least some of the textbooks they used for the semester for a percentage of the purchase price (offsetting some of the cost of textbooks).

The ability to purchase used textbooks at the start of the semester and to sell back used textbooks at the end of the semester is beneficial to students on a budget. In fact, the market for used textbooks is a big business in terms of dollars and cents—approximately $3 billion in 2009. This market provides a convenient starting point for us to develop the concepts of consumer and producer surplus. We'll use these concepts to understand exactly how buyers and sellers benefit from a competitive market and how big those benefits are. In addition, these concepts assist in the analysis of what happens when competitive markets don't work well or there is interference in the market.

So let's begin by looking at the market for used textbooks, starting with the buyers. The key point, as we'll see in a minute, is that the demand curve is derived from their tastes or preferences—and that those same preferences also determine how much they gain from the opportunity to buy used books.

Willingness to Pay and the Demand Curve

A used book is not as good as a new book—it will be battered and coffee-stained, may include someone else's highlighting, and may not be completely up to date. How much this bothers you depends on your preferences. Some potential buyers would prefer to buy the used book even if it is only slightly cheaper than a new one, while others would buy the used book only if it is considerably cheaper.

A consumer's **willingness to pay** for a good is the maximum price at which he or she would buy that good.

Let's define a potential buyer's **willingness to pay** as the maximum price at which he or she would buy a good, in this case a used textbook. An individual won't buy the good if it costs more than this amount but is eager to do so if it costs less. If the price is just equal to an individual's willingness to pay, he or she is indifferent between buying and not buying. For the sake of simplicity, we'll assume that the individual buys the good in this case.

The table in Figure 11-1 shows five potential buyers of a used book that costs $100 new, listed in order of their willingness to pay. At one extreme is Aleisha, who will buy a second-hand book even if the price is as high as $59. Brad is less willing to have a used book and will buy one only if the price is $45 or less. Claudia is willing to pay only $35 and Darren only $25. Edwina, who really doesn't like the idea of a used book, will buy one only if it costs no more than $10.

How many of these five students will actually buy a used book? It depends on the price. If the price of a used book is $55, only Aleisha buys one; if the price is $40, Aleisha and Brad both buy used books, and so on. So the information in the table can be used to construct the *demand schedule* for used textbooks.

We can use this demand schedule to derive the market demand curve shown in Figure 11-1. Because we are considering only a small number of consumers, this curve doesn't look like the smooth demand curves we have seen previously, for markets that contained hundreds or thousands of consumers. This demand curve is step-shaped, with alternating horizontal and vertical segments. Each horizontal segment—each step—corresponds to one potential buyer's willingness to pay. However, we'll see

FIGURE 11-1 **The Demand Curve for Used Textbooks**

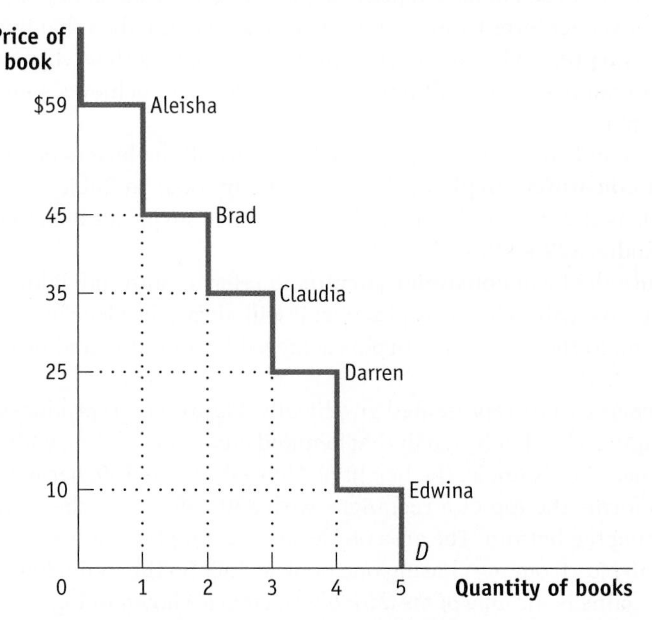

Potential buyers	Willingness to pay
Aleisha	$59
Brad	45
Claudia	35
Darren	25
Edwina	10

With only five potential consumers in this market, the demand curve is step-shaped. Each step represents one consumer, and its height indicates that consumer's willingness to pay—the maximum price at which each will buy a used textbook—as indicated in the table. Aleisha has the highest willingness to pay at $59, Brad has the next highest at $45, and so on down to Edwina with the lowest willingness to pay at $10. At a price of $59, the quantity demanded is one (Aleisha); at a price of $45, the quantity demanded is two (Aleisha and Brad); and so on until you reach a price of $10, at which all five students are willing to purchase a book.

shortly that for the analysis of consumer surplus it doesn't matter whether the demand curve is step-shaped, as in this figure, or whether there are many consumers, making the curve smooth.

Willingness to Pay and Consumer Surplus

Suppose that the campus bookstore makes used textbooks available at a price of $30. In that case Aleisha, Brad, and Claudia will buy used books. Do they gain from their purchases, and if so, how much?

The answer, shown in Table 11-1, is that each student who purchases a used book does achieve a net gain but that the amount of the gain differs among students.

TABLE 11-1

Consumer Surplus When the Price of a Used Textbook = $30

Potential buyer	Willingness to pay	Price paid	Individual consumer surplus = Willingness to pay − Price paid
Aleisha	$59	$30	$29
Brad	45	30	15
Claudia	35	30	5
Darren	25	—	—
Edwina	10	—	—
All buyers			Total consumer surplus = $49

Aleisha would have been willing to pay $59, so her net gain is $59 – $30 = $29. Brad would have been willing to pay $45, so his net gain is $45 – $30 = $15. Claudia would have been willing to pay $35, so her net gain is $35 – $30 = $5. Darren and Edwina, however, won't be willing to buy a used book at a price of $30, so they neither gain nor lose.

The net gain that a buyer achieves from the purchase of a good is called that buyer's **individual consumer surplus.** What we learn from this example is that whenever a buyer pays a price less than his or her willingness to pay, the buyer achieves some individual consumer surplus.

The sum of the individual consumer surpluses achieved by all the buyers of a good is known as the **total consumer surplus** achieved in the market. In Table 11-1, the total consumer surplus is the sum of the individual consumer surpluses achieved by Aleisha, Brad, and Claudia: $29 + $15 + $5 = $49.

Economists often use the term **consumer surplus** to refer to both individual and total consumer surplus. We will follow this practice; it will always be clear in context whether we are referring to the consumer surplus achieved by an individual or by all buyers.

Total consumer surplus can be represented graphically. Figure 11-2 reproduces the demand curve from Figure 11-1. Each step in that demand curve is one book wide and represents one consumer. For example, the height of Aleisha's step is $59, her willingness to pay. This step forms the top of a rectangle, with $30—the price she actually pays for a book—forming the bottom. The area of Aleisha's rectangle, ($59 – $30) × 1 = $29, is her consumer surplus from purchasing one book at $30. So the individual consumer surplus Aleisha gains is the *area of the dark blue rectangle* shown in Figure 11-2.

Individual consumer surplus is the net gain to an individual buyer from the purchase of a good. It is equal to the difference between the buyer's willingness to pay and the price paid.

Total consumer surplus is the sum of the individual consumer surpluses of all the buyers of a good in a market.

The term **consumer surplus** is often used to refer to both individual and to total consumer surplus.

In addition to Aleisha, Brad and Claudia will also each buy a book when the price is $30. Like Aleisha, they benefit from their purchases, though not as much, because they each have a lower willingness to pay. Figure 11-2 also shows the consumer surplus gained by Brad and Claudia; again, this can be measured by the areas of the appropriate rectangles. Darren and Edwina, because they do not buy books at a price of $30, receive no consumer surplus.

The total consumer surplus achieved in this market is just the sum of the individual consumer surpluses received by Aleisha, Brad, and Claudia. So total consumer surplus is equal to the combined area of the three rectangles—the entire shaded area

FIGURE 11-2 **Consumer Surplus in the Used-Textbook Market**

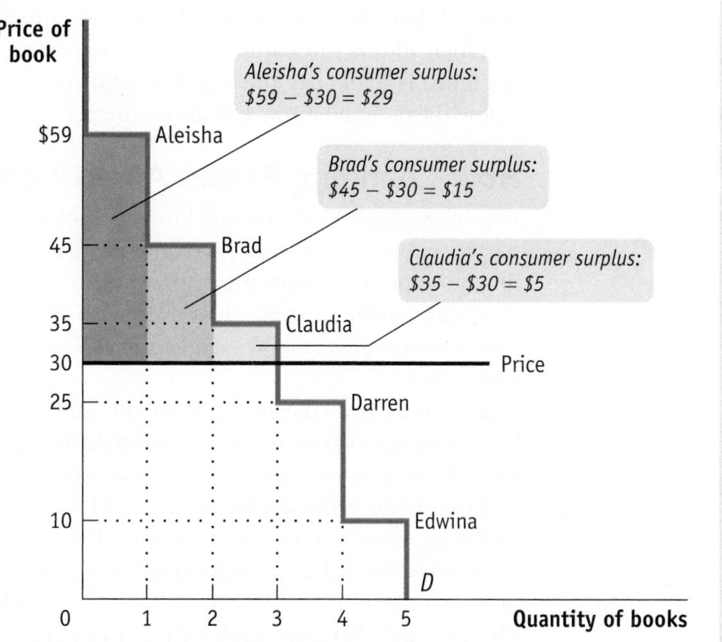

At a price of $30, Aleisha, Brad, and Claudia each buy a book but Darren and Edwina do not. Aleisha, Brad, and Claudia get individual consumer surpluses equal to the difference between their willingness to pay and the price, illustrated by the areas of the shaded rectangles. Both Darren and Edwina have a willingness to pay that is less than $30, so they are unwilling to buy a book at this market price; they receive zero consumer surplus. The total consumer surplus is given by the entire shaded area—the sum of the individual consumer surpluses of Aleisha, Brad, and Claudia—equal to $29 + $15 + $5 = $49.

in Figure 11-2. Another way to say this is that total consumer surplus is equal to the area below the demand curve but above the price.

This is worth repeating as a general principle: *The total consumer surplus generated by purchases of a good at a given price is equal to the area below the demand curve but above that price*. The same principle applies regardless of the number of consumers.

When we consider large markets, this graphical representation becomes particularly helpful. Consider, for example, the sales of iPads to millions of potential buyers. Each potential buyer has a maximum price that he or she is willing to pay. With so many potential buyers, the demand curve will be smooth, like the one shown in Figure 11-3.

FIGURE 11-3 **Consumer Surplus**

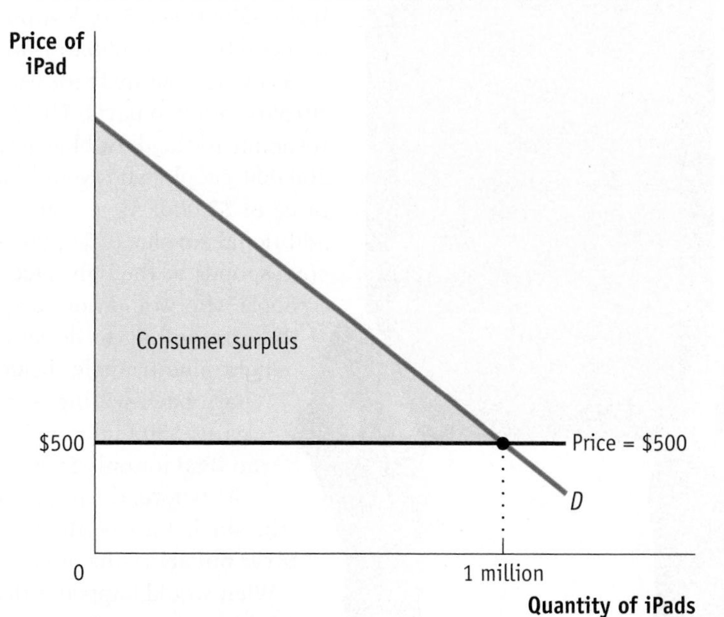

The demand curve for iPads is smooth because there are many potential buyers. At a price of $500, 1 million iPads are demanded. The consumer surplus at this price is equal to the shaded area: the area below the demand curve but above the price. This is the total net gain to consumers generated from buying and consuming iPads when the price is $500.

Suppose that at a price of $500 per iPad a total of 1 million iPads are purchased. How much do consumers gain from being able to buy those 1 million iPads? We could answer that question by calculating the individual consumer surplus of each buyer and then adding these numbers up to arrive at a total. But it is much easier just to look at Figure 11-3 and use the fact that total consumer surplus is equal to the shaded area below the demand curve but above the price.

How Changing Prices Affect Consumer Surplus

It is often important to know how price *changes* affect consumer surplus. For example, we may want to know how much consumers are hurt if a flood in Pakistan drives up cotton prices or how much consumers' gain from the introduction of fish farming that makes salmon steaks less expensive. The same approach we have used to derive consumer surplus can be used to answer questions about how changes in prices affect consumers.

Let's return to the example of the market for used textbooks. Suppose that the bookstore decided to sell used textbooks for $20 instead of $30. By how much would this fall in price increase consumer surplus?

The answer is illustrated in Figure 11-4. As shown in the figure, there are two parts to the increase in consumer surplus. The first part, shaded dark blue, is the gain of those who would have bought books even at the higher price of $30. Each of the students who would have bought a book at $30—Aleisha, Brad, and Claudia—now pays $10 less, and therefore each gains $10 in consumer surplus from the fall in price to $20. So the dark blue area represents the $10 × 3 = $30 increase in consumer surplus to those three buyers.

The second part, shaded light blue, is the gain to those who would not have bought a book at $30 but are willing to pay more than $20. In this case that gain goes to Darren, who would not have bought a book at $30 but does buy one at $20. He gains $5—the difference between his willingness to pay of $25 and the new price of $20. So the light blue area represents a further $5 gain in consumer surplus.

The total increase in consumer surplus is the sum of the shaded areas, $35. Likewise, a rise in price from $20 to $30 would decrease consumer surplus by an amount equal to the sum of the shaded areas.

Figure 11-4 illustrates that when the price of a good falls, the area under the demand curve but above the price—the total consumer surplus—increases. Figure 11-5 shows the same result for the case of a smooth demand curve, the demand for iPads. Here we assume that the price of iPads falls from $2,000 to $500, leading to an increase in the quantity demanded from 200,000 to 1 million units.

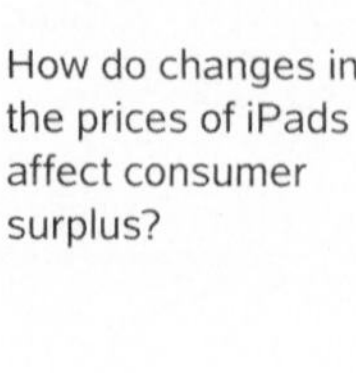

How do changes in the prices of iPads affect consumer surplus?

iStockphoto/Thinkstock

As in the used-textbook example, we divide the gain in consumer surplus into two parts. The dark blue rectangle in Figure 11-5 corresponds to the dark blue area in Figure 11-4: it is the gain to the 200,000 people who would have bought iPads even at the higher price of $2,000. As a result of the price reduction, each receives additional surplus of $1,500. The light blue triangle in Figure 11-5 corresponds to the light blue area in Figure 11-4: it is the gain to people who would not have bought the good at the higher price but are willing to do so at a price of $500. For example, the light blue triangle includes the gain to someone who would have been willing to pay $1,000 for an iPad and therefore gains $500 in consumer surplus when it is possible to buy an iPad for only $500.

As before, the total gain in consumer surplus is the sum of the shaded areas, the increase in the area under the demand curve but above the price.

What would happen if the price of a good were to rise instead of fall? We would do the same analysis in reverse. Suppose, for

FIGURE 11-4 **Consumer Surplus and a Fall in the Price of Used Textbooks**

There are two parts to the increase in consumer surplus generated by a fall in price from $30 to $20. The first is given by the dark blue rectangle: each person who would have bought at the original price of $30—Aleisha, Brad, and Claudia—receives an increase in consumer surplus equal to the total reduction in price, $10. So the area of the dark blue rectangle corresponds to an amount equal to 3 × $10 = $30. The second part is given by the light blue area: the increase in consumer surplus for those who would *not* have bought at the original price of $30 but who buy at the new price of $20—namely, Darren. Darren's willingness to pay is $25, so he now receives consumer surplus of $5. The total increase in consumer surplus is 3 × $10 + $5 = $35, represented by the sum of the shaded areas. Likewise, a rise in price from $20 to $30 would decrease consumer surplus by an amount equal to the sum of the shaded areas.

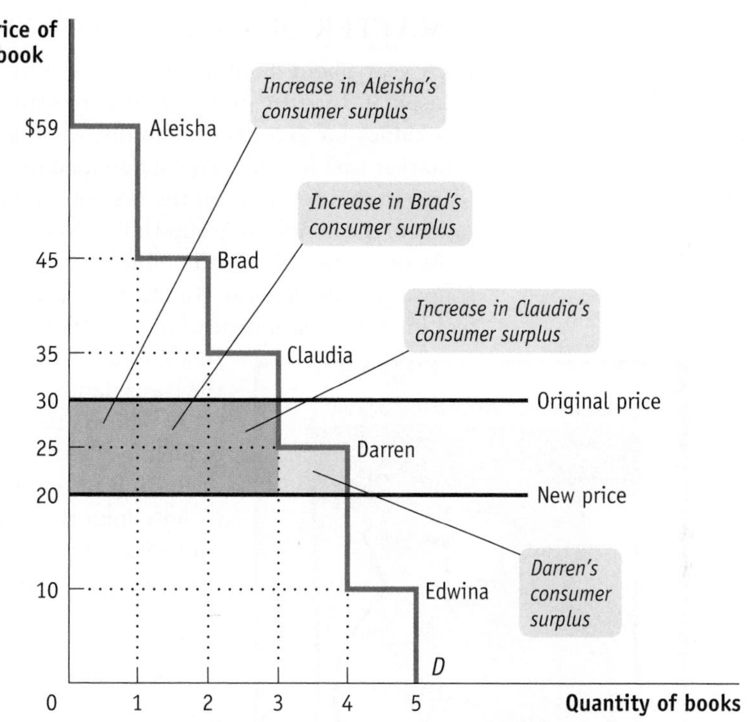

example, that for some reason the price of iPads rises from $500 to $2,000. This would lead to a fall in consumer surplus equal to the sum of the shaded areas in Figure 11-5. This loss consists of two parts. The dark blue rectangle represents the loss to consumers who would still buy an iPad, even at a price of $2,000. The light blue triangle represents the loss to consumers who decide not to buy an iPad at the higher price.

FIGURE 11-5 **A Fall in the Price Increases Consumer Surplus**

A fall in the price of an iPad from $2,000 to $500 leads to an increase in the quantity demanded and an increase in consumer surplus. The change in total consumer surplus is given by the sum of the shaded areas: the total area below the demand curve and between the old and new prices. Here, the dark blue area represents the increase in consumer surplus for the 200,000 consumers who would have bought an iPad at the original price of $2,000; they each receive an increase in consumer surplus of $1,500. The light blue area represents the increase in consumer surplus for those willing to buy at a price equal to or greater than $500 but less than $2,000. Similarly, a rise in the price of an iPad from $500 to $2,000 generates a decrease in consumer surplus equal to the sum of the two shaded areas.

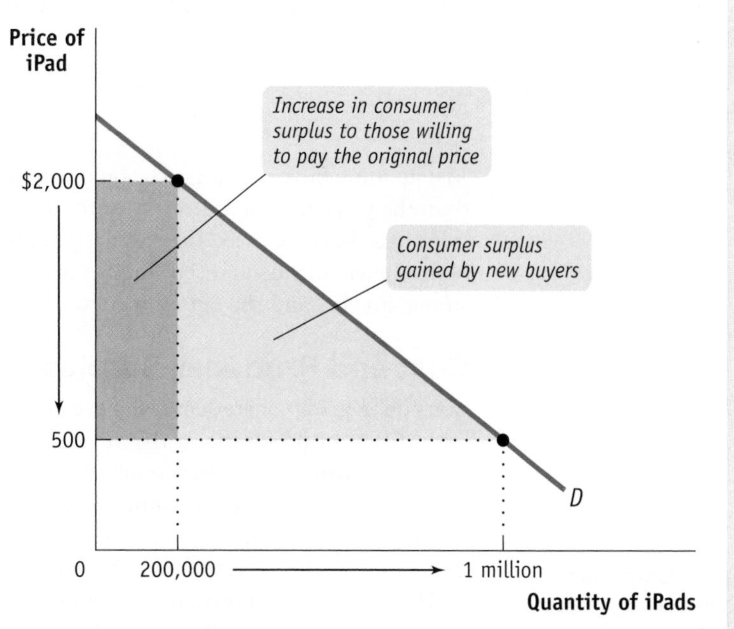

ECONOMICS ▶ IN ACTION

A MATTER OF LIFE AND DEATH

Each year about 4,000 people in the United States die while waiting for a kidney transplant. In 2013, over 90,000 were wait listed. Since the number of those in need of a kidney far exceeds availability, what is the best way to allocate available organs? A market isn't feasible. For understandable reasons, the sale of human body parts is illegal in this country. So the task of establishing a protocol for these situations has fallen to the nonprofit group United Network for Organ Sharing (UNOS).

At one time, UNOS guidelines stipulated that a donated kidney went to the person waiting the longest. An available kidney would go to a 75-year-old who had been waiting for 2 years instead of to a 25-year-old who had been waiting 6 months, even though the 25-year-old will likely live longer and benefit from the transplanted organ for a longer period of time.

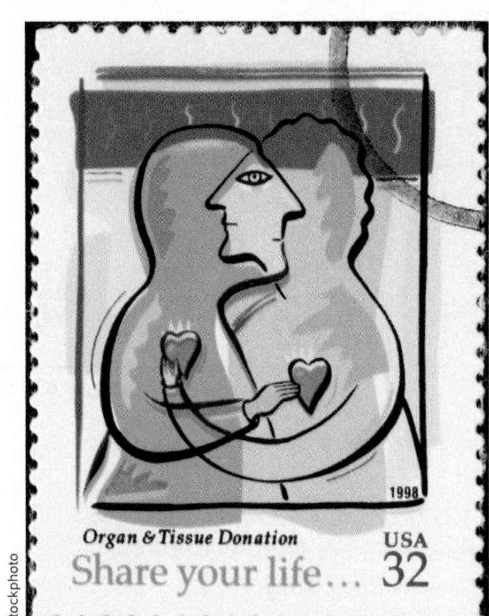

iStockphoto

To address this issue, in 2013 UNOS adopted a new set of guidelines based on a concept it called "net survival benefit." According to these guidelines, kidneys are ranked according to how long they are likely to last; similarly, recipients are ranked according to how long they are likely to live with the transplanted organ. Each kidney is then matched to the person expected to achieve the greatest survival time from it.

A kidney expected to last many decades will be allocated to a younger person, while older recipients will receive kidneys expected to last for fewer years. This way, UNOS tries to avoid situations in which (1) recipients outlive their transplants, creating the need for another transplant and reducing the pool of kidneys available and (2) a kidney "outlives" its recipient, thereby wasting years of kidney function that could have benefited someone else.

What does this have to do with consumer surplus? As you may have guessed, the UNOS concept of "net survival benefit" is a lot like individual consumer surplus—the individual consumer surplus generated from getting a new kidney. In essence, UNOS devised a system that allocates donated kidneys according to who gets the greatest individual consumer surplus from it. In this way, the new UNOS guidelines attempt to maximize the total consumer surplus available from the existing pool of kidneys. In terms of results, then, a "net survival benefit" system operates a lot like a competitive market.

Producer Surplus and the Supply Curve

Just as some buyers of a good would have been willing to pay more for their purchase than the price they actually pay, some sellers of a good would have been willing to sell it for less than the price they actually receive. We can therefore carry out an analysis of producer surplus and the supply curve that is almost exactly parallel to that of consumer surplus and the demand curve.

Cost and Producer Surplus

Consider a group of students who are potential sellers of used textbooks. Because they have different preferences, the various potential sellers differ in the price at which they are willing to sell their books. The table in Figure 11-6 shows the prices at which several different students would be willing to sell. Andrew is willing to sell the book as long as he can get at least $5; Betty won't sell unless she can get at least $15; Carlos requires $25; Donna requires $35; Engelbert $45.

A seller's **cost** is the lowest price at which he or she is willing to sell a good.

The lowest price at which a potential seller is willing to sell is called the seller's **cost.** So Andrew's cost is $5, Betty's is $15, and so on.

Using the term *cost,* which people normally associate with the monetary cost of producing a good, may sound a little strange when applied to sellers of used textbooks. The students don't have to manufacture the books, so it doesn't cost the student who sells a book anything to make that book available for sale, does it?

Yes, it does. A student who sells a book won't have it later, as part of his or her personal collection. So there is an *opportunity cost* to selling a textbook, even if the owner has completed the course for which it was required. And remember that one of the basic principles of economics is that the true measure of the cost of doing something is always its opportunity cost. That is, the real cost of something is what you must give up to get it.

So it is good economics to talk of the minimum price at which someone will sell a good as the "cost" of selling that good, even if he or she doesn't spend any money to make the good available for sale. Of course, in most real-world markets the sellers are also those who produce the good and therefore *do* spend money to make the good available for sale. In this case the cost of making the good available for sale *includes* monetary costs, but it may also include other opportunity costs.

Getting back to the example, suppose that Andrew sells his book for $30. Clearly he has gained from the transaction: he would have been willing to sell for only $5, so he has gained $25. This net gain, the difference between the price he actually gets and his cost—the minimum price at which he would have been willing to sell—is known as his **individual producer surplus.**

Individual producer surplus is the net gain to an individual seller from selling a good. It is equal to the difference between the price received and the seller's cost.

Just as we derived the demand curve from the willingness to pay of different consumers, we can derive the supply curve from the cost of different producers. The step-shaped curve in Figure 11-6 shows the supply curve implied by the costs shown in the accompanying table. At a price less than $5, none of the students are willing to sell; at a price between $5 and $15, only Andrew is willing to sell, and so on.

FIGURE 11-6 The Supply Curve for Used Textbooks

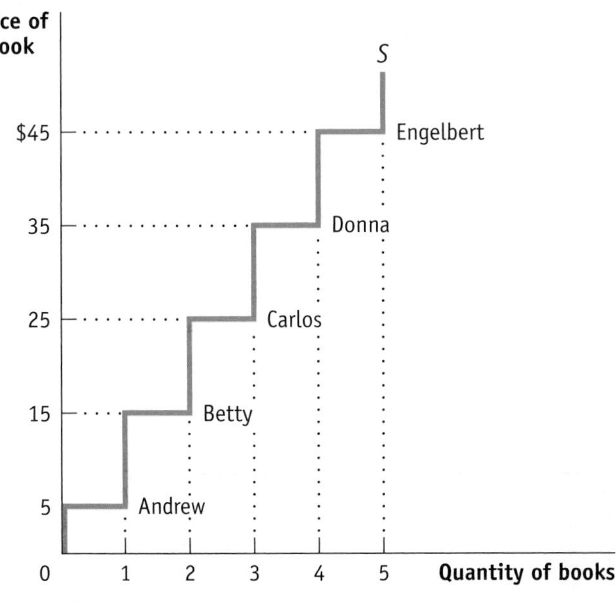

Potential sellers	Cost
Andrew	$5
Betty	15
Carlos	25
Donna	35
Engelbert	45

The supply curve illustrates sellers' cost, the lowest price at which a potential seller is willing to sell the good, and the quantity supplied at that price. Each of the five students has one book to sell and each has a different cost, as indicated in the accompanying table. At a price of $5 the quantity supplied is one (Andrew), at $15 it is two (Andrew and Betty), and so on until you reach $45, the price at which all five students are willing to sell.

FIGURE 11-9 **A Rise in the Price Increases Producer Surplus**

A rise in the price of wheat from $5 to $7 leads to an increase in the quantity supplied and an increase in producer surplus. The change in total producer surplus is given by the sum of the shaded areas: the total area above the supply curve but between the old and new prices. The red area represents the gain to the farmers who would have supplied 1 million bushels at the original price of $5; they each receive an increase in producer surplus of $2 for each of those bushels. The triangular pink area represents the increase in producer surplus achieved by the farmers who supply the additional 500,000 bushels because of the higher price. Similarly, a fall in the price of wheat from $7 to $5 generates a reduction in producer surplus equal to the sum of the shaded areas.

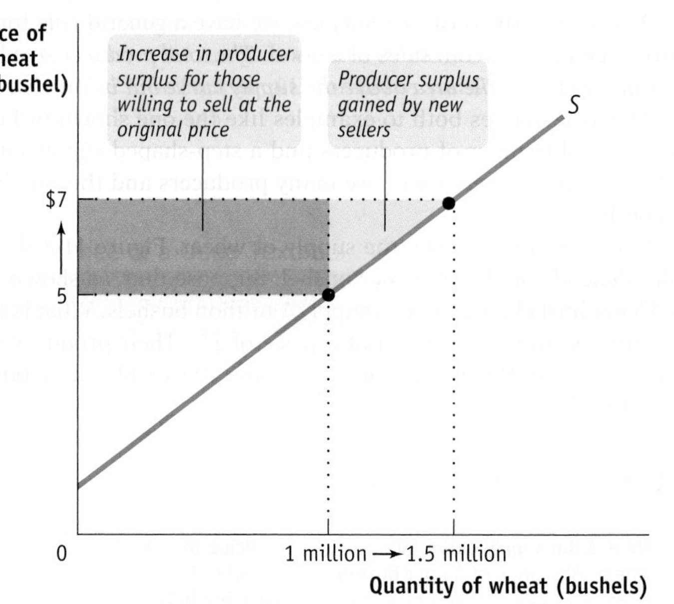

farmers who would not have supplied wheat at the original price but are drawn into the market by the higher price.

If the price were to fall from $7 to $5 per bushel, the story would run in reverse. The sum of the shaded areas would now be the decline in producer surplus, the decrease in the area above the supply curve but below the price. The loss would consist of two parts, the loss to farmers who would still grow wheat at a price of $5 (the red rectangle) and the loss to farmers who decide to no longer grow wheat because of the lower price (the pink triangle).

MODULE 11 Review

Solutions appear at the back of the book.

Check Your Understanding

1. Consider the market for cheese-stuffed jalapeno peppers. There are two consumers, Casey and Josey, and their willingness to pay for each pepper is given in the accompanying table. (Neither is willing to consume more than 4 peppers at any price.) Use the table (i) to construct the demand schedule for peppers for prices of $0.00, $0.10, and so on, up to $0.90, and (ii) to calculate the total consumer surplus when the price of a pepper is $0.40.

Quantity of peppers	Casey's willingness to pay	Josey's willingness to pay
1st pepper	$0.90	$0.80
2nd pepper	0.70	0.60
3rd pepper	0.50	0.40
4th pepper	0.30	0.30

2. Again consider the market for cheese-stuffed jalapeno peppers. There are two producers, Cara and Jamie, and their costs of producing each pepper are given in the accompanying table. (Neither is willing to produce more than 4 peppers at any price.) Use the table (i) to construct the supply schedule for peppers for prices of $0.00, $0.10, and so on, up to $0.90, and (ii) to calculate the total producer surplus when the price of a pepper is $0.70.

Quantity of peppers	Cara's cost	Jamie's cost
1st pepper	$0.10	$0.30
2nd pepper	0.10	0.50
3rd pepper	0.40	0.70
4th pepper	0.60	0.90

Multiple-Choice Questions

1. Refer to the following graph. What is the value of consumer surplus when the market price is $40?

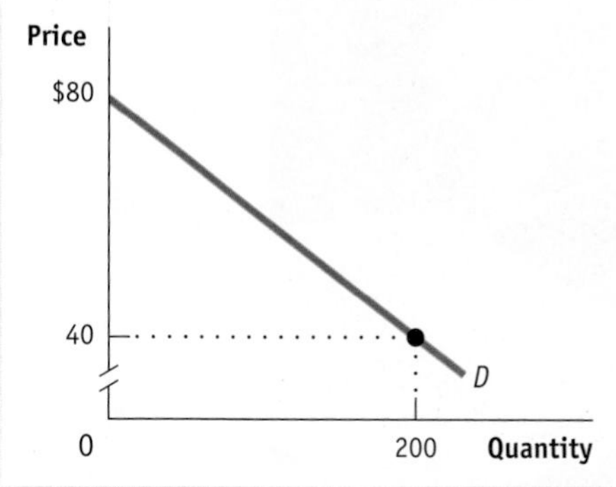

   a. $400
   b. $800
   c. $4,000
   d. $8,000
   e. $16,000

2. Refer to the graph below. What is the value of producer surplus when the market price is $60?

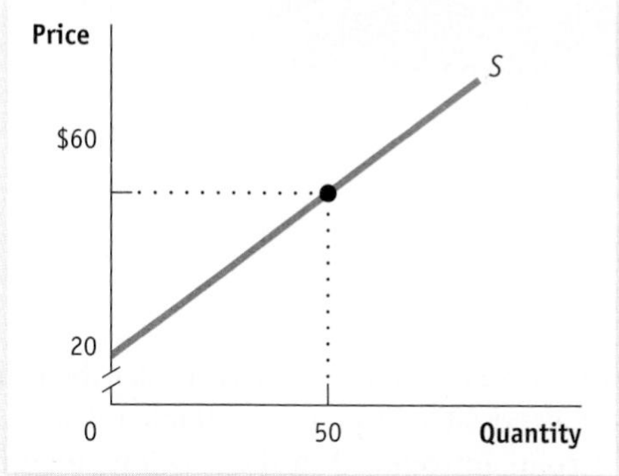

   a. $100
   b. $150
   c. $1,000
   d. $1,500
   e. $3,000

3. Other things equal, a rise in price will result in which of the following?
   a. Producer surplus will rise; consumer surplus will rise.
   b. Producer surplus will fall; consumer surplus will fall.
   c. Producer surplus will rise; consumer surplus will fall.
   d. Producer surplus will fall; consumer surplus will rise.
   e. Producer surplus will not change; consumer surplus will rise.

4. Consumer surplus is found as the area
   a. above the supply curve and below the price.
   b. below the demand curve and above the price.
   c. above the demand curve and below the price.
   d. below the supply curve and above the price.
   e. below the supply curve and above the demand curve.

5. Allocating kidneys to those with the highest net benefit (where net benefit is measured as the expected increase in life span from a transplant) is an attempt to maximize
   a. consumer surplus.
   b. producer surplus.
   c. profit.
   d. equity.
   e. respect for elders.

Critical-Thinking Question

Draw a correctly labeled graph showing a competitive market in equilibrium. On your graph, clearly indicate and label the area of consumer surplus and the area of producer surplus.

MODULE

12 Efficiency and Markets

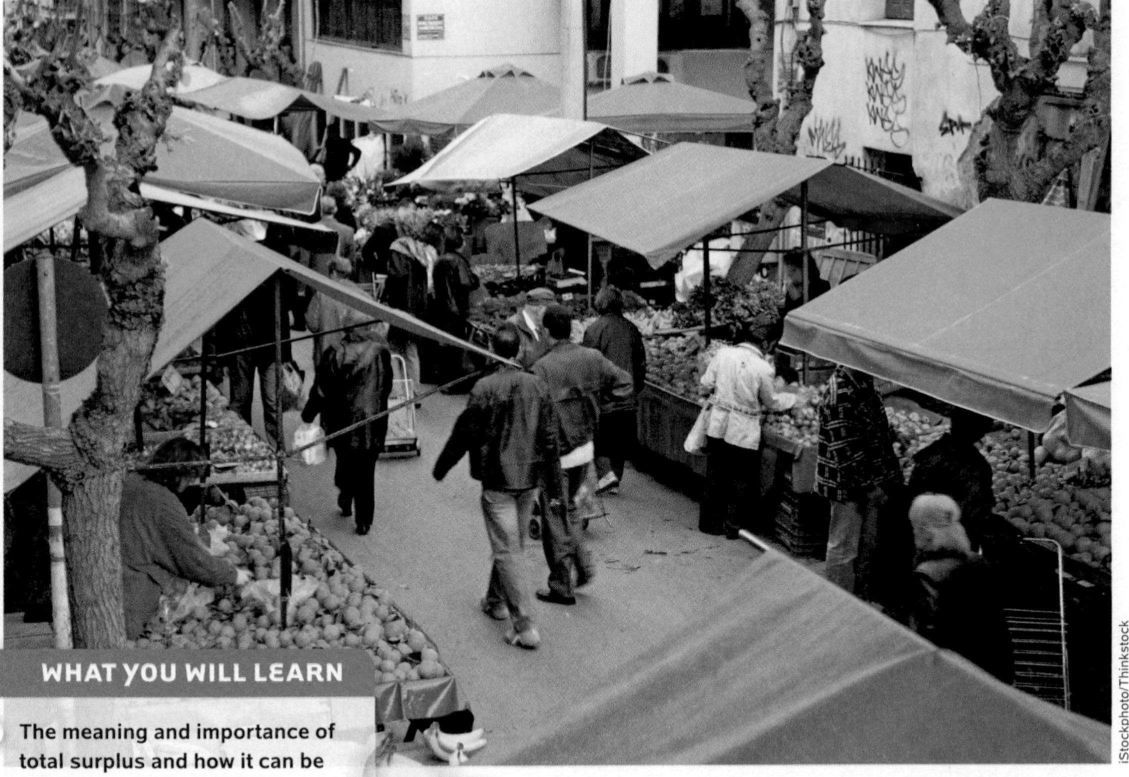
iStockphoto/Thinkstock

WHAT YOU WILL LEARN

1. **The meaning and importance of total surplus and how it can be used to illustrate efficiency in markets**
2. **Why property rights and prices as economic signals are critical to the smooth functioning of a market**
3. **Why markets typically lead to efficient outcomes despite the fact that they sometimes fail**

Consumer Surplus, Producer Surplus, and Efficiency

Markets are a remarkably effective way to organize economic activity: under the right conditions, they can make society as well off as possible given the available resources. The concepts of consumer and producer surplus introduced in the previous module can help us deepen our understanding of why this is so.

The Gains from Trade

Let's return to the market for used textbooks, but now consider a much bigger market—say, one at a large state university. There are many potential buyers and sellers, so the market is competitive. Let's line up incoming students who are potential buyers of a book in order of their willingness to pay, so that the entering student with the highest willingness to pay is potential buyer number 1, the student with the next highest willingness to pay is number 2, and so on. Then we can use their willingness to pay to derive a demand curve like the one in Figure 12-1.

Similarly, we can line up outgoing students, who are potential sellers of the book, in order of their cost, starting with the student with the lowest cost, then the student with the next lowest cost, and so on, to derive a supply curve like the one shown in the same figure.

As we have drawn the curves, the market reaches equilibrium at a price of $30 per book, and 1,000 books are bought and sold at that price. The two shaded triangles show the consumer surplus (blue) and the producer surplus (red) generated by this market. The sum of consumer and producer surplus is known as **total surplus.**

Total surplus is the total net gain to consumers and producers from trading in a market. It is the sum of producer and consumer surplus.

The striking thing about this picture is that both consumers and producers gain—that is, both consumers and producers are better off because there is a market for

FIGURE 12-1 Total Surplus

In the market for used textbooks, the equilibrium price is $30 and the equilibrium quantity is 1,000 books. Consumer surplus is given by the blue area, the area below the demand curve but above the price. Producer surplus is given by the red area, the area above the supply curve but below the price. The sum of the blue and the red areas is total surplus, the total benefit to society from the production and consumption of the good.

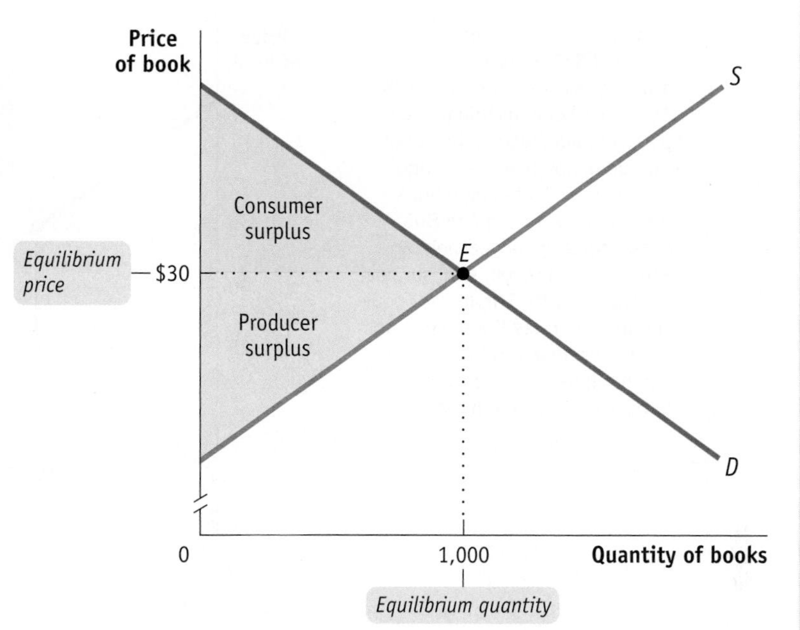

this good. But this should come as no surprise—because *there are gains from trade.* These gains from trade are the reason everyone is better off participating in a market economy than they would be if each individual tried to be self-sufficient.

But are we as well off as we could be? This brings us to the question of the efficiency of markets.

The Efficiency of Markets

A market is *efficient* if, once the market has produced its gains from trade, there is no way to make some people better off without making other people worse off. Note that market equilibrium is just *one* way of deciding who consumes a good and who sells a good. To better understand how markets promote efficiency, let's examine some alternatives.

Consider the example of kidney transplants discussed earlier in the Economics in Action in Module 11 (p. 108). There is not a market for kidneys, and available kidneys currently go to whoever has been on the waiting list the longest. Of course, those who have been waiting the longest aren't necessarily those who would benefit the most from a new kidney.

Similarly, imagine a committee charged with improving on the market equilibrium by deciding who gets and who gives up a used textbook. The committee's ultimate goal would be to bypass the market outcome and come up with another arrangement that would increase total surplus.

Let's consider three approaches the committee could take:

1. It could reallocate consumption among consumers.
2. It could reallocate sales among sellers.
3. It could change the quantity traded.

REALLOCATE CONSUMPTION AMONG CONSUMERS The committee might try to increase total surplus by selling books to different consumers. Figure 12-2 shows why this will result in lower surplus compared to the market equilibrium outcome. Points *A* and *B* show the positions on the demand curve of two potential buyers of used books, Ana and Bob. As we can see from the figure, Ana is willing to pay $35 for a

FIGURE 12-2 Reallocating Consumption Lowers Consumer Surplus

Ana (point A) has a willingness to pay of \$35. Bob (point B) has a willingness to pay of only \$25. At the market equilibrium price of \$30, Ana purchases a book but Bob does not. If we rearrange consumption by taking a book from Ana and giving it to Bob, consumer surplus declines by \$10 and, as a result, total surplus declines by \$10. The market equilibrium generates the highest possible consumer surplus by ensuring that those who consume the good are those who most value it.

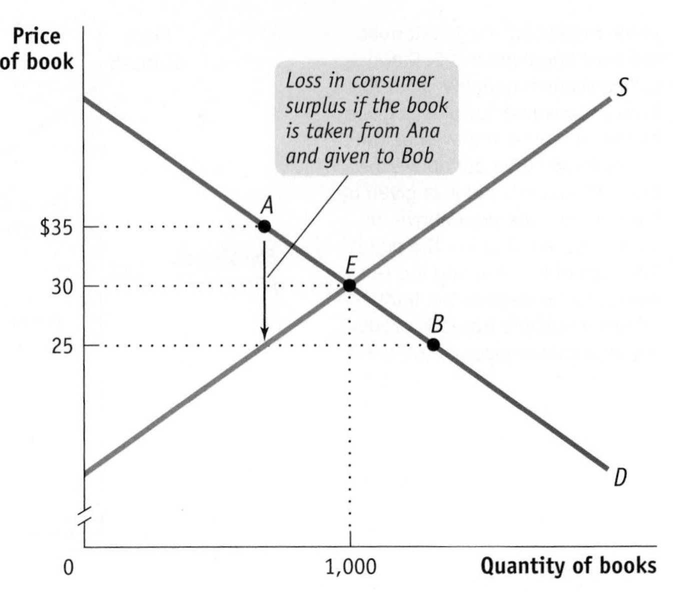

book, but Bob is willing to pay only \$25. Since the market equilibrium price is \$30, under the market outcome Ana gets a book and Bob does not.

Now suppose the committee reallocates consumption. This would mean taking the book away from Ana and giving it to Bob. Since the book is worth \$35 to Ana but only \$25 to Bob, this change *reduces total consumer surplus* by \$35 – \$25 = \$10. Moreover, this result doesn't depend on which two students we pick. Every student who buys a book at the market equilibrium price has a willingness to pay of \$30 or more, and every student who doesn't buy a book has a willingness to pay of less than \$30. So reallocating the good among consumers always means taking a book away from a student who values it more and giving it to one who values it less. This necessarily reduces total consumer surplus.

Viktor Cap/Alamy

REALLOCATE SALES AMONG SELLERS The committee might try to increase total surplus by altering who sells their books, taking sales away from sellers who would have sold their books in the market equilibrium and instead compelling those who would not have sold their books in the market equilibrium to sell them.

Figure 12-3 shows why this will result in lower surplus. Here points X and Y show the positions on the supply curve of Xavier, who has a cost of \$25, and Yvonne, who has a cost of \$35. At the equilibrium market price of \$30, Xavier would sell his book but Yvonne would not sell hers. If the committee reallocated sales, forcing Xavier to keep his book and Yvonne to sell hers, total producer surplus would be reduced by \$35 – \$25 = \$10.

Again, it doesn't matter which two students we choose. Any student who sells a book at the market equilibrium price has a lower cost than any student who keeps a book. So reallocating sales among sellers necessarily increases total cost and reduces total producer surplus.

CHANGE THE QUANTITY TRADED The committee might try to increase total surplus by compelling students to trade either more books or fewer books than the market equilibrium quantity.

Figure 12-4 shows why this will result in lower surplus. It shows all four students: potential buyers Ana and Bob, and potential sellers Xavier and Yvonne. To reduce sales, the committee will have to prevent a transaction that would have occurred in the market equilibrium—that is,

FIGURE 12-3 **Reallocating Sales Lowers Producer Surplus**

Yvonne (point Y) has a cost of \$35, \$10 more than Xavier (point X), who has a cost of \$25. At the market equilibrium price of \$30, Xavier sells a book but Yvonne does not. If we rearrange sales by preventing Xavier from selling his book and compelling Yvonne to sell hers, producer surplus declines by \$10 and, as a result, total surplus declines by \$10. The market equilibrium generates the highest possible producer surplus by assuring that those who sell the good are those who most value the right to sell it.

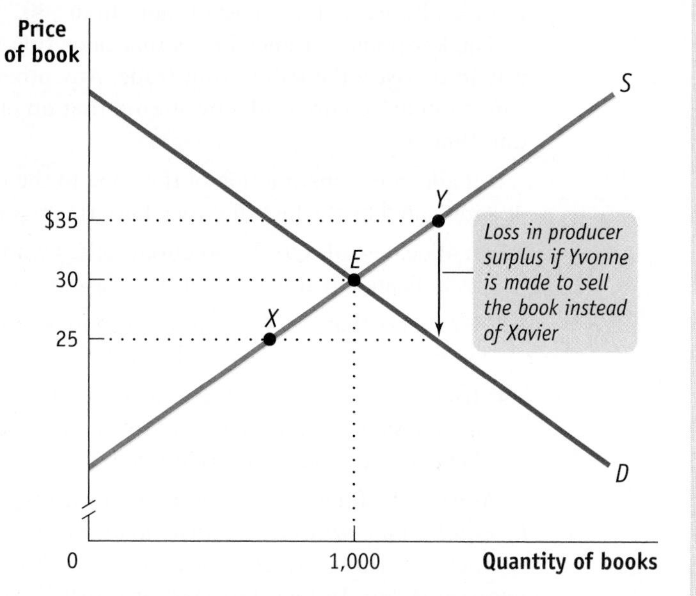

prevent Xavier from selling to Ana. Since Ana is willing to pay \$35 and Xavier's cost is \$25, preventing this transaction reduces total surplus by \$35 – \$25 = \$10.

Once again, this result doesn't depend on which two students we pick: any student who would have sold the book in the market equilibrium has a cost of \$30 or less, and any student who would have purchased the book in the market equilibrium has a willingness to pay of \$30 or more. So preventing any sale that would have occurred in the market equilibrium necessarily reduces total surplus.

Finally, the committee might try to increase sales by forcing Yvonne, who would not have sold her book in the market equilibrium, to sell it to someone like Bob, who would not have bought a book in the market equilibrium. Because Yvonne's cost is \$35, but Bob is only willing to pay \$25, this transaction reduces total surplus by \$10.

FIGURE 12-4 **Changing the Quantity Lowers Total Surplus**

If Xavier (point X) were prevented from selling his book to someone like Ana (point A), total surplus would fall by \$10, the difference between Ana's willingness to pay (\$35) and Xavier's cost (\$25). This means that total surplus falls whenever fewer than 1,000 books—the equilibrium quantity—are transacted. Likewise, if Yvonne (point Y) were compelled to sell her book to someone like Bob (point B), total surplus would also fall by \$10, the difference between Yvonne's cost (\$35) and Bob's willingness to pay (\$25). This means that total surplus falls whenever more than 1,000 books are transacted. These two examples show that at market equilibrium, all mutually beneficial transactions—and only mutually beneficial transactions—occur.

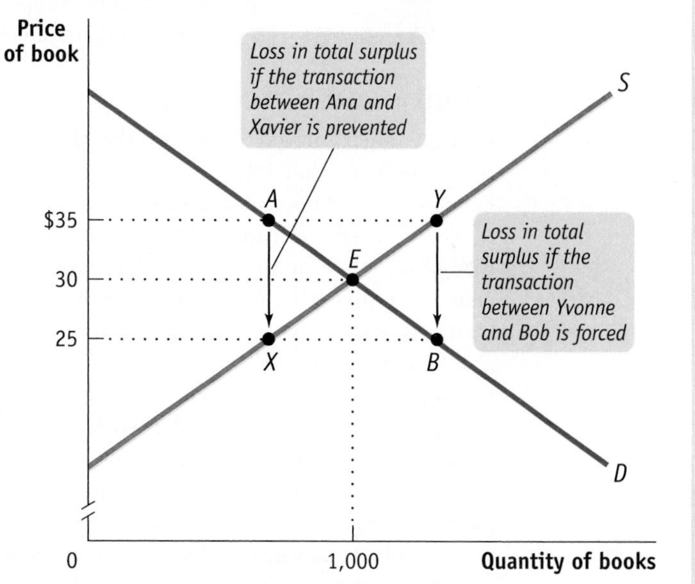

And once again it doesn't matter which two students we pick—anyone who wouldn't have bought the book has a willingness to pay of less than $30, and anyone who wouldn't have sold has a cost of more than $30.

The key point to remember is that once this market is in equilibrium, there is no way to increase the gains from trade. Any other outcome reduces total surplus. We can summarize our results by stating that an efficient market performs four important functions:

1. It allocates consumption of the good to the potential buyers who most value it, as indicated by the fact that they have the highest willingness to pay.
2. It allocates sales to the potential sellers who most value the right to sell the good, as indicated by the fact that they have the lowest cost.
3. It ensures that every consumer who makes a purchase values the good more than every seller who makes a sale, so that all transactions are mutually beneficial.
4. It ensures that every potential buyer who doesn't make a purchase values the good less than every potential seller who doesn't make a sale, so that no mutually beneficial transactions are missed.

As a result of these four functions, *any way of allocating the good other than the market equilibrium outcome will lower total surplus.*

There are three caveats, however. First, although a market may be efficient, it isn't necessarily *fair.* In fact, fairness, or *equity,* is often in conflict with efficiency. We'll discuss this next.

The second caveat is that markets sometimes *fail.* Under some well-defined conditions, markets can fail to deliver efficiency. When this occurs, markets no longer maximize total surplus. We'll take a closer look at market failures in later modules.

iStockphoto

Third, even when the market equilibrium maximizes total surplus, this does not mean that it results in the best outcome for every *individual* consumer and producer. Other things equal, each buyer would like to pay a lower price and each seller would like to receive a higher price. So if the government were to intervene in the market—say, by lowering the price below the equilibrium price to make consumers happy or by raising the price above the equilibrium price to make producers happy—the outcome would no longer be efficient. Although some people would be happier, society as a whole would be worse off because total surplus would be lower.

Equity and Efficiency

It's easy to get carried away with the idea that markets are always good and that economic policies that interfere with efficiency are bad. But that would be misguided because there is another factor to consider: society cares about equity, or what's "fair."

There is often a trade-off between equity and efficiency: policies that promote equity often come at the cost of decreased efficiency, and policies that promote efficiency often result in decreased equity. So it's important to realize that a society's choice to sacrifice some efficiency for the sake of equity, however it defines equity, may well be a valid one.

Consider, for example, patients who need kidney transplants. For them, the guidelines proposed by the United Network for Organ Sharing (UNOS), covered earlier, will be unwelcome news. Those who have waited years for a transplant will no doubt find the guidelines, which give precedence to younger patients, . . . well . . . unfair. And the guidelines raise other questions about fairness: Why limit potential transplant recipients to only Americans? Why not give precedence to those who have made recognized contributions to society? And so on.

The point is that efficiency is about *how to achieve goals, not what those goals should be.* For example, UNOS decided that its goal is to maximize the life span of kidney recipients. Some might have argued for a different goal, and efficiency does not address which goal is the best. *What efficiency does address is the best way to achieve a goal once it has been determined.*

It's important to understand that fairness, unlike efficiency, can be very hard to define. Fairness is a concept about which well-intentioned people often disagree.

Property rights are the rights of owners of valuable items, whether resources or goods, to dispose of those items as they choose.

An **economic signal** is any piece of information that helps people make better economic decisions.

A Market Economy

As we learned earlier, in a market economy decisions about production and consumption are made via markets. In fact, the economy as a whole is made up of many *interrelated markets*. Up until now, to learn how markets work, we've been examining a single market—the market for used textbooks. But in reality, consumers and producers do not make decisions in isolated markets. For example, a student's decision in the market for used textbooks might be affected by how much interest must be paid on a student loan; thus, the decision in the used-textbook market would be influenced by what is going on in the market for money.

We know that an efficient market equilibrium maximizes total surplus—the gains to buyers and sellers in that market. Is there a comparable result for an economy as a whole, an economy composed of a vast number of individual markets? The answer is yes, but with qualifications.

When each and every market in the economy maximizes total surplus, then the economy as a whole is efficient. This is a very important result: just as it is impossible to make someone better off without making other people worse off in a single market when it is efficient, the same is true when each and every market in that economy is efficient. However, it is virtually impossible to find an economy in which every market is efficient.

For now, let's examine why markets and market economies typically work so well. Once we understand why, we can then briefly address why markets sometimes get it wrong.

Why Markets Typically Work So Well

Economists have written volumes about why markets are an effective way to organize an economy. In the end, well-functioning markets owe their effectiveness to two powerful features: *property rights* and the role of prices as *economic signals*.

Property rights are a system in which valuable items in the economy have specific owners who can dispose of them as they choose. In a system of property rights, by purchasing a good you receive "ownership rights": the right to use and dispose of the good as you see fit. Property rights are what make the mutually beneficial transactions in the used-textbook market, or any market, possible.

To see why property rights are crucial, imagine that students do not have full property rights in their textbooks and are prohibited from reselling them when the semester ends. This restriction on property rights would prevent many mutually beneficial transactions. Some students would be stuck with textbooks they will never reread when they would be much happier receiving some cash instead. Other students would be forced to pay full price for brand-new books when they would be happier getting slightly battered copies at a lower price.

Once a system of well-defined property rights is in place, the second necessary feature of well-functioning markets—prices as economic signals—can operate. An **economic signal** is any piece of information that helps people make better economic

Price is the most important economic signal in a market economy.

Lifesize/Thinkstock

A market or an economy is **inefficient** if there are missed opportunities: some people could be made better off without making other people worse off.

Market failure occurs when a market fails to be efficient.

decisions. For example, business forecasters say that sales of cardboard boxes are a good early indicator of changes in industrial production: if businesses are buying lots of cardboard boxes, you can be sure that they will soon increase their production.

But prices are far and away the most important signals in a market economy, because they convey essential information about other people's costs and their willingness to pay. If the equilibrium price of used books is $30, this in effect tells everyone both that there are consumers willing to pay $30 and up and that there are potential sellers with a cost of $30 or less. The signal given by the market price ensures that total surplus is maximized by telling people whether to buy books, sell books, or do nothing at all.

This example shows that the market price "signals" to consumers with a willingness to pay equal to or more than the market price that they should buy the good, just as it signals to producers with a cost equal to or less than the market price that they should sell the good. And since, in equilibrium, the quantity demanded equals the quantity supplied, all willing consumers will find willing sellers.

Prices can sometimes fail as economic signals. Sometimes a price is not an accurate indicator of how desirable a good is. For example, you can't infer from the price alone whether a used car is good or a "lemon."

Why Markets Can Sometimes Get It Wrong

Although markets are an amazingly effective way to organize economic activity, as we've noted, markets can sometimes get it wrong—they can be *inefficient.* When markets are **inefficient,** there are missed opportunities—ways in which production or consumption can be rearranged that would make some people better off without making other people worse off. In other words, there are gains from trade that go unrealized: total surplus could be increased.

Markets can be inefficient for a number of reasons. Two of the most important are a lack of property rights and inaccuracy of prices as economic signals. When a market is inefficient, we have what is known as **market failure.** We will examine various types of market failure in later modules. For now, let's review the three main ways in which markets sometimes fall short of efficiency.

1. Markets can fail when, in an attempt to capture more surplus, one party prevents mutually beneficial trades from occurring. This situation arises, for instance, when a market contains only a single seller of a good, known as a *monopolist.* A monopolist creates inefficiency by manipulating the market price to increase profits.
2. Actions of individuals sometimes have side effects on the welfare of others that markets don't take into account. In economics, these side effects are known as *externalities,* and the best-known example is pollution. We can think of pollution as a problem of incomplete property rights; for example, existing property rights don't guarantee a right to ownership of clean air. Pollution and other externalities also give rise to inefficiency.
3. Markets for some goods fail because these goods, by their very nature, are unsuited for efficient management by markets. Falling into this category are goods for which some people possess information that others don't have. For example, the seller of a used car that is a "lemon" may have information that is unknown to potential buyers. Also in this category are goods for which there are problems limiting people's access to and consumption of the good; examples are fish in the sea and trees in the Amazonian rain forest. In these instances, markets generally fail due to incomplete property rights.

But even with these limitations, it's remarkable how well markets work at maximizing the gains from trade.

MODULE 12 Review

Solutions appear at the back of the book.

Check Your Understanding

1. Using the tables in Check Your Understanding in the preceding module, find the equilibrium price and quantity in the market for cheese-stuffed jalapeno peppers. What is the total surplus in the equilibrium in this market, and who receives it?

2. Using your answers from the previous question, show how each of the following three actions reduces total surplus:
   a. Having Josey consume one fewer pepper, and Casey one more pepper, than in the market equilibrium
   b. Having Cara produce one fewer pepper, and Jamie one more pepper, than in the market equilibrium
   c. Having Josey consume one fewer pepper, and Cara produce one fewer pepper, than in the market equilibrium

3. Suppose that in the market for used textbooks the equilibrium price is $30 but it is mistakenly announced that the equilibrium price is $300. How does this mistake affect the efficiency of the market?

Multiple-Choice Questions

1. At market equilibrium in a competitive market, which of the following is necessarily true?
   I. Consumer surplus is maximized.
   II. Producer surplus is maximized.
   III. Total surplus is maximized.
   a. I only
   b. II only
   c. III only
   d. I and II only
   e. I, II, and III

2. When a competitive market is in equilibrium, total surplus can be increased by
   I. reallocating consumption among consumers.
   II. reallocating sales among sellers.
   III. changing the quantity traded.
   a. I only
   b. II only
   c. III only
   d. I, II, and III
   e. None of the above

3. Which of the following is true regarding equity and efficiency in competitive markets?
   a. Competitive markets ensure equity and efficiency.
   b. There is often a trade-off between equity and efficiency.
   c. Competitive markets lead to neither equity nor efficiency.
   d. There is generally agreement about the level of equity and efficiency in a market.
   e. None of the above.

4. What features are essential to well-functioning markets?
   I. A system of property rights
   II. Externalities
   III. Economic signals
   a. I only
   b. II only
   c. III only
   d. I and III only
   e. I, II, and III

5. Which of the following is an example of the failure of a system of property rights to assign ownership to the appropriate party?
   I. The ability of one student to sell a used textbook to another student.
   II. The ability of some fishermen to fish as much as they wish in open waters
   III. The ability of a car salesman to make a sale to an interested buyer.
   a. I only
   b. II only
   c. I and ll only
   d. III only
   e. I, II, and III

Critical-Thinking Questions

1. Suppose UNOS alters its proposed guidelines for allocating donated kidneys to give preference to patients with young children, no longer relying solely on the concept of "net benefit." If total surplus in this case is defined as the total life span of kidney recipients, is this new guideline likely to reduce, increase, or leave total surplus unchanged? How might you justify this new guideline?

2. What is wrong with the following statement? "Markets are always the best way to organize economic activity. Any policies that interfere with markets reduce society's welfare."

BUSINESS CASE • StubHub Shows Up The Boss

Back in 1965, long before Ticketmaster, StubHub, and TicketsNow, legendary rock music promoter Bill Graham noticed that mass parties erupted wherever local rock groups played. Graham realized that fans would pay for the experience of the concert, in addition to paying for a recording of the music. He went on to create the business of rock concert promoting—booking and managing multicity tours for bands and selling lots of tickets. Those tickets were carefully rationed, a single purchaser allowed to buy only a limited number. Fans would line up at box offices, sometimes camping out the night before for popular bands.

AP Photo/Jason DeCrow

Wanting to maintain the aura of the 1960s that made rock concerts accessible to all their fans, many top bands choose to price their tickets below the market equilibrium level. For example, in 2009 Bruce Springsteen sold tickets at his concerts in New Jersey (his home state and home to his most ardent fans) for between $65 and $95. Tickets for Springsteen concerts could have sold for far more: economists Alan Krueger and Marie Connolly analyzed a 2002 Springsteen concert for which every ticket sold for $75 and concluded that The Boss forfeited about $4 million by not charging the market price, about $280 at the time.

So what was The Boss thinking? Cheap tickets can ensure that a concert sells out, making it a better experience for both band and audience. But it is believed that other factors are at work—that cheap tickets are a way for a band to reward fans' loyalty as well as a means to seem more "authentic" and less commercial. As Bruce Springsteen has said, "In some fashion, I help people hold on to their own humanity—if I'm doing my job right."

But the rise of the Internet has made things much more complicated. Now, rather than line up for tickets at the venue, fans buy tickets online, either from a direct seller like Ticketmaster (which obtains tickets directly from the concert producer) or a reseller like StubHub or TicketsNow. Resellers (otherwise known as scalpers) can—and do—make lots of money by scooping up large numbers of tickets at the box office price and reselling them at the market price. StubHub, for example, made $1 billion in the resale market for tickets in 2010.

This practice has infuriated fans as well as the bands. But resellers have cast the issue as one of the freedom to dispose of one's ticket as one chooses. In recent years, both sides—bands and their fans versus ticket resellers—have been lobbying government officials to shape ticket-reselling laws to their advantage.

Questions for Thought

1. Using the concepts of consumer surplus and producer surplus, draw a diagram to illustrate the exchange between The Boss and his fans. Explain your findings. (Hint: ticket supply is perfectly inelastic.)
2. How has the rise of Internet resellers changed the allocation of surplus between The Boss and his fans?
3. Using your diagram from the the first question, explain the effect of resellers on the allocation of consumer surplus and producer surplus in the market for concert tickets. What are the implications of the Internet for all such exchanges?

SECTION 4 REVIEW

Summary

Consumer and Producer Surplus

1. The **willingness to pay** of each individual consumer determines the shape of the demand curve. When price is less than or equal to the willingness to pay, the potential consumer purchases the good. The difference between willingness to pay and price is the net gain to the consumer, the **individual consumer surplus.**
2. **Total consumer surplus** in a market, which is the sum of all individual consumer surpluses in a market, is equal to the area below the market demand curve but above the price. A rise in the price of a good reduces consumer surplus; a fall in the price increases consumer surplus. The term **consumer surplus** is often used to refer to both individual and total consumer surplus.
3. The **cost** of each potential producer of a good, the lowest price at which he or she is willing to supply a unit of that good, determines the supply curve. If the price of a good is above a producer's cost, a sale generates a net gain to the producer, known as the **individual producer surplus.**
4. **Total producer surplus** in a market, the sum of the individual producer surpluses in a market, is equal to the area above the market supply curve but below the price. A rise in the price of a good increases producer surplus; a fall in the price reduces producer surplus. The term **producer surplus** is often used to refer to both individual and total producer surplus.

Efficiency and Markets

5. **Total surplus,** the total gain to society from the production and consumption of a good, is the sum of consumer and producer surplus.
6. Usually, markets are efficient and achieve the maximum total surplus. Any possible reallocation of consumption or sales, or change in the quantity bought and sold, reduces total surplus. However, society also cares about equity. So government intervention in a market that reduces efficiency but increases equity can be a valid choice by society.
7. An economy composed of efficient markets is also efficient, although this is virtually impossible to achieve in reality. The keys to the efficiency of a market economy are **property rights** and the operation of prices as **economic signals.**
8. Under certain conditions, **market failure** occurs, making a market **inefficient.** There are three principal sources of market failure: attempts to capture more surplus that create inefficiencies, side effects of some transactions, and problems in the nature of the good.

Key Terms

Problems

1. Determine the amount of consumer surplus generated in each of the following situations.

   a. Leon goes to the clothing store to buy a new T-shirt, for which he is willing to pay up to \$10. He picks out one he likes with a price tag of exactly \$10. When he is paying for it, he learns that the T-shirt has been discounted by 50%.

   b. Alberto goes online to the iTunes store hoping to find Mumford & Son's new album, and is willing to pay up to \$12. He sees that iTunes is selling the album for \$11.99, so he purchases it.

   c. After soccer practice, Stacey is willing to pay \$2 for a bottle of mineral water. The 7-Eleven sells mineral water for \$2.25 per bottle, so she declines to purchase it.

2. Determine the amount of producer surplus generated in each of the following situations.

   a. Gordon lists his old Lionel electric trains on eBay. He sets a minimum acceptable price, known as his *reserve price*, of $75. After five days of bidding, the final high bid is exactly $75. He accepts the bid.

   b. So-Hee advertises her car for sale in the used-car section of the student newspaper for $2,000, but she is willing to sell the car for any price higher than $1,500. The best offer she gets is $1,200, which she declines.

   c. Sanjay likes his job so much that he would be willing to do it for free. However, his annual salary is $80,000.

3. There are six potential consumers of computer games, each willing to buy only one game. Consumer 1 is willing to pay $40 for a computer game, consumer 2 is willing to pay $35, consumer 3 is willing to pay $30, consumer 4 is willing to pay $25, consumer 5 is willing to pay $20, and consumer 6 is willing to pay $15.

   a. Suppose the market price is $29. What is the total consumer surplus?

   b. The market price decreases to $19. What is the total consumer surplus now?

   c. When the price fell from $29 to $19, how much did each consumer's individual consumer surplus change? How does total consumer surplus change?

4. You are the manager of Fun World, a small amusement park. The accompanying diagram shows the demand curve of a typical customer at Fun World.

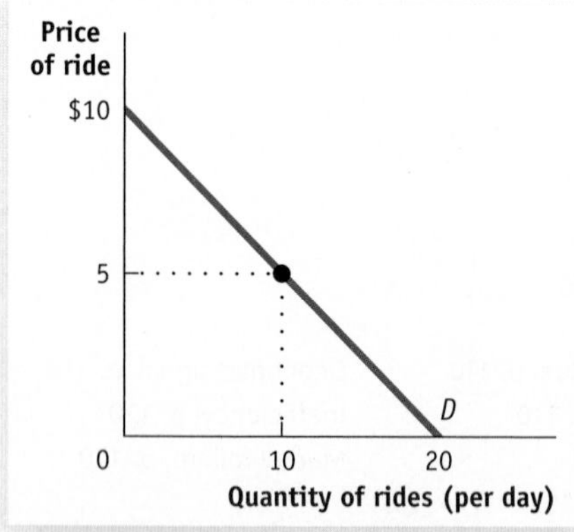

   a. Suppose that the price of each ride is $5. At that price, how much consumer surplus does an individual consumer get? (Note that the area of a right triangle is ½ × the height of the triangle × the base of the triangle.)

   b. Suppose that Fun World considers charging an admission fee, even though it maintains the price of each ride at $5. What is the maximum admission fee it could charge? (Assume that all potential customers have enough money to pay the fee.)

   c. Suppose that Fun World lowered the price of each ride to zero. How much consumer surplus does an individual consumer get? What is the maximum admission fee Fun World could charge?

5. The accompanying diagram illustrates a taxi driver's individual supply curve (assume that each taxi ride is the same distance).

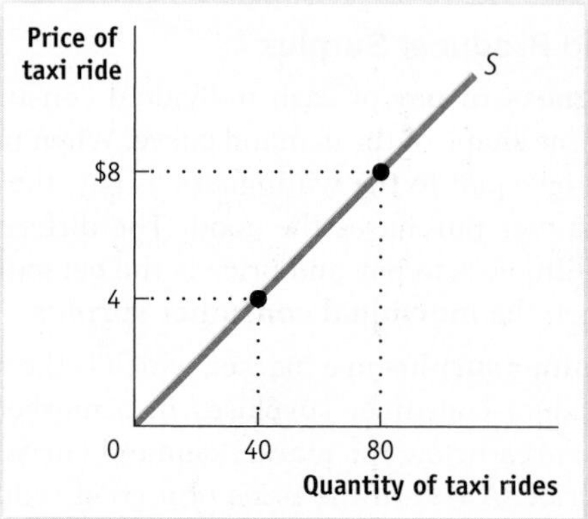

   a. Suppose the city sets the price of taxi rides at $4 per ride, and at $4 the taxi driver is able to sell as many taxi rides as he desires. What is this taxi driver's producer surplus? (Note that the area of a right triangle is ½ × the height of the triangle × the base of the triangle.)

   b. Suppose that the city keeps the price of a taxi ride set at $4, but it decides to charge taxi drivers a special fee. What is the maximum special fee the city could extract from this taxi driver?

   c. Suppose that the city allowed the price of taxi rides to increase to $8 per ride. Again assume that, at this price, the taxi driver sells as many rides as he is willing to offer. How much producer surplus does an individual taxi driver now get? What is the maximum special fee the city could charge this taxi driver?

6. The accompanying table shows the supply and demand schedules for used copies of the second edition of this textbook. The supply schedule is derived from offers at Amazon.com. The demand schedule is hypothetical.

Price of book	Quantity of books demanded	Quantity of books supplied
$55	50	0
60	35	1
65	25	3
70	17	3
75	14	6
80	12	9
85	10	10
90	8	18
95	6	22
100	4	31
105	2	37
110	0	42

   a. Calculate consumer and producer surplus at the equilibrium in this market.

b. Now the third edition of this textbook becomes available. As a result, the willingness to pay of each potential buyer for a second-hand copy of the second edition falls by $20. In a table, show the new demand schedule and again calculate consumer and producer surplus at the new equilibrium.

7. Suppose that Hollywood screenwriters negotiate a new agreement with movie producers stipulating that they will receive 10% of the revenue from every video rental of a movie they authored. They have no such agreement for movies shown on on-demand television.

a. When the new writers' agreement comes into effect, what will happen in the market for video rentals—that is, will supply or demand shift, and how? As a result, how will consumer surplus in the market for video rentals change? Illustrate with a diagram. Do you think the writers' agreement will be popular with consumers who rent videos?

b. Consumers consider video rentals and on-demand movies substitutable to some extent. When the new writers' agreement comes into effect, what will happen in the market for on-demand movies—that is, will supply or demand shift, and how? As a result, how will producer surplus in the market for on-demand movies change? Illustrate with a diagram. Do you think the writers' agreement will be popular with cable television companies that show on-demand movies?

8. A few years ago a New York district judge ruled in a copyright infringement lawsuit against the popular file-sharing website LimeWire and in favor of the 13 major record companies that had brought the lawsuit. The record companies, including Sony, Virgin, and Warner Brothers, had alleged that the file-sharing service encourages users to make illegal copies of copyrighted material. Allowing Internet users to obtain music for free limits the record companies' right to give access to their music only to those who have paid for it. In other words, it limits the record companies' property rights.

a. If everyone obtained music and video content for free from websites such as LimeWire, instead of paying the record companies, what would happen to the record companies' producer surplus from music sales? What are the implications for record companies' incentive to produce music content in the future?

b. If the record companies had lost the lawsuit and music could be freely downloaded from the Internet, what do you think would happen to mutually beneficial transactions (the producing and buying of music) in the future?

9. EAuction and EMarketplace are two competing Internet auction sites, where buyers and sellers transact goods. Each auction site earns money by charging sellers for listing their goods. Over time, because EAuction provides much better technical service than its rival, EMarketplace, buyers and sellers come to prefer EAuction. Eventually, EMarketplace closes down, leaving EAuction as the sole provider of this service (it becomes a monopolist). EAuction also owns a site that handles payments over the Internet, called PayForIt. It is competing with another Internet payment site, called PayBuddy. EAuction has now stipulated that any transaction on its auction site must use PayForIt, rather than PayBuddy, for the payment. What is the impact on market efficiency, producer surplus, and consumer surplus from EAuction's position in the market as the only provider of the service?

Module 13: Price Controls (Ceilings and Floors)
Module 14: Quantity Controls (Quotas)
Module 15: Taxes

SECTION 5

Government Policy and Taxes

BIG CITY, NOT-SO-BRIGHT IDEAS

New York City is a place where you can find almost anything—that is, almost anything, except a taxicab when you need one or a decent apartment at a rent you can afford. You might think that New York's notorious shortages of cabs and apartments are the inevitable price of big-city living. However, they are largely the product of government policies—specifically, of government policies that have, in one way or another, tried to prevail over the market forces of supply and demand.

In Section 2, we learned the principle that a market moves to equilibrium—that the market price rises or falls to the level at which the quantity of a good that people are willing to supply is equal to the quantity that other people demand.

But sometimes governments try to defy that principle. Whenever a government tries to dictate either a market price or a market quantity that's different from the equilibrium price or quantity, the market strikes back in predictable ways.

The shortages of apartments and taxicabs in New York are two examples of what happens when the logic of the market is defied. New York's housing shortage is the result of *rent control,* a law that prevents landlords from raising rents except when specifically given permission. Rent control was introduced during World War II to protect the interests of tenants, and it still remains in force. Many other American cities have had rent control at one time or another, but with the notable exceptions of New York and San Francisco, these controls have largely been done away with.

Similarly, New York's limited supply of taxis is the result of a licensing system introduced in the 1930s. New York taxi licenses are known as "medallions," and only taxis with medallions are allowed to pick up passengers. Although this system was originally intended to protect the interests of both drivers and customers, it has generated a shortage of taxis in the city.

In this section, we begin by examining what happens when governments try to control prices in a competitive market, keeping the price in a market either below its equilibrium level—a *price ceiling* such as rent control—or above it—a *price floor* such as the minimum wage paid to workers in many countries. We then turn to schemes such as taxi medallions that attempt to dictate the quantity of a good bought and sold. We conclude with a discussion of what happens when governments tax goods and services.

MODULE 13

Price Controls (Ceilings and Floors)

Thinkstock/Photodisc

WHAT YOU WILL LEARN

1. The meaning of price controls, one way government intervenes in markets
2. How price controls can create problems and make a market inefficient
3. Why economists are often deeply skeptical of attempts to intervene in markets
4. Who benefits and who loses from price controls, and why they are used despite their well-known problems

Why Governments Control Prices

As you've learned, a market moves to equilibrium—that is, the market price moves to the level at which the quantity supplied equals the quantity demanded. But this equilibrium price does not necessarily please either buyers or sellers.

After all, buyers would always like to pay less if they could, and sometimes they can make a strong moral or political case that they should pay lower prices. For example, what if the equilibrium between supply and demand for apartments in a major city leads to rental rates that an average working person can't afford? In that case, a government might well be under pressure to impose limits on the rents landlords can charge.

Sellers, however, would always like to get more money for what they sell, and sometimes they can make a strong moral or political case that they should receive higher prices. For example, consider the labor market: the price for an hour of a worker's time is the wage rate. What if the equilibrium between supply and demand for less skilled workers leads to wage rates that yield an income below the poverty level? In that case, a government might well be pressured to require employers to pay a rate no lower than some specified minimum wage.

In other words, there is often a strong political demand for governments to intervene in markets. And powerful interests can make a compelling case that a market intervention favoring them is "fair." When a government intervenes to regulate prices, we say that it imposes **price controls.** These controls typically take the form of either an upper limit, a **price ceiling,** or a lower limit, a **price floor.**

Price controls are legal restrictions on how high or low a market price may go. They can take two forms: a **price ceiling,** a maximum price sellers are allowed to charge for a good or service, or a **price floor,** a minimum price buyers are required to pay for a good or service.

Unfortunately, it's not that easy to tell a market what to do. As we will now see, when a government tries to legislate prices—whether it legislates them *down* by imposing a price ceiling or *up* by imposing a price floor—there are certain predictable and unpleasant side effects.

We make an important assumption in this module: the markets in question are efficient before price controls are imposed. Markets can sometimes be inefficient—for example, a market dominated by a monopolist, a single seller who has the power to influence the market price. When markets are inefficient, price controls don't necessarily cause problems and can potentially move the market closer to efficiency. In practice, however, price controls often *are* imposed on efficient markets—like the New York City apartment market. And so the analysis in this module applies to many important real-world situations.

Price Ceilings

Aside from rent control, there are not many price ceilings in the United States today. But at times they have been widespread. Price ceilings are typically imposed during crises—wars, harvest failures, natural disasters—because these events often lead to sudden price increases that hurt many people but produce big gains for a lucky few. The U.S. government imposed ceilings on many prices during World War II: the war sharply increased demand for raw materials, such as aluminum and steel, and price controls prevented those with access to these raw materials from earning huge profits. Price controls on oil were imposed in 1973, when an embargo by Arab oil-exporting countries seemed likely to generate huge profits for U.S. oil companies. Price controls were instituted again in 2012 by New York and New Jersey authorities in the aftermath of Hurricane Sandy, as gas shortages led to rampant price-gouging.

Rent control in New York is a legacy of World War II: it was imposed because wartime production created an economic boom, which increased demand for apartments at a time when the labor and raw materials that might have been used to build them were being used to win the war instead. Although most price controls were removed soon after the war ended, New York's rent limits were retained and gradually extended to buildings not previously covered, leading to some very strange situations.

You can rent a one-bedroom apartment in Manhattan on fairly short notice—if you are able and willing to pay several thousand dollars a month and live in a less-than-desirable area. Yet some people pay only a small fraction of this for comparable apartments, and others pay hardly more for bigger apartments in better locations.

Aside from producing great deals for some renters, however, what are the broader consequences of New York's rent-control system? To answer this question, we turn to the supply and demand model.

Modeling a Price Ceiling

To see what can go wrong when a government imposes a price ceiling on an efficient market, consider Figure 13-1, which shows a simplified model of the market for apartments in New York. For the sake of simplicity, we imagine that all apartments are exactly the same and so would rent for the same price in an unregulated market.

The table in the figure shows the demand and supply schedules; the demand and supply curves are shown on the left. We show the quantity of apartments on the horizontal axis and the monthly rent per apartment on the vertical axis. You can see that in an unregulated market the equilibrium would be at point *E:* 2 million apartments would be rented for $1,000 each per month.

Now suppose that the government imposes a price ceiling, limiting rents to a price below the equilibrium price—say, no more than $800.

Figure 13-2 shows the effect of the price ceiling, represented by the line at $800. At the enforced rental rate of $800, landlords have less incentive to offer apartments, so they won't be willing to supply as many as they would at the equilibrium rate of $1,000. They will choose point *A* on the supply curve, offering only 1.8 million apartments for rent, 200,000 fewer than in the unregulated market. At the same time, more

FIGURE 13-1 **The Market for Apartments in the Absence of Government Controls**

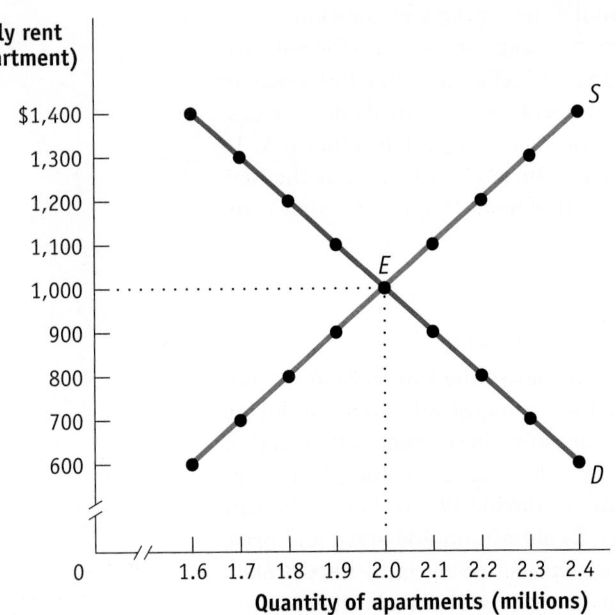

Monthly rent (per apartment)	Quantity of apartments (millions)	
	Quantity demanded	Quantity supplied
$1,400	1.6	2.4
1,300	1.7	2.3
1,200	1.8	2.2
1,100	1.9	2.1
1,000	2.0	2.0
900	2.1	1.9
800	2.2	1.8
700	2.3	1.7
600	2.4	1.6

Without government intervention, the market for apartments reaches equilibrium at point *E* with a market rent of $1,000 per month and 2 million apartments rented.

people will want to rent apartments at a price of $800 than at the equilibrium price of $1,000; as shown at point *B* on the demand curve, at a monthly rent of $800 the quantity of apartments demanded rises to 2.2 million, 200,000 more than in the unregulated market and 400,000 more than are actually available at the price of $800. So there is now a persistent shortage of rental housing: at that price, 400,000 more people want to rent than are able to find apartments.

FIGURE 13-2 **The Effects of a Price Ceiling**

The black horizontal line represents the government-imposed price ceiling on rents of $800 per month. This price ceiling reduces the quantity of apartments supplied to 1.8 million, point *A*, and increases the quantity demanded to 2.2 million, point *B*. This creates a persistent shortage of 400,000 units: 400,000 people who want apartments at the legal rent of $800 but cannot get them.

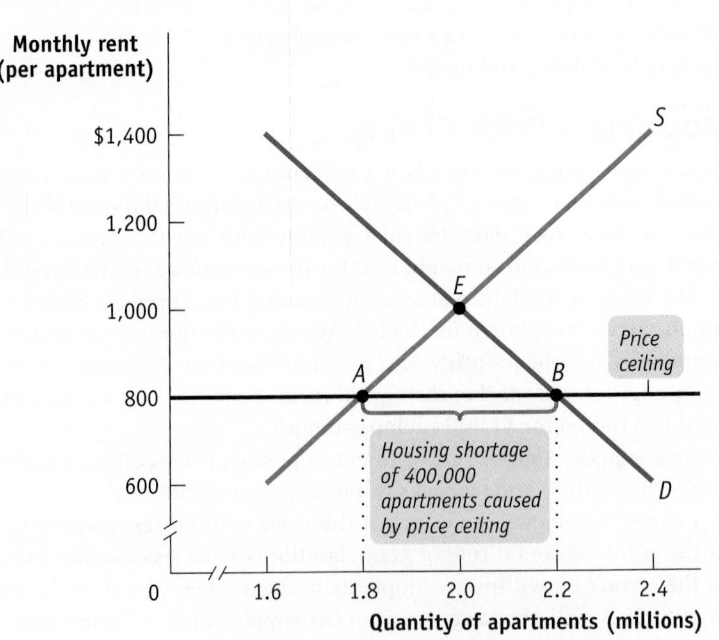

Do price ceilings always cause shortages? No. If a price ceiling is set above the equilibrium price, it won't have any effect. Suppose that the equilibrium rental rate on apartments is $1,000 per month and the city government sets a ceiling of $1,200. Who cares? In this case, the price ceiling won't be binding—it won't actually constrain market behavior—and it will have no effect.

How a Price Ceiling Causes Inefficiency

The housing shortage shown in Figure 13-2 is not merely annoying: like any shortage induced by price controls, it can be seriously harmful because it leads to inefficiency.

Rent control, like all price ceilings, creates inefficiency in at least three distinct ways. It typically leads to an inefficient allocation of apartments among would-be renters; it leads to wasted time and effort as people search for apartments; and it leads landlords to maintain apartments in inefficiently low quality or condition. In addition to inefficiency, price ceilings give rise to illegal behavior as people try to circumvent them. We should also add that price ceilings (as well as price floors) cause inefficiency in the form of *deadweight loss* by discouraging some mutually beneficial transactions from taking place. We'll learn more about deadweight loss in the upcoming two modules.

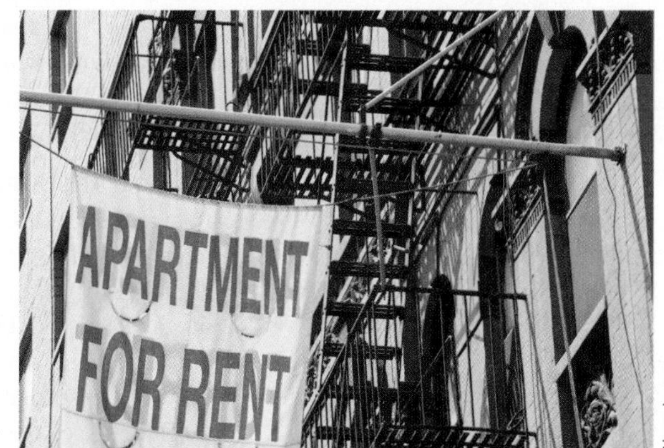

Alamy Images

Rent control often leads to the misallocation of available apartments.

INEFFICIENT ALLOCATION TO CONSUMERS Rent control doesn't just lead to too few apartments being available. It can also lead to misallocation of the apartments that are available: people who badly need a place to live may not be able to find an apartment, while some apartments may be occupied by people with much less urgent needs.

In the case shown in Figure 13-2, 2.2 million people would like to rent an apartment at $800 per month, but only 1.8 million apartments are available. Of those 2.2 million who are seeking an apartment, some want an apartment badly and are willing to pay a high price to get one. Others have a less urgent need and are only willing to pay a low price, perhaps because they have alternative housing. An efficient allocation of apartments would reflect these differences: people who really want an apartment will get one and people who aren't all that eager to find an apartment won't. In an inefficient distribution of apartments, the opposite will happen: some people who are not especially eager to find an apartment will get one and others who are very eager to find an apartment won't.

Because people usually get apartments through luck or personal connections under rent control, it generally results in an **inefficient allocation to consumers** of the few apartments available.

To see the inefficiency involved, consider the Lees, a family with young children who have no alternative housing and would be willing to pay up to $1,500 for an apartment—but are unable to find one. Also consider George, a retiree who lives most of the year in Florida but still has a lease on the New York apartment he moved into 40 years ago. George pays $800 per month for this apartment, but if the rent were even slightly more—say, $850—he would give it up and stay with his children when he is in New York.

This allocation of apartments—George has one and the Lees do not—is a missed opportunity: there is a way to make the Lees and George both better off at no additional cost. The Lees would be happy to pay George, say, $1,200 a month to sublease his apartment, which he would happily accept since the apartment is worth no more than $849 a month to him. George would prefer the money he gets from the Lees to keeping his apartment; the Lees would prefer to have the apartment rather than the money. So both would be made better off by this transaction—and nobody else would be made worse off.

Price ceilings often lead to inefficiency in the form of **inefficient allocation to consumers:** people who want the good badly and are willing to pay a high price don't get it, and those who care relatively little about the good and are only willing to pay a relatively low price do get it.

Generally, if people who really want apartments could sublease them from people who are less eager to live there, both those who gain apartments and those who trade

Price ceilings typically lead to inefficiency in the form of **wasted resources:** people expend money, effort, and time to cope with the shortages caused by the price ceiling.

Price ceilings often lead to inefficiency in that the goods being offered are of **inefficiently low quality:** sellers offer low quality goods at a low price even though buyers would prefer a higher quality at a higher price.

A **black market** is a market in which goods or services are bought and sold illegally—either because it is illegal to sell them at all or because the prices charged are legally prohibited by a price ceiling.

their occupancy for money would be better off. However, subletting is illegal under rent control because it would occur at prices above the price ceiling.

The fact that subletting is illegal doesn't mean it never happens. In fact, chasing down illegal subletting is a major business for New York private investigators, who have been known to use hidden cameras and other tricks to prove that the legal tenants in rent-controlled apartments actually live somewhere else and have sublet their apartments at two or three times the controlled rent. This subletting is a kind of illegal activity, which we will discuss shortly. For now, just notice that the aggressive pursuit of illegal subletting surely discourages the practice, so there isn't enough subletting to eliminate the inefficient allocation of apartments.

WASTED RESOURCES Another reason a price ceiling causes inefficiency is that it leads to **wasted resources:** people expend money, effort, and time to cope with the shortages caused by the price ceiling. Back in 1979, U.S. price controls on gasoline led to shortages that forced millions of Americans to spend hours each week waiting in lines at gas stations. The opportunity cost of the time spent in gas lines—the wages not earned, the leisure time not enjoyed—constituted wasted resources from the point of view of consumers and of the economy as a whole.

Because of rent control, the Lees will spend all their spare time for several months searching for an apartment, time they would rather have spent working or engaged in family activities. That is, there is an opportunity cost to the Lees' prolonged search for an apartment—the leisure or income they had to forgo. If the market for apartments worked freely, the Lees would quickly find an apartment at the equilibrium rent of $1,000, leaving them time to earn more or to enjoy themselves—an outcome that would make them better off without making anyone else worse off. Again, rent control creates missed opportunities.

INEFFICIENTLY LOW QUALITY Yet another way a price ceiling causes inefficiency is by causing goods to be of inefficiently low quality. **Inefficiently low quality** means that sellers offer low-quality goods at a low price even though buyers would rather have higher quality and are willing to pay a higher price for it.

Again, consider rent control. Landlords have no incentive to provide better conditions because they cannot raise rents to cover their repair costs but are able to find tenants easily. In many cases, tenants would be willing to pay much more for improved conditions than it would cost for the landlord to provide them—for example, the upgrade of an antiquated electrical system that cannot safely run air conditioners or computers. But any additional payment for such improvements would be legally considered a rent increase, which is prohibited. Indeed, rent-controlled apartments are notoriously badly maintained, rarely painted, subject to frequent electrical and plumbing problems, and sometimes even hazardous to inhabit.

This whole situation is a missed opportunity—some tenants would be happy to pay for better conditions, and landlords would be happy to provide them for payment. But such an exchange would occur only if the market were allowed to operate freely.

BLACK MARKETS And that leads us to a last aspect of price ceilings: the incentive they provide for illegal activities, specifically the emergence of **black markets.** We have already described one kind of black market activity—illegal subletting by tenants. But it does not stop there. Clearly, there is a temptation for a landlord to say to a potential tenant, "Look, you can have the place if you slip me an extra few hundred in cash each month"—and for the tenant to agree, if he or she is one of those people who would be willing to pay much more than the maximum legal rent.

What's wrong with black markets? In general, it's a bad thing if people break *any* law, because it encourages disrespect for the law in general. Worse yet, in this case illegal activity worsens the position of those who try to be honest. If the Lees are scrupulous about upholding the rent-control law but other people—who may need an apartment less than the Lees—are willing to bribe landlords, the Lees may *never* find an apartment.

So Why Are There Price Ceilings?

We have seen three common results of price ceilings:

- a persistent shortage of the good
- inefficiency arising from this persistent shortage in the form of inefficiently low quantity, inefficient allocation of the good to consumers, resources wasted in searching for the good, and the inefficiently low quality of the good offered for sale
- the emergence of illegal, black market activity

Given the unpleasant consequences of price ceilings, why do governments sometimes impose them?

One answer is that although price ceilings may have adverse effects, they do benefit some people. In practice, New York's rent-control rules—which are more complex than our simple model—hurt most residents but give a small minority of renters much cheaper housing than they would get in an unregulated market. And those who benefit from the controls may be better organized and more vocal than those who are harmed by them.

Also, when price ceilings have been in effect for a long time, buyers may not have a realistic idea of what would happen without them. In our previous example, the rental rate in an unregulated market (Figure 13-1) would be only 25% higher than in the regulated market (Figure 13-2): $1,000 instead of $800. But how would renters know that? Indeed, they might have heard about black market transactions at much higher prices—the Lees or some other family paying George $1,200 or more—and would not realize that these black market prices are much higher than the price that would prevail in a fully unregulated market.

A last answer is that government officials often do not understand supply and demand analysis! It is a great mistake to suppose that economic policies in the real world are always sensible or well informed.

ECONOMICS ▶ *IN ACTION*

HUNGER AND PRICE CONTROLS IN VENEZUELA

Something was rotten in the state of Venezuela—specifically, 30,000 tons of decomposing food in Puerto Cabello in June 2010. The discovery was particularly embarrassing for then President Hugo Chávez. He was elected in 1998 on a platform denouncing the country's economic elite and promising policies favoring the poor and working classes. Among those policies were price controls on basic foodstuffs, which led to shortages that began in 2003 and had become severe by 2006.

Generous government policies led to higher spending by consumers and sharply rising prices for goods that weren't subject to price controls or were bought on the black market. The result was a big increase in the demand for price-controlled goods. But a sharp decline in the value of Venezuela's currency led to a fall in imports of foreign food, and the result was empty shelves in the nation's food stores.

As the shortages persisted and inflation of food prices worsened (in the first five months of 2010, the prices of food and drink rose by 21%), Chávez declared "economic war" on the private sector, berating it for "hoarding and smuggling." The government expropriated farms, food manufacturers, and grocery stores, creating in their place government-owned ones, which were corrupt and inefficient. It was the government-owned food-distribution company, PDVAL, that left tens of thousands of tons of food to rot in Venezuelan ports. Food production also fell, forcing Venezuela to import 70% of its food.

Venezuela's food shortages offer a lesson in why price ceilings, however well intentioned, are usually never a good idea.

Reuters/Daniel Aguilar/Landov

The **minimum wage** is a legal floor on the wage rate, which is the market price of labor.

Not surprisingly, the shelves were far more bare in government-run grocery stores than in those still in private hands. The food shortages were so severe that they greatly diminished Chávez's popularity among working-class Venezuelans and halted his expropriation plans. As an old Venezuelan saying has it, "Love with hunger doesn't last."

Price Floors

Sometimes governments intervene to push market prices up instead of down. *Price floors* have been widely legislated for agricultural products, such as wheat and milk, as a way to support the incomes of farmers. Historically, there were also price floors on such services as trucking and air travel, although these were phased out by the U.S. government in the 1970s. If you have ever worked in a fast-food restaurant, you are likely to have encountered a price floor: governments in the United States and many other countries maintain a lower limit on the hourly wage rate of a worker's labor—that is, a floor on the price of labor—called the **minimum wage.**

Just like price ceilings, price floors are intended to help some people but generate predictable and undesirable side effects. Figure 13-3 shows hypothetical supply and demand curves for butter. Left to itself, the market would move to equilibrium at point *E*, with 10 million pounds of butter bought and sold at a price of $1 per pound.

Now suppose that the government, in order to help dairy farmers, imposes a price floor on butter of $1.20 per pound. Its effects are shown in Figure 13-4, where the line at $1.20 represents the price floor. At a price of $1.20 per pound, producers would want to supply 12 million pounds (point *B* on the supply curve) but consumers would want to buy only 9 million pounds (point *A* on the demand curve). So the price floor leads to a persistent surplus of 3 million pounds of butter.

FIGURE 13-3 The Market for Butter in the Absence of Government Controls

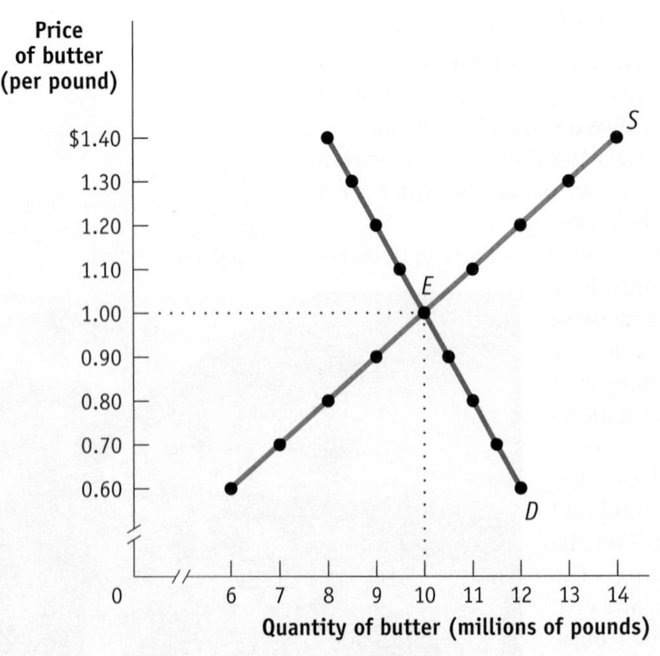

Price of butter (per pound)	Quantity of butter (millions of pounds)	
	Quantity demanded	Quantity supplied
$1.40	8.0	14.0
1.30	8.5	13.0
1.20	9.0	12.0
1.10	9.5	11.0
1.00	10.0	10.0
0.90	10.5	9.0
0.80	11.0	8.0
0.70	11.5	7.0
0.60	12.0	6.0

Without government intervention, the market for butter reaches equilibrium at a price of $1 per pound with 10 million pounds of butter bought and sold.

FIGURE 13-4 **The Effects of a Price Floor**

The dark horizontal line represents the government-imposed price floor of $1.20 per pound of butter. The quantity of butter demanded falls to 9 million pounds, and the quantity supplied rises to 12 million pounds, generating a persistent surplus of 3 million pounds of butter.

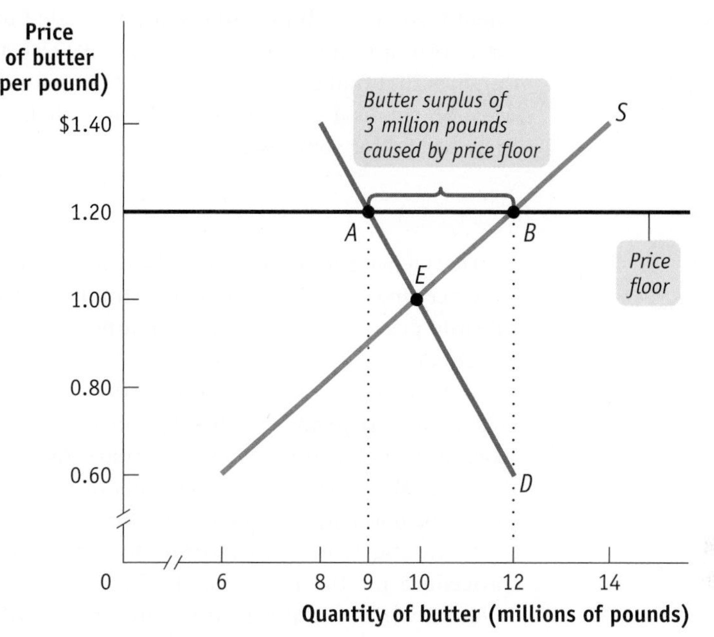

ECONOMICS IN ACTION

PRICE FLOORS AND SCHOOL LUNCHES

When you were in grade school, did your school offer free or very cheap lunches? If so, you were probably a beneficiary of price floors.

Where did all the cheap food come from? During the 1930s, when the U.S. economy was going through the Great Depression, a prolonged economic slump, prices were low and farmers were suffering severely. In an effort to help rural Americans, the U.S. government imposed price floors on a number of agricultural products. The system of agricultural price floors—officially called price support programs—continues to this day. Among the products subject to price support are sugar and various dairy products; at times grains, beef, and pork have also had a minimum price.

The big problem with any attempt to impose a price floor is that it creates a surplus. To some extent the U.S. Department of Agriculture has tried to head off surpluses by taking steps to reduce supply; for example, by paying farmers *not* to grow crops. As a last resort, however, the U.S. government has been willing to buy up the surplus, taking the excess supply off the market.

But then what? The government can't just sell the agricultural products: that would depress market prices, forcing the government to buy the stuff right back. So it has to give it away in ways that don't depress market prices. One way to do this is by giving surplus food, free, to school lunch programs. These gifts are known as "bonus foods." Along with financial aid, bonus foods allow many school districts to provide free or very cheap lunches to their students. Is this a story with a happy ending?

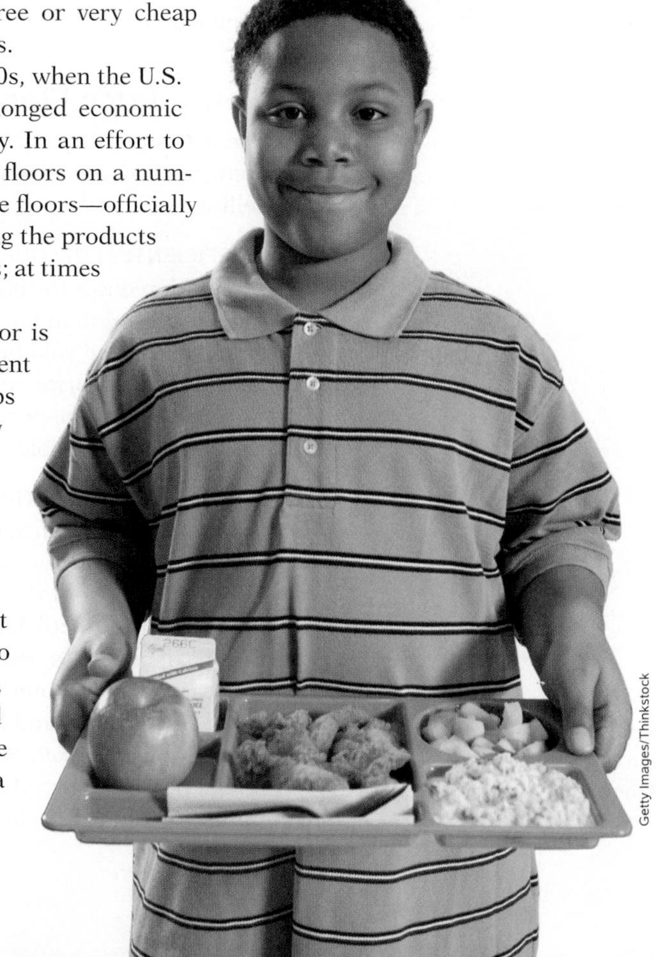

Getty Images/Thinkstock

Not really. Nutritionists, concerned about growing child obesity in the United States, place part of the blame on those bonus foods. Schools get whatever the government has too much of—and that has tended to include a lot of dairy products, beef, and corn, and not much in the way of fresh vegetables or fruit. As a result, school lunches that make extensive use of bonus foods tend to be very high in fat and calories. So this is a case in which there is such a thing as a free lunch—but this lunch may be bad for your health.

Does a price floor always lead to an unwanted surplus? No. Just as in the case of a price ceiling, the floor may not be binding—that is, it may be irrelevant. If the equilibrium price of butter is \$1 per pound but the floor is set at only \$0.80, the floor has no effect.

But suppose that a price floor *is* binding: what happens to the unwanted surplus? The answer depends on government policy. In the case of agricultural price floors, governments buy up unwanted surplus. As a result, the U.S. government has at times found itself warehousing thousands of tons of butter, cheese, and other farm products. The government then has to find a way to dispose of these unwanted goods.

Some countries pay exporters to sell products at a loss overseas; this is standard procedure for the European Union. The United States gives surplus food away to schools, which use the products in school lunches. In some cases, governments have actually destroyed the surplus production. To avoid the problem of dealing with the unwanted surplus, the U.S. government often pays farmers not to produce the products at all.

When the government is not prepared to purchase the unwanted surplus, a price floor means that would-be sellers cannot find buyers. This is what happens when there is a price floor on the wage rate paid for an hour of labor, the *minimum wage:* when the minimum wage is above the equilibrium wage rate, some people who are willing to work—that is, sell labor—cannot find buyers—that is, employers—willing to give them jobs.

How a Price Floor Causes Inefficiency

The persistent surplus that results from a price floor creates missed opportunities—inefficiencies—that resemble those created by the shortage that results from a price ceiling.

INEFFICIENTLY LOW QUANTITY Because a price floor raises the price of a good to consumers, it reduces the quantity of that good demanded; because sellers can't sell more units of a good than buyers are willing to buy, a price floor reduces the quantity of a good bought and sold below the market equilibrium quantity. Notice that this is the *same* effect as a price ceiling. You might be tempted to think that a price floor and a price ceiling have opposite effects, but both have the effect of reducing the quantity of a good bought and sold.

INEFFICIENT ALLOCATION OF SALES AMONG SELLERS Like a price ceiling, a price floor can lead to *inefficient allocation*—but in this case **inefficient allocation of sales among sellers** rather than inefficient allocation to consumers.

An episode from the Belgian movie *Rosetta,* a realistic fictional story, illustrates the problem of inefficient allocation of selling opportunities quite well. Like many European countries, Belgium has a high minimum wage, and jobs for young people are scarce. At one point Rosetta, a young woman who is very eager to work, loses her job at a fast-food stand because the owner of the stand replaces her with his son—a very reluctant worker. Rosetta would be willing to work for less money, and with the money he would save, the owner could give his son an allowance and let him do something else. But to hire Rosetta for less than the minimum wage would be illegal.

Price floors lead to **inefficient allocation of sales among sellers:** those who would be willing to sell the good at the lowest price are not always those who manage to sell it.

WASTED RESOURCES Also like a price ceiling, a price floor generates inefficiency by *wasting resources.* The most graphic examples involve government purchases of the unwanted surpluses of agricultural products caused by price floors. When the surplus production is simply destroyed, and when the stored produce goes, as officials euphemistically put it, "out of condition" and must be thrown away, it is pure waste.

Price floors also lead to wasted time and effort. Consider the minimum wage. Would-be workers who spend many hours searching for jobs, or waiting in line in the hope of getting jobs, play the same role in the case of price floors as hapless families searching for apartments in the case of price ceilings.

Vanbeets/Dreamstime.com

Since airline deregulation in the 1970s, American passengers have seen ticket prices decrease along with the quality of in-flight service.

INEFFICIENTLY HIGH QUALITY Again like price ceilings, price floors lead to inefficiency in the quality of goods produced.

We've seen that when there is a price ceiling, suppliers produce goods that are of inefficiently low quality: buyers prefer higher-quality products and are willing to pay for them, but sellers refuse to improve the quality of their products because the price ceiling prevents their being compensated for doing so. This same logic applies to price floors, but in reverse: suppliers offer goods of **inefficiently high quality.**

How can this be? Isn't high quality a good thing? Yes, but only if it is worth the cost. Suppose that suppliers spend a lot to make goods of very high quality but that this quality isn't worth much to consumers, who would rather receive the money spent on that quality in the form of a lower price. This represents a missed opportunity: suppliers and buyers could make a mutually beneficial deal in which buyers got goods of lower quality for a much lower price.

A good example of the inefficiency of excessive quality comes from the days when transatlantic airfares were set artificially high by international treaty. Forbidden to compete for customers by offering lower ticket prices, airlines instead offered expensive services, like lavish in-flight meals that went largely uneaten.

ILLEGAL ACTIVITY Finally, like price ceilings, price floors provide incentives for illegal activity. For example, in countries where the minimum wage is far above the equilibrium wage rate, workers desperate for jobs sometimes agree to work off the books for employers who conceal their employment from the government—or bribe the government inspectors. This practice, known in Europe as "black labor," is especially common in southern European countries such as Italy and Spain.

So Why Are There Price Floors?

To sum up, a price floor creates various negative side effects:

- a persistent surplus of the good
- inefficiency arising from the persistent surplus in the form of inefficiently low quantity, inefficient allocation of sales among sellers, wasted resources, and an inefficiently high level of quality offered by suppliers
- the temptation to engage in illegal activity, particularly bribery and corruption of government officials

So why do governments impose price floors when they have so many negative side effects? The reasons are similar to those for imposing price ceilings. Government officials often disregard warnings about the consequences of price floors either because they believe that the relevant market is poorly described by the supply and demand model or, more often, because they do not understand the model. Above all, just as price ceilings are often imposed because they benefit some influential buyers of a good, price floors are often imposed because they benefit some influential sellers.

Price floors often lead to inefficiency in that goods of **inefficiently high quality** are offered: sellers offer high-quality goods at a high price, even though buyers would prefer a lower quality at a lower price.

MODULE 13 Review

Solutions appear at the back of the book.

Check Your Understanding

1. On game days, homeowners near Middletown University's stadium used to rent parking spaces in their driveways to fans at a going rate of $11. A new town ordinance now sets a maximum parking fee of $7. Use the accompanying supply and demand diagram to explain how each of the following can result from the price ceiling.

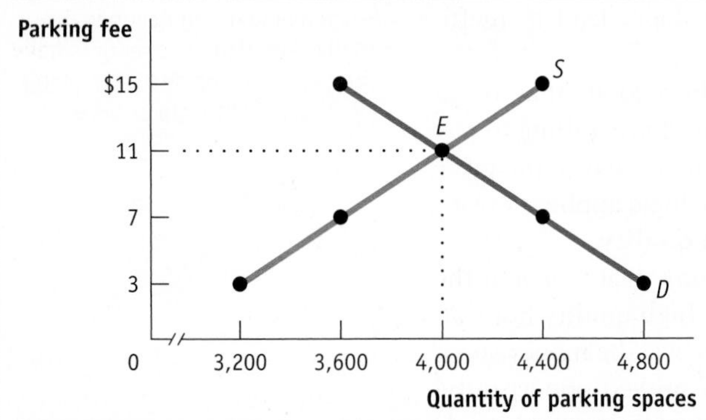

   a. Some homeowners now think it's not worth the hassle to rent out spaces.
   b. Some fans who used to carpool to the game now drive alone.
   c. Some fans can't find parking and leave without seeing the game.

   Explain how each of the following adverse effects arises from the price ceiling.

   d. Some fans now arrive several hours early to find parking.
   e. Friends of homeowners near the stadium regularly attend games, even if they aren't big fans. But some serious fans have given up because of the parking situation.
   f. Some homeowners rent spaces for more than $7 but pretend that the buyers are nonpaying friends or family.

2. True or false? Explain your answer. A price ceiling below the equilibrium price in an otherwise efficient market does the following:
   a. increases quantity supplied
   b. makes some people who want to consume the good worse off
   c. makes all producers worse off

3. The state legislature mandates a price floor for gasoline of P_F per gallon. Assess the following statements and illustrate your answer using the figure provided.

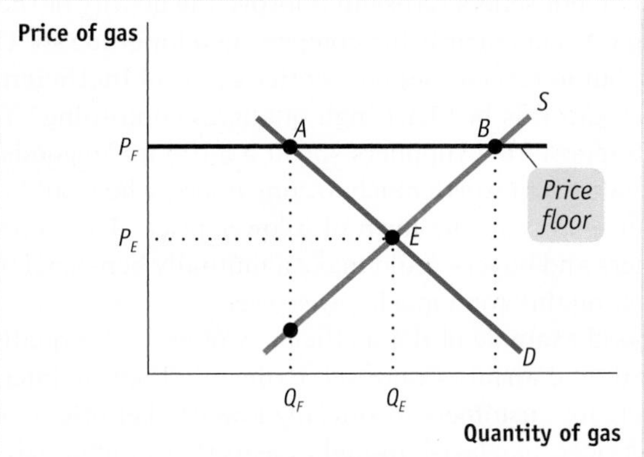

   a. Proponents of the law claim it will increase the income of gas station owners. Opponents claim it will hurt gas station owners because they will lose customers.
   b. Proponents claim consumers will be better off because gas stations will provide better service. Opponents claim consumers will be generally worse off because they prefer to buy gas at cheaper prices.
   c. Proponents claim that they are helping gas station owners without hurting anyone else. Opponents claim that consumers are hurt and will end up doing things like buying gas in a nearby state or on the black market.

Multiple-Choice Questions

1. To be effective, a price ceiling must be set
   I. above the equilibrium price.
   II. in the housing market.
   III. to achieve the equilibrium market quantity.

   a. I
   b. II
   c. III
   d. I, II, and III
   e. None of the above

2. Refer to the graph provided. A price floor set at $5 will result in

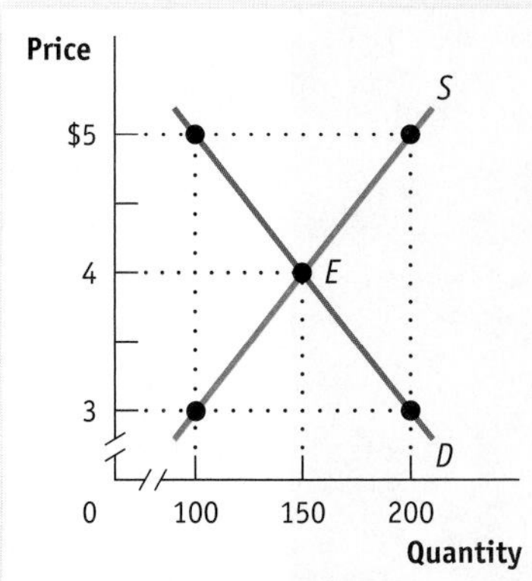

a. a shortage of 100 units.
b. a surplus of 100 units.
c. a shortage of 200 units.
d. a surplus of 200 units.
e. a surplus of 50 units.

3. Effective price ceilings are inefficient because they
a. create shortages.
b. lead to wasted resources.
c. decrease quality.
d. create black markets.
e. do all of the above.

4. Refer to the graph provided. If the government establishes a minimum wage at $10, how many workers will benefit from the higher wage?

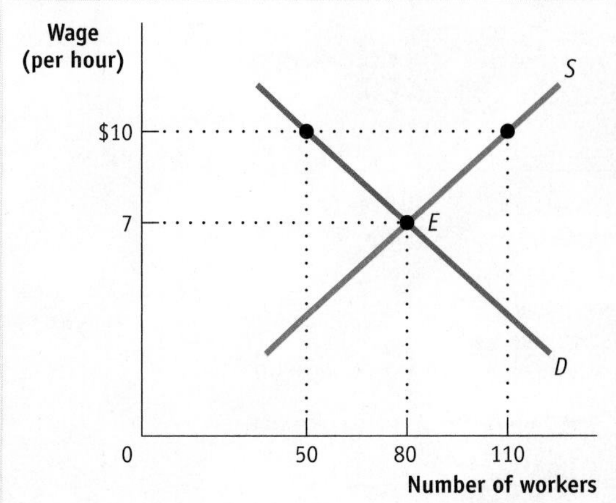

a. 30
b. 50
c. 60
d. 80
e. 110

5. Refer to the graph for question 4. With a minimum wage of $10, how many workers are unemployed (they would like to work, but are unable to find a job)?
a. 30
b. 50
c. 60
d. 80
e. 110

Critical-Thinking Question

Draw a correctly labeled graph of a housing market in equilibrium. On your graph, illustrate an effective legal limit (ceiling) on rent. Identify the quantity of housing demanded, the quantity of housing supplied, and the size of the resulting surplus or shortage.

PITFALLS

CEILINGS, FLOORS, AND QUANTITIES

? A price ceiling pushes the price of a good *down*. A price floor pushes the price of a good *up*. So it looks like we can assume that the effects of a price floor are the opposite of the effects of a price ceiling. Put another way, if a price ceiling reduces the quantity of a good bought and sold, doesn't a price floor increase the quantity?

> NO, IT DOESN'T, BECAUSE BOTH FLOORS AND CEILINGS REDUCE THE QUANTITY BOUGHT AND SOLD. Why? When the quantity of a good supplied isn't equal to the quantity demanded, the actual quantity sold is determined by the "short side" of the market—whichever quantity is less. If sellers don't want to sell as much as buyers want to buy, it's the sellers who determine the actual quantity sold, because buyers can't force unwilling sellers to sell. If buyers don't want to buy as much as sellers want to sell, it's the buyers who determine the actual quantity sold, because sellers can't force unwilling buyers to buy.

To learn more, see pp. 130–132 and 136–137, on price ceilings, floors, and inefficiency.

MODULE 14 Quantity Controls (Quotas)

Alamy Images

WHAT YOU WILL LEARN

1. The meaning of quantity controls, another way government intervenes in markets
2. How quantity controls create problems and can make a market inefficient
3. Who benefits and who loses from quantity controls, and why they are used despite their well-known problems

Controlling Quantities

In the 1930s, New York City instituted a system of licensing for taxicabs: only taxis with a "medallion" were allowed to pick up passengers. Because this system was intended to ensure quality, medallion owners were supposed to maintain certain standards, including safety and cleanliness. A total of 11,787 medallions were issued, with taxi owners paying $10 for each medallion.

In 1995, there were still only 11,787 licensed taxicabs in New York, even though the city had meanwhile become the financial capital of the world, a place where hundreds of thousands of people in a hurry tried to hail a cab every day. That same year, an additional 400 medallions were issued, and after several rounds of sales of additional medallions, today there are 13,237 medallions.

The result of this restriction on the number of taxis was that a New York City taxi medallion became very valuable. In 2012, the price of a medallion was about $700,000! If you wanted to operate a taxi in New York, you had to lease a medallion from someone else or buy one for a going price.

It turns out that this story is not unique; other cities introduced similar medallion systems in the 1930s and, like New York, have issued few new medallions since. In San Francisco and Boston, as in New York, taxi medallions trade for six-figure prices.

A taxi medallion system is a form of **quantity control,** or **quota,** by which the government regulates the quantity of a good that can be bought and sold rather than regulating the price. Typically, the government limits quantity in a market by issuing **licenses;** only people with a license can legally supply the good. A taxi medallion is just such a license. The government of New York City limits the number of taxi rides that can be sold by limiting the number of taxis to only those who hold medallions. There are many other cases of quantity controls, ranging from limits on how much

A **quantity control,** or **quota,** is an upper limit on the quantity of some good that can be bought or sold.

A **license** gives its owner the right to supply a good or service.

foreign currency (for instance, British pounds or Mexican pesos) people are allowed to buy to the quantity of clams New Jersey fishing boats are allowed to catch.

Some attempts to control quantities are undertaken for good economic reasons, some for bad ones. In many cases, as we will see, quantity controls introduced to address a temporary problem become politically hard to remove later because the beneficiaries don't want them abolished, even after the original reason for their existence is long gone. But whatever the reasons for such controls, they have certain predictable—and usually undesirable—economic consequences.

The **demand price** of a given quantity is the price at which consumers will demand that quantity.

How Quantity Controls Work

To understand why a New York taxi medallion is worth so much money, we consider a simplified version of the market for taxi rides, shown in Figure 14-1. Just as we assumed in the analysis of rent control that all apartments were the same, we now suppose that all taxi rides are the same—ignoring the real-world complication that some taxi rides are longer, and so more expensive, than others. The table in the figure shows supply and demand schedules. The equilibrium—indicated by point *E* in the figure and by the shaded entries in the table—is a fare of \$5 per ride, with 10 million rides taken per year.

Ed Rooney/Alamy

The New York medallion system limits the number of taxis, but each taxi driver can offer as many rides as he or she can manage. (Now you know why New York taxi drivers are so aggressive!) To simplify our analysis, however, we will assume that a medallion system limits the number of taxi rides that can legally be given to 8 million per year.

Until now, we have derived the demand curve by answering questions of the form: "How many taxi rides will passengers want to take if the price is \$5 per ride?" But it is possible to reverse the question and ask instead: "At what price will consumers want to buy 10 million rides per year?" The price at which consumers want to buy a given quantity—in this case, 10 million rides at \$5 per ride—is the **demand price** of that quantity. You can see from the demand schedule in Figure 14-1 that the demand price of 6 million rides is \$7 per ride, the demand price of 7 million rides is \$6.50 per ride, and so on.

FIGURE 14-1 The Market for Taxi Rides in the Absence of Government Controls

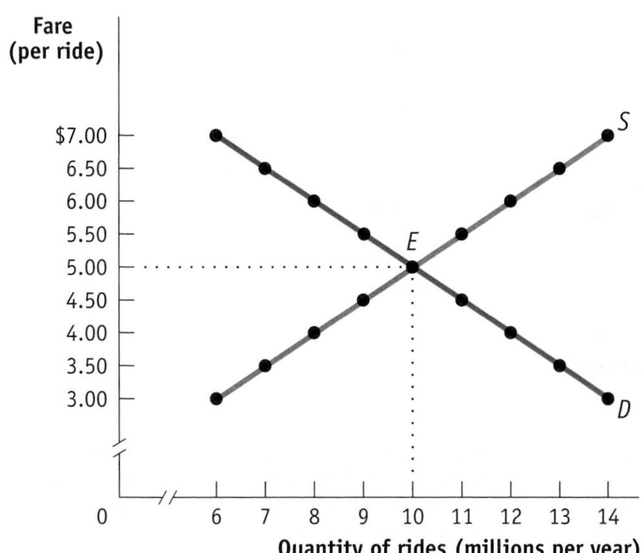

Fare (per ride)	Quantity of rides (millions per year): Quantity demanded	Quantity supplied
\$7.00	6	14
6.50	7	13
6.00	8	12
5.50	9	11
5.00	10	10
4.50	11	9
4.00	12	8
3.50	13	7
3.00	14	6

Without government intervention, the market reaches equilibrium with 10 million rides taken per year at a fare of \$5 per ride.

Deadweight loss is the lost gains associated with transactions that do not occur due to market intervention.

The Costs of Quantity Controls

Like price controls, quantity controls can have some predictable and undesirable side effects. The first is the by-now-familiar problem of inefficiency due to missed opportunities: quantity controls prevent mutually beneficial transactions from occurring, transactions that would benefit both buyers and sellers. Looking back at Figure 14-2, you can see that starting at the quota of 8 million rides, New Yorkers would be willing to pay at least $5.50 per ride for an additional 1 million rides and that taxi drivers would be willing to provide those rides as long as they got at least $4.50 per ride. These are rides that would have taken place if there had been no quota.

The same is true for the next 1 million rides: New Yorkers would be willing to pay at least $5 per ride when the quantity of rides is increased from 9 to 10 million, and taxi drivers would be willing to provide those rides as long as they got at least $5 per ride. Again, these rides would have occurred without the quota.

Only when the market has reached the unregulated market equilibrium quantity of 10 million rides are there no "missed-opportunity rides"—the quota of 8 million rides has caused 2 million "missed-opportunity rides." A buyer would be willing to buy the good at a price that the seller would be willing to accept, but such a transaction does not occur because it is forbidden by the quota.

Economists have a special term for the lost gains from missed opportunities such as these: **deadweight loss.** Generally, when the demand price exceeds the supply price, there is a deadweight loss. Figure 14-2 illustrates the deadweight loss with a shaded triangle between the demand and supply curves. This triangle represents the missed gains from taxi rides prevented by the quota, a loss that is experienced by both disappointed would-be riders and frustrated would-be drivers.

Because there are transactions that people would like to make but are not allowed to, quantity controls generate an incentive to evade them or even to break the law. New York's taxi industry again provides clear examples. Taxi regulation applies only to those drivers who are hailed by passengers on the street. A car service that makes prearranged pickups does not need a medallion. As a result, such hired cars provide much of the service that might otherwise be provided by taxis, as in other cities. In addition, there are substantial numbers of unlicensed cabs that simply defy the law by picking up passengers without a medallion. Because these cabs are illegal, their drivers are unregulated, and they generate a disproportionately large share of traffic accidents in New York City.

ECONOMICS IN ACTION

THE CLAMS OF THE JERSEY SHORE

One industry that New Jersey *really* dominates is clam fishing. The Garden State typically supplies about 70% of the country's surf clams, whose tongues are used in fried-clam dinners, and about 90% of the quahogs, which are used to make clam chowder.

In the 1980s, however, excessive fishing threatened to wipe out New Jersey's clam beds. To save the resource, the U.S. government introduced a clam quota, which sets an overall limit on the number of bushels of clams that may be caught and allocates licenses to owners of fishing boats based on their historical catches.

Notice, by the way, that this is an example of a quota that is probably justified by broader economic and environmental considerations—unlike the New York taxicab quota, which has long since lost any economic rationale. Still, whatever its rationale, the New Jersey clam quota works the same way as any other quota.

Once the quota system was established, many boat owners stopped fishing for clams. They realized that rather than operate a boat part time, it was more profitable to sell or rent their licenses to someone else, who could then assemble enough licenses to operate a boat full time. Today, there are about 50 New Jersey boats fishing for clams; the license required to operate one is worth more than the boat itself.

iStockphoto

Clam quotas were introduced in New Jersey to help save a threatened natural resource.

MODULE 14 Review

Solutions appear at the back of the book.

Check Your Understanding

1. Suppose that the supply and demand for taxi rides is given by Figure 14-1 and a quota is set at 6 million rides. Replicate the graph from Figure 14-1, and identify each of the following on your graph:
   a. the price of a ride
   b. the quota rent
   c. the deadweight loss resulting from the quota

   Suppose the quota on taxi rides is increased to 9 million.

   d. What happens to the quota rent and the deadweight loss?

2. Again replicate the graph from Figure 14-1. Suppose that the quota is 8 million rides and that demand decreases due to a decline in tourism. Show on your graph the smallest parallel leftward shift in demand that would result in the quota no longer having an effect on the market.

Multiple-Choice Questions

Refer to the graph provided to answer questions 1–3.

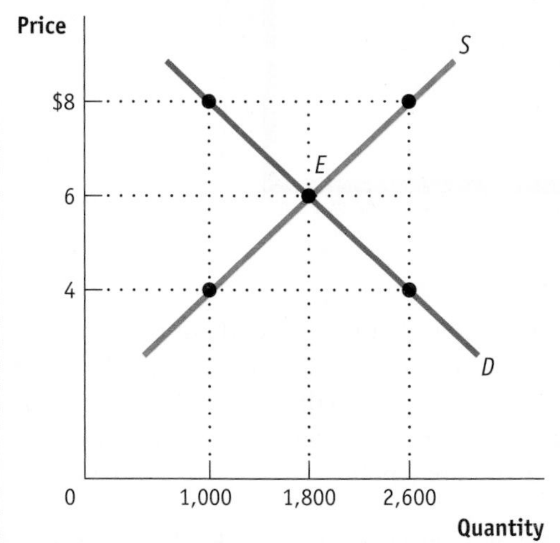

1. If the government established a quota of 1,000 in this market, the demand price would be
   a. less than $4.
   b. $4.
   c. $6.
   d. $8.
   e. more than $8.

2. If the government established a quota of 1,000 in this market, the supply price would be
   a. less than $4.
   b. $4.
   c. $6.
   d. $8.
   e. more than $8.

3. If the government established a quota of 1,000 in this market, the quota rent would be
   a. $2.
   b. $4.
   c. $6.
   d. $8.
   e. more than $8.

4. Quotas lead to which of the following?
   I. inefficiency due to missed opportunities
   II. incentives to evade or break the law
   III. a surplus in the market

   a. I
   b. II
   c. III
   d. I and II
   e. I, II, and III

5. Which of the following would decrease the effect of a quota on a market? A(n)
   a. decrease in demand
   b. increase in supply
   c. increase in demand
   d. price ceiling above the equilibrium price
   e. none of the above

Critical-Thinking Question

Draw a correctly labeled graph of the market for taxicab rides. On the graph, draw and label a vertical line showing the level of an effective quota. Label the demand price, the supply price, and the quota rent.

MODULE 15 Taxes

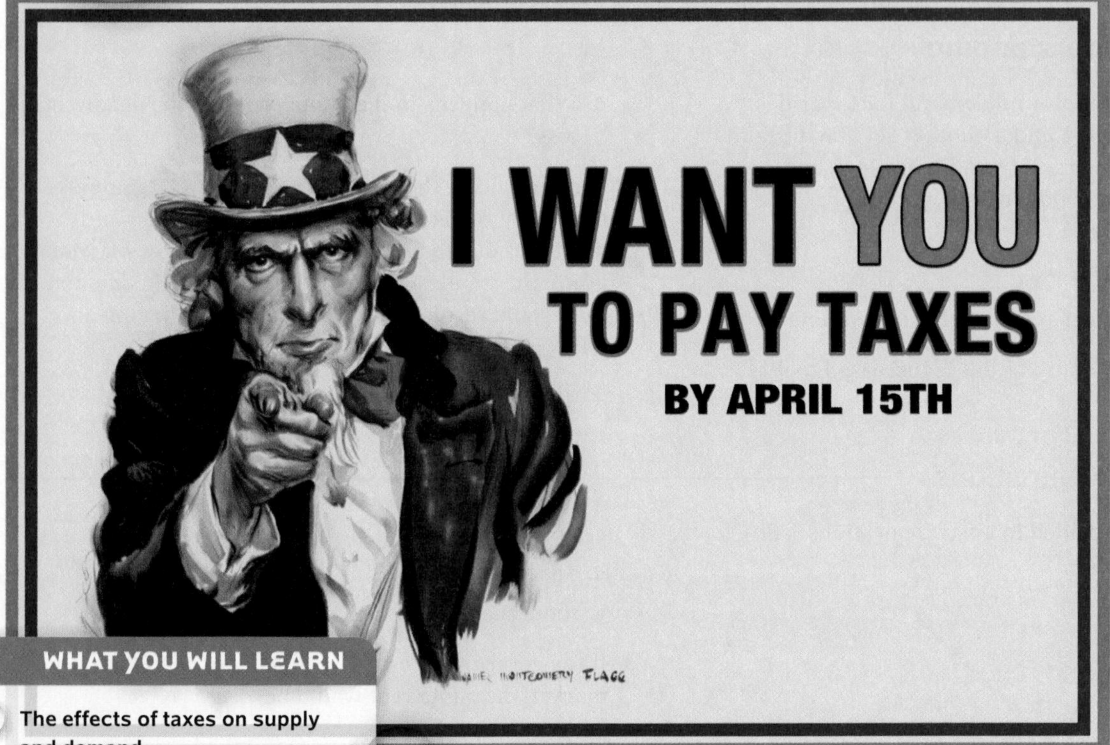

I WANT YOU
TO PAY TAXES
BY APRIL 15TH

Uncle Sam image courtesy of Library of Congress

WHAT YOU WILL LEARN

1. The effects of taxes on supply and demand
2. How taxes affect total surplus and can create deadweight loss

Taxes are necessary: all governments need money to function. Without taxes, governments could not provide the services we want, from national defense to public parks. But taxes have a cost that normally exceeds the money actually paid to the government. That's because taxes distort incentives to engage in mutually beneficial transactions.

Making tax policy isn't easy—in fact, if you are a politician, it can be dangerous to your professional health.

One principle used for guiding tax policy is efficiency: taxes should be designed to distort incentives as little as possible. But efficiency is not the only concern when designing tax rates. It's also important that a tax be seen as fair. Tax policy always involves striking a balance between the pursuit of efficiency and the pursuit of perceived fairness.

In this module, we will look at how taxes affect efficiency and fairness.

Equity, Efficiency, and Taxes

It's easy to get carried away with the idea that markets are always good and that economic policies that interfere with efficiency are bad. But that would be misguided because there is another factor to consider: society cares about equity, or what's "fair." There is often a trade-off between equity and efficiency: policies that promote equity often come at the cost of decreased efficiency, and policies that promote efficiency often result in decreased equity. Creating tax policy is no different. So it's important to realize that a society's choice to sacrifice some efficiency for the sake of equity, however it defines equity, may well be a valid one. It's important to understand that fairness, unlike efficiency, can be very hard to define, and it is a concept about which well-intentioned people often disagree.

In fact, the debate about equity and efficiency is at the core of most debates about taxation. Proponents of taxes that redistribute income from the rich to the poor often argue for the fairness of such redistributive taxes. Opponents of taxation often argue that phasing out certain taxes would make the economy more efficient.

Because taxes are ultimately paid out of income, economists classify taxes according to how they vary with the income of individuals. A tax that rises more than in proportion to income, so that high-income taxpayers pay a larger percentage of their income than low-income taxpayers, is a **progressive tax.** A tax that rises less than in proportion to income, so that high-income taxpayers pay a smaller percentage of their income than low-income taxpayers, is a **regressive tax.** A tax that rises in proportion to income, so that all taxpayers pay the same percentage of their income, is a **proportional tax.** The U.S. tax system contains a mixture of progressive and regressive taxes, though it is somewhat progressive overall.

A **progressive tax** rises more than in proportion to income. A **regressive tax** rises less than in proportion to income. A **proportional tax** rises in proportion to income.

An **excise tax** is a tax on sales of a particular good or service.

The Effects of Taxes on Total Surplus

To understand the economics of taxes, it's helpful to look at a simple type of tax known as an **excise tax**—a tax charged on each unit of a good or service that is sold. Most tax revenue in the United States comes from other kinds of taxes, but excise taxes are common. For example, there are excise taxes on gasoline, cigarettes, and foreign-made trucks, and many local governments impose excise taxes on services such as hotel room rentals. The lessons we'll learn from studying excise taxes apply to other, more complex taxes as well.

The Effect of an Excise Tax on Quantities and Prices

Suppose that the supply and demand for hotel rooms in the city of Potterville are as shown in Figure 15-1. We'll make the simplifying assumption that all hotel rooms are the same. In the absence of taxes, the equilibrium price of a room is $80 per night and the equilibrium quantity of hotel rooms rented is 10,000 per night.

Now suppose that Potterville's government imposes an excise tax of $40 per night on hotel rooms—that is, every time a room is rented for the night, the owner of the hotel must pay the city $40. For example, if a customer pays $80, $40 is collected as a

FIGURE 15-1 The Supply and Demand for Hotel Rooms in Potterville

In the absence of taxes, the equilibrium price of hotel rooms is $80 a night, and the equilibrium number of rooms rented is 10,000 per night, as shown by point *E*. The supply curve, *S*, shows the quantity supplied at any given price, pre-tax. At a price of $60 a night, hotel owners are willing to supply 5,000 rooms, as shown by point *B*. But post-tax, hotel owners are willing to supply the same quantity only at a price of $100: $60 for themselves plus $40 paid to the city as tax.

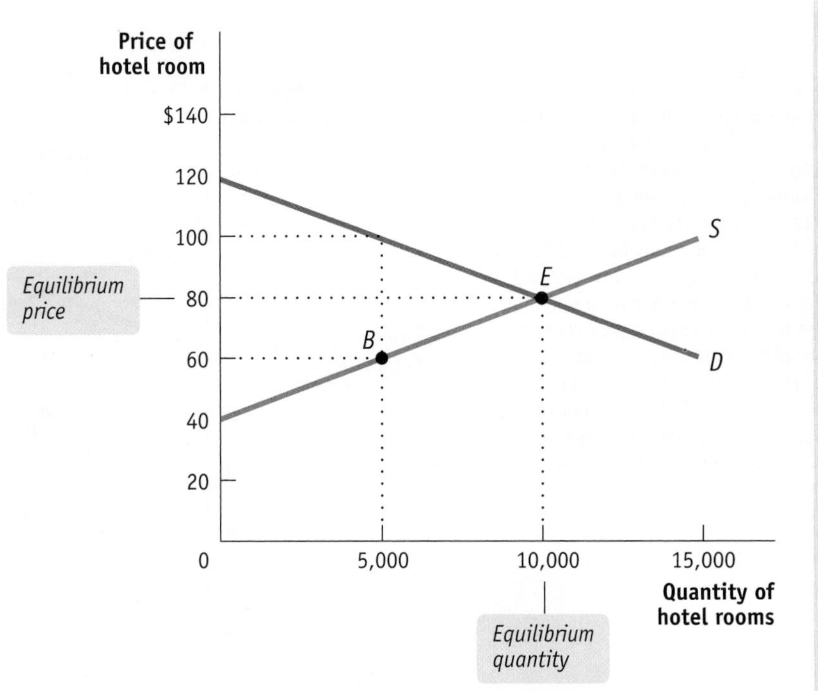

tax, leaving the hotel owner with only $40. As a result, hotel owners are less willing to supply rooms at any given price.

What does this imply about the supply curve for hotel rooms in Potterville? To answer this question, we must compare the incentives of hotel owners *pre-tax* (before the tax is levied) to their incentives *post-tax* (after the tax is levied).

From Figure 15-1 we know that pre-tax, hotel owners are willing to supply 5,000 rooms per night at a price of $60 per room. But after the $40 tax per room is levied, they are willing to supply the same amount, 5,000 rooms, only if they receive $100 per room—$60 for themselves plus $40 paid to the city as tax. In other words, in order for hotel owners to be willing to supply the same quantity post-tax as they would have pre-tax, they must receive an additional $40 per room, the amount of the tax. This implies that the post-tax supply curve shifts up by the amount of the tax compared to the pre-tax supply curve. At every quantity supplied, the supply price—the price that producers must receive to produce a given quantity—has increased by $40.

The upward shift of the supply curve caused by the tax is shown in Figure 15-2, where S_1 is the pre-tax supply curve and S_2 is the post-tax supply curve. As you can see, the market equilibrium moves from *E*, at the equilibrium price of $80 per room and 10,000 rooms rented each night, to *A*, at a market price of $100 per room and only 5,000 rooms rented each night. *A* is, of course, on both the demand curve *D* and the new supply curve S_2. In this case, $100 is the demand price of 5,000 rooms—but in effect hotel owners receive only $60, when you account for the fact that they have to pay the $40 tax. From the point of view of hotel owners, it is as if they were on their original supply curve at point *B*.

Let's check this again. How do we know that 5,000 rooms will be supplied at a price of $100? Because the price *net of tax* is $60, and according to the original supply curve, 5,000 rooms will be supplied at a price of $60, as shown by point *B* in Figure 15-2.

An excise tax *drives a wedge* between the price paid by consumers and the price received by producers. As a result of this wedge, consumers pay more and producers receive less.

In our example, consumers—people who rent hotel rooms—end up paying $100 a night, $20 more than the pre-tax price of $80. At the same time, producers—the hotel owners—receive a price net of tax of $60 per room, $20 less than the pre-tax price. In addition, the tax creates missed opportunities: 5,000 potential consumers who would

FIGURE 15-2 **An Excise Tax Imposed on Hotel Owners**

A $40 per room tax imposed on hotel owners shifts the supply curve from S_1 to S_2, an upward shift of $40. The equilibrium price of hotel rooms rises from $80 to $100 a night, and the equilibrium quantity of rooms rented falls from 10,000 to 5,000. Although hotel owners pay the tax, they actually bear only half the burden: the price they receive net of tax falls only $20, from $80 to $60. Guests who rent rooms bear the other half of the burden because the price they pay rises by $20, from $80 to $100.

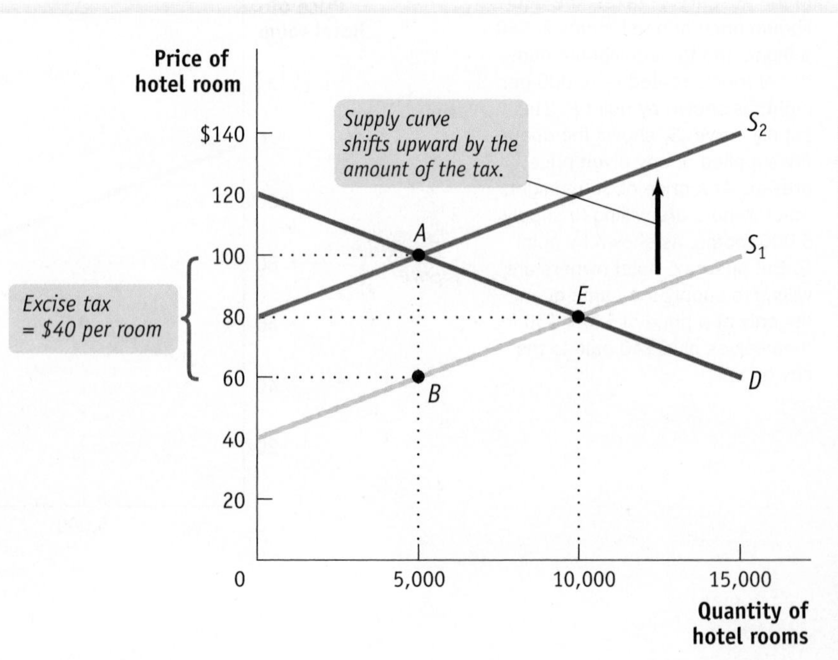

have rented hotel rooms—those willing to pay $80 but not $100 per night—are discouraged from renting rooms. Correspondingly, 5,000 rooms that would have been made available by hotel owners when they receive $80 are not offered when they receive only $60.

Tax incidence is the distribution of the tax burden.

Like a quota on sales, discussed in Module 14, this tax leads to inefficiency by distorting incentives and creating missed opportunities for mutually beneficial transactions.

It's important to recognize that as we've described it, Potterville's hotel tax is a tax on the hotel owners, not their guests—it's a tax on the producers, not the consumers. Yet the price received by producers, net of tax, is down by only $20, half the amount of the tax, and the price paid by consumers is up by $20. In effect, half the tax is being paid by consumers.

What would happen if the city levied a tax on consumers instead of producers? That is, suppose that instead of requiring hotel owners to pay $40 a night for each room they rent, the city required hotel *guests* to pay $40 for each night they stayed in a hotel. The answer is shown in Figure 15-3. If a hotel guest must pay a tax of $40 per night, then the price for a room paid by that guest must be reduced by $40 in order for the quantity of hotel rooms demanded post-tax to be the same as that demanded pre-tax. So the demand curve shifts *downward,* from D_1 to D_2, by the amount of the tax.

At every quantity demanded, the demand price—the price that consumers must be offered to demand a given quantity—has fallen by $40. This shifts the equilibrium from *E* to *B,* where the market price of hotel rooms is $60 and 5,000 hotel rooms are bought and sold. In effect, hotel guests pay $100 when you include the tax. So from the point of view of guests, it is as if they were on their original demand curve at point *A.*

If you compare Figures 15-2 and 15-3, you will notice that the effects of the tax are the same even though different curves are shifted. In each case, consumers pay $100 per unit (including the tax, if it is their responsibility), producers receive $60 per unit (after paying the tax, if it is their responsibility), and 5,000 hotel rooms are bought and sold. *In fact, it doesn't matter who officially pays the tax—the equilibrium outcome is the same.*

This example illustrates a general principle of **tax incidence,** a measure of who really pays a tax: the burden of a tax cannot be determined by looking at who writes the check to the government. In this particular case, a $40 tax on hotel rooms brings about a $20 increase in the price paid by consumers and a $20 decrease in the price

FIGURE 15-3 An Excise Tax Imposed on Hotel Guests

A $40 per room tax imposed on hotel guests shifts the demand curve from D_1 to D_2, a downward shift of $40. The equilibrium price of hotel rooms falls from $80 to $60 a night, and the quantity of rooms rented falls from 10,000 to 5,000. Although in this case the tax is officially paid by consumers, while in Figure 15-2 the tax was paid by producers, the outcome is the same: after taxes, hotel owners receive $60 per room but guests pay $100. This illustrates a general principle: *The incidence of an excise tax doesn't depend on whether consumers or producers officially pay the tax.*

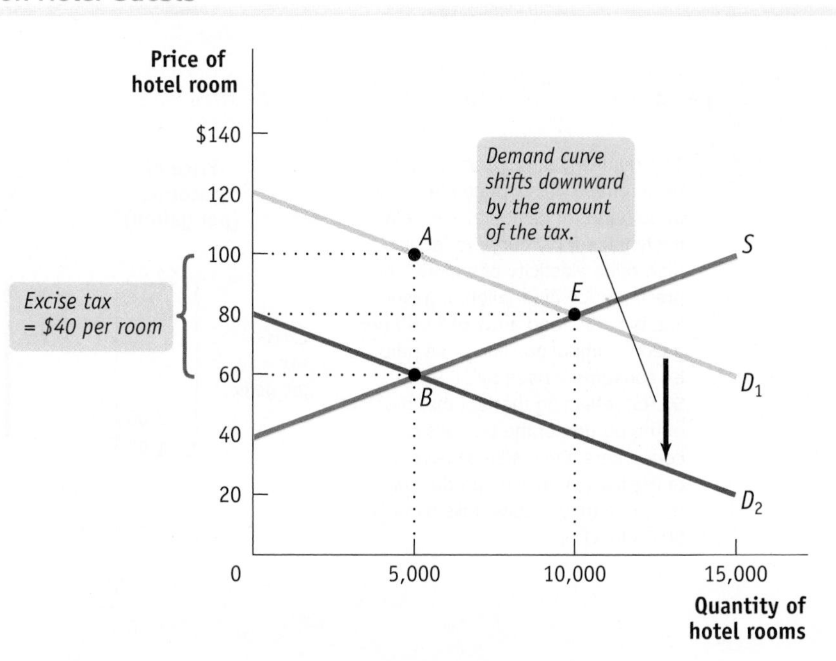

received by producers. Regardless of whether the tax is levied on consumers or producers, the incidence of the tax is the same. As we will see next, the burden of a tax depends on the price elasticities of supply and demand.

Price Elasticities and Tax Incidence

We've just learned that the incidence of an excise tax doesn't depend on who officially pays it. In the example shown in Figures 15-1 through 15-3, a tax on hotel rooms falls equally on consumers and producers, no matter on whom the tax is levied. But it's important to note that this 50–50 split between consumers and producers is a result of our assumptions in this example. In the real world, the incidence of an excise tax usually falls unevenly between consumers and producers: one group bears more of the burden than the other.

What determines how the burden of an excise tax is allocated between consumers and producers? The answer depends on the shapes of the supply and the demand curves. *More specifically, the incidence of an excise tax depends on the price elasticity of supply and the price elasticity of demand.* We can see this by looking first at a case in which consumers pay most of an excise tax, and then at a case in which producers pay most of the tax.

WHEN AN EXCISE TAX IS PAID MAINLY BY CONSUMERS Figure 15-4 shows an excise tax that falls mainly on consumers: an excise tax on gasoline, which we set at $1 per gallon. (There really is a federal excise tax on gasoline, though it is actually only about $0.18 per gallon in the United States. In addition, states impose excise taxes between $0.08 and $0.37 per gallon.) According to Figure 15-4, in the absence of the tax, gasoline would sell for $2 per gallon.

Two key assumptions are reflected in the shapes of the supply and demand curves in Figure 15-4. First, the price elasticity of demand for gasoline is assumed to be very low, so the demand curve is relatively steep. Recall that a low price elasticity of demand means that the quantity demanded changes little in response to a change in price. Second, the price elasticity of supply of gasoline is assumed to be very high, so the supply curve is relatively flat. A high price elasticity of supply means that the quantity supplied changes a lot in response to a change in price.

We have just learned that an excise tax drives a wedge, equal to the size of the tax, between the price paid by consumers and the price received by producers. This wedge

FIGURE 15-4 An Excise Tax Paid Mainly by Consumers

The relatively steep demand curve here reflects a low price elasticity of demand for gasoline. The relatively flat supply curve reflects a high price elasticity of supply. The pre-tax price of a gallon of gasoline is $2.00, and a tax of $1.00 per gallon is imposed. The price paid by consumers rises by $0.95 to $2.95, reflecting the fact that most of the burden of the tax falls on consumers. Only a small portion of the tax is borne by producers: the price they receive falls by only $0.05 to $1.95.

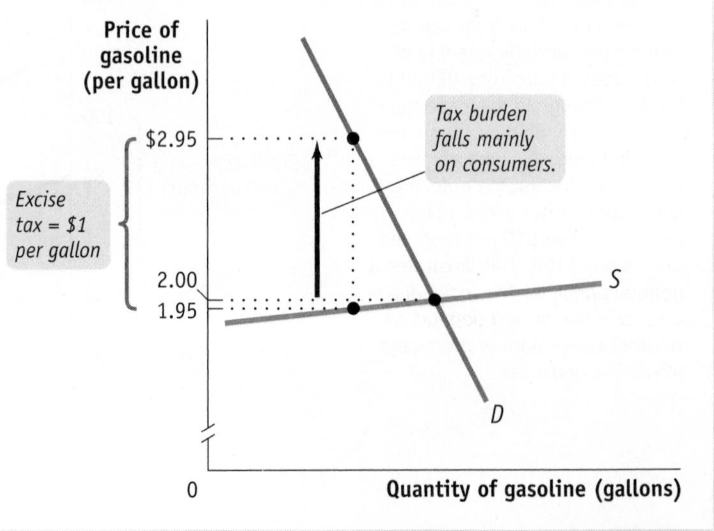

drives the price paid by consumers up and the price received by producers down. But as we can see from Figure 15-4, in this case those two effects are very unequal in size. The price received by producers falls only slightly, from $2.00 to $1.95, but the price paid by consumers rises by a lot, from $2.00 to $2.95. This means that consumers bear the greater share of the tax burden.

This example illustrates another general principle of taxation: *When the price elasticity of demand is low and the price elasticity of supply is high, the burden of an excise tax falls mainly on consumers.* Why? A low price elasticity of demand means that consumers have few substitutes and, therefore, little alternative to buying higher-priced gasoline. In contrast, a high price elasticity of supply results from the fact that producers have many production substitutes for their gasoline (that is, other uses for the crude oil from which gasoline is refined). This gives producers much greater flexibility in refusing to accept lower prices for their gasoline. And, not surprisingly, the party with the least flexibility—in this case, consumers—gets stuck paying most of the tax. This is a good description of how the burden of the most significant excise taxes actually collected in the United States today, such as those on cigarettes and alcoholic beverages, is allocated between consumers and producers.

WHEN AN EXCISE TAX IS PAID MAINLY BY PRODUCERS Figure 15-5 shows an example of an excise tax paid mainly by producers, a $5.00 per day tax on downtown parking in a small city. In the absence of the tax, the market equilibrium price of parking is $6.00 per day.

We've assumed in this case that the price elasticity of supply is very low because the lots used for parking have very few alternative uses. This makes the supply curve for parking spaces relatively steep. The price elasticity of demand, however, is assumed to be high: consumers can easily switch from the downtown spaces to other parking spaces a few minutes' walk from downtown, spaces that are not subject to the tax. This makes the demand curve relatively flat.

The tax drives a wedge between the price paid by consumers and the price received by producers. In this example, however, the tax causes the price paid by consumers to rise only slightly, from $6.00 to $6.50, but the price received by producers falls a lot, from $6.00 to $1.50. In the end, a consumer bears only $0.50 of the $5 tax burden, with a producer bearing the remaining $4.50.

Again, this example illustrates a general principle: *When the price elasticity of demand is high and the price elasticity of supply is low, the burden of an excise tax falls mainly on producers.* A real-world example is a tax on purchases of existing houses. In

FIGURE 15-5 **An Excise Tax Paid Mainly by Producers**

The relatively flat demand curve here reflects a high price elasticity of demand for downtown parking, and the relatively steep supply curve results from a low price elasticity of supply. The pre-tax price of a daily parking space is $6.00 and a tax of $5.00 is imposed. The price received by producers falls a lot, to $1.50, reflecting the fact that they bear most of the tax burden. The price paid by consumers rises a small amount, $0.50, to $6.50, so they bear very little of the burden.

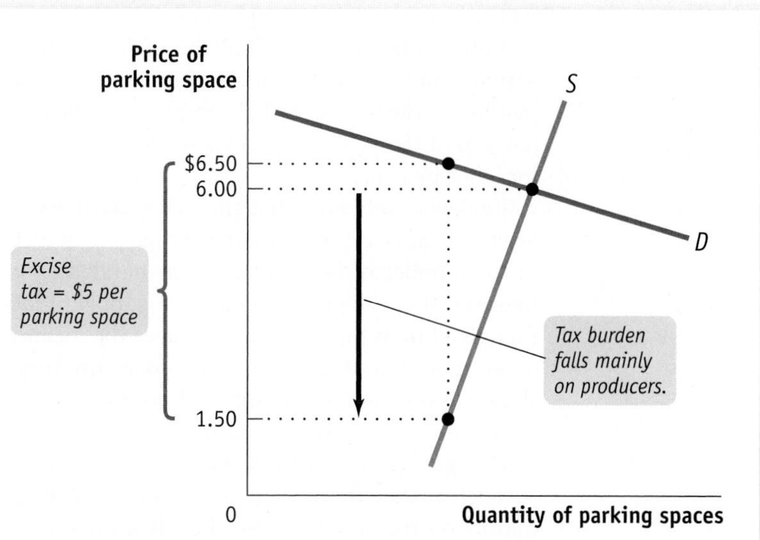

many American towns, house prices in desirable locations have risen as well-off outsiders have moved in and purchased homes from the less well-off original occupants, a phenomenon called gentrification. Some of these towns have imposed taxes on house sales intended to extract money from the new arrivals. But this ignores the fact that the price elasticity of demand for houses in a particular town is often high because potential buyers can choose to move to other towns. Furthermore, the price elasticity of supply is often low because most sellers must sell their houses due to job transfers or to provide funds for their retirement. So taxes on home purchases are actually paid mainly by the less well-off sellers—not, as town officials imagine, by wealthy buyers.

PUTTING IT ALL TOGETHER We've just seen that when the price elasticity of supply is high and the price elasticity of demand is low, an excise tax falls mainly on consumers. And when the price elasticity of supply is low and the price elasticity of demand is high, an excise tax falls mainly on producers. This leads us to the general rule: *When the price elasticity of demand is higher than the price elasticity of supply, an excise tax falls mainly on producers. When the price elasticity of supply is higher than the price elasticity of demand, an excise tax falls mainly on consumers.*

So elasticity—not who officially pays the tax—determines the incidence of an excise tax.

ECONOMICS ▶ IN ACTION

WHO PAYS THE FICA?

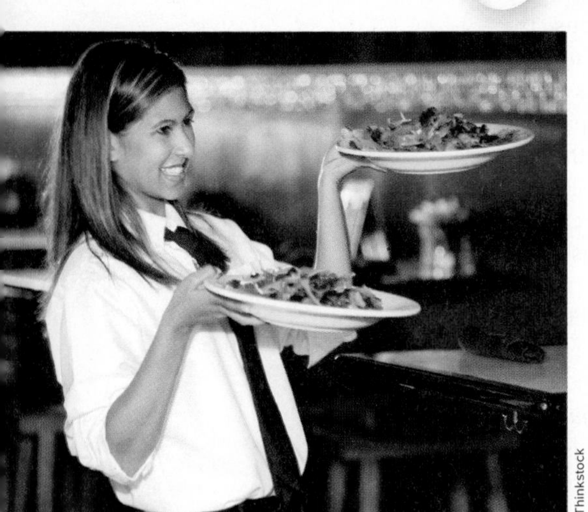

For 70% of Americans it's the FICA, not the income tax, that takes the biggest bite from their paychecks.

Anyone who works for an employer receives a paycheck that itemizes not only the wages paid but also the money deducted from the paycheck for various taxes. For most people, one of the big deductions is *FICA*, also known as the payroll tax. FICA, which stands for the Federal Insurance Contributions Act, pays for the Social Security and Medicare systems, federal social insurance programs that provide income and medical care to retired and disabled Americans.

In 2013, most American workers paid 7.65% of their earnings in FICA. (During 2011–2012, there was a temporary reduction in workers' tax rate to 5.65%, but that ended in 2012.) But this is literally only the half of it: each employer is required to pay an amount equal to the contributions of its employees.

How should we think about FICA? Is it really shared equally by workers and employers? We can use our previous analysis to answer that question, because FICA is like an excise tax—a tax on the sale and purchase of labor. Half of it is a tax levied on the sellers—that is, workers. The other half is a tax levied on the buyers—that is, employers.

But we already know that the incidence of a tax does not really depend on who actually makes out the check. Almost all economists agree that FICA is a tax actually paid by workers, not by their employers. The reason for this conclusion lies in a comparison of the price elasticities of the supply of labor by households and the demand for labor by firms.

Evidence indicates that the price elasticity of demand for labor is quite high, at least 3. That is, an increase in average wages of 1% would lead to at least a 3% decline in the number of hours of work demanded by employers. Labor economists believe, however, that the price elasticity of supply of labor is very low. The reason is that although a fall in the wage rate reduces the incentive to work more hours, it also makes people poorer and less able to afford leisure time. The strength of this second effect is shown in the data: the number of hours people are willing to work falls very little—if at all—when the wage per hour goes down.

Our general rule of tax incidence says that when the price elasticity of demand is much higher than the price elasticity of supply, the burden of an excise tax falls mainly on the suppliers. So the FICA falls mainly on the suppliers of labor, that is, workers—even though on paper half the tax is paid by employers. In other words, the FICA is largely borne by workers in the form of lower wages, rather than by employers in the form of lower profits.

This conclusion tells us something important about the American tax system: the FICA, rather than the much-maligned income tax, is the main tax burden on most families. For most workers, FICA is 15.3% of all wages and salaries up to $113,700 per year for 2013 (note that 7.65% + 7.65% = 15.3%). That is, the great majority of workers in the United States pay 15.3% of their wages in FICA. Only a minority of American families pay more than 15% of their income in income tax. In fact, according to estimates by the Congressional Budget Office, for more than 70% of families FICA is Uncle Sam's main bite out of their income.

The Benefits and Costs of Taxation

When a government is considering whether to impose a tax or how to design a tax system, it has to weigh the benefits of a tax against its costs. We may not think of a tax as something that provides benefits, but governments need money to provide things people want, such as streets, schools, national defense, and health care for those unable to afford it. The benefit of a tax is the revenue it raises for the government to pay for these services. Unfortunately, this benefit comes at a cost—a cost that is normally larger than the amount consumers and producers pay. Let's look first at what determines how much money a tax raises and then at the costs a tax imposes.

"What taxes would you like to see imposed on other people?"

The Revenue from an Excise Tax

How much revenue does the government collect from an excise tax? In our hotel tax example, the revenue is equal to the area of the shaded rectangle in Figure 15-6.

To see why this area represents the revenue collected by a $40 tax on hotel rooms, notice that the *height* of the rectangle is $40, equal to the tax per room. It is also, as we've seen, the size of the wedge that the tax drives between the supply price (the price received by producers) and the demand price (the price paid by consumers). Meanwhile, the *width* of the rectangle is 5,000 rooms, equal

FIGURE 15-6 The Revenue from an Excise Tax

The revenue from a $40 excise tax on hotel rooms is $200,000, equal to the tax rate, $40—the size of the wedge that the tax drives between the supply price and the demand price—multiplied by the number of rooms rented, 5,000. This is equal to the area of the shaded rectangle.

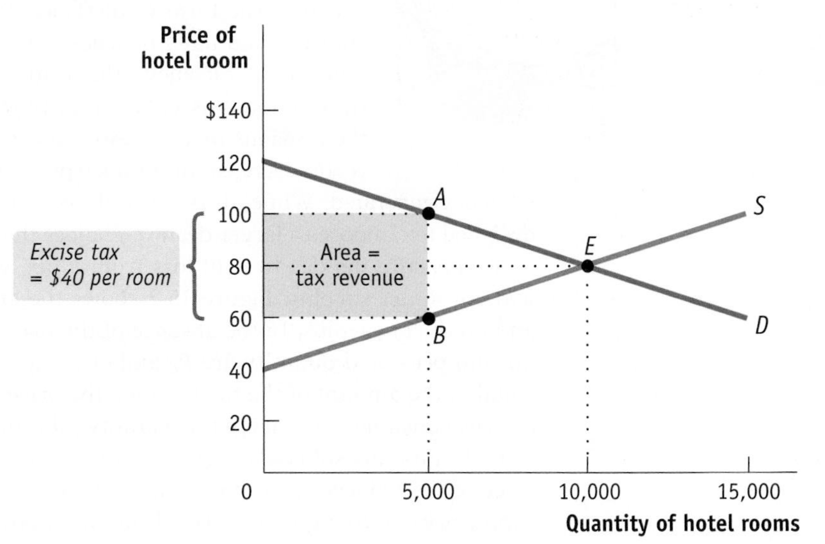

to the equilibrium quantity of rooms given the $40 tax. With that information, we can make the following calculations.

The tax revenue collected is:

Tax revenue = $40 per room × 5,000 rooms = $200,000

The area of the shaded rectangle is:

Area = Height × Width = $40 per room × 5,000 rooms = $200,000

or

Tax revenue = Area of shaded rectangle

This is a general principle: *The revenue collected by an excise tax is equal to the area of a rectangle with the height of the tax wedge between the supply price and the demand price and the width of the quantity sold under the tax.*

The Costs of Taxation

What is the cost of a tax? You might be inclined to answer that it is the amount of money taxpayers pay to the government—the tax revenue collected. But suppose the government uses the tax revenue to provide services that taxpayers want. Or suppose that the government simply hands the tax revenue back to taxpayers. Would we say in those cases that the tax didn't actually cost anything?

No—because a tax, like a quota, prevents mutually beneficial transactions from occurring. Consider Figure 15-6 once more. Here, with a $40 tax on hotel rooms, guests pay $100 per room but hotel owners receive only $60 per room. Because of the wedge created by the tax, we know that some transactions didn't occur that would have occurred without the tax. More specifically, we know from the supply and demand curves that there are some potential guests who would be willing to pay up to $90 per night and some hotel owners who would be willing to supply rooms if they received at least $70 per night.

If these two sets of people were allowed to trade with each other without the tax, they would engage in mutually beneficial transactions—hotel rooms would be rented. But such deals would be illegal because the $40 tax would not be paid. In our example, 5,000 potential hotel room rentals that would have occurred in the absence of the tax, to the mutual benefit of guests and hotel owners, do not take place because of the tax.

Like price controls and quantity controls, taxes create inefficiency by preventing mutually beneficial transactions from occurring.

©Visions of America, LLC/Alamy

So an excise tax imposes costs over and above the tax revenue collected in the form of inefficiency, which occurs because the tax discourages mutually beneficial transactions. The cost to society of this kind of inefficiency—the value of the forgone mutually beneficial transactions—is called *deadweight loss*, which you learned about in the previous module. More specifically, the *deadweight loss from a tax* is the decrease in total surplus resulting from the tax, minus the tax revenues generated. While all real-world taxes impose some deadweight loss, a badly designed tax imposes a larger deadweight loss than a well-designed one.

To measure the deadweight loss from a tax, we turn to the concepts of producer and consumer surplus. Figure 15-7 shows the effects of an excise tax on consumer and producer surplus. In the absence of the tax, the equilibrium is at E and the equilibrium price and quantity are P_E and Q_E, respectively. An excise tax drives a wedge equal to the amount of the tax between the price received by producers and the price paid by consumers, reducing the quantity sold. In this case, with a tax of T dollars per unit, the quantity sold falls to Q_T. The price paid by consumers rises to P_C, the demand price of the reduced quantity, Q_T, and the price received by producers falls to P_P, the supply price of that quantity. The difference between these prices, $P_C - P_P$, is equal to the excise tax, T.

FIGURE 15-7 A Tax Reduces Consumer and Producer Surplus

Before the tax, the equilibrium price and quantity are P_E and Q_E, respectively. After an excise tax of T per unit is imposed, the price to consumers rises to P_C and consumer surplus falls by the sum of the dark blue rectangle, labeled A, and the light blue triangle, labeled B. The tax also causes the price to producers to fall to P_P; producer surplus falls by the sum of the dark red rectangle, labeled C, and the light red triangle, labeled F. The government receives revenue from the tax, $Q_T \times T$, which is given by the sum of the areas A and C. Areas B and F represent the losses to consumer and producer surplus that are not collected by the government as revenue; they are the deadweight loss to society of the tax.

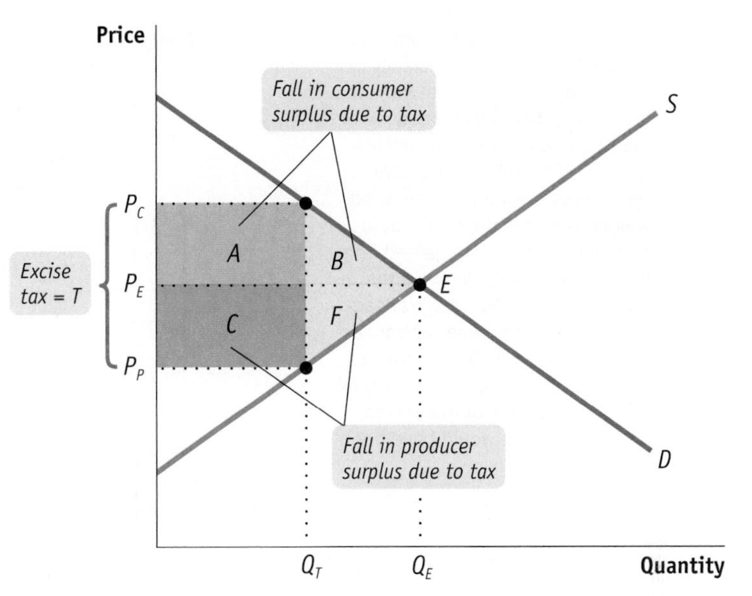

Using the concepts of producer and consumer surplus, we can show exactly how much surplus producers and consumers lose as a result of the tax. We learned previously that a fall in the price of a good generates a gain in consumer surplus that is equal to the sum of the areas of a rectangle and a triangle. Similarly, a price increase causes a loss to consumers that is represented by the sum of the areas of a rectangle and a triangle. So it's not surprising that in the case of an excise tax, the rise in the price paid by consumers causes a loss equal to the sum of the areas of a rectangle and a triangle: the dark blue rectangle labeled A and the area of the light blue triangle labeled B in Figure 15-7.

Meanwhile, the fall in the price received by producers leads to a fall in producer surplus. This, too, is equal to the sum of the areas of a rectangle and a triangle. The loss in producer surplus is the sum of the areas of the dark red rectangle labeled C and the light red triangle labeled F in Figure 15-7.

Of course, although consumers and producers are hurt by the tax, the government gains revenue. The revenue the government collects is equal to the tax per unit sold, T, multiplied by the quantity sold, Q_T. This revenue is equal to the area of a rectangle Q_T wide and T high. And we already have that rectangle in the figure: it is the sum of rectangles A and C. So the government gains part of what consumers and producers lose from an excise tax.

But a portion of the loss to producers and consumers from the tax is not offset by a gain to the government—specifically, the two triangles B and F. The deadweight loss caused by the tax is equal to the combined area of these two triangles. It represents the total surplus lost to society because of the tax—that is, the amount of surplus that would have been generated by transactions that now do not take place because of the tax.

Figure 15-8 is a version of Figure 15-7 that leaves out rectangles A (the surplus shifted from consumers to the government) and C (the surplus shifted from producers to the government) and shows only the deadweight loss, drawn here as a triangle shaded yellow. The base of that triangle is equal to the tax wedge, T; the height of the triangle is equal to the reduction in the quantity transacted due to the tax, $Q_E - Q_T$. Clearly, the larger the tax wedge and the larger the reduction in the quantity transacted, the greater the inefficiency from the tax.

But also note an important, contrasting point: if the excise tax somehow *didn't* reduce the quantity bought and sold in this market—if Q_T remained equal to Q_E after

FIGURE 15-8 The Deadweight Loss of a Tax

A tax leads to a deadweight loss because it creates inefficiency: some mutually beneficial transactions never take place because of the tax, namely the transactions $Q_E - Q_T$. The yellow area here represents the value of the deadweight loss: it is the total surplus that would have been gained from the $Q_E - Q_T$ transactions. If the tax had not discouraged transactions—had the number of transactions remained at Q_E because of either perfectly inelastic supply or perfectly inelastic demand—no deadweight loss would have been incurred.

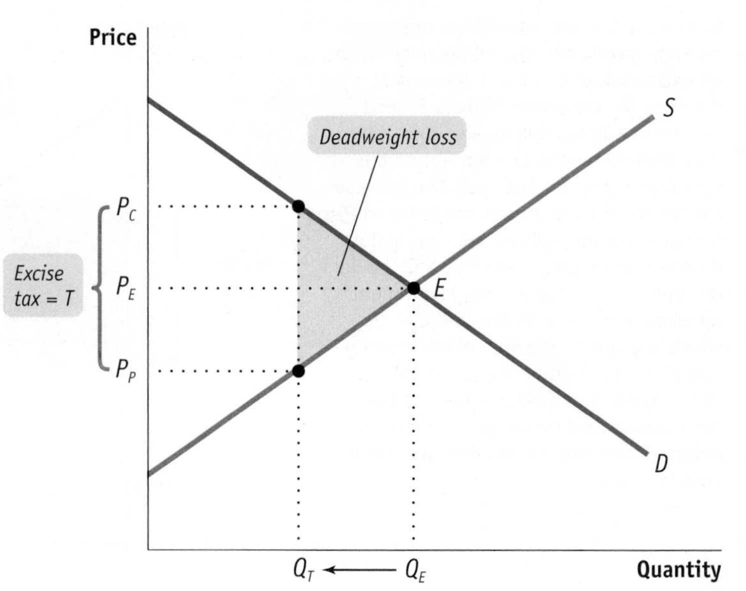

the tax was levied—the yellow triangle would disappear and the deadweight loss from the tax would be zero. So if a tax does *not* discourage transactions, which would be true if either supply or demand were perfectly inelastic, it causes no deadweight loss. In this case, the tax simply shifts surplus straight from consumers and producers to the government.

Using a triangle to measure deadweight loss is a technique used in many economic applications. For example, triangles are used to measure the deadweight loss produced by types of taxes other than excise taxes. They are also used to measure the deadweight loss produced by monopoly, another kind of market distortion. And deadweight-loss triangles are often used to evaluate the benefits and costs of public policies besides taxation—such as whether to impose stricter safety standards on a product.

In considering the total amount of inefficiency caused by a tax, we must also take into account something not shown in Figure 15-8: the resources actually used by the government to collect the tax, and by taxpayers to pay it, over and above the amount of the tax. These lost resources are called the **administrative costs** of the tax. The most familiar administrative cost of the U.S. tax system is the time individuals spend filling out their income tax forms or the money they spend on accountants to prepare their tax forms for them. (The latter is considered an inefficiency from the point of view of society because accountants could instead be performing other, non-tax-related services.)

Included in the administrative costs that taxpayers incur are resources used to evade the tax, both legally and illegally. The costs of operating the Internal Revenue Service, the arm of the federal government tasked with collecting the federal income tax, are actually quite small in comparison to the administrative costs paid by taxpayers. The total inefficiency caused by a tax is the sum of its deadweight loss and its administrative costs.

The **administrative costs** of a tax are the resources used by government to collect the tax, and by taxpayers to pay (or to evade) it, over and above the amount collected.

A **lump-sum tax** is a tax of a fixed amount paid by all taxpayers.

Some extreme forms of taxation, such as the *poll tax* instituted by the government of British Prime Minister Margaret Thatcher in 1989, are notably unfair but very efficient. A poll tax is an example of a **lump-sum tax,** a tax that is the same for everyone regardless of any actions people take. The poll tax in Britain was widely perceived as much less fair than the tax structure it replaced, in which local taxes were proportional to property values.

Under the old system, the highest local taxes were paid by the people with the most expensive houses. Because these people tended to be wealthy, they were also best able to bear the burden. But the old system definitely distorted incentives to engage in mutually beneficial transactions and created deadweight loss. People who were considering home improvements knew that such improvements, by making their property more valuable, would increase their tax bills. The result, surely, was that some home improvements that would have taken place without the tax did not take place because of it.

In contrast, a lump-sum tax does not distort incentives. Because under a lump-sum tax people have to pay the same amount of tax regardless of their actions, it does not cause them to substitute untaxed goods for a good whose price has been artificially inflated by a tax, as occurs with an excise tax. So lump-sum taxes, although unfair, are better than other taxes at promoting economic efficiency.

15 Review

Solutions appear at the back of the book.

Check Your Understanding

1. Consider the market for butter, shown in the accompanying figure. The government imposes an excise tax of $0.30 per pound of butter. What is the price paid by consumers post-tax? What is the price received by producers post-tax? What is the quantity of butter sold? How is the incidence of the tax allocated between consumers and producers? Show this on the figure.

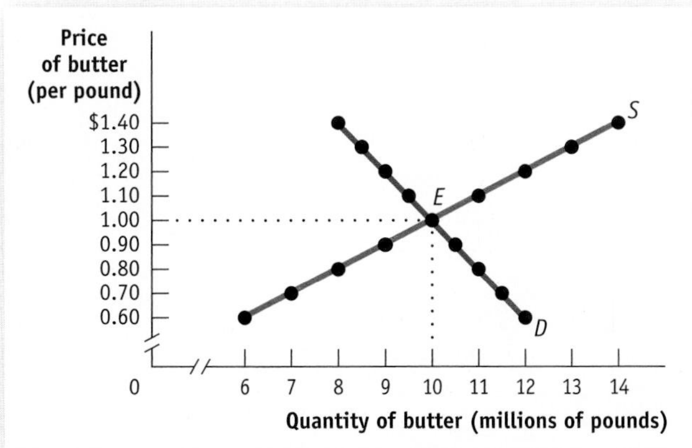

2. The accompanying table shows five consumers' willingness to pay for one can of diet soda each as well as five producers' costs of selling one can of diet soda each. Each consumer buys at most one can of soda; each producer sells at most one can of soda. The government asks your advice about the effects of an excise tax of $0.40 per can of diet soda. Assume that there are no administrative costs from the tax.

Consumer	Willingness to Pay	Producer	Cost
Ana	$0.70	Zhang	$0.10
Bernice	0.60	Yves	0.20
Chizuko	0.50	Xavier	0.30
Dagmar	0.40	Walter	0.40
Ella	0.30	Vern	0.50

a. Without the excise tax, what is the equilibrium price and the equilibrium quantity of soda?

b. The excise tax raises the price paid by consumers post-tax to $0.60 and lowers the price received by producers post-tax to $0.20. With the excise tax, what is the quantity of soda sold?

c. Without the excise tax, how much individual consumer surplus does each of the consumers gain? How much individual consumer surplus does each consumer gain with the tax? How much total consumer surplus is lost as a result of the tax?

d. Without the excise tax, how much individual producer surplus does each of the producers gain? How much individual producer surplus does each producer gain with the tax? How much total producer surplus is lost as a result of the tax?

e. How much government revenue does the excise tax create?

f. What is the deadweight loss from the imposition of this excise tax?

Multiple-Choice Questions

1. An excise tax imposed on sellers in a market will result in which of the following?
   - I. an upward shift of the supply curve
   - II. a downward shift of the demand curve
   - III. deadweight loss

   a. I only
   b. II only
   c. III only
   d. I and III only
   e. I, II, and III

2. An excise tax will be paid mainly by producers when
   a. it is imposed on producers.
   b. it is imposed on consumers.
   c. the price elasticity of supply is low and the price elasticity of demand is high.
   d. the price elasticity of supply is high and the price elasticity of demand is low.
   e. the price elasticity of supply is perfectly elastic.

Critical-Thinking Question

Draw a correctly labeled graph of a competitive market in equilibrium. Use your graph to illustrate the effect of an excise tax imposed on consumers. Indicate each of the following on your graph:

a. the equilibrium price and quantity without the tax, labeled P_E and Q_E
b. the quantity sold in the market post-tax, labeled Q_T
c. the price paid by consumers post-tax, labeled P_C
d. the price received by producers post-tax, labeled P_P
e. the tax revenue generated by the tax, labeled "Tax revenue"
f. the deadweight loss resulting from the tax, labeled "DWL"
g. the wedge created by the tax between P_C and P_P, labeled "Excise tax"

BUSINESS CASE: Medallion Financial: Cruising Right Along

Owaki/Kulla/Corbis

Back in 1937, before New York City froze its number of taxi medallions, Andrew Murstein's immigrant grandfather bought his first one for $10. Over time, the grandfather accumulated 500 medallions, which he rented to other drivers. Those 500 taxi medallions became the foundation for Medallion Financial: the company that would eventually pass to Andrew, its current president.

With a market value of almost $300 million in early 2013, Medallion Financial has shifted its major line of business from renting out medallions to financing the purchase of new ones, lending money to those who want to buy a medallion but don't have the sizable amount of cash required to do so. Murstein believes that he is helping people who, like his Polish immigrant grandfather, want to buy a piece of the American dream.

Andrew Murstein carefully watches the value of a New York City taxi medallion: the more one costs, the more demand there is for loans from Medallion Financial, and the more interest the company makes on the loan. A loan from Medallion Financial is secured by the value of the medallion itself. If the borrower is unable to repay the loan, Medallion Financial takes possession of his or her medallion and resells it to offset the cost of the loan default. As of 2012, the value of a medallion has risen faster than stocks, oil, and gold. Since 1990, the value of a medallion rose 555% compared to only 330% for an index of stocks.

But medallion prices can fluctuate dramatically, threatening profits. During periods of a very strong economy, such as 1999 and 2001, the price of New York taxi medallions fell as drivers found jobs in other sectors. When the New York economy tanked in the aftermath of 9/11, the price of a medallion fell to $180,000, its lowest level in 12 years. In 2004, medallion owners were concerned about the impending sale by the New York City Taxi and Limousine Commission of an additional 900 medallions. As Peter Hernandez, a worried New York cabdriver who financed his medallion with a loan from Medallion Financial, said at the time: "If they pump new taxis into the industry, it devalues my medallion. It devalues my daily income, too."

Yet Murstein has always been optimistic that medallions would hold their value. He believed that a 25% fare increase would offset potential losses in their value caused by the sale of new medallions. In addition, more medallions would mean more loans for his company. As of early 2013, Murstein's optimism had been justified. Because of the financial crisis of 2007–2009, many New York companies cut back the limousine services they ordinarily provided to their employees, forcing them to take taxis instead. As a result, the price of a medallion rose to an astonishing $917,000 in March 2013. And investors have noticed the value in Medallion Financial's line of business: from March 2012 to March 2013, shares of Medallion Financial have risen 40%.

Questions for Thought

1. How does Medallion Financial benefit from the restriction on the number of New York taxi medallions?
2. What will be the effect on Medallion Financial if New York companies resume widespread use of limousine services for their employees? What is the economic motivation that prompts companies to offer this perk to their employees? (Note that it is very difficult and expensive to own a personal car in New York City.)
3. What would happen to Medallion Financial's business if New York City eliminated restrictions on the number of taxis?

SECTION 5 REVIEW

Summary

Price Controls (Ceilings and Floors)

1. Even when a market is efficient, governments often intervene to pursue greater fairness or to please a powerful interest group. Interventions can take the form of **price controls** or **quantity controls,** both of which generate predictable and undesirable side effects, consisting of various forms of inefficiency and illegal activity.

2. A **price ceiling,** a maximum market price below the equilibrium price, benefits successful buyers but creates persistent shortages. Because the price is maintained below the equilibrium price, the quantity demanded is increased and the quantity supplied is decreased compared to the equilibrium quantity. This leads to predictable problems including **inefficient allocation to consumers, wasted resources,** and **inefficiently low quality.** It also encourages illegal activity as people turn to **black markets** to get the good. Because of these problems, price ceilings have generally lost favor as an economic policy tool. But some governments continue to impose them either because they don't understand the effects or because the price ceilings benefit some influential group.

3. A **price floor,** a minimum market price above the equilibrium price, benefits successful sellers but creates a persistent surplus: because the price is maintained above the equilibrium price, the quantity demanded is decreased and the quantity supplied is increased compared to the equilibrium quantity. This leads to predictable problems: inefficiencies in the form of **inefficient allocation of sales among sellers,** wasted resources, and **inefficiently high quality.** It also encourages illegal activity such as black markets. The most well known kind of price floor is the **minimum wage,** but price floors are also commonly applied to agricultural products.

Quantity Controls (Quotas)

4. Quantity controls, or **quotas,** limit the quantity of a good that can be bought or sold. The government issues **licenses** to individuals, the right to sell a given quantity of the good. The owner of a license earns a **quota rent,** earnings that accrue from ownership of the right to sell the good. It is equal to the difference between the **demand price** at the quota amount, what consumers are willing to pay for that amount, and the **supply price** at the quota amount, what suppliers are willing to accept for that amount. Economists say that a quota drives a **wedge** between the demand price and the supply price; this wedge is equal to the quota rent. By limiting mutually beneficial transactions, quantity controls generate inefficiency. Like price controls, quantity controls lead to **deadweight loss** and encourage illegal activity.

Taxes

5. A tax that rises more than in proportion to income is a **progressive tax.** A tax that rises less than in proportion to income is a **regressive tax.** A tax that rises in proportion to income is, you guessed it, a **proportional tax.**

6. An **excise tax**—a tax on the purchase or sale of a good—raises the price paid by consumers and reduces the price received by producers, driving a wedge between the two. The **incidence** of the tax—how the burden of the tax is divided between consumers and producers—does not depend on who officially pays the tax.

7. The incidence of an excise tax depends on the price elasticities of supply and demand. If the price elasticity of demand is higher than the price elasticity of supply, the tax falls mainly on producers; if the price elasticity of supply is higher than the price elasticity of demand, the tax falls mainly on consumers.

8. The tax revenue generated by a tax depends on the **tax rate** and on the number of units sold with the tax. Excise taxes cause inefficiency in the form of deadweight loss because they discourage some mutually beneficial transactions. Taxes also impose **administrative costs:** resources used to collect the tax, to pay it (over and above the amount of the tax), and to evade it.

9. An excise tax generates revenue for the government but lowers total surplus. The loss in total surplus exceeds the tax revenue, resulting in a deadweight loss to society. This deadweight loss is represented by a triangle, the area of which equals the value of the transactions discouraged by the tax. The greater the elasticity of demand or supply, or both, the larger the deadweight loss from a tax. If either demand or supply is perfectly inelastic, there is no deadweight loss from a tax.

10. A **lump-sum tax** is a tax of a fixed amount paid by all taxpayers. Because a lump-sum tax does not depend on the behavior of taxpayers, it does not discourage mutually beneficial transactions and therefore causes no deadweight loss.

Key Terms

Problems

1. Suppose it is decided that rent control in New York City will be abolished and that market rents will now prevail. Assume that all rental units are identical and are therefore offered at the same rent. To address the plight of residents who may be unable to pay the market rent, an income supplement will be paid to all low-income households equal to the difference between the old controlled rent and the new market rent.

a. Use a diagram to show the effect on the rental market of the elimination of rent control. What will happen to the quality and quantity of rental housing supplied?

b. Now use a second diagram to show the additional effect of the income-supplement policy on the market, namely the resulting increase in demand. What effect does it have on the market rent and quantity of rental housing supplied in comparison to your answers to part a?

c. Are tenants better or worse off as a result of these policies? Are landlords better or worse off?

d. From a political standpoint, why do you think cities have been more likely to resort to rent control rather than a policy of income supplements to help low-income people pay for housing?

2. In the late eighteenth century, the price of bread in New York City was controlled, set at a predetermined price above the market price.

a. Draw a diagram showing the effect of the policy. Did the policy act as a price ceiling or a price floor?

b. What kinds of inefficiencies were likely to have arisen when the controlled price of bread was above the market price? Explain in detail.

One year during this period, a poor wheat harvest caused a leftward shift in the supply of bread and therefore an increase in its market price. New York bakers found that the controlled price of bread in New York was below the market price.

c. Draw a diagram showing the effect of the price control on the market for bread during this one-year period. Did the policy act as a price ceiling or a price floor?

d. What kinds of inefficiencies do you think occurred during this period? Explain in detail.

3. Suppose the U.S. government decides that the incomes of dairy farmers should be maintained at a level that allows the traditional family dairy farm to survive. It therefore implements a price floor of $1 per pint by buying surplus milk until the market price is $1 per pint. Use the accompanying diagram to answer the following questions.

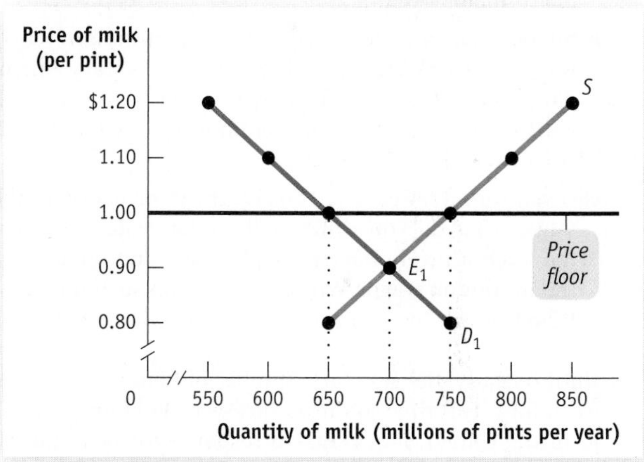

a. How much surplus milk will be produced as a result of this policy?

b. What will be the cost to the government of this policy?

c. Since milk is an important source of protein and calcium, the government decides to provide the surplus milk it purchases to elementary schools at a price of only $0.60 per pint. Assume that schools will buy any amount of milk available at this low price. But parents now reduce their purchases of milk at any price by 50 million pints per year because they know their children are getting milk at school. How much will the dairy program now cost the government?

d. Give two examples of inefficiencies arising from wasted resources that are likely to result from this policy. What is the missed opportunity in each case?

4. European governments tend to make greater use of price controls than the U.S. government. For example, the French government sets minimum starting yearly wages for new hires who have completed *le bac,* certification roughly equivalent to a high school diploma. The demand schedule for new hires with *le bac* and the supply schedule for similarly credentialed new job seekers are given in the accompanying table. The price here—given in euros, the currency used in France—is the same as the yearly wage.

Wage (per year)	Quantity demanded (new job offers per year)	Quantity supplied (new job seekers per year)
€45,000	200,000	325,000
40,000	220,000	320,000
35,000	250,000	310,000
30,000	290,000	290,000
25,000	370,000	200,000

a. In the absence of government interference, what is the equilibrium wage and number of graduates hired per year? Illustrate with a diagram. Will there be anyone seeking a job at the equilibrium wage who is unable to find one—that is, will there be anyone who is involuntarily unemployed?

b. Suppose the French government sets a minimum yearly wage of 35,000 euros. Is there any involuntary unemployment at this wage? If so, how much? Illustrate with a diagram. What if the minimum wage is set at 40,000 euros? Also illustrate with a diagram.

c. Given your answer to part b and the information in the table, what do you think is the relationship between the level of involuntary unemployment and the level of the minimum wage? Who benefits from such a policy? Who loses? What is the missed opportunity here?

5. Until recently, the standard number of hours worked per week for a full-time job in France was 39 hours, similar to in the United States. But in response to social unrest over high levels of involuntary unemployment, the French government instituted a 35-hour workweek—a worker could not work more than 35 hours per week even if both the worker and employer wanted it. The motivation behind this policy was that if current employees worked fewer hours, employers would be forced to hire more new workers. Assume that it is costly for employers to train new workers. French employers were greatly opposed to this policy and threatened to move their operations to neighboring countries that did not have such employment restrictions. Can you explain their attitude? Give an example of both an inefficiency and an illegal activity that are likely to arise from this policy.

6. The waters off the north Atlantic coast were once teeming with fish. Now, due to overfishing by the commercial fishing industry, the stocks of fish are seriously depleted. In 1991, the National Marine Fishery Service of the U.S. government implemented a quota to allow fish stocks to recover. The quota limited the amount of swordfish caught per year by all U.S.-licensed fishing boats to 7 million pounds. As soon as the U.S. fishing fleet had met the quota, the swordfish catch was closed down for the rest of the year. The accompanying table gives the hypothetical demand and supply schedules for swordfish caught in the United States per year.

Price of swordfish (per pound)	Quantity of swordfish (millions of pounds per year)	
	Quantity demanded	Quantity supplied
$20	6	15
18	7	13
16	8	11
14	9	9
12	10	7

a. Use a diagram to show the effect of the quota on the market for swordfish in 1991.

b. How do you think fishermen will change how they fish in response to this policy?

7. Consider the original market for pizza in Collegetown, illustrated in the accompanying table. Collegetown officials decide to impose an excise tax on pizza of $4 per pizza.

Price of pizza	Quantity of pizza demanded	Quantity of pizza supplied
10	0	6
9	1	5
8	2	4
7	3	3
6	4	2
5	5	1
4	6	0
3	7	0
2	8	0
1	9	0

a. What is the quantity of pizza bought and sold after the imposition of the tax? What is the price paid by consumers? What is the price received by producers?

b. Calculate the consumer surplus and the producer surplus after the imposition of the tax. By how much has the imposition of the tax reduced consumer surplus? By how much has it reduced producer surplus?

c. How much tax revenue does Collegetown earn from this tax?

d. Calculate the deadweight loss from this tax.

8. The state needs to raise money, and the governor has a choice of imposing an excise tax of the same amount on one of two previously untaxed goods: either restaurant meals or gasoline. Both the demand for and the supply of restaurant meals are more elastic than the demand for and the supply of gasoline. If the governor wants to minimize the deadweight loss caused by the tax, which good should be taxed? For each good, draw a diagram that illustrates the deadweight loss from taxation.

9. The U.S. government would like to help the American auto industry compete against foreign automakers that sell trucks in the United States. It can do this by imposing an excise tax on each foreign truck sold in the United States. The hypothetical pre-tax demand and supply schedules for imported trucks are given in the accompanying table.

Price of imported truck	Quantity of imported trucks (thousands)	
	Quantity demanded	Quantity supplied
$32,000	100	400
31,000	200	350
30,000	300	300
29,000	400	250
28,000	500	200
27,000	600	150

a. In the absence of government interference, what is the equilibrium price of an imported truck? The equilibrium quantity? Illustrate with a diagram.

b. Assume that the government imposes an excise tax of $3,000 per imported truck. Illustrate the effect of this excise tax in your diagram from part a. How many imported trucks are now purchased and at what price? How much does the foreign automaker receive per truck?

c. Calculate the government revenue raised by the excise tax in part b. Illustrate it on your diagram.

d. How does the excise tax on imported trucks benefit American automakers? Whom does it hurt? How does inefficiency arise from this government policy?

10. In 1990, the United States began to levy a tax on sales of luxury cars. For simplicity, assume that the tax was an excise tax of $6,000 per car. The accompanying figure shows hypothetical demand and supply curves for luxury cars.

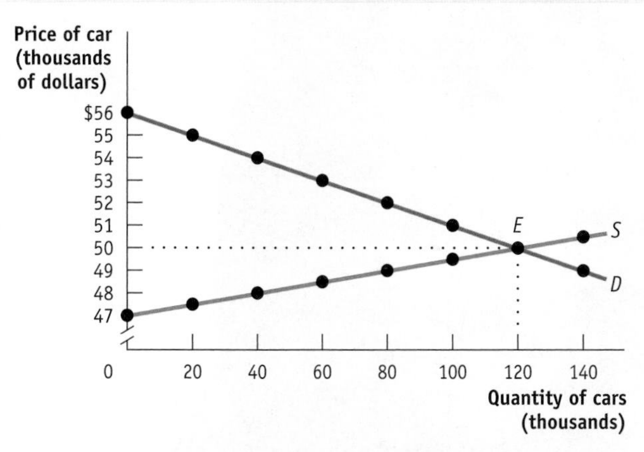

a. Under the tax, what is the price paid by consumers? What is the price received by producers? What is the government tax revenue from the excise tax?

Over time, the tax on luxury automobiles was slowly phased out (and completely eliminated in 2002). Suppose that the excise tax falls from $6,000 per car to $4,500 per car.

b. After the reduction in the excise tax from $6,000 to $4,500 per car, what is the price paid by consumers? What is the price received by producers? What is tax revenue now?

c. Compare the tax revenue created by the taxes in parts a and b. What accounts for the change in tax revenue from the reduction in the excise tax?

11. All states impose excise taxes on gasoline. According to data from the Federal Highway Administration, one year the state of California imposed an excise tax of $0.18 per gallon of gasoline. That same year, gasoline sales in California totaled 14.8 billion gallons. What was California's tax revenue from the gasoline excise tax? If California doubled the excise tax, would tax revenue double? Why or why not?

12. In each of the following cases involving taxes, explain: (i) whether the incidence of the tax falls more heavily on consumers or producers, (ii) why government revenue raised from the tax is not a good indicator of the true cost of the tax, and (iii) how deadweight loss arises as a result of the tax.

a. The government imposes an excise tax on the sale of all college textbooks. Before the tax was imposed, 1 million textbooks were sold every year at a price of $50. After the tax is imposed, 600,000 books are sold yearly; students pay $55 per book, $30 of which publishers receive.

b. The government imposes an excise tax on the sale of all airline tickets. Before the tax was imposed, 3 million airline tickets were sold every year at a price of $500. After the tax is imposed, 1.5 million tickets are sold yearly; travelers pay $550 per ticket, $450 of which the airlines receive.

c. The government imposes an excise tax on the sale of all toothbrushes. Before the tax, 2 million toothbrushes were sold every year at a price of $1.50. After the tax is imposed, 800,000 toothbrushes are sold every year; consumers pay $2 per toothbrush, $1.25 of which producers receive.

Module 16: Gains from Trade

Module 17: Supply, Demand, and International Trade

SECTION 6

International Trade

CAR PARTS AND SUCKING SOUNDS

Stop in an auto showroom, and odds are that the majority of cars on display were produced in the United States. Even if they're Nissans, Hondas, or Volkswagens, most cars sold in this country were made here by the Big Three U.S. auto firms or by subsidiaries of foreign firms.

Although that car you're looking at may have been made in America, a significant part of what's inside was probably made elsewhere, very likely in Mexico. Since the 1980s, U.S. auto production has increasingly relied on factories in Mexico to produce *labor-intensive* auto parts, such as seat parts—products that use a relatively high amount of labor in their production.

Changes in economic policy over the years have contributed greatly to the emergence of large-scale U.S. imports of auto parts from Mexico. Until the 1980s, Mexico had a system of *trade protection*—taxes and regulations limiting imports—that kept out U.S. manufactured goods and encouraged Mexican industry to focus on selling to Mexican consumers rather than to a wider market. In 1985, however, the Mexican government began dismantling much of its trade protection, boosting trade with the United States.

A further boost came in 1993, when the United States, Mexico, and Canada signed the North American Free Trade Agreement (NAFTA), which eliminated most taxes on trade among the three nations and provided guarantees that business investments in Mexico would be protected from arbitrary changes in government policy.

NAFTA was deeply controversial when it went into effect: Mexican workers were paid only about 10% as much as their U.S. counterparts, and many expressed concern that U.S. jobs would be lost to low-wage competition. And although apocalyptic predictions about NAFTA's impact haven't come to pass, the agreement remains controversial even now.

Most economists disagreed with those who saw NAFTA as a threat to the U.S. economy. We saw in Module 4 how international trade can lead to mutual *gains from trade*. Economists, for the most part, believed that the same logic applied to NAFTA, that the treaty would make both the United States and Mexico richer. But making a nation as a whole richer isn't the same thing as improving the welfare of everyone living in a country, and there were and are reasons to believe that NAFTA hurts some U.S. citizens.

Until now, we have analyzed the economy as if it were self-sufficient, producing all the goods and services it consumes, and vice versa. This is, of course, true for the world economy as a whole. But it's not true for any individual country. Assuming self-sufficiency would have been far more accurate 50 years ago, when the United States exported only a small fraction of what it produced and imported only a small fraction of what it consumed.

Since then, however, both U.S. imports and exports have grown dramatically. Moreover, compared to the United States, other countries engage in far more foreign trade relative to the size of their economies.

To have a full picture of how national economies work, we must understand the economics of international trade, which we will examine in this section. We start by revisiting the model of comparative advantage, which, as we saw in Module 4, explains why there are gains from international trade. We then extend our study to address deeper questions about international trade, such as why some individuals can be hurt by international trade while the country, as a whole, gains. At the conclusion of the section, we'll look at the effects of policies that countries use to limit imports or promote exports. And we'll look at the challenges nations face as a result of the forward march of globalization.

it no longer produces auto parts, because it can import parts from Mexico. Mexico can also consume more of both goods, even though it no longer produces airplanes, because it can import airplanes from the United States.

The key to this mutual gain is the fact that trade liberates both countries from self-sufficiency—from the need to produce the same mixes of goods they consume. Because each country can concentrate on producing the good in which it has a comparative advantage, total world production rises, making a higher standard of living possible in both nations.

Comparative Advantage versus Absolute Advantage

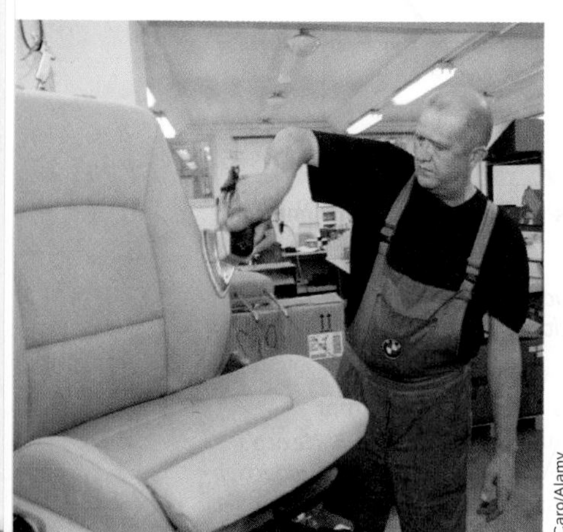
Caro/Alamy

The opportunity cost of producing auto parts is higher in the United States than in Mexico.

There's nothing about Mexico's climate or resources that makes it especially good at manufacturing auto parts. In fact, it almost surely takes *fewer* hours of labor to produce an auto seat in the United States than in Mexico. Why, then, do we buy Mexican auto parts?

Because the gains from trade depend on *comparative advantage,* not *absolute advantage.* Yes, it takes less labor to produce an auto seat in the United States than in Mexico. That is, the productivity of Mexican auto parts workers is less than that of their U.S. counterparts. But what determines comparative advantage is not the amount of resources used to produce a good but the opportunity cost of that good—here, the quantity of other goods given up in order to produce an auto seat. And the opportunity cost of auto parts is lower in Mexico than in the United States.

Here's how it works: Mexican workers have low productivity compared with U.S. workers in the auto parts industry. But Mexican workers have even lower productivity compared with U.S. workers in other industries. Because Mexican labor productivity in industries other than auto parts is relatively lower, producing an auto seat in Mexico, even though it takes a lot of labor, does not require forgoing the production of large quantities of other goods.

In the United States, the opposite is true: very high productivity in other industries (such as high-technology goods) means that producing an auto seat in the United States, even though it doesn't require much labor, requires sacrificing lots of other goods. So the opportunity cost of producing auto parts is less in Mexico than in the United States. Despite its lower labor productivity, Mexico has a comparative advantage in the production of auto parts, although the United States has an absolute advantage.

Mexico's comparative advantage in auto parts is reflected in global markets by the wages Mexican workers are paid. That's because a country's wage rates, in general, reflect its labor productivity. In countries where labor is highly productive in many industries, employers are willing to pay high wages to attract workers, so competition among employers leads to an overall high wage rate. In countries where labor is less productive, competition for workers is less intense and wage rates are correspondingly lower.

International trade that depends on low-wage exports can raise a country's standard of living, as it has in Mexico and elsewhere.

Bloomberg via Getty Images

The kind of trade that takes place between low-wage, low-productivity economies like Mexico and high-wage, high-productivity economies like the United States gives rise to two common misperceptions. One, the *pauper labor fallacy,* is the belief that when a country with high wages imports goods produced by workers who are paid low wages, this must hurt the standard of living of workers in the importing country. The other, the *sweatshop labor fallacy,* is the belief that trade must be bad for workers in poor exporting countries because those workers are paid very low wages by our standards.

Both fallacies miss the nature of gains from trade: it's to the advantage of *both* countries if the poorer, lower-wage country exports goods in which it has a comparative advantage, even if its cost advantage in these goods depends on low wages. That is, both countries are able to achieve a higher standard of living through trade.

It's particularly important to understand that buying a good made by someone who is paid much lower wages than most U.S. workers doesn't necessarily imply that you're taking advantage of that person. It depends on the alternatives. Because workers in poor countries have low productivity across the board, they are offered low wages whether they produce goods exported to America or goods sold in local markets. A job that looks terrible by rich-country standards can be a step up for someone in a poor country.

International trade that depends on low-wage exports can nonetheless raise a country's standard of living. This is especially true of very-low-wage nations. For example, Bangladesh and similar countries would be much poorer than they are—their citizens might even be starving—if they weren't able to export goods such as clothing based on their low wage rates.

The **factor intensity** of production of a good is a measure of which factor is used in relatively greater quantities than other factors in production.

According to the **Heckscher–Ohlin model,** a country has a comparative advantage in a good whose production is intensive in the factors that are abundantly available in that country.

Sources of Comparative Advantage

International trade is driven by comparative advantage, but where does comparative advantage come from? Economists who study international trade have found three main sources of comparative advantage:

1. international differences in *climate*
2. international differences in *factor endowments*
3. international differences in *technology*

1. DIFFERENCES IN CLIMATE In general, differences in climate play a significant role in international trade. Tropical countries export tropical products like coffee, sugar, bananas, and shrimp. Countries in the temperate zones export crops like wheat and corn. Some trade is even driven by the difference in seasons between the northern and southern hemispheres: winter deliveries of Chilean grapes and New Zealand apples have become commonplace in U.S. and European supermarkets.

2. DIFFERENCES IN FACTOR ENDOWMENTS Canada is a major exporter of forest products—lumber and products derived from lumber, like pulp and paper—to the United States. These exports don't reflect the special skill of Canadian lumberjacks. Canada has a comparative advantage in forest products because its forested area is much greater compared to the size of its labor force than the ratio of forestland to the labor force in the United States.

Forestland, like labor and capital, is a *factor of production:* an input used to produce goods and services. (Recall that the factors of production are land, labor, physical capital, and human capital.) Due to history and geography, the mix of available factors of production differs among countries, providing an important source of comparative advantage. The relationship between comparative advantage and factor availability is found in an influential model of international trade, the *Heckscher–Ohlin model,* developed by two Swedish economists in the first half of the twentieth century.

Two key concepts in the model are *factor abundance* and *factor intensity.* Factor abundance refers to how large a country's supply of a factor is relative to its supply of other factors. Factor intensity refers to the fact that producers use different ratios of factors of production in the production of different goods. For example, oil refineries use much more capital per worker than clothing factories. Economists use the term **factor intensity** to describe this difference among goods: oil refining is capital-intensive, because it tends to use a high ratio of capital to labor, but auto seats production is labor-intensive, because it tends to use a high ratio of labor to capital.

According to the **Heckscher–Ohlin model,** *a country that has an abundant supply of a factor of production will have a comparative advantage in goods whose production is intensive in that factor.* So a country that has a relative abundance of capital will have a comparative advantage in capital-intensive industries such as oil refining, but a country that has a relative abundance of labor will have a comparative advantage in labor-intensive industries such as auto seats production.

iStockphoto

Canada's comparative advantage in forest production has little to do with the skill of its storied lumberjacks and a lot to do with the size of its forests.

The basic intuition behind this result is simple and based on opportunity cost. The opportunity cost of a given factor—the value that the factor would generate in alternative uses—is low for a country when it is relatively abundant in that factor. Relative to the United States, Mexico has an abundance of low-skilled labor. As a result, the opportunity cost of the production of low-skilled, labor-intensive goods is lower in Mexico than in the United States.

The most dramatic example of the validity of the Heckscher–Ohlin model is world trade in clothing. Clothing production is a labor-intensive activity: it doesn't take much physical capital, nor does it require a lot of human capital in the form of highly educated workers. So you would expect labor-abundant countries such as China and Bangladesh to have a comparative advantage in clothing production. And they do.

Corbis/Photolibrary

3. DIFFERENCES IN TECHNOLOGY In the 1970s and 1980s, Japan became by far the world's largest exporter of automobiles, selling large numbers to the United States and the rest of the world. Japan's comparative advantage in automobiles wasn't the result of climate. Nor can it easily be attributed to differences in factor endowments: aside from a scarcity of land, Japan's mix of available factors is quite similar to that in other advanced countries. Instead, as we discussed in the Section 1 Business Case on lean production at Toyota and Boeing, Japan's comparative advantage in automobiles was based on the superior production techniques developed by its manufacturers, which allowed them to produce more cars with a given amount of labor and capital than their American or European counterparts.

Lean production involves organizing workers and parts to ensure a smooth work flow, minimize waste, and allow for flexibility to change.

Japan's comparative advantage in automobiles was a case of comparative advantage caused by differences in technology—the techniques used in production.

ECONOMICS ▶ *IN ACTION*

WORLD VIEW

SKILL AND COMPARATIVE ADVANTAGE

In 1953 U.S. workers were clearly better equipped with machinery than their counterparts in other countries. Most economists at the time thought that America's comparative advantage lay in capital-intensive goods. But Wassily Leontief made a surprising discovery: America's comparative advantage was in something other than capital-intensive goods. In fact, goods that the United States exported were slightly less capital-intensive than goods the country imported. This discovery came to be known as the *Leontief paradox,* and it led to a sustained effort to make sense of U.S. trade patterns.

The main resolution of this paradox, it turns out, depends on the definition of *capital.* U.S. exports aren't intensive in *physical* capital—machines and buildings. Instead, they are *skill-intensive*—that is, they are intensive in *human* capital. U.S. exporting industries use a substantially higher ratio of highly educated workers to other workers than is found in U.S. industries that compete against imports. For example, one of America's biggest export sectors is aircraft; the aircraft industry employs large numbers of engineers and other people with graduate degrees relative to the number of manual laborers. Conversely, we import a lot of clothing, which is often produced by workers with little formal education.

In general, countries with highly educated workforces tend to export skill-intensive goods, while countries with less educated workforces tend to export goods whose production requires little skilled labor.

Figure 16-4 illustrates this point by comparing the goods the United States imports from Germany, a country with a highly educated labor force, with the goods the United States imports from Bangladesh, where about half of the adult population is still illiterate. In each country industries are ranked, first, according to how skill-intensive they are. Next, for each industry, we calculate its share of U.S. imports. This allows us to plot, for each country, various industries according to their skill intensity and their share of U.S. imports.

In Figure 16-4, the horizontal axis shows a measure of the skill intensity of different industries, and the vertical axes show the share of U.S. imports in each industry coming from Germany (on the left) and Bangladesh (on the right). As you can see, each country's share of U.S. imports reflects its skill level. The curve representing Germany slopes upward: the more skill-intensive a German industry is, the higher its share of U.S. imports. In contrast, the curve representing Bangladesh slopes downward: the less skill-intensive a Bangladeshi industry is, the higher its share of U.S. imports.

FIGURE 16-4 Education, Skill Intensity, and Trade

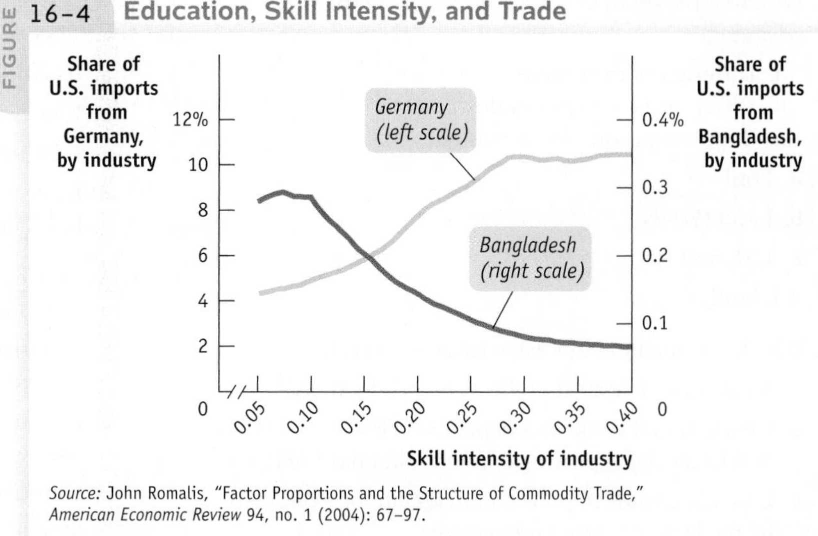

Source: John Romalis, "Factor Proportions and the Structure of Commodity Trade," *American Economic Review* 94, no. 1 (2004): 67–97.

MODULE 16 Review

Solutions appear at the back of the book.

Check Your Understanding

1. In the United States, the opportunity cost of 1 ton of corn is 50 bicycles. In China, the opportunity cost of 1 bicycle is 0.01 ton of corn.
   a. Determine the pattern of comparative advantage.
   b. In autarky, the United States can produce 200,000 bicycles if no corn is produced, and China can produce 3,000 tons of corn if no bicycles are produced. Draw each country's production possibility curve assuming constant opportunity cost, with tons of corn on the vertical axis and bicycles on the horizontal axis.
   c. With trade, each country specializes its production. The United States consumes 1,000 tons of corn and 200,000 bicycles; China consumes 3,000 tons of corn and 100,000 bicycles. Indicate the production and consumption points on your diagrams, and use them to explain the gains from trade.
2. Explain the following patterns of trade using the Heckscher–Ohlin model.
   a. France exports wine to the United States, and the United States exports movies to France.
   b. Brazil exports shoes to the United States, and the United States exports shoe-making machinery to Brazil.

Multiple-Choice Questions

1. Globalization can be defined as
   a. the growing number of multinational companies.
   b. the growth of various forms of economic linkages among countries.
   c. the value of imports and exports as a percentage of a country's GDP.
   d. the price of goods in world markets.

2. Which of the following are sources of comparative advantage?

   I. Differences in climate
   II. Differences in factor endowments
   III. Superior production techniques

   a. I only
   b. I and II only
   c. I, II, and III
   d. III only

3. Which statement about wage rates is correct?
   a. A country's wage rate reflects its productivity.
   b. International trade that depends on low-wage exports will lower the exporting country's standard of living.
   c. Low wage rates in poor countries can be explained by the lack of factor endowments.
   d. All of the above are correct.

4. Which of the following best describes a country in autarky?
   a. Its workers are highly productive in many industries.
   b. It does not trade with other countries.
   c. It benefits from trading with only one other country.
   d. It specializes in the production of goods in which it has a comparative advantage.

5. According to the Heckscher–Ohlin model of international trade,
   a. countries have a comparative advantage in the good that can be imported the most cheaply.
   b. countries have a comparative advantage in the good they want to produce.
   c. countries have a comparative advantage in the good produced with the country's most abundant resources.
   d. All of the above are true.

Critical-Thinking Question

In autarky, the equilibrium price of a good in the domestic market is $10. If the world price of the same good is $8 and the country opens up to trade, how will the domestic quantity supplied and demanded be affected? Will the country be an importer or an exporter of the good?

Supply, Demand, and International Trade

Glow Images/Superstock

WHAT YOU WILL LEARN

1. How tariffs and import quotas cause inefficiency and reduce total surplus
2. Why governments often engage in trade protection to shelter domestic industries from imports
3. About the challenges that have been created by globalization

Imports, Exports, and Wages

Simple models of comparative advantage are helpful for understanding the fundamental causes of international trade. However, to analyze the effects of international trade at a more detailed level and to understand trade policy, it helps to return to the supply and demand model. We'll start by looking at the effects of imports on domestic producers and consumers, then turn to the effects of exports.

The Effects of Imports

Figure 17-1 shows the U.S. market for auto seats, ignoring international trade for a moment. It introduces a few new concepts: the *domestic demand curve,* the *domestic supply curve,* and the domestic or autarky price.

The **domestic demand curve** shows how the quantity of a good demanded by residents of a country depends on the price of that good. Why "domestic"? Because people living in other countries may demand the good, too. Once we introduce international trade, we need to distinguish between purchases of a good by domestic consumers and purchases by foreign consumers. So the domestic demand curve reflects only the demand of residents of our own country. Similarly, the **domestic supply curve** shows how the quantity of a good supplied by producers inside our own country depends on the price of that good. Once we introduce international trade, we need to distinguish between the supply of domestic producers and foreign supply—supply brought in from abroad.

In autarky, with no international trade in auto seats, the equilibrium in this market would be determined by the intersection of the domestic demand and domestic

The **domestic demand curve** shows how the quantity of a good demanded by domestic consumers depends on the price of that good.

The **domestic supply curve** shows how the quantity of a good supplied by domestic producers depends on the price of that good.

FIGURE 17-1 **Consumer and Producer Surplus in Autarky**

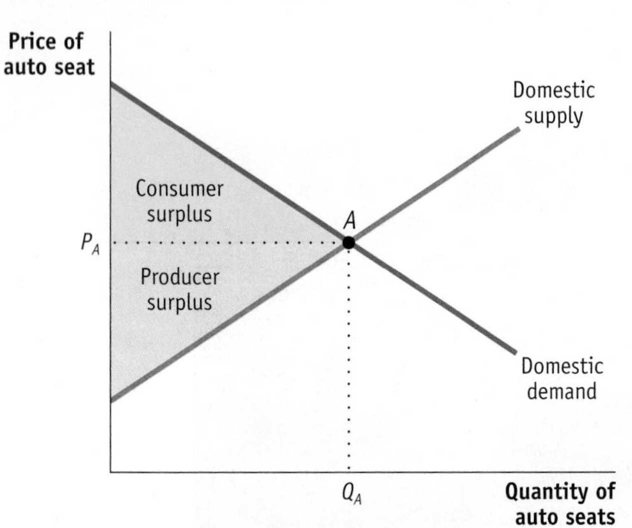

In the absence of trade, the domestic price is P_A, the autarky price at which the domestic supply curve and the domestic demand curve intersect. The quantity produced and consumed domestically is Q_A. Consumer surplus is represented by the blue-shaded area, and producer surplus is represented by the red-shaded area.

supply curves, point A. The equilibrium price of auto seats would be P_A, and the equilibrium quantity of auto seats produced and consumed would be Q_A. As always, both consumers and producers gain from the existence of the domestic market. In autarky, consumer surplus would be equal to the area of the blue-shaded triangle in Figure 17-1. Producer surplus would be equal to the area of the red-shaded triangle. And total surplus would be equal to the sum of these two shaded triangles.

Now let's imagine opening up this market to imports. To do this, we must make an assumption about the supply of imports. The simplest assumption, which we will adopt here, is that unlimited quantities of auto seats can be purchased from abroad at a fixed price, known as the **world price** of auto seats. Figure 17-2 shows a situation in which the world price of an auto seat, P_W, is lower than the price of an auto seat that would prevail in the domestic market in autarky, P_A.

Given that the world price is below the domestic price of an auto seat, it is profitable for importers to buy auto seats abroad and resell them domestically. The imported auto seats increase the supply of auto seats in the domestic market, driving down the domestic market price. Auto seats will continue to be imported until the domestic price falls to a level equal to the world price.

The **world price** of a good is the price at which that good can be bought or sold abroad.

The result is shown in Figure 17-2. Because of imports, the domestic price of an auto seat falls from P_A to P_W. The quantity of auto seats demanded by domestic consumers rises from Q_A to Q_D, and the quantity supplied by domestic producers falls from Q_A to Q_S. The difference between the domestic quantity demanded and the domestic quantity supplied, $Q_D - Q_S$, is filled by imports.

Now let's turn to the effects of imports on consumer surplus and producer surplus. Because imports of auto seats lead to a fall in their domestic price, consumer surplus

FIGURE 17-2 **The Domestic Market with Imports**

Here the world price of auto seats, P_W, is below the autarky price, P_A. When the economy is opened to international trade, imports enter the domestic market, and the domestic price falls from the autarky price, P_A, to the world price, P_W. As the price falls, the domestic quantity demanded rises from Q_A to Q_D and the domestic quantity supplied falls from Q_A to Q_S. The difference between domestic quantity demanded and domestic quantity supplied at P_W, the quantity $Q_D - Q_S$, is filled by imports.

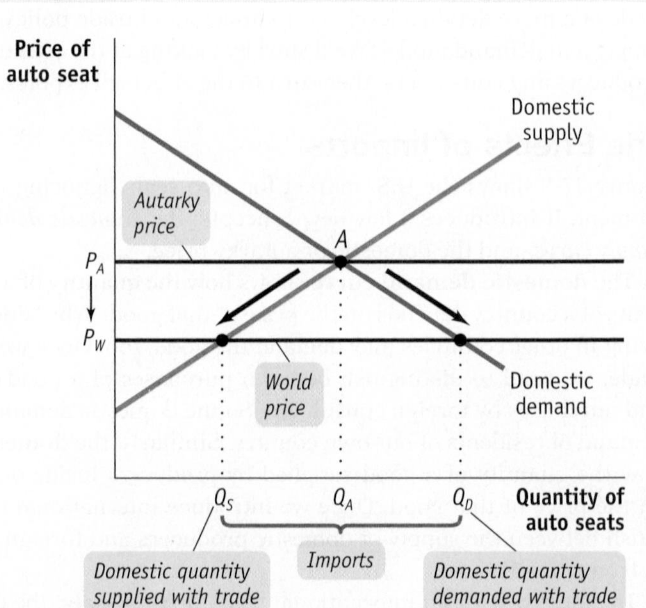

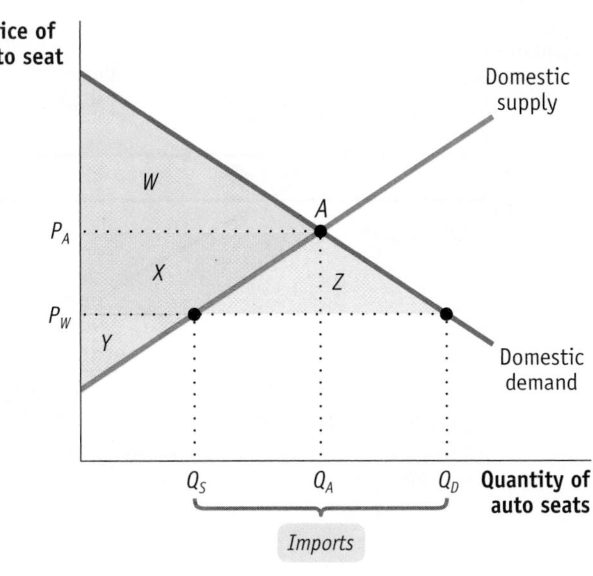

	Changes in surplus	
	Gain	**Loss**
Consumer surplus	$X + Z$	
Producer surplus		$-X$
Change in total surplus	$+Z$	

When the domestic price falls to P_W as a result of international trade, consumers gain additional surplus (areas $X + Z$) and producers lose surplus (area X). Because the gains to consumers outweigh the losses to producers, there is an increase in the total surplus in the economy as a whole (area Z).

rises and producer surplus falls. Figure 17-3 shows how this works. We label four areas: *W, X, Y,* and *Z*. The autarky consumer surplus we identified in Figure 17-1 corresponds to *W*, and the autarky producer surplus corresponds to the sum of *X* and *Y*. The fall in the domestic price to the world price leads to an increase in consumer surplus; it increases by *X* and *Z*, so consumer surplus now equals the sum of *W, X,* and *Z*. At the same time, producers lose *X* in surplus, so producer surplus now equals only *Y*.

The table in Figure 17-3 summarizes the changes in consumer and producer surplus when the auto seats market is opened to imports. Consumers gain surplus equal to the areas $X + Z$. Producers lose surplus equal to *X*. So the sum of producer and consumer surplus—the total surplus generated in the auto seats market—increases by *Z*. As a result of trade, consumers gain and producers lose, but the gain to consumers exceeds the loss to producers.

This is an important result. We have just shown that opening up a market to imports leads to a net gain in total surplus, which is what we should have expected given the proposition that there are gains from international trade.

However, we have also learned that although the country as a whole gains, some groups—in this case, domestic producers of auto parts—lose as a result of international trade. As we'll see shortly, the fact that international trade typically creates losers as well as winners is crucial for understanding the politics of trade policy.

We turn next to the case in which a country exports a good.

Thinkstock

Opening up a market to imports and exports leads to a net gain in total surplus, but creates losers as well as winners.

The Effects of Exports

Figure 17-4 shows the effects on a country when it exports a good, in this case airplanes. For this example, we assume that unlimited quantities of airplanes can be sold abroad at a given world price, P_W, which is higher than the price that would prevail in the domestic market in autarky, P_A.

The higher world price makes it profitable for exporters to buy airplanes domestically and sell them overseas. The purchases of domestic airplanes drive the domestic price up until it is equal to the world price. As a result, the quantity demanded by domestic consumers falls from Q_A to Q_D and the quantity supplied by domestic producers rises from Q_A to Q_S. This difference between domestic production and domestic consumption, $Q_S - Q_D$, is exported.

FIGURE **17-4 The Domestic Market with Exports**

Here the world price, P_W, is greater than the autarky price, P_A. When the economy is opened to international trade, some of the domestic supply is now exported. The domestic price rises from the autarky price, P_A, to the world price, P_W. As the price rises, the domestic quantity demanded falls from Q_A to Q_D and the domestic quantity supplied rises from Q_A to Q_S. The portion of domestic production that is not consumed domestically, $Q_S - Q_D$, is exported.

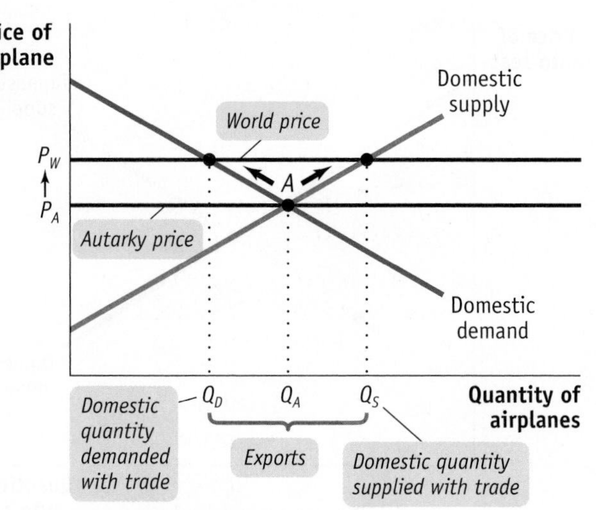

Like imports, exports lead to an overall gain in total surplus for the exporting country but also create losers as well as winners. Figure 17-5 shows the effects of airplane exports on producer and consumer surplus. In the absence of trade, the price of each airplane would be P_A. Consumer surplus in the absence of trade is the sum of areas *W* and *X*, and producer surplus is area *Y*. As a result of trade, price rises from P_A to P_W, consumer surplus falls to *W*, and producer surplus rises to $Y + X + Z$. So producers gain $X + Z$, consumers lose *X*, and, as shown in the table accompanying the figure, the economy as a whole gains total surplus in the amount of *Z*.

We have learned, then, that imports of a particular good hurt domestic producers of that good but help domestic consumers, whereas exports of a particular good hurt domestic consumers of that good but help domestic producers. In each case, the gains are larger than the losses.

International Trade and Wages

So far we have focused on the effects of international trade on producers and consumers in a particular industry. For many purposes this is a very helpful approach. How-

FIGURE **17-5 The Effects of Exports on Surplus**

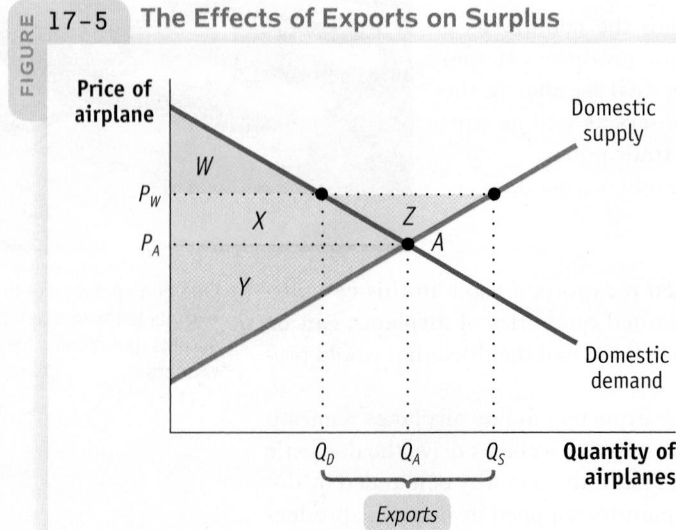

	Changes in surplus	
	Gain	Loss
Consumer surplus		$-X$
Producer surplus	$X + Z$	
Change in total surplus	$+Z$	

When the domestic price rises to P_W as a result of trade, producers gain additional surplus (areas $X + Z$) but consumers lose surplus (area *X*). Because the gains to producers outweigh the losses to consumers, there is an increase in the total surplus in the economy as a whole (area *Z*).

ever, producers and consumers are not the only parts of society affected by trade—so are the owners of factors of production. In particular, the owners of labor, land, and capital employed in producing goods that are exported, or goods that compete with imported goods, can be deeply affected by trade.

Moreover, the effects of trade aren't limited to just those industries that export or compete with imports because *factors of production can often move between industries*. So now we turn our attention to the long-run effects of international trade on income distribution—how a country's total income is allocated among its various factors of production.

To begin our analysis, consider the position of Maria, an accountant at Midwest Auto Parts, Inc. If the economy is opened up to imports of auto parts from Mexico, the domestic auto parts industry will contract, and it will hire fewer accountants.

But accounting is a profession with employment opportunities in many industries, and Maria might well find a better job in the aircraft industry, which expands as a result of international trade. So it may not be appropriate to think of her as a producer of auto parts who is hurt by competition from imported parts. Rather, we should think of her as an accountant who is affected by auto part imports only to the extent that these imports change the wages of accountants in the economy as a whole.

The wage rate of accountants is a *factor price*—the price employers have to pay for the services of a factor of production. One key question about international trade is how it affects factor prices—not just narrowly defined factors of production like accountants, but broadly defined factors such as capital, unskilled labor, and college-educated labor.

In the previous module we described the Heckscher–Ohlin model of trade, which states that comparative advantage is determined by a country's factor endowment. This model also suggests how international trade affects factor prices in a country: compared to autarky, international trade tends to raise the prices of factors that are abundantly available and reduce the prices of factors that are scarce.

We won't work this out in detail, but the idea is simple. The prices of factors of production, like the prices of goods and services, are determined by supply and demand. If international trade increases the demand for a factor of production, that factor's price will rise; if international trade reduces the demand for a factor of production, that factor's price will fall.

Now think of a country's industries as consisting of two kinds: **exporting industries,** which produce goods and services that are sold abroad, and **import-competing industries,** which produce goods and services that are also imported from abroad. Compared with autarky, international trade leads to higher production in exporting industries and lower production in import-competing industries. This indirectly increases the demand for the factors used by exporting industries and decreases the demand for factors used by import-competing industries.

In addition, the Heckscher–Ohlin model says that a country tends to export goods that are intensive in its abundant factors and to import goods that are intensive in its scarce factors. So *international trade tends to increase the demand for factors that are abundant in our country compared with other countries, and to decrease the demand for factors that are scarce in our country compared with other countries.* As a result, *the prices of abundant factors tend to rise, and the prices of scarce factors tend to fall as international trade grows.* In other words, international trade tends to redistribute income toward a country's abundant factors and away from its less abundant factors.

As we've seen, U.S. exports tend to be human-capital-intensive and U.S. imports tend to be unskilled-labor-intensive. This suggests that the effect of international trade on U.S. factor markets is to raise the wage rate of highly educated American workers and reduce the wage rate of unskilled American workers.

Exporting industries produce goods and services that are sold abroad.

Import-competing industries produce goods and services that are also imported.

Dreamstime

Trade affects factor markets by raising the wages of highly educated workers and lowering them for unskilled workers.

An economy has **free trade** when the government does not attempt either to reduce or to increase the levels of exports and imports that occur naturally as a result of supply and demand.

Policies that limit imports are known as **trade protection** or simply as **protection.**

A **tariff** is a tax levied on imports.

This effect has been a source of much concern in recent years. Wage inequality—the gap between the wages of high-paid and low-paid workers—has increased substantially over the last 30 years. Some economists believe that growing international trade is an important factor in that trend. If international trade has the effects predicted by the Heckscher–Ohlin model, its growth raises the wages of highly educated American workers, who already have relatively high wages, and lowers the wages of less educated American workers, who already have relatively low wages. But keep in mind another phenomenon: trade reduces the income inequality *between* countries as poor countries improve their standard of living by exporting to rich countries.

The effects of trade on wages in the United States have generated considerable controversy in recent years. Most economists who have studied the issue agree that growing imports of labor-intensive products from newly industrializing economies, and the export of high-technology goods in return, have helped cause a widening wage gap between highly educated and less educated workers in this country. However, most economists believe that it is only one of several forces explaining the growth in American wage inequality.

The Effects of Trade Protection

Ever since the principle of comparative advantage was laid out in the early nineteenth century, most economists have advocated **free trade.** That is, they have argued that government policy should not attempt either to reduce or to increase the levels of exports and imports that occur naturally as a result of supply and demand.

Despite the free-trade arguments of economists, however, many governments use taxes and other restrictions to limit imports. Less frequently, governments offer subsidies to encourage exports. Policies that limit imports, usually with the goal of protecting domestic producers in import-competing industries from foreign competition, are known as **trade protection** or simply as **protection.**

Let's look at the two most common protectionist policies, tariffs and import quotas, then turn to the reasons governments follow these policies.

The Effects of a Tariff

A **tariff** is a form of excise tax, one that is levied only on sales of imported goods. For example, the U.S. government could declare that anyone bringing in auto seats must pay a tariff of $100 per unit. In the distant past, tariffs were an important source of government revenue because they were relatively easy to collect. But in the modern world, tariffs are usually intended to discourage imports and protect import-competing domestic producers rather than to serve as a source of government revenue.

The tariff raises both the price received by domestic producers and the price paid by domestic consumers. Suppose, for example, that our country imports auto seats, and an auto seat costs $200 on the world market. As we saw earlier, under free trade the domestic price would also be $200. But if a tariff of $100 per unit is imposed, the domestic price will rise to $300, because it won't be profitable to import auto seats unless the price in the domestic market is high enough to compensate importers for the cost of paying the tariff.

Figure 17-6 illustrates the effects of a tariff on imports of auto seats. As before, we assume that P_W is the world price of an auto seat. Before the tariff is imposed, imports have driven the domestic price down to P_W, so that pre-tariff domestic production is Q_S, pre-tariff domestic consumption is Q_D, and pre-tariff imports are $Q_D - Q_S$.

Now suppose that the government imposes a tariff on each auto seat imported. As a consequence, it is no longer profitable to import auto seats unless the domestic price received by the importer is greater than or equal to the world price *plus* the tariff. So the domestic price rises to P_T, which is equal to the world price, P_W, plus the tariff. Domestic production rises to Q_{ST}, domestic consumption falls to Q_{DT}, and imports fall to $Q_{DT} - Q_{ST}$.

FIGURE **17-6 The Effect of a Tariff**

A tariff raises the domestic price of the good from P_W to P_T. The domestic quantity demanded shrinks from Q_D to Q_{DT}, and the domestic quantity supplied increases from Q_S to Q_{ST}. As a result, imports—which had been $Q_D - Q_S$ before the tariff was imposed—shrink to $Q_{DT} - Q_{ST}$ after the tariff is imposed.

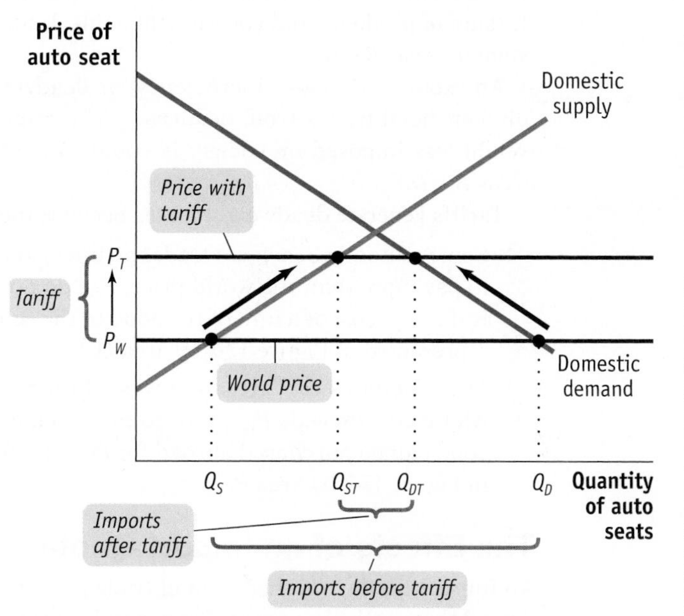

A tariff, then, raises domestic prices, leading to increased domestic production and reduced domestic consumption compared to the situation under free trade. Figure 17-7 shows the effects on surplus. There are three effects:

1. The higher domestic price increases producer surplus, a gain equal to area *A*.
2. The higher domestic price reduces consumer surplus, a reduction equal to the sum of areas *A*, *B*, *C*, and *D*.
3. The tariff yields revenue to the government. How much revenue? The government collects the tariff—which, remember, is equal to the difference between P_T and P_W on each of the $Q_{DT} - Q_{ST}$ units imported. So total revenue is $(P_T - P_W) \times (Q_{DT} - Q_{ST})$. This is equal to area *C*.

FIGURE **17-7 A Tariff Reduces Total Surplus**

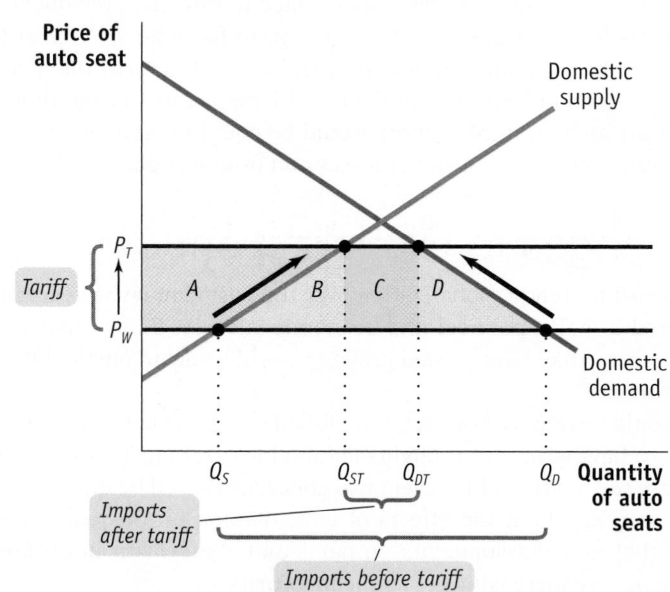

	Changes in surplus	
	Gain	Loss
Consumer surplus		$-(A + B + C + D)$
Producer surplus	A	
Government revenue	C	
Change in total surplus		$-(B + D)$

When the domestic price rises as a result of a tariff, producers gain additional surplus (area *A*), the government gains revenue (area *C*), and consumers lose surplus (areas $A + B + C + D$). Because the losses to consumers outweigh the gains to producers and the government, the economy as a whole loses surplus (areas $B + D$).

An **import quota** is a legal limit on the quantity of a good that can be imported.

The welfare effects of a tariff are summarized in the table in Figure 17-7. Producers gain, consumers lose, and the government gains. But consumer losses are greater than the sum of producer and government gains, leading to a net reduction in total surplus equal to areas $B + D$.

An excise tax creates inefficiency, or deadweight loss, because it prevents mutually beneficial trades from occurring. The same is true of a tariff, where the deadweight loss imposed on society is equal to the loss in total surplus represented by areas $B + D$.

Tariffs generate deadweight losses because they create inefficiencies in two ways:

1. Some mutually beneficial trades go unexploited: some consumers who are willing to pay more than the world price, P_W, do not purchase the good, even though P_W is the true cost of a unit of the good to the economy. The cost of this inefficiency is represented in Figure 17-7 by area D.
2. The economy's resources are wasted on inefficient production: some producers whose cost exceeds P_W produce the good, even though an additional unit of the good can be purchased abroad for P_W. The cost of this inefficiency is represented in Figure 17-7 by area B.

The Effects of an Import Quota

An **import quota,** another form of trade protection, is a legal limit on the quantity of a good that can be imported. For example, a U.S. import quota on Mexican auto seats might limit the quantity imported each year to 500,000 units. Import quotas are usually administered through licenses: a number of licenses are issued, each giving the license-holder the right to import a limited quantity of the good each year.

A quota on sales has the same effect as an excise tax, with one difference: the money that would otherwise have accrued to the government as tax revenue under an excise tax becomes license-holders' revenue under a quota—this revenue is also known as *quota rents.* Similarly, an import quota has the same effect as a tariff, with one difference: the money that would otherwise have been government revenue becomes quota rents to license-holders.

Look again at Figure 17-7. An import quota that limits imports to $Q_{DT} - Q_{ST}$ will raise the domestic price of auto parts by the same amount as the tariff we considered previously. That is, it will raise the domestic price from P_W to P_T. However, area C will now represent quota rents rather than government revenue.

Who receives import licenses and so collects the quota rents? In the case of U.S. import protection, the answer may surprise you: the most important import licenses—mainly for clothing, to a lesser extent for sugar—are granted to foreign governments.

Because the quota rents for most U.S. import quotas go to foreigners, the cost to the nation of such quotas is larger than that of a comparable tariff (a tariff that leads to the same level of imports). In Figure 17-7 the net loss to the United States from such an import quota would be equal to areas $B + C + D$, the difference between consumer losses and producer gains.

Economists and policy makers view growing world trade as a positive, but not everyone agrees.

© FC_Italy/Alamy

Challenges to Globalization

The forward march of globalization over the past century is generally considered a major political and economic success. Economists and policy makers alike have viewed growing world trade, in particular, as a good thing.

We would be remiss, however, if we failed to acknowledge that many people are having second thoughts about globalization. To a large extent, these second thoughts reflect two concerns shared by many economists: worries about the effects of globalization on inequality and worries that new developments, in particular the growth in *offshore outsourcing,* are increasing economic insecurity.

Globalization and Inequality

We've already mentioned the implications of international trade for factor prices, such as wages: when wealthy countries like the United States export skill-intensive products like aircraft while importing labor-intensive products like clothing, they can expect to see the wage gap between more educated and less educated domestic workers widen. Thirty years ago, this wasn't a significant concern, because most of the goods wealthy countries imported from poorer countries were raw materials or goods where comparative advantage depended on climate. Today, however, many manufactured goods are imported from relatively poor countries, with a potentially much larger effect on the distribution of income.

Trade with China, in particular, raises concerns among labor groups trying to maintain wage levels in rich countries. Although China has experienced spectacular economic growth since the economic reforms that began in the late 1970s, it remains a poor, low-wage country: wages in Chinese manufacturing are estimated to be only about 6% of U.S. wages. Meanwhile, imports from China have soared. In 1983 less than 1% of U.S. imports came from China; by 2012, the figure was 18%. There's not much question that these surging imports from China put at least some downward pressure on the wages of less educated American workers.

Outsourcing

Chinese exports to the United States overwhelmingly consist of labor-intensive manufactured goods. However, some U.S. workers have recently found themselves facing another form of international competition. *Outsourcing,* in which a company hires another company to perform some task, such as running the corporate computer system, is a long-standing business practice. Until recently, however, outsourcing was normally done locally, with a company hiring another company in the same city or country.

Now, modern telecommunications make it possible to engage in **offshore outsourcing,** in which businesses hire people in another country to perform various tasks. The classic example is a call center: the person answering the phone when you call a company's 1-800 help line may well be in India, which has taken the lead in attracting offshore outsourcing. Offshore outsourcing has also spread to fields such as software design and even health care: the radiologist examining your X-rays, like the person giving you computer help, may be on another continent.

Offshore outsourcing is relatively small compared with more traditional trade.

Although offshore outsourcing has come as a shock to some U.S. workers, such as programmers whose jobs have been outsourced to India, it's still relatively small compared with more traditional trade. Some economists have warned, however, that millions or even tens of millions of workers who have never thought they could face foreign competition for their jobs may face unpleasant surprises in the not-too-distant future.

Concerns about income distribution and outsourcing, as we've said, are shared by many economists. There is also, however, widespread opposition to globalization in general, particularly among college students.

What motivates the antiglobalization movement? To some extent it's the sweatshop labor fallacy: it's easy to get outraged about the low wages paid to the person who made your shirt, and harder to appreciate how much worse off that person would be if denied the opportunity to sell goods in rich countries' markets.

Offshore outsourcing takes place when businesses hire people in another country to perform various tasks.

It's also true, however, that the movement represents a backlash against supporters of globalization who have oversold its benefits. Countries in Latin America, in particular, were promised that reducing their tariff rates would produce an economic takeoff; instead, they have experienced disappointing results.

Do these challenges to globalization undermine the argument that international trade is a good thing? The great majority of economists would argue that the gains from reducing trade protection still exceed the losses. However, it has become more important than before to make sure that the gains from international trade are widely spread. And the politics of international trade is becoming increasingly difficult as the extent of trade has grown.

ECONOMICS IN ACTION

WORLD VIEW

BEEFING UP EXPORTS

In December 2010, negotiators from the United States and South Korea reached final agreement on a free-trade deal that would phase out many of the tariffs and other restrictions on trade between the two nations. The deal also involved changes in a variety of business regulations that were expected to make it easier for U.S. companies to operate in South Korea. This was, literally, a fairly big deal: South Korea's economy is comparable in size to Mexico's, so this was the most important free-trade agreement that the United States had been party to since NAFTA. (As you'll recall, the North American Free Trade Agreement, or NAFTA, is an agreement signed in 1993 by the United States, Mexico, and Canada, that removes all barriers to trade among these three countries.)

Kyodo via AP Images

The 2010 trade agreement between South Korea and the United States was the most important free-trade deal since NAFTA.

What made this deal possible? Estimates by the U.S. International Trade Commission found that the deal would raise average American incomes, although modestly: the commission put the gains at around one-tenth of one percent. Not bad when you consider the fact that South Korea, despite its relatively large economy, is still only America's seventh-most-important trading partner.

These overall gains played little role in the politics of the deal, however, which hinged on losses and gains for particular U.S. constituencies. Some opposition to the deal came from labor, especially from autoworkers, who feared that eliminating the 8% U.S. tariff on imports of Korean automobiles would lead to job losses.

But there were also interest groups in America that badly wanted the deal, most notably the beef industry: Koreans are big beef-eaters, yet American access to that market was limited by a 38% Korean tariff.

And the Obama administration definitely wanted a deal, in part for reasons unrelated to economics: South Korea is an important U.S. ally, and military tensions with North Korea had been ratcheting up. So a trade deal was viewed in part as a symbol of U.S.–South Korean cooperation. Even labor unions weren't as opposed as they might have been.

It also helped that South Korea—unlike Mexico when NAFTA was signed—is both a fairly high-wage country and not right on the U.S. border, which meant less concern about massive shifts of manufacturing. In the end, the balance of interests was just favorable enough to make the deal politically possible.

MODULE 17 Review

Solutions appear at the back of the book.

Check Your Understanding

1. Suppose the world price of butter is $0.50 per pound and the domestic price in autarky is $1.00 per pound. Use a diagram similar to Figure 17-7 to show the following.
   a. If there is free trade, domestic butter producers want the government to impose a tariff of no less than $0.50 per pound.
   b. What happens if a tariff greater than $0.50 per pound is imposed?
2. Suppose the government imposes an import quota rather than a tariff on butter. What quota limit would generate the same quantity of imports as a tariff of $0.50 per pound?
3. Due to a strike by truckers, trade in food between the United States and Mexico is halted. In autarky, the price of Mexican grapes is lower than that of U.S. grapes. Using a diagram of the U.S. domestic demand curve and the U.S. domestic supply curve for grapes, explain the effect of these events on the following.
   a. U.S. grape consumers' surplus
   b. U.S. grape producers' surplus
   c. U.S. total surplus
4. What effect do you think the event described in question 3 will have on Mexican grape producers? Mexican grape pickers? Mexican grape consumers? U.S. grape pickers?

Multiple-Choice Questions

1. When a country imports a good,
   a. the domestic quantity supplied equals zero.
   b. the domestic quantity demanded equals zero.
   c. the domestic quantity demanded equals the quantity of imports.
   d. the domestic quantity demanded is greater than the domestic quantity supplied.
   e. the domestic quantity demanded is less than the domestic quantity supplied.
2. When a country exports a good,
   a. the domestic quantity supplied equals zero.
   b. the domestic quantity demanded equals zero.
   c. the domestic quantity supplied equals the quantity of exports.
   d. the domestic quantity demanded is greater than the domestic quantity supplied.
   e. the domestic quantity demanded is less than the domestic quantity supplied.
3. When a country opens up to trade and begins to export a particular good, the domestic quantity supplied of the good will ___________ and the wages of the workers who produce the good will ___________.
   a. increase; increase
   b. increase; decrease
   c. decrease; decrease
   d. decrease; increase
   e. remain unchanged; remain unchanged
4. If the world price is higher than the domestic autarky price, then when the economy opens up to trade, the country will become an ___________ of the good and the price in the domestic market will ___________.
   a. exporter; decrease
   b. importer; decrease
   c. importer; increase
   d. exporter; increase
   e. exporter; remain unchanged
5. A tariff or quota will increase deadweight loss because
   a. some mutually beneficial trades are unexploited.
   b. countries tend to focus on the most efficient production.
   c. countries are prevented from retaliating against each other.
   d. A and B are both correct.

Critical-Thinking Question

A few years ago, the United States imposed tariffs on steel imports, which are an input in a large number and variety of U.S. industries. Explain why political lobbying to eliminate these tariffs is more likely to be effective than political lobbying to eliminate tariffs on consumer goods such as sugar or clothing.

BUSINESS CASE: Li & Fung: From Guangzhou to You

Daniel J. Groshong/Bloomberg via Getty Images

It's a very good bet that as you read this, you're wearing something manufactured in Asia. And if you are, it's also a good bet that the Hong Kong company Li & Fung was involved in getting your garment designed, produced, and shipped to your local store. From Levi's to The Limited to Walmart, Li & Fung is a critical conduit from factories around the world to the shopping mall nearest you.

The company was founded in 1906 in Guangzhou, China. According to Victor Fung, the company's chairman, his grandfather's "value added" was that he spoke English, allowing him to serve as an interpreter in business deals between Chinese and foreigners. When Mao's Communist Party seized control in mainland China, the company moved to Hong Kong. There, as Hong Kong's market economy took off during the 1960s and 1970s, Li & Fung grew as an export broker, bringing together Hong Kong manufacturers and foreign buyers.

The real transformation of the company came, however, as Asian economies grew and changed. Hong Kong's rapid growth led to rising wages, making Li & Fung increasingly uncompetitive in garments, its main business. So the company reinvented itself: rather than being a simple broker, it became a "supply chain manager." Not only would it allocate production of a good to a manufacturer, it would also break production down, allocate production of the inputs, and then allocate final assembly of the good among its 12,000+ suppliers around the globe. Sometimes production would be done in sophisticated economies like those of Hong Kong or even Japan, where wages are high but so is quality and productivity; sometimes it would be done in less advanced locations like mainland China or Thailand, where labor is less productive but cheaper.

For example, suppose you own a U.S. retail chain and want to sell garment-washed blue jeans. Rather than simply arrange for production of the jeans, Li & Fung will work with you on their design, providing you with the latest production and style information, like what materials and colors are hot. After the design has been finalized, Li & Fung will arrange for the creation of a prototype, find the most cost-effective way to manufacture it, and then place an order on your behalf. Through Li & Fung, the yarn might be made in Korea and dyed in Taiwan, and the jeans sewn in Thailand or mainland China. And because production is taking place in so many locations, Li & Fung provides transport logistics as well as quality control.

Li & Fung has been enormously successful. In late 2013, the company had a market value of approximately $12.5 billion, with offices and distribution centers in more than 40 countries. Year after year, it continues to post sizeable profits.

Questions for Thought

1. Why do you think it was profitable for Li & Fung to go beyond brokering exports to becoming a supply chain manager, breaking down the production process and sourcing the inputs from various suppliers across many countries?
2. What principle do you think underlies Li & Fung's decisions on how to allocate production of a good's inputs and its final assembly among various countries?
3. Why do you think a retailer prefers to have Li & Fung arrange international production of its jeans rather than purchase them directly from a jeans manufacturer in mainland China?
4. What is the source of Li & Fung's success? Is it based on human capital, on ownership of a natural resource, or on ownership of capital?

SECTION 6 REVIEW

Summary

Gains from Trade

1. International trade is of growing importance to the United States and of even greater importance to most other countries. International trade, like trade among individuals, arises from comparative advantage: the opportunity cost of producing an additional unit of a good is lower in some countries than in others. Goods and services purchased abroad are **imports;** those sold abroad are **exports.** Foreign trade, like other economic linkages between countries, has been growing rapidly, a phenomenon called **globalization.**
2. There are gains from trade: two countries are better off with trade than in **autarky,** a situation in which a country does not trade with other countries.
3. In practice, comparative advantage reflects differences between countries in climate, factor endowments, and technology. The **Heckscher–Ohlin** model shows how differences in factor endowments determine comparative advantage: goods differ in **factor intensity,** and countries tend to export goods that are intensive in the factors they have in relative abundance.
4. The **domestic demand curve** and the **domestic supply curve** determine the price of a good in autarky. When international trade occurs, the domestic price is driven to equality with the **world price,** the price at which the good is bought and sold abroad.
5. If the world price is below the autarky price, a good is imported. This leads to an increase in consumer surplus, a fall in producer surplus, and a gain in total surplus. If the world price is above the autarky price, a good is exported. This leads to an increase in producer surplus, a fall in consumer surplus, and a gain in total surplus.

Supply, Demand, and International Trade

6. International trade leads to expansion in **exporting industries** and contraction in **import-competing industries.** This raises the domestic demand for abundant factors of production, reduces the demand for scarce factors, and so affects factor prices, such as wages.
7. Most economists advocate **free trade,** but in practice many governments engage in **trade protection.** The two most common forms of **protection** are tariffs and quotas. On rare occasions, export industries are subsidized.
8. A **tariff** is a tax levied on imports. It raises the domestic price above the world price, hurting consumers, benefiting domestic producers, and generating government revenue. As a result, total surplus falls. An **import quota** is a legal limit on the quantity of a good that can be imported. It has the same effects as a tariff, except that the revenue goes not to the government but to those who receive import licenses.
9. In the past few years, many concerns have been raised about the effects of globalization. One issue is the increase in income inequality due to the surge in imports from relatively poor countries over the past 20 years. Another is the increase in **offshore outsourcing,** as many jobs, once considered safe from foreign competition, have been moved abroad.

Key Terms

Problems

1. Assume Saudi Arabia and the United States face the production possibilities for oil and cars shown in the accompanying table.

   a. What is the opportunity cost of producing a car in Saudi Arabia? In the United States? What is the opportunity cost of producing a barrel of oil in Saudi Arabia? In the United States?

Saudi Arabia		United States	
Quantity of oil (millions of barrels)	Quantity of cars (millions)	Quantity of oil (millions of barrels)	Quantity of cars (millions)
0	4	0	10.0
200	3	100	7.5
400	2	200	5.0
600	1	300	2.5
800	0	400	0

b. Which country has the comparative advantage in producing oil? In producing cars?

c. Suppose that in autarky, Saudi Arabia produces 200 million barrels of oil and 3 million cars; similarly, that the United States produces 300 million barrels of oil and 2.5 million cars. Without trade, can Saudi Arabia produce more oil *and* more cars? Without trade, can the United States produce more oil *and* more cars?

2. The production possibilities for the United States and Saudi Arabia are given in Problem 1. Suppose now that each country specializes in the good in which it has the comparative advantage, and the two countries trade.

a. What is the total quantity of oil produced? What is the total quantity of cars produced?

b. Is it possible for Saudi Arabia to consume 400 million barrels of oil and 5 million cars and for the United States to consume 400 million barrels of oil and 5 million cars?

c. Suppose that, in fact, Saudi Arabia consumes 300 million barrels of oil and 4 million cars and the United States consumes 500 million barrels of oil and 6 million cars. How many barrels of oil does the United States import? How many cars does the United States export? Suppose a car costs $10,000 on the world market. How much, then, does a barrel of oil cost on the world market?

3. Both Canada and the United States produce lumber and music CDs with constant opportunity costs. The United States can produce either 10 tons of lumber and no CDs, or 1,000 CDs and no lumber, or any combination in between. Canada can produce either 8 tons of lumber and no CDs, or 400 CDs and no lumber, or any combination in between.

a. Draw the U.S. and Canadian production possibility curves in two separate diagrams, with CDs on the horizontal axis and lumber on the vertical axis.

b. In autarky, if the United States wants to consume 500 CDs, how much lumber can it consume at most? Label this point *A* in your diagram. Similarly, if Canada wants to consume 1 ton of lumber, how many CDs can it consume in autarky? Label this point *C* in your diagram.

c. Which country has the absolute advantage in lumber production?

d. Which country has the comparative advantage in lumber production?

Suppose each country specializes in the good in which it has the comparative advantage, and there is trade.

e. How many CDs does the United States produce? How much lumber does Canada produce?

f. Is it possible for the United States to consume 500 CDs and 7 tons of lumber? Label this point *B* in your diagram. Is it possible for Canada at the same time to consume 500 CDs and 1 ton of lumber? Label this point *D* in your diagram.

4. For each of the following trade relationships, explain the likely source of the comparative advantage of each of the exporting countries.

a. The United States exports software to Venezuela, and Venezuela exports oil to the United States.

b. The United States exports airplanes to China, and China exports clothing to the United States.

c. The United States exports wheat to Colombia, and Colombia exports coffee to the United States.

5. Shoes are labor-intensive and satellites are capital-intensive to produce. The United States has abundant capital. China has abundant labor. According to the Heckscher–Ohlin model, which good will China export? Which good will the United States export? In the United States, what will happen to the price of labor (the wage) and to the price of capital?

6. Before the North American Free Trade Agreement (NAFTA) gradually eliminated import tariffs on goods traded by the United States, Mexico, and Canada, the autarky price of tomatoes in Mexico was below the world price and in the United States was above the world price. Similarly, the autarky price of poultry in Mexico was above the world price and in the United States was below the world price. Draw diagrams with domestic supply and demand curves for each country and each of the two goods. As a result of NAFTA, the United States now imports tomatoes from Mexico and the United States now exports poultry to Mexico. How would you expect the following groups to be affected?

a. Mexican and U.S. consumers of tomatoes. Illustrate the effect on consumer surplus in your diagram.

b. Mexican and U.S. producers of tomatoes. Illustrate the effect on producer surplus in your diagram.

c. Mexican and U.S. tomato workers.

d. Mexican and U.S. consumers of poultry. Illustrate the effect on consumer surplus in your diagram.

e. Mexican and U.S. producers of poultry. Illustrate the effect on producer surplus in your diagram.

f. Mexican and U.S. poultry workers.

7. The accompanying table indicates the U.S. domestic demand schedule and domestic supply schedule for commercial jet airplanes. Suppose that the world price of a commercial jet airplane is $100 million.

Price of jet (millions)	Quantity of jets demanded	Quantity of jets supplied
$120	100	1,000
110	150	900
100	200	800
90	250	700
80	300	600
70	350	500
60	400	400
50	450	300
40	500	200

a. In autarky, how many commercial jet airplanes does the United States produce, and at what price are they bought and sold?

b. With trade, what will the price for commercial jet airplanes be? Will the United States import or export airplanes? How many?

8. The accompanying table shows the U.S. domestic demand schedule and domestic supply schedule for oranges. Suppose that the world price of oranges is $0.30 per orange.

Price of orange	Quantity of oranges demanded (thousands)	Quantity of oranges supplied (thousands)
$1.00	2	11
0.90	4	10
0.80	6	9
0.70	8	8
0.60	10	7
0.50	12	6
0.40	14	5
0.30	16	4
0.20	18	3

a. Draw the U.S. domestic supply curve and domestic demand curve.

b. With free trade, how many oranges will the United States import or export?

Suppose that the U.S. government imposes a tariff on oranges of $0.20 per orange.

c. How many oranges will the United States import or export after introduction of the tariff?

d. In your diagram, shade the gain or loss to the economy as a whole from the introduction of this tariff.

9. The U.S. domestic demand schedule and domestic supply schedule for oranges was given in Problem 8. Suppose that the world price of oranges is $0.30. The United States introduces an import quota of 3,000 oranges and assigns the quota rents to foreign orange exporters.

a. Draw the domestic demand and supply curves.

b. What will the domestic price of oranges be after introduction of the quota?

c. What is the value of the quota rents that foreign exporters of oranges receive?

10. The accompanying diagram illustrates the U.S. domestic demand curve and domestic supply curve for beef.

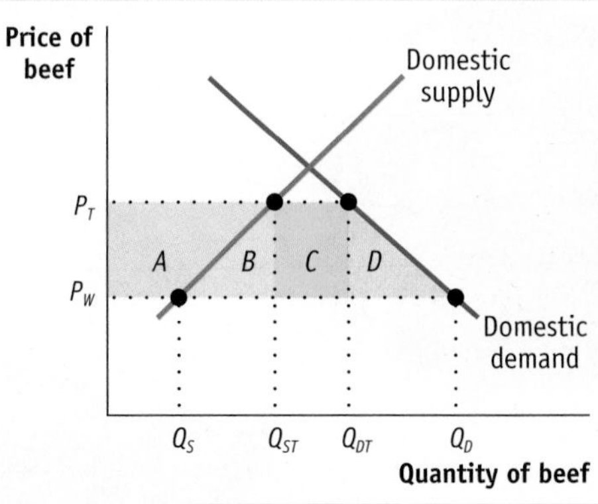

The world price of beef is P_W. The United States currently imposes an import tariff on beef, so the price of beef is P_T. Congress decides to eliminate the tariff. In terms of the areas marked in the diagram, answer the following questions.

a. What is the gain/loss in consumer surplus?

b. What is the gain/loss in producer surplus?

c. What is the gain/loss to the government?

d. What is the gain/loss to the economy as a whole?

11. As the United States has opened up to trade, it has lost many of its low-skill manufacturing jobs, but it has gained jobs in high-skill industries, such as the software industry. Explain whether the United States as a whole has been made better off by trade.

12. If a country agrees to reduce trade barriers (tariffs or quotas), is doing so a *concession* to other countries? Do you think that this terminology is appropriate?

13. Producers in import-competing industries often make the following argument: "Other countries have an advantage in production of certain goods purely because workers abroad are paid lower wages. In fact, American workers are much more productive than foreign workers. So import-competing industries need to be protected." Is this a valid argument? Explain your answer.

NORTH
This way
That

Module 18: Making Decisions
Module 19: Behavioral Economics
Module 20: Maximizing Utility

SECTION 7

Economics and Decision Making

GOING BACK TO SCHOOL

In the spring of 2010, Ashley Hildreth, a class of 2008 journalism major at the University of Oregon, was deeply frustrated. After working for 18 months in what she described as a "dead-end, part-time job" in the food industry, she decided to apply to a master's degree program in teaching.

In explaining her decision, she pointed to the many job applications she submitted without a single call back for an interview. What she hoped for was an entry-level opportunity in advertising and marketing or an administrative position with a nonprofit. What she got instead was silence or gentle rejections. After considering her options, she decided to apply for graduate school.

Hildreth was far from alone in her decision. In the spring of 2010, colleges and universities across the country were reporting a record number of applications for bachelor and associate degree programs. And as Hildreth's story illustrates, they also soared for graduate and continuing education programs.

Why did so many people make a similar choice in the spring of 2010? We'll answer that question shortly. Before we do, note that every year millions of people—just like you—face a choice about work versus continued schooling: should I continue another year (or semester, or quarter) in school, or should I get a job? That is, they are making a decision.

This section is about the economics of making decisions: how to make a decision that results in the best possible economic outcome. Economists have formulated principles of decision making that lead to the best possible—often called "optimal"—outcome, regardless of whether the decision maker is a consumer or a producer.

We start by examining three different types of economic decisions. For each of these types, there is a corresponding principle, or method, of decision making that leads to the best possible economic outcome. We'll also see why economists consider decision making to be the very essence of microeconomics.

Despite the fact that people *should* use the principles of economic decision making to achieve the best possible economic outcome, they sometimes fail to do so. In other words, people are not always rational when making decisions. For example, a shopper in pursuit of a bargain may knowingly spend more on gasoline than he or she saves. In this section, we'll learn about these tendencies when we discuss *behavioral economics,* the branch of economics that studies predictably irrational economic behavior.

The section concludes with a discussion of *utility,* a measure of satisfaction from consumption, and how individuals make consumption decisions when faced with a limited budget.

MODULE 18

Making Decisions

Vividpixel/Dreamstime

WHAT YOU WILL LEARN

1. Why good decision making begins with accurately understanding costs and benefits
2. The difference between accounting profit and economic profit, and why economic profit is the correct basis for decisions
3. That there are three different types of economic decisions: "either–or" decisions, "how much" decisions, and decisions involving sunk costs
4. The principles of decision making that correspond to each type of economic decision

Costs, Benefits, and Profits

In making any type of decision, it's critical to define the costs and benefits of that decision accurately. If you don't know the costs and benefits, it is nearly impossible to make a good decision. So that is where we begin.

An important first step is to recognize the role of *opportunity cost,* a concept we first encountered in Section 1, where we learned that opportunity costs arise because *resources are scarce*. Because resources are scarce, the true cost of anything is what you must give up to get it—its opportunity cost.

When making decisions, it is crucial to think in terms of opportunity cost, because the opportunity cost of an action is often considerably more than the cost of any outlays of money. Economists use the concepts of *explicit costs* and *implicit costs* to compare the relationship between monetary outlays and opportunity costs. We'll discuss these two concepts first. Then we'll define the concepts of *accounting profit* and *economic profit,* which are *ways of measuring whether the benefit of an action is greater than the cost.* Armed with these concepts for assessing costs and benefits, we will be in a position to consider three principles of economic decision making.

Explicit versus Implicit Costs

Suppose that, after graduating from college, you have two options: to go to school for an additional year to get an advanced degree or to take a job immediately. You would like to enroll in the extra year in school but are concerned about the cost.

What exactly is the cost of that additional year of school? Here is where it is important to remember the concept of opportunity cost: the cost of the year spent getting an advanced degree includes what you forgo by not taking a job for that year. The opportunity cost of an additional year of school, like any cost, can be broken into two parts: the *explicit* cost of the year's schooling and the *implicit* cost.

An **explicit cost** is a cost that requires an outlay of money. For example, the explicit cost of the additional year of schooling includes tuition. An **implicit cost,** though, does not involve an outlay of money; instead, it is measured by the value, in dollar terms, of the benefits that are forgone. For example, the implicit cost of the year spent in school includes the income you would have earned if you had taken a job instead.

An **explicit cost** is a cost that requires an outlay of money.

An **implicit cost** does not require an outlay of money; it is measured by the value, in dollar terms, of benefits that are forgone.

Accounting profit is equal to revenue minus explicit cost.

A common mistake, both in economic analysis and in life—whether individual or business—is to ignore implicit costs and focus exclusively on explicit costs. But often the implicit cost of an activity is quite substantial—indeed, sometimes it is much larger than the explicit cost.

Table 18-1 gives a breakdown of hypothetical explicit and implicit costs associated with spending an additional year in school instead of taking a job. The explicit cost consists of tuition, books, supplies, and a computer for doing assignments—all of which require you to spend money. The implicit cost is the salary you would have earned if you had taken a job instead. As you can see, the total cost of attending an additional year of schooling is $44,500, the sum of the total implicit cost—$35,000 in forgone salary, and the total explicit cost—$9,500 in outlays on tuition, supplies, and computer. Because the implicit cost is more than three times as much as the explicit cost, ignoring the implicit cost would lead to a seriously misguided decision.

TABLE 18-1

Opportunity Cost of an Additional Year of School

Explicit cost		Implicit cost	
Tuition	$7,000	Forgone salary	$35,000
Books and supplies	1,000		
Computer	1,500		
Total explicit cost	**9,500**	**Total implicit cost**	**35,000**
Total opportunity cost = Total explicit cost + Total implicit cost = $44,500			

A slightly different way of looking at the implicit cost in this example can deepen our understanding of opportunity cost. The forgone salary is the cost of using your own resources—your time—in going to school rather than working. The use of your time for more schooling, despite the fact that you don't have to spend any money on it, is still costly to you. This illustrates an important aspect of opportunity cost: in considering the cost of an activity, you should include the cost of using any of your own resources for that activity. You can calculate the cost of using your own resources by determining what they would have earned in their next best use.

Accounting Profit versus Economic Profit

Let's return to Ashley Hildreth. Assume that Ashley faces the choice of either completing a two-year full-time graduate program in teaching or spending those two years working in her original field of advertising. We'll also assume that in order to be certified as a teacher, she must complete the entire two years of the graduate program. Which choice should she make?

To get started, let's consider what Ashley gains by getting the teaching degree—what we might call her *revenue* from the teaching degree. Once she has completed her degree two years from now, she will receive earnings from her degree valued at $600,000 over the rest of her lifetime. In contrast, if she doesn't get the degree and stays in advertising, two years from now her future lifetime earnings will be valued at $500,000. The cost of the tuition for her teaching degree program is $40,000, which she pays for with a student loan that costs her $4,000 in interest.

At this point, what she should do might seem obvious: if she chooses the teaching degree, she gets a lifetime increase in the value of her earnings of $600,000 – $500,000 = $100,000, and she pays $40,000 in tuition plus $4,000 in interest. Doesn't that mean she makes a profit of $100,000 – $40,000 – $4,000 = $56,000 by getting her teaching degree? This $56,000 is Ashley's **accounting profit** from obtaining her teaching degree: her revenue minus her explicit cost. In this example her explicit cost of getting the degree is $44,000, the amount of her tuition plus student loan interest.

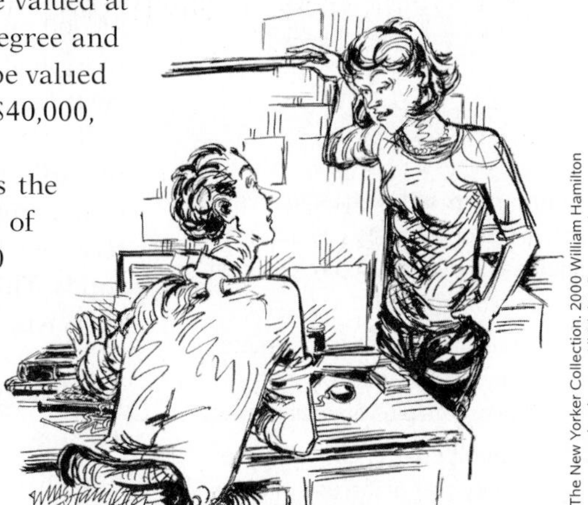

"I've done the numbers, and I will marry you."

Although accounting profit is a useful measure, it would be misleading for Ashley to use it alone in making her decision. To make the right decision, the one that leads to the best possible economic outcome for her, she needs to calculate her **economic profit**—the revenue she receives from the teaching degree minus her opportunity cost of staying in school (which is equal to her explicit cost *plus* her implicit cost). In general, the economic profit of a given project will be less than the accounting profit because there are almost always implicit costs in addition to explicit costs.

When economists use the term *profit,* they are referring to *economic* profit, not *accounting* profit. This will be our convention in the rest of the book: when we use the term *profit,* we mean economic profit.

How does Ashley's economic profit from staying in school differ from her accounting profit? We've already encountered one source of the difference: her two years of forgone job earnings. This is an implicit cost of going to school full time for two years. We assume that Ashley's total forgone earnings for the two years is $57,000.

TABLE 18-2

Ashley's Economic Profit from Acquiring a Teaching Degree

Value of increase in lifetime earnings	$100,000
Explicit cost:	
Tuition	–40,000
Interest paid on student loan	– 4,000
Accounting Profit	**56,000**
Implicit cost:	
Income forgone during 2 years spent in school	–57,000
Economic Profit	**–1,000**

Once we factor in implicit costs and calculate her economic profit, we see that she is better off not getting a teaching degree. You can see this in Table 18-2: her economic profit from getting the teaching degree is –$1,000. In other words, she incurs an *economic loss* of $1,000 if she gets the degree. Clearly, she is better off sticking to advertising and going to work now.

To make sure that the concepts of opportunity costs and economic profit are well understood, let's consider a slightly different scenario. Let's suppose that Ashley does not have to take out $40,000 in student loans to pay her tuition. Instead, she can pay for it with an inheritance from her grandmother. As a result, she doesn't have to pay $4,000 in interest. In this case, her accounting profit is $60,000 rather than $56,000. Would the right decision now be for her to get the teaching degree? Wouldn't the economic profit of the degree now be $60,000 – $57,000 = $3,000?

The answer is no, because Ashley is using her own *capital* to finance her education, and the use of that capital has an opportunity cost even when she owns it. **Capital** is the total value of the assets of an individual or a firm. An individual's capital usually consists of cash in the bank, stocks, bonds, and the ownership value of real estate such as a house. In the case of a business, capital also includes its equipment, its tools, and its inventory of unsold goods and used parts. (Economists like to distinguish between *financial assets,* such as cash, stocks, and bonds, and *physical assets,* such as buildings, equipment, tools, and inventory.)

The point is that even if Ashley owns the $40,000, using it to pay tuition incurs an opportunity cost—what she forgoes in the next best use of that $40,000. If she hadn't used the money to pay her tuition, her next best use of the money would have been to deposit it in a bank to earn interest. To keep things simple, let's assume that she earns $4,000 on that $40,000 once it is deposited in a bank. Now, rather than pay $4,000 in explicit costs in the form of student loan interest, Ashley incurs $4,000 in implicit costs from the forgone interest she could have earned.

This $4,000 in forgone interest earnings is what economists call the **implicit cost of capital**—the income the owner of the capital could have earned if the capital had been employed in its next best alternative use. The net effect is that it makes no difference whether Ashley finances her tuition with a student loan or by using her own funds. This comparison reinforces how carefully you must keep track of opportunity costs when making a decision.

Economic profit is equal to revenue minus the opportunity cost of resources used. It is usually less than the accounting profit.

Capital is the total value of assets owned by an individual or firm—physical assets plus financial assets.

The **implicit cost of capital** is the opportunity cost of the use of one's own capital—the income earned if the capital had been employed in its next best alternative use.

Making "Either–Or" Decisions

An "either–or" decision is one in which you must choose between two activities. That's in contrast to a "how much" decision, which requires you to choose how much of a given activity to undertake. For example, Ashley faced an "either–or" decision: to spend two years in graduate school to obtain a teaching degree, or to work. In contrast, a "how much" decision would be deciding how many hours to study or how many hours to work at a job. Table 18-3 contrasts a variety of "either–or" and "how much" decisions.

In making economic decisions, as we have already emphasized, it is vitally important to calculate opportunity costs correctly. The best way to make an "either–or" decision, the method that leads to the best possible economic outcome, is the straightforward **principle of "either–or" decision making.** According to this principle, *when making an "either–or" choice between two activities, choose the one with the positive economic profit.*

TABLE 18-3

"How Much" versus "Either–Or" Decisions

"Either–or" decisions	"How much" decisions
Do the laundry with Tide or Cheer?	How many days before you do your laundry?
Buy a car or not?	How many miles do you go before an oil change in your car?
An order of nachos or a sandwich?	How many jalapeños on your nachos?
Run your own business or work for someone else?	How many workers should you hire in your company?
Prescribe drug A or drug B for your patients?	How much should a patient take of a drug that generates side effects?
Graduate school or not?	How many hours to study?

Let's examine Ashley's dilemma from a different angle to understand how this principle works. If she continues with advertising and goes to work immediately, the total value of her lifetime earnings is \$57,000 (her earnings over the next two years) + \$500,000 (the value of her lifetime earnings thereafter) = \$557,000. If she gets her teaching degree instead and works as a teacher, the total value of her lifetime earnings is \$600,000 (value of her lifetime earnings after two years in school) – \$40,000 (tuition) – \$4,000 (interest payments) = \$556,000. The economic profit from continuing in advertising versus becoming a teacher is \$557,000 – \$556,000 = \$1,000.

So the right choice for Ashley is to begin work in advertising immediately, which gives her an economic profit of \$1,000, rather than become a teacher, which would give her an economic profit of –\$1,000. In other words, by becoming a teacher she loses the \$1,000 economic profit she would have gained by working in advertising immediately.

In making "either–or" decisions, mistakes most commonly arise when people or businesses use their own assets in projects rather than rent or borrow assets. That's because they fail to account for the implicit cost of using self-owned capital. In contrast, when they rent or borrow assets, these rental or borrowing costs show up as explicit costs. If, for example, a restaurant owns its equipment and tools, it would have to compute its implicit cost of capital by calculating how much the equipment could be sold for and how much could be earned by using those funds in the next best alternative project. In addition, businesses run by the owner (an *entrepreneur)* often fail to calculate the opportunity cost of the owner's time in running the business. In that way, small businesses often underestimate their opportunity costs and overestimate their economic profit of staying in business.

Making "How Much" Decisions: The Role of Marginal Analysis

Although many decisions in economics are "either–or," many others are "how much." Not many people will give up their cars if the price of gasoline goes up, but many people will drive less. How much less? A rise in corn prices won't necessarily persuade a lot of people to take up farming for the first time, but it will persuade farmers who are already growing corn to plant more. How much more?

To understand "how much" decisions, we will use an approach known as **marginal analysis.** Marginal analysis involves comparing the benefit of doing a little bit more of some activity with the cost of doing a little bit more of that activity. The benefit of doing a little bit more of something is what economists call its *marginal benefit*, and the cost of doing a little bit more of something is its *marginal cost*.

Why is this called "marginal" analysis? A margin is an edge; what you do in marginal analysis is push out the edge a bit and see whether that is a good move. We will study marginal analysis by considering a hypothetical decision of how many years of school to complete. We'll consider the case of Alex, who studies computer

According to the **principle of "either–or" decision making,** when faced with an "either–or" choice between two activities, choose the one with the positive economic profit.

Marginal analysis involves comparing the benefit of doing a little bit more of some activity with the cost of doing a little bit more of that activity.

Wavebreakmedia/Shutterstock

To make his decision, Alex will need to compare the benefit of additional years of schooling with the cost of spending more time in school.

programming and design. Since there are many computer languages, app design methods, and graphics programs that can be learned one year at a time, each year Alex can decide whether to continue his studies or not.

Unlike Ashley, who faced an "either–or" decision of whether to get a teaching degree, Alex faces a "how much" decision of how many years to study computer programming and design. For example, he could study one more year, or five more years, or any number of years in between. We'll begin our analysis of Alex's decision problem by defining Alex's *marginal cost* of another year of study.

Marginal Cost

We'll assume that each additional year of schooling costs Alex $10,000 in explicit costs—tuition, interest on a student loan, and so on. In addition to the explicit costs, he also has implicit costs—the income forgone by spending one more year in school. Unlike Alex's explicit costs, which are constant (that is, the same each year), Alex's implicit cost changes each year. That's because each year he spends in school leaves him better trained than the year before; and the better trained he is, the higher the salary he can command. Consequently, the income he forgoes by not working rises each additional year he stays in school.

Table 18-4 contains the data on how Alex's cost of an additional year of schooling changes as he completes more years. The second column shows how his total cost of schooling changes as the number of years he has completed increases. For example, Alex's first year has a total cost of $30,000: $10,000 in explicit costs of tuition and the like as well as $20,000 in forgone salary.

TABLE 18-4

Alex's Marginal Cost of Additional Years in School

Quantity of schooling (years)	Total cost	Marginal cost
0	$0	
		$30,000
1	30,000	
		40,000
2	70,000	
		60,000
3	130,000	
		90,000
4	220,000	
		130,000
5	350,000	

The second column also shows that the total cost of attending two years is $70,000: $30,000 for his first year plus $40,000 for his second year. During his second year in school, his explicit costs have stayed the same ($10,000) but his implicit cost of forgone salary has gone up to $30,000. That's because he's a more valuable worker with one year of schooling under his belt than with no schooling. Likewise, the total cost of three years of schooling is $130,000: $30,000 in explicit cost for three years of tuition (at $10,000 per year), plus $100,000 in implicit cost of three years of forgone salary. The total cost of attending four years is $220,000, and $350,000 for five years.

The change in Alex's total cost of schooling when he goes to school an additional year is his *marginal cost* of the one-year increase in years of schooling. In general, the **marginal cost** of producing a good or service (in this case, producing one's own education) is the additional cost incurred by producing one more unit of that good or service. The arrows, which zigzag between the total costs in the second column and the marginal costs in the third column, are there to help you to see how marginal cost is calculated from total cost, and vice versa.

The **marginal cost** of producing a good or service is the additional cost incurred by producing one more unit of that good or service.

Production of a good or service has **increasing marginal cost** when each additional unit costs more to produce than the previous one.

The **marginal cost curve** shows how the cost of producing one more unit depends on the quantity that has already been produced.

Production of a good or service has **constant marginal cost** when each additional unit costs the same to produce as the previous one.

Alex's marginal costs of more years of schooling have a clear pattern: they are increasing. They go from $30,000, to $40,000, to $60,000, to $90,000, and finally to $130,000 for the fifth year of schooling. That's because each year of schooling would make Alex a more valuable and highly paid employee if he were to work. As a result, forgoing a job becomes more and more costly as he becomes more educated. This is an example of what economists call **increasing marginal cost,** which occurs when each unit of a good costs more to produce than the previous unit.

Figure 18-1 shows a **marginal cost curve,** a graphic representation of Alex's marginal costs. The height of each shaded bar corresponds to the marginal cost of a given year of schooling. The red line connecting the dots at the midpoint of the top of each bar is Alex's marginal cost curve. Alex has an upward-sloping marginal cost curve because he has increasing marginal cost of additional years of schooling.

Although increasing marginal cost is a frequent phenomenon in real life, it's not the only possibility. **Constant marginal cost** occurs when the cost of producing an

FIGURE 18-1 Marginal Cost

The height of each shaded bar corresponds to Alex's marginal cost of an additional year of schooling. The height of each bar is higher than the preceding one because each year of schooling costs more than the previous years. As a result, Alex has increasing marginal cost and the marginal cost curve, the line connecting the midpoints at the top of each bar, is upward sloping.

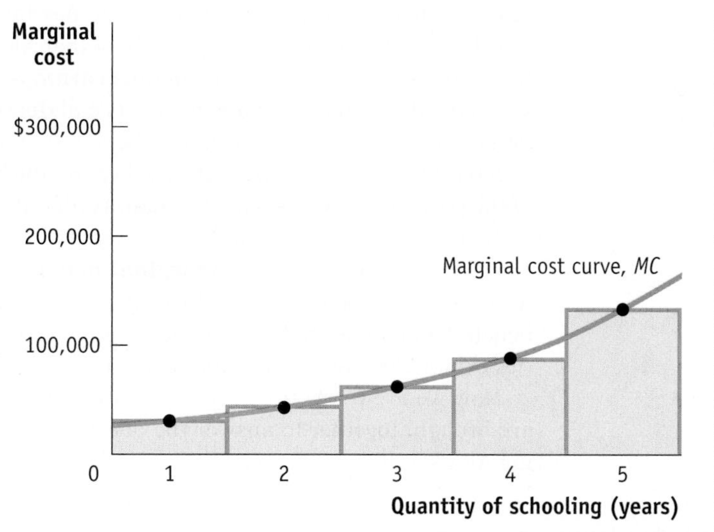

additional unit is the same as the cost of producing the previous unit. Plant nurseries, for example, typically have constant marginal cost—the cost of growing one more plant is the same, regardless of how many plants have already been produced. With constant marginal cost, the marginal cost curve is a horizontal line.

There can also be **decreasing marginal cost,** which occurs when marginal cost falls as the number of units produced increases. With decreasing marginal cost, the marginal cost line is downward sloping. Decreasing marginal cost is often due to *learning effects* in production: for complicated tasks, such as assembling a new model of a car, workers are often slow and mistake-prone when assembling the earliest units, making for higher marginal cost on those units. But as workers gain experience, assembly time and the rate of mistakes fall, generating lower marginal cost for later units. As a result, overall production has decreasing marginal cost.

Finally, for the production of some goods and services the shape of the marginal cost curve changes as the number of units produced increases. For example, auto production is likely to have decreasing marginal costs for the first batch of cars produced as workers iron out kinks and mistakes in production. Then production has constant marginal costs for the next batch of cars as workers settle into a predictable pace. But at some point, as workers produce more and more cars, marginal cost begins to increase as they run out of factory floor space and the auto company incurs costly overtime wages. This gives rise to what we call a "swoosh"-shaped marginal cost curve—a topic we will discuss in more detail in the next section. For now, we'll stick to the simpler example of an increasing marginal cost curve.

Production of a good or service has **decreasing marginal cost** when each additional unit costs less to produce than the previous one.

The **marginal benefit** of a good or service is the additional benefit derived from producing one more unit of that good or service.

Marginal Benefit

Alex benefits from higher lifetime earnings as he completes more years of school. Exactly how much he benefits is shown in Table 18-5. Column 2 shows Alex's total benefit according to the number of years of school completed, expressed as the value of the increase in lifetime earnings. The third column shows Alex's *marginal benefit* from an additional year of schooling. In general, the **marginal benefit** of producing a good or service is the additional benefit earned from producing one more unit.

As in Table 18-4, the data in the third column of Table 18-5 show a clear pattern. However, this time the numbers are decreasing rather than increasing. The first year of schooling gives

TABLE 18-5

Alex's Marginal Benefit of Additional Years in School

Quantity of schooling (years)	Total benefit	Marginal benefit
0	$0	
		$300,000
1	300,000	
		150,000
2	450,000	
		90,000
3	540,000	
		60,000
4	600,000	
		50,000
5	650,000	

Alex a $300,000 increase in the value of his lifetime earnings. The second year also gives him a positive return, but the size of that return has fallen to $150,000; the third year's return is also positive, but its size has fallen yet again to $90,000; and so on. In other words, the more years of school that Alex has already completed, the smaller the increase in the value of his lifetime earnings from attending one more year. Alex's schooling decision has what economists call **decreasing marginal benefit:** each additional year of school yields a smaller benefit than the previous year. Or, to put it slightly differently, with decreasing marginal benefit, the benefit from producing one more unit of the good or service falls as the quantity already produced rises.

Just as marginal cost can be represented by a marginal cost curve, marginal benefit can be represented by a **marginal benefit curve,** shown in blue in Figure 18-2. Alex's marginal benefit curve slopes downward because he faces decreasing marginal benefit from additional years of schooling. Note, however that not all goods or activities exhibit decreasing marginal benefit.

Now we are ready to see how the concepts of marginal benefit and marginal cost are brought together to answer the question of how many years of additional schooling Alex should undertake.

FIGURE 18-2 Marginal Benefit

The height of each shaded bar corresponds to Alex's marginal benefit of an additional year of schooling. The height of each bar is lower than the one preceding it because an additional year of schooling has decreasing marginal benefit. As a result, Alex's marginal benefit curve, the curve connecting the midpoints at the top of each bar, is downward sloping.

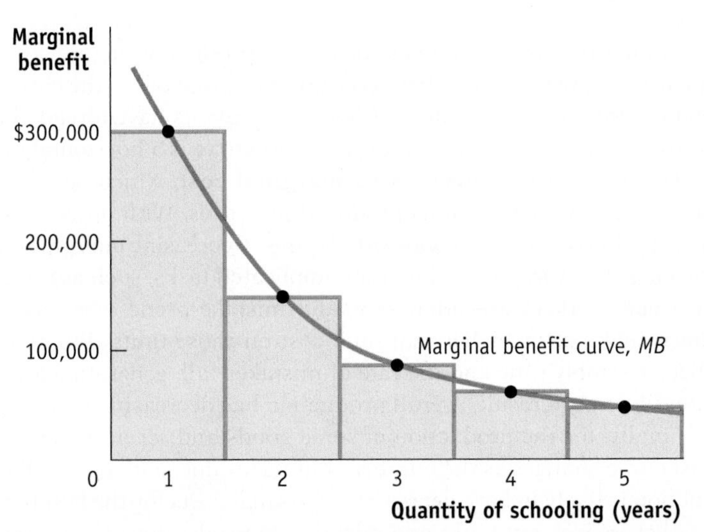

Marginal Analysis

Table 18-6 shows the marginal cost and marginal benefit numbers from Tables 18-4 and 18-5. It also adds an another column: the additional profit to Alex from staying in school one more year, equal to the difference between the marginal benefit and the marginal cost of that additional year in school. (Remember that it is Alex's economic profit that we care about, not his accounting profit.) We can now use Table 18-6 to determine how many additional years of schooling Alex should undertake in order to maximize his total profit.

There is **decreasing marginal benefit** from an activity when each additional unit of the activity yields less benefit than the previous unit.

The **marginal benefit curve** shows how the benefit from producing one more unit depends on the quantity that has already been produced.

First, imagine that Alex chooses not to attend any additional years of school. We can see from column 4 that this is a mistake if Alex wants to achieve the highest total profit from his schooling—the sum of the additional profits generated by another year of schooling. If he attends one additional year of school, he increases the value of his lifetime earnings by $270,000, the profit from the first additional year attended.

Now, let's consider whether Alex should attend the second year of school. The additional profit from the second year is $110,000, so Alex should attend the second year as well. What about the third year? The additional profit from that year is $30,000; so, yes, Alex should attend the third year as well. What about a fourth year? In this case, the additional profit is negative: it is –$30,000. Clearly, Alex is worse off by attending the fourth additional year rather than taking a job. And the same is true for the fifth year as well: it has a negative additional profit of –$80,000.

TABLE 18-6

Alex's Profit from Additional Years of Schooling

Quantity of schooling (years)	Marginal benefit	Marginal cost	Additional profit
0			
	$300,000	$30,000	$270,000
1			
	150,000	40,000	110,000
2			
	90,000	60,000	30,000
3			
	60,000	90,000	–30,000
4			
	50,000	130,000	–80,000
5			

What have we learned? That Alex should attend three additional years of school and stop at that point. Although the first, second, and third years of additional schooling increase the value of his lifetime earnings, the fourth and fifth years diminish it. So three years of additional schooling lead to the quantity that generates the maximum possible total profit. It is what economists call the **optimal quantity**—the quantity that generates the maximum possible total profit.

Figure 18-3 shows how the optimal quantity can be determined graphically. Alex's marginal benefit and marginal cost curves are shown together. If Alex chooses fewer than three additional years (that is, years 0, 1, or 2), he will choose a level of schooling at which his marginal benefit curve lies *above* his marginal cost curve. He can make himself better off by staying in school. If instead he chooses more than three additional years (years 4 or 5), he will choose a level of schooling at which his marginal benefit curve lies *below* his marginal cost curve. He can make himself better off by not attending the additional year of school and taking a job instead.

The table in Figure 18-3 confirms our result. The second column repeats information from Table 18-6, showing Alex's marginal benefit minus marginal cost—the additional profit per additional year of schooling. The third column shows Alex's total

The **optimal quantity** is the quantity that generates the highest possible total profit.

FIGURE 18-3 Alex's Optimal Quantity of Years of Schooling

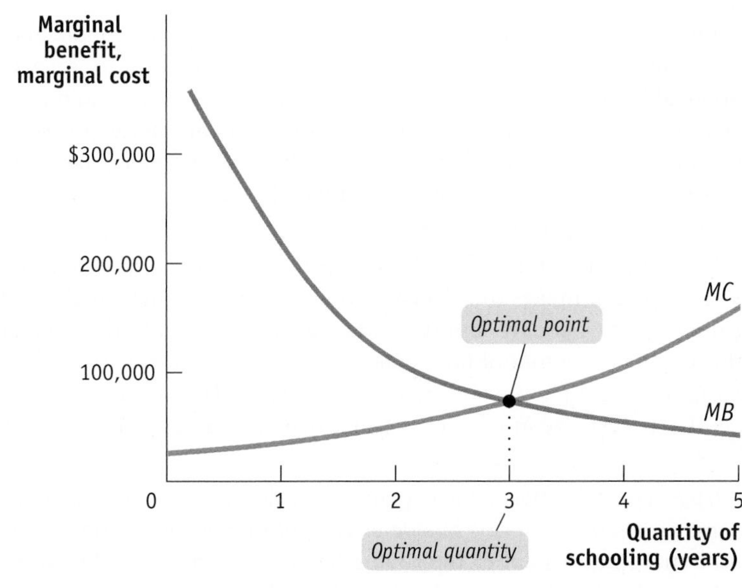

Quantity of schooling (years)	Additional profit	Total profit
0		$0
	$270,000	
1		270,000
	110,000	
2		380,000
	30,000	
3		410,000
	–30,000	
4		380,000
	–80,000	
5		300,000

The optimal quantity is the quantity that generates the highest possible total profit. It is the quantity at which marginal benefit is greater than or equal to marginal cost. Equivalently, it is the quantity at which the marginal benefit and marginal cost curves intersect. Here, they intersect at 3 additional years of schooling. The table confirms that 3 is indeed the optimal quantity: it leads to the maximum total profit of $410,000.

profit for different years of schooling. The total profit, for each possible year of schooling is simply the sum of numbers in the second column up to and including that year. For example, Alex's profit from additional years of schooling is $270,000 for the first year and $110,000 for the second year. So the total profit for two additional years of schooling is $270,000 + $110,000 = $380,000. Similarly, the total profit for three additional years is $270,000 + $110,000 + $30,000 = $410,000. Our claim that three years is the optimal quantity for Alex is confirmed by the data in the table in Figure 18-3: at three years of additional schooling, Alex reaps the greatest total profit, $410,000.

Alex's decision problem illustrates how you go about finding the optimal quantity when the choice involves a small number of quantities. (In this example, one through five years.) With small quantities, the rule for choosing the optimal quantity is: *increase the quantity as long as the marginal benefit from one more unit is greater than the marginal cost, but stop before the marginal benefit becomes less than the marginal cost.*

Purestock/Thinkstock

How many years of schooling will maximize your total profit?

In contrast, when a "how much" decision involves relatively large quantities, the rule for choosing the optimal quantity simplifies to this: *The optimal quantity is the quantity at which marginal benefit is equal to marginal cost.*

With very large quantities, increasing output by one unit will produce very small changes in marginal benefit and marginal cost. To see why this is so, consider the example of a farmer who finds that her optimal quantity of wheat produced is 5,000 bushels. Typically, she will find that in going from 4,999 to 5,000 bushels, her marginal benefit is only very slightly greater than her marginal cost—that is, the difference between marginal benefit and marginal cost is close to zero. Similarly, in going from 5,000 to 5,001 bushels, her marginal cost is only very slightly greater than her marginal benefit—again, the difference between marginal cost and marginal benefit is very close to zero. So a simple rule in choosing the optimal quantity is to produce the quantity at which the difference between marginal benefit and marginal cost is approximately zero—that is, the quantity at which marginal benefit equals marginal cost.

Now we are ready to state the general rule for choosing the optimal quantity—one that applies for decisions involving either small quantities or large quantities. This general rule is known as the **profit-maximizing principle of marginal analysis:** *When making a profit-maximizing "how much" decision, the optimal quantity is the largest quantity at which marginal benefit is greater than or equal to marginal cost.*

The profit-maximizing principle of marginal analysis can be applied to just about any "how much" decision in which you want to maximize the total profit for an activity. It is equally applicable to production decisions, consumption decisions, and policy decisions. Furthermore, decisions where the benefits and costs are not expressed in dollars and cents can also be made using marginal analysis, as long as benefits and costs can be measured in some type of common units. Here are a few examples of decisions that are suitable for marginal analysis:

- A producer, the retailer PalMart, must decide on the size of the new store it is constructing in Beijing. It makes this decision by comparing the marginal benefit of enlarging the store by 1 square foot (the value of the additional sales it makes from that additional square foot of floor space) to the marginal cost (the cost of constructing and maintaining the additional square foot). The optimal store size for PalMart is the largest size at which marginal benefit is greater than or equal to marginal cost.
- Many useful drugs have side effects that depend on the dosage. So a physician must consider the marginal cost, in terms of side effects, of increasing the dosage of a drug versus the marginal benefit of improving health by increasing the dosage. The optimal dosage level is the largest level at which the marginal benefit of disease amelioration is greater than or equal to the marginal cost of side effects.
- A farmer must decide how much fertilizer to apply. More fertilizer increases crop yield but also costs more. The optimal amount of fertilizer is the largest quantity at which the marginal benefit of higher crop yield is greater than or equal to the marginal cost of purchasing and applying more fertilizer.

According to the **profit-maximizing principle of marginal analysis,** when faced with a profit-maximizing "how much" decision, the optimal quantity is the largest quantity at which marginal benefit is greater than or equal to marginal cost.

ECONOMICS ▶ IN ACTION WORLD VIEW

THE COST OF A LIFE

What's the marginal benefit to society of saving a human life? You might be tempted to answer that human life is infinitely precious. If in the real world resources are scarce, then we must decide how much to spend on saving lives since we cannot spend infinite amounts. After all, we could surely reduce highway deaths by dropping the speed limit on interstates to 40 miles per hour, but the cost of such a lower speed limit—in time and money—is more than most people are willing to pay.

Generally, people are reluctant to talk in a straightforward way about comparing the marginal cost of a life saved with the marginal benefit—it sounds too callous. Sometimes, however, the question becomes unavoidable.

For example, the cost of saving a life became an object of intense discussion in the United Kingdom after a horrible train crash near London's Paddington Station killed 31 people. There were accusations that the British government was spending too little on rail safety. However, the government estimated that improving rail safety would cost an additional $4.5 million per life saved.

But if that amount were worth spending—that is, if the estimated marginal benefit of saving a life exceeded $4.5 million—then the implication was that the British government was spending far too little on traffic safety. In contrast, the estimated marginal cost per life saved through highway improvements was only $1.5 million, making it a much better deal than saving lives through greater rail safety.

Sunk Costs

When making decisions, knowing what to ignore can be as important as what to include. Although we have devoted much attention in this module to costs that are important to take into account when making a decision, some costs should be ignored when doing so. Let's now look at the kinds of costs that people should ignore when making decisions—what economists call *sunk costs*—and why they should be ignored.

Daniel Grill/Getty Images

The $250 you already spent on brake pads is irrelevant because it is a sunk cost.

To gain some intuition, consider the following scenario. You own a car that is a few years old, and you have just replaced the brake pads at a cost of $250. But then you find out that the entire brake system is defective and also must be replaced. This will cost you an additional $1,500. Alternatively, you could sell the car and buy another of comparable quality, but with no brake defects, by spending an additional $1,600. What should you do: fix your old car, or sell it and buy another?

Some might say that you should take the latter option. After all, this line of reasoning goes, if you repair your car, you will end up having spent $1,750: $1,500 for the brake system and $250 for the brake pads. If instead you sell your old car and buy another, you would spend only $1,600.

But this reasoning, although it sounds plausible, is wrong. It is wrong because it ignores the fact that you have *already* spent $250 on brake pads, and that $250 cannot be recovered. Therefore, it should be ignored and should have no effect on your decision whether or not to repair your car and keep it. From a rational viewpoint, the real cost at this time of repairing and keeping your car is $1,500, not $1,750. So the correct decision is to repair your car and keep it rather than spend $1,600 on a new car.

In this example, the $250 that has already been spent and cannot be recovered is what economists call a **sunk cost.** Sunk costs should be ignored in making decisions about future actions because they have no influence on their actual costs and benefits. It's like the old saying, "There's no use crying over spilled milk": once something can't be recovered, it is irrelevant in making decisions about what to do in the future.

A **sunk cost** is a cost that has already been incurred and is nonrecoverable. A sunk cost should be ignored in decisions about future actions.

It is often psychologically hard to ignore sunk costs. And if, in fact, you haven't yet incurred the costs, then you should take them into consideration. That is, if you had known at the beginning that it would cost $1,750 to repair your car, then the right choice at that time would have been to replace the car for $1,600. But once you have already paid the $250 for brake pads, you should no longer include it in your decision making about your next actions. It may be hard to accept that "bygones are bygones," but it is the right way to make a decision.

MODULE 18 Review

Solutions appear at the back of the book.

Check Your Understanding

1. Karma and Don run a furniture-refinishing business from their home. Which of the following represent an explicit cost of the business and which represent an implicit cost?
   - **a.** Supplies such as paint stripper, varnish, polish, sandpaper, and so on
   - **b.** Basement space that has been converted into a workroom
   - **c.** Wages paid to a part-time helper
   - **d.** A van that they inherited and use only for transporting furniture
   - **e.** The job at a larger furniture restorer that Karma gave up in order to run the business
2. Ashley Hildreth faced the choice of either completing a two-year graduate program in teaching or working at a job in advertising. Assume that she has a third alternative to consider: entering a two-year apprenticeship program for skilled machinists that would, upon completion, make her a licensed machinist. During the apprenticeship, she earns a reduced salary of $15,000 per year. At the end of the apprenticeship, the value of her lifetime earnings is $725,000. What is Ashley's best career choice?
3. Suppose you have three alternatives—A, B, and C—and you can undertake only one of them. In comparing A versus B, you find that B has an economic profit and A yields an economic loss. But in comparing A versus C, you find that C has an economic profit and A yields an economic loss. How do you decide what to do?
4. For each of the "how much" decisions listed in Table 18-3, describe the nature of the marginal cost and of the marginal benefit.
5. Suppose that Alex's school charges a fixed fee of $70,000 for four years of schooling. If Alex drops out before he finishes those four years, he still has to pay the $70,000. Alex's total cost for different years of schooling is now given by the data in the accompanying table. Assume that Alex's total benefit and marginal benefit remain as reported in Table 18-5.

   Use this information to calculate (i) Alex's new marginal cost, (ii) his new profit, and (iii) his new optimal years of schooling. What kind of marginal cost does Alex now have—constant, increasing, or decreasing?

Quantity of schooling (years)	Total cost
0	$0
1	90,000
2	120,000
3	170,000
4	250,000
5	370,000

6. You have decided to go into the ice-cream business and have bought a used ice-cream truck for $8,000. Now you are reconsidering. What is your sunk cost in the following scenarios?
   - **a.** The truck cannot be resold.
   - **b.** The truck can be resold, but only at a 50% discount.
7. You have gone through two years of medical school but are suddenly wondering whether you wouldn't be happier as a musician. Which of the following statements are potentially valid arguments and which are not?
   - **a.** "I can't give up now, after all the time and money I've put in."
   - **b.** "If I had thought about it from the beginning, I never would have gone to med school, so I should give it up now."
   - **c.** "I wasted two years, but never mind—let's start from here."
   - **d.** "My parents would kill me if I stopped now." (*Hint:* We're discussing your decision-making ability, not your parents'.)

Multiple-Choice Questions

1. Which of the following is NOT considered an explicit cost of attending college?
   a. Tuition
   b. Room and board
   c. Lab and student fees
   d. Lost income from a job you had to quit

2. Suppose that at your current level of consumption, marginal benefit of the most recent unit is 6, and marginal cost is 5. Which of the following is true?
   a. You must be maximizing economic profit.
   b. If possible, you should consume more units until marginal benefit equals marginal cost.
   c. If possible, you should consume more units until marginal benefits are less than marginal cost.
   d. You must reduce consumption until the difference between marginal benefit and marginal cost is greatest.

3. In her previous job, Mei was earning $38,000 a year. She now has a new job where she is paid an annual salary of $42,000. What was Mei's economic profit when she switched jobs?
   a. $42,000
   b. $38,000
   c. $4,000
   d. $0

4. Which of the following is true about accounting profit and economic profit?
   a. Accounting profit considers both explicit and implicit costs.
   b. Accounting profit considers only implicit costs.
   c. Economic profit considers only explicit costs.
   d. Economic profit considers both explicit and implicit costs.

5. Which of the following is an example of increasing marginal cost?
   a. On-the-job training makes it easier for workers to produce.
   b. Planting a second field with crops costs the same as planting the first field.
   c. The further Steven goes in his education, the more difficult the schoolwork becomes.
   d. Learning a new production technique allows workers to produce more than they ever could in the past.

Critical-Thinking Question

You and your friend are at the stadium watching your favorite football team. But they are losing so badly that you can't bear to watch anymore and want to leave. Your friend, however, says, "But we paid $100 for these seats. Shouldn't we stay and get our money's worth?" How do you respond?

PITFALLS

MUDDLED AT THE MARGIN

? The idea of setting marginal benefit equal to marginal cost sometimes confuses people. Aren't we trying to maximize the *difference* between benefits and costs? And don't we wipe out our gains by setting benefits and costs equal to each other?

> THE ANSWER TO BOTH QUESTIONS IS YES. BUT THIS IS NOT WHAT WE ARE DOING. RATHER, WHAT WE ARE DOING IS SETTING *MARGINAL*, NOT *TOTAL*, BENEFIT AND COST EQUAL TO EACH OTHER. Once again, the point is to maximize the total profit from an activity. If the marginal benefit from the activity is greater than the marginal cost, doing a bit more will increase that profit. If the marginal benefit is less than the marginal cost, doing a bit less will increase the total profit. So only when the *marginal* benefit and *marginal* cost are equal is the difference between *total* benefit and *total* cost at a maximum.

To learn more about the idea of setting marginal benefit equal to marginal cost, see pages 198–200 on marginal analysis, and Figure 18-3.

MODULE 19 Behavioral Economics

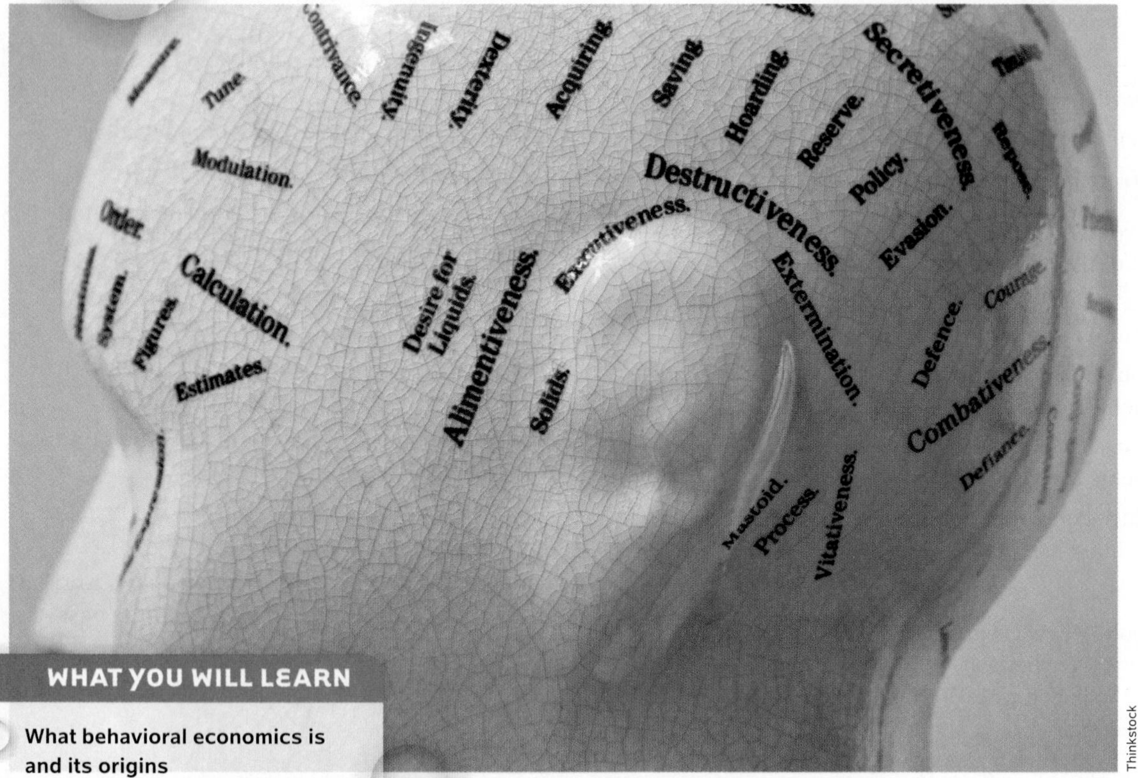

Thinkstock

WHAT YOU WILL LEARN

1. What behavioral economics is and its origins
2. What economists consider to be rational and irrational behavior
3. Why people sometimes behave irrationally in predictable ways

How People Make Economic Choices

Most economic models assume that people make choices based on achieving the best possible economic outcome for themselves. Human behavior, however, is often not so simple. Rather than acting like economic computing machines, people often make choices that fall short—sometimes far short—of the greatest possible economic outcome, or payoff. Why people sometimes make less-than-perfect choices is the subject of behavioral economics, a branch of economics that combines economic modeling with insights from human psychology. Behavioral economics grew out of economists' and psychologists' attempts to understand how people actually make economic choices in real life (instead of in theory).

It's well documented that people consistently engage in *irrational* behavior, choosing an option that leaves them worse off than other available options. Yet, as we'll soon learn, sometimes it's entirely *rational* for people to make a choice that is different from the one that generates the highest possible profit for themselves. For example, Ashley Hildreth, who we read about in Module 18, may decide to earn a teaching degree because she enjoys teaching more than advertising, even though the profit from the teaching degree is less than that from continuing with advertising.

The study of irrational economic behavior was largely pioneered by Daniel Kahneman and Amos Tversky. Kahneman won the 2002 Nobel Prize in economics for his work integrating insights from the psychology of human judgment and decision making into economics. Their work and the insights of others into why people often behave irrationally are having a significant influence on how economists analyze financial markets, labor markets, and other economic concerns.

Rational, but Human, Too

If you are **rational,** you will choose the available option that leads to the outcome you most prefer. But is the outcome you most prefer always the same as the one that gives you the best possible economic payoff? No. It can be entirely rational to choose an option that gives you a worse economic payoff because you care about something other than the size of the economic payoff. There are three principal reasons why people might prefer a worse economic payoff: concerns about fairness, bounded rationality, and risk aversion.

A **rational** decision maker chooses the available option that leads to the outcome he or she most prefers.

A decision maker operating with **bounded rationality** makes a choice that is close to but not exactly the one that leads to the best possible economic outcome.

Risk aversion is the willingness to sacrifice some economic payoff in order to avoid a potential loss.

An **irrational** decision maker chooses an option that leaves him or her worse off than choosing another available option.

CONCERNS ABOUT FAIRNESS In social situations, people often care about fairness as well as about the economic payoff to themselves. For example, no law requires you to tip a waiter or waitress. But concern for fairness leads most people to leave a tip (unless they've had outrageously bad service) because a tip is seen as fair compensation for good service according to society's norms. Tippers are reducing their own economic payoff in order to be fair to waiters and waitresses.

BOUNDED RATIONALITY Being an economic computing machine—choosing the option that gives you the best economic payoff—can require a fair amount of work: sizing up the options, computing the opportunity costs, calculating the marginal amounts, and so on. The mental effort required has its own opportunity cost. This realization led economists to the concept of **bounded rationality**—making a choice that is close to but not exactly the one that leads to the highest possible profit because the effort of finding the best payoff is too costly. In other words, bounded rationality is the "good enough" method of decision making.

Retailers are particularly good at exploiting their customers' tendency to engage in bounded rationality. For example, pricing items in units ending in 99¢ takes advantage of shoppers' tendency to interpret an item that costs, say, $2.99 as significantly cheaper than one that costs $3.00. Bounded rationality leads them to give more weight to the $2 part of the price (the first number they see) than the 99¢ part.

RISK AVERSION Because life is uncertain and the future unknown, sometimes a choice comes with significant risk. Although you may receive a high payoff if things turn out well, the possibility also exists that things may turn out badly and leave you worse off. So even if you think a choice will give you the best payoff of all your available options, you may forgo it because you find the possibility that things could turn out badly too, well, risky. This is called **risk aversion**—the willingness to sacrifice some potential economic payoff in order to avoid a potential loss. Because risk makes most people uncomfortable, it's rational for them to give up some potential economic gain in order to avoid it.

Irrationality: An Economist's View

Sometimes, though, instead of being rational, people are **irrational**—they make choices that leave them worse off in terms of economic payoff *and* other considerations like fairness than if they had chosen another available option. Is there anything systematic that economists and psychologists can say about economically irrational behavior? Yes, because most people are irrational in predictable ways. People's irrational behavior *typically* stems from six mistakes they make when thinking about economic decisions. The mistakes are listed in Table 19-1, and we will discuss each in turn.

TABLE 19-1

Six Common Mistakes in Economic Decision Making

1. Misperceiving opportunity costs
2. Being overconfident
3. Having unrealistic expectations about future behavior
4. Counting dollars unequally
5. Being loss-averse
6. Having a bias toward the status quo

MISPERCEPTIONS OF OPPORTUNITY COSTS As we've seen, people tend to ignore nonmonetary opportunity costs also known as *implicit costs.* These are opportunity costs that don't involve an outlay of cash. Likewise,

Mental accounting is the habit of mentally assigning dollars to different accounts so that some dollars are worth more than others.

a misperception of what exactly constitutes an opportunity cost (and what does not) is at the root of the tendency to count sunk costs in one's decision making. In this case, someone takes an opportunity cost into account when none actually exists.

OVERCONFIDENCE It's a function of ego: we tend to think we know more than we actually do. And even if alerted to how widespread overconfidence is, people tend to think that it's someone else's problem, not theirs. (Certainly not yours or mine!) For example, a 1994 study asked students to estimate how long it would take them to complete their thesis "if everything went as well as it possibly could" and "if everything went as poorly as it possibly could." The results: the typical student thought it would take him or her 33.9 days to finish, with an average estimate of 27.4 days if everything went well and 48.6 days if everything went poorly. In fact, the average time it took to complete a thesis was much longer, 55.5 days. Students were, on average, from 14% to 102% more confident than they should have been about the time it would take to complete their theses.

Jack Watts/Alamy

Overconfidence can be bad for your financial health.

Overconfidence can cause trouble by having a strong adverse effect on people's financial health. Overconfidence often persuades people that they are in better financial shape than they actually are. It can also lead to bad investment and spending decisions. For example, nonprofessional investors who engage in a lot of speculative investing—such as quickly buying and selling stocks—on average have significantly worse results than professional brokers because of their misguided faith in their ability to spot a winner. Similarly, overconfidence can lead people to make a large spending decision, such as buying a car, without doing research on the pros and cons, relying instead on anecdotal evidence. Even worse, people tend to remain overconfident because they remember their successes and explain away or forget their failures.

UNREALISTIC EXPECTATIONS ABOUT FUTURE BEHAVIOR Another form of overconfidence is being overly optimistic about your future behavior: tomorrow you'll study, tomorrow you'll give up ice cream, tomorrow you'll spend less and save more, and so on. Of course, as we all know, when tomorrow arrives, it's still just as hard to study or give up something that you like as it is right now.

Strategies that keep a person on the straight-and-narrow over time are often, at their root, ways to deal with the problem of unrealistic expectations about one's future behavior. Examples are automatic payroll deduction savings plans, diet plans with prepackaged foods, and mandatory attendance at study groups. By providing a way for someone to commit today to an action tomorrow, such plans counteract the habit of pushing difficult actions off into the future.

COUNTING DOLLARS UNEQUALLY If you tend to spend more when you pay with a credit card than when you pay with cash, particularly if you tend to splurge, then you are very likely engaging in **mental accounting.** This is the habit of mentally assigning dollars to different accounts, making some dollars worth more than others. By spending more with a credit card, you are in effect treating dollars in your wallet as more valuable than dollars on your credit card balance, although in reality they count equally in your budget.

A dollar is a dollar, whether it's in your wallet or on your credit card balance.

discpicture/Alamy

Credit card overuse is the most recognizable form of mental accounting. However, there are other forms as well, such as splurging after receiving a windfall, like an unexpected inheritance, or overspending at sales, buying something that seemed like a great bargain at the time whose purchase you later regretted. It's the failure to understand that, regardless of the form it comes in, a dollar is a dollar.

LOSS AVERSION An oversensitivity to loss, leading to an unwillingness to recognize a loss and move on, is called **loss aversion.** In fact, in the lingo of the financial markets, "selling discipline"—being able and willing to quickly acknowledge when a stock you've bought is a loser and sell it—is a highly desirable trait to have. Many investors, though, are reluctant to acknowledge that they've lost money on a stock and won't make it back.

Although it's rational to sell the stock at that point and redeploy the remaining funds, most people find it so painful to admit a loss that they avoid selling for much longer than they should. According to Daniel Kahneman and Amos Tversky, most people feel the misery of losing $100 about twice as keenly as they feel the pleasure of gaining $100.

Loss aversion can help explain why sunk costs are so hard to ignore: ignoring a sunk cost means recognizing that the money you spent is unrecoverable and therefore lost.

Loss aversion is an oversensitivity to loss, leading to unwillingness to recognize a loss and move on.

The **status quo bias** is the tendency to avoid making a decision and stick with existing conditions.

STATUS QUO BIAS Another irrational behavior is **status quo bias,** the tendency to avoid making a decision altogether. A well-known example is the way that employees make decisions about investing in their employer-directed retirement accounts, known as 401(k)s. With a 401(k), employees can, through payroll deductions, set aside part of their salary tax-free, a practice that saves a significant amount of money every year in taxes. Some companies operate on an opt-in basis: employees have to actively choose to participate in a 401(k). Other companies operate on an opt-out basis: employees are automatically enrolled in a 401(k) unless they choose to opt out.

If everyone behaved rationally, then the proportion of employees enrolled in 401(k) accounts at opt-in companies would be roughly equal to the proportion enrolled at opt-out companies. In other words, your decision about whether to participate in a 401(k) should be independent of the default choice at your company. But, in reality, when companies switch to automatic enrollment and an opt-out system, employee enrollment rises dramatically. Clearly, people tend to just go with the status quo.

Why do people exhibit status quo bias? Some claim it's a form of "decision paralysis": when given many options, people find it harder to make a decision. Others claim it's due to loss aversion and the fear of regret, to thinking that "if I do nothing, then I won't have to regret my choice." Irrational, yes. But not altogether surprising. However, rational people know that, in the end, the act of not making a choice is still a choice.

Rational Models for Irrational People?

So why do economists still use models based on rational behavior when people are at times manifestly irrational? For one thing, models based on rational behavior still provide mostly accurate predictions about how people behave in most markets. For example, the great majority of farmers will use less fertilizer when it becomes more expensive—a result consistent with rational behavior.

Another explanation is that sometimes market forces can compel people to behave more rationally over time. For example, if you are a small-business owner who exaggerates your abilities or refuses to acknowledge that your favorite line of items is a loser, then sooner or later you will be out of business unless you learn to correct your mistakes. As a result, it is reasonable to assume that when people are disciplined for their mistakes, as happens in most markets, rationality will win out over time.

Finally, economists depend on the assumption of rationality for the simple but fundamental reason that it makes modeling so much simpler. Remember that models are built on generalizations, and it's much harder to extrapolate from messy, irrational behavior. Even behavioral economists, in their research, search for *predictably* irrational behavior in an attempt to build better models of how people behave. Clearly, there is an ongoing dialogue between behavioral economists and the rest of the economics profession, and economics itself has been irrevocably changed by it.

ECONOMICS IN ACTION

"THE JINGLE MAIL BLUES"

It's called jingle mail—when a homeowner seals the keys to his or her house in an envelope and leaves them with the bank that holds the mortgage on the house. (A mortgage is a loan taken out to buy a house.) By leaving the keys with the bank, the homeowner is walking away not only from the house but also from the obligation to continue paying the mortgage. And to their great consternation, banks have lately been flooded with jingle mail.

To default on a mortgage—that is, to walk away from one's obligation to repay the loan and lose the house to the bank in the process—used to be a fairly rare phenomenon. For decades, continually rising home values made homeownership a good investment for the typical household.

"Officer, that couple is just walking away from their mortgage!"

In recent years, though, an entirely different phenomenon—called "strategic default"—has appeared. In a strategic default, a homeowner who is financially capable of paying the mortgage instead chooses not to, voluntarily walking away. Strategic defaults account for a significant proportion of jingle mail; in March 2010, they accounted for 31% of all foreclosures, up from 22% in 2009. And there is little indication that number will change dramatically: in the spring of 2011, strategic defaults still accounted for 30% of all defaults.

What happened? The Great American Housing Bust happened. After decades of huge increases, house prices began a precipitous fall in 2008. Prices dropped so much that a significant proportion of homeowners found their homes "underwater"—they owed more on their homes than the homes were worth. And with house prices projected to stay depressed for several years, possibly a decade, there appeared to be little chance that an underwater house would recover its value enough in the foreseeable future to move "abovewater."

Many homeowners suffered a major loss. They lost their down payment, money spent on repairs and renovation, moving expenses, and so on. And because they were paying a mortgage that was greater than the house was now worth, they found they could rent a comparable dwelling for less than their monthly mortgage payments. In the words of Benjamin Koellmann, who paid $215,000 for an apartment in Miami where similar units were now selling for $90,000, "There is no financial sense in staying."

Realizing their losses were sunk costs, underwater homeowners walked away. Perhaps they hadn't made the best economic decision when purchasing their houses, but in leaving them they showed impeccable economic logic.

MODULE 19 Review

Solutions appear at the back of the book.

Check Your Understanding

1. Which of the types of irrational behavior are suggested by the following events?
   - **a.** Although the housing market has fallen and Jenny wants to move, she refuses to sell her house for any amount less than what she paid for it.
   - **b.** Dan worked more overtime hours last week than he had expected. Although he is strapped for cash, he spends his unexpected overtime earnings on a weekend getaway rather than trying to pay down his student loan.
   - **c.** Carol has just started her first job and deliberately decided to opt out of the company's savings plan. Her reasoning is that she is very young and there is plenty of time in the future to start saving. Why not enjoy life now?
   - **d.** Jeremy's company requires employees to download and fill out a form if they want to participate in the company-sponsored savings plan. One year after starting the job, Jeremy had still not submitted the form needed to participate in the plan.

Multiple-Choice Questions

1. Kookie's friends give her gift cards that she forgets to use before they expire. However, she is very careful about how she spends her cash. Kookie has made which of the following mistakes in economic decision making?
   a. Status quo bias
   b. Unrealistic expectations about future behavior
   c. Counting dollars unequally
   d. Loss aversion

2. Why would decision makers choose an option that doesn't give them the best possible economic payoff?
   a. Concerns about fairness
   b. Concerns about taking risks
   c. Because the effort to find the best possible payoff is too costly
   d. All of the above

3. Which of the following is unlikely to lead to an irrational decision?
   a. Counting sunk costs
   b. Overconfidence
   c. Committing today to an action tomorrow
   d. Splurging after winning the lottery

4. Despite the fact that some people are irrational, why do economists continue to assume that people behave rationally?
   a. Because economists want everyone to behave rationally
   b. Because markets don't require rationality
   c. Because people will behave rationally in most markets
   d. Because models of rationality are much more complex and reflect the real world

5. Which of the following would be an example of irrational behavior?
   a. Ignoring opportunity cost in your calculation of economic cost
   b. Not being overconfident, even when others around you encourage you to be overconfident
   c. Treating your credit card in the same way you do cash
   d. Considering sunk costs as irrelevant for decision making

Critical-Thinking Question

How would you determine whether a decision you made was rational or irrational?

MODULE

20 Maximizing Utility

craftvision/Getty Images

WHAT YOU WILL LEARN

1. Why consumers' general goal is to maximize utility
2. Why the principle of diminishing marginal utility applies to the consumption of most goods and services
3. How to use marginal analysis to find the optimal consumption bundle

Earlier in this section we learned about principles for rational economic decision making that lead to the best possible outcomes. In this module, we will show how economists analyze the decisions of rational consumers, those who know what they want and make the most of available opportunities. We begin with the concept of utility—a measure of consumer satisfaction.

Utility: It's All About Getting Satisfaction

When analyzing consumer behavior, we're looking into how people pursue their needs and wants and the subjective feelings that motivate purchases. Yet there is no simple way to measure subjective feelings. How much satisfaction do I get from my third cookie? Is it less or more than the satisfaction you receive from your first cookie? Does it even make sense to ask that question?

Luckily, we don't need to make comparisons between your feelings and mine. An analysis of consumer behavior requires only the assumption that individuals try to maximize some personal measure of the satisfaction gained from consumption. That measure of satisfaction is known as **utility,** a concept we use to understand behavior but don't expect to measure in practice.

Utility and Consumption

We can think of consumers as using consumption to "produce" utility, much in the same way that producers use inputs to produce output. As consumers, we do not make explicit calculations of the utility generated by consumption choices, but we must make choices, and we usually base them on at least a rough attempt to achieve greater satisfaction. I can have either soup or salad with my dinner. Which will I enjoy more? I can go to Disney World this year or put the money toward buying a new

Utility is a measure of personal satisfaction.

car. Which will make me happier? These are the types of questions that go into utility maximization.

The concept of utility offers a way to study choices that are made in a more or less rational way.

How do we measure utility? For the sake of simplicity, it is useful to suppose that we can measure utility in hypothetical units called—what else?—**utils.** A *utility function* shows the relationship between a consumer's utility and the combination of goods and services—the *consumption bundle*—he or she consumes.

A **util** is a hypothetical unit of utility.

Figure 20-1 illustrates a utility function. It shows the total utility that Cassie, who likes fried clams, gets from an all-you-can-eat clam dinner. We suppose that her consumption bundle consists of a side of coleslaw, which comes with the meal, plus a number of clams to be determined. The table that accompanies the figure shows how Cassie's total utility depends on the number of clams; the curve in panel (a) of the figure shows that same information graphically.

FIGURE 20-1 **Cassie's Total Utility and Marginal Utility**

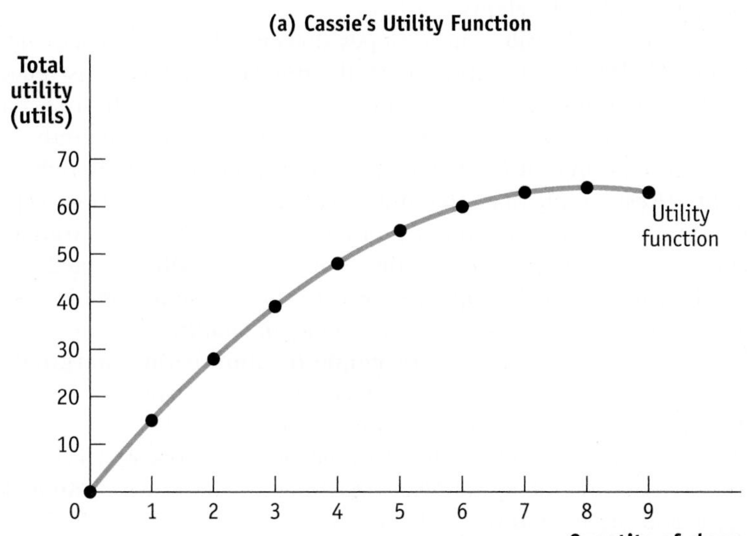

(b) Cassie's Marginal Utility Curve

Marginal utility per clam (utils)

16 14 12 10 8 6 4 2 0 −2

1 2 3 4 5 6 7 8 9

Quantity of clams

Marginal utility curve

Quantity of clams	Total utility (utils)	Marginal utility per clam (utils)
0	0	
		15
1	15	
		13
2	28	
		11
3	39	
		9
4	48	
		7
5	55	
		5
6	60	
		3
7	63	
		1
8	64	
		−1
9	63	

Panel (a) shows how Cassie's total utility depends on her consumption of fried clams. It increases until it reaches its maximum utility level of 64 utils at 8 clams consumed and decreases after that. Marginal utility is calculated in the table. Panel (b) shows the marginal utility curve, which slopes downward due to diminishing marginal utility. That is, each additional clam gives Cassie less utility than the previous clam.

Cassie's utility function slopes upward over most of the range shown, but it gets flatter as the number of clams consumed increases. And in this example it eventually turns downward. According to the information in the table in Figure 20-1, nine clams is a clam too many. Adding that additional clam actually makes Cassie worse off: it would lower her total utility. If she's rational, of course, Cassie will realize that and not consume the ninth clam.

So when Cassie chooses how many clams to consume, she will make this decision by considering the *change* in her total utility from consuming one more clam. This illustrates the general point: to maximize *total* utility, consumers must focus on *marginal* utility.

The Principle of Diminishing Marginal Utility

In addition to showing how Cassie's total utility depends on the number of clams she consumes, the table in Figure 20-1 also shows the **marginal utility** generated by consuming each additional clam—that is, the *change* in total utility from consuming one additional clam. The **marginal utility curve** is constructed by plotting points at the midpoint between the numbered quantities since marginal utility is found as consumption levels change. For example, when consumption rises from 1 to 2 clams, marginal utility is 13. Therefore, we place the point corresponding to marginal utility of 13 halfway between 1 and 2 clams.

iStockphoto

When is more of a good thing too much?

The marginal utility curve slopes downward because each successive clam adds less to total utility than the previous clam. This is reflected in the table: marginal utility falls from a high of 15 utils for the first clam consumed to –1 for the ninth clam consumed. The fact that the ninth clam has negative marginal utility means that consuming it actually reduces total utility. (Restaurants that offer all-you-can-eat meals depend on the proposition that you can have too much of a good thing.) Not all marginal utility curves eventually become negative. But it is generally accepted that marginal utility curves do slope downward—that consumption of most goods and services is subject to *diminishing marginal utility.*

The basic idea behind the **principle of diminishing marginal utility** is that the additional satisfaction a consumer gets from one more unit of a good or service declines as the amount of that good or service consumed rises. Or, to put it slightly differently, the more of a good or service you consume, the closer you are to being satiated—reaching a point at which an additional unit of the good adds nothing to your satisfaction.

The principle of diminishing marginal utility doesn't always apply, but it does apply in the great majority of cases, enough to serve as a foundation for our analysis of consumer behavior.

Budgets and Optimal Consumption

The **marginal utility** of a good or service is the change in total utility generated by consuming one additional unit of that good or service.

The **marginal utility curve** shows how marginal utility depends on the quantity of a good or service consumed.

According to the **principle of diminishing marginal utility,** each successive unit of a good or service consumed adds less to total utility than does the previous unit.

The principle of diminishing marginal utility explains why most people eventually reach a limit, even at an all-you-can-eat buffet where the cost of another clam is measured only in future indigestion. Under ordinary circumstances, however, it costs some additional resources to consume more of a good, and consumers must take that cost into account when making choices.

What do we mean by cost? As always, the fundamental measure of cost is *opportunity cost.* Because the amount of money a consumer can spend is limited, a decision to consume more of one good is also a decision to consume less of some other good.

Budget Constraints and Budget Lines

Consider Sammy, whose appetite is exclusively for clams and potatoes. (There's no accounting for tastes.) He has a weekly income of $20 and since, given his appetite, more of either good is better than less, he spends all of it on clams and potatoes. We will assume that clams cost \$4 per pound and potatoes cost \$2 per pound. What are his possible choices?

Whatever Sammy chooses, we know that the cost of his consumption bundle cannot exceed the amount of money he has to spend. That is,

(20-1) *Expenditure on clams + Expenditure on potatoes ≤ Total income*

Consumers always have limited income, which constrains how much they can consume. So the requirement illustrated by Equation 20-1—that a consumer must choose a consumption bundle that costs no more than his or her income—is known as the consumer's **budget constraint.** It's a simple way of saying that a consumer can't spend more than the total amount of income available to him or her. We call the set of all of Sammy's affordable consumption bundles his **consumption possibilities.** In general, whether or not a particular consumption bundle is included in a consumer's consumption possibilities depends on the consumer's income and the prices of goods and services.

A **budget constraint** limits the cost of a consumer's consumption bundle to no more than the consumer's income.

A consumer's **consumption possibilities** is the set of all consumption bundles that are affordable, given the consumer's income and prevailing prices.

Figure 20-2 shows Sammy's consumption possibilities. The quantity of clams in his consumption bundle is measured on the horizontal axis and the quantity of potatoes on the vertical axis. The downward-sloping line connecting points *A* through *F* shows which consumption bundles are affordable and which are not. Every bundle on or inside this line (the shaded area) is affordable; every bundle outside this line is unaffordable.

As an example of one of the points, let's look at point *C*, representing 2 pounds of clams and 6 pounds of potatoes, and check whether it satisfies Sammy's budget constraint. The cost of bundle *C* is 6 pounds of potatoes × \$2 per pound + 2 pounds of clams × \$4 per pound = \$12 + \$8 = \$20. So bundle *C* does indeed satisfy Sammy's budget constraint: it costs no more than his weekly income of \$20. In fact, bundle *C* costs exactly as much as Sammy's income. By doing the arithmetic, you can check

FIGURE 20-2 **The Budget Line**

Consumption bundle	Quantity of clams (pounds)	Quantity of potatoes (pounds)
A	0	10
B	1	8
C	2	6
D	3	4
E	4	2
F	5	0

The *budget line* represents all the possible combinations of quantities of potatoes and clams that Sammy can purchase if he spends all of his income. Also, it is the boundary between the set of affordable consumption bundles (the *consumption possibilities*) and the unaffordable ones. Given that clams cost \$4 per pound and potatoes cost \$2 per pound, if Sammy spends all of his income on clams (bundle *F*), he can purchase 5 pounds of clams. If he spends all of his income on potatoes (bundle *A*), he can purchase 10 pounds of potatoes.

A consumer' consumptio consumer w income.

A consumer' **bundle** is th that maximiz total utility g constraint.

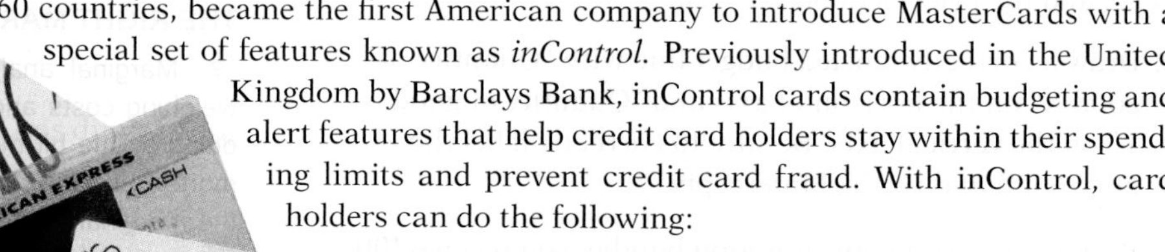

BUSINESS CASE: Citi Puts Card Holders "inControl"

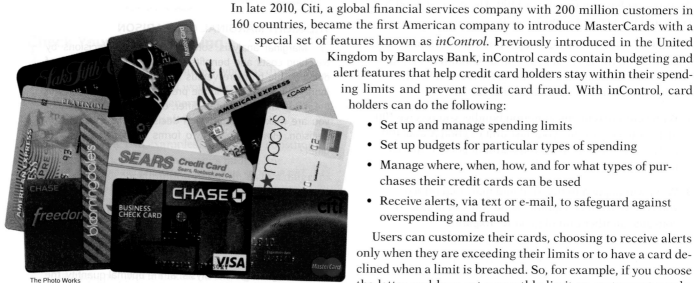

The Photo Works

In late 2010, Citi, a global financial services company with 200 million customers in 160 countries, became the first American company to introduce MasterCards with a special set of features known as *inControl.* Previously introduced in the United Kingdom by Barclays Bank, inControl cards contain budgeting and alert features that help credit card holders stay within their spending limits and prevent credit card fraud. With inControl, card holders can do the following:

- Set up and manage spending limits
- Set up budgets for particular types of spending
- Manage where, when, how, and for what types of purchases their credit cards can be used
- Receive alerts, via text or e-mail, to safeguard against overspending and fraud

Users can customize their cards, choosing to receive alerts only when they are exceeding their limits or to have a card declined when a limit is breached. So, for example, if you choose the latter and have set a monthly limit on restaurant meals, your card will be rejected for restaurant bills above your pre-set cap. Card holders can also arrange to have their credit cards shut off once a limit is reached that corresponds to monthly disposable income.

inControl is not the first product that alerts card holders when they have exceeded their limit. Mint.com offers such a service, but you have to log into your bank's website to retrieve updates, and those sites are updated only every 24 hours. In contrast, alerts from inControl happen in real time. Until inControl was introduced, no other product allowed you to completely cut off certain types of spending. "The personalization of consumer products has reached far deeper than it ever has before," says Ed McLaughlin, chief payments officer of MasterCard.

But what about the obvious question of whether credit card companies are hurting or helping themselves by introducing this product? After all, if consumers get serious about budgeting and place caps on their credit card spending, won't that reduce the interest that credit card companies profit from? In answer to this question, McLaughlin replied, "I think anyone knows that having a superior offering wins out in the long run."

The service, though, is not ironclad—having hit the self-imposed limit, a customer can turn the card back on with a phone call or text message. The thinking goes, however, that having your card rejected will make a significant enough impression to put a damper on your urge to splurge.

In the end, how well inControl does, and whether something like it is adopted by competitors like VISA, depends on whether customers actually use the service *and* how much customers' newfound discipline hurts credit card companies' bottom lines.

Questions for Thought

1. What aspects of decision making does the inControl card address? Be specific.
2. Consider credit scores, the scores assigned to individuals by credit-rating agencies, based on whether you pay your bills on time, how many credit cards you have (too many is a bad sign), whether you have ever declared bankruptcy, and so on. Now consider people who choose inControl cards and those who don't. Which group do you think has better credit scores *before* they adopt the inControl cards? After adopting the inControl cards? Explain.
3. What do you think explains Ed McLaughlin's optimism that his company will profit from the introduction of inControl?

TABLE 2

Sammy's

Utili
Quantity (pou
(

SECTION 7 REVIEW

Summary

Making Decisions

1. All economic decisions involve the allocation of scarce resources. Some decisions are "either–or" decisions, in which the question is whether or not to do something. Other decisions are "how much" decisions, in which the question is how much of a resource to put into a given activity.
2. The cost of using a resource for a particular activity is the opportunity cost of that resource. Some opportunity costs are **explicit costs;** they involve a direct outlay of money. Other opportunity costs, however, are **implicit costs;** they involve no outlay of money but are measured by the dollar value of the benefits that are forgone. Both explicit and implicit costs should be taken into account in making decisions. Many decisions involve the use of **capital** and time, for both individuals and firms. So they should base decisions on **economic profit,** which takes into account implicit costs such as the opportunity cost of time and the **implicit cost of capital.** Making decisions based on **accounting profit** can be misleading. It is often considerably larger than the economic profit because it includes only explicit costs and not implicit costs.
3. According to the **principle of "either–or" decision making,** when faced with an "either–or" choice between two activities, one should choose the activity with the positive economic profit.
4. A **"how much" decision** is made using marginal analysis, which involves comparing the benefit to the cost of doing an additional unit of an activity. The **marginal cost** of producing a good or service is the additional cost incurred by producing one more unit of that good or service. The **marginal benefit** of producing a good or service is the additional benefit earned by producing one more unit. The **marginal cost curve** is the graphical illustration of marginal cost, and the **marginal benefit curve** is the graphical illustration of marginal benefit.
5. In the case of **constant marginal cost,** each additional unit costs the same amount to produce as the previous unit. However, marginal cost and marginal benefit typically depend on how much of the activity has already been done. With **increasing marginal cost,** each unit costs more to produce than the previous unit and is represented by an upward-sloping marginal cost curve. With **decreasing marginal cost,** each unit costs less to produce than the previous unit, leading to a downward-sloping marginal cost curve. In the case of **decreasing marginal benefit,** each additional unit produces a smaller benefit than the unit before.
6. The **optimal quantity** is the quantity that generates the highest possible total profit. According to the **profit-maximizing principle of marginal analysis,** the optimal quantity is the highest quantity at which marginal benefit is greater than or equal to marginal cost. It is the quantity at which the marginal cost curve and the marginal benefit curve intersect.
7. A cost that has already been incurred and that is nonrecoverable is a **sunk cost.** Sunk costs should be ignored in decisions about future actions because they have no effect on future benefits and costs.

Behavioral Economics

8. With **rational** behavior, individuals will choose the available option that leads to the outcome they most prefer. **Bounded rationality** occurs because the effort needed to find the best economic payoff is costly. **Risk aversion** causes individuals to sacrifice some economic payoff in order to avoid a potential loss. People might also prefer outcomes with worse economic payoffs because they are concerned about fairness.
9. An **irrational** choice leaves someone worse off than if they had chosen another available option. It takes the form of misperceptions of opportunity cost; overconfidence; unrealistic expectations about future behavior; **mental accounting,** in which dollars are valued unequally; **loss aversion,** an oversensitivity to loss; and **status quo bias,** avoiding a decision by sticking with the status quo.

Maximizing Utility

10. Consumers maximize a measure of satisfaction called **utility.** We measure utility in hypothetical units called **utils.**
11. A good's or service's **marginal utility** is the additional utility generated by consuming one more unit of the good or service. We usually assume that the **principle of diminishing marginal utility** holds: consumption of another unit of a good or service yields less additional utility than the previous unit. As a result, the **marginal utility curve** slopes downward.
12. A **budget constraint** limits a consumer's spending to no more than his or her income. It defines the consumer's **consumption possibilities,** the set of all affordable consumption bundles. A consumer who spends all of his or her income will choose a consumption bundle on the **budget line.** An individual chooses the consumption bundle that maximizes total utility, the **optimal consumption bundle.**

13. We use marginal analysis to find the optimal consumption bundle by analyzing how to allocate the marginal dollar. According to the **optimal consumption rule,** with the optimal consumption bundle, the **marginal utility per dollar** spent on each good and service—the marginal utility of a good divided by its price—is the same.

Key Terms

Explicit cost, p. 193
Implicit cost, p. 193
Accounting profit, p. 193
Economic profit, p. 194
Capital, p. 194
Implicit cost of capital, p. 194
Principle of "either-or" decision making, p. 195
Marginal analysis, p. 195
Marginal cost, p. 196
Increasing marginal cost, p. 196
Marginal cost curve, p. 196
Constant marginal cost, p. 196
Decreasing marginal cost, p. 197
Marginal benefit, p. 197
Decreasing marginal benefit, p. 198
Marginal benefit curve, p. 198
Optimal quantity, p. 199
Profit-maximizing principle of marginal analysis, p. 200
Sunk cost, p. 201
Rational, p. 205
Bounded rationality, p. 205
Risk aversion, p. 205
Irrational, p. 205
Mental accounting, p. 206
Loss aversion. p. 207
Status quo bias, p. 207
Utility, p. 210
Util, p. 211
Marginal utility, p. 212
Marginal utility curve, p. 212
Principle of diminishing marginal utility, p. 212
Budget constraint, p. 213
Consumption possibilities, p. 213
Budget line, p. 214
Optimal consumption bundle, p. 214
Marginal utility per dollar, p. 216
Optimal consumption rule, p. 219

Problems

1. Hiro owns and operates a small business that provides economic consulting services. During the year he spends $57,000 on travel to clients and other expenses. In addition, he owns a computer that he uses for business. If he didn't use the computer, he could sell it and earn yearly interest of $100 on the money created through this sale. Hiro's total revenue for the year is $100,000. Instead of working as a consultant for the year, he could teach economics at a small local college and make a salary of $50,000.

   a. What is Hiro's accounting profit?

   b. What is Hiro's economic profit?

   c. Should Hiro continue working as a consultant, or should he teach economics instead?

2. Jackie owns and operates a web-design business. To keep up with new technology, she spends $5,000 per year upgrading her computer equipment. She runs the business out of a room in her home. If she didn't use the room as her business office, she could rent it out for $2,000 per year. Jackie knows that if she didn't run her own business, she could return to her previous job at a large software company that would pay her a salary of $60,000 per year. Jackie has no other expenses.

   a. How much total revenue does Jackie need to make in order to break even in the eyes of her accountant? That is, how much total revenue would give Jackie an accounting profit of just zero?

   b. How much total revenue does Jackie need to make in order for her to want to remain self-employed? That is, how much total revenue would give Jackie an economic profit of just zero?

3. You own and operate a bike store. Each year, you receive revenue of $200,000 from your bike sales, and it costs you $100,000 to obtain the bikes. In addition, you pay $20,000 for electricity, taxes, and other expenses per year. Instead of running the bike store, you could become an accountant and receive a yearly salary of $40,000. A large clothing retail chain wants to expand and offers to rent the store from you for $50,000 per year. How do you explain to your friends that despite making a profit, it is too costly for you to continue running your store?

4. Suppose you have just paid a nonrefundable fee of $1,000 for your meal plan for this academic term. This allows you to eat dinner in the cafeteria every evening.

   a. You are offered a part-time job in a restaurant where you can eat for free each evening. Your parents say that you should eat dinner in the cafeteria anyway, since you have already paid for those meals. Are your parents right? Explain why or why not.

   b. You are offered a part-time job in a different restaurant where, rather than being able to eat for free, you receive only a large discount on your meals. Each meal there will cost you $2; if you eat there each evening this semester, it will add up to $200. Your roommate says that you should eat in the restaurant since it costs less than the $1,000 that you paid for the meal plan. Is your roommate right? Explain why or why not.

5. You have bought a $10 ticket in advance for the college soccer game, a ticket that cannot be resold. You know that going to the soccer game will give you a benefit equal to $20. After you have bought the ticket, you hear that there will be a professional baseball post-season game at the same time. Tickets to the baseball game cost $20, and you know that going to the baseball game will give you a benefit equal to $35. You tell your friends the following: "If I had known about the baseball game before buying the ticket to the soccer game, I would have gone to the baseball game instead. But now that I already have the ticket to the soccer game, it's better for me to just go to the soccer game." Are you making the correct decision? Justify your answer by calculating the benefits and costs of your decision.

6. Amy, Bill, and Carla all mow lawns for money. Each of them operates a different lawn mower. The accompanying table shows the total cost to Amy, Bill, and Carla of mowing lawns.

Quantity of lawns mowed	Amy's total cost	Bill's total cost	Carla's total cost
0	$0	$0	$0
1	20	10	2
2	35	20	7
3	45	30	17
4	50	40	32
5	52	50	52
6	53	60	82

a. Calculate Amy's, Bill's, and Carla's marginal costs, and draw each of their marginal cost curves.

b. Who has increasing marginal cost, who has decreasing marginal cost, and who has constant marginal cost?

7. You are the manager of a gym, and you have to decide how many customers to admit each hour. Assume that each customer stays exactly one hour. Customers are costly to admit because they inflict wear and tear on the exercise equipment. Moreover, each additional customer generates more wear and tear than the customer before. As a result, the gym faces increasing marginal cost. The accompanying table shows the marginal costs associated with each number of customers per hour.

Quantity of customers per hour	Marginal cost of customer
0	
	$14.00
1	
	14.50
2	
	15.00
3	
	15.50
4	
	16.00
5	
	16.50
6	
	17.00
7	

a. Suppose that each customer pays $15.25 for a one-hour workout. Use the profit-maximizing principle of marginal analysis to find the optimal number of customers that you should admit per hour.

b. You increase the price of a one-hour workout to $16.25. What is the optimal number of customers per hour that you should admit now?

8. Georgia and Lauren are economics students who go to a karate class together. Both have to choose how many classes to go to per week. Each class costs $20. The accompanying table shows Georgia's and Lauren's estimates of the marginal benefit that each of them gets from each class per week.

Quantity of classes	Lauren's marginal benefit of each class	Georgia's marginal benefit of each class
0		
	$23	$28
1		
	19	22
2		
	14	15
3		
	8	7
4		

a. Use marginal analysis to find Lauren's optimal number of karate classes per week. Explain your answer.

b. Use marginal analysis to find Georgia's optimal number of karate classes per week. Explain your answer.

9. The Centers for Disease Control and Prevention (CDC) recommended against vaccinating the whole population against the smallpox virus because the vaccination has undesirable, and sometimes fatal, side effects. Suppose the accompanying table gives the data that are available about the effects of a smallpox vaccination program.

Percent of population vaccinated	Deaths due to smallpox	Deaths due to vaccination side effects
0%	200	0
10	180	4
20	160	10
30	140	18
40	120	33
50	100	50
60	80	74

a. Calculate the marginal benefit (in terms of lives saved) and the marginal cost (in terms of lives lost) of each 10% increment of smallpox vaccination. Calculate the net increase in human lives for each 10% increment in population vaccinated.

b. Using marginal analysis, determine the optimal percentage of the population that should be vaccinated.

Production and Costs

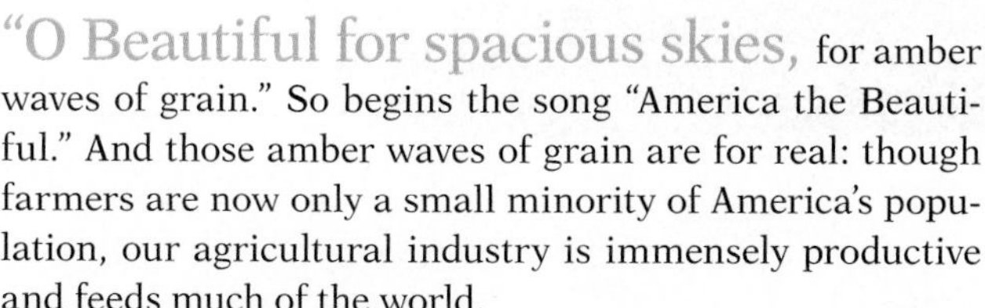

THE FARMER'S MARGIN

"O Beautiful for spacious skies, for amber waves of grain." So begins the song "America the Beautiful." And those amber waves of grain are for real: though farmers are now only a small minority of America's population, our agricultural industry is immensely productive and feeds much of the world.

If you look at agricultural statistics, however, something may seem a bit surprising: when it comes to yield per acre, U.S. farmers are often nowhere near the top. For example, farmers in Western European countries grow about three times as much wheat per acre as their U.S. counterparts. Are the Europeans better at growing wheat than we are?

No: European farmers are very skillful, but no more so than Americans. They produce more wheat per acre because they employ more inputs—more fertilizer and, especially, more labor—per acre. Of course, this means that European farmers have higher costs than their American counterparts. But because of government policies, European farmers receive a much higher price for their wheat than American farmers. This gives them an incentive to use more inputs and to expend more effort at the margin to increase the crop yield per acre.

Notice our use of the phrase "at the margin." Like most decisions that involve a comparison of benefits and costs, decisions about inputs and production involve a comparison of marginal quantities—the marginal cost versus the marginal benefit of producing a bit more from each acre.

In Module 18 we considered the case of Alex, who had to choose the number of years of schooling that maximized his profit from schooling. There we used the profit-maximizing principle of marginal analysis to find the optimal quantity of years of schooling. In this chapter, we will encounter producers who have to make similar "how much" decisions: choosing the quantity of output produced to maximize profit.

In this section, we will show how marginal analysis can be used to understand these output decisions—decisions that lie behind the supply curve.

The first step in this analysis is to show how the relationship between a firm's inputs and its output—its *production function*—determines its *cost curves,* the relationship between cost and quantity of output produced. That is what we do in Module 21. In Modules 22 and 23, we will use our understanding of the firm's cost curves to derive the individual and the market supply curves.

MODULE 21 The Production Function

© Terrance Klassen/AgeFotostock

WHAT YOU WILL LEARN

1. The importance of the firm's production function, the relationship between the quantity of inputs and the quantity of output
2. Why production is often subject to diminishing returns to inputs

The Production Function

A *firm* produces goods or services for sale. To do this, it must transform inputs into output. The quantity of output a firm produces depends on the quantity of inputs; this relationship is known as the firm's **production function.** As we'll see, a firm's production function underlies its *cost curves.* As a first step, let's look at the characteristics of a hypothetical production function.

Inputs and Output

To understand the concept of a production function, let's consider a farm that we assume, for the sake of simplicity, produces only one output, wheat, and uses only two inputs, land and labor. This particular farm is owned by a couple named George and Martha. They hire workers to do the actual physical labor on the farm. Moreover, we will assume that all potential workers are of the same quality—they are all equally knowledgeable and capable of performing farmwork.

A **production function** is the relationship between the quantity of inputs a firm uses and the quantity of output it produces.

A **fixed input** is an input whose quantity is fixed for a period of time and cannot be varied.

A **variable input** is an input whose quantity the firm can vary at any time.

The **long run** is the time period in which all inputs can be varied.

The **short run** is the time period in which at least one input is fixed.

George and Martha's farm sits on 10 acres of land; no more acres are available to them, and they are currently unable to either increase or decrease the size of their farm by selling, buying, or leasing acreage. Land here is what economists call a **fixed input**—an input whose quantity is fixed for a period of time and cannot be varied. George and Martha are, however, free to decide how many workers to hire. The labor provided by these workers is called a **variable input**—an input whose quantity the firm can vary at any time.

In reality, whether or not the quantity of an input is really fixed depends on the time horizon. In the **long run**—that is, given that a long enough period of time has elapsed—firms can adjust the quantity of any input. So there are no fixed inputs in the long run. In contrast, the **short run** is defined as the time period during which at least one input is fixed. Later, we'll look more carefully at the distinction between the short run and the long run. But for now, we will restrict our attention to the short run and assume that at least one input (land) is fixed.

George and Martha know that the quantity of wheat they produce depends on the number of workers they hire. Using modern farming techniques, one worker can cultivate the 10-acre farm, albeit not very intensively. When an additional worker is added, the land is divided equally among all the workers: each worker has 5 acres to cultivate when 2 workers are employed, each cultivates 3⅓ acres when 3 are employed, and so on. So as additional workers are employed, the 10 acres of land are cultivated more intensively and more bushels of wheat are produced.

The **total product curve** shows how the quantity of output depends on the quantity of the variable input, for a given quantity of the fixed input.

The **marginal product** of an input is the additional quantity of output produced by using one more unit of that input.

The relationship between the quantity of labor and the quantity of output, for a given amount of the fixed input, constitutes the farm's production function. The production function for George and Martha's farm, where land is the fixed input and labor is the variable input, is shown in the first two columns of the table in Figure 21-1; the diagram there depicts the same information graphically. The curve in Figure 21-1 shows how the quantity of output depends on the quantity of the variable input for a given quantity of the fixed input; it is called the farm's **total product curve.** The physical quantity of output, bushels of wheat, is measured on the vertical axis; the quantity of the variable input, labor (that is, the number of workers employed), is measured on the horizontal axis. The total product curve here slopes upward, reflecting the fact that more bushels of wheat are produced as more workers are employed.

Although the total product curve in Figure 21-1 slopes upward along its entire length, the slope isn't constant: as you move up the curve to the right, it flattens out. To understand this changing slope, look at the third column of the table in Figure 21-1, which shows the *change in the quantity of output* generated by adding one more worker. That is, it shows the **marginal product** of labor, or *MPL*: the additional quantity of output from using one more unit of labor (one more worker).

FIGURE 21-1 **Production Function and Total Product Curve for George and Martha's Farm**

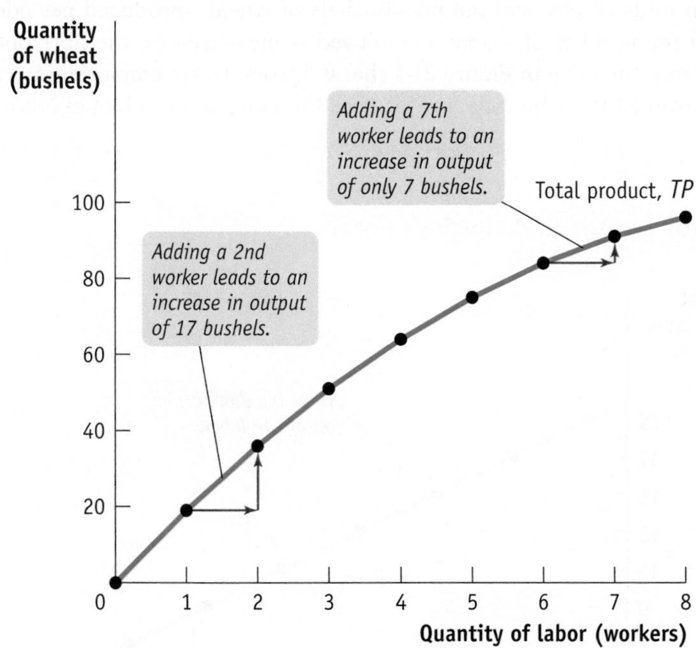

Quantity of labor *L* (workers)	Quantity of wheat *Q* (bushels)	Marginal product of labor $MPL = \Delta Q/\Delta L$ (bushels per worker)
0	0	
		19
1	19	
		17
2	36	
		15
3	51	
		13
4	64	
		11
5	75	
		9
6	84	
		7
7	91	
		5
8	96	

The table shows the production function, the relationship between the quantity of the variable input (labor, measured in number of workers) and the quantity of output (wheat, measured in bushels) for a given quantity of the fixed input. It also shows the marginal product of labor on George and Martha's farm. The total product curve shows the production function graphically. It slopes upward because more wheat is produced as more workers are employed. It also becomes flatter because the marginal product of labor declines as more and more workers are employed.

In this example, we have data at intervals of 1 worker—that is, we have information on the quantity of output when there are 3 workers, 4 workers, and so on. Sometimes data aren't available in increments of 1 unit—for example, you might have information on the quantity of output only when there are 40 workers and when there are 50 workers. In this case, you can use the following equation to calculate the marginal product of labor:

$$\text{(21-1)} \quad \begin{array}{c}\text{Marginal}\\\text{product}\\\text{of labor}\end{array} = \begin{array}{c}\text{Change in quantity of}\\\text{output produced by one}\\\text{additional unit of labor}\end{array} = \frac{\text{Change in quantity of output}}{\text{Change in quantity of labor}}$$

or

$$MPL = \frac{\Delta Q}{\Delta L}$$

Note that Δ, the Greek uppercase delta, represents the change in a variable.

Now we can explain the significance of the slope of the total product curve: it is equal to the marginal product of labor. The slope of a line is equal to "rise" over "run." This implies that the slope of the total product curve is the change in the quantity of output (the "rise") divided by the change in the quantity of labor (the "run"). And this, as we can see from Equation 21-1, is simply the marginal product of labor. So in Figure 21-1, the fact that the marginal product of the first worker is 19 also means that the slope of the total product curve in going from 0 to 1 worker is 19. Similarly, the slope of the total product curve in going from 1 to 2 workers is the same as the marginal product of the second worker, 17, and so on.

In this example, the marginal product of labor steadily declines as more workers are hired—that is, each successive worker adds less to output than the previous worker. So as employment increases, the total product curve gets flatter.

Figure 21-2 shows how the marginal product of labor depends on the number of workers employed on the farm. The marginal product of labor, *MPL*, is measured on the vertical axis in units of physical output—bushels of wheat—produced per additional worker, and the number of workers employed is measured on the horizontal axis. You can see from the table in Figure 21-1 that if 5 workers are employed instead of 4, output rises from 64 to 75 bushels; in this case the marginal product of labor is

FIGURE 21-2 Marginal Product of Labor Curve for George and Martha's Farm

The marginal product of labor curve plots each worker's marginal product, the increase in the quantity of output generated by each additional worker. The change in the quantity of output is measured on the vertical axis and the number of workers employed on the horizontal axis. The first worker employed generates an increase in output of 19 bushels, the second worker generates an increase of 17 bushels, and so on. The curve slopes downward due to diminishing returns to labor.

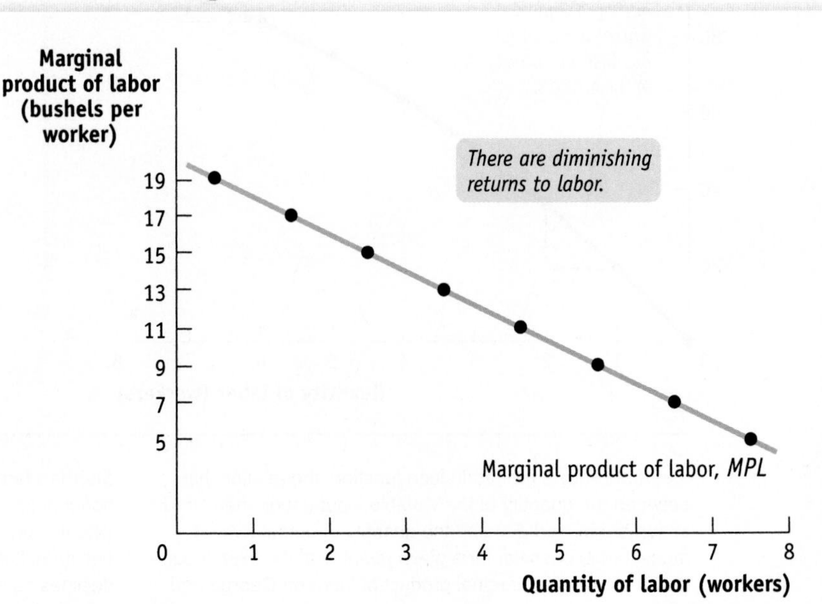

11 bushels—the same number found in Figure 21-2. To indicate that 11 bushels is the marginal product when employment rises from 4 to 5, we place the point corresponding to that information halfway between 4 and 5 workers.

In this example the marginal product of labor falls as the number of workers increases. That is, there are *diminishing returns to labor* on George and Martha's farm. In general, there are **diminishing returns to an input** when an increase in the quantity of that input, holding the quantity of all other inputs fixed, reduces that input's marginal product. Due to diminishing returns to labor, the *MPL* curve is negatively sloped.

There are **diminishing returns to an input** when an increase in the quantity of that input, holding the levels of all other inputs fixed, leads to a decline in the marginal product of that input.

Cultura Limited/Superstock

As more workers are added to a fixed amount of land, each worker adds less to total output than the previous worker.

To grasp why diminishing returns can occur, think about what happens as George and Martha add more and more workers without increasing the number of acres. As the number of workers increases, the land is farmed more intensively and the number of bushels increases. But each additional worker is working with a smaller share of the 10 acres—the fixed input—than the previous worker. As a result, the additional worker cannot produce as much output as the previous worker. So it's not surprising that the marginal product of the additional worker falls.

The crucial point to emphasize about diminishing returns is that, like many propositions in economics, it is an "other things equal" proposition: each successive unit of an input will raise production by less than the last *if the quantity of all other inputs is held fixed.*

What would happen if the levels of other inputs were allowed to change? You can see the answer illustrated in Figure 21-3. Panel (a) shows two total product curves, TP_{10} and TP_{20}. TP_{10} is the farm's total product curve when its total area is 10 acres (the same curve as in Figure 21-1). TP_{20} is the total product curve when the farm's area

FIGURE 21-3 Total Product, Marginal Product, and the Fixed Input

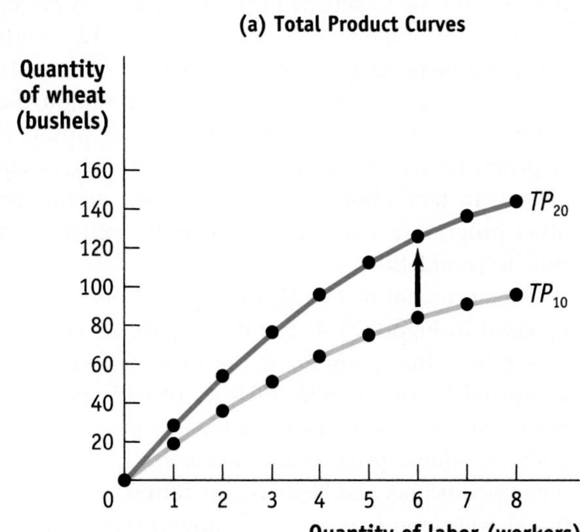

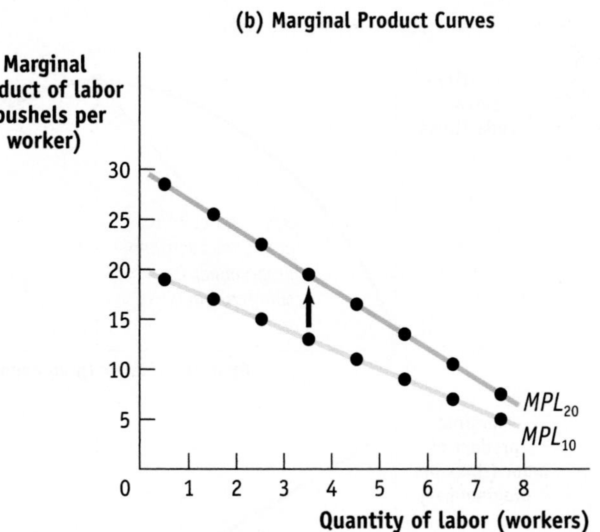

This figure shows how the quantity of output—illustrated by the total product curve—and marginal product depend on the level of the fixed input. Panel (a) shows two total product curves for George and Martha's farm, TP_{10} when their farm is 10 acres and TP_{20} when it is 20 acres. With more land, each worker can produce more wheat. So an increase in the fixed input shifts the total product curve up from TP_{10} to TP_{20}. This also implies that the marginal product of each worker is higher when the farm is 20 acres than when it is 10 acres. As a result, an increase in acreage also shifts the marginal product of labor curve up from MPL_{10} to MPL_{20}. Panel (b) shows the marginal product of labor curves. Note that both marginal product of labor curves still slope downward due to diminishing returns to labor.

has increased to 20 acres. Except when 0 workers are employed, TP_{20} lies everywhere above TP_{10} because with more acres available, any given number of workers produces more output. Panel (b) shows the corresponding marginal product of labor curves. MPL_{10} is the marginal product of labor curve given 10 acres to cultivate (the same curve as in Figure 21-2), and MPL_{20} is the marginal product of labor curve given 20 acres. Both curves slope downward because, in each case, the amount of land is fixed, although at different levels. But MPL_{20} lies everywhere above MPL_{10}, reflecting the fact that the marginal product of the same worker is higher when he or she has more of the fixed input to work with.

Figure 21-3 demonstrates a general result: the position of the total product curve depends on the quantities of other inputs. If you change the quantities of the other inputs, both the total product curve and the marginal product curve of the remaining input will shift.

ECONOMICS IN ACTION

THE MYTHICAL MAN-MONTH

The concept of diminishing returns to an input was first formulated by economists during the late eighteenth century. These economists, notably including Thomas Malthus, drew their inspiration from agricultural examples. Although still valid, examples drawn from agriculture can seem somewhat musty and old-fashioned in our modern economy.

However, the idea of diminishing returns to an input applies with equal force to the most modern of economic activities—such as, say, the design of software. In 1975 Frederick P. Brooks Jr., a project manager at IBM during the days when it dominated the computer business, published a book titled *The Mythical Man-Month* that soon became a classic.

The chapter that gave its title to the book is basically about diminishing returns to labor in the writing of software. Brooks observed that multiplying the number of programmers assigned to a project did not produce a proportionate reduction in the time it took to get the program written. A project that could be done by one programmer in 12 months could *not* be done by 12 programmers in one month. The "mythical man-month" is the false notion that the number of lines of programming code produced is proportional to the number of code writers employed. In fact, above a certain number, adding another programmer on a project actually *increased* the time to completion.

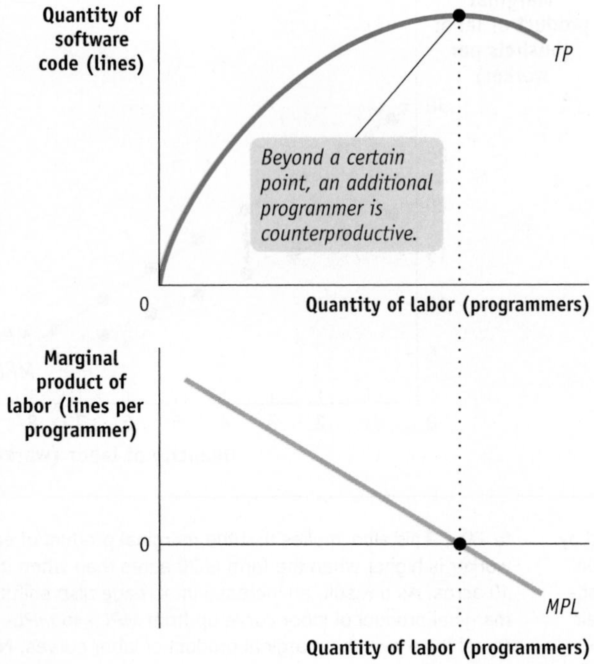

The argument of *The Mythical Man-Month* is summarized in Figure 21-4. The upper part of the figure shows how the quantity of the project's output, as measured by the number of lines of code produced per month, varies with the number of programmers. Each additional programmer accomplishes less than the previous one, and beyond a certain point an additional programmer is actually counterproductive. The lower part of the figure shows the marginal product of each successive programmer, which falls as more programmers are employed and eventually becomes negative.

In other words, programming is subject to diminishing returns so severe that at some point more programmers actually have negative marginal product.

FIGURE 21-4 Mythical Man-Month

The source of the diminishing returns lies in the nature of the production function for a programming project: each programmer must coordinate his or her work with that of all the other programmers on the project, leading to each person spending more time communicating with others—exchanging e-mails, devising project plans, attending meetings, and so on. In other words, other things equal, there are diminishing returns to labor. It is likely, however, that if fixed inputs devoted to programming projects are increased—say, installing a faster *Wiki system*—the problem of diminishing returns for additional programmers can be mitigated.

21 Review

Solutions appear at the back of the book.

Check Your Understanding

1. Bernie's ice-making company produces ice cubes using a 10-ton machine and electricity (along with water, which we will ignore as an input for simplicity). The quantity of output, measured in pounds of ice, is given in the accompanying table.
   a. What is the fixed input? What is the variable input?
   b. Construct a table showing the marginal product of the variable input. Does it show diminishing returns?
   c. Suppose a 50% increase in the size of the fixed input increases output by 100% for any given amount of the variable input. What is the fixed input now? Construct a table showing the quantity of output and the marginal product in this case.

Quantity of electricity (kilowatts)	Quantity of ice (pounds)
0	0
1	1,000
2	1,800
3	2,400
4	2,800

Multiple-Choice Questions

1. A production function shows the relationship between inputs and
   a. fixed costs.
   b. variable costs.
   c. total revenue.
   d. output.
   e. profit.
2. Which of the following defines the short run?
   a. less than a year
   b. when all inputs are fixed
   c. when no inputs are variable
   d. when only one input is variable
   e. when at least one input is fixed
3. The slope of the total product curve is also known as
   a. marginal product.
   b. marginal cost.
   c. average product.
   d. average revenue.
   e. profit.
4. Diminishing returns to an input means that as a firm continues to produce, the total product curve will have what kind of slope?
   a. negative decreasing
   b. positive decreasing
   c. negative increasing
   d. positive increasing
   e. positive constant
5. Historically, the limits imposed by diminishing returns have been alleviated by
   a. investment in capital.
   b. increases in the population.
   c. discovery of more land.
   d. Thomas Malthus.
   e. economic models.

Critical-Thinking Question

Use the data in the table below to graph the production function and the marginal product of labor. Do the data illustrate diminishing returns to labor? Explain.

Quantity of labor	Quantity of output
L	Q
0	0
1	19
2	36
3	51
4	64
5	75
6	84
7	91
8	96

PITFALLS

WHAT ARE THE RIGHT UNITS TO USE?

? The marginal product of labor (or any other input) is defined as the increase in the quantity of output when you increase the quantity of that input by one unit. But when we say a "unit" of labor, do we mean an additional hour of labor, an additional week, or a person-year?

> IT DOESN'T MATTER, *AS LONG AS YOU ARE CONSISTENT.* WHATEVER UNITS YOU USE, ALWAYS BE CAREFUL THAT YOU USE THE SAME UNITS THROUGHOUT YOUR ANALYSIS OF ANY PROBLEM. One common source of error in economics is getting units confused—say, comparing the output added by an additional *hour* of labor with the cost of employing a worker for a *week*.

To learn more, review the definition of marginal product of labor *on pages 231–232.*

Firm Costs

WHAT YOU WILL LEARN

1. The various types of cost a firm faces, including fixed cost, variable cost, and total cost
2. How a firm's costs generate marginal cost curves and average cost curves

From the Production Function to Cost Curves

Now that we have learned about the firm's production function, we can use that knowledge to develop its cost curves. To see how a firm's production function is related to its cost curves, let's turn once again to George and Martha's farm.

Once George and Martha know their production function, they know the relationship between inputs of labor and land and output of wheat. But if they want to maximize their profits, they need to translate this knowledge into information about the relationship between the quantity of output and cost. Let's see how they can do this.

To translate information about a firm's production function into information about its cost, we need to know how much the firm must pay for its inputs. We will assume that George and Martha face either an explicit or an implicit cost of $400 for the use of the land. As we learned previously, it is irrelevant whether George and Martha must rent the land for $400 from someone else or whether they own the land themselves and forgo earning $400 from renting it to someone else. Either way, they pay an opportunity cost of $400 by using the land to grow wheat. Moreover, since the land is a fixed input for which George and Martha pay $400 whether they grow one bushel of wheat or one hundred, its cost is a **fixed cost,** denoted by *FC*—a cost that does not depend on the quantity of output produced. In business, a fixed cost is often referred to as an *overhead cost*.

We also assume that George and Martha must pay each worker $200. Using their production function, George and Martha know that the number of workers they must hire depends on the amount of wheat they intend to produce. So the cost of labor, which is equal to the number of workers multiplied by $200, is a **variable cost,** denoted by *VC*—a cost that depends on the quantity of output produced. Adding the fixed cost and the variable cost of a given quantity of output gives the **total cost,** or

A **fixed cost** is a cost that does not depend on the quantity of output produced. It is the cost of the fixed input.

A **variable cost** is a cost that depends on the quantity of output produced. It is the cost of the variable input.

The **total cost** of producing a given quantity of output is the sum of the fixed cost and the variable cost of producing that quantity of output.

FIGURE 22-3 Average Total Cost Curve for Selena's Gourmet Salsas

The average total cost curve at Selena's Gourmet Salsas is U-shaped. At low levels of output, average total cost falls because the "spreading effect" of falling average fixed cost dominates the "diminishing returns effect" of rising average variable cost. At higher levels of output, the opposite is true and average total cost rises. At point *M*, corresponding to an output of three cases of salsa per day, average total cost is at its minimum level, the minimum average total cost.

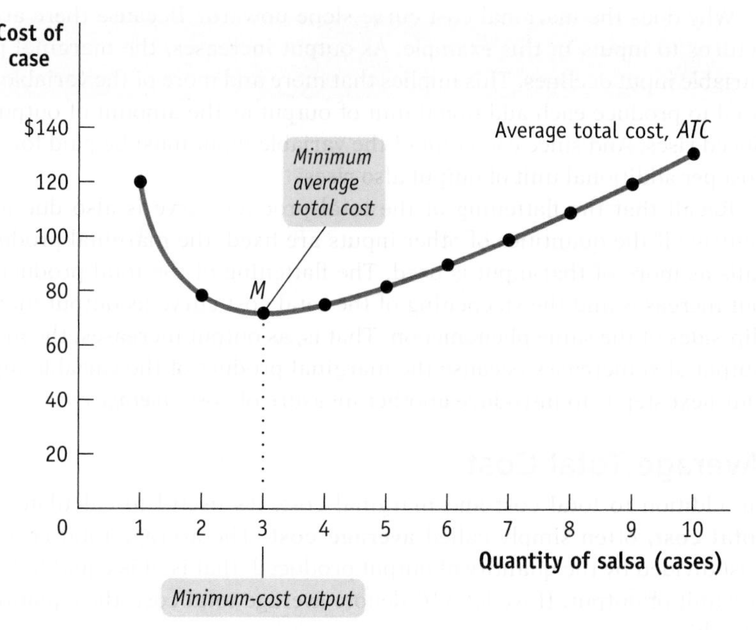

Figure 22-3 plots that data to yield the *average total cost curve,* which shows how average total cost depends on output. As before, cost in dollars is measured on the vertical axis and quantity of output is measured on the horizontal axis. The average total cost curve has a distinctive U shape that corresponds to how average total cost first falls and then rises as output increases. Economists believe that such **U-shaped average total cost curves** are the norm for firms in many industries.

To help our understanding of why the average total cost curve is U-shaped, Table 22-2 breaks average total cost into its two underlying components, *average fixed cost* and *average variable cost.* **Average fixed cost,** or *AFC,* is fixed cost divided by the quantity of output, also known as the fixed cost per unit of output. For example, if Selena's Gourmet Salsas produces 4 cases of salsa, average fixed cost is $108/4 = $27 per case. **Average variable cost,** or *AVC,* is variable cost divided by the quantity of output, also known as variable cost per unit of output. At an output of 4 cases, average variable cost is $192/4 = $48 per case. Writing these in the form of equations:

$$\textbf{(22-4)}\quad AFC = \frac{\text{Fixed cost}}{\text{Quantity of output}} = \frac{FC}{Q}$$

$$AVC = \frac{\text{Variable cost}}{\text{Quantity of output}} = \frac{VC}{Q}$$

Average total cost is the sum of average fixed cost and average variable cost; it has a U shape because these components move in opposite directions as output rises.

Average fixed cost falls as more output is produced because the numerator (the fixed cost) is a fixed number but the denominator (the quantity of output) increases as more is produced. Another way to think about this relationship is that, as more output is produced, the fixed cost is spread over more units of output; the end result is that the fixed cost *per unit of output*—the average fixed cost—falls.

A **U-shaped average total cost curve** falls at low levels of output and then rises at higher levels.

Average fixed cost is the fixed cost per unit of output.

Average variable cost is the variable cost per unit of output.

You can see this effect in the fourth column of Table 22-2: average fixed cost drops continuously as output increases.

Average variable cost, however, rises as output increases. As we've seen, this reflects diminishing returns to the variable input: each additional unit of output adds more to variable cost than the previous unit because increasing amounts of the variable input are required to make another unit.

So increasing output has two opposing effects on average total cost—the "spreading effect" and the "diminishing returns effect":

1. *The spreading effect.* The larger the output, the greater the quantity of output over which fixed cost is spread, leading to lower average fixed cost.
2. *The diminishing returns effect.* The larger the output, the greater the amount of variable input required to produce additional units, leading to higher average variable cost.

At low levels of output, the spreading effect is very powerful because even small increases in output cause large reductions in average fixed cost. So at low levels of output, the spreading effect dominates the diminishing returns effect and causes the average total cost curve to slope downward.

But when output is large, average fixed cost is already quite small, so increasing output further has only a very small spreading effect. Diminishing returns, however, usually grow increasingly important as output rises. As a result, when output is large, the diminishing returns effect dominates the spreading effect, causing the average total cost curve to slope upward.

At the bottom of the U-shaped average total cost curve, point *M* in Figure 22-3, the two effects exactly balance each other. At this point average total cost is at its minimum level, the minimum average total cost.

Figure 22-4 brings together in a single picture the four other cost curves that we have derived from the total cost curve for Selena's Gourmet Salsas: the marginal cost curve (*MC*), the average total cost curve (*ATC*), the average variable cost curve (*AVC*), and the average fixed cost curve (*AFC*). All are based on the information in Tables 22-1 and 22-2. As before, cost is measured on the vertical axis and the quantity of output is measured on the horizontal axis.

Let's take a moment to note some features of the various cost curves. First of all, marginal cost slopes upward—the result of diminishing returns that make an additional unit of output more costly to produce than the one before. Average variable cost also slopes upward—again, due to diminishing returns—but is flatter than the marginal cost curve. This is because the higher cost of an additional

Photodisc

FIGURE 22-4 Marginal Cost and Average Cost Curves for Selena's Gourmet Salsas

Here we have the family of cost curves for Selena's Gourmet Salsas: the marginal cost curve (*MC*), the average total cost curve (*ATC*), the average variable cost curve (*AVC*), and the average fixed cost curve (*AFC*). Note that the average total cost curve is U-shaped and the marginal cost curve crosses the average total cost curve at the bottom of the U, point *M*, corresponding to the minimum average total cost from Table 22-2 and Figure 22-3.

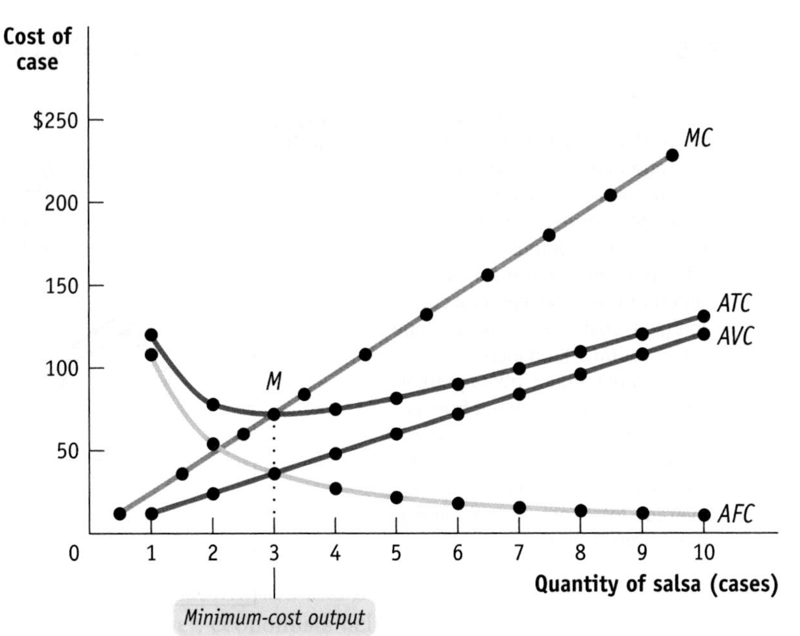

BUSINESS CASE: Kiva Systems' Robots versus Humans: The Challenge of Holiday Order Fulfillment

For those who like to procrastinate when it comes to holiday shopping, the rise of e-commerce has been a welcome phenomenon. Amazon.com boasts that in 2012, customers living in 11 cities in the United States could receive same-day delivery for orders placed on the day before Christmas.

Courtesy Kiva Systems

E-commerce retailers like Amazon.com and CrateandBarrel.com can see their sales quadruple for the holidays. With advances in order fulfillment technology that get customers' orders to them quickly, e-commerce sellers have been able to capture an ever-greater share of sales from brick-and-mortar retailers. Holiday sales at e-commerce sites grew by over 13% from 2011 to 2012.

Behind these technological advances, however, lies an intense debate: people versus robots. Amazon has relied on a large staff of temporary workers to get it through the previous holiday seasons, often quadrupling its staff and operating 24 hours a day. In contrast, Crate and Barrel only doubled its workforce, thanks to a cadre of orange robots that allows each worker to do the work of six people.

But, Amazon is set to increase its robotic work force in the future. In May of 2012, Amazon bought Kiva Systems, the leader in order fulfillment robotics, for $775 million, with the hope of tailoring Kiva's systems to best fit Amazon's warehouse and fulfillment needs.

Although many retailers—Staples, Gap, Saks Fifth Avenue, and Walgreens, for example—also use Kiva equipment, installation of a robotic system can be expensive, with some installations costing as much as $20 million. Yet hiring workers has a cost, too: during the 2010 holiday season, before it had installed an extensive robotic system, Amazon hired some 12,500 temporary workers at its 20 distribution centers around the United States.

As one industry analyst noted, an obstacle to the purchase of a robotic system for many e-commerce retailers is that it often doesn't make economic sense: it's too expensive to buy sufficient robots for the busiest time of the year because they would be idle at other times. Before Amazon's purchase, Kiva was testing a program to rent out its robots seasonally so that retailers could "hire" enough robots to handle their holiday orders just like Amazon used to hire more humans.

Questions for Thought

1. Assume that a firm can sell a robot, but that the sale takes time and the firm is likely to get less than what it paid. Other things equal, which system, human-based or robotic, will have a higher fixed cost? Which will have a higher variable cost? Explain.
2. What pattern of off-holiday sales versus holiday sales would induce a retailer to keep a human-based system? What pattern would induce a retailer to move to a robotic system?
3. How would a "robot-for-hire" program affect your answer to Question 2? Explain.

SECTION 8 REVIEW

Summary

The Production Function

1. The relationship between inputs and output is represented by a firm's **production function.** In the **short run,** the quantity of a **fixed input** cannot be varied but the quantity of a **variable input,** by definition, can. In the **long run,** the quantities of all inputs can be varied. For a given amount of the fixed input, the **total product curve** shows how the quantity of output changes as the quantity of the variable input changes. The **marginal product** of an input is the increase in output that results from using one more unit of that input.
2. There are **diminishing returns to an input** when its marginal product declines as more of the input is used, holding the quantity of all other inputs fixed.

Firm Costs

3. **Total cost,** represented by the **total cost curve,** is equal to the sum of **fixed cost,** which does not depend on output, and **variable cost,** which does depend on output. Due to diminishing returns, marginal cost, the increase in total cost generated by producing one more unit of output, normally increases as output increases.
4. **Average total cost** (also known as **average cost**) is the total cost divided by the quantity of output. Economists believe that **U-shaped average total cost curves** are typical because average total cost consists of two parts: **average fixed cost,** which falls when output increases (the spreading effect), and **average variable cost,** which rises with output (the diminishing returns effect).
5. When average total cost is U-shaped, the bottom of the U is the level of output at which average total cost is minimized, the point of **minimum-cost output.** This is also the point at which the **marginal cost curve** crosses the average total cost curve from below. Due to gains from specialization, the marginal cost curve may slope downward initially before sloping upward, giving it a "swoosh" shape.

Long-Run Costs and Economies of Scale

6. In the long run, a firm can change its fixed input and its level of fixed cost. By accepting higher fixed cost, a firm can lower its variable cost for any given output level, and vice versa. The **long-run average total cost curve** shows the relationship between output and average total cost when fixed cost has been chosen to minimize average total cost at each level of output. A firm moves along its short-run average total cost curve as it changes the quantity of output, and it returns to a point on both its short-run and long-run average total cost curves once it has adjusted fixed cost to its new output level.
7. As output increases, long-run average total cost changes. There are **increasing returns to scale** if long-run average total cost falls as output rises; **decreasing returns to scale** if long-run average cost rises as output rises; and **constant returns to scale** if long-run average total cost does not change as output rises.

Key Terms

Production function, p. 230
Fixed input, p. 230
Variable input, p. 230
Long run, p. 230
Short run, p. 230
Total product curve, p. 231
Marginal product, p. 231
Diminishing returns to an input, p. 233
Fixed cost, p. 237
Variable cost, p. 237
Total cost, p. 237
Total cost curve, p. 238
Average total cost, p. 241
Average cost, p. 241
U-shaped average total cost curve, p. 242
Average fixed cost, p. 242
Average variable cost, p. 242
Minimum-cost output, p. 244
Long-run average total cost curve, p. 250
Increasing returns to scale, p. 251
Decreasing returns to scale, p. 251
Constant returns to scale, p. 251

Problems

1. Changes in the prices of key commodities can have a significant impact on a company's bottom line. According to an article in the *Wall Street Journal,* "Now, with oil, gas and electricity prices soaring, companies are beginning to realize that saving energy can translate into dramatically lower costs." Another *Wall Street Journal* article states, "Higher grain prices are taking an increasing financial toll." Energy is an input into virtually all types of production; corn is an input into the production of beef, chicken, high-fructose corn syrup, and ethanol (the gasoline substitute fuel).

   a. Explain how the cost of energy can be both a fixed cost and a variable cost for a company.

b. Suppose energy is a fixed cost and energy prices rise. What happens to the company's average total cost curve? What happens to its marginal cost curve? Illustrate your answer with a diagram.

c. Explain why the cost of corn is a variable cost but not a fixed cost for an ethanol producer.

d. When the cost of corn goes up, what happens to the average total cost curve of an ethanol producer? What happens to its marginal cost curve? Illustrate your answer with a diagram.

2. Marty's Frozen Yogurt is a small shop that sells cups of frozen yogurt in a university town. Marty owns three frozen-yogurt machines. His other inputs are refrigerators, frozen-yogurt mix, cups, sprinkle toppings, and, of course, workers. He estimates that his daily production function when he varies the number of workers employed (and at the same time, of course, yogurt mix, cups, and so on) is as shown in the accompanying table.

Quantity of labor (workers)	Quantity of frozen yogurt (cups)
0	0
1	110
2	200
3	270
4	300
5	320
6	330

a. What are the fixed inputs and variable inputs in the production of cups of frozen yogurt?

b. Draw the total product curve. Put the quantity of labor on the horizontal axis and the quantity of frozen yogurt on the vertical axis.

c. What is the marginal product of the first worker? The second worker? The third worker? Why does marginal product decline as the number of workers increases?

3. The production function for Marty's Frozen Yogurt is given in Problem 2. Marty pays each of his workers \$80 per day. The cost of his other variable inputs is \$0.50 per cup of yogurt. His fixed cost is \$100 per day.

a. What is Marty's variable cost and total cost when he produces 110 cups of yogurt? 200 cups? Calculate variable and total cost for every level of output given in Problem 2.

b. Draw Marty's variable cost curve. On the same diagram, draw his total cost curve.

c. What is the marginal cost per cup for the first 110 cups of yogurt? For the next 90 cups? Calculate the marginal cost for all remaining levels of output.

4. The production function for Marty's Frozen Yogurt is given in Problem 2. The costs are given in Problem 3.

a. For each of the given levels of output, calculate the average fixed cost (*AFC*), average variable cost (*AVC*), and average total cost (*ATC*) per cup of frozen yogurt.

b. On one diagram, draw the *AFC*, *AVC*, and *ATC* curves.

c. What principle explains why the *AFC* declines as output increases? What principle explains why the *AVC* increases as output increases? Explain your answers.

d. How many cups of frozen yogurt are produced when average total cost is minimized?

5. The accompanying table shows a car manufacturer's total cost of producing cars.

Quantity of cars	*TC*
0	\$500,000
1	540,000
2	560,000
3	570,000
4	590,000
5	620,000
6	660,000
7	720,000
8	800,000
9	920,000
10	1,100,000

a. What is this manufacturer's fixed cost?

b. For each level of output, calculate the variable cost (*VC*). For each level of output except zero, calculate the average variable cost (*AVC*), average total cost (*ATC*), and average fixed cost (*AFC*). What is the minimum-cost output?

c. For each level of output, calculate this manufacturer's marginal cost (*MC*).

d. On one diagram, draw the manufacturer's *AVC*, *ATC*, and *MC* curves.

6. Labor costs represent a large percentage of total costs for many firms. Assume that in September 2013 U.S. labor costs were up 0.9% during the preceding three months and 0.8% over the three months preceding those.

a. When labor costs increase, what happens to average total cost and marginal cost? Consider a case in which labor costs are only variable costs and a case in which they are both variable and fixed costs.

An increase in labor productivity means each worker can produce more output. Recent data on productivity show that labor productivity in the U.S. nonfarm business sector grew 2% for each of the years 2011, 2012, and 2013. Annual growth in labor productivity averaged 1.5% from the mid-1970s to mid-1990s, 2.6% in the past decade, and 4% for a couple of years in the early 2000s.

b. When productivity growth is positive, what happens to the total product curve and the marginal product of labor curve? Illustrate your answer with a diagram.

c. When productivity growth is positive, what happens to the marginal cost curve and the average total cost curve? Illustrate your answer with a diagram.

d. If labor costs are rising over time on average, why would a company want to adopt equipment and methods that increase labor productivity?

7. Magnificent Blooms is a florist specializing in floral arrangements for weddings, graduations, and other events. The firm has a fixed cost associated with space and equipment of $100 per day. Each worker is paid $50 per day. The daily production function for Magnificent Blooms is shown in the accompanying table.

Quantity of labor (workers)	Quantity of floral arrangements
0	0
1	5
2	9
3	12
4	14
5	15

a. Calculate the marginal product of each worker. What principle explains why the marginal product per worker declines as the number of workers employed increases?

b. Calculate the marginal cost of each level of output. What principle explains why the marginal cost per floral arrangement increases as the number of arrangements increases?

8. You have the information shown in the accompanying table about a firm's costs. Complete the missing data.

Quantity	*TC*	*MC*	*ATC*	*AVC*
0	$20		—	—
		$20		
1	?		?	?
		10		
2	?		?	?
		16		
3	?		?	?
		20		
4	?		?	?
		24		
5	?		?	?

9. Evaluate each of the following statements. If a statement is true, explain why; if it is false, identify the mistake and try to correct it.

a. A decreasing marginal product tells us that marginal cost must be rising.

b. An increase in fixed cost increases the minimum-cost output.

c. An increase in fixed cost increases marginal cost.

d. When marginal cost is above average total cost, average total cost must be falling.

10. Mark and Jeff operate a small company that produces souvenir footballs. Their fixed cost is $2,000 per month. They can hire workers for $1,000 per worker per month. Their monthly production function for footballs is as given in the accompanying table.

Quantity of labor (workers)	Quantity of footballs
0	0
1	300
2	800
3	1,200
4	1,400
5	1,500

a. For each quantity of labor, calculate average variable cost (*AVC*), average fixed cost (*AFC*), average total cost (*ATC*), and marginal cost (*MC*).

b. On one diagram, draw the *AVC*, *ATC*, and *MC* curves.

c. At what level of output is Mark and Jeff's average total cost minimized?

11. You produce widgets. Currently you produce four widgets at a total cost of $40.

a. What is your average total cost?

b. Suppose you could produce one more (the fifth) widget at a marginal cost of $5. If you do produce that fifth widget, what will your average total cost be? Has your average total cost increased or decreased? Why?

c. Suppose instead that you could produce one more (the fifth) widget at a marginal cost of $20. If you do produce that fifth widget, what will your average total cost be? Has your average total cost increased or decreased? Why?

Coca-Cola
ORGANIC!
TOMATOES!
FIRST OF SEASON

Module 24: Introduction to Market Structure
Module 25: Perfect Competition
Module 26: Graphing Perfect Competition
Module 27: Long-Run Outcomes in Perfect Competition

SECTION 9

Market Structure and Perfect Competition

DOING WHAT COMES NATURALLY

Food consumers in the United States are concerned about health issues. Demand for natural foods and beverages, such as bottled water and organically grown fruits and vegetables, increased rapidly over the past 25 years at an average growth rate of about 20% per year. The small group of farmers who had pioneered organic farming techniques prospered thanks to higher prices.

But everyone knew that the high prices of organic produce were unlikely to persist even if the new, higher demand for naturally grown food continued: the supply of organic food, although relatively price-inelastic in the short run, was surely price-elastic in the long run. Over time, farms already producing organically would increase their capacity, and conventional farmers would enter the organic food business. So the increase in the quantity supplied in response to the increase in price would be much larger in the long run than in the short run.

Where does the market supply curve come from? Why is there a difference between the short-run and the long-run supply curve? In this section we will use our understanding of costs, developed in Section 8, as the basis for an analysis of the market supply curve. As we'll see, this will require that we understand the behavior both of individual firms and of an entire industry, composed of these many individual firms.

Our analysis in this section assumes that the industry in question is characterized by *perfect competition*. We begin with an introduction to *market structures*, a system economists use to classify markets and industries according to two main dimensions. Perfect competition is actually one particular type of market structure, along with monopoly, oligopoly, and monopolistic competition (we will look at these three other types of market structures in upcoming sections). We continue by explaining the concept of perfect competition, providing a brief introduction to the conditions that give rise to a perfectly competitive industry. Then we show how a producer under perfect competition decides how much to produce. Finally, we use the cost curves of the individual producers to derive the *industry supply curve* under perfect competition.

By analyzing the way a competitive industry evolves over time, we will come to understand the distinction between the short-run and long-run effects of changes in demand on a competitive industry—for example, the effect of America's new taste for organic food on the organic farming industry. We conclude with a more in-depth discussion of the conditions necessary for an industry to be perfectly competitive.

MODULE 24

Introduction to Market Structure

Richard B. Levine/Alamy

WHAT YOU WILL LEARN

1. The meaning and dimensions of market structure
2. The four principal types of market structure—perfect competition, monopoly, oligopoly, and monopolistic competition

To discuss the supply curve in a market, we need to identify the type of market we are looking at. In this module we will learn about the basic characteristics of the four major types of markets in the economy.

Types of Market Structure

The real world holds a mind-boggling array of different markets. Patterns of firm behavior vary as widely as the markets themselves: in some markets firms are extremely competitive; in others, they seem somehow to coordinate their actions to limit competition; and some markets are monopolies in which there is no competition at all.

In order to develop principles and make predictions about markets and firm behavior, economists have developed four primary models of market structure: *perfect competition, monopoly, oligopoly,* and *monopolistic competition*. This system of market structure is based on two dimensions:

1. the number of firms in the market (one, few, or many)
2. whether the goods offered are identical or *differentiated*.

Differentiated goods are goods that are different but considered at least somewhat substitutable by consumers—think Coke versus Pepsi.

Figure 24-1 provides a simple visual summary of the types of market structure classified according to the two dimensions. In *perfect competition* many firms each sell an identical product. In *monopoly,* a single firm sells a single, undifferentiated product. In *oligopoly,* a few firms—more than one but not a large number—sell products that may be either identical or differentiated. And in *monopolistic competition,* many firms each sell a differentiated product—think of producers of economics textbooks.

FIGURE 24-1 Types of Market Structure

The behavior of any given firm and the market it occupies are analyzed using one of four models of market structure—monopoly, oligopoly, perfect competition, or monopolistic competition. This system for categorizing market structure is based on two dimensions: (1) whether products are differentiated or identical and (2) the number of firms in the industry—one, a few, or many.

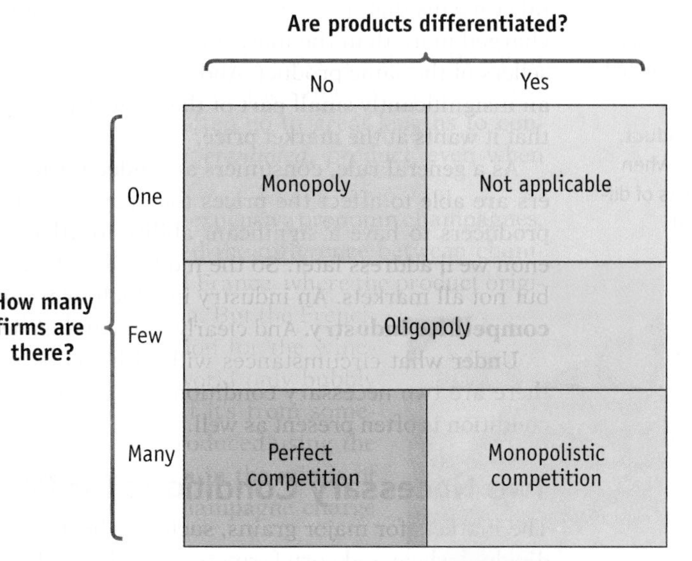

Perfect Competition

Suppose that Yves and Zoe are neighboring farmers, both of whom grow organic tomatoes. Both sell their output to the same grocery store chains that carry organic foods; so, in a real sense, Yves and Zoe compete with each other.

Does this mean that Yves should try to stop Zoe from growing tomatoes or that Yves and Zoe should form an agreement to grow fewer? Almost certainly not: there are hundreds or thousands of organic tomato farmers, and Yves and Zoe are competing with all those other growers as well as with each other. Because so many farmers sell organic tomatoes, if any one of them produced more or fewer, there would be no measurable effect on market prices.

When people talk about business competition, they often imagine a situation in which two or three rival firms are struggling for advantage. But economists know that when a business focuses on a few main competitors, it's actually a sign that competition is fairly limited. As the example of organic tomatoes suggests, when the number of competitors is large, it doesn't even make sense to identify rivals and engage in aggressive competition because each firm is too small within the scope of the market to make a significant difference.

We can put it another way: Yves and Zoe are *price-takers.* A firm or producer is a **price-taker** when its actions cannot affect the market price of the good or service it sells. As a result, a price-taking firm takes the market price as given. When there is enough competition—when competition is what economists call "perfect"—then every firm is a price-taker. There is a similar definition for consumers: a **price-taking consumer** is a consumer who cannot influence the market price of the good or service by his or her actions. That is, the market price is unaffected by how much or how little of the good the consumer buys.

The actions of a **price-taking firm** have no effect on the market price of the good or service it sells.

A **price-taking consumer** is a consumer whose actions have no effect on the market price of the good or service he or she buys.

Defining Perfect Competition

In a **perfectly competitive market,** all market participants, both consumers and producers, are price-takers. That is, neither consumption decisions by individual consumers nor production decisions by individual producers affect the market price of the good.

A **perfectly competitive market** is a market in which all market participants are price-takers.

The supply and demand model is a model of a perfectly competitive market. It depends fundamentally on the assumption that no individual buyer or seller of a good,

A **monopolist** is the only producer of a good that has no close substitutes. An industry controlled by a monopolist is known as a **monopoly.**

To earn economic profits, a monopolist must be protected by a **barrier to entry**—something that prevents other firms from entering the industry.

A **natural monopoly** exists when economies of scale provide a large cost advantage to a single firm that produces all of an industry's output.

mines and consolidated them into a single company, De Beers. By 1889, De Beers controlled almost all of the world's diamond production.

De Beers, in other words, became a *monopolist*. But what does it mean to be a monopolist? And what do monopolists do?

Defining Monopoly

As we mentioned earlier, the supply and demand model of a market is not universally valid. Instead, it's a model of perfect competition, which is only one of several types of market structure. A market will be perfectly competitive only if there are many firms, all of which produce the same good. Monopoly is the most extreme departure from perfect competition.

A **monopolist** is a firm that is the only producer of a good that has no close substitutes. An industry controlled by a monopolist is known as a **monopoly.**

In practice, true monopolies are hard to find in the modern American economy, partly because of legal obstacles. A contemporary entrepreneur who tried to consolidate all the firms in an industry the way Rhodes did would soon find himself in court, accused of breaking *antitrust* laws, which are intended to prevent monopolies from emerging. Monopolies do, however, play an important role in some sectors of the economy.

Why Do Monopolies Exist?

A monopolist making profits will not go unnoticed by others. (Recall that we mean "economic profit," revenue over and above the opportunity costs of the firm's resources.) But won't other firms crash the party, grab a piece of the action, and drive down prices and profits in the long run?

If possible, yes, they will. For a profitable monopoly to persist, something must keep others from going into the same business; that "something" is known as a **barrier to entry.** There are four principal types of barriers to entry: control of a scarce resource or input, economies of scale, technological superiority, and government-created barriers.

CONTROL OF A SCARCE RESOURCE OR INPUT A monopolist that controls a resource or input crucial to an industry can prevent other firms from entering its market. Cecil Rhodes made De Beers into a monopolist by establishing control over the mines that produced the bulk of the world's diamonds.

ECONOMIES OF SCALE Many Americans have natural gas piped into their homes for cooking and heating. Invariably, the local gas company is a monopolist. But why don't rival companies compete to provide gas?

In the early nineteenth century, when the gas industry was just starting up, companies did compete for local customers. But this competition didn't last long; soon local gas companies became monopolists in almost every town because of the large fixed cost of providing a town with gas lines. The cost of laying gas lines didn't depend on how much gas a company sold, so a firm with a larger volume of sales had a cost advantage: because it was able to spread the fixed cost over a larger volume, it had a lower average total cost than smaller firms.

The natural gas industry is one in which average total cost falls as output increases, resulting in economies of scale and encouraging firms to grow larger. In an industry characterized by economies of scale, larger firms are more profitable and drive out smaller ones. For the same reason, established firms have a cost advantage over any potential entrant—a potent barrier to entry. So economies of scale can both give rise to and sustain a monopoly.

A monopoly created and sustained by economies of scale is called a **natural monopoly.** The defining characteristic of a natural monopoly is that it possesses economies of scale over the range of output that is relevant for the industry. The source of this condition is large fixed costs: when large fixed costs are required to operate, a given quantity of output is produced at lower average total cost by one large firm than by two or more smaller firms.

The most visible natural monopolies in the modern economy are local utilities—water, gas, electricity, local land line phone service, and, in most locations, cable television. As we'll see later, natural monopolies pose a special challenge to public policy.

TECHNOLOGICAL SUPERIORITY A firm that maintains a consistent technological advantage over potential competitors can establish itself as a monopolist. For example, from the 1970s through the 1990s, the chip manufacturer Intel was able to maintain a consistent advantage over potential competitors in both the design and production of microprocessors, the chips that run computers. But technological superiority is typically not a barrier to entry over the longer term: over time competitors will invest in upgrading their technology to match that of the technology leader. In fact, in the last few years Intel found its technological superiority eroded by a competitor, Advanced Micro Devices (also known as AMD), which was able to produce chips approximately as fast and as powerful as Intel chips.

We should note, however, that in certain high-tech industries, technological superiority is not a guarantee of success against competitors. Some high-tech industries are characterized by *network externalities,* a condition that arises when the value of a good to a consumer rises as the number of other people who also use the good rises. In these industries, the firm possessing the largest network—the largest number of consumers currently using its product—has an advantage over its competitors in attracting new customers. For example, think about the number of people who use Facebook. What value would Facebook have to consumers if only a few people had pages instead of the current 1 billion users worldwide? Users are attracted to Facebook precisely because so many other people are using it as well. Facebook has been cited as an example of a company with the potential to gain significant monopoly power in its industry through the phenomenon of network externalities.

Stephanie Pilick/picture-alliance/dpa/AP Images

Top social-media sites like Twitter (500 million users) and Tumblr (over 200 million users) have an advantage over their competition in attracting new customers.

GOVERNMENT-CREATED BARRIERS In 1998 the pharmaceutical company Merck introduced Propecia, a drug effective against baldness. Despite the fact that Propecia was very profitable and other drug companies had the know-how to produce it, no other firms challenged Merck's monopoly. That's because the U.S. government had given Merck the sole legal right to produce the drug in the United States. Propecia is an example of a monopoly protected by government-created barriers.

The most important legally created monopolies today arise from *patents* and *copyrights.* A **patent** gives an inventor the sole right to make, use, or sell that invention for a period that in most countries lasts between 16 and 20 years. Patents are given to the creators of new products, such as drugs or mechanical devices. Similarly, a **copyright** gives the creator of a literary or artistic work the sole right to profit from that work, usually for a period equal to the creator's lifetime plus 70 years.

The justification for patents and copyrights is a matter of incentives. If inventors were not protected by patents, they would gain little reward from their efforts: as soon as a valuable invention was made public, others would copy it and sell products based on it. And if inventors could not expect to profit from their inventions, then there would be no incentive to incur the costs of invention in the first place. Likewise for the creators of literary or artistic works. So the law allows a monopoly to exist temporarily by granting property rights that encourage invention and creation.

A **patent** gives an inventor a temporary monopoly in the use or sale of an invention.

A **copyright** gives the creator of a literary or artistic work the sole right to profit from that work.

Patents and copyrights are temporary because the law strikes a compromise. The higher price for the good that holds while the legal protection is in effect compensates inventors for the cost of invention; conversely, the lower price that results once the legal protection lapses benefits consumers.

An **oligopoly** is an industry with only a small number of firms. A producer in such an industry is known as an **oligopolist.**

When no one firm has a monopoly, but producers nonetheless realize that they can affect market prices, an industry is characterized by **imperfect competition.**

Because the lifetime of the temporary monopoly cannot be tailored to specific cases, this system is imperfect and leads to some missed opportunities. In some cases there can be significant welfare issues. For example, the violation of American drug patents by pharmaceutical companies in poor countries has been a major source of controversy, pitting the needs of poor patients who cannot afford to pay retail drug prices against the interests of drug manufacturers who have incurred high research costs to discover these drugs. To solve this problem, some American drug companies and poor countries have negotiated deals in which the patents are honored but the American companies sell their drugs at deeply discounted prices. (This is an example of *price discrimination,* which we'll learn more about in the next section.)

Oligopoly

An industry with only a few firms is known as an **oligopoly;** a producer in such an industry is known as an **oligopolist.**

Oligopolists compete with each other for sales. But oligopolists aren't like producers in a perfectly competitive industry, who take the market as given. Oligopolists know their decisions about how much to produce will affect the market price. That is, like monopolists, oligopolists have some *market power.*

Economists refer to a situation in which firms compete but also possess market power—which enables them to affect market prices—as **imperfect competition.** There are two important forms of imperfect competition: oligopoly and *monopolistic competition.* Of these, oligopoly is probably the more important in practice.

© Colin Underhill/Alamy

Oligopolies supply familiar goods and services in a market with only a few competing sellers.

Many familiar goods and services are supplied by only a few competing sellers, which means the industries in question are oligopolies. For example, most air routes are served by only two or three airlines: in recent years, regularly scheduled shuttle service between New York and either Boston or Washington, D.C., has been provided only by Delta and US Airways. Three firms—Chiquita, Dole, and Del Monte, which own huge banana plantations in Central America—control 65% of world banana exports. Most cola beverages are sold by Coca-Cola and Pepsi. This list could go on for many pages.

It's important to realize that an oligopoly isn't necessarily made up of large firms. What matters isn't size per se; the question is how many competitors there are. When a small town has only two grocery stores, grocery service there is just as much an oligopoly as air shuttle service between New York and Washington.

Why are oligopolies so prevalent? Essentially, an oligopoly is the result of the same factors that sometimes produce a monopoly, but in somewhat weaker form. Probably the most important source of oligopolies is the existence of economies of scale, which give bigger firms a cost advantage over smaller ones. When these effects are very strong, as we have seen, they lead to a monopoly; when they are not that strong, they lead to an industry with a small number of firms. For example, larger grocery stores typically have lower costs than smaller stores. But the advantages of large scale taper off once grocery stores are reasonably large, which is why two or three stores often survive in small towns.

Is It an Oligopoly or Not?

In practice, it is not always easy to determine an industry's market structure just by looking at the number of sellers. Many oligopolistic industries contain a number of small "niche" firms, which don't really compete with the major players. For example, the U.S. airline industry includes a number of regional airlines such as New Mexico Airlines, which flies propeller planes between Albuquerque and Carlsbad, New Mexico; if you count these carriers, the U.S. airline industry contains nearly one hundred firms, which doesn't sound like competition among a small group. But there are only a handful of national competitors like American and United, and on many routes, as we've seen, there are only two or three competitors.

To get a better picture of market structure, economists often use a measure called the **Herfindahl–Hirschman Index,** or HHI. The HHI for an industry is the square of each firm's share of market sales summed over the firms in the industry. The HHI takes into account the distribution of market sales among the top firms by squaring each firm's market share, thereby giving more weight to larger firms. For example, if an industry contains only 3 firms and their market shares are 60%, 25%, and 15%, then the HHI for the industry is:

Herfindahl–Hirschman Index, or HHI, is the square of each firm's share of market sales summed over the industry. It gives a picture of the industry market structure.

$$HHI = 60^2 + 25^2 + 15^2 = 4{,}450$$

By squaring each market share, the HHI calculation produces numbers that are much larger when a larger share of an industry output is dominated by fewer firms. So it's a better measure of just how concentrated the industry is. This is confirmed by the data in Table 24-1. Here, the indices for industries dominated by a small number of firms, like the personal computer operating systems industry or the wide-body aircraft industry, are many times larger than the index for the retail grocery industry, which has numerous firms of approximately equal size.

TABLE 24-1

The HHI for Some Oligopolistic Industries

Industry	HHI	Largest firms
PC operating systems	9,182	Microsoft, Linux
Wide-body aircraft	5,098	Boeing, Airbus
Diamond mining	2,338	De Beers, Alrosa, Rio Tinto
Automobiles	1,432	GM, Ford, Chrysler, Toyota, Honda, Nissan, VW
Movie distributors	1,096	Buena Vista, Sony Pictures, 20th Century Fox, Warner Bros., Universal, Paramount, Lionsgate
Internet service providers	750	SBC, Comcast, AOL, Verizon, Road Runner, Earthlink, Charter, Qwest
Retail grocers	321	Walmart, Kroger, Sears, Target, Costco, Walgreens, Ahold, Albertsons

Sources: Canadian Government; Diamond Facts 2006; www.w3counter.com; Planet retail; Autodata; Reuters; ISP Planet; Swivel. Data cover 2006–2007.

Monopolistic Competition

Leo manages the Wonderful Wok stand in the food court of a big shopping mall. He offers the only Chinese food there, but there are more than a dozen alternatives, from Bodacious Burgers to Pizza Paradise. When deciding what to charge for a meal, Leo knows that he must take those alternatives into account: even people who normally prefer stir-fry won't order a $15 lunch from Leo when they can get a burger, fries, and drink for $4.

But Leo also knows that he won't lose all his business even if his lunches cost a bit more than the alternatives. Chinese food isn't the same thing as burgers or pizza. Some people will really be in the mood for Chinese that day, and they will buy from Leo even if they could have dined more cheaply on burgers. Of course, the reverse is also true: even if Chinese is a bit cheaper, some people will choose burgers instead. In other words, Leo does have some market power: he has *some* ability to set his own price.

So how would you describe Leo's situation? He definitely isn't a price-taker, so he isn't in a situation of perfect competition. But you wouldn't exactly call him a monopolist, either. Although he's the only seller of Chinese food in that food court, he does face competition from other food vendors.

Yet it would also be wrong to call him an oligopolist. Oligopoly, remember, involves competition among a small number of interdependent firms in an industry protected

Monopolistic competition is a market structure in which there are many competing firms in an industry, each firm sells a differentiated product, and there is free entry into and exit from the industry in the long run.

by some—albeit limited—barriers to entry and whose profits are highly interdependent. Because their profits are highly interdependent, oligopolists have an incentive to collude, tacitly or explicitly. But in Leo's case there are *lots* of vendors in the shopping mall, too many to make tacit collusion feasible.

Defining Monopolistic Competition

Economists describe Leo's situation as one of **monopolistic competition.** Monopolistic competition is particularly common in service industries such as the restaurant and gas station industries, but it also exists in some manufacturing industries. It involves three conditions:

1. a large number of competing firms,
2. differentiated products, and
3. free entry into and exit from the industry in the long run.

In a monopolistically competitive industry, each producer has some ability to set the price of her differentiated product. But exactly how high she can set it is limited by the competition she faces from other existing and potential firms that produce close, but not identical, products.

LARGE NUMBERS In a monopolistically competitive industry there are many firms. Such an industry does not look either like a monopoly, where the firm faces no competition, or like an oligopoly, where each firm has only a few rivals. Instead, each seller has many competitors. For example, there are many vendors in a big food court, many gas stations along a major highway, and many hotels at a popular beach resort.

DIFFERENTIATED PRODUCTS In a monopolistically competitive industry, each firm has a product that consumers view as somewhat distinct from the products of competing firms. Such product differentiation can come in the form of different styles or types, different locations, or different levels of quality. At the same time, though, consumers see these competing products as close substitutes. If Leo's food court contained 15 vendors selling exactly the same kind and quality of food, there would be perfect competition: any seller who tried to charge a higher price would have no customers. But suppose that Wonderful Wok is the only Chinese food vendor, Bodacious Burgers is the only hamburger stand, and so on. The result of this differentiation is that each vendor has some ability to set his or her own price: each firm has some—albeit limited—market power.

© imac/Alamy

You'll find monopolistic competition in action in any food court, where restaurants like Burger King, TCBY, Popeyes, and others vie for your food dollar.

FREE ENTRY AND EXIT IN THE LONG RUN In monopolistically competitive industries, new firms, with their own distinct products, can enter the industry freely in the long run. For example, other food vendors would open outlets in the food court if they thought it would be profitable to do so. In addition, firms will exit the industry if they find they are not covering their costs in the long run.

Monopolistic competition, then, differs from the three market structures we have examined so far. It's not the same as perfect competition: firms have some power to set prices. It's not pure monopoly: firms face some competition. And it's not the same as oligopoly: there are many firms and free entry, which eliminates the potential for collusion that is so important in oligopoly. As we'll see in a later section, competition among the sellers of differentiated products is the key to understanding how monopolistic competition works.

Now that we have introduced the idea of market structure and presented the four principal models of market structure, we can proceed to explain and predict firm behavior (e.g., price and quantity determination) and analyze individual markets.

MODULE 24 Review

Solutions appear at the back of the book.

Check Your Understanding

1. In each of the following situations, what type of market structure do you think the industry represents?
   a. There are three producers of aluminum in the world, a good sold in many places.
   b. There are thousands of farms that produce indistinguishable soybeans to thousands of buyers.
   c. Many designers sell high-fashion clothes. Each designer has a distinctive style and a somewhat loyal clientele.
   d. A small town in the middle of Alaska has one bicycle shop.

Multiple-Choice Questions

1. Which of the following is true for a perfectly competitive industry?
   I. There are many firms, each with a large market share.
   II. The firms in the industry produce a standardized product.
   III. There are barriers to entry and exit.
   a. I only
   b. II only
   c. III only
   d. I and II only
   e. I, II, and III
2. Which of the following is true for a monopoly?
   I. There is only one firm.
   II. The firm produces a product with many close substitutes.
   III. The industry has free entry and exit.
   a. I only
   b. II only
   c. III only
   d. I and II only
   e. I, II, and III
3. Which of the following is true for an oligopoly?
   I. There are a few firms, each with a large market share.
   II. The firms in the industry are interdependent.
   III. The industry experiences diseconomies of scale.
   a. I only
   b. II only
   c. III only
   d. I and II only
   e. I, II, and III
4. Which of the following is true for a monopolistically competitive industry?
   I. There are many firms, each with a small market share.
   II. The firms in the industry produce a standardized product.
   III. Firms are price-takers.
   a. I only
   b. II only
   c. III only
   d. I and II only
   e. I, II, and III
5. Which of the following is an example of differentiated products?
   a. Coke and Pepsi
   b. automobiles and bicycles
   c. trucks and gasoline
   d. stocks and bonds
   e. gold and silver

Critical-Thinking Questions

1. Draw a correctly labeled graph of a perfectly competitive firm's demand curve if the market price is $10.
2. What does the firm's marginal revenue equal any time it sells one more unit of its output?

Module 25 Perfect Competition

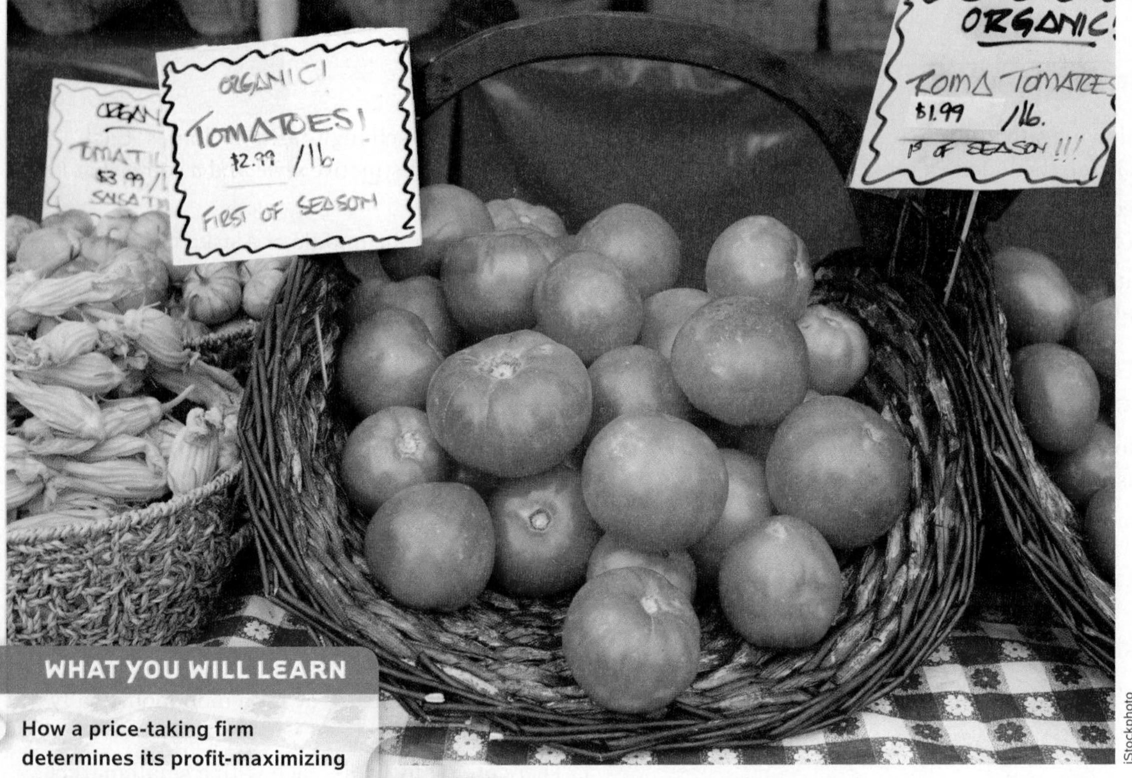

iStockphoto

WHAT YOU WILL LEARN

1. How a price-taking firm determines its profit-maximizing quantity of output
2. How to assess whether or not a competitive firm is profitable

Recall the example of the market for organic tomatoes from the previous module. There, Yves and Zoe run organic tomato farms. But many other organic tomato farmers sell their output to the same grocery store chains. Since organic tomatoes are a standardized product, consumers don't care which farmer produces the organic tomatoes they buy. And because so many farmers sell organic tomatoes, no individual farmer has a large market share, which means that no individual farmer can have a measurable effect on market prices. These farmers are price-takers and their customers are price-taking consumers. The market for organic tomatoes meets the two necessary conditions for perfect competition: there are many producers each with a small market share, and the firms produce a standardized product. In this module we learn how to determine the quantity of output that would maximize a producer's profit as we build the model of perfect competition and use it to look at a representative firm in the market.

Production and Profits

Let's now consider Jennifer and Jason, who, like Yves and Zoe, run an organic tomato farm. Suppose that the market price of organic tomatoes is $18 per bushel and that Jennifer and Jason can sell as many as they would like at that price. We can use the data in Table 25-1 to find their profit-maximizing level of output.

The first column shows the quantity of output in bushels, and the second column shows Jennifer and Jason's total revenue from their output: the market value of their output. Total revenue, *TR*, is equal to the market price multiplied by the quantity of output:

$$\textbf{(25-1)}\quad TR = P \times Q$$

TABLE 25-1

Profit for Jennifer and Jason's Farm When the Market Price Is $18

Quantity of tomatoes Q (bushels)	Total revenue TR	Total cost TC	Profit $TR - TC$
0	$0	$14	−$14
1	18	30	−12
2	36	36	0
3	54	44	10
4	72	56	16
5	90	72	18
6	108	92	16
7	126	116	10

In this example, total revenue is equal to $18 per bushel times the quantity of output in bushels.

The third column of Table 25-1 shows Jennifer and Jason's total cost, *TC*. The fourth column shows their profit, equal to total revenue minus total cost:

(25-2) $\text{Profit} = TR - TC$

As indicated by the numbers in the table, profit is maximized at an output of five bushels, where profit is equal to $18. But we can gain more insight into the profit-maximizing choice of output by viewing it as a problem of marginal analysis, a task we'll dive into next.

Using Marginal Analysis to Choose the Profit-Maximizing Quantity of Output

Recall from Module 18 the *profit-maximizing principle of marginal analysis:* the optimal amount of an activity is the level at which marginal benefit equals marginal cost. To apply this principle, consider the effect on a producer's profit of increasing output by one unit. The marginal benefit of that unit is the additional revenue generated by selling it; this measure has a name—it is called the **marginal revenue** of that unit of output. The general formula for marginal revenue is:

(25-3) $$\text{Marginal revenue} = \begin{array}{l}\text{Change in total}\\ \text{revenue generated}\\ \text{by one additional}\\ \text{unit of output}\end{array} = \frac{\text{Change in total revenue}}{\text{Change in quantity of output}}$$

or

$$MR = \Delta TR/\Delta Q$$

In this equation, the Greek uppercase delta (the triangular symbol) represents the change in a variable.

So Jennifer and Jason maximize their profit by producing bushels up to the point at which marginal revenue is equal to marginal cost. We can summarize this result as the producer's **optimal output rule,** which states that profit is maximized by producing the quantity at which the marginal revenue of the last unit produced is equal to its marginal cost. That is, $MR = MC$ at the optimal quantity of output.

Note that there may not be any particular quantity at which marginal revenue exactly equals marginal cost. In this case the producer should produce until one more unit would cause marginal benefit to fall below marginal cost. As a common simplification, we can think of marginal cost as rising steadily, rather than jumping from

Marginal revenue is the change in total revenue generated by an additional unit of output.

The **optimal output rule** says that profit is maximized by producing the quantity of output at which the marginal revenue of the last unit produced is equal to its marginal cost.

TABLE 25-2

Short-Run Costs for Jennifer and Jason's Farm

Quantity of tomatoes Q (bushels)	Total cost TC	Marginal cost of bushel $MC = \Delta TC/\Delta Q$	Marginal revenue of bushel MR	Net gain of bushel = $MR - MC$
0	$14			
		$16	$18	$2
1	30			
		6	18	12
2	36			
		8	18	10
3	44			
		12	18	6
4	56			
		16	18	2
5	72			
		20	18	−2
6	92			
		24	18	−6
7	116			

one level at one quantity to a different level at the next quantity. This ensures that marginal cost will equal marginal revenue at some quantity. We will now employ this simplified approach.

Consider Table 25-2, which provides cost and revenue data for Jennifer and Jason's farm. The second column contains the farm's total cost of output. The third column shows their marginal cost. Notice that, in this example, marginal cost initially falls as output rises but then begins to increase, so that the marginal cost curve has a "swoosh" shape. (Later you will see that this shape has important implications for short-run production decisions.)

The fourth column contains the farm's marginal revenue, which has an important feature: Jennifer and Jason's marginal revenue is assumed to be constant at $18 for every output level. The fifth and final column shows the calculation of the net gain per bushel of tomatoes, which is equal to marginal revenue minus marginal cost. As you can see, it is positive for the first through fifth bushels; producing each of these bushels raises Jennifer and Jason's profit. For the sixth and seventh bushels, however, net gain is negative: producing them would decrease, not increase, profit. (You can verify this by reexamining Table 25-1.) So five bushels are Jennifer and Jason's profit-maximizing output; it is the level of output at which marginal cost is equal to the market price, $18.

iStockphoto/Thinkstock

This example, in fact, illustrates an application of the optimal output rule to the particular case of a price-taking firm—the price-taking firm's optimal output rule, which says that a price-taking firm's profit is maximized by producing the quantity of output at which the market price is equal to the marginal cost of the last unit produced. That is, *$P = MC$ at the price-taking firm's optimal quantity of output.*

In fact, the price-taking firm's optimal output rule is just an application of the optimal output rule to the particular case of a price-taking firm. Why? Because *in the case of a price-taking firm, marginal revenue is equal to the market price.*

A price-taking firm cannot influence the market price by its actions. It always takes the market price as given because it cannot lower the market price by selling more or raise the market price by selling less. So, for a price-taking firm, the additional revenue generated by producing one more unit is always the market price. We will need to keep this fact in mind when we turn to Sections 10 and 11, where we will learn that marginal revenue is not equal to the market price if the industry is not perfectly competitive. As a result, firms are not price-takers when an industry is not perfectly competitive.

According to the **price-taking firm's optimal output rule**, a price-taking firm's profit is maximized by producing the quantity of output at which the market price is equal to the marginal cost of the last unit produced.

FIGURE 25-1 The Firm's Profit-Maximizing Quantity of Output

At the profit-maximizing quantity of output, marginal revenue is equal to marginal cost. It is located at the point where the marginal cost curve crosses the marginal revenue curve, which is a horizontal line at the market price. Here, the profit-maximizing point is at an output of 5 bushels of tomatoes, the output quantity at point *E*.

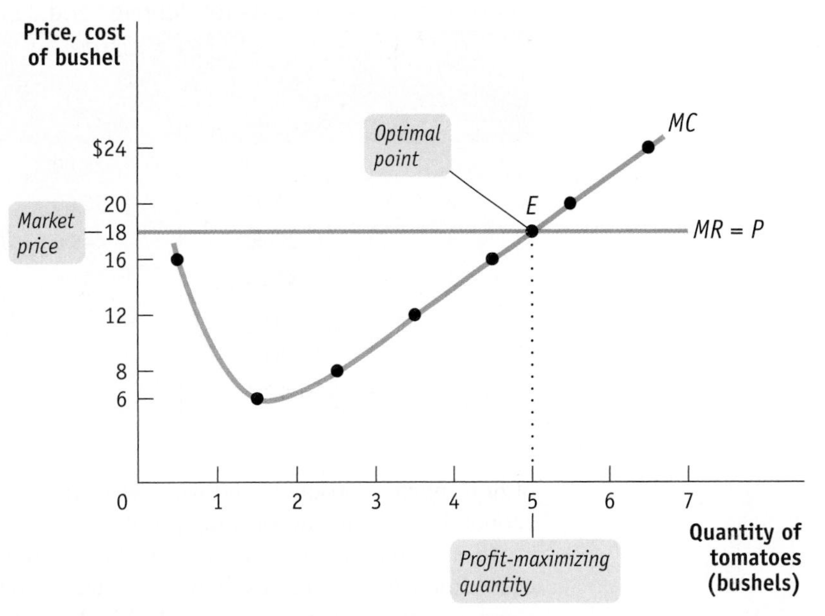

Figure 25-1 shows that Jennifer and Jason's profit-maximizing quantity of output is, indeed, the number of bushels at which the marginal cost of production is equal to price. The figure shows the *marginal cost curve, MC,* drawn from the data in the third column of Table 25-2. Recall that the marginal cost curve shows how the cost of producing one more unit depends on the quantity that has already been produced.

We plot the marginal cost of increasing output from one to two bushels halfway between one and two, and so on. The horizontal line at $18 is Jennifer and Jason's **marginal revenue curve,** which shows how marginal revenue varies as output varies. Note that marginal revenue stays the same regardless of how much Jennifer and Jason sell because we have assumed marginal revenue is constant.

The **marginal revenue curve** shows how marginal revenue varies as output varies.

Does this mean that the firm's production decision can be entirely summed up as "produce up to the point where the marginal cost of production is equal to the price"? No, not quite. Before applying the price-taking firm's optimal output rule to determine how much to produce, a potential producer must, as a first step, answer an "either–or" question: Should I produce at all? If the answer to that question is yes, the producer then proceeds to the second step—a "how much" decision: maximizing profit by choosing the quantity of output at which marginal cost is equal to price.

To understand why the first step in the production decision involves an "either–or" question, we need to ask how we determine whether it is profitable or unprofitable to produce at all.

When Is Production Profitable?

Remember that firms make their production decisions with the goal of maximizing *economic profit*—a measure based on the opportunity cost of resources used by the firm. In the calculation of economic profit, a firm's total cost incorporates the *implicit cost*—the benefits forgone in the next best use of the firm's resources—as well as the *explicit cost* in the form of actual cash outlays.

In contrast, *accounting profit* is profit calculated using only the explicit costs incurred by the firm. This means that economic profit incorporates all of the opportunity cost of resources owned by the firm and used in the production of output, while accounting profit does not.

A firm may make positive accounting profit while making zero or even negative economic profit. It's important to understand that a firm's decisions

iStockphoto

TABLE 25-3

Short-Run Average Costs for Jennifer and Jason's Farm

Quantity of tomatoes *Q* (bushels)	Variable cost *VC*	Total cost *TC*	Short-run average variable cost of bushel *AVC = VC/Q*	Short-run average total cost of bushel *ATC = TC/Q*
1	$16.00	$30.00	$16.00	$30.00
2	22.00	36.00	11.00	18.00
3	30.00	44.00	10.00	14.67
4	42.00	56.00	10.50	14.00
5	58.00	72.00	11.60	14.40
6	78.00	92.00	13.00	15.33
7	102.00	116.00	14.57	16.57

of how much to produce, and whether or not to stay in business, should be based on economic profit, not accounting profit.

So we will assume, as usual, that the cost numbers given in Table 25-1 include all costs, implicit as well as explicit. What determines whether Jennifer and Jason's farm earns a profit or generates a loss? This depends on the market price of tomatoes—specifically, *whether the market price is more or less than the farm's minimum average total cost.*

In Table 25-3 we calculate short-run average variable cost and short-run average total cost for Jennifer and Jason's farm. These are short-run values because we take fixed cost as given. (We'll turn to the effects of changing fixed cost shortly.) The short-run average total cost curve, *ATC,* is shown in Figure 25-2, along with the marginal cost curve, *MC,* from Figure 25-1. As you can see, average total cost is minimized at point *C,* corresponding to an output of 4 bushels—the *minimum-cost output*—and an average total cost of $14 per bushel.

To see how these curves can be used to decide whether production is profitable or unprofitable, recall that profit is equal to total revenue minus total cost, $TR - TC$. This means:

- If the firm produces a quantity at which $TR > TC$, the firm is profitable.
- If the firm produces a quantity at which $TR = TC$, the firm earns neither a profit nor a loss—it *breaks even.*
- If the firm produces a quantity at which $TR < TC$, the firm incurs a loss.

We can also express this idea in terms of revenue and cost per unit of output. If we divide profit by the number of units of output, Q, we obtain the following expression for profit per unit of output:

(25-4) $\text{Profit}/Q = TR/Q - TC/Q$

TR/Q is average revenue, which is the market price. TC/Q is average total cost. So a firm is profitable if the market price for its product is more than the average total cost of the quantity the firm produces; a firm experiences losses if the market price is less than the average total cost of the quantity the firm produces. This means:

- If the firm produces a quantity at which $P > ATC$, the firm is profitable.
- If the firm produces a quantity at which $P = ATC$, the firm earns neither a profit nor a loss—it breaks even.
- If the firm produces a quantity at which $P < ATC$, the firm incurs a loss.

In summary, in the short run a firm will maximize profit by producing the quantity of output at which $MC = MR$. A perfectly competitive firm is a price-taker, so it can sell

FIGURE 25-2 Costs and Production in the Short Run

This figure shows the marginal cost curve, *MC*, and the short-run average total cost curve, *ATC*. When the market price is $14, output will be 4 bushels of tomatoes (the minimum-cost output), represented by point *C*. The price of $14 is equal to the firm's minimum average total cost, so at this price the firm earns neither a profit nor a loss (it breaks even).

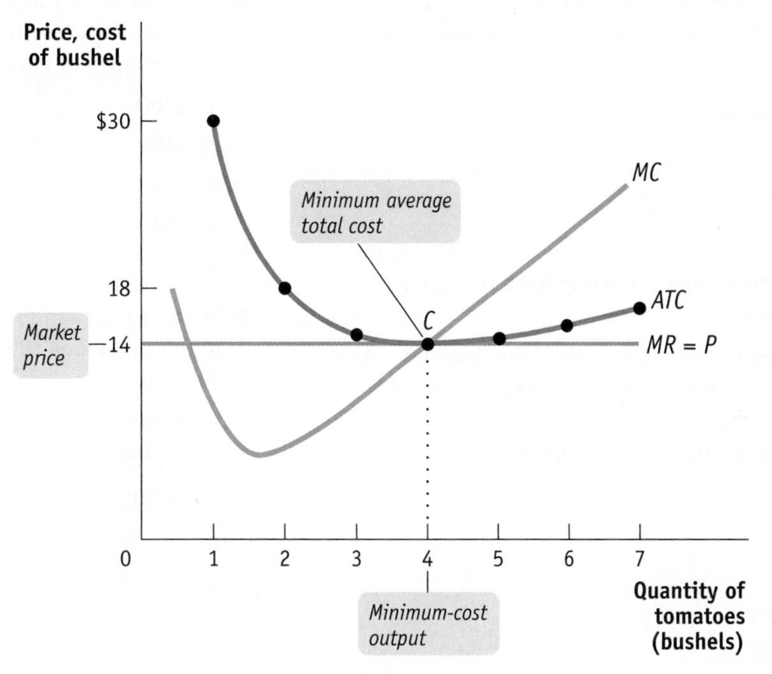

as many units of output as it would like at the market price. For a perfectly competitive firm then, it is always true that $MR = P$. The firm is profitable, or breaks even, as long as the market price is greater than, or equal to, average total cost. In the next module, we develop the perfect competition model using graphs to analyze the firm's level of profit.

MODULE 25 Review

Solutions appear at the back of the book.

Check Your Understanding

1. Refer to the graph provided to answer the questions that follow.

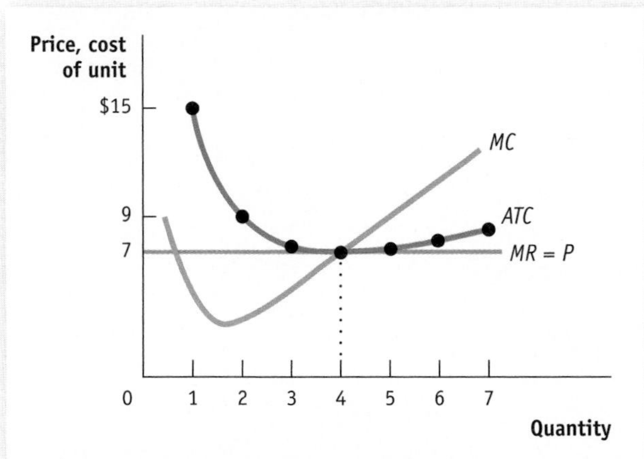

   a. At what level of output does the firm maximize profit? Explain how you know.
   b. At the profit-maximizing quantity of output, is the firm profitable, does it just break even, or does it earn a loss? Explain.

2. If a firm has a total cost of $500 at a quantity of 50 units, and it is at that quantity that average total cost is minimized for the firm, what is the lowest price that would allow the firm to break even? Explain.

Multiple-Choice Questions

1. A perfectly competitive firm will maximize profit at the quantity at which the firm's marginal revenue equals
   a. price.
   b. average revenue.
   c. total cost.
   d. marginal cost.
   e. demand.

2. Which of the following is correct for a perfectly competitive firm?
   I. The marginal revenue curve is the demand curve.
   II. The firm maximizes profit when price equals marginal cost.
   III. The demand curve is horizontal.
   a. I only
   b. II only
   c. III only
   d. I and II only
   e. I, II, and III

3. A firm is profitable if
   a. $TR < TC$.
   b. $AR < ATC$.
   c. $MC < ATC$.
   d. $ATC < P$.
   e. $ATC > MC$.

4. If a firm has a total cost of $200, its profit-maximizing level of output is 10 units, and it is breaking even (that is, earning a normal profit), what is the market price?
   a. $200
   b. $100
   c. $20
   d. $10
   e. $2

5. What is the firm's profit if the price of its product is $5 and it produces 500 units of output at a total cost of $1,000?
   a. $5,000
   b. $2,500
   c. $1,500
   d. −$1,500
   e. −$2,500

Critical-Thinking Questions

The table provided presents the short-run costs for Jennifer and Jason's farm. Price is equal to $14. Using the table:

1. calculate the firm's marginal cost at each quantity.
2. determine the firm's profit-maximizing level of output.
3. calculate the firm's profit at the profit-maximizing level of output.

Quantity of tomatoes *Q* (bushels)	Variable cost *VC*	Total cost *TC*
0	$0	$14
1	16	30
2	22	36
3	30	44
4	42	56
5	58	72
6	78	92
7	102	116

PITFALLS

WHAT'S A FIRM TO DO?

? The optimal output rule says that to maximize profit, a firm should produce the quantity at which marginal revenue is equal to marginal cost. But what should a firm do if there is no output level at which marginal revenue equals marginal cost?

> IN THIS CASE, A FIRM WOULD PRODUCE THE LARGEST QUANTITY FOR WHICH MARGINAL REVENUE EXCEEDS MARGINAL COST. This is the case in Table 25-2 at an output of 5 bushels. However, a simpler version of the optimal output rule applies when production involves much larger numbers, such as hundreds or thousands of units. In such cases, marginal cost comes in small increments, and there is always a level of output at which marginal cost almost exactly equals marginal revenue.

To learn more, see pages 271–273, and Table 25-2.

Graphing Perfect Competition

iStockphoto

WHAT YOU WILL LEARN

1. How to evaluate a perfectly competitive firm's situation using a graph
2. How to determine a perfect competitor's profit or loss
3. How a firm decides whether to produce or shut down in the short run

In the previous module we learned how to compare market price and average total cost to determine whether or not a competitive firm is profitable. Now we can evaluate the profitability of perfectly competitive firms in a variety of situations.

Interpreting Perfect Competition Graphs

Figure 26-1 illustrates how the market price determines whether a firm is profitable. It also shows how profits are depicted graphically. Each panel shows the marginal cost curve, *MC*, and the short-run average total cost curve, *ATC*. Average total cost is minimized at point *C*. Panel (a) shows the case in which the market price of tomatoes is \$18 per bushel. Panel (b) shows the case in which the market price of tomatoes is lower, \$10 per bushel.

In panel (a), we see that at a price of \$18 per bushel the profit-maximizing quantity of output is 5 bushels, indicated by point *E*, where the marginal cost curve, *MC*, intersects the marginal revenue curve, *MR*—which for a price-taking firm is a horizontal line at the market price. At that quantity of output, average total cost is \$14.40 per bushel, indicated by point *Z*. Since the price per bushel exceeds the average total cost per bushel, Jennifer and Jason's farm is profitable.

Jennifer and Jason's total profit when the market price is \$18 is represented by the area of the shaded rectangle in panel (a). To see why, notice that total profit can be expressed in terms of profit per unit:

(26-1) $\text{Profit} = TR - TC = (TR/Q - TC/Q) \times Q$

FIGURE 26-1 **Profitability and the Market Price**

In panel (a) the market price is $18. The farm is profitable because price exceeds minimum average total cost, the break-even price, $14. The farm's optimal output choice is indicated by point *E*, corresponding to an output of 5 bushels. The average total cost of producing 5 bushels is indicated by point *Z* on the *ATC* curve, corresponding to an amount of $14.40. The vertical distance between *E* and *Z* corresponds to the farm's per-unit profit, $18.00 – $14.40 = $3.60. Total profit is given by the area of the shaded rectangle, 5 × $3.60 = $18.00. In panel (b) the market price is $10; the farm is unprofitable because the price falls below the minimum average total cost, $14. The farm's optimal output choice when producing is indicated by point *A*, corresponding to an output of 3 bushels. The farm's per-unit loss, $14.67 – $10.00 = $4.67, is represented by the vertical distance between *A* and *Y*. The farm's total loss is represented by the shaded rectangle, 3 × $4.67 = $14.00 (adjusted for rounding error).

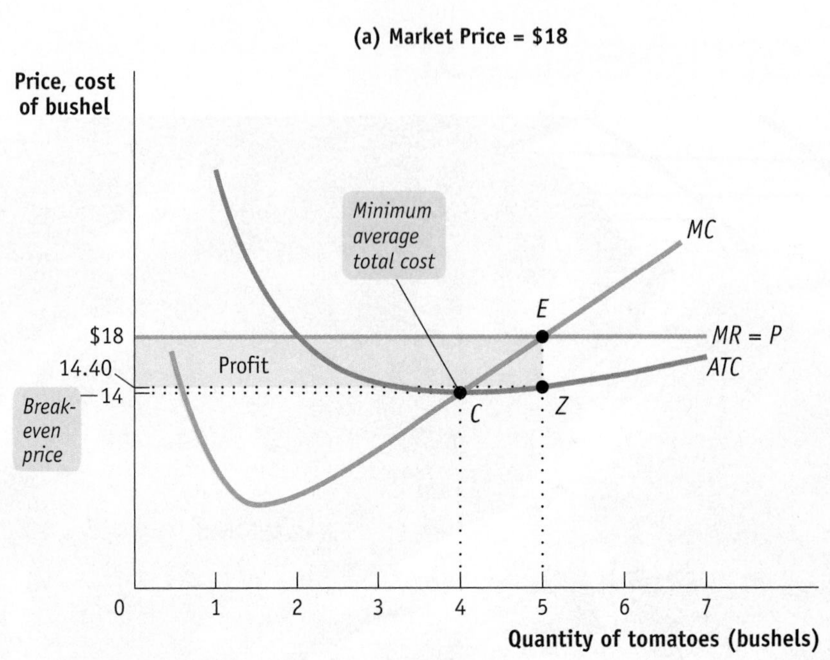

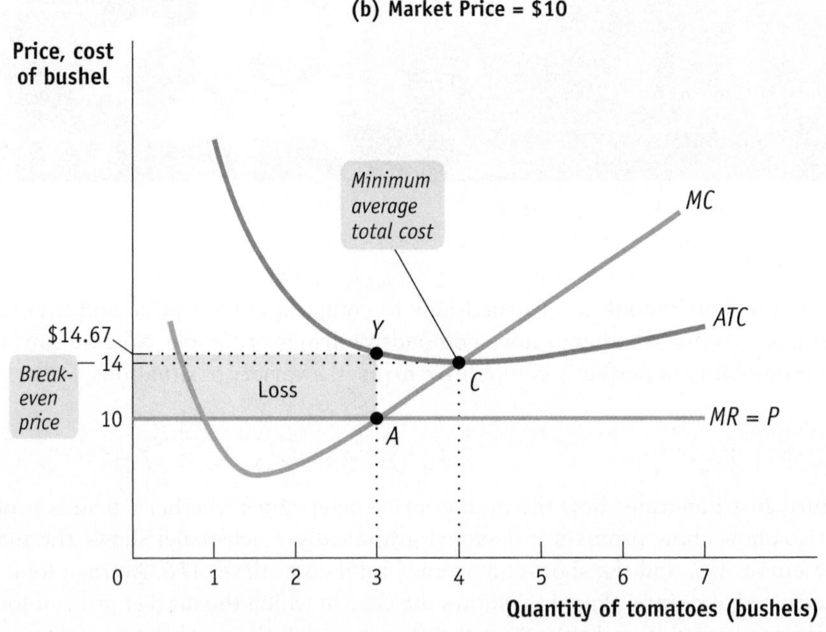

or, equivalently, because *P* is equal to *TR*/*Q* and *ATC* is equal to *TC*/*Q*,

$$\text{Profit} = (P - ATC) \times Q$$

The height of the shaded rectangle in panel (a) corresponds to the vertical distance between points *E* and *Z*. It is equal to $P - ATC$ = $18.00 – $14.40 = $3.60 per bushel. The shaded rectangle has a width equal to the output: Q = 5 bushels. So the area of that rectangle is equal to Jennifer and Jason's profit: 5 bushels × $3.60 profit per bushel = $18.

What about the situation illustrated in panel (b)? Here the market price of tomatoes is $10 per bushel. Producing until price equals marginal cost leads to a profit-maximizing output of 3 bushels, indicated by point *A*. At this output, Jennifer and Jason have an average total cost of $14.67 per bushel, indicated by point *Y*. At their profit-maximizing output quantity—3 bushels—average total cost exceeds the market price. This means that Jennifer and Jason's farm generates a loss, not a profit.

How much do they lose by producing when the market price is $10? On each bushel they lose $ATC - P$ = $14.67 – $10.00 = $4.67, an amount corresponding to the vertical distance between points *A* and *Y*. And they produce 3 bushels, which corresponds to the width of the shaded rectangle. So the total value of the losses is $4.67 × 3 = $14.00 (adjusted for rounding error), an amount that corresponds to the area of the shaded rectangle in panel (b).

But how does a producer know, in general, whether or not its business will be profitable? It turns out that the crucial test lies in a comparison of the market price to the firm's *minimum average total cost*. On Jennifer and Jason's farm, average total cost reaches its minimum, $14, at an output of 4 bushels, indicated by point *C*. Whenever the market price exceeds the minimum average total cost, there are output levels for which the average total cost is less than the market price. In other words, the producer can find a level of output at which the firm makes a profit. So Jennifer and Jason's farm will be profitable whenever the market price exceeds $14. And they will achieve the highest possible profit by producing the quantity at which marginal cost equals price.

Conversely, if the market price is less than the minimum average total cost, there is no output level at which price exceeds average total cost. As a result, the firm will be unprofitable at any quantity of output. As we saw, at a price of $10—an amount less than the minimum average total cost—Jennifer and Jason did indeed lose money. By producing the quantity at which marginal cost equaled price, Jennifer and Jason did the best they could, but the best they could do was a loss of $14. Any other quantity would have increased the size of their loss.

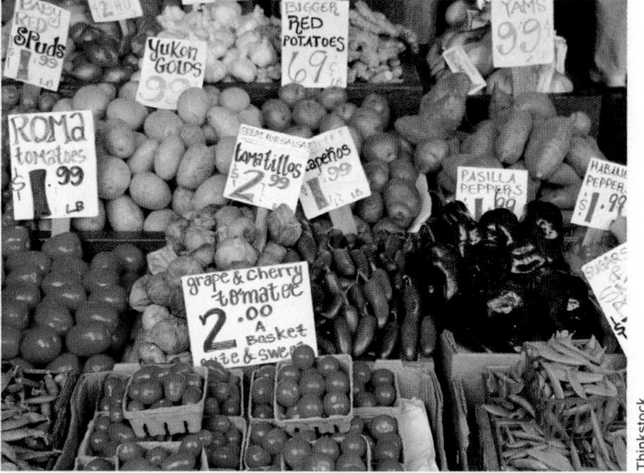

Thinkstock

A firm will earn positive profit when the market price is above the break-even price.

The minimum average total cost of a price-taking firm is called its **break-even price,** the market price at which it earns zero economic profit. A firm will earn positive profit when the market price is above the break-even price, and it will suffer losses when the market price is below the break-even price. Jennifer and Jason's break-even price of $14 is the price at point *C* in Figure 26-1.

So the rule for determining whether a firm is profitable depends on a comparison of the market price of the good to the firm's break-even price—its minimum average total cost:

- Whenever the market price exceeds the minimum average total cost, the producer is profitable.
- Whenever the market price equals the minimum average total cost, the producer breaks even.
- Whenever the market price is less than the minimum average total cost, the producer is unprofitable.

The Short-Run Production Decision

You might be tempted to say that if a firm is unprofitable because the market price is below its minimum average total cost, it shouldn't produce any output. In the short run, however, this conclusion isn't right. In the short run, sometimes the firm should produce even if price falls below minimum average total cost. The reason is that total cost includes *fixed cost*—cost that does not depend on the amount of output produced and can be altered only in the long run. In the short run, fixed cost must still be paid,

The **break-even price** of a price-taking firm is the market price at which it earns zero economic profit.

regardless of whether or not a firm produces. For example, if Jennifer and Jason have rented a tractor for the year, they have to pay the rent on the tractor regardless of whether they produce any tomatoes. *Since it cannot be changed in the short run, their fixed cost is irrelevant to their decision about whether to produce or shut down in the short run.*

Although fixed cost should play no role in the decision about whether to produce in the short run, another type of cost—variable cost—does matter. Part of the variable cost for Jennifer and Jason is the wage cost of workers who must be hired to help with planting and harvesting. Variable cost can be eliminated by *not* producing, which makes it a critical consideration when determining whether or not to produce in the short run.

Let's turn to Figure 26-2: it shows both the short-run average total cost curve, *ATC*, and the short-run average variable cost curve, *AVC*, drawn from the information in Table 25-3. Recall that the difference between the two curves—the vertical distance between them—represents average fixed cost, the fixed cost per unit of output, *FC/Q*. Because the marginal cost curve has a "swoosh" shape—falling at first before rising—the short-run average variable cost curve is U-shaped: the initial fall in marginal cost causes average variable cost to fall as well, and then the rise in marginal cost eventually pulls average variable cost up again. The short-run average variable cost curve reaches its minimum value of $10 at point *A*, at an output of 3 bushels.

FIGURE 26-2 **The Short-Run Individual Supply Curve**

When the market price equals or exceeds Jennifer and Jason's *shut-down price* of $10, the minimum average variable cost indicated by point *A*, they will produce the output quantity at which marginal cost is equal to price. So at any price equal to or above the minimum average *variable* cost, the short-run individual supply curve is the firm's marginal cost curve; this corresponds to the upward-sloping segment of the individual supply curve. When market price falls below minimum average variable cost, the firm ceases operation in the short run. This corresponds to the vertical segment of the individual supply curve along the vertical axis.

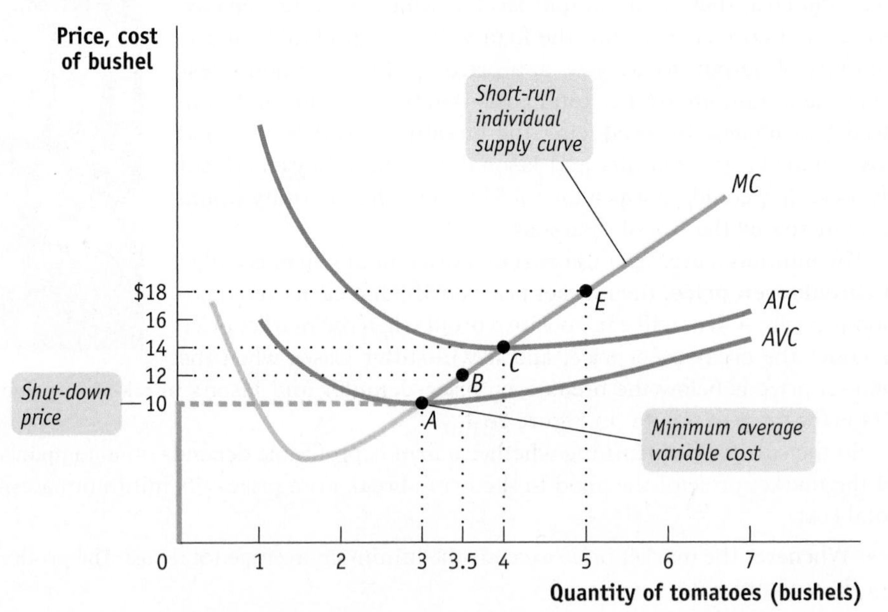

The Shut-Down Price

We are now prepared to analyze the optimal production decision in the short run. We have two cases to consider:

- When the market price is below the minimum average *variable* cost
- When the market price is greater than or equal to the minimum average *variable* cost

When the market price is below the minimum average variable cost, the price the firm receives per unit is not covering its variable cost per unit. A firm in this situation should cease production immediately. Why? Because there is no level of output at which the firm's total revenue covers its variable cost—the cost it can avoid by not operating. In this case the firm maximizes its profit by not producing at all—by, in effect, minimizing its loss. It will still incur a fixed cost in the short run, but it will no longer incur any variable cost. This means that the minimum average variable cost determines the **shut-down price,** the price at which the firm ceases production in the short run.

A firm will cease production in the short run if the market price falls below the **shut-down price,** which is equal to minimum average variable cost.

When price is greater than minimum average variable cost, however, the firm should produce in the short run. In this case, the firm maximizes profit—or minimizes loss—by choosing the output level at which its marginal cost is equal to the market price. For example, if the market price of tomatoes is $18 per bushel, Jennifer and Jason should produce at point *E* in Figure 26-2, corresponding to an output of 5 bushels. Note that point *C* in Figure 26-2 corresponds to the farm's break-even price of $14 per bushel. Since *E* lies above *C*, Jennifer and Jason's farm will be profitable; they will generate a per-bushel profit of $18.00 – $14.40 = $3.60 when the market price is $18.

But what if the market price lies between the shut-down price and the break-even price—that is, between the minimum average *variable* cost and the minimum average *total* cost? In the case of Jennifer and Jason's farm, this corresponds to prices anywhere between $10 and $14—say, a market price of $12. At $12, Jennifer and Jason's farm is not profitable; since the market price is below the minimum average total cost, the farm is losing (on average) the difference between price and average total cost on every unit produced. Yet even though the market price isn't covering Jennifer and Jason's average total cost, it is covering their average variable cost and some—but not all—of the average fixed cost. If a firm in this situation shuts down, it will incur no variable cost but it will incur the *full* fixed cost. As a result, shutting down will generate an even greater loss than continuing to operate.

This means that whenever price falls between minimum average total cost and minimum average variable cost, the firm is better off producing some output in the short run. The reason is that by producing, it can cover its variable cost and at least some of its fixed cost, even though it is incurring a loss. In this case, the firm maximizes profit—that is, minimizes loss—by choosing the quantity of output at which its marginal cost is equal to the market price. So if Jennifer and Jason face a market price of $12 per bushel, their profit-maximizing output is given by point *B* in Figure 26-2, corresponding to an output of 3.5 bushels.

Anthony Masterson/Digital Vision/Getty Images

In the short-run production decision, a firm's fixed cost is essentially a sunk cost.

It's worth noting that the decision to produce when the firm is covering its variable cost but not all of its fixed cost is similar to the decision to ignore a *sunk cost,* a concept we studied previously. You may recall that a sunk cost is a cost that has already been incurred and cannot be recouped; and because it cannot be changed, it should have no effect on any current decision. In the short-run production decision, fixed cost is, in effect, like a sunk cost—it has been spent, and it can't be recovered in the short run. This comparison also illustrates why variable cost does indeed matter in the short run: it can be avoided by not producing.

And what happens if the market price is exactly equal to the shut-down price, the minimum average variable cost? In this instance, the firm is indifferent between producing 3 units or 0 units. As we'll see shortly, this is an important point when looking at the behavior of an industry as a whole. For the sake of clarity, we'll assume that the firm, although indifferent, does indeed produce output when price is equal to the shut-down price.

Putting everything together, we can now draw the *short-run individual supply curve* of Jennifer and Jason's farm, the red line in Figure 26-2; it shows how the profit-maximizing quantity of output in the short run depends on the price. As you can see, the curve is in two segments. The upward-sloping red segment starting at point *A* shows the short-run profit-maximizing output when market price is equal to or above the shut-down price of $10 per bushel.

As long as the market price is equal to or above the shut-down price, Jennifer and Jason will produce the quantity of output at which marginal cost is equal to the market price. So at market prices equal to or above the shut-down price, the firm's short-run supply curve corresponds to its marginal cost curve. But at any market price below the minimum average variable cost, in this case, $10 per bushel—the firm shuts down and output drops to zero in the short run. This corresponds to the vertical segment of the curve that lies on top of the vertical axis.

V.e.r.i.k/Dreamstime.com

Some firms shut down temporarily without going out of business.

Do firms sometimes shut down temporarily without going out of business? Yes. In fact, in some industries temporary shut-downs are routine. The most common examples are industries in which demand is highly seasonal, like outdoor amusement parks in climates with cold winters. Such parks would have to offer very low prices to entice customers during the colder months—prices so low that the owners would not cover their variable cost (principally wages and electricity). The wiser choice economically is to shut down until warm weather brings enough customers who are willing to pay a higher price.

Changing Fixed Cost

Although fixed cost cannot be altered in the short run, in the long run firms can acquire or get rid of machines, buildings, and so on. In the long run the level of fixed cost is a matter of choice, and a firm will choose the level of fixed cost that minimizes the average total cost for its desired output level. Now we will focus on an even bigger question facing a firm when choosing its fixed cost: whether to incur *any* fixed cost at all by continuing to operate.

In the long run, a firm can always eliminate fixed cost by selling off its plant and equipment. If it does so, of course, it can't produce any output—it has exited the industry. In contrast, a new firm can take on some fixed cost by acquiring machines and other resources, which puts it in a position to produce—it can enter the industry. In most perfectly competitive industries the set of firms, although fixed in the short run, changes in the long run as some firms enter or exit the industry.

Consider Jennifer and Jason's farm once again. In order to simplify our analysis, we will sidestep the issue of choosing among several possible levels of fixed cost. Instead, we will assume that if they operate at all, Jennifer and Jason have only one possible choice of fixed cost: $14. Alternatively, they can choose a fixed cost of zero if they exit the industry. It is changes in fixed cost that cause short-run average total cost curves to differ from long-run average total cost curves, so with this assumption, Jennifer and Jason's short-run and long-run average total cost curves are one and the same.

Suppose that the market price of organic tomatoes is consistently less than the break-even price of $14 over an extended period of time. In that case, Jennifer and Jason never fully cover their total cost: their business runs at a persistent loss. In the long run, then, they can do better by closing their business and leaving the industry. In other words, *in the long run* firms will exit an industry if the market price is consistently less than their break-even price—their minimum average total cost.

Conversely, suppose that the price of organic tomatoes is consistently above the break-even price, $14, for an extended period of time. Because their farm is profitable, Jennifer and Jason will remain in the industry and continue producing.

But things won't stop there. The organic tomato industry meets the criterion of *free entry*: there are many potential organic tomato producers because the necessary inputs are easy to obtain. And the cost curves of those potential producers are likely to be similar to those of Jennifer and Jason, since the technology used by other producers is likely to be very similar to that used by Jennifer and Jason. If the price is high enough to generate profits for existing producers, it will also attract some of these potential producers into the industry. So *in the long run* a price in excess of $14 should lead to entry: new producers will come into the organic tomato industry.

As we will see shortly, exit and entry lead to an important distinction between the *short-run industry supply curve* and the *long-run industry supply curve*.

ECONOMICS ▶ IN ACTION

PRICES ARE UP . . . BUT SO ARE COSTS

Because of the Energy Policy Act of 2005, 7.5 billion gallons of alternative fuel, mostly corn-based ethanol, was added to the American fuel supply to help reduce gasoline consumption. The unsurprising result of this mandate: the demand for corn skyrocketed, along with its price. In August 2012, a bushel of corn hit a high of $8.32, nearly quadruple the January 2005 price of $2.09.

This sharp rise in the price of corn caught the eye of American farmers like Ronnie Gerik of Aquilla, Texas, who, in response to surging corn prices, reduced the size of his cotton crop and increased his corn acreage by 40%. He was not alone; overall, the U.S. corn acreage planted in 2011 was 9% more than the average planted over the previous decade. And 4% more was planted in 2012.

Although this sounds like a sure way to make a profit, Gerik was actually taking a big gamble: even though the price of corn increased, so did the cost of the raw materials needed to grow it—by 20%. Consider the cost of just two inputs: fertilizer and fuel. Corn requires more fertilizer than other crops and, with more farmers planting corn, the increased demand for fertilizer led to a price increase.

Moreover, corn is much more sensitive to the amount of rainfall than a crop like cotton. So farmers who plant corn in drought-prone places like Texas are increasing their risk of loss. Gerik had to incorporate into his calculations his best guess of what a dry spell would cost him.

Courtesy of Ronnie Gerik.

Although Gerik was taking a big gamble when he cut the size of his cotton crop to plant more corn, his decision made good economic sense.

Despite all of this, what Gerik did made complete economic sense. By planting more corn, he was moving up his individual short-run supply curve for corn production. And because his individual supply curve is his marginal cost curve, his costs also went up because he had to use more inputs—inputs that had become more expensive to obtain.

So the moral of this story is that farmers will increase their corn acreage until the marginal cost of producing corn is approximately equal to the market price of corn—which shouldn't come as a surprise because corn production satisfies all the requirements of a perfectly competitive industry.

Summing Up: The Perfectly Competitive Firm's Profitability and Production Conditions

In this module we've studied what's behind the supply curve for a perfectly competitive, price-taking firm. A perfectly competitive firm maximizes profit, or minimizes loss, by producing the quantity that equates price and marginal cost. The exception is if price is below minimum average variable cost in the short run, or below minimum average total cost in the long run, in which case the firm is better off shutting down. Table 26-1 summarizes the perfectly competitive firm's profitability and production conditions. It also relates them to entry into and exit from the industry in the long run. Now that we understand how a perfectly competitive *firm* makes its decisions, we can go on to look at the supply curve for a perfectly competitive *market* and the long-run market equilibrium in perfect competition.

TABLE 26-1

Summary of the Perfectly Competitive Firm's Profitability and Production Conditions

Profitability condition (minimum *ATC* = break-even price)	Result
P > minimum *ATC*	Firm profitable. Entry into industry in the long run.
P = minimum *ATC*	Firm breaks even. No entry into or exit from industry in the long run.
P < minimum *ATC*	Firm unprofitable. Exit from industry in the long run.
Production condition (minimum *AVC* = shut-down price)	**Result**
P > minimum *AVC*	Firm produces in the short run. If *P* < minimum *ATC*, firm covers variable cost and some but not all of fixed cost. If *P* > minimum *ATC*, firm covers all variable cost and fixed cost.
P = minimum *AVC*	Firm indifferent between producing in the short run or not. Just covers variable cost.
P < minimum *AVC*	Firm shuts down in the short run. It cannot cover variable cost.

MODULE 26 Review

Solutions appear at the back of the book.

Check Your Understanding

1. Draw a short-run diagram showing a U-shaped average total cost curve, a U-shaped average variable cost curve, and a "swoosh"-shaped marginal cost curve. On it, indicate the range of prices for which the following actions are optimal. Explain your answers.
   a. The firm shuts down immediately.
   b. The firm operates in the short run despite sustaining a loss.
   c. The firm operates while making a profit.

2. The state of Maine has a very active lobster industry, which harvests lobsters during the summer months. During the rest of the year, lobsters can be obtained by restaurants from producers in other parts of the world, but at a much higher price. Maine is also full of "lobster shacks," roadside restaurants serving lobster dishes that are open only during the summer. Supposing that the market demand for lobster dishes remains the same throughout the year, explain why it is optimal for lobster shacks to operate only during the summer.

Multiple-Choice Questions

To answer questions 1–3, refer to the graph provided.

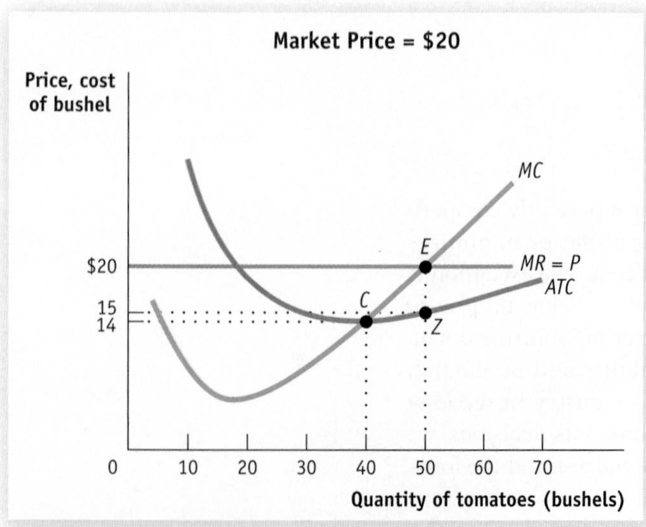

1. The firm's total revenue is equal to
   a. $14.
   b. $20.
   c. $560.
   d. $750.
   e. $1,000.

2. The firm's total cost is equal to
   a. $14.
   b. $15.
   c. $560.
   d. $750.
   e. $1,000.

3. The firm is earning a
   a. profit equal to $5.
   b. profit equal to $250.
   c. loss equal to $15.
   d. loss equal to $750.
   e. loss equal to $250.

4. A firm should continue to produce in the short run as long as price is at least equal to
   a. *MR*.
   b. *MC*.
   c. minimum *ATC*.
   d. minimum *AVC*.
   e. *AFC*.

5. At prices that motivate the firm to produce at all, the short-run supply curve for a perfect competitor corresponds to which curve?
   a. the *ATC* curve
   b. the *AVC* curve
   c. the *MC* curve
   d. the *AFC* curve
   e. the *MR* curve

Critical-Thinking Questions

Refer to the graph provided to answer the questions that follow.

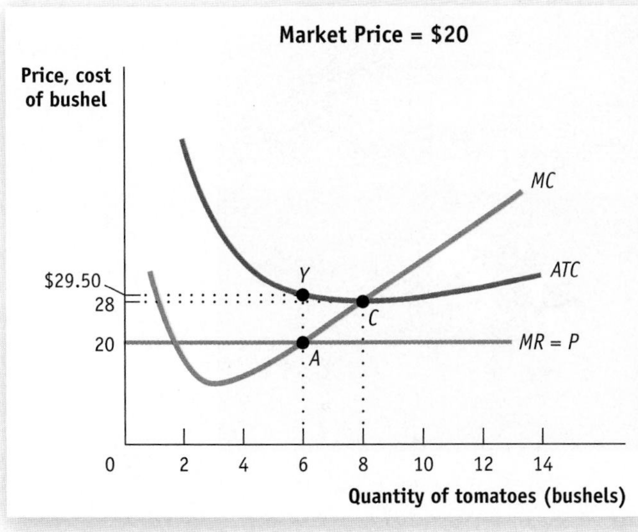

1. Assuming it is appropriate for the firm to produce in the short run, what is the firm's profit-maximizing level of output?
2. Calculate the firm's total revenue.
3. Calculate the firm's total cost.
4. Calculate the firm's profit or loss.
5. If *AVC* were $22 at the profit-maximizing level of output, would the firm produce in the short run? Explain why or why not.

Long-Run Outcomes in Perfect Competition

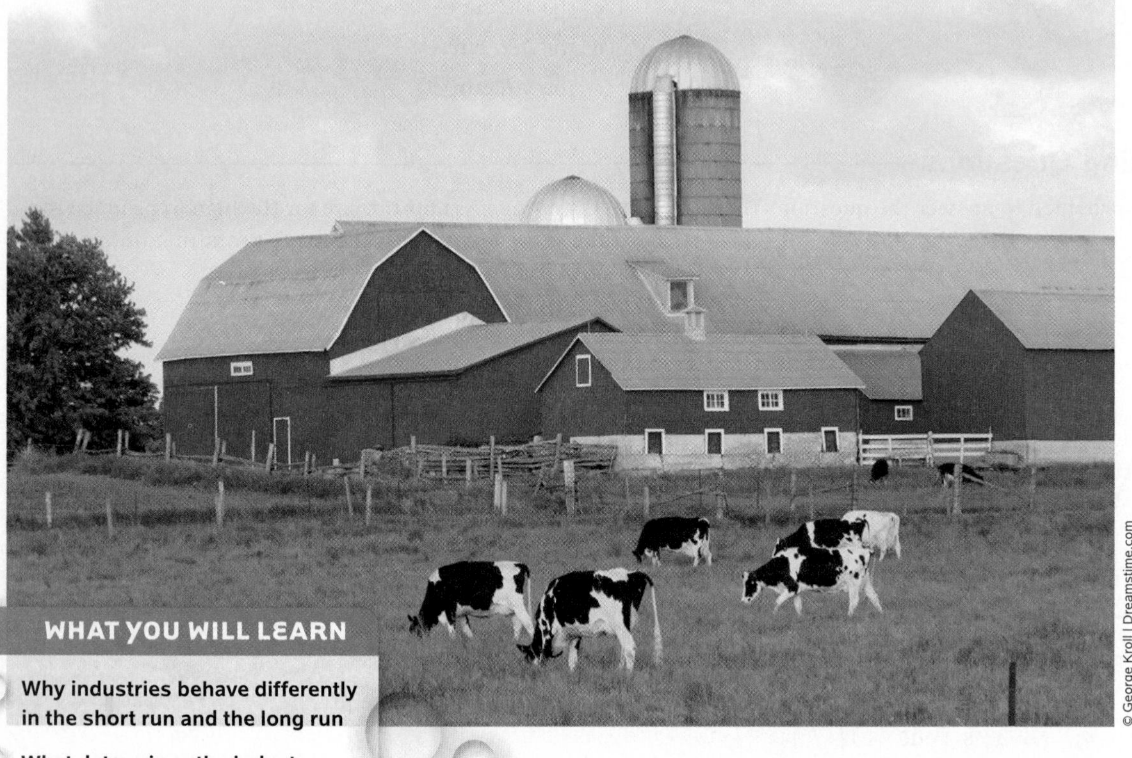

© George Kroll | Dreamstime.com

WHAT YOU WILL LEARN

1. Why industries behave differently in the short run and the long run
2. What determines the industry supply curve in both the short run and the long run

Up to this point we have been discussing the perfectly competitive firm's short-run situation—whether to produce or not, and if so, whether the firm earns a positive profit, breaks even, or takes a loss. In this module, we look at the long-run situation in a perfectly competitive market. We will see that perfect competition leads to some interesting and desirable market outcomes. In upcoming sections, we will contrast these outcomes with the outcomes in monopolistic and imperfectly competitive markets.

The Industry Supply Curve

Why will an increase in the demand for organic tomatoes lead to a large price increase at first but a much smaller increase in the long run? The answer lies in the behavior of the **industry supply curve**—the relationship between the price and the total output of an industry as a whole. The industry supply curve is what we referred to in earlier modules as the supply curve or the market supply curve. But here we take some extra care to distinguish between the *individual supply curve* of a single firm and the supply curve of the industry as a whole.

As you might guess from the previous module, the industry supply curve must be analyzed in somewhat different ways for the short run and the long run. Let's start with the short run.

The **industry supply curve** shows the relationship between the price of a good and the total output of the industry as a whole.

The Short-Run Industry Supply Curve

Recall that in the short run the number of firms in an industry is fixed—there is no entry or exit. And you may also remember from Section 2 that the market supply

FIGURE 27-1 The Short-Run Individual Supply Curve

When the market price equals or exceeds Jennifer and Jason's *shut-down price* of $10, the minimum average variable cost indicated by point *A*, they will produce the output quantity at which marginal cost is equal to price. So at any price equal to or above the minimum average *variable* cost, the short-run individual supply curve is the firm's marginal cost curve; this corresponds to the upward-sloping segment of the individual supply curve. When market price falls below minimum average variable cost, the firm ceases operation in the short run. This corresponds to the vertical segment of the individual supply curve along the vertical axis.

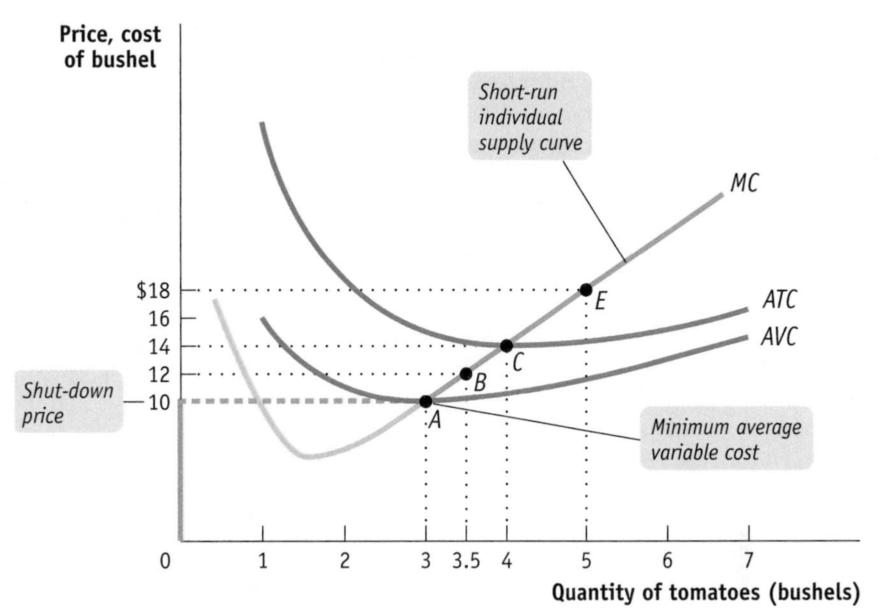

curve is the horizontal sum of the individual supply curves of all firms—you find it by summing the total output across all suppliers at every given price. We will do that exercise here under the assumption that all the firms are alike—an assumption that makes the derivation particularly simple. So let's assume that there are 100 organic tomato farms, each with the same costs as Jennifer and Jason's farm.

Each of these 100 farms will have an individual short-run supply curve like the one in Figure 26-2 from the previous module, which appears again here, as Figure 27-1 for your convenience.

At a price below $10, no farms will produce. At a price of more than $10, each farm will produce the quantity of output at which its marginal cost is equal to the market price. As you can see from Figure 27-1, this will lead each farm to produce 4 bushels if the price is $14 per bushel, 5 bushels if the price is $18, and so on.

So if there are 100 organic tomato farms and the price of organic tomatoes is $18 per bushel, the industry as a whole will produce 500 bushels, corresponding to 100 farms × 5 bushels per farm. The result is the **short-run industry supply curve,** shown as *S* in Figure 27-2. This curve shows the quantity that producers will supply at each price, *taking the number of farms as given.*

The market demand curve, labeled *D* in Figure 27-2, crosses the short-run industry supply curve at E_{MKT}, corresponding to a price of $18 and a quantity of 500 bushels. Point E_{MKT} is a **short-run market equilibrium:** the quantity supplied equals the quantity demanded, taking the number of farms as given. But the long run may look quite different because in the long run farms may enter or exit the industry.

The **short-run industry supply curve** shows how the quantity supplied by an industry depends on the market price, given a fixed number of firms.

There is a **short-run market equilibrium** when the quantity supplied equals the quantity demanded, taking the number of producers as given.

The Long-Run Industry Supply Curve

Suppose that in addition to the 100 farms currently in the organic tomato business, there are many other potential organic tomato farms. Suppose also that each of these potential farms would have the same cost curves as existing farms, like the one owned by Jennifer and Jason, upon entering the industry.

When will additional farms enter the industry? Whenever existing farms are making a profit—that is, whenever the market price is above the break-even price of $14

FIGURE 27-2 The Short-Run Market Equilibrium

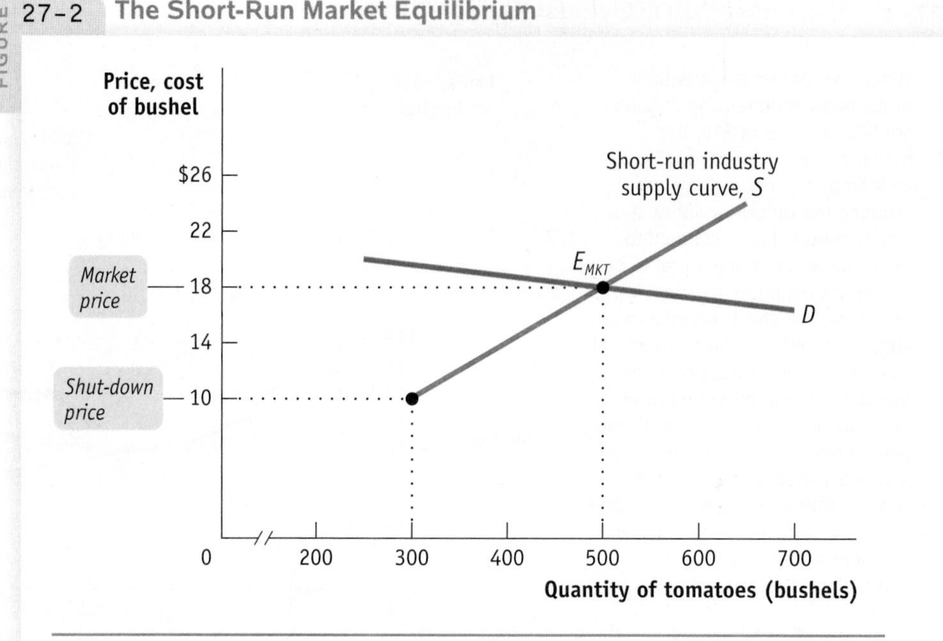

The short-run industry supply curve, *S*, is the industry supply curve taking the number of producers—here, 100—as given. It is generated by adding together the individual supply curves of the 100 producers. Below the shut-down price of $10, no producer wants to produce in the short run. Above $10, the short-run industry supply curve slopes upward, as each producer increases output as price increases. It intersects the demand curve, *D*, at point E_{MKT}, the point of short-run market equilibrium, corresponding to a market price of $18 and a quantity of 500 bushels.

per bushel, the minimum average total cost of production. For example, at a price of $18 per bushel, new farms will enter the industry.

What will happen as additional farms enter the industry? Clearly, the quantity supplied at any given price will increase. The short-run industry supply curve will shift to the right. This will, in turn, alter the market equilibrium and result in a lower market price. Existing farms will respond to the lower market price by reducing their output, but the total industry output will increase because of the larger number of farms in the industry.

Figure 27-3 illustrates the effects of this chain of events on an existing farm and on the market; panel (a) shows how the market responds to entry, and panel (b) shows how an individual existing farm responds to entry. (Note that these two graphs have been rescaled in comparison to Figures 27-1 and 27-2 to better illustrate how profit changes in response to price.) In panel (a), S_1 is the initial short-run industry supply curve, based on the existence of 100 producers. The initial short-run market equilibrium is at E_{MKT}, with an equilibrium market price of $18 and a quantity of 500 bushels. At this price existing farms are profitable, which is reflected in panel (b): an existing farm makes a total profit represented by the green shaded rectangle labeled A when the market price is $18.

These profits will induce new producers to enter the industry, shifting the short-run industry supply curve to the right. For example, the short-run industry supply curve when the number of farms has increased to 167 is S_2. Corresponding to this supply curve is a new short-run market equilibrium labeled D_{MKT}, with a market price of $16 and a quantity of 750 bushels. At $16, each farm produces 4.5 bushels, so that industry output is 167 × 4.5 = 750 bushels (rounded). From panel (b) you can see the

FIGURE 27-3 The Long-Run Market Equilibrium

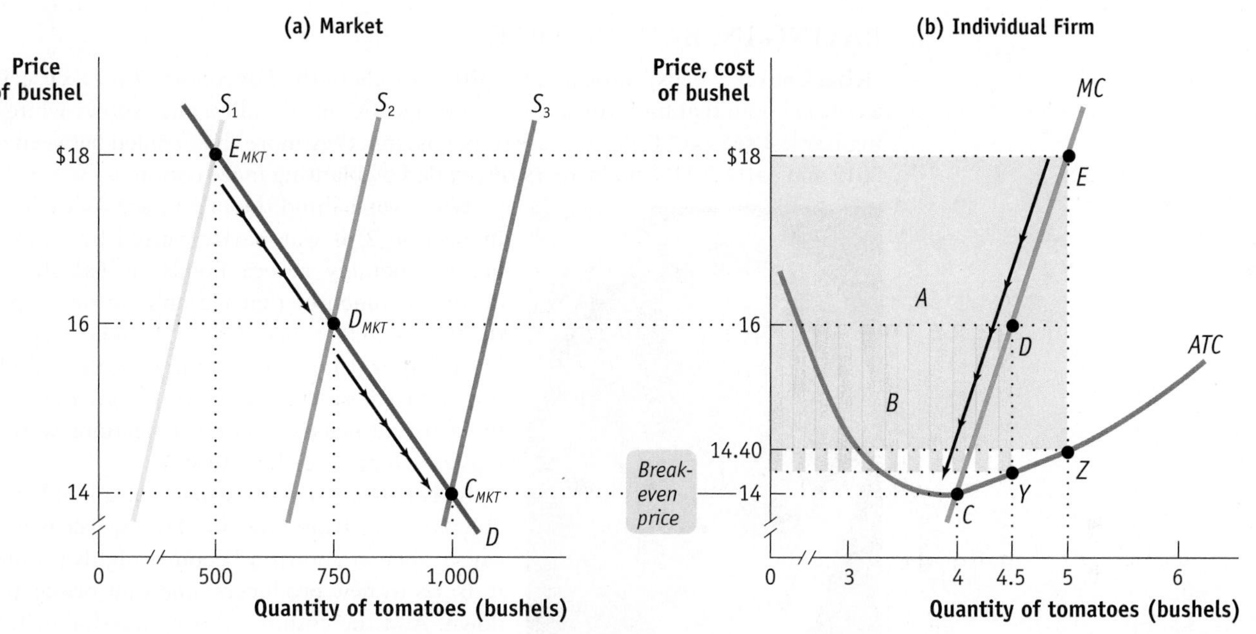

Point E_{MKT} of panel (a) shows the initial short-run market equilibrium. Each of the 100 existing producers makes an economic profit, illustrated in panel (b) by the green rectangle labeled *A*, the profit of an existing firm. Profits induce entry by additional producers, shifting the short-run industry supply curve outward from S_1 to S_2 in panel (a), resulting in a new short-run equilibrium at point D_{MKT}, at a lower market price of $16 and higher industry output. Existing firms reduce output and profit falls to the area given by the striped rectangle labeled *B* in panel (b). Entry continues to shift out the short-run industry supply curve, as price falls and industry output increases yet again. Entry ceases at point C_{MKT} on supply curve S_3 in panel (a). Here market price is equal to the break-even price; existing producers make zero economic profits and there is no incentive for entry or exit. Therefore C_{MKT} is also a long-run market equilibrium.

effect of the entry of 67 new farms on an existing farm: the fall in price causes it to reduce its output, and its profit falls to the area represented by the striped rectangle labeled *B*.

Although diminished, the profit of existing farms at D_{MKT} means that entry will continue and the number of farms will continue to rise. If the number of farms rises to 250, the short-run industry supply curve shifts out again to S_3, and the market equilibrium is at C_{MKT}, with a quantity supplied and demanded of 1,000 bushels and a market price of $14 per bushel.

Like E_{MKT} and D_{MKT}, C_{MKT} is a short-run equilibrium. But it is also something more. Because the price of $14 is each farm's break-even price, an existing producer makes zero economic profit—neither a profit nor a loss, earning only the opportunity cost of the resources used in production—when producing its profit-maximizing output of 4 bushels. At this price there is no incentive either for potential producers to enter or for existing producers to exit the industry. So C_{MKT} corresponds to a **long-run market equilibrium**—a situation in which the quantity supplied equals the quantity demanded, given that sufficient time has elapsed for producers to either enter or exit the industry. In a long-run market equilibrium, all existing and potential producers have fully adjusted to their optimal long-run choices; as a result, no producer has an incentive to either enter or exit the industry.

A market is in **long-run market equilibrium** when the quantity supplied equals the quantity demanded, given that sufficient time has elapsed for entry into and exit from the industry to occur.

ECONOMICS IN ACTION

WORLD VIEW

BALING IN, BAILING OUT

"King Cotton is back," proclaimed a 2010 article in the *Los Angeles Times*, describing a cotton boom that had "turned great swaths of Central California a snowy white during harvest season." Cotton prices were soaring: they more than tripled between early 2010 and early 2011. And farmers responded by planting more cotton.

King Cotton's reign will inevitably end as new producers enter the market and bring prices down.

PhotoAlto/Superstock

What was behind the price rise? As we learned in Section 2, it was partly caused by temporary factors, notably severe floods in Pakistan that destroyed much of that nation's cotton crop. But there was also a big rise in demand, especially from China, whose burgeoning textile and clothing industries demanded ever more raw cotton to weave into cloth. And all indications were that higher demand was here to stay.

So is cotton farming going to be a highly profitable business from now on? The answer is no, because when an industry becomes highly profitable, it draws in new producers, and that brings prices down. And the cotton industry was following the standard script.

For it wasn't just the Central Valley of California that had turned "snowy white." Farmers around the world were moving into cotton growing. "This summer, cotton will stretch from Queensland through northern NSW [New South Wales] all the way down to the Murrumbidgee valley in southern NSW," declared an Australian report.

And by 2012, the entry of all these new producers had a big effect. By the summer of 2012, cotton prices were only about a third of their peak in early 2011. It was clear that the cotton boom had reached its limit—and that at some point in the not too distant future some of the farmers who had rushed into the industry would leave it again.

To explore further the difference between short-run and long-run equilibrium, consider the effect of an increase in demand on an industry with free entry that is initially in long-run equilibrium. Panel (b) in Figure 27-4 shows the market adjustment; panels (a) and (c) show how an existing individual firm behaves during the process.

In panel (b) of Figure 27-4, D_1 is the initial demand curve and S_1 is the initial short-run industry supply curve. Their intersection at point X_{MKT} is both a short-run and a long-run market equilibrium because the equilibrium price of \$14 leads to zero economic profit—and therefore neither entry nor exit. It corresponds to point X in panel (a), where an individual existing firm is operating at the minimum of its average total cost curve.

Now suppose that the demand curve shifts out for some reason to D_2. As shown in panel (b), in the short run, industry output moves along the short-run industry supply curve, S_1, to the new short-run market equilibrium at Y_{MKT}, the intersection of S_1 and D_2. The market price rises to \$18 per bushel, and industry output increases from Q_X to Q_Y. This corresponds to an existing firm's movement from X to Y in panel (a) as the firm increases its output in response to the rise in the market price.

But we know that Y_{MKT} is not a long-run equilibrium because \$18 is higher than minimum average total cost, so existing firms are making economic profits. This will lead additional firms to enter the industry. Over time entry will cause the short-run industry supply curve to shift to the right. In the long run, the short-run industry

FIGURE 27-4 The Effect of an Increase in Demand in the Short Run and the Long Run

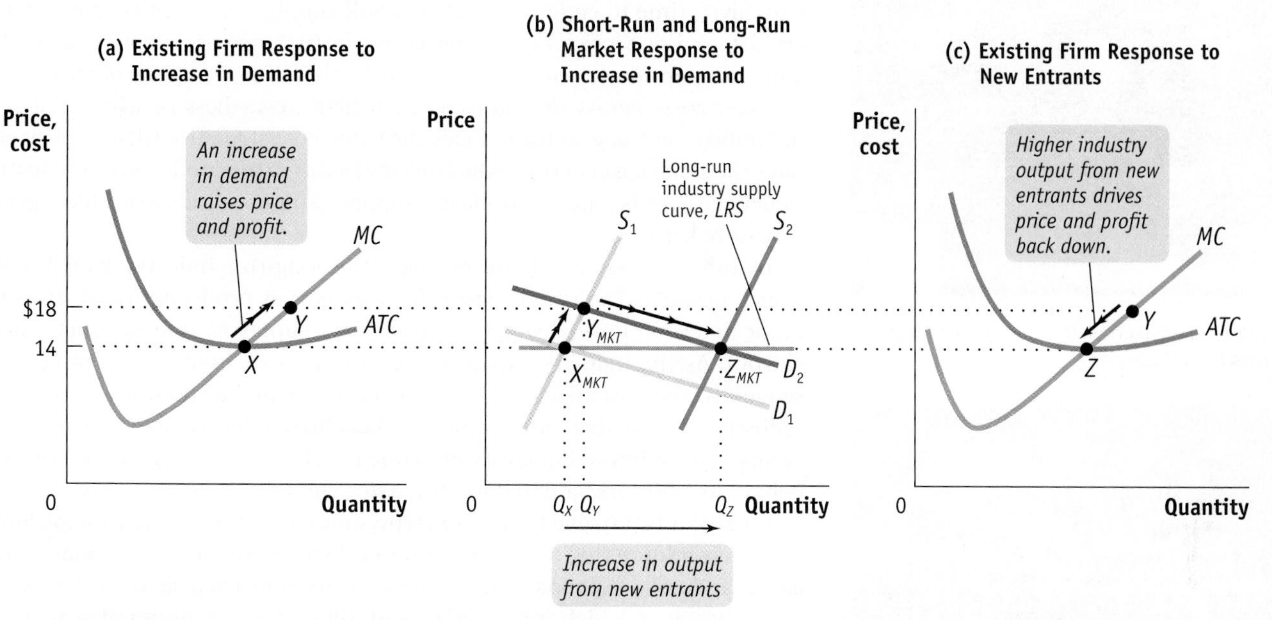

Panel (b) shows how an industry adjusts in the short and long run to an increase in demand; panels (a) and (c) show the corresponding adjustments by an existing firm. Initially the market is at point X_{MKT} in panel (b), a short-run and long-run equilibrium at a price of \$14 and industry output of Q_X. An existing firm makes zero economic profit, operating at point *X* in panel (a) at minimum average total cost. Demand increases as D_1 shifts rightward to D_2, in panel (b), raising the market price to \$18. Existing firms increase their output, and industry output moves along the short-run industry supply curve S_1 to a short-run equilibrium at Y_{MKT}. Correspondingly, the existing firm in panel (a) moves from point *X* to point *Y*. But at a price of \$18 existing firms are profitable. As shown in panel (b), in the long run new entrants arrive and the short-run industry supply curve shifts rightward, from S_1 to S_2. There is a new equilibrium at point Z_{MKT}, at a lower price of \$14 and higher industry output of Q_Z. An existing firm responds by moving from *Y* to *Z* in panel (c), returning to its initial output level and zero economic profit. Production by new entrants accounts for the total increase in industry output, $Q_Z - Q_X$. Like X_{MKT}, Z_{MKT} is also a short-run and long-run equilibrium: with existing firms earning zero economic profit, there is no incentive for any firms to enter or exit the industry. The horizontal line passing through X_{MKT} and Z_{MKT}, *LRS*, is the *long-run industry supply curve:* at the break-even price of \$14, producers will produce any amount that consumers demand in the long run.

supply curve will have shifted out to S_2, and the equilibrium will be at Z_{MKT}—with the price falling back to \$14 per bushel and industry output increasing yet again, from Q_Y to Q_Z. Like X_{MKT} before the increase in demand, Z_{MKT} is both a short-run and a long-run market equilibrium.

The effect of entry on an existing firm is illustrated in panel (c), in the movement from *Y* to *Z* along the firm's individual supply curve. The firm reduces its output in response to the fall in the market price, ultimately arriving back at its original output quantity, corresponding to the minimum of its average total cost curve. In fact, every firm that is now in the industry—the initial set of firms and the new entrants—will operate at the minimum of its average total cost curve, at point *Z*. This means that the entire increase in industry output, from Q_X to Q_Z, comes from production by new entrants.

The line *LRS* that passes through X_{MKT} and Z_{MKT} in panel (b) is the **long-run industry supply curve.** It shows how the quantity supplied by an industry responds to the price, given that firms have had time to enter or exit the industry.

The **long-run industry supply curve** shows how the quantity supplied responds to the price once producers have had time to enter or exit the industry.

iStockphoto

For firms like bakeries, there are constant costs across the industry.

iStockphoto

Firms like beachfront resorts face increasing costs across the industry.

Simon Turner/Alamy

Firms producing electric cars enjoy decreasing costs across the industry.

In this particular case, the long-run industry supply curve is horizontal at $14. In other words, in this industry supply is *perfectly elastic* in the long run: given time to enter or exit, firms will supply any quantity that consumers demand at a price of $14. Perfectly elastic long-run supply is actually a good assumption for many industries. In this case we speak of there being *constant costs across the industry*: each firm, regardless of whether it is an incumbent or a new entrant, faces the same cost structure (that is, they each have the same cost curve). Industries that satisfy this condition are industries in which there is a perfectly elastic supply of inputs—industries like agriculture or bakeries.

In other industries, however, even the long-run industry supply curve slopes upward. The usual reason for this is that producers must use some input that is in limited supply (that is, their supply is at least somewhat inelastic). As the industry expands, the price of that input is driven up. Consequently, the cost structure for firms becomes higher than it was when the industry was smaller. An example is beachfront resort hotels, which must compete for a limited quantity of prime beachfront property. Industries that behave like this are said to have *increasing costs across the industry.*

Finally, it is possible for the long-run industry supply curve to slope downward, a condition that occurs when the cost structure for firms becomes lower as the industry expands. This is the case in industries such as the electric car industry, in which increased output allows for economies of scale in the production of lithium batteries and other specialized inputs, and thus lower input prices. A downward-sloping industry supply curve indicates *decreasing costs across the industry.*

Regardless of whether the long-run industry supply curve is horizontal, upward sloping, or downward sloping, the long-run price elasticity of supply is *higher* than the short-run price elasticity whenever there is free entry and exit. As shown in Figure 27-5, the long-run industry supply curve is always flatter than the short-run industry supply curve. The reason is entry and exit: a high price caused by an increase in demand attracts entry by new firms, resulting in a rise in industry output and an eventual fall in price; a low price caused by a decrease in demand induces existing firms to exit, leading to a fall in industry output and an eventual increase in price.

The distinction between the short-run industry supply curve and the long-run industry supply curve is very important in practice. We often see a sequence of events like that shown in Figure 27-4: an increase in demand initially leads to a large price increase, but prices return to their initial level once new firms have entered the industry. Or we see the sequence in reverse: a fall in demand reduces prices in the short run, but they return to their initial level as producers exit the industry.

The Cost of Production and Efficiency in Long-Run Equilibrium

Our analysis leads us to three conclusions about the cost of production and efficiency in the long-run equilibrium of a perfectly competitive industry. These results will be important in our upcoming discussion of how monopoly gives rise to inefficiency.

First, in a perfectly competitive industry in equilibrium, the value of marginal cost is the same for all firms. That's because all firms produce the quantity of output at which marginal cost equals the market price, and as price-takers they all face the same market price.

Second, in a perfectly competitive industry with free entry and exit, each firm will have zero economic profit in the long-run equilibrium. Each firm produces the quantity of output that minimizes its average total cost—corresponding to point Z in panel (c) of Figure 27-4. So the total cost of producing the industry's output is minimized in a perfectly competitive industry.

FIGURE 27-5 **Comparing the Short-Run and Long-Run Industry Supply Curves**

The long-run industry supply curve may slope upward, but it is always flatter—more elastic—than the short-run industry supply curve. This is because of entry and exit: a higher price attracts new entrants in the long run, resulting in a rise in industry output and a fall in price; a lower price induces existing producers to exit in the long run, generating a fall in industry output and a rise in price.

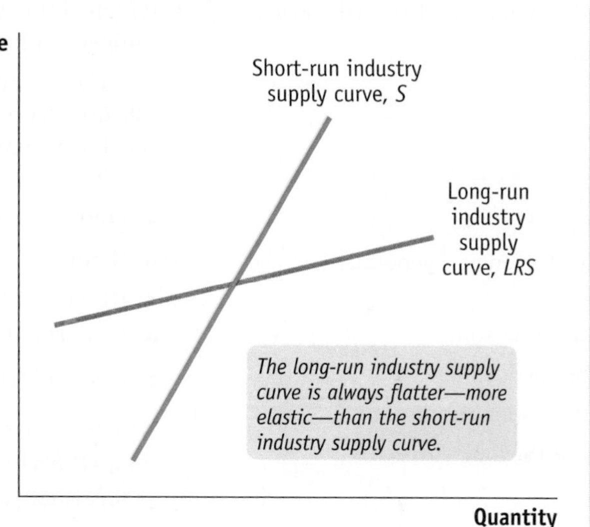

The third and final conclusion is that the long-run market equilibrium of a perfectly competitive industry is efficient: no mutually beneficial transactions go unexploited. To understand this, recall a fundamental requirement for efficiency: all consumers who are willing to pay an amount greater than or equal to the sellers' cost actually get the good. We also learned that when a market is efficient (except under certain, well-defined conditions), the market price matches all consumers willing to pay at least the market price with all sellers who have a cost of production that is less than or equal to the market price.

So in the long-run equilibrium of a perfectly competitive industry, production is efficient: costs are minimized and no resources are wasted. In addition, the allocation of goods to consumers is efficient: every consumer willing to pay the cost of producing the good gets it. Indeed, no mutually beneficial transaction is left unexploited. Moreover, this condition tends to persist over time as the environment changes: the force of competition makes producers responsive to changes in consumers' desires and to changes in technology.

MODULE 27 Review

Solutions appear at the back of the book.

Check Your Understanding

1. Which of the following events will induce firms to enter an industry? Which will induce firms to exit? When will entry or exit cease? Explain your answer.
   a. A technological advance lowers the fixed cost of production of every firm in the industry.
   b. The wages paid to workers in the industry go up for an extended period of time.
   c. A permanent change in consumer tastes increases demand for the good.
   d. The price of a key input rises due to a long-term shortage of that input.

2. Assume that the egg industry is perfectly competitive and is in long-run equilibrium with a perfectly elastic long-run industry supply curve. Health concerns about cholesterol then lead to a decrease in demand. Construct a figure similar to Figure 27-4, showing the short-run behavior of the industry and how long-run equilibrium is reestablished.

Multiple-Choice Questions

1. In the long run, a perfectly competitive firm will earn
   a. a negative market return.
   b. a positive profit.
   c. a loss.
   d. zero economic profit.
   e. excess profit.

2. With perfect competition, efficiency is generally attained in
   a. the short run but not the long run.
   b. the long run but not the short run.
   c. both the short run and the long run.
   d. neither the short run nor the long run.
   e. specific firms only.

3. Compared to the short-run industry supply curve, the long-run industry supply curve will be more
   a. elastic.
   b. inelastic.
   c. steeply sloped.
   d. profitable.
   e. accurate.

4. Which of the following is generally true for perfect competition?
   I. There is free entry and exit.
   II. Long-run market equilibrium is efficient.
   III. Firms maximize profits at the output level where $P = MC$.
   a. I only
   b. II only
   c. III only
   d. I and II only
   e. I, II, and III

5. Which of the following will happen if perfectly competitive firms are earning positive economic profit?
   a. Firms will exit the industry.
   b. The short-run industry supply curve will shift right.
   c. The short-run industry supply curve will shift left.
   d. Firm output will increase.
   e. Market price will increase.

Critical-Thinking Question

Draw correctly labeled side-by-side graphs to show the long-run adjustment that would take place if perfectly competitive firms were earning a profit.

BUSINESS CASE • TheFind Finds the Cheapest Price

Courtesy of The Find, Inc.

In Sunnyvale, California, Tri Trang walked into a Best Buy and found the perfect gift for his girlfriend, a $184.85 Garmin GPS system. A year earlier, he would have put the item in his cart and purchased it. Instead, he whipped out his Android phone; using an app that instantly compared Best Buy's price to those of other retailers, he found the same item on Amazon.com for $106.75, with no shipping charges and no sales tax. Trang proceeded to buy it from Amazon, right there on the spot.

It doesn't stop there. TheFind, the most popular of the price-comparison sites, will also provide users with a map to the store with the best price, coupon codes and shipping deals, and other tools to help organize purchases. *Terror* has been the word used to describe the reaction of brick-and-mortar retailers.

Before the advent of apps like TheFind's, a retailer could lure customers into its store with enticing specials, and reasonably expect them to buy other, more profitable things, too—with some prompting from salespeople. But those days are disappearing. According to one study, 73% of customers with mobile devices prefer to shop by phone rather than talk to a salesperson. Best Buy recently settled a lawsuit alleging that it posted web prices at in-store kiosks faster than the ones customers saw on their home computers, a maneuver that would have been quickly discovered by users of TheFind's app.

Not surprisingly, use of TheFind's app has increased at an extremely fast clip. The number of people making purchases on their phones nearly doubled between 2011 and 2012. Indeed, retailers are expecting even more shoppers to use their phones to make purchases in the coming years. The accompanying figure illustrates their projections for dramatic growth in cell phone sales through 2016. On TheFind, the most frequently searched items in stores are iPhones, iPads, video games, and other electronics.

Expected Growth in Cell Phone Purchases in the United States, 2010–2016

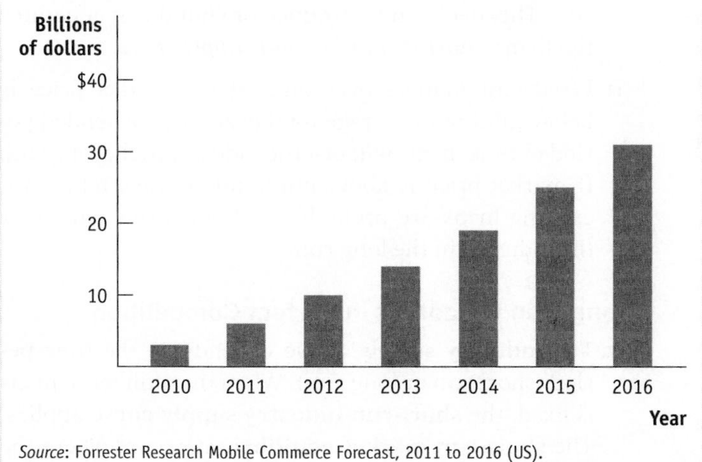

Source: Forrester Research Mobile Commerce Forecast, 2011 to 2016 (US).

According to e-commerce experts, U.S. retailers have begun to alter their selling strategies in response. One strategy involves stocking products that manufacturers have slightly modified for the retailer, which allows the retailer to be their exclusive seller. In addition, when confronted by an in-store customer wielding a lower price on a mobile device, some retailers will lower their price to avoid losing the sale.

Yet retailers are clearly frightened. As one analyst said, "Only a couple of retailers can play the lowest-price game. This is going to accelerate the demise of retailers who do not have either competitive pricing or stand-out store experience."

Questions for Thought

1. What do the details in the case suggest about whether or not the retail market for electronics was perfectly competitive before the advent of mobile-device comparison shopping?
2. What effect will the introduction of TheFind's and similar apps have on competition in the retail market for electronics? On the profitability of brick-and-mortar retailers like Best Buy? What, on average, will be the effect on the consumer surplus of purchasers of these items?
3. Why are some retailers responding by having manufacturers make exclusive versions of products for them? Is this trend likely to increase or diminish?

SECTION 9 REVIEW

Summary

Introduction to Market Structure

1. There are four main types of market structure based on the number of firms in the industry and product differentiation: perfect competition, monopoly, oligopoly, and monopolistic competition.
2. In a **perfectly competitive market** all firms are **price-taking firms** and all consumers are **price-taking consumers**—no one's actions can influence the market price. Consumers are normally price-takers, but firms often are not. In a **perfectly competitive industry,** every firm in the industry is a price-taker.
3. A **monopolist** is a producer who is the sole supplier of a good without close substitutes. An industry controlled by a monopolist is a **monopoly.**
4. To persist, a monopoly must be protected by a **barrier to entry.** This can take the form of control of a natural resource or input, increasing returns to scale that give rise to a **natural monopoly,** technological superiority, or government rules that prevent entry by other firms, such as **patents** or **copyrights.**
5. There are two necessary conditions for a perfectly competitive industry: there are many firms, none of which has a large **market share,** and the industry produces a **standardized product** or **commodity**—goods that consumers regard as equivalent. A third condition is often satisfied as well: **free entry and exit** into and from the industry.
6. Many industries are **oligopolies:** there are only a few sellers, called **oligopolists.** Oligopolies exist for more or less the same reasons that monopolies exist, but in weaker form. They are characterized by **imperfect competition:** firms compete but possess some market power.
7. **Monopolistic competition** is a market structure in which there are many competing firms, each producing a differentiated product, and there is free entry and exit in the long run. Product differentiation takes three main forms: by style or type, by location, and by quality. The extent of imperfect competition can be measured by the **Herfindahl–Hirschman Index.**

Perfect Competition

8. A producer chooses output according to the **optimal output rule:** produce the quantity at which **marginal revenue** equals marginal cost. For a price-taking firm, marginal revenue is equal to price and its **marginal revenue curve** is a horizontal line at the market price. It chooses output according to the **price-taking firm's optimal output rule:** produce the quantity at which price equals marginal cost. However, a firm that produces the optimal quantity may not be profitable.

Graphing Perfect Competition

9. A firm is profitable if total revenue exceeds total cost or, equivalently, if the market price exceeds its **break-even price**—minimum average total cost. If market price exceeds the break-even price, the firm is profitable. If market price is less than minimum average total cost, the firm is unprofitable. If market price is equal to minimum average total cost, the firm breaks even. When profitable, the firm's per-unit profit is $P - ATC$; when unprofitable, its per-unit loss is $ATC - P$.
10. Fixed cost is irrelevant to the firm's optimal short-run production decision. The short-run production decision depends on the firm's **shut-down price**—its minimum average variable cost—and the market price. When the market price is equal to or exceeds the shut-down price, the firm produces the output quantity at which marginal cost equals the market price. When the market price falls below the shut-down price, the firm ceases production in the short run. This decision to produce or shut down generates the firm's *short-run individual supply curve.*
11. Fixed cost matters over time. If the market price is below minimum average total cost for an extended period of time, firms will exit the industry in the long run. If market price is above minimum average total cost, existing firms are profitable and new firms will enter the industry in the long run.

Long-Run Outcomes in Perfect Competition

12. The **industry supply curve** depends on the time period (short run or long run). When the number of firms is fixed, the **short-run industry supply curve** applies. The **short-run market equilibrium** occurs where the short-run industry supply curve and the demand curve intersect.
13. With sufficient time for entry into and exit from an industry, the **long-run industry supply curve** applies. The **long-run market equilibrium** occurs at the intersection of the long-run industry supply curve and the demand curve. At this point, no producer has an incentive to enter or exit. The long-run industry supply curve is often horizontal. It may slope upward if there is limited supply of an input, resulting in increasing costs across the industry. It may even slope downward, as in the case of decreasing costs across the industry. But the long-run industry supply curve is always more elastic than the short-run industry supply curve.

14. In the long-run market equilibrium of a competitive industry, profit maximization leads each firm to produce at the same marginal cost, which is equal to the market price. Free entry and exit means that each firm earns zero economic profit—producing the output corresponding to its minimum average total cost. So the total cost of production of an industry's output is minimized. The outcome is efficient because every consumer with willingness to pay greater than or equal to marginal cost gets the good.

Key Terms

Price-taking firm, p. 261
Price-taking consumer, p. 261
Perfectly competitive market, p. 261
Perfectly competitive industry, p. 262
Market share, p. 262
Standardized product, p. 262
Commodity, p. 262
Free entry and exit, p. 263
Monopolist, p. 264
Monopoly, p. 264
Barrier to entry, p. 264
Natural monopoly, p. 264
Patent, p. 265
Copyright, p. 265
Oligopoly, p. 266
Oligopolist, p. 266
Imperfect competition, p. 266
Herfindahl–Hirschman Index p. 267
Monopolistic competition, p. 268
Marginal revenue, p. 271
Optimal output rule, p. 271
Price-taking firm's optimal output rule, p. 272
Marginal revenue curve, p. 273
Break-even price, p. 279
Shut-down price, p. 281
Industry supply curve, p. 286
Short-run industry supply curve, p. 287
Short-run market equilibrium, p. 287
Long-run market equilibrium, p. 289
Long-run industry supply curve, p. 291

Problems

1. For each of the following, is the industry perfectly competitive? Referring to market share, standardization of the product, and/or free entry and exit, explain your answers.
   a. aspirin
   b. Alicia Keys concerts
   c. SUVs

2. Kate's Katering provides catered meals, and the catered meals industry is perfectly competitive. Kate's machinery costs $100 per day and is the only fixed input. Her variable cost consists of the wages paid to the cooks and the food ingredients. The variable cost per day associated with each level of output is given in the accompanying table.

Quantity of meals	VC
0	$0
10	200
20	300
30	480
40	700
50	1,000

   a. Calculate the total cost, the average variable cost, the average total cost, and the marginal cost for each quantity of output.
   b. What is the break-even price? What is the shut-down price?
   c. Suppose that the price at which Kate can sell catered meals is $21 per meal. In the short run, will Kate earn a profit? In the short run, should she produce or shut down?
   d. Suppose that the price at which Kate can sell catered meals is $17 per meal. In the short run, will Kate earn a profit? In the short run, should she produce or shut down?
   e. Suppose that the price at which Kate can sell catered meals is $13 per meal. In the short run, will Kate earn a profit? In the short run, should she produce or shut down?

3. Bob produces DVD movies for sale, which requires a building and a machine that copies the original movie onto a DVD. Bob rents a building for $30,000 per month and rents a machine for $20,000 a month. Those are his fixed costs. His variable costs per month are given in the accompanying table.

Quantity of DVDs	VC
0	$0
1,000	5,000
2,000	8,000
3,000	9,000
4,000	14,000
5,000	20,000
6,000	33,000
7,000	49,000
8,000	72,000
9,000	99,000
10,000	150,000

   a. Calculate Bob's average variable cost, average total cost, and marginal cost for each quantity of output.
   b. There is free entry into the industry, and anyone who enters will face the same costs as Bob. Suppose that currently the price of a DVD is $25. What will Bob's profit be? Is this a long-run equilibrium? If not, what will the price of DVD movies be in the long run?

4. Consider Bob's DVD company described in Problem 3. Assume that DVD production is a perfectly competitive industry. For each of the following questions, explain your answers.

a. What is Bob's break-even price? What is his shut-down price?

b. Suppose the price of a DVD is $2. What should Bob do in the short run?

c. Suppose the price of a DVD is $7. What is the profit-maximizing quantity of DVDs that Bob should produce? What will his total profit be? Will he produce or shut down in the short run? Will he stay in the industry or exit in the long run?

d. Suppose instead that the price of DVDs is $20. Now what is the profit-maximizing quantity of DVDs that Bob should produce? What will his total profit be now? Will he produce or shut down in the short run? Will he stay in the industry or exit in the long run?

5. Consider again Bob's DVD company described in Problem 3.

a. Draw Bob's marginal cost curve.

b. Over what range of prices will Bob produce no DVDs in the short run?

c. Draw Bob's individual supply curve.

6. a. A profit-maximizing business incurs an economic loss of $10,000 per year. Its fixed cost is $15,000 per year. Should it produce or shut down in the short run? Should it stay in the industry or exit in the long run?

b. Suppose instead that this business has a fixed cost of $6,000 per year. Should it produce or shut down in the short run? Should it stay in the industry or exit in the long run?

7. The first sushi restaurant opens in town. Initially, people are very cautious about eating tiny portions of raw fish, as this is a town where large portions of grilled meat have always been popular. Soon, however, an influential health report warns consumers against grilled meat and suggests that they increase their consumption of fish, especially raw fish. The sushi restaurant becomes very popular and its profit increases.

a. What will happen to the short-run profit of the sushi restaurant? What will happen to the number of sushi restaurants in town in the long run? Will the first sushi restaurant be able to sustain its short-run profit over the long run? Explain your answers.

b. Local steakhouses suffer from the popularity of sushi and start incurring losses. What will happen to the number of steakhouses in town in the long run? Explain your answer.

8. A perfectly competitive firm has the following short-run total costs:

Quantity	*TC*
0	$5
1	10
2	13
3	18
4	25
5	34
6	45

Market demand for the firm's product is given by the following market demand schedule:

Price	Quantity demanded
$12	300
10	500
8	800
6	1,200
4	1,800

a. Calculate this firm's marginal cost and, for all output levels except zero, the firm's average variable cost and average total cost.

b. There are 100 firms in this industry that all have costs identical to those of this firm. Draw the short-run industry supply curve. In the same diagram, draw the market demand curve.

c. What is the market price, and how much profit will each firm make?

9. A new vaccine against a deadly disease has just been discovered. Presently, 55 people die from the disease each year. The new vaccine will save lives, but it is not completely safe. Some recipients of the shots will die from adverse reactions. The projected effects of the inoculation are given in the accompanying table:

Percent of population inoculated	Total deaths due to disease	Total deaths due to inoculation	Marginal benefit of inoculation	Marginal cost of inoculation	"Profit" of inoculation
0	55	0			
			___	___	___
10	45	0			
			___	___	___
20	36	1			
			___	___	___
30	28	3			
			___	___	___
40	21	6			
			___	___	___
50	15	10			
			___	___	___
60	10	15			
			___	___	___
70	6	20			
			___	___	___
80	3	25			
			___	___	___
90	1	30			
			___	___	___
100	0	35			

a. What are the interpretations of "marginal benefit" and "marginal cost" here? Calculate marginal benefit and marginal cost per each 10% increase in the rate of inoculation. Write your answers in the table.

b. What proportion of the population should optimally be inoculated?

c. What is the interpretation of "profit" here? Calculate the profit for all levels of inoculation.

10. The production of agricultural products like wheat is one of the few examples of a perfectly competitive industry. In this question, we analyze results from a hypothetical study about wheat production in the United States in 2001 and make some comparisons to wheat production in 2013.

a. The average variable cost per acre planted with wheat was $107 per acre. Assuming a yield of 50 bushels per acre, calculate the average variable cost per bushel of wheat.

b. The average price of wheat received by a farmer in 1998 was $2.65 per bushel. Do you think the average farm would have shut down in the short run? Explain.

c. With a yield of 50 bushels of wheat per acre, the average total cost per farm was $3.80 per bushel. The harvested acreage for rye (a type of wheat) in the United States fell from 418,000 acres in 1998 to 250,000 in 2010. Using the information on prices and costs here and in parts a and b, explain why this might have happened.

d. Using the above information, do you think the price of wheat was higher or lower than $2.65 per bushel prior to 1998? Why?

M0-M1-M2
M3-M4-M5

Monopoly

EVERYBODY MUST GET STONES

A few years back De Beers, the world's main supplier of diamonds, ran an ad urging men to buy their wives diamond jewelry. "She married you for richer, for poorer," read the ad. "Let her know how it's going."

Crass? Yes. Effective? No question. For generations diamonds have been a symbol of luxury, valued not only for their appearance but also for their rarity.

But geologists will tell you that diamonds aren't all that rare. In fact, according to the *Dow Jones-Irwin Guide to Fine Gems and Jewelry,* diamonds are "more common than any other gem-quality colored stone. They only seem rarer . . ."

Why do diamonds seem rarer than other gems? Part of the answer is a brilliant marketing campaign. But mainly diamonds seem rare because De Beers *makes* them rare: the company controls most of the world's diamond mines and limits the quantity of diamonds supplied to the market.

In the previous section we concentrated on perfectly competitive markets—those in which the producers are perfect competitors. But De Beers isn't like the producers we've studied so far: it is a *monopolist,* the sole (or almost sole) producer of a good.

Monopolists behave differently from producers in perfectly competitive industries: whereas perfect competitors take the price at which they can sell their output as given, monopolists know that their actions affect market prices and take that effect into account when deciding how much to produce.

In this section we examine how monopolies function and differ from industries in perfect competition. We'll also look at the policies governments adopt in response to monopoly behavior. We conclude with a discussion of how monopolists use *price discrimination*—charging different types of consumers different prices for the same good—to increase profits.

MODULE 28 Monopoly in Practice

iStockphoto

WHAT YOU WILL LEARN

1. **How a monopolist determines the profit-maximizing price and quantity**
2. **How to determine whether a monopoly is earning a profit or a loss**

In this module we turn to monopoly, the market structure at the opposite end of the spectrum from perfect competition. A monopolist's profit-maximizing decision is subtly different from that of a price-taking producer, yet it has large implications for the output produced and the welfare created. We will see the crucial role that market demand plays in leading a monopolist to behave differently from a firm in a perfectly competitive industry.

The Monopolist's Demand Curve and Marginal Revenue

Recall the firm's *optimal output rule:* a profit-maximizing firm produces the quantity of output at which the marginal cost of producing the last unit of output equals marginal revenue—the change in total revenue generated by the last unit of output. That is, $MR = MC$ at the profit-maximizing quantity of output.

Although the optimal output rule holds for *all* firms, decisions about price and the quantity of output differ between monopolies and perfectly competitive industries due to differences in the demand curves faced by monopolists and perfectly competitive firms.

We have learned that even though the *market* demand curve always slopes downward, each of the firms that make up a perfectly competitive industry faces a horizontal, *perfectly elastic* demand curve, like D_C in panel (a) of Figure 28-1. Any attempt by an individual firm in a perfectly competitive industry to charge more than the going market price will cause the firm to lose all its sales. It can, however, sell as much as it likes at the market price.

FIGURE 28-1 Comparing the Demand Curves of a Perfectly Competitive Producer and a Monopolist

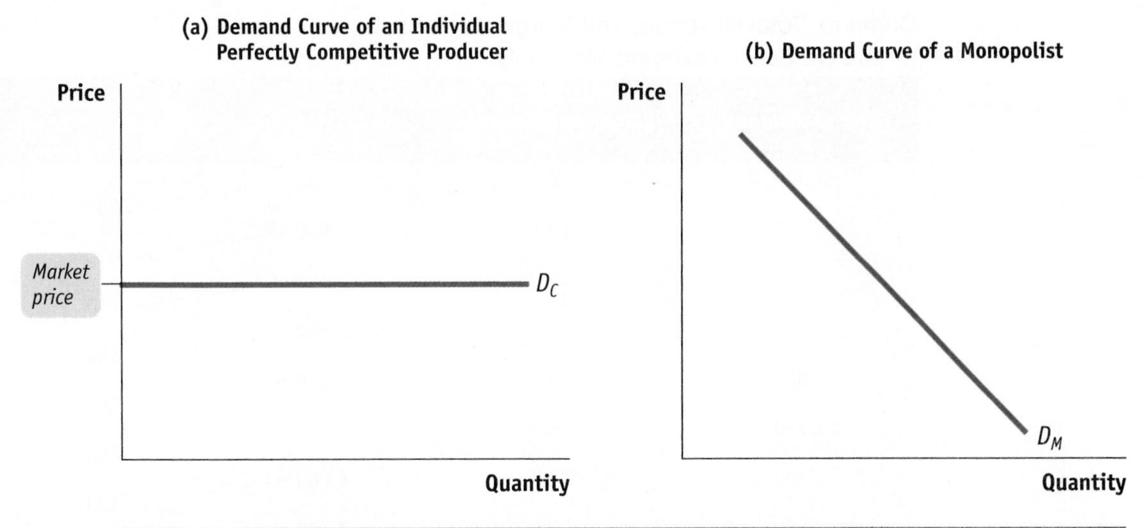

Because an individual perfectly competitive producer cannot affect the market price of the good, it faces a horizontal demand curve D_C, as shown in panel (a). A monopolist, on the other hand, can affect the price. Because it is the sole supplier in the industry, its demand curve is the market demand curve D_M, as shown in panel (b). To sell more output, it must lower the price; by reducing output, it can raise the price.

We saw that the marginal revenue of a perfectly competitive firm is simply the market price. As a result, the price-taking firm's optimal output rule is to produce the output level at which the marginal cost of the last unit produced is equal to the market price.

A monopolist, in contrast, is the sole supplier of its good. So its demand curve is simply the market demand curve, which slopes downward, like D_M in panel (b) of Figure 28-1. This downward slope creates a "wedge" between the price of the good and the marginal revenue of the good.

Table 28-1 shows how this wedge develops. The first two columns of Table 28-1 show a hypothetical demand schedule for De Beers diamonds. For the sake of simplicity, we assume that all diamonds are exactly alike. And to make the arithmetic easy, we suppose that the number of diamonds sold is far smaller than is actually the case. For instance, at a price of $500 per diamond, we assume that only 10 diamonds are sold. The demand curve implied by this schedule is shown in panel (a) of Figure 28-2.

The third column of Table 28-1 shows De Beers's total revenue from selling each quantity of diamonds—the price per diamond multiplied by the number of diamonds sold. The last column shows marginal revenue, the change in total revenue from producing and selling another diamond.

Clearly, after the first diamond, the marginal revenue a monopolist receives from selling one more unit is less than the price at which that unit is sold. For example, if De Beers sells 10 diamonds, the price at which the 10th diamond is sold is $500. But the marginal revenue—the change in total revenue in going from 9 to 10 diamonds—is only $50.

Why is the marginal revenue from that 10th diamond less than the price? Because an increase in production by a monopolist has two opposing effects on revenue:

1. *A quantity effect.* One more unit is sold, increasing total revenue by the price at which the unit is sold (in this case, +$500).
2. *A price effect.* In order to sell that last unit, the monopolist must cut the market price on *all* units sold. This decreases total revenue (in this case, by $9 \times (-\$50) = -\$450$).

TABLE 28-1

Demand, Total Revenue, and Marginal Revenue for the De Beers Diamond Monopoly

Price of diamond P	Quantity of diamonds demanded Q	Total revenue $TR = P \times Q$	Marginal revenue $MR = \Delta TR/\Delta Q$
$1,000	0	$0	
			$950
950	1	950	
			850
900	2	1,800	
			750
850	3	2,550	
			650
800	4	3,200	
			550
750	5	3,750	
			450
700	6	4,200	
			350
650	7	4,550	
			250
600	8	4,800	
			150
550	9	4,950	
			50
500	10	5,000	
			−50
450	11	4,950	
			−150
400	12	4,800	
			−250
350	13	4,550	
			−350
300	14	4,200	
			−450
250	15	3,750	
			−550
200	16	3,200	
			−650
150	17	2,550	
			−750
100	18	1,800	
			−850
50	19	950	
			−950
0	20	0	

The quantity effect and the price effect are illustrated by the two shaded areas in panel (a) of Figure 28-2. Increasing diamond sales from 9 to 10 means moving down the demand curve from *A* to *B,* reducing the price per diamond from $550 to $500. The green-shaded area represents the quantity effect: De Beers sells the 10th diamond at a price of $500. This is offset, however, by the price effect, represented by the orange-shaded area. In order to sell that 10th diamond, De Beers must reduce the price on all its diamonds from $550 to $500. So it loses 9 × $50 = $450 in revenue, the orange-shaded area. So, as point *C* indicates, the total effect on revenue of selling one more diamond—the marginal revenue—derived from an increase in diamond sales from 9 to 10 is only $50.

Point *C* lies on the monopolist's marginal revenue curve, labeled *MR* in panel (a) of Figure 28-2 and taken from the last column of Table 28-1. The crucial point about the monopolist's marginal revenue curve is that it is always *below* the demand curve. That's because of the price effect, which means that a monopolist's marginal revenue from selling an additional unit is always less than the price the monopolist receives

FIGURE 28-2 A Monopolist's Demand, Total Revenue, and Marginal Revenue Curves

Panel (a) shows the monopolist's demand and marginal revenue curves for diamonds from Table 28-1. The marginal revenue curve lies below the demand curve. To see why, consider point *A* on the demand curve, where 9 diamonds are sold at $550 each, generating total revenue of $4,950. To sell a 10th diamond, the price on all 10 diamonds must be cut to $500, as shown by point *B*. As a result, total revenue increases by the green area (the quantity effect: +$500) but decreases by the orange area (the price effect: –$450). So the marginal revenue from the 10th diamond is $50 (the difference between the green and orange areas), which is much lower than its price, $500. Panel (b) shows the monopolist's total revenue curve for diamonds. As output goes from 0 to 10 diamonds, total revenue increases. It reaches its maximum at 10 diamonds—the level at which marginal revenue is equal to 0—and declines thereafter. When the quantity effect dominates the price effect, total revenue rises. When the price effect dominates the quantity effect, total revenue falls.

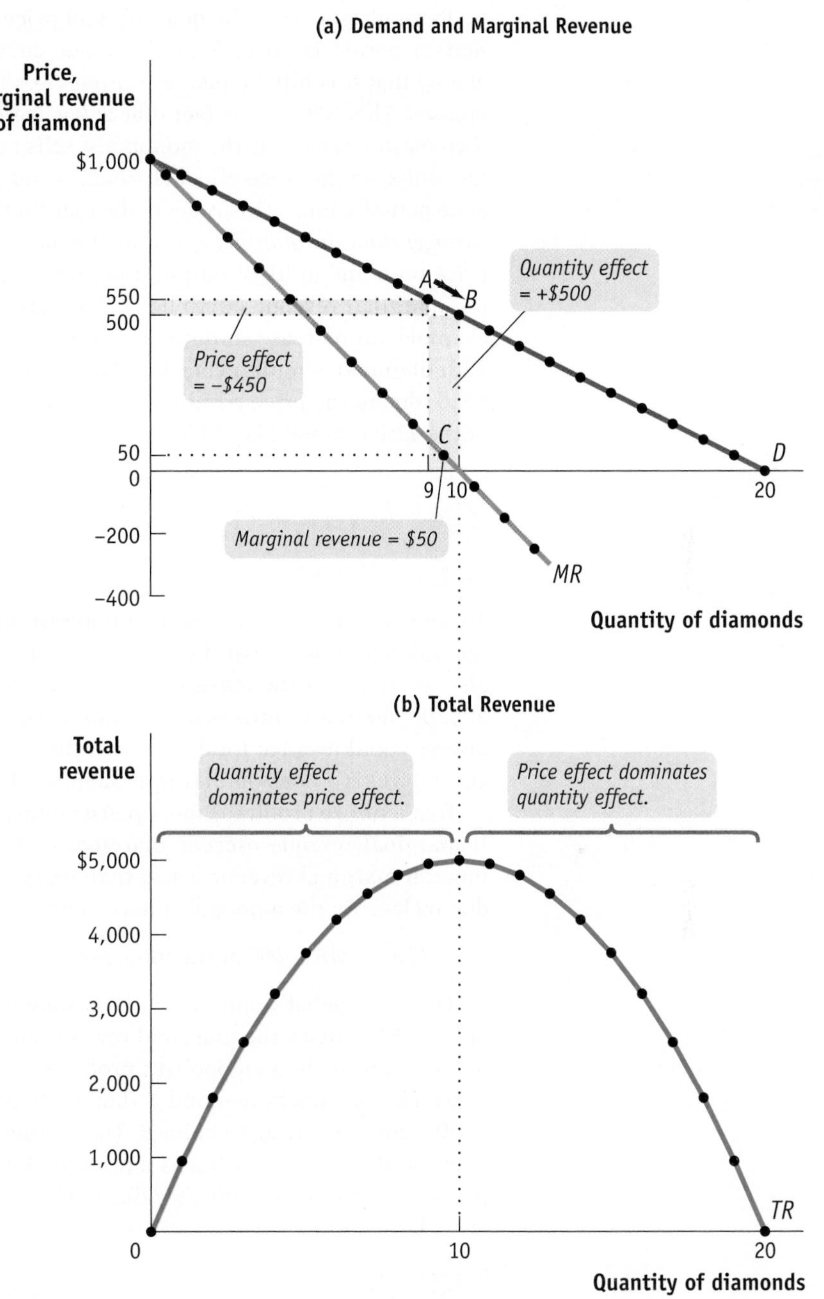

for that unit. It is the price effect that creates the wedge between the monopolist's marginal revenue curve and the demand curve: in order to sell an additional diamond, De Beers must cut the market price on all units sold.

In fact, this wedge exists for any firm that possesses market power, such as an oligopolist. Having market power means that the firm faces a downward-sloping demand curve. As a result, there will always be a price effect from an increase in output for a firm with market power that charges every customer the same price. So for such a firm, the marginal revenue curve always lies below the demand curve.

Take a moment to compare the monopolist's marginal revenue curve with the marginal revenue curve for a perfectly competitive firm, which has no market power. For such a firm there is no price effect from an increase in output: its marginal revenue curve is simply its horizontal demand curve. So for a perfectly competitive firm, market price and marginal revenue are always equal.

To emphasize how the quantity and price effects offset each other for a firm with market power, De Beers's total revenue curve is shown in panel (b) of Figure 28-2. Notice that it is hill-shaped: as output rises from 0 to 10 diamonds, total revenue increases. This reflects the fact that *at low levels of output, the quantity effect is stronger than the price effect:* as the monopolist sells more, it has to lower the price on only very few units, so the price effect is small. As output rises beyond 10 diamonds, total revenue actually falls. This reflects the fact that *at high levels of output, the price effect is stronger than the quantity effect:* as the monopolist sells more, it now has to lower the price on many units of output, making the price effect very large. Correspondingly, the marginal revenue curve lies below zero at output levels above 10 diamonds. For example, an increase in diamond production from 11 to 12 yields only $400 for the 12th diamond, simultaneously reducing the revenue from diamonds 1 through 11 by $550 (due to the price per diamond falling by $50). As a result, the marginal revenue of the 12th diamond is –$150.

The Monopolist's Profit-Maximizing Output and Price

To complete the story of how a monopolist maximizes profit, we now bring in the monopolist's marginal cost. Let's assume that there is no fixed cost of production; we'll also assume that the marginal cost of producing an additional diamond is constant at $200, no matter how many diamonds De Beers produces. Then marginal cost will always equal average total cost, and the marginal cost curve (and the average total cost curve) is a horizontal line at $200, as shown in Figure 28-3.

To maximize profit, the monopolist compares marginal cost with marginal revenue. If marginal revenue exceeds marginal cost, De Beers increases profit by producing more; if marginal revenue is less than marginal cost, De Beers increases profit by producing less. So the monopolist maximizes its profit by using the optimal output rule:

(28-1) $MR = MC$ at the monopolist's profit-maximizing quantity of output

The monopolist's optimal point is shown in Figure 28-3. At *A*, the marginal cost curve, *MC*, crosses the marginal revenue curve, *MR*. The corresponding output level, 8 diamonds, is the monopolist's profit-maximizing quantity of output, Q_M. The price at which consumers demand 8 diamonds is $600, so the monopolist's price, P_M, is $600—corresponding to point *B*. The average total cost of producing each diamond is $200, so the monopolist earns a profit of $600 – $200 = $400 per diamond, and total profit is 8 × $400 = $3,200, as indicated by the shaded area.

Monopoly versus Perfect Competition

In the 1880s, when Cecil Rhodes consolidated many independent diamond producers into the company he founded, De Beers, he converted a perfectly competitive industry into a monopoly. We can now use our analysis to see the effects of such a consolidation.

Let's look again at Figure 28-3 and ask how this same market would work if, instead of being a monopoly, the industry were perfectly competitive. We will continue to assume that there is no fixed cost and that marginal cost is constant, so average total cost and marginal cost are equal.

If the diamond industry consists of many perfectly competitive firms, each of those producers takes the market price as given. That is, each producer acts as if its marginal revenue is equal to the market price. So each firm within the industry uses the price-taking firm's optimal output rule:

(28-2) $P = MC$ at the perfectly competitive firm's profit-maximizing quantity of output.

FIGURE 28-3 **The Monopolist's Profit-Maximizing Output and Price**

This figure shows the demand, marginal revenue, and marginal cost curves. Marginal cost per diamond is constant at $200, so the marginal cost curve is horizontal at $200. According to the optimal output rule, the profit-maximizing quantity of output for the monopolist is at *MR* = *MC*, shown by point *A*, where the marginal cost and marginal revenue curves cross at an output of 8 diamonds. The price De Beers can charge per diamond is found by going to the point on the demand curve directly above point *A*, which is point *B* here—a price of $600 per diamond. It makes a profit of $400 × 8 = $3,200. A perfectly competitive industry produces the output level at which *P* = *MC*, given by point *C*, where the demand curve and marginal cost curves cross. So a competitive industry produces 16 diamonds, sells at a price of $200, and makes zero economic profit.

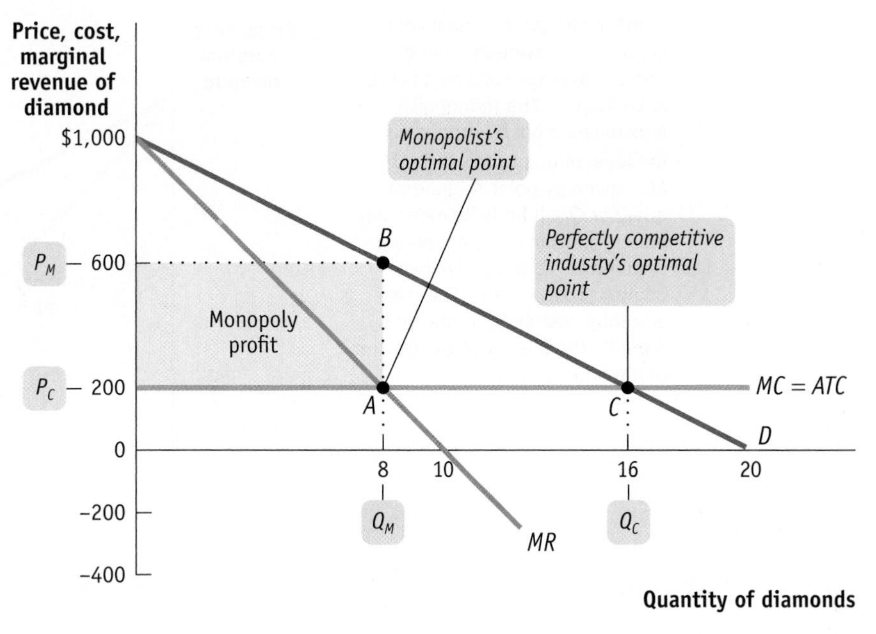

In Figure 28-3, this would correspond to producing at *C*, where the price per diamond, P_C, is $200, equal to the marginal cost of production. So the profit-maximizing output of an industry under perfect competition, Q_C, is 16 diamonds.

But does the perfectly competitive industry earn any profit at *C*? No: the price of $200 is equal to the average total cost per diamond. So there is no economic profit for this industry when it produces at the perfectly competitive output level.

We've already seen that once the industry is consolidated into a monopoly, the result is very different. The monopolist's marginal revenue is influenced by the price effect, so that marginal revenue is less than the price. That is,

(28-3) $P > MR = MC$ at the monopolist's profit-maximizing quantity of output

As shown in Figure 28-3, the monopolist produces less than the competitive industry—8 diamonds rather than 16. The price under monopoly is $600, compared with only $200 under perfect competition. The monopolist earns a positive profit, but the competitive industry does not.

So, we can see that compared with a competitive industry, a monopolist does the following:

- produces a smaller quantity: $Q_M < Q_C$
- charges a higher price: $P_M > P_C$
- earns a profit

Monopoly: The General Picture

Figure 28-3 involved specific numbers and assumed that marginal cost was constant, there was no fixed cost, and therefore, that the average total cost curve was a horizontal line. Figure 28-4 shows a more general picture of monopoly in action: *D* is the market demand curve; *MR*, the marginal revenue curve; *MC*, the marginal cost curve; and *ATC*, the average total cost curve. Here we return to the usual assumption

Compared with competitive firms, monopolies produce less, charge more, and earn a profit.

FIGURE 28-4 The Monopolist's Profit

In this case, the marginal cost curve has a "swoosh" shape and the average total cost curve is U-shaped. The monopolist maximizes profit by producing the level of output at which $MR = MC$, given by point A, generating quantity Q_M. It finds its monopoly price, P_M, from the point on the demand curve directly above point A, point B here. The average total cost of Q_M is shown by point C. Profit is given by the area of the shaded rectangle.

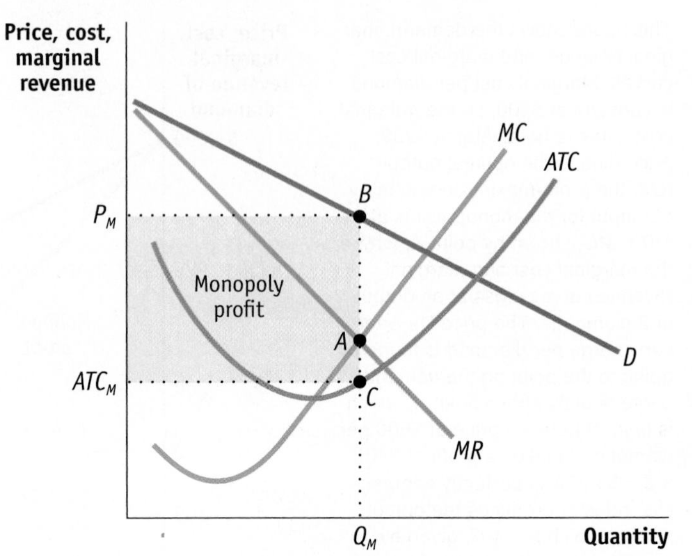

that the marginal cost curve has a "swoosh" shape and the average total cost curve is U-shaped.

Applying the optimal output rule, we see that the profit-maximizing level of output, identified as the quantity at which marginal revenue and marginal cost intersect (see point A), is Q_M. The monopolist charges the highest price possible for this quantity, P_M, found at the height of the demand curve at Q_M (see point B). At the profit-maximizing level of output, the monopolist's average total cost is ATC_M (see point C).

Profit is equal to the difference between total revenue and total cost. So we have

$$\textbf{(28-4)}\quad \text{Profit} = TR - TC = (P_M \times Q_M) - (ATC_M \times Q_M) = (P_M - ATC_M) \times Q_M$$

Profit is equal to the area of the shaded rectangle in Figure 28-4, with a height of $P_M - ATC_M$ and a width of Q_M.

We learned that a perfectly competitive industry can have profits *in the short run but not in the long run.* In the short run, price can exceed average total cost, allowing a perfectly competitive firm to make a profit. But we also know that this cannot persist. In the long run, any profit in a perfectly competitive industry will be competed away as new firms enter the market. In contrast, while a monopoly can earn a profit or a loss in the short run, barriers to entry make it possible for a monopolist to make positive profits in the long run.

ECONOMICS *IN ACTION*

SHOCKED BY THE HIGH PRICE OF ELECTRICITY

Historically, electric utilities were recognized as natural monopolies. As you'll recall, these are monopolies that are created and sustained by economies of scale. A utility serviced a defined geographical area, owning the plants that generated electricity as well as the transmission lines that delivered it to retail customers. The rates charged customers were regulated by the government, set at a level to cover the utility's cost of operation plus a modest return on capital to its shareholders.

In the late 1990s, however, there was a move toward deregulation, based on the belief that competition would result in lower retail electricity prices. Competition was introduced at two junctures in the channel from power generation to retail customers: (1) distributors would compete to sell electricity to retail customers, and (2) power generators would compete to supply power to the distributors.

That was the theory, at least. According to one detailed report, 92% of households in states claiming to have retail choice actually cannot choose an alternative supplier of electricity because their wholesale market is still dominated by one power generator.

What proponents of deregulation failed to realize is that the bulk of power generation still entails large up-front fixed costs. Although many small, gas-fired power generators have been built in the last decade, massive, coal-fired plants are still the cheapest and most plentiful form of electricity generation.

In addition, deregulation and the lack of genuine competition enabled power generators to engage in market manipulation—intentionally reducing the amount of power they supplied to distributors in order to drive up prices.

Brand X Pictures

Although electric utilities were deregulated in the 1990s, there's been a trend toward reregulating them.

The most shocking case occurred during the California energy crisis of 2000–2001 that brought blackouts and billions of dollars in electricity surcharges to homes and businesses. On audiotapes later acquired by regulators, workers could be heard discussing plans to shut down power plants during times of peak energy demand, joking about how they were "stealing" more than $1 million a day from California.

According to a Michigan State University study, from 2002 to 2006, average retail electricity prices rose 21% in regulated states versus 36% in fully deregulated states. Another study found that from 1999 to 2007, the difference between prices charged to industrial retail customers in deregulated states and regulated states tripled. And data through 2011 indicate that customers in deregulated states continue to pay more for electricity than those in regulated states.

Angry customers have prompted several states to change the way they regulate their industries, slow down the process of deregulation, or move to reregulate their industries. California has gone so far as to mandate that its electricity distributors reacquire their generation plants (and has plans to reregulate the industry). In addition, regulators continue to be on the lookout for price manipulation in energy markets.

MODULE 28 Review

Solutions appear at the back of the book.

Check Your Understanding

1. Use the accompanying total revenue schedule of Emerald, Inc., a monopoly producer of 10-carat emeralds, to calculate the items listed in parts a–d. Then answer part e.

Quantity of emeralds demanded	Total revenue
1	$100
2	186
3	252
4	280
5	250

a. the demand schedule (Hint: the average revenue at each quantity indicates the price at which that quantity would be demanded.)

b. the marginal revenue schedule

c. the quantity effect component of marginal revenue at each output level

d. the price effect component of marginal revenue at each output level

e. What additional information is needed to determine Emerald, Inc.'s profit-maximizing output?

2. Using the price, quantity, and marginal revenue information from Table 28-1, and a marginal cost of $200, replicate Figure 28-3. Let the marginal cost of diamond production rise to $400. On your graph, show what happens to each of the following:
    a. the marginal cost curve
    b. the profit-maximizing price and quantity
    c. the profit of the monopolist
    d. the quantity that would be produced if the diamond industry were perfectly competitive, and the associated profit

Multiple-Choice Questions

Refer to the graph provided for questions 1–4.

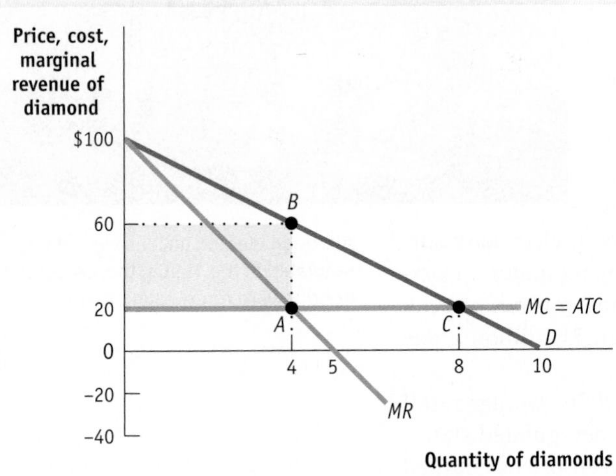

1. The monopolist's profit-maximizing output is
    a. 0.
    b. 4.
    c. 5.
    d. 8.
    e. 10.

2. The monopolist's total revenue equals
    a. $80.
    b. $160.
    c. $240.
    d. $300.
    e. $480.

3. The monopolist's total cost equals
    a. $20.
    b. $80.
    c. $160.
    d. $240.
    e. $480.

4. The monopolist is earning a profit equal to
    a. $0.
    b. $40.
    c. $80.
    d. $160.
    e. $240.

5. How does a monopoly differ from a perfectly competitive industry with the same costs?
    I. It produces a smaller quantity.
    II. It charges a higher price.
    III. It earns zero economic profit in the long run.
    a. I only
    b. II only
    c. III only
    d. I and II only
    e. I, II, and III

Critical-Thinking Questions

1. Draw a graph showing a monopoly earning zero economic profit in the short run.

2. Can a monopoly earn zero economic profit in the long run? Explain.

PITFALLS

IS THERE A MONOPOLY SUPPLY CURVE?

? Given that a monopolist applies its optimal output rule in the same way as a perfectly competitive industry, can we then conclude that a monopolist's supply curve can be calculated in the same way as the supply curve for the industry in perfect competition?

> No, *BECAUSE MONOPOLISTS DON'T HAVE SUPPLY CURVES!* Remember that a supply curve shows the quantity that producers are willing to supply for any given market price. A monopolist, however, does not take the price as given; it chooses a profit-maximizing quantity, taking into account its own ability to influence the price.

To learn more, see pages 302–306.

Monopoly and Public Policy

WHAT YOU WILL LEARN

1. **The effects of the difference between perfect competition and monopoly on society's welfare**
2. **How policy makers address the problems posed by monopoly**

It's good to be a monopolist, but it's not so good to be a monopolist's customer. A monopolist, by reducing output and raising prices, benefits at the expense of consumers. But buyers and sellers always have conflicting interests. Is the conflict of interest under monopoly any different from what it is under perfect competition?

The answer is yes, because monopoly is a source of inefficiency: the losses to consumers from monopoly behavior are larger than the gains to the monopolist. Because monopoly leads to net losses for the economy, governments often try to adopt policies that either prevent the emergence of monopolies or limit their effects. In this module, we will see why monopoly leads to inefficiency and examine the policies governments turn to in response.

Welfare Effects of Monopoly

By holding output below the level at which marginal cost is equal to the market price, a monopolist increases its profit but hurts consumers. To assess whether this is a net benefit or loss to society, we must compare the monopolist's gain in profit to the consumers' loss. And what we learn is that the consumers' loss is larger than the monopolist's gain. Monopoly causes a net loss for society.

To see why, let's return to the case in which the marginal cost curve is horizontal, as shown in the two panels of Figure 29-1. Here the marginal cost curve is *MC*, the demand curve is *D*, and, in panel (b), the marginal revenue curve is *MR*.

Panel (a) shows what happens if this industry is perfectly competitive. Equilibrium output is Q_C; the price of the good, P_C, is equal to marginal cost, and marginal cost is also equal to average total cost because there is no fixed cost and marginal cost is constant. Each firm is earning exactly its average total cost per unit of output, so there is no producer surplus in this equilibrium. The consumer surplus generated by the market is equal to the area of the blue-shaded triangle CS_C shown in panel (a). Since there

FIGURE 29-1 Monopoly Causes Inefficiency

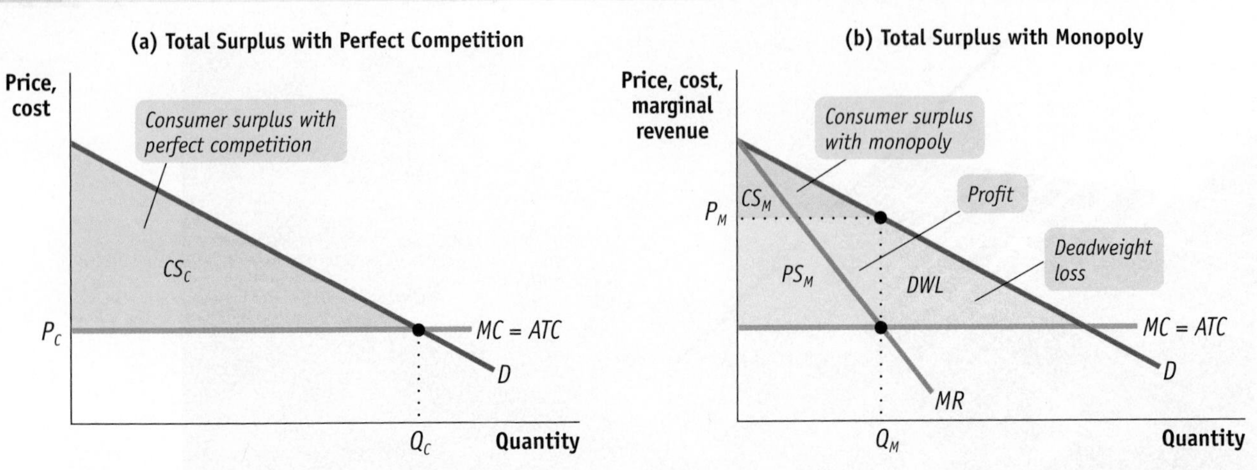

Panel (a) depicts a perfectly competitive industry: output is Q_C, and market price, P_C, is equal to *MC*. Since price is exactly equal to each producer's average total cost of production, there is no producer surplus. So total surplus is equal to consumer surplus, the entire shaded area. Panel (b) depicts the industry under monopoly: the monopolist decreases output to Q_M and charges P_M. Consumer surplus (blue area) has shrunk: a portion of it has been captured as profit (green area), and a portion of it has been lost to deadweight loss (yellow area), the value of mutually beneficial transactions that do not occur because of monopoly behavior. As a result, total surplus falls.

is no producer surplus when the industry is perfectly competitive, CS_C also represents the total surplus.

Panel (b) shows the results for the same market, but this time assuming that the industry is a monopoly. The monopolist produces the level of output, Q_M, at which marginal cost is equal to marginal revenue, and it charges the price, P_M. The industry now earns profit—which is also the producer surplus in this case—equal to the area of the green rectangle, PS_M. Note that this profit is part of what was consumer surplus in the perfectly competitive market, and consumer surplus with the monopoly shrinks to the area of the blue triangle, CS_M.

By comparing panels (a) and (b), we see that in addition to the redistribution of surplus from consumers to the monopolist, another important change has occurred: the sum of profit and consumer surplus—total surplus—is *smaller* under monopoly than under perfect competition. That is, the sum of CS_M and PS_M in panel (b) is less than the area CS_C in panel (a).

Previously, we analyzed how taxes could cause *deadweight loss* for society. Here we show that a monopoly creates deadweight loss equal to the area of the yellow triangle, *DWL*. So monopoly produces a net loss for society.

This net loss arises because some mutually beneficial transactions do not occur. There are people for whom an additional unit of the good is worth more than the marginal cost of producing it but who don't consume it because they are not willing to pay the monopoly price, P_M. Indeed, by driving a wedge between price and marginal cost, a monopoly acts much like a tax on consumers and produces the same kind of inefficiency.

So monopoly power detracts from the welfare of society as a whole and is a source of market failure. Is there anything government policy can do about it?

Preventing Monopoly

Policy toward monopolies depends crucially on whether or not the industry in question is a natural monopoly. As you know, a *natural monopoly* is one in which increasing returns to scale ensure that a bigger producer has lower average total cost. If the industry is *not* a natural monopoly, the best policy is to prevent a monopoly from arising or break it up if it already exists.

Dealing with a Natural Monopoly

Breaking up a monopoly that isn't natural is clearly a good idea: the gains to consumers outweigh the loss to the producer. But it's not so clear whether a natural monopoly, one in which large producers have lower average total costs than small producers, should be broken up, because this would raise average total cost. For example, a town government that tried to prevent a single company from dominating local gas supply—which, as we've discussed, is almost surely a natural monopoly—would raise the cost of providing gas to its residents.

Yet even in the case of a natural monopoly, a profit-maximizing monopolist acts in a way that causes inefficiency—it charges consumers a price that is higher than marginal cost and, by doing so, prevents some potentially beneficial transactions. Also, it can seem unfair that a firm that has managed to establish a monopoly position earns a large profit at the expense of consumers.

What can public policy do about this? There are two common answers:

1. Public ownership
2. Regulation

Public Ownership

In many countries, the preferred answer to the problem of natural monopoly has been **public ownership.** Instead of allowing a private monopolist to control an industry, the government establishes a public agency to provide the good and protect consumers' interests.

There are some examples of public ownership in the United States. Passenger rail service is provided by the public company Amtrak; regular mail delivery is provided by the U.S. Postal Service; some cities, including Los Angeles, have publicly owned electric power companies.

The advantage of public ownership, in principle, is that a publicly owned natural monopoly can set prices based on the criterion of efficiency rather than profit maximization. In a perfectly competitive industry, profit-maximizing behavior *is* efficient because producers set price equal to marginal cost; that is why there is no economic argument for public ownership of, say, wheat farms.

Richard Elliot/AA World Travel/Topfoto/The Image Works

Amtrak, a public company, has provided train service, at a loss, to destinations that attract few passengers.

Experience suggests, however, that public ownership as a solution to the problem of natural monopoly often works badly in practice. One reason is that publicly owned firms are often less eager than private companies to keep costs down or offer high-quality products. Another is that publicly owned companies all too often end up serving political interests—providing contracts or jobs to people with the right connections.

Regulation

In the United States, the more common answer to the existence of natural monopolies has been to leave the industry in private hands but subject it to regulation. In particular, most local utilities, like electricity, telephone service, natural gas, and so on, are covered by **price regulation** that limits the prices they can charge.

Figure 29-2 shows an example of price regulation of a natural monopoly—a highly simplified version of a local gas company. The company faces a demand curve, *D*, with an associated marginal revenue curve, *MR*. For simplicity, we assume that the firm's total cost consists of two parts: a fixed cost and a variable cost that is the same for every unit. So marginal cost is constant in this case, and the marginal cost curve (which here is also the average variable cost curve) is the horizontal line *MC*. The average total cost curve is the downward-sloping curve *ATC;* it slopes downward because the higher the output, the lower the average fixed cost (the fixed cost per unit of

In **public ownership** of a monopoly, the good is supplied by the government or by a firm owned by the government.

Price regulation limits the price that a monopolist is allowed to charge.

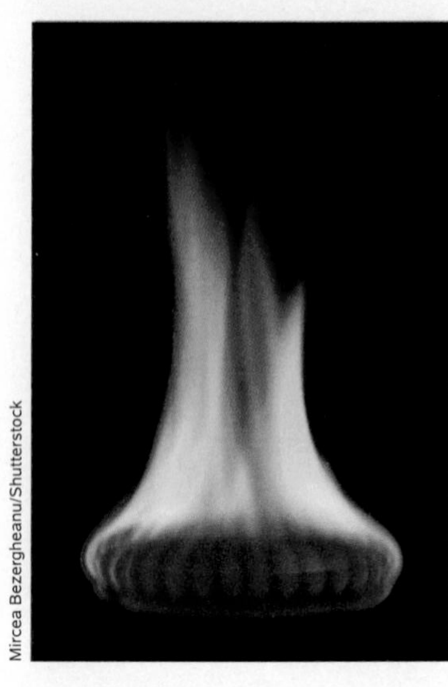
Mircea Bezergheanu/Shutterstock

output). Because average total cost slopes downward over the range of output relevant for market demand, this is a natural monopoly.

Panel (a) illustrates a case of natural monopoly without regulation. The unregulated natural monopolist chooses the monopoly output Q_M and charges the price P_M. Since the monopolist receives a price greater than average total cost, it earns a profit, represented by the green-shaded rectangle in panel (a). Consumer surplus is given by the blue-shaded triangle.

Now suppose that regulators impose a price ceiling on local gas deliveries—one that falls below the monopoly price P_M but above average total cost, say, at P_R in panel (a). At that price the quantity demanded is Q_R.

Does the company have an incentive to produce that quantity? Yes. If the price the monopolist can charge is fixed at P_R by regulators, the firm can sell any quantity between zero and Q_R for the same price, P_R. Because it doesn't have to lower its price to sell more (up to Q_R), there is no price effect to bring marginal revenue below price, so the regulated price becomes the marginal revenue for the monopoly just like the market price is the marginal revenue for a perfectly competitive firm. With marginal revenue being above marginal cost and price exceeding average cost, the firm expands output to meet the quantity demanded, Q_R. This policy has appeal because at the regulated price, the monopolist produces more at a lower price.

Of course, the monopolist will not be willing to produce at all in the long run if the regulated price means producing at a loss. That is, the price ceiling has to be set high enough to allow the firm to cover its average total cost. Panel (b) shows a situation in which regulators have pushed the price down as far as possible, at the level where the average total cost curve crosses the demand curve. At any lower price the firm loses money. The price here, P_R^*, is the best regulated price: the monopolist is just willing to operate because profits are zero and produces Q_R^*, the quantity demanded at that price. Consumers and society gain as a result.

The welfare effects of this regulation can be seen by comparing the shaded areas in the two panels of Figure 29-2. Consumer surplus is increased by the regulation, with the gains coming from two sources. First, profits are eliminated and added instead

FIGURE 29-2 **Unregulated and Regulated Natural Monopoly**

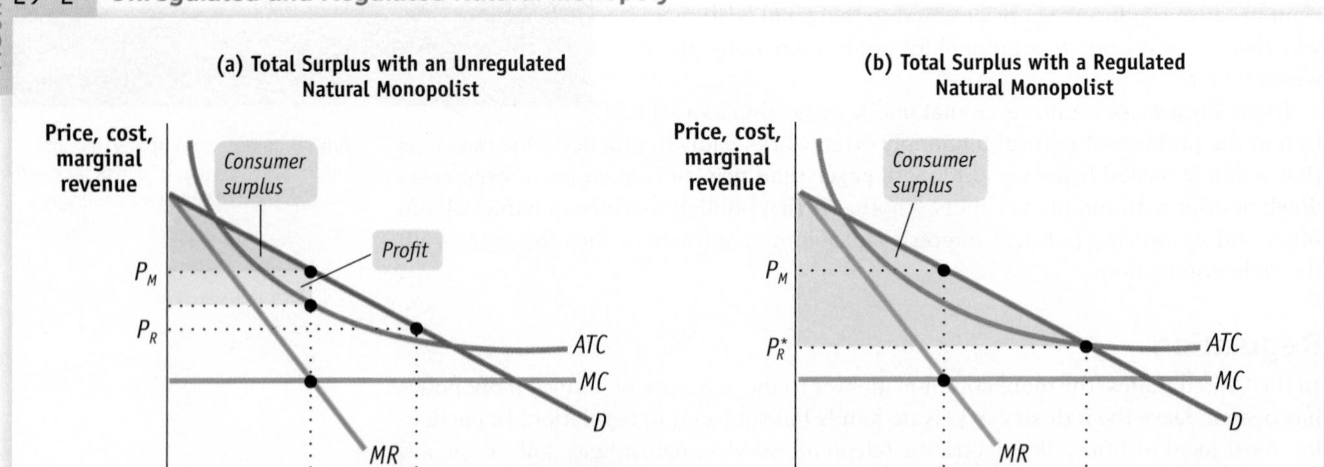

This figure shows the case of a natural monopolist. In panel (a), if the monopolist is allowed to charge P_M, it makes a profit, shown by the green area; consumer surplus is shown by the blue area. If it is regulated and must charge the lower price, P_R, output increases from Q_M to Q_R, profit falls, and consumer surplus increases.

Panel (b) shows what happens when the monopolist must charge a price equal to average total cost, the price P_R^*. Output expands to Q_R^*, and consumer surplus is now the entire blue area. The monopolist makes zero profit. This is the greatest total surplus possible without the monopoly incurring losses.

to consumer surplus. Second, the larger output and lower price leads to an overall welfare gain—an increase in total surplus. In fact, panel (b) illustrates the largest total surplus possible.

Must Monopoly Be Controlled?

Sometimes the cure is worse than the disease. Some economists have argued that the best solution, even in the case of a natural monopoly, may be to live with it. The case for doing nothing is that attempts to control monopoly will, one way or another, do more harm than good.

The following Economics in Action describes the case of cable television, a natural monopoly that has been alternately regulated and deregulated as politicians change their minds about the appropriate policy.

ECONOMICS IN ACTION

CHAINED BY YOUR CABLE

The old saying "you can't escape death and taxes" now has a modern twist: "you can't escape death, taxes, and *cable price increases*." Over the last 10 years consumers have seen their cable prices increase by around 3% every year, an amount exceeding the rate of inflation.

Until 1984, cable prices were regulated locally. Because running a cable through a town entailed large fixed costs, cable TV was considered a natural monopoly. However, in 1984 Congress passed a law prohibiting most local governments from regulating cable prices. The result: prices increased sharply, and in 1992 the ensuing consumer backlash led to a new law that once again allowed local governments to set limits on cable prices. But cable operators found ways to circumvent the restrictions.

PhotoAlto/Alamy

Cable prices have increased by around 3% every year, an amount that exceeds the rate of inflation.

What went wrong? One possible explanation is that the 1992 law applied only to "basic" packages, and those prices did indeed level off. In response, cable operators began offering fewer channels in the basic package and charging more for premium channels like HBO.

Cable operators have defended their pricing policies, claiming they have been forced to pay higher prices to content providers for popular shows. For example, Time Warner Cable and the Fox network fought fiercely when their contract ended in late 2009, with Fox demanding to be paid $1 per subscriber to their content. When a deal was reached, it was reported that Time Warner had agreed to pay Fox more than 50 cents per subscriber.

Yet critics counter that this defense is largely invalid because about 40% of the channels that command the highest prices are owned in whole or in part by the cable operators themselves. So in paying high prices for content, cable operators are actually profiting.

Cable operators also claim they need to raise prices to pay for system upgrades. Critics, however, once again dismiss the claim, asserting that upgrades pay for themselves through premium pricing and so should not have any effect on the price of non-upgraded services.

Critics also point to evidence that cable operators are exploiting their monopoly power. For example, a study by the Federal Communications Commission showed that cable operators have increased their take per subscriber by over 30% after factoring out all operating costs, including the cost of content. Similarly, the General Accounting Office found that prices are on average 17% lower in communities with two cable operators compared to one.

TV-watchers should not give up hope just yet. Telephone companies Verizon and AT&T are increasingly using their fiber-optic networks to compete with cable operators in many communities. And technological advances in streaming video services are beginning to make a dent in cable's subscriber base. Stay tuned.

MODULE 29 Review

Solutions appear at the back of the book.

Check Your Understanding

1. What policy should the government adopt in the following cases? Explain.
   a. Internet service in Anytown, OH, is provided by cable. Customers feel they are being overcharged, but the cable company claims it must charge prices that let it recover the costs of laying cable.
   b. The only two airlines that currently fly to Alaska need government approval to merge. Other airlines wish to fly to Alaska but need government-allocated landing slots to do so.

2. True or false? Explain your answer.
   a. Society's welfare is lower under monopoly because some consumer surplus is transformed into profit for the monopolist.
   b. A monopolist causes inefficiency because there are consumers who are willing to pay a price greater than or equal to marginal cost but less than the monopoly price.

3. Suppose a monopolist mistakenly believes that its marginal revenue is always equal to the market price. Assuming constant marginal cost and no fixed cost, draw a diagram comparing the level of profit, consumer surplus, total surplus, and deadweight loss for this misguided monopolist compared to a smart monopolist. Explain your findings.

Multiple-Choice Questions

1. Which of the following statements is true of a monopoly as compared to a perfectly competitive market with the same costs?
   I. Consumer surplus is smaller.
   II. Profit is smaller.
   III. Deadweight loss is smaller.
   a. I only
   b. II only
   c. III only
   d. I and II only
   e. I, II, and III

2. Which of the following is true of a natural monopoly?
   a. It experiences diseconomies of scale.
   b. *ATC* is lower if there is a single firm in the market.
   c. It occurs in a market that relies on natural resources for its production.
   d. There are decreasing returns to scale in the industry.
   e. The government must provide the good or service to achieve efficiency.

3. Which of the following government actions is the most common for a natural monopoly in the United States?
   a. prevent its formation
   b. break it up using antitrust laws
   c. use price regulation
   d. public ownership
   e. elimination of the market

4. Which of the following markets is an example of a regulated natural monopoly?
   a. local cable TV
   b. gasoline
   c. cell phone service
   d. organic tomatoes
   e. diamonds

5. Which of the following is most likely to be higher for a regulated natural monopoly than for an unregulated natural monopoly?
   a. product variety
   b. quantity
   c. price
   d. profit
   e. deadweight loss

Critical-Thinking Question

Draw a correctly labeled graph of a natural monopoly. Use your graph to identify each of the following:

a. consumer surplus if the market were somehow able to operate as a perfectly competitive market
b. consumer surplus with the monopoly
c. monopoly profit
d. deadweight loss with the monopoly

Price Discrimination

Exactostock/Superstock

WHAT YOU WILL LEARN

1. The meaning of price discrimination
2. Why price discrimination is so prevalent when producers have market power

Up to this point, we have considered only the case of a monopolist who charges all consumers the same price. However, monopolists want to maximize their profits and often they do so by charging different prices for the same product. In this module we look at how monopolists increase their profits by engaging in *price discrimination*.

Price Discrimination Defined

A monopolist that charges everyone the same price is known as a **single-price monopolist.** As the term suggests, not all monopolists do this. In fact, many monopolists find that they can increase their profits by selling the same good to different customers for different prices: they practice **price discrimination.**

An example of price discrimination that travelers encounter regularly involves airline tickets. Although there are a number of airlines, most routes in the United States are serviced by only one or two carriers, which, as a result, have market power and can influence prices. So any regular airline passenger quickly becomes aware that the simple question "How much will it cost me to fly there?" rarely has a simple answer.

If you are willing to buy a nonrefundable ticket a month in advance and stay over a Saturday night, the round trip may cost only $150—or less if you are a senior citizen or a student. But if you have to go on a business trip tomorrow, which happens to be Tuesday, and want to come back on Wednesday, the same round trip might cost $550. Yet the business traveler and the visiting grandparent receive the same product.

You might object that airlines are not usually monopolies—that in most flight markets the airline industry is an oligopoly. In fact, price discrimination takes place under oligopoly and monopolistic competition as well as monopoly. But it doesn't happen under perfect competition. And once we've seen why monopolists sometimes price-discriminate, we'll be in a good position to understand why it happens in other cases, too.

A **single-price monopolist** charges all consumers the same price.

Sellers engage in **price discrimination** when they charge different prices to different consumers for the same good.

The Logic of Price Discrimination

To get a preliminary view of why price discrimination might be more profitable than charging all consumers the same price, imagine that Air Sunshine offers the only non-stop flights between Bismarck, North Dakota, and Ft. Lauderdale, Florida. Assume that there are no capacity problems—the airline can fly as many planes as the number of passengers warrants. Also assume that there is no fixed cost. The marginal cost to the airline of providing a seat is $125 however many passengers it carries.

Further assume that the airline knows there are two kinds of potential passengers. First, there are business travelers, 2,000 of whom want to travel between the destinations each week. Second, there are high school students, 2,000 of whom also want to travel each week.

Will potential passengers take the flight? It depends on the price. The business travelers, it turns out, really need to fly; they will take the plane as long as the price is no more than $550. Since they are flying purely for business, we assume that cutting the price below $550 will not lead to any increase in business travel. The students, however, have less money and more time; if the price goes above $150, they will take the bus. The implied demand curve is shown in Figure 30-1.

So what should the airline do? If it has to charge everyone the same price, its options are limited. It could charge $550; that way it would get as much as possible out of the business travelers but lose the student market. Or it could charge only $150; that way it would get both types of travelers but would make significantly less money from sales to business travelers.

We can quickly calculate the profits from each of these alternatives. If the airline charged $550, it would sell 2,000 tickets to the business travelers, earning a total revenue of 2,000 × $550 = $1.1 million and incurring costs of 2,000 × $125 = $250,000; so its profit would be $850,000, illustrated by the shaded area B in Figure 30-1. If the airline charged only $150, it would sell 4,000 tickets, receiving revenue of 4,000 × $150 = $600,000 and incurring costs of 4,000 × $125 = $500,000; so its profit would be $100,000. If the airline must charge everyone the same price, charging the higher price and forgoing sales to students is clearly more profitable.

What the airline would really like to do, however, is charge the business travelers the full $550 but offer $150 tickets to the students. That's a lot less than the price paid by business travelers, but it's still above marginal cost; so if the airline could sell those

FIGURE 30-1 **Two Types of Airline Customers**

Air Sunshine has two types of customers, business travelers willing to pay at most $550 per ticket and students willing to pay at most $150 per ticket. There are 2,000 of each kind of customer. Air Sunshine has constant marginal cost of $125 per seat. If Air Sunshine could charge these two types of customers different prices, it would maximize its profit by charging business travelers $550 and students $150 per ticket. It would capture all of the consumer surplus as profit.

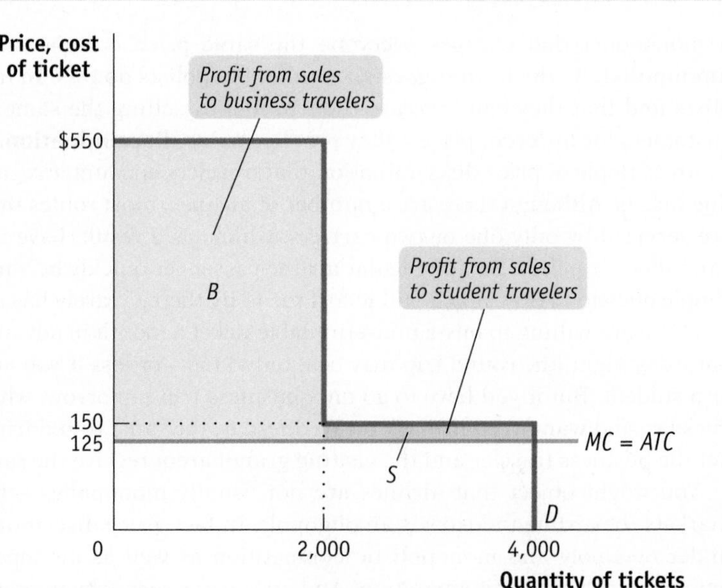

extra 2,000 tickets to students, it would make an additional $50,000 in profit. That is, it would make a profit equal to the areas *B* plus *S* in Figure 30-1.

It would be more realistic to suppose that there is some "give" in the demand of each group: at a price below $550, there would be some increase in business travel; and at a price above $150, some students would still purchase tickets. But this, it turns out, does not do away with the argument for price discrimination. The important point is that the two groups of consumers differ in their *sensitivity to price*—that a high price has a larger effect in discouraging purchases by students than by business travelers. As long as different groups of customers respond differently to the price, a monopolist will find that it can capture more consumer surplus and increase its profit by charging them different prices.

Price Discrimination and Elasticity

A more realistic description of the demand that airlines face would not specify particular prices at which different types of travelers would choose to fly. Instead, it would distinguish between the groups on the basis of their sensitivity to the price—their price elasticity of demand.

Suppose that a company sells its product to two easily identifiable groups of people—business travelers and students. It just so happens that business travelers are very insensitive to the price: there is a certain amount of the product they just have to have whatever the price, but they cannot be persuaded to buy much more than that no matter how cheap it is. Students, though, are more flexible: offer a good enough price and they will buy quite a lot, but raise the price too high and they will switch to something else. What should the company do?

The answer is the one already suggested by our simplified example: the company should charge business travelers, with their low price elasticity of demand, a higher price than it charges students, with their high price elasticity of demand.

The actual situation of the airlines is very much like this hypothetical example. Business travelers typically place a high priority on being in the right place at the right time and are not very sensitive to the price. But leisure travelers are fairly sensitive to the price: faced with a high price, they might take the bus, drive to another airport to get a lower fare, or skip the trip altogether.

Ostill/Shutterstock

On many airline routes, the fare you pay depends on the type of traveler you are.

So why doesn't an airline simply announce different prices for business and leisure customers? First, this would probably be illegal. (U.S. law places some limits on the ability of companies to practice blatant price discrimination.) Second, even if it were legal, it would be a hard policy to enforce: business travelers might be willing to wear casual clothing and claim they were visiting family in Ft. Lauderdale in order to save $400.

So what the airlines do—quite successfully—is impose rules that indirectly have the effect of charging business and leisure travelers different fares. Business travelers usually travel during the week and want to be home on the weekend, so the round-trip fare is much higher if you don't stay over a Saturday night. The requirement of a weekend stay for a cheap ticket effectively separates business travelers from leisure travelers. Similarly, business travelers often visit several cities in succession rather than make a simple round trip; so round-trip fares are much lower than twice the one-way fare. Many business trips are scheduled on short notice, so fares are much lower if you book far in advance. Fares are also lower if you travel standby, taking your chances on whether you actually get a seat—business travelers have to make it to that meeting; people visiting their relatives don't.

Because customers must show their ID at check-in, airlines make sure there are no resales of tickets between the two groups that would undermine their ability to price-discriminate—students can't buy cheap tickets and resell them to business travelers. Look at the rules that govern ticket pricing, and you will see an ingenious implementation of profit-maximizing price discrimination.

Perfect price discrimination takes place when a monopolist charges each consumer his or her willingness to pay—the maximum that the consumer is willing to pay.

Perfect Price Discrimination

Let's return to the example of business travelers and students traveling between Bismarck and Ft. Lauderdale, illustrated in Figure 30-1, and ask what would happen if the airline could distinguish between the two groups of customers in order to charge each a different price.

Clearly, the airline would charge each group its *willingness to pay*—that is, the maximum that each group is willing to pay. For business travelers, the willingness to pay is \$550; for students, it is \$150. As we have assumed, the marginal cost is \$125 and does not depend on output, making the marginal cost curve a horizontal line. And as we noted earlier, we can easily determine the airline's profit: it is the sum of the areas of rectangle B and rectangle S.

In this case, the consumers do not get any consumer surplus! The entire surplus is captured by the monopolist in the form of profit. When a monopolist is able to capture the entire surplus in this way, we say that the monopolist achieves **perfect price discrimination.**

Fernando Jose V. Soares/Shutterstock

Perfect price discrimination is almost impossible to achieve in practice.

In general, the greater the number of different prices charged, the closer the monopolist is to perfect price discrimination. Figure 30-2 shows a monopolist facing a downward-sloping demand curve, a monopolist who we assume is able to charge different prices to different groups of consumers, with the consumers who are willing to pay the most being charged the most. In panel (a) the monopolist charges two different prices; in panel (b) the monopolist charges three different prices. Two things are apparent:

- The greater the number of prices the monopolist charges, the lower the lowest price—that is, some consumers will pay prices that approach marginal cost.
- The greater the number of prices the monopolist charges, the more surplus extracted from consumers.

With a very large number of different prices, the picture would look like panel (c), a case of perfect price discrimination. Here, every consumer pays the most he or she is willing to pay, and the entire consumer surplus is extracted as profit.

Both our airline example and the example in Figure 30-2 can be used to make another point: a monopolist that can engage in perfect price discrimination doesn't cause any inefficiency! The reason is that the source of inefficiency is eliminated: all potential consumers who are willing to purchase the good at a price equal to or above marginal cost are able to do so. The perfectly price-discriminating monopolist manages to "scoop up" all consumers by offering some of them lower prices than others.

Perfect price discrimination is almost never possible in practice. At a fundamental level, the inability to achieve perfect price discrimination is a problem of prices as economic signals. When prices work as economic signals, they convey the information needed to ensure that all mutually beneficial transactions will indeed occur: the market price signals the seller's cost, and a consumer signals willingness to pay by purchasing the good whenever that willingness to pay is at least as high as the market price.

The problem in reality, however, is that prices are often not perfect signals: a consumer's true willingness to pay can be disguised, as by a business traveler who claims to be a student when buying a ticket in order to obtain a lower fare. When such disguises work, a monopolist cannot achieve perfect price discrimination.

However, monopolists do try to move in the direction of perfect price discrimination through a variety of pricing strategies. Common techniques for price discrimination include the following:

- *Advance purchase restrictions.* Prices are lower for those who purchase well in advance (or in some cases for those who purchase at the last minute). This separates those who are likely to shop for better prices from those who won't.
- *Volume discounts.* Often the price is lower if you buy a large quantity. For a consumer who plans to consume a lot of a good, the cost of the last unit—the marginal cost to the consumer—is considerably less than the average price. This

separates those who plan to buy a lot, and so are likely to be more sensitive to price, from those who don't.

- *Two-part tariffs.* In a discount club like Costco or Sam's Club (which are not monopolists but monopolistic competitors), you pay an annual fee (the first part of the tariff) in addition to the price of the item(s) you purchase (the second part of the tariff). So the full price of the first item you buy is in effect much higher than that of subsequent items, making the two-part tariff behave like a volume discount.

Our discussion also helps explain why government policies on monopoly typically focus on preventing deadweight loss, not preventing price discrimination—unless it causes serious issues of equity. Compared to a single-price monopolist, price discrimination—even when it is not perfect—can increase the efficiency of the market.

Consider the case of consumers formerly priced out of the market who can now purchase the good at a lower price. If they generate enough surplus to offset the loss in surplus to those facing a higher price and no longer buying the good, then total surplus will increase when price discrimination is introduced.

FIGURE 30-2 Price Discrimination

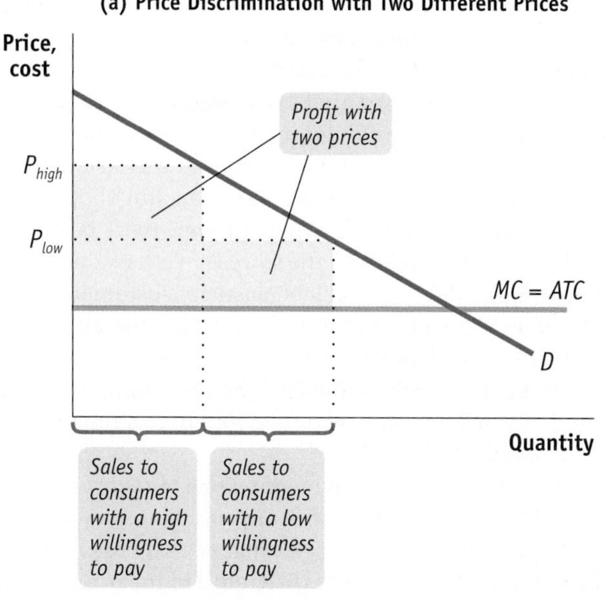

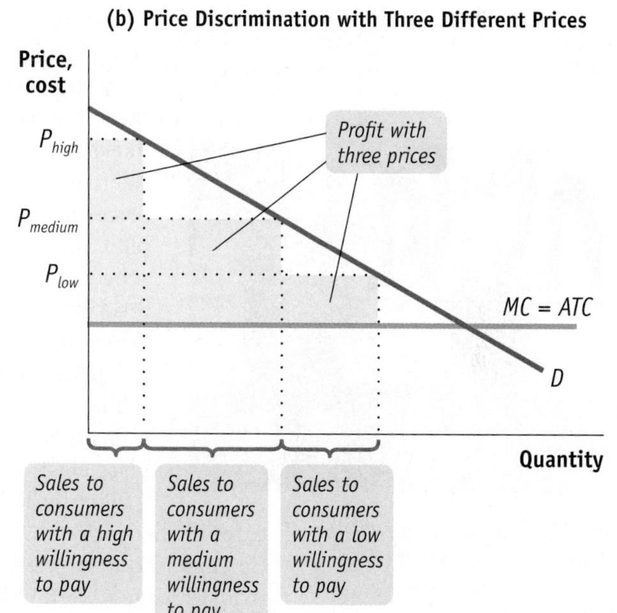

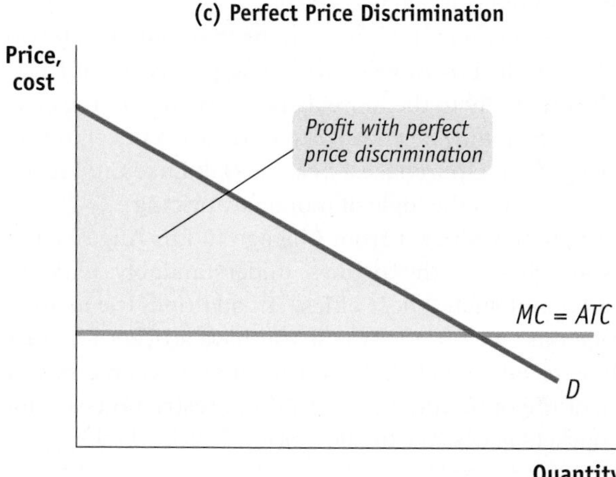

Panel (a) shows a monopolist that charges two different prices; its profit is shown by the shaded area. Panel (b) shows a monopolist that charges three different prices; its profit, too, is shown by the shaded area. It is able to capture more of the consumer surplus and to increase its profit. That is, by increasing the number of different prices charged, the monopolist captures more of the consumer surplus and makes a larger profit. Panel (c) shows the case of perfect price discrimination, where a monopolist charges each consumer his or her willingness to pay; the monopolist's profit is given by the shaded triangle.

Consider the example of a drug that is disproportionately prescribed to senior citizens, who are often on fixed incomes and so are very sensitive to price. A policy that allows a drug company to charge senior citizens a low price and everyone else a high price will serve more consumers and create more total surplus than a situation in which everyone is charged the same price.

But price discrimination that creates serious concerns about equity is likely to be prohibited—for example, an ambulance service that charges patients based on the severity of their emergency.

ECONOMICS IN ACTION

SALES, FACTORY OUTLETS, AND GHOST CITIES

Have you ever wondered why department stores occasionally hold sales, offering their merchandise for considerably less than the usual prices? Or why, driving along America's highways, you sometimes encounter clusters of "factory outlet" stores, often a couple of hours' drive from the nearest city?

These familiar features of the economic landscape are actually rather peculiar if you think about them: why should sheets and towels be cheaper for a week each winter, or raincoats be offered for less in Freeport, Maine, than in Boston? In each case the answer is that the sellers—who are often oligopolists or monopolistic competitors—are engaged in a subtle form of price discrimination.

Periodic sales allow stores to price-discriminate between their high-elasticity and low-elasticity customers.

As for sheets and towels, stores are aware that some consumers buy these goods only when they discover that they need them; they are not likely to put a lot of effort into searching for the best price and so have a relatively low price elasticity of demand. So the store wants to charge high prices for customers who come in on an ordinary day. But shoppers who plan ahead, looking for the lowest price, will wait until there is a sale. By scheduling such sales only now and then, the store is in effect able to price-discriminate between high-elasticity and low-elasticity customers.

An outlet store serves the same purpose: by offering merchandise for low prices, but only at a considerable distance away, a seller is able to establish a separate market for those customers who are willing to make an effort to search out lower prices—and who therefore have a relatively high price elasticity of demand.

Finally, let's return to airline tickets to mention one of the truly odd features of their prices. Often a flight from one major destination to another—say, from Chicago to Los Angeles—is cheaper than a much shorter flight to a smaller city—say, from Chicago to Salt Lake City. Again, the reason is a difference in the price elasticity of demand: customers have a choice of many airlines between Chicago and Los Angeles, so the demand for any one flight is quite elastic; customers have very little choice in flights to a small city, so the demand is much less elastic.

But often there is a flight between two major destinations that makes a stop along the way—say, a flight from Chicago to Los Angeles with a stop in Salt Lake City. In these cases, it is sometimes cheaper to fly to the more distant city than to the city that is a stop along the way. For example, it may be cheaper to purchase a ticket to Los Angeles and get off in Salt Lake City than to purchase a ticket to Salt Lake City! It sounds ridiculous but makes perfect sense given the logic of monopoly pricing.

So why don't passengers simply buy a ticket from Chicago to Los Angeles, but get off at Salt Lake City? Well, some do—but the airlines, understandably, make it difficult for customers to find out about such "ghost cities." In addition, the airline will not allow you to check baggage only part of the way if you have a ticket for the final destination. And airlines refuse to honor tickets for return flights when a passenger has not completed all the legs of the outbound flight. All these restrictions are meant to enforce the separation of markets necessary to allow price discrimination.

MODULE 30 Review

Solutions appear at the back of the book.

Check Your Understanding

1. True or false? Explain your answer.
   a. A single-price monopolist sells to some customers that would not find the product affordable if purchasing from a price-discriminating monopolist.
   b. A price-discriminating monopolist creates more inefficiency than a single-price monopolist because it captures more of the consumer surplus.
   c. Under price discrimination, a customer with highly elastic demand will pay a lower price than a customer with inelastic demand.

2. Which of the following are cases of price discrimination and which are not? In the cases of price discrimination, identify the consumers with high price elasticity of demand and those with low price elasticity of demand.
   a. Damaged merchandise is marked down.
   b. Restaurants have senior citizen discounts.
   c. Food manufacturers place discount coupons for their merchandise in newspapers.
   d. Airline tickets cost more during the summer peak flying season.

Multiple-Choice Questions

1. Which of the following characteristics is necessary for a firm to price-discriminate?
   a. free entry and exit
   b. differentiated product
   c. many sellers
   d. some control over price
   e. horizontal demand curve

2. Price discrimination
   a. is the opposite of volume discounts.
   b. is a practice limited to movie theaters and the airline industry.
   c. can lead to increased efficiency in the market.
   d. rarely occurs in the real world.
   e. helps to increase the profits of perfect competitors.

3. With perfect price discrimination, consumer surplus
   a. is maximized.
   b. equals zero.
   c. is increased.
   d. cannot be determined.
   e. is the area below the demand curve above *MC*.

4. Which of the following is a technique used by price discriminating monopolists?
   I. advance purchase restrictions
   II. two-part tariffs
   III. volume discounts
   a. I only
   b. II only
   c. III only
   d. I and II only
   e. I, II, and III

5. A price discriminating monopolist will charge a higher price to consumers with
   a. a more inelastic demand.
   b. a less inelastic demand.
   c. higher income.
   d. lower willingness to pay.
   e. less experience in the market.

Critical-Thinking Question

Draw a correctly labeled graph showing a monopoly practicing perfect price discrimination. On your graph, identify the monopoly's profit. What does consumer surplus equal in this case? Explain.

BUSINESS CASE • Newly Emerging Markets: A Diamond Monopolist's Best Friend

Daniel Acker/Bloomberg via Getty Images

When Cecil Rhodes created the De Beers monopoly in 1888, it was a particularly opportune moment. The new diamond mines in South Africa dwarfed all previous sources, so almost all of the world's diamond production was concentrated in a few square miles.

For almost a century, De Beers was able to extend its control of resources even as new mines opened. De Beers either bought out new producers or entered into agreements with local governments that controlled some of the new mines, effectively making them part of the De Beers monopoly. The most remarkable of these was an agreement with the former Soviet Union, which ensured that Russian diamonds would be marketed through De Beers, preserving its ability to control retail prices. De Beers also went so far as to stockpile a year's supply of diamonds in its London vaults so that when demand dropped, newly mined stones would be stored rather than sold, restricting retail supply until demand and prices recovered.

However, the De Beers monopoly has been under assault. Until the 1980s, De Beers accounted for 90% of all rough diamond sales. Today, that share has dropped to about 40%, courtesy of dramatic changes in the industry.

Government regulators have forced De Beers to loosen its control of the market. For the first time, De Beers has competition: a number of independent companies have begun mining for diamonds in other African countries, including Alrosa, a Russian-based mining company, BHP Billiton of Australia, and Anglo-Australian mining group Rio Tinto. The growing market share of these companies has helped to erode De Beers's dominance. In addition, high-quality, inexpensive synthetic diamonds have become an alternative to real gems, eating into De Beers's profits. So does this mean an end to high diamond prices and De Beers's high profits?

Not really. Although today's De Beers is more of a "near-monopolist" than a true monopolist, it still mines more of the world's supply of diamonds than any other single producer. And it has been benefiting from newly emerging markets. Consumer demand for diamonds has soared in countries like China and India, leading to price increases.

Although the economic crisis of 2009 put a serious dent in worldwide demand for diamonds, forcing De Beers to cut production by 20% (compared to 2008), affluent Chinese continue to be heavy buyers of diamonds. In fact, in 2011, China surpassed Japan to become the biggest diamond-consuming nation behind the United States. Buyers in China and India made up about 20% of global demand in 2011, and estimates are that number will rise to 28% in 2016. De Beers is anticipating that Asian demand will accelerate the depletion of the world's existing diamond mines. As a result, diamond analysts predict rough diamond prices to rise by at least 6% per year through 2020.

In the end, although a diamond monopoly may not be forever, a near-monopoly with rising demand in newly emerging markets may be just as profitable.

Questions for Thought

1. What will happen to the demand for De Beers's diamonds when consumers start seeing high-quality, inexpensive synthetic diamonds as a substitute? Explain.
2. Using the concept of monopoly profits, explain what would happen if demand for De Beers's diamonds decreases. Also explain what would happen to the market price and market quantity of De Beers's diamonds.
3. What effect will the market entry of other diamond-mining firms have on the extent of De Beers's market power?
4. Given that the depletion of existing diamond mines will make it more costly to produce (mine) diamonds, draw a graph to illustrate the effects of this development on De Beers's prices and quantities. Explain your findings.

SECTION 10 REVIEW

Summary

Monopoly in Practice

1. The key difference between a monopoly and a perfectly competitive industry is that a single, perfectly competitive firm faces a horizontal demand curve but a monopolist faces a downward-sloping demand curve. This gives the monopolist market power, the ability to raise the market price by reducing output.
2. The marginal revenue of a monopolist is composed of a quantity effect (the price received from the additional unit) and a price effect (the reduction in the price at which all units are sold). Because of the price effect, a monopolist's marginal revenue is always less than the market price, and the marginal revenue curve lies below the demand curve.
3. At the monopolist's profit-maximizing output level, marginal cost equals marginal revenue, which is less than market price. At the perfectly competitive firm's profit-maximizing output level, marginal cost equals the market price. So in comparison to perfectly competitive industries, monopolies produce less, charge higher prices, and can earn profits in both the short run and the long run.

Monopoly and Public Policy

4. A monopoly creates deadweight losses by charging a price above marginal cost: the loss in consumer surplus exceeds the monopolist's profit. This makes monopolies a source of market failure and governments often make policies to prevent or end them.
5. Natural monopolies also cause deadweight losses. To limit these losses, governments sometimes impose **public ownership** and at other times impose **price regulation.** A price ceiling on a monopolist, as opposed to a perfectly competitive industry, need not cause shortages and can increase total surplus.

Price Discrimination

6. Not all monopolists are **single-price monopolists.** Monopolists, as well as oligopolists and monopolistic competitors, often engage in **price discrimination** to make higher profits, using various techniques to differentiate consumers based on their sensitivity to price and charging those with less elastic demand higher prices. A monopolist that achieves **perfect price discrimination** charges each consumer a price equal to his or her willingness to pay and captures the total surplus in the market. Although perfect price discrimination creates no inefficiency, it is practically impossible to implement.

Key Terms

Public ownership, p. 313
Price regulation, p. 313
Single-price monopolist, p. 317
Price discrimination, p. 317
Perfect price discrimination, p. 320

Problems

1. Skyscraper City has a subway system for which a one-way fare is $1.50. There is pressure on the mayor to reduce the fare by one-third, to $1.00. The mayor is dismayed, thinking that this will mean Skyscraper City is losing one-third of its revenue from sales of subway tickets. The mayor's economic adviser reminds her that she is focusing only on the price effect and ignoring the quantity effect. Explain why the mayor's estimate of a one-third loss of revenue is likely to be an overestimate. Illustrate with a diagram.
2. Consider an industry with the demand curve (*D*) and marginal cost curve (*MC*) shown in the accompanying diagram. There is no fixed cost. If the industry is a single-price monopoly, the monopolist's marginal revenue curve would be *MR*. Answer the following questions by naming the appropriate points or areas.

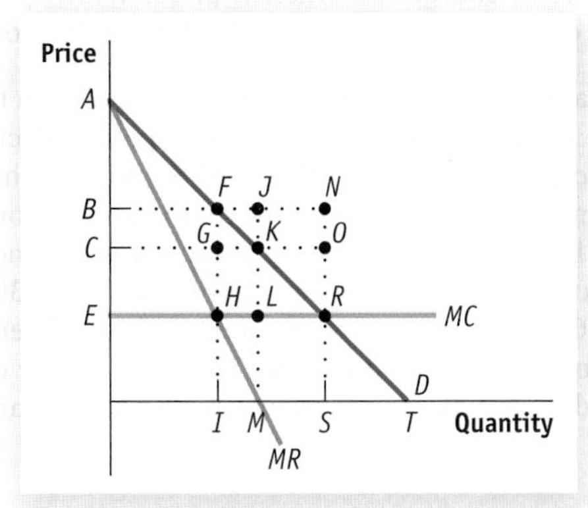

Mobil
EXXON
Carvel
CINNABON

Module 31: Oligopoly
Module 32: Game Theory
Module 33: Oligopoly in Practice
Module 34: Monopolistic Competition
Module 35: Product Differentiation and Advertising

SECTION 11

Imperfect Competition

ILLEGAL AND LEGAL PRACTICES

The agricultural products company Archer Daniels Midland (also known as ADM) has often described itself as "supermarket to the world." Its name is familiar to many Americans not only because of its important role in the economy but also because of its advertising and sponsorship of public television programs. But in 1993, ADM itself was on camera as executives from ADM and its Japanese competitor Ajinomoto met to discuss the market for lysine, an additive used in animal feed. In this and subsequent meetings, the two companies joined with several other producers to set targets for the price of lysine, behavior known as *price-fixing*. Each company agreed to limit its production to achieve the price targets, with the goal of raising industry profits.

But what the companies were doing was illegal, and the FBI had bugged the meeting room with a camera hidden in a lamp. Over the past few years, there have been numerous investigations and some convictions for price-fixing in a variety of industries, from insurance to college education to computer chips. Despite its illegality, some firms continue to attempt to fix the price of their products.

In the fast-food market, it is the legal practice of *product differentiation* that occupies the minds of marketing executives. Fast-food producers go to great lengths to convince you they have something special to offer beyond the ordinary burger: it's flame broiled or 100% beef or super-thick or lathered with special sauce. Or maybe they offer chicken or fish or roast beef. And the differentiation dance goes on in the pizza industry as well. Domino's offers their never-frozen handmade pan pizza. At Pizza Hut they "make it great." Papa John's claims "better ingredients." The slogans and logos for fast-food restaurants often seem to differ more than the food itself.

To understand why ADM engaged in illegal price-fixing and why fast-food restaurants go to great lengths to differentiate their patties and pizzas, we need to understand the two market structures in between perfect competition and monopoly in the spectrum of market power: *oligopoly* and *monopolistic competition*. The models of these two market structures are at the same time more complicated and more realistic than those we studied previously. Indeed, they describe the behavior of most firms in the real world.

MODULE

31 Oligopoly

Martin Barraud/Getty Images

WHAT YOU WILL LEARN

1. **Why oligopolists have an incentive to act in ways that reduce their combined profit**
2. **Why oligopolies can benefit from collusion**

Although much that we have learned about both perfect competition and monopoly is relevant to oligopoly, oligopoly also raises some entirely new issues. Among other things, firms in an oligopoly are often tempted to engage in the kind of behavior that got ADM, Ajinomoto, and other lysine producers into trouble with the law. We will devote three modules to the study of oligopoly, beginning here, where we examine what oligopoly is and why it is so important.

Interdependence and Oligopoly

Earlier we learned that an oligopoly is an industry with only a few sellers. But what number constitutes a "few"? There is no universal answer, and it is not always easy to determine an industry's market structure just by looking at the number of sellers. Economists use various measures to gain a better picture of market structure, such as the *Herfindahl–Hirschman Index,* as explained in Module 24.

In addition to having a small number of sellers in the industry, an oligopoly is characterized by **interdependence,** a relationship in which the outcome (profit) of each firm depends on the actions of the other firms in the market. This is not true for monopolies because, by definition, they have no other firms to consider. And competitive markets contain so many firms that no one firm has a significant effect on the outcome of the others.

However, in an oligopoly, an industry with few sellers, the outcome for each seller depends on the behavior of the others. Interdependence makes studying a market much more interesting because firms must observe and predict the behavior of other firms. But it is also more complicated. To understand the strategies of oligopolists, we must do more than find the point where the *MC* and *MR* curves intersect!

Firms are **interdependent** when the outcome (profit) of each firm depends on the actions of the other firms in the market.

Understanding Oligopoly

How much will a firm produce? Up to this point, we have always answered: the quantity that maximizes its profit. When a firm is a perfect competitor or a monopolist, we can assume that the firm will use its cost curves to determine its profit-maximizing output. When it comes to oligopoly, however, we run into some difficulties. In fact, economists often describe the behavior of oligopolistic firms as a "puzzle."

An oligopoly consisting of only two firms is a **duopoly.** Each firm is known as a **duopolist.**

Sellers engage in **collusion** when they cooperate to raise their joint profits. A **cartel** is a group of producers that agree to restrict output in order to increase prices and their joint profits.

A Duopoly Example

Let's begin looking at the puzzle of oligopoly with the simplest version, an industry in which there are only two firms—a **duopoly**—and each is known as a **duopolist.**

Going back to our opening story, imagine that ADM and Ajinomoto are the only two producers of lysine. To make things even simpler, suppose that once a company has incurred the fixed cost needed to produce lysine, the marginal cost of producing another pound is zero. So the companies are concerned only with the revenue they receive from sales.

Table 31-1 shows a hypothetical demand schedule for lysine and the total revenue of the industry at each price–quantity combination.

TABLE 31-1

Demand Schedule for Lysine

Price of lysine (per pound)	Quantity of lysine demanded (millions of pounds)	Total revenue (millions)
$12	0	$0
11	10	110
10	20	200
9	30	270
8	40	320
7	50	350
6	60	360
5	70	350
4	80	320
3	90	270
2	100	200
1	110	110
0	120	0

If this were a perfectly competitive industry, each firm would have an incentive to produce more as long as the market price was above marginal cost. Since the marginal cost is assumed to be zero, this would mean that at equilibrium, lysine would be provided for free. Firms would produce until price equals zero, yielding a total output of 120 million pounds and zero revenue for both firms.

However, surely the firms would not be foolish enough to allow price and revenue to plummet to zero. Each would realize that by producing more, it drives down the market price. So each firm would, like a monopolist, see that profits would be higher if it and its rival limited their production.

So how much will the two firms produce?

One possibility is that the two companies will engage in **collusion**—they will cooperate to raise their joint profits. The strongest form of collusion is a **cartel,** a group of producers with an agreement to work together to limit output and increase price, and therefore profit. The world's most famous cartel is the Organization of Petroleum Exporting Countries (OPEC), whose members routinely meet to try to set targets for oil production.

As its name indicates, OPEC is actually a cartel made up of governments rather than firms. There's a reason for this: cartels among firms are illegal in the United States and many other jurisdictions. But let's ignore the law for a moment (which is, of course, what ADM and Ajinomoto did in real life—to their own detriment).

Suppose that ADM and Ajinomoto were to form a cartel and that this cartel decided to act as if it were a monopolist, maximizing total industry profits. We can see from Table 31-1 that in order to maximize the combined profits of the firms, this cartel should set total industry output at 60 million pounds of lysine, which would sell at a price of $6 per pound, leading to revenue of $360 million, the maximum possible. Then the only question would be how much of that 60 million pounds each firm gets to produce. A "fair" solution might be for each firm to produce 30 million pounds and receive revenues of $180 million.

But even if the two firms agreed on such a deal, they might have a problem: each of the firms would have an incentive to break its word and produce more than the agreed-upon quantity.

It is in OPEC's interest to keep oil prices high and output low.

iStockphoto/Thinkstock

When firms ignore the effects of their actions on each other's profits, they engage in **noncooperative behavior.**

Collusion and Competition

Suppose that the presidents of ADM and Ajinomoto were to agree that each would produce 30 million pounds of lysine over the next year. Both would understand that this plan maximizes their combined profits. And both would have an incentive to cheat.

To see why, consider what would happen if Ajinomoto honored its agreement, producing only 30 million pounds, but ADM ignored its promise and produced 40 million pounds. This increase in total output would drive the price down from $6 to $5 per pound, the price at which 70 million pounds are demanded. The industry's total revenue would fall from $360 million ($6 × 60 million pounds) to $350 million ($5 × 70 million pounds). However, ADM's revenue would *rise*, from $180 million to $200 million. Since we are assuming a marginal cost of zero, this would mean a $20 million increase in ADM's profits.

But Ajinomoto's president might make exactly the same calculation. And if *both* firms were to produce 40 million pounds of lysine, the price would drop to $4 per pound. So each firm's profits would fall, from $180 million to $160 million.

The incentive to cheat motivates ADM and Ajinomoto to produce more than the quantity that maximizes their joint profits rather than limiting output as a true monopolist would. We know that a profit-maximizing monopolist sets marginal cost (which in this case is zero) equal to marginal revenue. But what is marginal revenue? Recall that producing an additional unit of a good has two effects:

1. A positive *quantity* effect: one more unit is sold, increasing total revenue by the price at which that unit is sold.
2. A negative *price* effect: in order to sell one more unit, the monopolist must cut the market price on *all* units sold.

The negative price effect is the reason marginal revenue for a monopolist is less than the market price. But when considering the effect of increasing production, a firm is concerned only with the price effect on its *own* units of output, not on those of its fellow oligopolists. Both ADM and Ajinomoto suffer a negative price effect if ADM decides to produce extra lysine and so drives down the price. But ADM cares only about the negative price effect on the units it produces, not about the loss to Ajinomoto.

This tells us that an individual firm in an oligopolistic industry faces a smaller price effect from an additional unit of output than a monopolist; therefore, the marginal revenue that such a firm calculates is higher. So it will seem to be profitable for any one firm in an oligopoly to increase production, even if that increase reduces the profits of the industry as a whole. But if everyone thinks that way, the result is that everyone earns a lower profit!

Because collusion is more profitable than noncooperative behavior, firms have an incentive to collude if they can.

Until now, we have been able to analyze producer behavior by asking what a producer should do to maximize profits. But even if our duopolists, ADM and Ajinomoto, are both trying to maximize profits, what does this predict about their behavior? Will they engage in collusion, reaching and holding to an agreement that maximizes their combined profits? Or will they engage in **noncooperative behavior,** with each firm acting in its own self-interest, even though this has the effect of driving down everyone's profits? Both strategies can be carried out with a goal of profit maximization. Which will actually describe their behavior?

Moodboard/Alamy

Now you see why oligopoly presents a puzzle: there are only a small number of players, making collusion a real possibility. If there were dozens or hundreds of firms, it would be safe to assume they would behave noncooperatively. Yet, when there are only a handful of firms in an industry, it's hard to determine whether collusion will actually occur.

Since collusion is ultimately more profitable than noncooperative behavior, firms have an incentive to collude if they can. One way to do so is to formalize it—sign an agreement (maybe even make a legal contract) or establish some financial incentives for the companies to set their prices high. But in the United States and many other nations, firms can't do that—at least not legally. A contract among firms to keep prices high would be unenforceable, and it could be a one-way ticket to jail. The same goes for an informal agreement.

In fact, executives from rival firms rarely meet without lawyers present, who make sure that the conversation does not stray into inappropriate territory. Even hinting at how nice it would be if prices were higher can bring an unwelcome interview with the Justice Department or the Federal Trade Commission. For example, in 2003 the Justice Department launched a price-fixing case against Monsanto and other large producers of genetically modified seed. The Justice Department was alerted by a series of meetings held between Monsanto and Pioneer Hi-Bred International, two companies that account for 60% of the U.S. market in maize and soybean seed. These companies, parties to a licensing agreement involving genetically modified seed, claimed that no illegal discussions of price-fixing occurred in those meetings. But the fact that the two firms discussed prices as part of the licensing agreement was enough to trigger action by the Justice Department.

ECONOMICS IN ACTION

WORLD VIEW

BITTER CHOCOLATE?

Millions of chocolate lovers around the world have been spending more to satisfy their cravings, and regulators in Germany, Canada, and the United States have become suspicious. They have been investigating whether the seven leading chocolate companies—including Mars, Kraft Foods, Nestlé, Hershey, and Cadbury—have been colluding to raise prices. The amount of money involved could well run into the billions of dollars.

Many of the nation's largest grocery stores and snack retailers are convinced that they have been the victims of collusion. They claim that the chocolate industry has responded to stagnant consumer sales by price-fixing, an allegation the chocolate makers have vigorously denied.

In 2010, one of those stores, Supervalu, filed a lawsuit against Mars, Hershey, Nestlé, and Cadbury, who together control about 76% of the U.S. chocolate market. Supervalu claimed that the confectioners had been fixing prices since 2002, regularly increasing prices by mid-single to double-digit amounts. Supervalu also claimed that grocers who resisted or refused to raise prices were systematically penalized with delayed or insufficient product deliveries.

What's clear is that chocolate candy prices have been soaring while sales fell. Chocolate makers defend their actions, contending that they were simply passing on increases in their costs.

iStockphoto/Thinkstock

Are chocolate makers engaging in price-fixing?

But, as antitrust experts point out, price collusion is often very difficult to prove because it is not illegal for businesses to increase their prices at the same time. To prove collusion, there must be some evidence of conversations or written agreements.

Such evidence did emerge in our chocolate case. According to the Canadian press, 13 Cadbury executives voluntarily provided information to the courts about contacts between the companies. And, according to affidavits submitted to a Canadian court, top executives at Hershey, Mars, and Nestlé met secretly in coffee shops, in restaurants, and at conventions to set prices.

More recently, in 2013, Nestlé, Mars, and others were accused of conspiring to fix the prices of popular chocolate bars in Canada. This episode came not too long after similar charges were filed against chocolate sellers in Germany, including Nestlé and Mars, that resulted in multi-million-dollar fines for the companies involved.

Critics of the chocolate makers may get some sweet vindication in the end.

MODULE 31 Review

Solutions appear at the back of the book.

Check Your Understanding

1. Explain whether each of the following factors will increase or decrease the likelihood that a firm will collude with other firms in an oligopoly to restrict output.
   a. The firm's initial market share is small. (Hint: think about the price effect.)
   b. The firm has a cost advantage over its rivals.
   c. The firm's customers face additional costs when they switch from one firm's product to another firm's product.
   d. The firm and its rivals are currently operating at maximum production capacity, which cannot be altered in the short run.

Multiple-Choice Questions

1. When firms cooperate to raise their joint profits, they are necessarily
   a. colluding.
   b. in a cartel.
   c. a monopoly.
   d. in a duopoly.
   e. in a competitive industry.

2. Use the information in the accompanying table on market shares in the search engine industry and measures of market power (defined in Module 24) to determine which of the following statements are correct.

Search engine	Market share
Google	44%
Yahoo	29
MSN	13
AOL	6
Ask	5
Other	3

   I. The Herfindahl–Hirschman Index is 3,016.
   II. The industry is likely to be an oligopoly.
   a. I only
   b. II only
   c. Both I and II
   d. Neither I nor II

3. An agreement among several producers to restrict output and increase profit is necessary for
   a. cooperation.
   b. collusion.
   c. monopolization.
   d. a cartel.
   e. competition.

4. Oligopolists engage in which of the following types of behavior?
   I. quantity competition
   II. price competition
   III. cooperative behavior
   a. I only
   b. II only
   c. III only
   d. I and II only
   e. I, II, and III

5. Which of the following will make it easier for firms in an industry to maintain positive economic profit?
   a. a ban on cartels
   b. a small number of firms in the industry
   c. a lack of product differentiation
   d. low start-up costs for new firms
   e. the assumption by firms that other firms have variable output levels

Critical-Thinking Question

What are the two major reasons we don't see cartels among oligopolistic industries in the United States today?

Game Theory

Photosindia/Getty Images

WHAT YOU WILL LEARN

1. How our understanding of oligopoly can be enhanced by using game theory
2. The concept of the prisoners' dilemma
3. How repeated interactions among oligopolists can result in collusion in the absence of any formal agreement

Games Oligopolists Play

In our duopoly example (from the previous module) and in real life, each oligopolistic firm realizes both that its profit depends on what its competitor does and that its competitor's profit depends on what it does. That is, the two firms are in a situation of *interdependence,* whereby each firm's decision significantly affects the profit of the other firm (or firms, in the case of more than two).

In effect, the two firms are playing a "game" in which the profit of each player depends not only on its own actions but on those of the other player (or players). In order to understand more fully how oligopolists behave, economists, along with mathematicians, developed the area of study of such games, known as **game theory.** It has many applications, not just to economics but also to military strategy, politics, and other social sciences.

Let's see how game theory helps us understand how oligopolies behave.

The Prisoners' Dilemma

Game theory deals with any situation in which the reward to any one player—the **payoff**—depends not only on his or her own actions but also on those of other players in the game. In the case of oligopolistic firms, the payoff is simply the firm's profit.

When there are only two players, as in a lysine duopoly, the interdependence between the players can be represented with a **payoff matrix** like that shown in Figure 32-1. Each row corresponds to an action by one player (in this case, ADM); each column corresponds to an action by the other (in this case, Ajinomoto). For simplicity, let's assume that each of our firms can pick only one of two alternatives: produce 30 million pounds of lysine or produce 40 million pounds.

The matrix contains four boxes, each divided by a diagonal line. Each box shows the payoff to the two firms that results from a pair of choices; the number below the diagonal shows ADM's profits, the number above the diagonal shows Ajinomoto's profits.

The study of behavior in situations of interdependence is known as **game theory.**

The reward received by a player in a game, such as the profit earned by an oligopolist, is that player's **payoff.**

A **payoff matrix** shows how the payoff to each of the participants in a two-player game depends on the actions of both. Such a matrix helps us analyze situations of interdependence.

FIGURE 32-1 A Payoff Matrix

Two firms, ADM and Ajinomoto, must decide how much lysine to produce. The profits of the two firms are *interdependent:* each firm's profit depends not only on its own decision but also on the other's decision. Each row represents an action by ADM, each column, one by Ajinomoto. Both firms will be better off if they both choose the lower output, but it is in each firm's individual interest to choose the higher output.

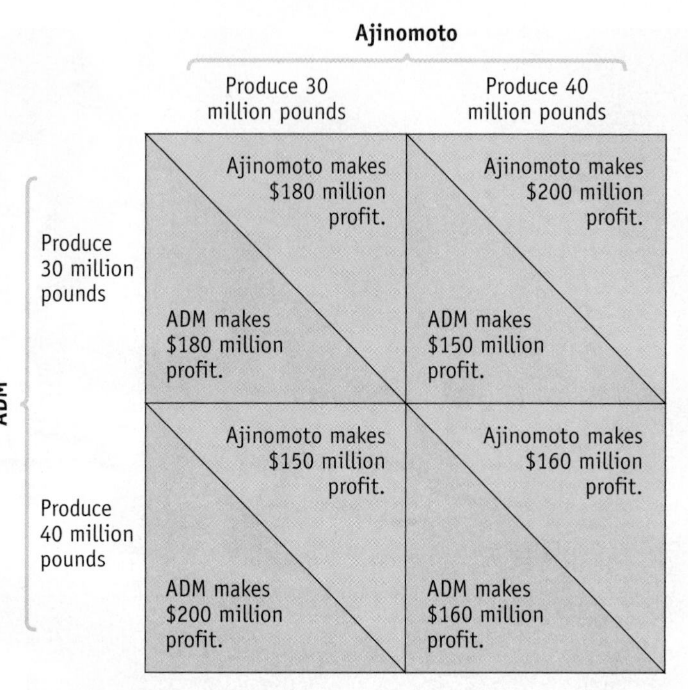

These payoffs show what we concluded from our earlier analysis: the combined profit of the two firms is maximized if they each produce 30 million pounds. Either firm can, however, increase its own profits by producing 40 million pounds if the other produces only 30 million pounds. But if both produce the larger quantity, both will have lower profits than if they had both held their output down.

The particular situation shown here is a version of a famous—and paradoxical—case of interdependence that appears in many contexts. Known as the **prisoners' dilemma,** it is a type of game in which the payoff matrix implies the following:

- Each player has an incentive, regardless of what the other player does, to cheat—to take an action that benefits it at the other's expense.
- When both players cheat, both are worse off than they would have been if neither had cheated.

The original illustration of the prisoners' dilemma occurred in a fictional story about two accomplices in crime—let's call them Thelma and Louise—who have been caught by the police. The police have enough evidence to put them behind bars for 5 years. They also know that the pair have committed a more serious crime, one that carries a 20-year sentence; unfortunately, they don't have enough evidence to convict the women on that charge. To do so, they would need each of the prisoners to implicate the other in the second crime.

So the police put the miscreants in separate cells and say the following to each: "Here's the deal: if neither of you confesses, you know that we'll send you to jail for 5 years. If you confess and implicate your partner, and she doesn't do the same, we reduce your sentence from 5 years to 2. But if your partner confesses and you don't, you'll get the maximum 20 years. And if both of you confess, we'll give you both 15 years."

The **prisoners' dilemma** is a game based on two premises: (1) Each player has an incentive to choose an action that benefits itself at the other player's expense; and (2) When both players act in this way, both are worse off than if they had acted cooperatively.

Figure 32-2 shows the payoffs that face the prisoners, depending on the decision of each to remain silent or to confess. (Usually the payoff matrix reflects the players' payoffs, and higher payoffs are better than lower payoffs. This case is an exception: a higher number of years in prison is bad, not good!) Let's assume that the prisoners have no way to communicate and that they have not sworn an oath not to harm each other or anything of that sort. So each acts in her own self-interest. What will they do?

FIGURE 32-2 The Prisoners' Dilemma

Each of two prisoners, held in separate cells, is offered a deal by the police—a light sentence if she confesses and implicates her accomplice but her accomplice does not do the same, a heavy sentence if she does not confess but her accomplice does, and so on. It is in the joint interest of both prisoners not to confess; it is in each one's individual interest to confess.

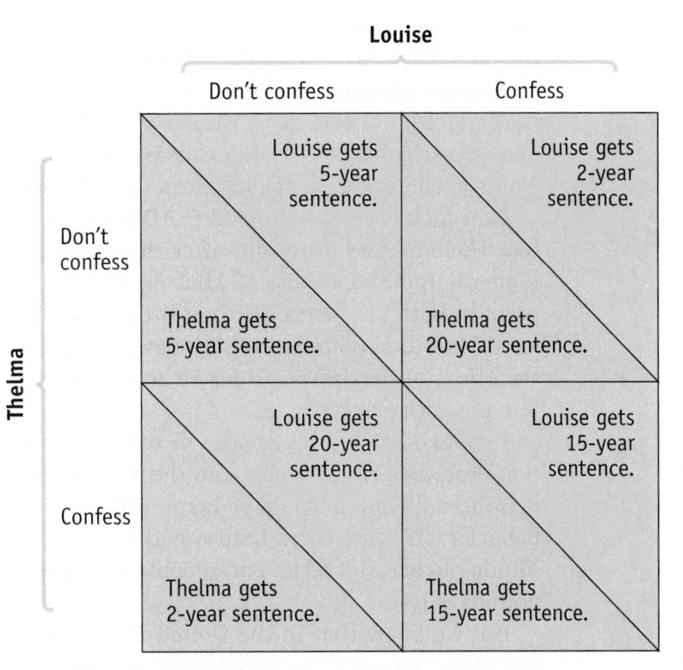

The answer is clear: both will confess. Look at it first from Thelma's point of view: she is better off confessing, regardless of what Louise does. If Louise doesn't confess, Thelma's confession reduces her own sentence from 5 years to 2. If Louise *does* confess, Thelma's confession reduces her sentence from 20 to 15 years. Either way, it's clearly in Thelma's interest to confess. And because she faces the same incentives, it's clearly in Louise's interest to confess, too. To confess in this situation is a type of action that economists call a *dominant strategy.* An action is a **dominant strategy** when it is the player's best action regardless of the action taken by the other player.

It's important to note that not all games have a dominant strategy—it depends on the structure of payoffs in the game. But in the case of Thelma and Louise, it is clearly in the interest of the police to structure the payoffs so that confessing is a dominant strategy for each person. As long as the two prisoners have no way to make an enforceable agreement that neither will confess (something they can't do if they can't communicate, and the police certainly won't allow them to do so because the police want to compel each one to confess), the dominant strategy exists as the best alternative.

So if each prisoner acts rationally in her own interest, both will confess. Yet if neither of them had confessed, both would have received a much lighter sentence! In a prisoners' dilemma, each player has a clear incentive to act in a way that hurts the other player—but when both make that choice, it leaves both of them worse off.

When Thelma and Louise both confess, they reach an *equilibrium* of the game. We have used the concept of equilibrium many times in this book; it is an outcome in which no individual or firm has any incentive to change his or her action. In game theory, this kind of equilibrium, in which each player takes the action that is best for her, given the actions taken by other players, is known as a **Nash equilibrium,** after the mathematician and Nobel Laureate John Nash. Because the players in a Nash equilibrium do not take into account the effect of their actions on others, this is also known as a **noncooperative equilibrium.**

An action is a **dominant strategy** when it is a player's best action regardless of the action taken by the other player.

A **Nash equilibrium,** also known as a **noncooperative equilibrium,** is the result when each player in a game chooses the action that maximizes his or her payoff, given the actions of other players.

In the prisoners' dilemma, the Nash equilibrium happens to be an equilibrium of two dominant strategies—a *dominant strategy equilibrium*—but Nash equilibria can exist when there is no dominant strategy at all. For example, suppose that after serving time in jail, Thelma and Louise are disheartened by the mutual distrust that led them to confess, and each wants nothing more than to avoid seeing the other. On a Saturday night, they might each have to choose between going to the nightclub and going to the movie theater. Neither has a dominant strategy because the best strategy for each depends on what the other is doing. However, Thelma going to the nightclub and Louise going to the movie theater is a Nash equilibrium because each player takes the action that is best given the action of the other. Thelma going to the movie theater and Louise going to the nightclub is also a Nash equilibrium, because again, neither wants to change her behavior given what the other is doing.

Now look back at Figure 32-1: ADM and Ajinomoto face a prisoners' dilemma just like Thelma and Louise did after the crimes. Each firm is better off producing the higher output, regardless of what the other firm does. Yet if both produce 40 million pounds, both are worse off than if they had followed their agreement and produced only 30 million pounds. In both cases, then, the pursuit of individual self-interest—the effort to maximize profits or to minimize jail time—has the perverse effect of hurting both players.

Prisoners' dilemmas appear in many situations. The following Economics in Action describes an example from the days of the Cold War. Clearly, the players in any prisoners' dilemma would be better off if they had some way of enforcing cooperative behavior: if Thelma and Louise had both sworn to a code of silence, or if ADM and Ajinomoto had signed an enforceable agreement not to produce more than 30 million pounds of lysine.

But we know that in the United States an agreement setting the output levels of two oligopolists isn't just unenforceable, it's illegal. So it seems that a noncooperative equilibrium is the only possible outcome. Or is it?

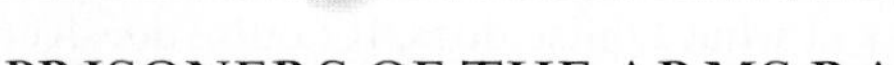

PRISONERS OF THE ARMS RACE

TASS/Sovfoto

Caught in the prisoners' dilemma: heavy military spending hastened the collapse of the Soviet Union.

Between World War II and the late 1980s, the United States and the Soviet Union were locked in a seemingly endless struggle that never broke out into open war. During this Cold War, both countries spent huge sums on arms, sums that were a significant drain on the U.S. economy and eventually proved a crippling burden for the Soviet Union, whose underlying economic base was much weaker. Yet neither country was ever able to achieve a decisive military advantage.

As many people pointed out, both nations would have been better off if they had both spent less on arms. Yet the arms race continued for 40 years.

Why? As political scientists were quick to notice, one way to explain the arms race was to suppose that the two countries were locked in a classic prisoners' dilemma. Each government would have liked to achieve decisive military superiority, and each feared military inferiority. But both would have preferred a stalemate with low military spending to one with high spending. However, each government rationally chose to engage in high spending. If its rival did not spend heavily, this would lead to military superiority; not spending heavily would lead to inferiority if the other government continued its arms buildup. So the countries were trapped.

The answer to this trap could have been an agreement not to spend as much; indeed, the two sides tried repeatedly to negotiate limits on some kinds of weapons. But these agreements weren't very effective. In the end the issue was resolved as heavy military spending hastened the collapse of the Soviet Union in 1991.

Unfortunately, the logic of an arms race has not disappeared. A nuclear arms race has developed between Pakistan and India, neighboring countries with a history of mutual antagonism. In 1998 the two countries confirmed the unrelenting logic of the prisoners' dilemma: both publicly tested their nuclear weapons in a tit-for-tat sequence, each seeking to prove to the other that it could inflict just as much damage as its rival.

Overcoming the Prisoners' Dilemma: Repeated Interaction and Tacit Collusion

A firm engages in **strategic behavior** when it attempts to influence the future behavior of other firms.

A strategy of **tit for tat** involves playing cooperatively at first, then doing whatever the other player did in the previous period.

Thelma and Louise are playing what is known as a *one-shot* game—they play the game with each other only once. They get to choose once and for all whether to confess or deny, and that's it. However, most of the games that oligopolists play aren't one-shot games; instead, the players expect to play the game repeatedly with the same rivals. An oligopolist usually expects to be in business for many years, and knows that a decision today about whether to cheat is likely to affect the decisions of other firms in the future. So a smart oligopolist doesn't just decide what to do based on the effect on profit in the short run. Instead, it engages in **strategic behavior,** taking into account the effects of its action on the future actions of other players. And under some conditions oligopolists that behave strategically can manage to behave as if they had a formal agreement to collude.

Suppose that ADM and Ajinomoto expect to be in the lysine business for many years and therefore expect to play the game of cheat versus collude shown in Figure 32-1 many times. Would they really betray each other time and again?

Probably not. Suppose that ADM considers two strategies. In one strategy it always cheats, producing 40 million pounds of lysine each year, regardless of what Ajinomoto does. In the other strategy, it starts with good behavior, producing only 30 million pounds in the first year, and watches to see what its rival does. If Ajinomoto also keeps its production down, ADM will stay cooperative, producing 30 million pounds again for the next year. But if Ajinomoto produces 40 million pounds, ADM will take the gloves off and also produce 40 million pounds next year. This latter strategy—start by behaving cooperatively, but thereafter do whatever the other player did in the previous period—is generally known as **tit for tat.**

Tit for tat is a form of strategic behavior because it is intended to influence the future actions of other players. The tit-for-tat strategy offers a reward to the other player for cooperative behavior—if you behave cooperatively, so will I. It also provides a punishment for cheating—if you cheat, don't expect me to be nice in the future.

The payoff to ADM of each of these strategies would depend on which strategy Ajinomoto chooses. Consider the four possibilities, shown in Figure 32-3:

1. If ADM plays tit for tat and so does Ajinomoto, both firms will make a profit of \$180 million each year.
2. If ADM plays always cheat but Ajinomoto plays tit for tat, ADM makes a profit of \$200 million the first year but only \$160 million per year thereafter.
3. If ADM plays tit for tat but Ajinomoto plays always cheat, ADM makes a profit of only \$150 million in the first year but \$160 million per year thereafter.
4. If ADM plays always cheat and Ajinomoto does the same, both firms will make a profit of \$160 million each year.

Which strategy is better? In the first year, ADM does better playing always cheat, whatever its rival's strategy: it assures itself that it will get either \$200 million or \$160 million. (Which of the two payoffs it actually receives depends on whether Ajinomoto plays tit for tat or always cheat.) This is better than what it would get in the first year if it played tit for tat: either \$180 million or \$150 million. But by the second year, a strategy of always cheat gains ADM only \$160 million per year for the second and all subsequent years, regardless of Ajinomoto's actions.

Over time, the total amount gained by ADM by playing always cheat is less than the amount gained by playing tit for tat: for the second and all subsequent years, it would never get any less than \$160 million and would get as much as \$180 million if Ajinomoto played tit for tat as well. Which strategy, always cheat or tit for tat, is more profitable depends on two things: how many years ADM expects to play the game and what strategy Ajinomoto follows.

FIGURE 32-3 **How Repeated Interaction Can Support Collusion**

A strategy of tit for tat involves playing cooperatively at first, then following the other player's move. This rewards good behavior and punishes bad behavior. If the other player cheats, playing tit for tat will lead to only a short-term loss in comparison to playing always cheat. But if the other player plays tit for tat, also playing tit for tat leads to a long-term gain. So a firm that expects other firms to play tit for tat may well choose to do the same, leading to successful tacit collusion.

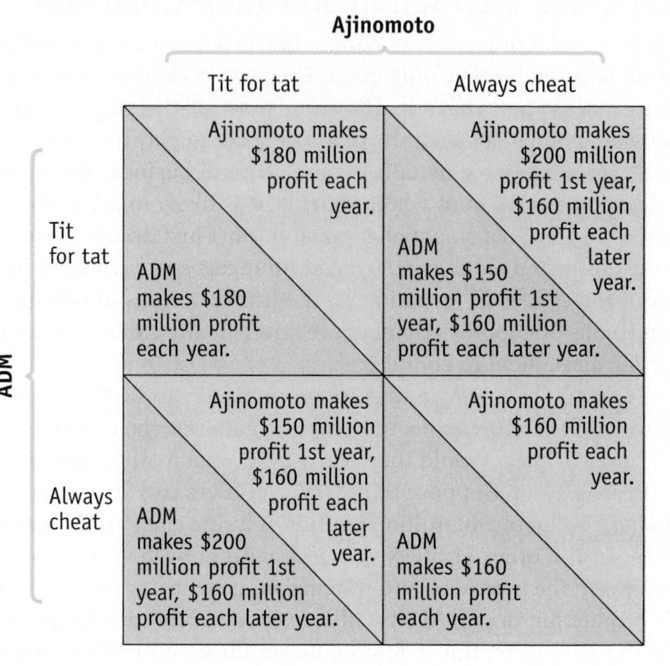

ADM \ Ajinomoto	Tit for tat	Always cheat
Tit for tat	Ajinomoto makes $180 million profit each year. ADM makes $180 million profit each year.	Ajinomoto makes $200 million profit 1st year, $160 million profit each later year. ADM makes $150 million profit 1st year, $160 million profit each later year.
Always cheat	Ajinomoto makes $150 million profit 1st year, $160 million profit each later year. ADM makes $200 million profit 1st year, $160 million profit each later year.	Ajinomoto makes $160 million profit each year. ADM makes $160 million profit each year.

When firms limit production and raise prices in a way that raises each other's profits, even though they have not made any formal agreement, they are engaged in **tacit collusion.**

If ADM expects the lysine business to end in the near future, it is in effect playing a one-shot game. So it might as well cheat and grab what it can. Even if ADM expects to remain in the lysine business for many years (therefore to find itself repeatedly playing this game with Ajinomoto) and, for some reason, expects Ajinomoto will always cheat, it should also always cheat. That is, ADM should follow the old rule, "Do unto others before they do unto you."

But if ADM expects to be in the business for a long time and thinks Ajinomoto is likely to play tit for tat, it will make more profits over the long run by playing tit for tat, too. It could have made some extra short-term profit by cheating at the beginning, but this would provoke Ajinomoto into cheating, too, and would, in the end, mean less profit.

Lucenet Patrice/Oredia Eurl/Superstock

Oligopolists engage in unspoken agreements that limit output and raise prices.

The lesson of this story is that when oligopolists expect to compete with each other over an extended period of time, each individual firm will often conclude that it is in its own best interest to be helpful to the other firms in the industry. So it will restrict its output in a way that raises the profit of the other firms, expecting them to return the favor. Despite the fact that firms have no way of making an enforceable agreement to limit output and raise prices (and are in legal jeopardy if they even discuss prices), they manage to act "as if" they had such an agreement. When this type of unspoken agreement comes about, we say that the firms are engaging in **tacit collusion.**

MODULE 32 Review

Solutions appear at the back of the book.

Check Your Understanding

1. Suppose world leaders Nikita and Margaret are engaged in an arms race and face the decision of whether to build a missile. Answer the following questions using the information in the payoff matrix below, which shows how each set of actions will affect the utility, a measure of personal satisfaction, of the players (the numbers represent utils gained or lost).

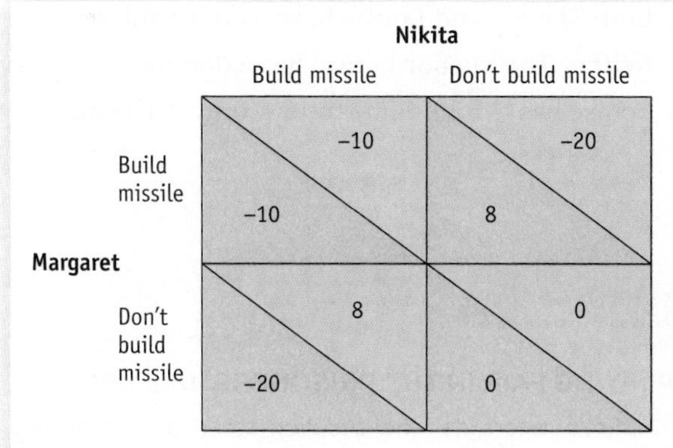

   a. Identify any Nash equilibria that exist in this game, and explain why they exist.

   b. Which set of actions maximizes the total payoff for Nikita and Margaret?

   c. Why is it unlikely that they will choose the payoff-maximizing set of actions without some communication?

2. Which of the following factors make it more likely that oligopolists will play noncooperatively? Which make it more likely that they will engage in tacit collusion? Explain.

   a. Each oligopolist expects several new firms to enter the market in the future.

   b. It is very difficult for a firm to detect whether another firm has raised output.

   c. The firms have coexisted while maintaining high prices for a long time.

Multiple-Choice Questions

1. Each player has an incentive to choose an action that, when both players choose it, makes them both worse off. This situation describes

   a. a dominant strategy.
   b. the prisoners' dilemma.
   c. interdependence.
   d. Nash equilibrium.
   e. tit for tat.

2. Which of the following types of oligopoly behavior is/are illegal?

   I. tacit collusion
   II. cartel formation
   III. tit for tat

   a. I only
   b. II only
   c. III only
   d. I and II only
   e. I, II, and III

3. A situation in which each player in a game chooses the action that maximizes his or her payoff, given the actions of the other players, ignoring the effects of his or her action on the payoffs received by others, is known as a

   a. dominant strategy.
   b. cooperative equilibrium.
   c. Nash equilibrium.
   d. strategic situation.
   e. prisoners' dilemma.

4. In the context of the Thelma and Louise story in the module, suppose that Louise discovers Thelma's action (confess or don't confess) before choosing her own action.

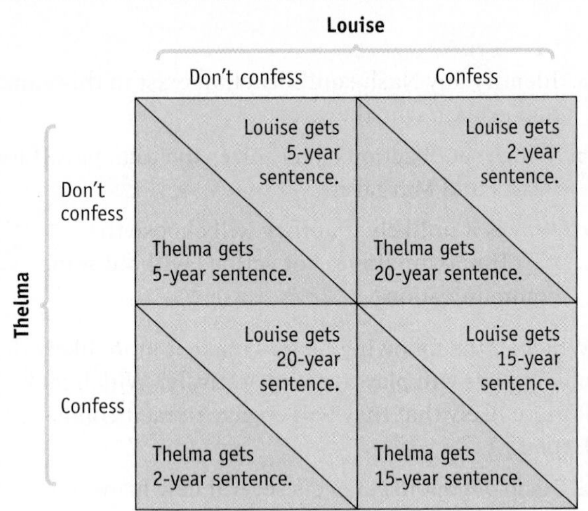

Based on the payoff matrix provided, Louise will

a. confess whether or not Thelma confessed.
b. not confess only if Thelma confessed.
c. not confess only if Thelma didn't confess.
d. not confess regardless of whether or not Thelma confessed.
e. confess only if Thelma did not confess.

5. Which of the following is true on the basis of the payoff matrix provided in Question 4?

a. Louise has no dominant strategy, but Thelma does.
b. Thelma has no dominant strategy, but Louise does.
c. Both Thelma and Louise have a dominant strategy.
d. Neither Thelma nor Louise has a dominant strategy.
e. Louise has a dominant strategy only if Thelma confesses.

Critical-Thinking Question

Draw a clearly labeled payoff matrix illustrating the following situation. There are two firms, "Firm A" and "Firm B." Each firm must decide whether to charge a high price or a low price. If one firm charges a high price and the other a low price, the firm charging the high price will earn low profits while the firm charging the low price will earn high profits. If both firms charge a high price, both earn high profits and if both firms charge low prices, both earn low profits.

PITFALLS

PLAYING FAIR IN THE PRISONERS' DILEMMA

? Let's reconsider the situation faced by our accomplices in crime, Thelma and Louise. Is it rational for them to confess in the prisoners' dilemma? They are both criminals, after all, and it's not unreasonable to think that they would keep their mouths shut out of fear that the other would take revenge for a confession.

> YES, IT IS RATIONAL FOR BOTH OF THEM TO CONFESS. TO UNDERSTAND THE DILEMMA, YOU HAVE TO PLAY FAIR AND IMAGINE PRISONERS WHO CARE *ONLY* ABOUT THE LENGTH OF THEIR SENTENCES. YOU CANNOT CHANGE THE PAYOFFS IN THE PAYOFF MATRIX! Doing so is a little bit like cheating. Luckily, when it comes to oligopoly, it's a lot easier to believe that the firms care only about their profits. There is no indication that anyone at ADM felt either fear of or affection for Ajinomoto, or vice versa; it was strictly about business.

To learn more, see pp. 335–336, especially Figure 32-1.

Oligopoly in Practice

(L) Tim Sloan/AFP/Getty Images/Newscom (R) AP Photo/Steven Senne

WHAT YOU WILL LEARN

1. The legal constraints of antitrust policy
2. The factors that limit tacit collusion
3. The cause and effect of product differentiation and price leadership
4. The importance of oligopoly in the real world

How do oligopolies usually work in practice? The answer depends both on the legal framework that limits what firms can do and on the underlying ability of firms in a given industry to cooperate without formal agreements. In this module we will explore a variety of oligopoly behaviors and how antitrust laws limit oligopolists' attempts to maximize their profits.

The Legal Framework

To understand oligopoly pricing in practice, we must be familiar with the legal constraints under which oligopolistic firms operate. In the United States, oligopoly first became an issue during the second half of the nineteenth century, when the growth of railroads—themselves an oligopolistic industry—created a national market for many goods. Large firms producing oil, steel, and many other products soon emerged. The industrialists quickly realized that profits would be higher if they could limit price competition. So many industries formed cartels—that is, they signed formal agreements to limit production and raise prices. Until 1890, when the first federal legislation against such cartels was passed, this was perfectly legal.

However, although these cartels were legal, their agreements weren't legally *enforceable*—members of a cartel couldn't ask the courts to force a firm that was violating its agreement to reduce its production. And firms often did violate their agreements, for the reason already suggested by our duopoly example in the two previous modules: there is always a temptation for each firm in a cartel to produce more than it is supposed to.

In 1881 clever lawyers at John D. Rockefeller's Standard Oil Company came up with a solution—the so-called *trust*. In a trust, shareholders of all the major companies in an industry placed their shares in the hands of a board of trustees who controlled the companies. This, in effect, merged the companies into a single firm that could then engage in monopoly pricing. In this way, the Standard Oil Trust established what was

HARD COAL TRUST
BEEF TRUST
STANDARD OIL TRUST
NO LACK OF BIG GAME
The President Seems to Have Scared Up Quite a Bunch of

The Sherman Antitrust Act went mostly unenforced until Theodore Roosevelt's presidency (1901–1909).

essentially a monopoly of the oil industry, and it was soon followed by trusts in sugar, whiskey, lead, cottonseed oil, and linseed oil.

Eventually, there was a public backlash, driven partly by concern about the economic effects of the trust movement and partly by fear that the owners of the trusts were simply becoming too powerful. The result was the Sherman Antitrust Act of 1890, which was intended both to prevent the creation of more monopolies and to break up existing ones. At first this law went largely unenforced. But over the decades that followed, the federal government became increasingly committed to making it difficult for oligopolistic industries either to become monopolies or to behave like them. Such efforts are known to this day as **antitrust policy.**

Antitrust policy involves efforts by the government to prevent oligopolistic industries from becoming or behaving like monopolies.

One of the most striking early actions of antitrust policy was the breakup of Standard Oil in 1911. Its components formed the nuclei of many of today's large oil companies—Standard Oil of New Jersey became Exxon, Standard Oil of New York became Mobil, and so on. In the 1980s a long-running case led to the breakup of Bell Telephone, which once had a monopoly on both local and long-distance phone service in the United States. As we mentioned earlier, the Justice Department reviews proposed mergers between companies in the same industry and will bar mergers that it believes will reduce competition.

Among advanced countries, the United States is unique in its long tradition of antitrust policy. Until recently, other advanced countries did not have policies against price-fixing, and some even supported the creation of cartels, believing that it would help their own firms compete against foreign rivals. But the situation has changed radically over the past 20 years, as the European Union (EU)—an international body with the duty of enforcing antitrust policy for its member countries—has converged toward U.S. practices. Today, EU and U.S. regulators often target the same firms because price-fixing has "gone global" as international trade has expanded.

During the early 1990s, the United States instituted an amnesty program in which a price-fixer receives a much-reduced penalty if it provides information on its co-conspirators. In addition, Congress substantially increased maximum fines levied upon conviction. These two new policies clearly made informing on cartel partners a dominant strategy, and it has paid off: in recent years, executives from Belgium, Britain, Canada, France, Germany, Italy, Mexico, the Netherlands, South Korea, and Switzerland, as well as from the United States, have been convicted in U.S. courts of cartel crimes. As one lawyer commented, "You get a race to the courthouse" as each conspirator seeks to be the first to come clean. (For an example out of the United Kingdom, see the Business Case at the end of the section.)

Life has gotten much tougher over the past few years if you want to operate a cartel. So what's an oligopolist to do?

Tacit Collusion and Price Wars

If real life were as simple as our lysine story, it probably wouldn't be necessary for the company presidents to meet or do anything that could land them in jail. Both firms would realize that it was in their mutual interest to restrict output to 30 million pounds each and that any short-term gains to either firm from producing more would be much less than the later losses as the other firm retaliated. So even without any explicit agreement, the firms would probably have achieved the tacit collusion needed to maximize their combined profits.

Real industries are nowhere near that simple; nonetheless, in most oligopolistic industries, most of the time, the sellers do appear to succeed in keeping prices above their noncooperative level. Tacit collusion, in other words, is the normal state of oligopoly.

Although tacit collusion is common, it rarely allows an industry to push prices all the way up to their monopoly level; collusion is usually far from perfect. Four factors make it hard for an industry to coordinate on high prices.

1. LARGE NUMBERS Suppose that there were three instead of two firms in the lysine industry and that each was currently producing only 20 million pounds. In that case any one firm that decided to produce an extra 10 million pounds would gain more in short-term profits—and lose less once another firm responded in kind—than in our original example because it has fewer units on which to feel the price effect. The general point is that the more firms there are in an oligopoly, the less is the incentive for any one firm to behave cooperatively, taking into account the impact of its actions on the profits of the other firms. Large numbers of firms, also known as less concentration in an industry, also make the monitoring of price and output levels more difficult, and typically indicate low barriers to entry.

2. COMPLEX PRODUCTS AND PRICING SCHEMES In our simplified lysine example the two firms produce only one product. In reality, however, oligopolists often sell thousands or even tens of thousands of different products. In these circumstances, as when there are a large number of firms, keeping track of what other firms are producing and what prices they are charging is difficult. This makes it hard to determine whether a firm is cheating on the tacit agreement.

3. DIFFERENCES IN INTERESTS In the lysine example, a tacit agreement for the firms to split the market equally is a natural outcome, probably acceptable to both firms. In other situations, however, firms often differ both in their perceptions about what is fair and in their real interests.

For example, suppose that Ajinomoto was a long-established lysine producer and ADM a more recent entrant into the industry. Ajinomoto might feel that it deserved to continue producing more than ADM, but ADM might feel that it was entitled to 50% of the business.

Alternatively, suppose that ADM's marginal costs were lower than Ajinomoto's. Even if they could agree on market shares, they would then disagree about the profit-maximizing level of output.

4. BARGAINING POWER OF BUYERS Often oligopolists sell not to individual consumers but to large buyers—other industrial enterprises, nationwide chains of stores, and so on. These large buyers are in a position to bargain for lower prices from the oligopolists: they can ask for a discount from an oligopolist, and warn that they will go to a competitor if they don't get it. An important reason large retailers like Walmart are able to offer lower prices to customers than small retailers is precisely their ability to use their size to extract lower prices from their suppliers.

These difficulties in enforcing tacit collusion have sometimes led companies to defy the law and create illegal cartels. We've already examined the cases of the lysine industry and the chocolate industry. An older, classic example was the U.S. electrical equipment conspiracy of the 1950s, which led to the indictment of and jail sentences for some executives. The industry was one in which tacit collusion was especially difficult because of all the reasons just mentioned. There were many firms—40 companies were indicted. They produced a very complex array of products, often more or less custom-built for particular clients. They differed greatly in size, from giants like General Electric to family firms with only a few dozen employees. And the customers in many cases were large buyers like electrical utilities, which would normally try to force suppliers to compete for their business. Tacit collusion just didn't seem practical—so executives met secretly and illegally to decide who would bid what price for which contract.

Because tacit collusion is often hard to achieve, most oligopolies charge prices that are well below what the same industry would charge if it were controlled by a monopolist—or what they would charge if they were able to collude explicitly. In addition, sometimes tacit collusion breaks down and aggressive price competition amounts to a **price war.** A price war sometimes precipitates a collapse of prices to their noncooperative level, or even lower, as sellers try to put each other out of business or at least punish what they regard as cheating.

A **price war** occurs when tacit collusion breaks down and aggressive price competition causes prices to collapse.

ECONOMICS ▶ IN ACTION

THE PRICE WARS OF CHRISTMAS

During the last several holiday seasons, the toy aisles of American retailers have been the scene of cutthroat competition: Target priced the latest Elmo doll at 89 cents less than Walmart (for those with a coupon), and $6 less than Toys "R" Us. So extreme is the price-cutting that since 2003 three toy retailers—KB Toys, FAO Schwarz, and Zany Brainy—have been forced into bankruptcy. Due to aggressive price-cutting by competitors, the market share of Toys "R" Us has fallen from first to third.

What is happening? The turmoil can be traced back to trouble in the toy industry itself as well as to changes in toy retailing. Every year for several years, overall toy sales have fallen a few percentage points as children increasingly turn to video games and the Internet. There have also been new entrants into the toy business: Walmart and Target have expanded their numbers of stores and have been aggressive price-cutters.

The result is much like a story of tacit collusion sustained by repeated interaction run in reverse: because the overall industry is in a state of decline and there are new entrants, the future payoff from collusion is shrinking. The predictable outcome is a price war.

Bloomberg via Getty Images

The price wars of Christmas now arrive earlier each year.

Since retailers depend on holiday sales for nearly half of their annual sales, the holidays are a time of intense price-cutting. Traditionally, the biggest shopping day of the year has been the day after Thanksgiving. But in an effort to expand sales and undercut rivals, retailers—particularly Walmart—have begun slashing prices earlier in the fall, well before Thanksgiving. In fact, in 2010, Walmart slashed its toy prices in early November to within a few cents of Target's prices. Target then placed about half of its toys on sale. Toys "R" Us instead relied on a selection of exclusive toys to avoid direct price competition.

With other retailers feeling as if they have no choice but to follow this pattern, we have the phenomenon known as "creeping Christmas": the price wars of Christmas arrive earlier each year.

Product Differentiation and Price Leadership

Lysine is lysine: there was no question in anyone's mind that ADM and Ajinomoto were producing the same good and that consumers would make their decision about which company's lysine to buy based on the price. In many oligopolies, however, firms produce products that consumers regard as similar but not identical. A $10 difference in the price won't make many customers switch from a Ford to a Chrysler, or vice versa. Sometimes the differences between products are real, like differences between Froot Loops and Wheaties; sometimes, they exist mainly in the minds of consumers, like differences between brands of vodka (which is *supposed* to be tasteless). Either way, the effect is to reduce the intensity of competition among the firms: consumers will not all rush to buy whichever product is cheapest.

As you might imagine, oligopolists welcome the extra market power that comes when consumers think that their product is different from that of competitors. So in many oligopolistic industries, firms make considerable efforts to create the perception that their product is different—that is, they engage in **product differentiation.**

A firm that tries to differentiate its product may do so by altering what it actually produces, adding "extras," or choosing a different design. It may also use advertising and marketing campaigns to create a differentiation in the minds of consumers, even though its product is more or less identical to the products of rivals.

Product differentiation is an attempt by a firm to convince buyers that its product is different from the products of other firms in the industry.

A classic case of how products may be perceived as different even when they are really pretty much the same is over-the-counter medication. For many years there were only three widely sold pain relievers—aspirin, ibuprofen, and acetaminophen. Yet each of these generic pain relievers was marketed under a number of brand names. And each brand used a marketing campaign implying some special superiority.

Whatever the nature of product differentiation, oligopolists producing differentiated products often reach a tacit understanding not to compete on price. For example, during the years when the great majority of cars sold in the United States were produced by the Big Three auto companies (General Motors, Ford, and Chrysler), there was an unwritten rule that none of the three companies would try to gain market share by making its cars noticeably cheaper than those of the other two.

But then who would decide on the overall price of cars? The answer was normally General Motors: as the biggest of the three, it would announce its prices for the year first; and the other companies would adopt similar prices. This pattern of behavior, in which one company tacitly sets prices for the industry as a whole, is known as **price leadership.**

Interestingly, firms that have a tacit agreement not to compete on price often engage in vigorous **nonprice competition**—adding new features to their products, spending large sums on ads that proclaim the inferiority of their rivals' offerings, and so on.

BW Folsom/ Shutterstock

Oligopolists enjoy extra market power when consumers view their product as superior to the competition.

Perhaps the best way to understand the mix of cooperation and competition in such industries is with a political analogy. During the long Cold War between the United States and the Soviet Union, the two countries engaged in intense rivalry for global influence. They not only provided financial and military aid to their allies; they sometimes supported forces trying to overthrow governments allied with their rival (as the Soviet Union did in Vietnam in the 1960s and early 1970s, and as the United States did in Afghanistan from 1979 until the collapse of the Soviet Union in 1991). They even sent their own soldiers to support allied governments against rebels (as the United States did in Vietnam and the Soviet Union did in Afghanistan). But they did not get into direct military confrontations with each other; open warfare between the two superpowers was regarded by both as too dangerous—and tacitly avoided.

Price wars aren't as serious as shooting wars, but the principle is the same.

How Important Is Oligopoly?

We have seen that, across industries, oligopoly is far more common than either perfect competition or monopoly. When we try to analyze oligopoly, the economist's usual way of thinking—asking how self-interested individuals would behave, then analyzing their interaction—does not work as well as we might hope because we do not know whether rival firms will engage in noncooperative behavior or manage to engage in some kind of collusion. Given the prevalence of oligopoly, then, is the analysis we developed in earlier modules, which was based on perfect competition, still useful?

The conclusion of the great majority of economists is yes. For one thing, important parts of the economy are fairly well described by perfect competition. And even though many industries are oligopolistic, in many cases the limits to collusion keep prices relatively close to marginal costs—in other words, the industry behaves "almost" as if it were perfectly competitive.

It is also true that predictions from supply and demand analysis are often valid for oligopolies. For example, we saw that price controls will produce shortages. Strictly speaking, this conclusion is certain only for perfectly competitive industries. But in the 1970s, when the U.S. government imposed price controls on the definitely oligopolistic oil industry, the result was indeed to produce shortages and lines at the gas pumps.

So how important is it to take account of oligopoly? Most economists adopt a pragmatic approach. As we have seen here, the analysis of oligopoly is far more difficult and messy than that of perfect competition; so in situations where they do not expect the complications associated with oligopoly to be crucial, economists prefer to adopt the working assumption of perfectly competitive markets. They always keep in mind the possibility that oligopoly might be important; they recognize that there are important issues, from antitrust policies to price wars, that make trying to understand oligopolistic behavior crucial.

In **price leadership**, one firm sets its price first, and other firms then follow.

Firms that have a tacit understanding not to compete on price often engage in intense **nonprice competition**, using advertising and other means to try to increase their sales.

MODULE 33 Review

Solutions appear at the back of the book.

Check Your Understanding

1. For each of the following industry practices, explain whether the practice supports the conclusion that there is tacit collusion in this industry.
   a. For many years the price in the industry has changed infrequently, and all the firms in the industry charge the same price. The largest firm publishes a catalog containing a "suggested" retail price. Changes in price coincide with changes in the catalog.
   b. There has been considerable variation in the market shares of the firms in the industry over time.
   c. Firms in the industry build into their products unnecessary features that make it hard for consumers to switch from one company's products to another's.
   d. Firms meet yearly to discuss their annual sales forecasts.
   e. Firms tend to adjust their prices upward at the same times.

Multiple-Choice Questions

1. Having which of the following makes it easier for oligopolies to coordinate on raising prices?
   a. a large number of firms
   b. differentiated products
   c. buyers with bargaining power
   d. identical perceptions of fairness
   e. complex pricing schemes
2. Which of the following led to the passage of the first antitrust laws?
   I. growth of the railroad industry
   II. the emergence of the Standard Oil Company
   III. increased competition in agricultural industries
   a. I only
   b. II only
   c. III only
   d. I and II only
   e. I, II, and III
3. When was the first federal legislation against cartels passed?
   a. 1776
   b. 1800
   c. 1890
   d. 1900
   e. 1980
4. Based on your reading about oligopoly in this section, firms in which of the following industries have been prosecuted for creating an illegal cartel?
   a. the lysine industry
   b. top firms in the chocolate industry
   c. the U.S. electrical equipment industry
   d. none of the above
   e. all of the above
5. Oligopolists engage in tacit collusion in order to
   a. raise prices.
   b. increase output.
   c. share profits.
   d. increase market share.
   e. all of the above

Critical-Thinking Question

List four factors that make it difficult for firms to form a cartel. Explain each.

Monopolistic Competition

iStockphoto

WHAT YOU WILL LEARN

1. **How prices and profits are determined in monopolistic competition, both in the short run and in the long run**
2. **How monopolistic competition can lead to inefficiency and excess capacity**

Understanding Monopolistic Competition

Suppose an industry is monopolistically competitive: it consists of many producers, all competing for the same consumers but offering differentiated products. There is also free entry into and exit from the industry in the long run. How does such an industry behave?

As the term *monopolistic competition* suggests, this market structure combines some features typical of monopoly with others typical of perfect competition. Because each firm is offering a distinct product, it is in a way like a monopolist: it faces a downward-sloping demand curve and has some market power—the ability within limits to determine the price of its product.

However, unlike a pure monopolist, a monopolistically competitive firm does face competition: the amount of its product it can sell depends on the prices and products offered by other firms in the industry.

The same, of course, is true of an oligopoly. In a monopolistically competitive industry, however, there are *many* producers, as opposed to the small number that defines an oligopoly. This means that the "puzzle" of oligopoly—whether firms will collude or behave noncooperatively—does not arise in the case of monopolistically competitive industries. True, if all the gas stations or all the restaurants in a town could agree—explicitly or tacitly—to raise prices, it would be in their mutual interest to do so. But such collusion is virtually impossible when the number of firms is large and, by implication, there are no barriers to entry.

So in situations of monopolistic competition, we can safely assume that firms behave noncooperatively and ignore the potential for collusion.

Monopolistic Competition in the Short Run

We introduced the distinction between short-run and long-run equilibrium when we studied perfect competition. The short-run equilibrium of an industry takes the number of firms as given. The long-run equilibrium, by contrast, is reached only after enough time has elapsed for firms to enter or exit the industry. To analyze monopolistic competition, we focus first on the short run and then on how an industry moves from the short run to the long run.

Panels (a) and (b) of Figure 34-1 show two possible situations that a typical firm in a monopolistically competitive industry might face in the short run. In each case, the firm looks like any monopolist: it faces a downward-sloping demand curve, which implies a downward-sloping marginal revenue curve.

We assume that every firm has an upward-sloping marginal cost curve but that it also faces some fixed costs, so that its average total cost curve is U-shaped. This assumption doesn't matter in the short run; but, as we'll see shortly, it is crucial to understanding the long-run equilibrium.

In each case the firm, in order to maximize profit, sets marginal revenue equal to marginal cost. So how do these two figures differ? In panel (a) the firm is profitable; in panel (b) it is unprofitable. (Recall that we are referring always to economic profit and not accounting profit—that is, a profit given that all factors of production are earning their opportunity costs.)

In panel (a) the firm faces the demand curve D_P and the marginal revenue curve MR_P. It produces the profit-maximizing output Q_P, the quantity at which marginal

FIGURE 34-1 The Monopolistically Competitive Firm in the Short Run

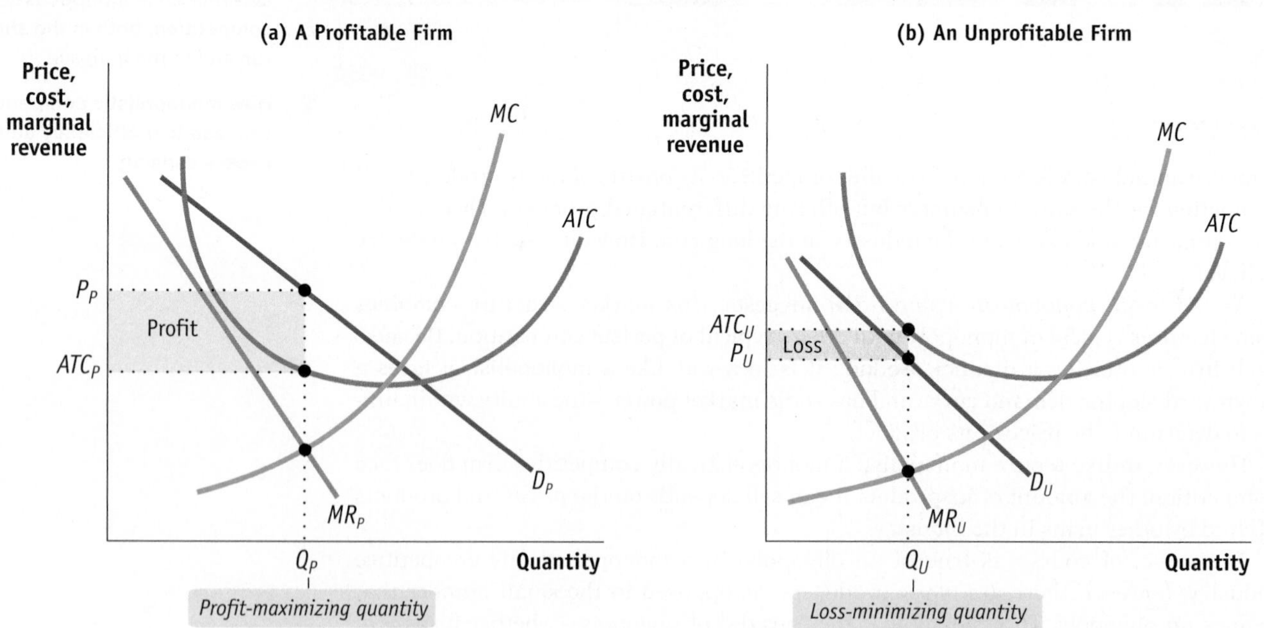

The firm in panel (a) can be profitable for some output quantities: the quantities for which its average total cost curve, *ATC*, lies below its demand curve, D_P. The profit-maximizing output quantity is Q_P, the output at which marginal revenue, MR_P, is equal to marginal cost, *MC*. The firm charges price P_P and earns a profit, represented by the area of the green shaded rectangle. The firm in panel (b), however, can never be profitable because its average total cost curve lies above its demand curve, D_U, for every output quantity. The best that it can do if it produces at all is to produce quantity Q_U and charge price P_U. This generates a loss, indicated by the area of the yellow shaded rectangle. Any other output quantity results in a greater loss.

revenue is equal to marginal cost, and sells it at the price P_P. This price is above the average total cost at this output, ATC_P. The firm's profit is indicated by the area of the shaded rectangle.

In panel (b) the firm faces the demand curve D_U and the marginal revenue curve MR_U. It chooses the quantity Q_U at which marginal revenue is equal to marginal cost. However, in this case the price P_U is *below* the average total cost ATC_U; so at this quantity the firm loses money. Its loss is equal to the area of the shaded rectangle. Since Q_U is the profit-maximizing quantity—which means, in this case, the loss-minimizing quantity—there is no way for a firm in this situation to make a profit. We can confirm this by noting that at any quantity of output, the average total cost curve in panel (b) lies above the demand curve D_U. Because $ATC > P$ at all quantities of output, this firm always suffers a loss.

As this comparison suggests, the key to whether a firm with market power is profitable or unprofitable in the short run lies in the relationship between its demand curve and its average total cost curve. In panel (a) the demand curve D_P crosses the average total cost curve, meaning that some of the demand curve lies above the average total cost curve. So there are some price–quantity combinations available at which price is higher than average total cost, indicating that the firm can choose a quantity at which it makes positive profit.

In panel (b), by contrast, the demand curve D_U does not cross the average total cost curve—it always lies below it. So the price corresponding to each quantity demanded is always less than the average total cost of producing that quantity. There is no quantity at which the firm can avoid losing money.

These figures, showing firms facing downward-sloping demand curves and their associated marginal revenue curves, look just like ordinary monopoly graphs. The "competition" aspect of monopolistic competition comes into play, however, when we move from the short run to the long run.

Monopolistic Competition in the Long Run

Obviously, an industry in which existing firms are losing money, like the one in panel (b) of Figure 34-1, is not in long-run equilibrium. When existing firms are losing money, some firms will *exit* the industry. The industry will not be in long-run equilibrium until the persistent losses have been eliminated by the exit of some firms.

It may be less obvious that an industry in which existing firms are earning profits, like the one in panel (a) of Figure 34-1, is also not in long-run equilibrium. Given there is *free entry* into the industry, persistent profits earned by the existing firms will lead to the entry of additional producers. The industry will not be in long-run equilibrium until the persistent profits have been eliminated by the entry of new producers.

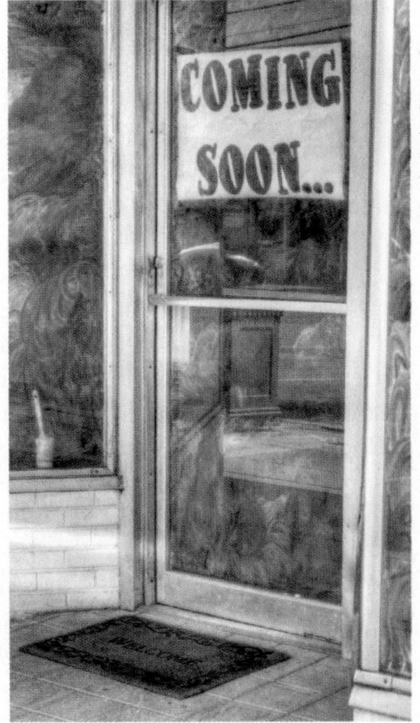

In the long run, profit lures new firms to enter an industry.

How will entry or exit by other firms affect the profit of a typical existing firm? Because the differentiated products offered by firms in a monopolistically competitive industry are available to the same set of customers, entry or exit by other firms will affect the demand curve facing every existing producer.

If new gas stations open along a highway, each of the existing gas stations will no longer be able to sell as much gas as before at any given price. So, as illustrated in

FIGURE 34-2 Entry and Exit Shift Existing Firms' Demand Curves and Marginal Revenue Curves

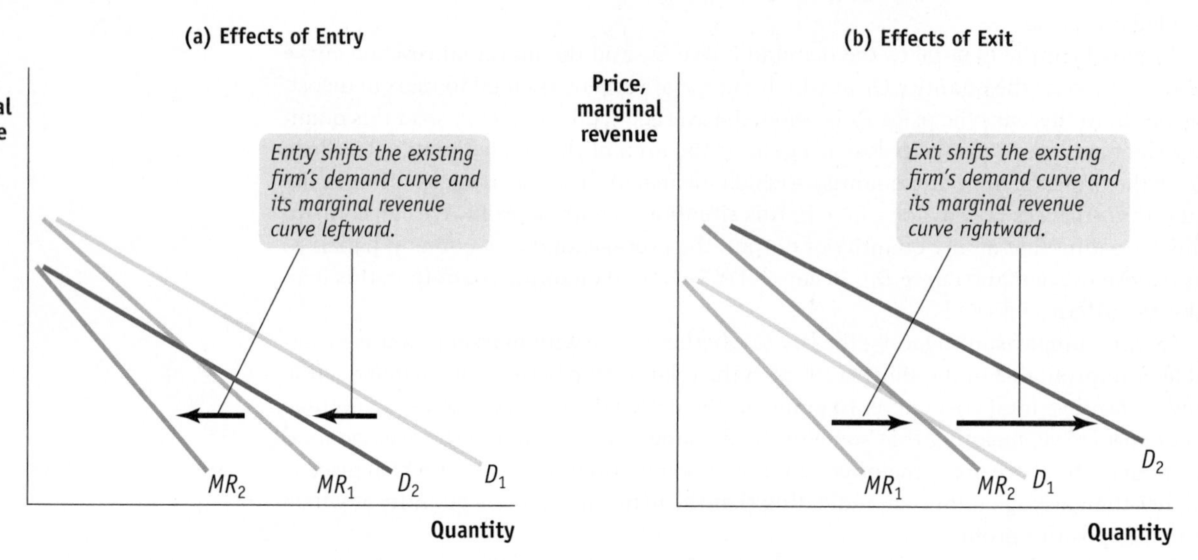

Entry will occur in the long run when existing firms are profitable. In panel (a), entry causes each existing firm's demand curve and marginal revenue curve to shift to the left. The firm receives a lower price for every unit it sells, and its profit falls. Entry will cease when firms make zero profit. Exit will occur in the long run when existing firms are unprofitable. In panel (b), exit from the industry shifts each remaining firm's demand curve and marginal revenue curve to the right. The firm receives a higher price for every unit it sells, and profit rises. Exit will cease when the remaining firms make zero profit.

panel (a) of Figure 34-2, entry of additional producers into a monopolistically competitive industry will lead to a *leftward* shift of the demand curve and the marginal revenue curve facing a typical existing producer.

Conversely, suppose that some of the gas stations along the highway close. Then each of the remaining stations will be able to sell more gasoline at any given price. So as illustrated in panel (b), exit of firms from an industry leads to a *rightward* shift of the demand curve and marginal revenue curve facing a typical remaining producer.

The industry will be in long-run equilibrium when there is neither entry nor exit. This will occur only when every firm earns zero profit. So in the long run, a monopolistically competitive industry will end up in **zero-profit equilibrium,** in which firms just manage to cover their costs at their profit-maximizing output quantities.

We have seen that a firm facing a downward-sloping demand curve will earn positive profit if any part of that demand curve lies above its average total cost curve; it will incur a loss if its entire demand curve lies below its average total cost curve. So in zero-profit equilibrium, the firm must be in a borderline position between these two cases; its demand curve must just touch its average total cost curve. That is, the demand curve must be just *tangent* to the average total cost curve (meaning it just touches the curve) at the firm's profit-maximizing output quantity—the output quantity at which marginal revenue equals marginal cost.

If this is not the case, the firm operating at its profit-maximizing quantity will find itself making either a profit or loss, as illustrated in the panels of Figure 34-1. But we also know that free entry and exit means that this cannot be a long-run equilibrium. Why?

In the long run, a monopolistically competitive industry ends up in **zero-profit equilibrium:** each firm makes zero profit at its profit-maximizing quantity.

In the case of a profit, new firms will enter the industry, shifting the demand curve of every existing firm leftward until all profit is eliminated. In the case of a loss, some existing firms exit and so shift the demand curve of every remaining firm to the right until all losses are eliminated. All entry and exit ceases only when every existing firm makes zero profit at its profit-maximizing quantity of output.

FIGURE 34-3 The Long-Run Zero-Profit Equilibrium

If existing firms are profitable, entry will occur and shift each existing firm's demand curve leftward. If existing firms are unprofitable, each remaining firm's demand curve shifts rightward as some firms exit the industry. Entry and exit will cease when every existing firm makes zero profit at its profit-maximizing quantity. So, in long-run zero-profit equilibrium, the demand curve of each firm is tangent to its average total cost curve at its profit-maximizing quantity: at the profit-maximizing quantity, Q_{MC}, price, P_{MC}, equals average total cost, ATC_{MC}. A monopolistically competitive firm is like a monopolist without monopoly profits.

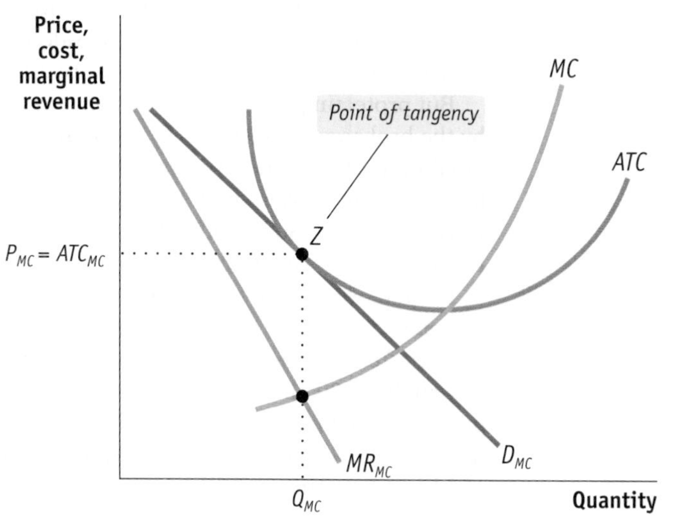

Figure 34-3 shows a typical monopolistically competitive firm in such a zero-profit equilibrium. The firm produces Q_{MC}, the output at which $MR_{MC} = MC$, and charges price P_{MC}. At this price and quantity, represented by point *Z*, the demand curve is just tangent to its average total cost curve. The firm earns zero profit because price, P_{MC}, is equal to average total cost, ATC_{MC}.

The normal long-run condition of a monopolistically competitive industry, then, is that each producer is in the situation shown in Figure 34-3. Each producer acts like a monopolist, facing a downward-sloping demand curve and setting marginal cost equal to marginal revenue so as to maximize profit. But this is just enough to achieve zero economic profit. The producers in the industry are like monopolists without monopoly profit.

ECONOMICS IN ACTION

THE HOUSING BUST AND THE DEMISE OF THE 6% COMMISSION

The vast majority of home sales in the United States are transacted with the use of real estate agents. A homeowner looking to sell hires an agent, who lists the house for sale and shows it to interested buyers. Correspondingly, prospective home buyers hire their own agent to arrange inspections of available houses.

Traditionally, agents were paid by the seller: a commission equal to 6% of the sales price of the house, which the seller's agent and the buyer's agent would split equally. If a house sold for $300,000, for example, the seller's agent and the buyer's agent each received $9,000 (equal to 3% of $300,000).

The real estate brokerage industry fits the model of monopolistic competition quite well: in any given local market, there are many real estate agents, all competing with one another, but the agents are differentiated by location and personality as well as by the type of home they sell (whether condominiums, very expensive homes, and so on). And the industry has free entry: it's relatively easy for someone to become a real estate agent (take a course and then pass a test to obtain a license).

But for a long time there was one feature that didn't fit the model of monopolistic competition: the fixed 6% commission that had not changed over time and was unaffected by the ups and downs of the housing market.

Shutterstock

iStockphoto

Consumers benefit from the diversity of products offered in a monopolistically competitive industry.

Furthermore, it is often argued that monopolistic competition is subject to a further kind of inefficiency: that the excess capacity of every monopolistic competitor implies *wasteful duplication* because monopolistically competitive industries offer too many varieties. According to this argument, it would be better if there were only two or three vendors in the food court, not six or seven. If there were fewer vendors, they would each have lower average total costs and so could offer food more cheaply.

Is this argument against monopolistic competition right—that it lowers total surplus by causing inefficiency? Not necessarily. It's true that if there were fewer gas stations along a highway, each gas station would sell more gasoline and so would have a lower cost per gallon. But there is a drawback: motorists would be inconvenienced because gas stations would be farther apart. The point is that the diversity of products offered in a monopolistically competitive industry is beneficial to consumers. So the higher price consumers pay because of excess capacity is offset to some extent by the value they receive from greater diversity.

There is, in other words, a trade-off: more producers mean higher average total costs but also greater product diversity. Does a monopolistically competitive industry arrive at the socially optimal point in this trade-off? Probably not—but it is hard to say whether there are too many firms or too few! Most economists now believe that duplication of effort and excess capacity in monopolistically competitive industries are not large problems in practice.

MODULE 34 Review

Solutions appear at the back of the book.

Check Your Understanding

1. Suppose a monopolistically competitive industry composed of firms with U-shaped average total cost curves is in long-run equilibrium. For each of the following changes, explain how the industry is affected in the short run and how it adjusts to a new long-run equilibrium.
   a. a technological change that increases fixed cost for every firm in the industry
   b. a technological change that decreases marginal cost for every firm in the industry
2. Why is it impossible for firms in a monopolistically competitive industry to join together to form a monopoly that is capable of maintaining positive economic profit in the long run?
3. Are the following statements true or false? Explain your answers.
   a. Like a firm in a perfectly competitive industry, a firm in a monopolistically competitive industry is willing to sell a good at any price that equals or exceeds marginal cost.
   b. Suppose there is a monopolistically competitive industry in long-run equilibrium that possesses excess capacity. All the firms in the industry would be better off if they merged into a single firm and produced a single product, but whether consumers would be made better off by this is ambiguous.
   c. Fads and fashions are more likely to arise in industries characterized by monopolistic competition or oligopoly than in those characterized by perfect competition or monopoly.

Multiple-Choice Questions

1. Which of the following is a characteristic of monopolistic competition?
   a. a standardized product
   b. many sellers
   c. barriers to entry
   d. positive long-run profits
   e. a perfectly elastic demand curve

2. Which of the following results is possible for a monopolistic competitor in the short run?
   I. positive economic profit
   II. normal profit
   III. loss
   a. I only
   b. II only
   c. III only
   d. I and II only
   e. I, II, and III

3. Which of the following results is possible for a monopolistic competitor in the long run?
   I. positive economic profit
   II. normal profit
   III. loss
   a. I only
   b. II only
   c. III only
   d. I and II only
   e. I, II, and III

4. Which of the following best describes a monopolistic competitor's demand curve?
   a. upward sloping
   b. downward sloping
   c. U-shaped
   d. horizontal
   e. vertical

5. The long-run outcome in a monopolistically competitive industry results in
   a. inefficiency because firms earn positive economic profits.
   b. efficiency due to excess capacity.
   c. inefficiency due to product diversity.
   d. efficiency because price exceeds marginal cost.
   e. a trade-off between higher average total cost and more product diversity.

Critical-Thinking Question

Draw a correctly labeled graph for a monopolistically competitive firm in long-run equilibrium. Label the distance on the quantity axis that represents excess capacity.

Product Differentiation and Advertising

Andrew Moore/Gallery Stock

WHAT YOU WILL LEARN

1. Why oligopolists and monopolistic competitors differentiate their products
2. The economic significance of advertising and brand names

In previous modules we learned that product differentiation often plays an important role in oligopolistic industries. In such industries, product differentiation reduces the intensity of competition between firms when tacit collusion cannot be achieved. It plays an even more crucial role in monopolistically competitive industries. Because tacit collusion is virtually impossible when there are many producers, product differentiation is the only way monopolistically competitive firms can acquire some market power.

In this module, we look at how oligopolists and monopolistic competitors differentiate their products in order to maximize profits.

How Firms Differentiate Their Products

How do firms in the same industry—such as fast-food vendors, gas stations, or chocolate makers—differentiate their products? Sometimes the difference is mainly in the minds of consumers rather than in the products themselves. We'll discuss the role of advertising and the importance of brand names in achieving this kind of product differentiation later. But, in general, firms differentiate their products by—surprise!—actually making them different.

The key to product differentiation is that consumers have different preferences and are willing to pay somewhat more to satisfy those preferences. Each producer can carve out a market niche by producing something that caters to the particular preferences of some group of consumers better than the products of other firms. There are three important forms of product differentiation:

- differentiation by style or type
- differentiation by location
- differentiation by quality.

Differentiation by Style or Type

Recall our discussion of Leo's Wonderful Wok in an earlier module. The sellers in Leo's food court offer different types of fast food: hamburgers, pizza, Chinese food, Mexican food, and so on. Each consumer arrives at the food court with some preference for one or another of these offerings. This preference may depend on the consumer's mood, her diet, or what she has already eaten that day. These preferences will not make consumers indifferent to price: if Wonderful Wok were to charge $15 for an egg roll, everybody would go to Bodacious Burgers or Pizza Paradise instead. But some people will choose a more expensive meal if that type of food is closer to their preference. So the products of the different vendors are substitutes, but they aren't *perfect* substitutes—they are *imperfect substitutes.*

Vendors in a food court or the restaurant chains in Times Square (shown in the photo at left) aren't the only sellers who differentiate their offerings by type. Clothing stores concentrate on women's or men's clothes, on business attire or sportswear, on trendy or classic styles, and so on. Auto manufacturers offer sedans, minivans, sport-utility vehicles, and sports cars, each type aimed at drivers with different needs and tastes.

Books offer yet another example of differentiation by type and style. Mysteries are differentiated from romances; among mysteries, we can differentiate among hard-boiled detective stories, whodunits, and police procedurals. And no two writers of hard-boiled detective stories are exactly alike: Raymond Chandler and Sue Grafton each have devoted fans.

In fact, product differentiation is characteristic of most consumer goods. As long as people differ in their tastes, producers find it possible and profitable to offer variety.

Differentiation by Location

Gas stations along a road offer differentiated products. True, the gas may be exactly the same. But the location of the stations is different, and location matters to consumers: it's more convenient to stop for gas near your home, near your workplace, or near wherever you are when the gas gauge gets low.

In fact, many monopolistically competitive industries supply goods differentiated by location. This is especially true in service industries, from dry cleaners to hairdressers, where customers often choose the seller who is closest rather than cheapest.

Buddy Mays/Alamy

For industries that differentiate by location, proximity is everything.

Differentiation by Quality

Do you have a craving for chocolate? How much are you willing to spend on it? You see, there's chocolate and then there's chocolate: although ordinary chocolate may not be very expensive, gourmet chocolate can cost several dollars per bite.

With chocolate, as with many goods, there is a range of possible qualities. You can get a usable bicycle for less than $100; you can get a much fancier bicycle for 10 times as much. It all depends on how much the additional quality matters to you and how much you will miss the other things you could have purchased with that money.

Because consumers vary in what they are willing to pay for higher quality, producers can differentiate their products by quality—some offering lower-quality, inexpensive products and others offering higher-quality products at a higher price.

Product differentiation, then, can take several forms. Whatever form it takes, however, there are two important features of industries with differentiated products: *competition among sellers* and *value in diversity.*

iStockphoto

Chocolate lovers know that there's ordinary chocolate and then there's *extraordinary* chocolate.

Competition among sellers means that even though sellers of differentiated products are not offering identical goods, they are to some extent competing for a limited market. If more businesses enter the market, each will find that it sells a lower quantity at any given price. For example, as we saw in the previous chapter, if a new gas station opens along a road, each of the existing gas stations will sell a bit less.

Value in diversity refers to the gain to consumers from the proliferation of differentiated products. A food court with eight vendors makes consumers happier than one with only six vendors, even if the prices are the same, because some customers will get a meal that is closer to what they had in mind. A road on which there is a gas station every two miles is more convenient for motorists than a road where gas stations are five miles apart. When a product is available in many different qualities, fewer people are forced to pay for more quality than they need or to settle for lower quality than they want. There are, in other words, benefits to consumers from a greater diversity of available products.

ECONOMICS IN ACTION

Science and Society/Superstock

ANY COLOR, SO LONG AS IT'S BLACK

The early history of the auto industry offers a classic illustration of the power of product differentiation.

The modern automobile industry was created by Henry Ford, who first introduced assembly-line production. This technique made it possible for him to offer the famous Model T at a far lower price than anyone else was charging for a car; by 1920, Ford dominated the automobile business.

Ford's strategy was to offer just one style of car, which maximized his economies of scale in production but made no concessions to differences in consumers' tastes. He supposedly declared that customers could get the Model T in "any color, so long as it's black."

This strategy was challenged by Alfred P. Sloan, who had merged a number of smaller automobile companies into General Motors. Sloan's strategy was to offer a range of car types, differentiated by quality and price. Chevrolets were basic cars that directly challenged the Model T, Buicks were bigger and more expensive, and so on up to Cadillacs. And you could get each model in several different colors.

By the 1930s the verdict was clear: customers preferred a range of styles, and General Motors, not Ford, became the dominant auto manufacturer for the rest of the twentieth century.

Controversies About Product Differentiation

Up to this point, we have assumed that products are differentiated in a way that corresponds to some real desire of consumers. There is real convenience in having a gas station in your neighborhood; Chinese food and Mexican food are really different from each other.

In the real world, however, some instances of product differentiation can seem puzzling if you think about them. What is the real difference between Crest and Colgate toothpaste? Between Energizer and Duracell batteries? Or a Marriott and a Hilton hotel room? Most people would be hard-pressed to answer any of these questions. Yet the producers of these goods make considerable efforts to convince consumers that their products are different from and better than those of their competitors.

No discussion of product differentiation is complete without spending at least a bit of time on the two related issues—and puzzles—of *advertising* and *brand names.*

The Role of Advertising

Wheat farmers don't advertise their wares on TV, but car dealers do. That's not because farmers are shy and car dealers are outgoing; it's because advertising is worthwhile only in industries in which firms have at least some market power.

The purpose of advertisements is to persuade people to buy more of a seller's product at the going price. A perfectly competitive firm, which can sell as much as it likes at the going market price, has no incentive to spend money persuading consumers to buy more. Only a firm that has some market power, and which therefore charges a price that is above marginal cost, can gain from advertising. Some industries that are more or less perfectly competitive, like the milk industry, do advertise—but these ads are sponsored by an association on behalf of the industry as a whole, not on behalf of a particular farm.

Given that advertising "works," it's not hard to see why firms with market power would spend money on it. But the big question about advertising is, *why* does it work? A related question is whether advertising is, from society's point of view, a waste of resources.

Not all advertising poses a puzzle. Much of it is straightforward: it's a way for sellers to inform potential buyers about what they have to offer (or, occasionally, for buyers to inform potential sellers about what they want). Nor is there much controversy about the economic usefulness of ads that provide information: the real estate ad that declares "sunny, charming, 2 bedrooms, 1 bath, a/c" tells you things you need to know (even if a few euphemisms are involved—"charming," of course, means "small").

But what information is being conveyed when a TV actress proclaims the virtues of one or another toothpaste or a sports hero declares that some company's batteries are better than those inside that pink mechanical rabbit? Surely nobody believes that the sports star is an expert on batteries—or that he chose the company that he personally believes makes the best batteries, as opposed to the company that offered to pay him the most. Yet companies believe, with good reason, that money spent on such promotions increases their sales—and that they would be in big trouble if they stopped advertising but their competitors continued to do so.

Why are consumers influenced by ads that do not really provide any information about the product? One answer is that consumers are not as rational as economists typically assume. Perhaps consumers' judgments, or even their tastes, can be influenced by things that economists think ought to be irrelevant, such as which company has hired the most charismatic celebrity to endorse its product. And there is surely some truth to this. Consumer rationality is a useful working assumption; it is not an absolute truth.

However, another answer is that consumer response to advertising is not entirely irrational because ads can serve as indirect "signals" in a world where consumers don't have good information about products. Suppose, to take a common example, that you need to avail yourself of some local service that you don't use regularly—body work on your car, say, or furniture moving. You can go online, as many of us do, or turn to the Yellow Pages, where you see a number of small listings and several large display ads. You know that those display ads are large because the firms paid extra for them; still, it may be quite rational to call one of the firms with a big display ad. After all, the big ad probably means that it's a relatively large, successful company—otherwise, the company wouldn't have found it worth spending the money for the larger ad.

The same principle may partly explain why ads feature celebrities. You don't really believe that the supermodel prefers that watch; but the fact that the watch manufacturer is willing and able to pay her fee tells you that it is a major company that is likely

BUSINESS CASE • Virgin Atlantic Blows the Whistle . . . or Blows It?

Ian Waldie/Getty Images

The United Kingdom is home to two long-haul airline carriers (carriers that fly between continents): British Airways and its rival, Virgin Atlantic. Although British Airways is the dominant company, with a market share generally between 50% and 100% on routes between London and various American cities, Virgin has been a tenacious competitor.

The rivalry between the two has ranged from relatively peaceable to openly hostile over the years. In the 1990s, British Airways lost a court case alleging it had engaged in "dirty tricks" to drive Virgin out of business. In April 2010, however, British Airways may well have wondered if the tables had been turned.

It all began in mid-July 2004, when oil prices were rising (long-haul airlines are especially vulnerable to oil price hikes). British prosecutors alleged that the two airlines had plotted to levy fuel surcharges on passengers. For the next two years, according to the prosecutors, the rivals had established a cartel through which they coordinated increases in surcharges. British Airways first introduced a £5 ($8.25) surcharge on long-haul flights when a barrel of oil traded at about $38. It increased the surcharge six times, so that by 2006, when oil was trading at about $69 a barrel, the surcharge was £70 ($115). At the same time, Virgin Atlantic also levied a £70 fee. These surcharges increased within days of each other.

Eventually, three Virgin executives decided to blow the whistle in exchange for immunity from prosecution. British Airways immediately suspended its executives under suspicion and paid fines of nearly $500 million to U.S. and U.K. authorities. And in 2010 four British Airways executives were prosecuted by British authorities for their alleged role in the conspiracy.

The lawyers for the executives argued that although the two airlines had swapped information, this was not proof of a criminal conspiracy. In fact, they argued, Virgin so feared American regulators that it had admitted to criminal behavior before confirming that it had committed an offense. One of the defense lawyers, Clare Montgomery, argued that because U.S. laws against anti-competitive behavior are much tougher than those in the United Kingdom, companies may be compelled to blow the whistle to avoid investigation. "It's a race," she said. "If you don't get to them and confess first, you can't get immunity. The only way to protect yourself is to go to the authorities, even if you haven't [done anything]." The result was that Virgin executives were given immunity in both the United States and the United Kingdom, but British Airways executives were subject to prosecution (and possible multiyear jail terms) in both countries.

In late 2011 the case came to a shocking end. Citing e-mails that Virgin had finally been forced by the court to turn over, the judge found insufficient evidence that there had ever been a conspiracy between the two airlines. The court was incensed enough to threaten to rescind the immunity granted to the three Virgin executives.

Questions for Thought

1. Explain why Virgin Atlantic and British Airlines might collude in response to increased oil prices. Was the market conducive to collusion or not?
2. How would you determine whether illegal behavior actually occurred? What might explain these events other than illegal behavior?
3. Did these two airlines and their individual executives face a prisoners' dilemma? Explain your answer.

SECTION 11 REVIEW

Summary

Oligopoly

1. Many industries are oligopolies, characterized by a small number of sellers. The smallest type of oligopoly, a **duopoly,** has only two sellers. Oligopolies exist for more or less the same reasons that monopolies exist, but in weaker form. They are characterized by imperfect competition: firms compete but possess market power.
2. Predicting the behavior of oligopolists poses something of a puzzle. The firms in an oligopoly could maximize their combined profits by acting as a **cartel,** setting output levels for each firm as if they were a single monopolist; to the extent that firms manage to do this, they engage in **collusion.** But each individual firm has an incentive to produce more than the agreed upon quantity of output—to engage in **noncooperative behavior.** Informal collusion is likely to be easier to achieve in industries in which firms face capacity constraints.

Game Theory

3. The situation of **interdependence,** in which each firm's profit depends noticeably on what other firms do, is the subject of **game theory.** In the case of a game with two players, the **payoff** of each player depends on both its own actions and on the actions of the other; this interdependence can be shown in a **payoff matrix.** Depending on the structure of payoffs in the payoff matrix, a player may have a **dominant strategy**—an action that is always the best regardless of the other player's actions.
4. Some **duopolists** face a particular type of game known as a **prisoners' dilemma;** if each acts independently in its own interest, the resulting **Nash equilibrium** or **noncooperative equilibrium** will be bad for both. However, firms that expect to play a game repeatedly tend to engage in **strategic behavior,** trying to influence each other's future actions. A particular strategy that seems to work well in such situations is **tit for tat,** which often leads to **tacit collusion.**

Oligopoly in Practice

5. In order to limit the ability of oligopolists to collude and act like monopolists, most governments pursue **antitrust policy** designed to make collusion more difficult. In practice, however, tacit collusion is widespread.
6. A variety of factors make tacit collusion difficult: a large numbers of firms, complex products and pricing, differences in interests, and buyers with bargaining power. When tacit collusion breaks down, there can be a **price war.** Oligopolists try to avoid price wars in various ways, such as through **product differentiation** and through **price leadership,** in which one firm sets prices for the industry. Another approach is **nonprice competition,** such as advertising.

Monopolistic Competition

7. Monopolistic competition is a market structure in which there are many competing producers, each producing a differentiated product, and there is free entry and exit in the long run.
8. Short-run profits will attract the entry of new firms in the long run. This reduces the quantity each existing producer sells at any given price and shifts its demand curve to the left. Short-run losses will induce exit by some firms in the long run. This shifts the demand curve of each remaining firm to the right.
9. In the long run, a monopolistically competitive industry is in **zero-profit equilibrium:** at its profit-maximizing quantity, the demand curve for each existing firm is tangent to its average total cost curve. There are zero profits in the industry and no entry or exit.
10. In long-run equilibrium, firms in a monopolistically competitive industry sell at a price greater than marginal cost. They also have **excess capacity** because they produce less than the minimum-cost output; as a result, they have higher costs than firms in a perfectly competitive industry. Whether or not monopolistic competition is inefficient is ambiguous because consumers value the product diversity that it creates.

Product Differentiation and Advertising

11. Product differentiation takes three main forms: style or type, location, and quality. Firms will engage in advertising to increase demand for their products and enhance their market power. Advertising and **brand names** that provide useful information to consumers are valuable to society. Advertisements can be wasteful from a societal standpoint when their only purpose is to create market power.

Key Terms

Problems

1. The accompanying table shows the demand schedule for vitamin D. Suppose that the marginal cost of producing vitamin D is zero.

Price of vitamin D (per ton)	Quantity of vitamin D demanded (tons)
$8	0
7	10
6	20
5	30
4	40
3	50
2	60
1	70

   a. Assume that BASF is the only producer of vitamin D and acts as a monopolist. It currently produces 40 tons of vitamin D at $4 per ton. If BASF were to produce 10 more tons, what would be the price effect for BASF? What would be the quantity effect? Would BASF have an incentive to produce those 10 additional tons?

   b. Now assume that Roche enters the market by also producing vitamin D and the market is now a duopoly. BASF and Roche agree to produce 40 tons of vitamin D in total, 20 tons each. BASF cannot be punished for deviating from the agreement with Roche. If BASF, on its own, were to deviate from that agreement and produce 10 more tons, what would be the price effect for BASF? What would be the quantity effect for BASF? Would BASF have an incentive to produce those 10 additional tons?

2. The market for olive oil in New York City is controlled by two families, the Sopranos and the Contraltos. Both families will ruthlessly eliminate any other family that attempts to enter the New York City olive oil market. The marginal cost of producing olive oil is constant and equal to $40 per gallon. There is no fixed cost. The accompanying table gives the market demand schedule for olive oil.

Price of olive oil (per gallon)	Quantity of olive oil demanded (gallons)
$100	1,000
90	1,500
80	2,000
70	2,500
60	3,000
50	3,500
40	4,000
30	4,500
20	5,000
10	5,500

   a. Suppose the Sopranos and the Contraltos form a cartel. For each of the quantities given in the table, calculate the total revenue for their cartel and the marginal revenue for each additional gallon. How many gallons of olive oil would the cartel sell in total and at what price? The two families share the market equally (each produces half of the total output of the cartel). How much profit does each family make?

   b. Uncle Junior, the head of the Soprano family, breaks the agreement and sells 500 more gallons of olive oil than under the cartel agreement. Assuming the Contraltos maintain the agreement, how does this affect the price for olive oil and the profits earned by each family?

   c. Anthony Contralto, the head of the Contralto family, decides to punish Uncle Junior by increasing his sales by 500 gallons as well. How much profit does each family earn now?

3. In France, the market for bottled water is controlled by two large firms, Perrier and Evian. Each firm has a fixed cost of €1 million and a constant marginal cost of €2 per liter of bottled water (€1 = 1 euro). The following table gives the market demand schedule for bottled water in France.

Price of bottled water (per liter)	Quantity of bottled water demanded (millions of liters)
€10	0
9	1
8	2
7	3
6	4
5	5
4	6
3	7
2	8
1	9

a. Suppose the two firms form a cartel and act as a monopolist. Calculate marginal revenue for the cartel. What will the monopoly price and output be? Assuming the firms divided the output evenly, how much will each produce and what will each firm's profits be?

b. Now suppose Perrier decides to increase production by 1 million liters. Evian doesn't change its production. What will the new market price and output be? What is Perrier's profit? What is Evian's profit?

c. What if Perrier increases production by 3 million liters? Evian doesn't change its production. What would its output and profits be relative to those in part b?

d. What do your results tell you about the likelihood of cheating on such agreements?

4. To preserve the North Atlantic fish stocks, it is decided that only two fishing fleets, one from the United States and the other from the European Union (EU), can fish in those waters. The accompanying table shows the market demand schedule per week for fish from these waters. The only costs are fixed costs, so fishing fleets maximize profit by maximizing revenue.

Price of fish (per pound)	Quantity of fish demanded (pounds)
$17	1,800
16	2,000
15	2,100
14	2,200
12	2,300

a. If both fishing fleets collude, what is the revenue-maximizing output for the North Atlantic fishery? What price will a pound of fish sell for?

b. If both fishing fleets collude and share the output equally, what is the revenue to the EU fleet? To the U.S. fleet?

c. Suppose the EU fleet cheats by expanding its own catch by 100 pounds per week. The U.S. fleet doesn't change its catch. What is the revenue to the U.S. fleet? To the EU fleet?

d. In retaliation for the cheating by the EU fleet, the U.S. fleet also expands its catch by 100 pounds per week. What is the revenue to the U.S. fleet? To the EU fleet?

5. Suppose that the fisheries agreement in Problem 4 breaks down, so that the fleets behave noncooperatively. Assume that the United States and the EU each can send out either one or two fleets. The more fleets in the area, the more fish they catch in total but the lower the catch of each fleet. The accompanying matrix shows the profit (in dollars) per week earned by the two sides.

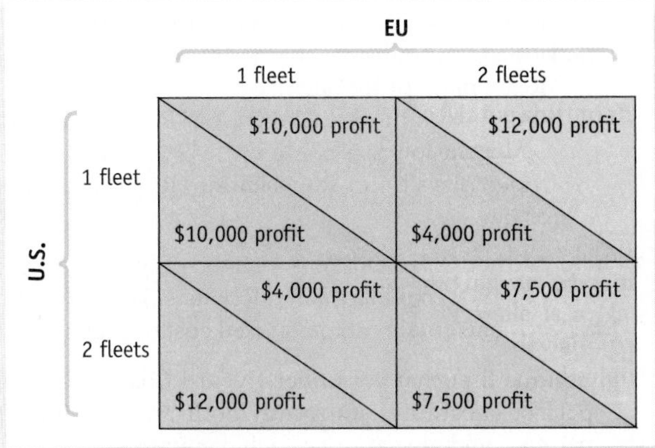

a. What is the noncooperative Nash equilibrium? Will each side choose to send out one or two fleets?

b. Suppose that the fish stocks are being depleted. Each region considers the future and comes to a tit-for-tat agreement whereby each side will send only one fleet out as long as the other does the same. If either of them breaks the agreement and sends out a second fleet, the other will also send out two and will continue to do so until its competitor sends out only one fleet. If both play this tit-for-tat strategy, how much profit will each make every week?

6. Untied and Air "R" Us are the only two airlines operating flights between Collegeville and Bigtown. That is, they operate in a duopoly. Each airline can charge either a high price or a low price for a ticket. The accompanying matrix shows their payoffs, in profits per seat (in dollars), for any choice that the two airlines can make.

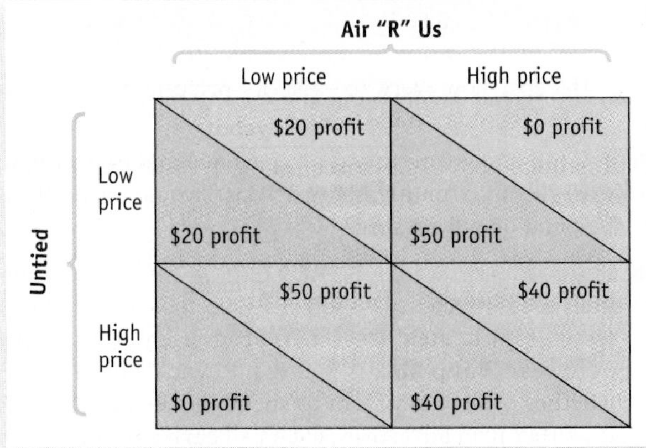

a. Suppose the two airlines play a one-shot game—that is, they interact only once and never again. What will be the Nash equilibrium in this one-shot game?

b. Now suppose the two airlines play this game twice. And suppose each airline can play one of two strategies: it can play either "always charge the low price" or "tit for tat"—that is, start off charging the high price in the first period, and then in the second period do whatever the other airline did in the previous period. Write down the payoffs to Untied from the following four possibilities:

i. Untied plays always charge the low price when Air "R" Us also plays always charge the low price.

ii. Untied plays always charge the low price when Air "R" Us plays tit for tat.

iii. Untied plays tit for tat when Air "R" Us plays always charge the low price.

iv. Untied plays tit for tat when Air "R" Us also plays tit for tat.

7. Suppose that Coke and Pepsi are the only two producers of cola drinks, making them duopolists. Both companies have zero marginal cost and a fixed cost of $100,000.

a. Assume first that consumers regard Coke and Pepsi as perfect substitutes. Currently both are sold for $0.20 per can, and at that price each company sells 4 million cans per day.

i. How large is Pepsi's profit?

ii. If Pepsi were to raise its price to $0.30 cents per can, and Coke did not respond, what would happen to Pepsi's profit?

b. Now suppose that each company advertises to differentiate its product from the other company's. As a result of advertising, Pepsi realizes that if it raises or lowers its price, it will sell less or more of its product, as shown by the demand schedule in the accompanying table.

Price of Pepsi (per can)	Quantity of Pepsi demanded (millions of cans)
$0.10	5
0.20	4
0.30	3
0.40	2
0.50	1

If Pepsi now were to raise its price to $0.30 per can, what would happen to its profit?

c. Comparing your answer to part a(i) and to part b, what is the maximum amount Pepsi would be willing to spend on advertising?

8. Philip Morris and R.J. Reynolds spend huge sums of money each year to advertise their tobacco products in an attempt to steal customers from each other. Suppose each year Philip Morris and R.J. Reynolds have to decide whether or not they want to spend money on advertising. If neither firm advertises, each will earn a profit of $2 million. If they both advertise, each will earn a profit of $1.5 million. If one firm advertises and the other does not, the firm that advertises will earn a profit of $2.8 million and the other firm will earn $1 million.

a. Use a payoff matrix to depict this problem.

b. Suppose Philip Morris and R.J. Reynolds can write an enforceable contract about what they will do. What is the cooperative solution to this game?

c. What is the Nash equilibrium without an enforceable contract? Explain why this is the likely outcome.

9. Use the three conditions for monopolistic competition discussed in this section to decide which of the following firms are likely to be operating as monopolistic competitors. If they are not monopolistically competitive firms, are they monopolists, oligopolists, or perfectly competitive firms?

a. a local band that plays for weddings, parties, and so on

b. Minute Maid, a producer of individual-serving juice boxes

c. a dry cleaner in a large metropolitan area

d. a farmer who produces soybeans

10. You are thinking of setting up a coffee shop. The market structure for coffee shops is monopolistic competition. There are three Starbucks shops, and two other coffee shops very much like Starbucks, in your town already. In order for you to have some degree of market power, you may want to differentiate your coffee shop. Thinking about the three different ways in which products can be differentiated, explain how you would decide whether you should copy Starbucks or whether you should sell coffee in a completely different way.

11. The restaurant business in town is a monopolistically competitive industry in long-run equilibrium. One restaurant owner asks for your advice. She tells you that, each night, not all tables in her restaurant are full. She also tells you that if she lowered the prices on her menu, she would attract more customers and that doing so would lower her average total cost. Should she lower her prices? Draw a diagram showing the demand curve, marginal revenue curve, marginal cost curve, and average total cost curve for this restaurant to explain your advice. Show in your diagram what would happen to the restaurant owner's profit if she were to lower the price so that she sells the minimum-cost output.

12. The local hairdresser industry has the market structure of monopolistic competition. Your hairdresser boasts that he is making a profit and that if he continues to do so, he will be able to retire in five years. Use a diagram to illustrate your hairdresser's current situation. Do you expect this to last? In a separate diagram, draw what you expect to happen in the long run. Explain your reasoning.

13. Magnificent Blooms is a florist in a monopolistically competitive industry. It is a successful operation, producing the quantity that minimizes its average total cost and making a profit. The owner also says that at its current level of output, its marginal cost is above marginal revenue. Illustrate the current situation of Magnificent Blooms in a diagram. Answer the following questions by illustrating with a diagram.

a. In the short run, could Magnificent Blooms increase its profit?

b. In the long run, could Magnificent Blooms increase its profit?

14. "In both the short run and in the long run, the typical firm in monopolistic competition and a monopolist each make a profit." Do you agree with this statement? Explain your reasoning.

15. The market for clothes has the structure of monopolistic competition. What impact will fewer firms in this industry have on you as a consumer? Address the following issues:

a. variety of clothes

b. differences in quality of service

c. price

16. For each of the following situations, decide whether advertising is directly informative about the product or simply an indirect signal of its quality. Explain your reasoning.

a. Star quarterback Peyton Manning drives a Buick in a TV commercial and claims that he prefers it to any other car.

b. A newspaper ad states, "For sale: 2006 Honda Civic, 160,000 miles, new transmission."

c. McDonald's spends millions of dollars on an advertising campaign that proclaims: "I'm lovin' it."

d. Subway advertises one of its sandwiches by claiming that it contains 6 grams of fat and fewer than 300 calories.

17. In each of the following cases, explain how the advertisement functions as a signal to a potential buyer. Explain what information the buyer lacks that is being supplied by the advertisement and how the information supplied by the advertisement is likely to affect the buyer's willingness to buy the good.

a. "Looking for work. Excellent references from previous employers available."

b. "Electronic equipment for sale. All merchandise carries a one-year, no-questions-asked warranty."

c. "Car for sale by original owner. All repair and maintenance records available."

An **emissions tax** is a tax that depends on the amount of pollution a firm produces.

vehicles to have catalytic converters, which reduce the emission of chemicals that can cause smog and lead to health problems. Other rules require communities to treat their sewage, factories to limit their pollution emissions, and homes to be painted with lead-free paint, among many other examples.

Environmental standards came into widespread use in the 1960s and 1970s with considerable success. Since the United States passed the Clean Air Act in 1970, for example, the emission of air pollutants has fallen by more than a third, even though the population has grown by a third and the size of the economy has more than doubled. Even in Los Angeles, still famous for its smog, the air has improved dramatically: in 1976 ozone levels in the South Coast Air Basin exceeded federal standards on 194 days; in 2010, on only 7 days. Improvements have continued in 2013.

Despite these successes, economists believe that when regulators can control a polluter's emissions directly, there are more efficient ways than environmental standards to deal with pollution. By using methods grounded in economic analysis, society can achieve a cleaner environment at lower cost.

Most current environmental standards are inflexible and don't allow reductions in pollution to be achieved at the lowest possible cost. For example, two power plants—plant A and plant B—might be ordered to reduce pollution by the same percentage, even if their costs of achieving that objective are very different.

iStockphoto

Environmental standards have helped reduce the Los Angeles smog and improve air quality.

How does economic theory suggest that pollution should be controlled? We'll examine two approaches: taxes and tradable permits. As we'll see, either approach can achieve the efficient outcome at the minimum feasible cost.

Emissions Taxes

One way to deal with pollution directly is to charge polluters an **emissions tax.** Emissions taxes depend on the amount of pollution a firm produces. For example, power plants might be charged $200 for every ton of sulfur dioxide they emit.

Consider the socially optimal quantity of pollution, Q_{OPT}, shown in Figure 37-1. At that quantity of pollution, the marginal social benefit and the marginal social cost of

FIGURE 37-1 In Pursuit of the Efficient Quantity of Pollution

The market determined quantity of pollution, Q_{MKT}, is too high because polluters don't pay the marginal social cost, and thus pollute beyond the socially optimal quantity, Q_{OPT}, at which marginal social cost equals marginal social benefit. A Pigouvian tax of $200—the value of the marginal social cost of pollution when it equals the marginal social benefit of pollution—gives polluters the incentive to emit only the socially optimal quantity of pollution. Another solution is to provide permits for only the socially optimal quantity of pollution.

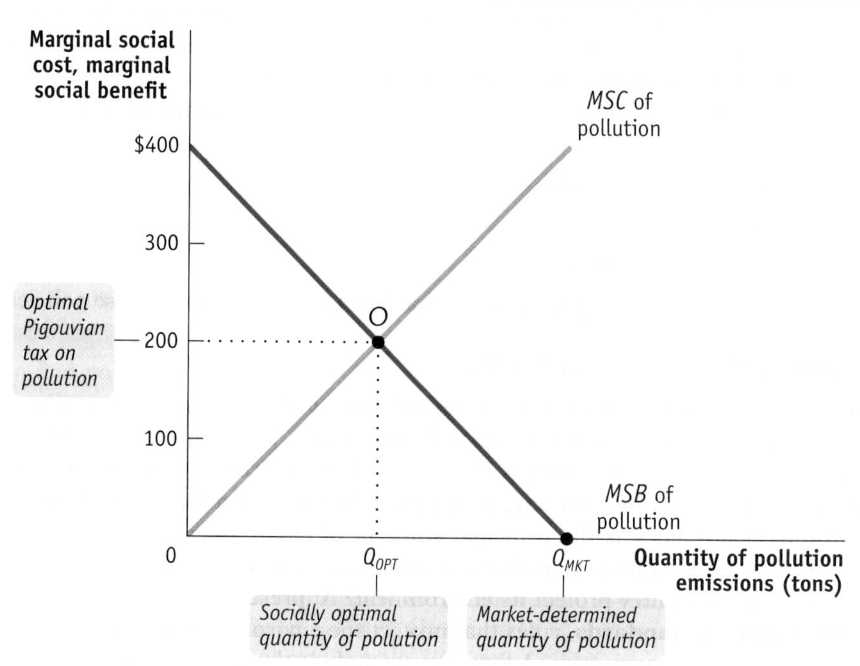

an additional ton of emissions are equal at $200. But in the absence of government intervention, power companies have no incentive to limit pollution to the socially optimal quantity Q_{OPT}; instead, they will push pollution up to the quantity Q_{MKT}, at which the marginal social benefit is zero.

It's now easy to see how an emissions tax can solve the problem. If power companies are required to pay a tax of $200 per ton of emissions, they face a marginal cost of $200 per ton and have an incentive to reduce emissions to Q_{OPT}, the socially optimal quantity. This illustrates a general result: an emissions tax equal to the marginal social cost at the socially optimal quantity of pollution induces polluters to internalize the externality—to take into account the true cost to society of their actions. (The Pigouvian tax noted in Figure 37-1 will be explained shortly.)

Why is an emissions tax an efficient way (that is, a cost-minimizing way) to reduce pollution but environmental standards generally are not? Because an emissions tax ensures that the marginal benefit of pollution is equal for all sources of pollution, but an environmental standard does not.

Figure 37-2 shows a hypothetical industry consisting of only two plants, plant A and plant B. We'll assume that plant A uses newer technology than plant B and so has a lower cost of reducing pollution. Reflecting this difference in costs, plant A's marginal benefit of pollution curve, MB_A, lies below plant B's marginal benefit of pollution curve, MB_B. Because it is more costly for plant B to reduce its pollution at any output quantity, an additional ton of pollution is worth more to plant B than to plant A.

FIGURE 37-2 Environmental Standards versus Emissions Taxes

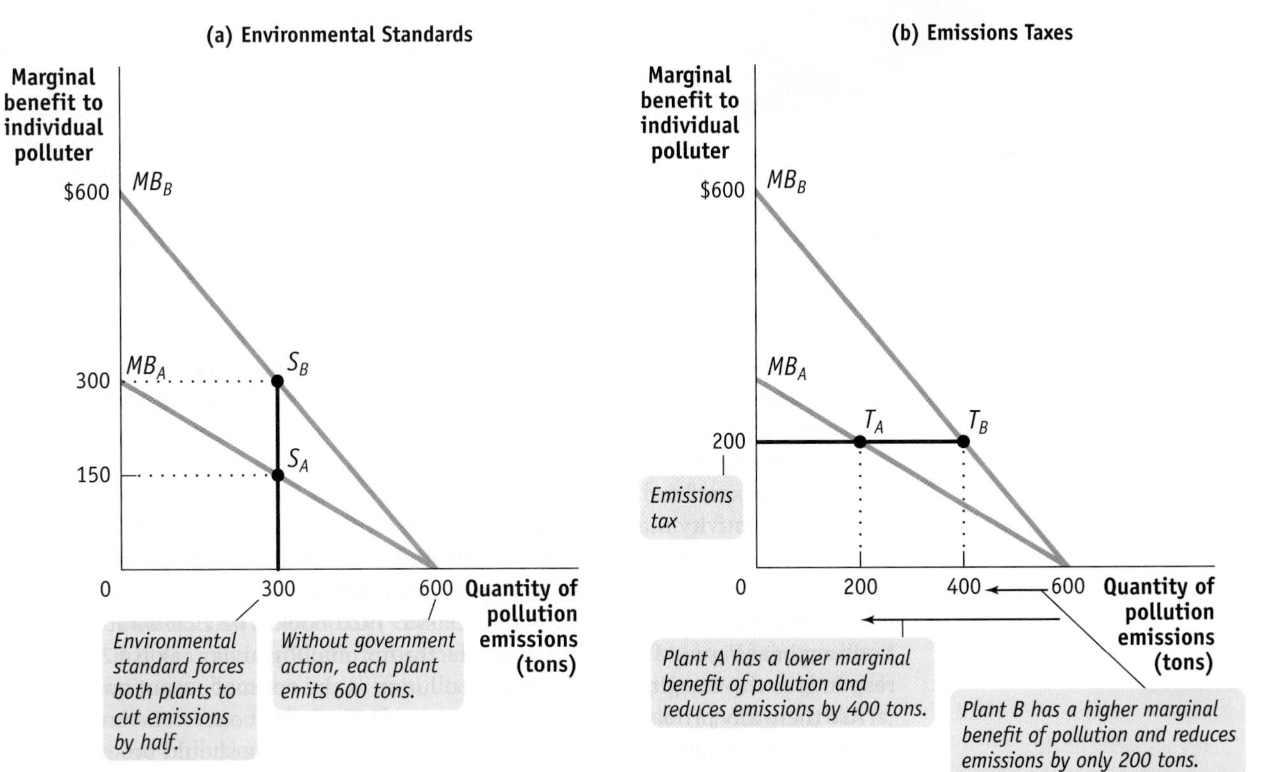

In both panels, MB_A shows the marginal benefit of pollution to plant A and MB_B shows the marginal benefit of pollution to plant B. In the absence of government intervention, each plant would emit 600 tons. However, the cost of reducing emissions is lower for plant A, as shown by the fact that MB_A lies below MB_B. Panel (a) shows the result of an environmental standard that requires both plants to cut emissions in half; this is inefficient, because it leaves the marginal benefit of pollution higher for plant B than for plant A. Panel (b) shows that an emissions tax achieves the same quantity of overall pollution efficiently: faced with an emissions tax of $200 per ton, both plants reduce pollution to the point where its marginal benefit is $200.

ECONOMICS ▶ IN ACTION WORLD VIEW

CAP AND TRADE

The tradable emissions permit systems for both acid rain in the United States and greenhouse gases in the European Union are examples of *cap and trade systems:* the government sets a *cap* (a maximum amount of pollutant that can be emitted), issues tradable emissions permits, and enforces a yearly rule that a polluter must hold a number of permits equal to the amount of pollutant emitted. The goal is to set the cap low enough to generate environmental benefits, while giving polluters flexibility in meeting environmental standards and motivating them to adopt new technologies that will lower the cost of reducing pollution.

AP Photo/Kin Cheung

Cap and trade systems can benefit the environment, but they are not a silver bullet against pollution.

In 1994 the United States began a cap and trade system for the sulfur dioxide emissions that cause acid rain by issuing permits to power plants based on their historical consumption of coal. Thanks to the system, air pollutants in the United States decreased by more than 40% from 1990 to 2008, and 2010 acid rain levels dropped to approximately 50% of their 1980 levels and they continue to drop.

Economists who have analyzed the sulfur dioxide cap and trade system point to another reason for its success: it would have been a lot more expensive—80% more to be exact—to reduce emissions by this much using a non-market-based regulatory policy.

The EU cap and trade scheme, covering all 28 member nations of the European Union (plus Iceland, Liechtenstein, and Norway), is the world's only mandatory trading scheme for greenhouse gases. It is scheduled to achieve a 21% reduction in greenhouse gases by 2020 compared to 2005 levels.

Despite all this good news, however, cap and trade systems are not silver bullets for the world's pollution problems for these reasons:

- Although they are appropriate for pollution that's geographically dispersed, like sulfur dioxide and greenhouse gases, they don't work for pollution that's localized, like mercury or lead contamination.
- The amount of overall reduction in pollution depends on the level of the cap. Under industry pressure, regulators run the risk of issuing too many permits, effectively eliminating the cap.
- There must be vigilant monitoring of compliance if the system is to work. Without oversight of a polluter's emissions, there is no way to know for sure that the rules are being followed.

Positive Externalities

New Jersey is the most densely populated state in the country, lying along the northeastern corridor, an area of almost continuous development stretching from Washington, D.C., to Boston. Yet a drive through New Jersey reveals a surprising feature: acre upon acre of farmland, growing everything from corn to pumpkins to the famous Jersey tomatoes. This situation is no accident: starting in 1961, New Jerseyans have voted in a series of measures that subsidize farmers to permanently preserve their farmland rather than sell it to developers.

Why have New Jersey citizens voted to raise their own taxes to subsidize the preservation of farmland? Because they believe that preserved farmland in an already heavily developed state provides external benefits, such as natural beauty, access to fresh food, and the conservation of wild bird populations. In addition, preservation alleviates the external costs that come with more development, such as pressure on roads, water supplies, and municipal services—and, inevitably, more pollution.

In this section we'll explore the topics of external benefits and positive externalities. They are, in many ways, the mirror images of external costs and negative externalities. Left on its own, the market will produce too little of a good (in this case, preserved New Jersey farmland) that confers external benefits on others. But society as a whole is better off when policies are adopted that increase the supply of such a good.

© Gene Ahrens/Alamy

Preserved farmland provides external benefits to an entire community.

Preserved Farmland: An External Benefit

Preserved farmland yields both benefits and costs to society. In the absence of government intervention, the farmer who wants to sell his land incurs all the costs of preservation—namely, the forgone profit to be made from selling the farmland to a developer. But the benefits of preserved farmland accrue not to the farmer but to neighboring residents, who have no right to influence how the farmland is disposed of.

Figure 37-3 illustrates society's problem. The marginal social cost of preserved farmland, shown by the *MSC* curve, is the additional cost imposed on society by an additional acre of such farmland. This represents the forgone profits that would have accrued to farmers if they had sold their land. The line is upward-sloping because when very few acres are preserved and there is plenty of land available for development, the profit that could be made from selling an acre to a developer is small. But as the number of preserved acres increases and few are left for development, the amount a developer is willing to pay for them, and therefore the forgone profit, increases as well.

The *MSB* curve represents the marginal social benefit of preserved farmland. It is the additional benefit that accrues to society—in this case, the farmer's neighbors—when an additional acre of farmland is preserved. The curve is downward sloping because as more farmland is preserved, the benefit to society of preserving another acre falls. As Figure 37-3 shows, the socially optimal point, *O*, occurs when the marginal social cost and the marginal social benefit are equalized—here, at a price of $10,000 per acre. At the socially optimum point, Q_{OPT} acres of farmland are preserved.

FIGURE 37-3 **Why a Market Economy Preserves Too Little Farmland**

Without government intervention, the quantity of preserved farmland will be zero, the level at which the marginal social cost of preservation is zero. This is an inefficiently low quantity of preserved farmland: the marginal social benefit is $20,000, but the marginal social cost is zero. An optimal Pigouvian subsidy of $10,000, the value of the marginal social benefit of preservation when it equals the marginal social cost, can move the market to the socially optimal level of preservation, Q_{OPT}.

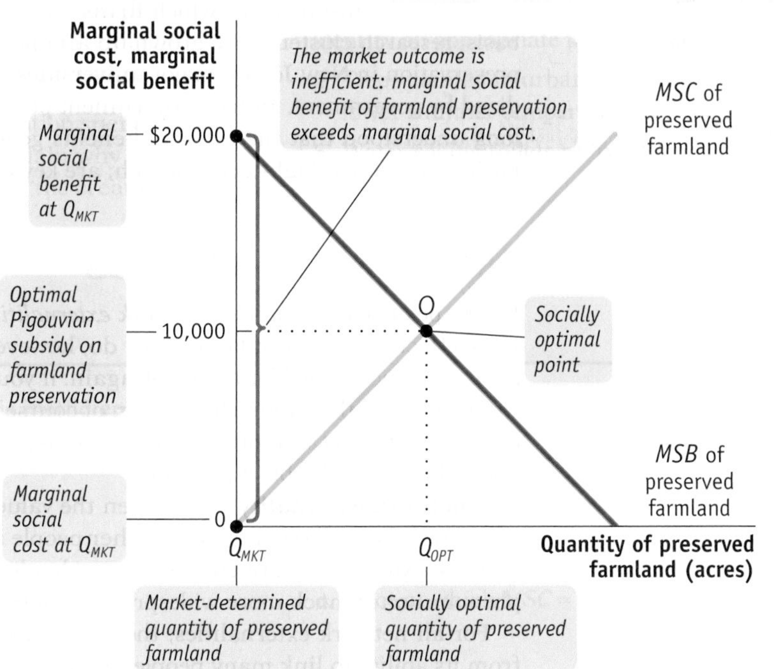

SECTION 12 REVIEW

Summary

Externalities

1. When pollution can be directly observed and controlled, government policies should be geared directly to producing the **socially optimal quantity of pollution,** the quantity at which the **marginal social cost of pollution** is equal to the **marginal social benefit of pollution.** In the absence of government intervention, a market produces too much pollution because polluters take only their benefit from polluting into account, not the costs imposed on others.
2. The cost to society of pollution from a power plant is an example of an **external cost;** the benefit to neighbors of beautiful flowers planted in your yard is an example of an **external benefit.** External costs and benefits are jointly known as **externalities,** with external costs called **negative externalities** and external benefits called **positive externalities.**
3. According to the **Coase theorem,** when externalities exist, bargaining will cause individuals to **internalize the externalities,** making government intervention unnecessary, as long as property rights are clearly defined and **transaction costs**—the costs of making a deal—are sufficiently low. However, in many cases transaction costs are too high to permit such deals.

Externalities and Public Policy

4. Governments often deal with pollution by imposing **environmental standards,** an approach, economists argue, that is usually inefficient. Two efficient (cost-minimizing) methods for reducing pollution are **emissions taxes,** a form of **Pigouvian tax,** and **tradable emissions permits.** The optimal Pigouvian tax on pollution is equal to its marginal social cost at the socially optimal quantity of pollution. These methods also provide incentives for the creation and adoption of production technologies that cause less pollution.
5. When a good or activity yields external benefits, or positive externalities, such as **technology spillovers,** then an optimal **Pigouvian subsidy** to producers moves the market to the socially optimal quantity of production.
6. High-technology goods are frequently subject to **network externalities,** which arise when the value of the good to an individual is greater when a large number of people use the good. Such goods are likely to be subject to **positive feedback:** if large numbers of people buy the good, other people are more likely to buy it, too. So success breeds greater success and failure breeds failure: the good with the larger network will eventually dominate, and competing products will disappear.

Public Goods and Common Resources

7. Goods may be classified according to whether or not they are **excludable,** meaning that people can be prevented from consuming them, and whether or not they are **rival in consumption,** meaning that one person's consumption of them affects another person's consumption of them.
8. Free markets can deliver efficient levels of production and consumption for **private goods,** which are both excludable and rival in consumption. When goods are nonexcludable, nonrival in consumption, or both, free markets cannot achieve efficient outcomes.
9. When goods are **nonexcludable,** there is a **free-rider problem:** consumers will not pay for the good, leading to inefficiently low production. When goods are **nonrival in consumption,** any positive price leads to inefficiently low consumption.
10. A **public good** is nonexcludable and nonrival in consumption. In most cases a public good must be supplied by the government. The marginal social benefit of a public good is equal to the sum of the marginal benefits to each consumer. The efficient quantity of a public good is the quantity at which marginal social benefit equals the marginal social cost of providing the good. As with a positive externality, the marginal social benefit is greater than any one individual's marginal benefit, so no individual is willing to provide the efficient quantity.
11. A **common resource** is rival in consumption but nonexcludable. It is subject to **overuse,** because an individual does not take into account the fact that his or her use depletes the amount available for others. This is similar to the problem with a negative externality: the marginal social cost of an individual's use of a common resource is always higher than his or her individual marginal cost. Pigouvian taxes, the creation of a system of tradable licenses, and the assignment of property rights are possible solutions.
12. **Artificially scarce goods** are excludable but nonrival in consumption. Because no marginal cost arises from allowing another individual to consume the good, the efficient price is zero. A positive price compensates the producer for the cost of production but leads to inefficiently low consumption.

The Economics of the Welfare State

13. The **welfare state** absorbs a large share of government spending in all wealthy countries. **Government transfers** are the payments made by the government to individuals and families. **Poverty programs** alleviate

income inequality by helping the poor; **social insurance programs** alleviate economic insecurity. Welfare state programs also deliver external benefits to society through poverty reduction and improved access to health care, particularly for children.

14. Despite the fact that the **poverty threshold** is adjusted according to the cost of living but not according to the standard of living, and that the average American income has risen substantially over the last 30 years, the **poverty rate,** the percentage of the population with an income below the poverty threshold, is no lower than it was 30 years ago. There are various causes of poverty: lack of education, the legacy of discrimination, and bad luck. The consequences of poverty are particularly harmful for children.

15. **Median household income,** the income of a family at the center of the income distribution, is a better indicator of the income of the typical household than **mean household income** because it is not distorted by the inclusion of a small number of very wealthy households. The **Gini coefficient,** a number that summarizes a country's level of income inequality based on how unequally income is distributed across quintiles, is used to compare income inequality across countries.

16. Both **means-tested** and non-means-tested programs reduce poverty. The major **in-kind benefits** programs are Medicare and Medicaid, which pay for medical care. Due to concerns about the effects on incentives to work and on family cohesion, aid to poor families has become significantly less generous even as the **negative income tax** has become more generous. Social Security, the largest U.S. welfare state program, has significantly reduced poverty among the elderly. Unemployment insurance is also a key social insurance program.

17. Most Americans are covered by employment-based private health insurance; the majority of the remaining are covered by Medicare (for those over 65) or Medicaid (for those with low incomes). The Patient Protection and Affordable Care Act (ACA) was passed in 2010 with the objectives of reducing the number of uninsured and reducing the rate of growth of health care costs.

18. Debates over the size of the welfare state are based on philosophical and equity-versus-efficiency considerations. Although high marginal tax rates to finance an extensive welfare state can reduce the incentive to work, means-testing of programs in order to reduce the cost of the welfare state can also reduce the incentive to work unless carefully designed to avoid notches.

19. Politicians on the left tend to favor a bigger welfare state and those on the right to oppose it. This left–right distinction is central to today's politics.

Key Terms

Marginal social cost of pollution, p. 373
Marginal social benefit of pollution, p. 373
Socially optimal quantity of pollution, p. 373
External cost, p. 375
External benefit, p. 375
Externalities, p. 375
Negative externalities, p. 375
Positive externalities, p. 375
Coase theorem, p. 376
Transaction costs, p. 376
Internalize the externalities, p. 376
Environmental standards, p. 379
Emissions taxes, p. 380
Pigouvian taxes, p. 382
Tradable emissions permits, p. 382
Pigouvian subsidy, p. 386
Technology spillover, p. 386
Network externality, p. 386
Positive feedback, p. 387
Excludable, p. 390
Rival in consumption, p. 390
Private good, p. 390
Nonexcludable, p. 390
Nonrival in consumption, p. 390
Free-rider problem, p. 391
Public good, p. 392
Common resource, p. 395
Overuse, p. 395
Artificially scarce good, p. 397
Welfare state, p. 400
Government transfer, p. 400
Poverty program, p. 401
Social insurance program, p. 401
Poverty threshold, p. 401
Poverty rate, p. 402
Mean household income, p. 404
Median household income, p. 404
Gini coefficient, p. 405
Means-tested, p. 408
In-kind benefit, p. 408
Negative income tax, p. 409

Problems

1. What type of externality (positive or negative) is present in each of the following examples? Is the marginal social benefit of the activity greater than or equal to the marginal benefit to the individual? Is the marginal social cost of the activity greater than or equal to the marginal cost to the individual? Without intervention, will there be too little or too much (relative to what would be socially optimal) of this activity?

   a. Mr. Chau plants lots of colorful flowers in his front yard.

   b. Your next-door neighbor likes to build bonfires in his backyard, and sparks often drift onto your house.

   c. Maija, who lives next to an apple orchard, decides to keep bees to produce honey.

   d. Justine buys a large SUV that consumes a lot of gasoline.

2. The loud music coming from the sorority next to your dorm is a negative externality that can be directly quantified. The accompanying table shows the marginal social benefit and the marginal social cost per decibel (dB, a measure of volume) of music.

Volume of music (dB)	Marginal social benefit of dB	Marginal social cost of dB
90		
	$36	$0
91		
	30	2
92		
	24	4
93		
	18	6
94		
	12	8
95		
	6	10
96		
	0	12
97		

a. Draw the marginal social benefit curve and the marginal social cost curve. Use your diagram to determine the socially optimal volume of music.

b. Only the members of the sorority benefit from the music and they bear none of the cost. Which volume of music will they choose?

c. The college imposes a Pigouvian tax of $3 per decibel of music played. From your diagram, determine the volume of music the sorority will now choose.

3. Many dairy farmers in California are adopting a new technology that allows them to produce their own electricity from methane gas captured from animal wastes. (One cow can produce up to 2 kilowatts a day.) This practice reduces the amount of methane gas released into the atmosphere. In addition to reducing their own utility bills, the farmers are allowed to sell any electricity they produce at favorable rates.

a. Explain how the ability to earn money from capturing and transforming methane gas behaves like a Pigouvian tax on methane gas pollution and can lead dairy farmers to emit the efficient amount of methane gas pollution.

b. Suppose some dairy farmers have lower costs of transforming methane into electricity than others. Explain how this system leads to an efficient allocation of emissions reduction among farmers.

4. According to a report from the U.S. Census Bureau, "the average [lifetime] earnings of a full-time, year round worker with a high school education are about $1.2 million compared with $2.1 million for a college graduate." This indicates that there is a considerable benefit to a graduate from investing in his or her own education. Tuition at most state universities covers only about two-thirds to three-quarters of the cost, so the state applies a Pigouvian subsidy to college education.

If a Pigouvian subsidy is appropriate, is the externality created by a college education a positive or a negative externality? What does this imply about the differences between the costs and benefits to students compared to social costs and benefits? What are some reasons for the differences?

5. The city of Falls Church, Virginia, subsidizes trees planted in homeowners' front yards when they are within 15 feet of the street.

a. Using concepts from this section, explain why a municipality would subsidize trees planted on private property, but near the street.

b. Draw a diagram similar to Figure 37-3 that shows the marginal social benefit, the marginal social cost, and the optimal Pigouvian subsidy on trees.

6. Smoking produces a negative externality because it imposes a health risk on others who inhale second-hand smoke. Cigarette smoking also causes productivity losses to the economy due to the shorter expected life span of a smoker. The U.S. Centers for Disease Control and Prevention (CDC) has estimated the average social cost of smoking a single pack of cigarettes for different states by taking these negative externalities into account. Assume that the accompanying table provides the price of cigarettes and the estimated average social cost of smoking in five states.

State	Cigarette retail price with taxes (per pack)	CDC estimate of smoking cost in 2013 (per pack)
California	$4.40	$15.10
New York	5.82	21.91
Florida	3.80	10.14
Texas	4.76	9.94
Ohio	4.60	9.19

a. At the current level of consumption, what is the optimal retail price of a pack of cigarettes in the different states? Is the current price below or above this optimal price? Does this suggest that the current level of consumption is too high or too low? Explain your answer.

b. In order to deal with negative externalities, state governments currently impose excise taxes on cigarettes. Are current taxes set at the optimal level? Justify your answer.

c. What is the correct size of an additional Pigouvian tax on cigarette sales in the different states if the CDC's estimate for smoking cost does not change with an increase in the retail price of cigarettes?

7. Fishing for sablefish has been so intensive that sablefish were threatened with extinction. After several years of banning such fishing, the government is now proposing to introduce tradable vouchers, each of which entitles its holder to a catch of a certain size. Explain how fishing generates a negative externality and how the voucher scheme may overcome the inefficiency created by this externality.

8. Which of the following are characterized by network externalities? Which are not? Explain.

a. the choice between installing 110-volt electrical current in structures rather than 220-volt

b. the choice between purchasing a Toyota versus a Ford

c. the choice of a printer, where each printer requires its own specific type of ink cartridge

d. the choice of whether to purchase an iPod Touch or an iPod Nano.

9. The government is involved in providing many goods and services. For each of the goods or services listed, determine whether it is rival or nonrival in consumption and whether it is excludable or nonexcludable. What type of good is it? Without government involvement, would the quantity provided be efficient, inefficiently low, or inefficiently high?

a. street signs

b. Amtrak rail service

c. regulations limiting pollution

d. an interstate highway without tolls

e. a lighthouse on the coast

10. A residential community has 100 residents who are concerned about security. The accompanying table gives the total cost of hiring a 24-hour security service as well as each individual resident's total benefit.

Quantity of security guards	Total cost	Total individual benefit to each resident
0	$ 0	$ 0
1	150	10
2	300	16
3	450	18
4	600	19

a. Explain why the security service is a public good for the residents of the community.

b. Calculate the marginal cost, the individual marginal benefit for each resident, and the marginal social benefit.

c. If an individual resident were to decide about hiring and paying for security guards on his or her own, how many guards would that resident hire?

d. If the residents act together, how many security guards will they hire?

11. The accompanying table shows Tanisha's and Ari's individual marginal benefit of different numbers of street cleanings per month. Suppose that the marginal cost of street cleanings is constant at $9 each.

Quantity of street cleanings per month	Tanisha's individual marginal benefit	Ari's individual marginal benefit
0		
	$10	$8
1		
	6	4
2		
	2	1
3		

a. If Tanisha had to pay for street cleaning on her own, how many street cleanings would there be?

b. Calculate the marginal social benefit of street cleaning. What is the optimal number of street cleanings?

c. Consider the optimal number of street cleanings. The last street cleaning of that number costs $9. Is Tanisha willing to pay for that last cleaning on her own? Is Ari willing to pay for that last cleaning on his own?

12. Anyone with a radio receiver can listen to public radio, which is funded largely by donations.

a. Is public radio excludable or nonexcludable? Is it rival in consumption or nonrival? What type of good is it?

b. Should the government support public radio? Explain your reasoning.

c. In order to finance itself, public radio decides to transmit only to satellite radios, for which users have to pay a fee. What type of good is public radio then? Will the quantity of radio listening be efficient? Why or why not?

13. Your economics teacher assigns a group project for the course. Describe the free-rider problem that can lead to a suboptimal outcome for your group. To combat this problem, the instructor asks you to evaluate the contribution of your peers in a confidential report. Will this evaluation have the desired effects?

14. The accompanying table shows six consumers' willingness to pay (his or her individual marginal benefit) for one MP3 file copy of a Jay-Z album. The marginal cost of making the file accessible to one additional consumer is constant, at zero.

Consumer	Individual marginal benefit
Adriana	$ 2
Bhagesh	15
Chizuko	1
Denzel	10
Emma	5
Frank	4

a. What would be the efficient price to charge for a download of the file?

b. All six consumers are able to download the file for free from a file-sharing service, Pantster. Which consumers will download the file? What will be the total consumer surplus to those consumers?

c. Pantster is shut down for copyright law infringement. In order to download the file, consumers now have to pay $4.99 at a commercial music site. Which consumers will download the file? What will be the total consumer surplus to those consumers? How much producer surplus accrues to the commercial music site? What is the total surplus? What is the deadweight loss from the new pricing policy?

15. Software has historically been an artificially scarce good—it is nonrival because the cost of replication is negligible once the investment to write the code is made, but software companies make it excludable by charging for user licenses. Recently, however, open-source software has emerged, most of which is free to download and can be modified and maintained by anyone.

a. Discuss the free-rider problem that might exist in the development of open-source software. What effect might this have on quality? Why does this problem not exist for proprietary software, such as the products of a company like Microsoft or Adobe?

b. Some argue that open-source software serves an unsatisfied market demand that proprietary software ignores. Draw a typical diagram that illustrates how proprietary software may be underproduced. Put the price and marginal cost of software on the vertical axis and the quantity of software on the horizontal axis. Draw a typical demand curve and a marginal cost curve (*MC*) that is always equal to zero. Assume that the software company charges a positive price, *P*, for the software. Label the equilibrium point and the efficient point.

16. The two dry-cleaning companies in Collegetown, College Cleaners and Big Green Cleaners, are a major source of air pollution. Together they currently produce 350 units of air pollution, which the town wants to reduce to 200 units. The accompanying table shows the current pollution level produced by each company and each company's marginal cost of reducing its pollution. The marginal cost is constant.

Company	Initial pollution level (units)	Marginal cost of reducing pollution (per unit)
College Cleaners	230	$5
Big Green Cleaners	120	2

a. Suppose that Collegetown passes an environmental standards law that limits each company to 100 units of pollution. What would be the total cost to the two companies of each reducing its pollution emissions to 100 units?

Suppose instead that Collegetown issues 100 pollution vouchers to each company, each entitling the company to one unit of pollution, and that these vouchers can be traded.

b. How much is each pollution voucher worth to College Cleaners? to Big Green Cleaners? (That is, how much would each company, at most, be willing to pay for one more voucher?)

c. Who will sell vouchers and who will buy them? How many vouchers will be traded?

d. What is the total cost to the two companies of the pollution controls under this voucher system?

17. Ronald owns a cattle farm at the source of a long river. His cattle's waste flows into the river and down many miles to where Carla lives. Carla gets her drinking water from the river. By allowing his cattle's waste to flow into the river, Ronald imposes a negative externality on Carla. In each of the two following cases, do you think that through negotiation, Ronald and Carla can find an efficient solution? What might this solution look like?

a. There are no telephones, and for Carla to talk to Ronald, she has to travel for two days on a rocky road.

b. Carla and Ronald both have e-mail access, making it costless for them to communicate.

18. In the city of Metropolis, there are 100 residents, each of whom lives until age 75. Residents of Metropolis have the following incomes over their lifetime: Through age 14, they earn nothing. From age 15 until age 29, they earn 200 metros (the currency of Metropolis) per year. From age 30 to age 49, they earn 400 metros. From age 50 to age 64, they earn 300 metros. Finally, at age 65 they retire and are paid a pension of 100 metros per year until they die at age 75. Each year, everyone consumes whatever their income is that year (that is, there is no saving and no borrowing). Currently, 20 residents are 10 years old, 20 residents are 20 years old, 20 residents are 40 years old, 20 residents are 60 years old, and 20 residents are 70 years old.

a. Study the income distribution among all residents of Metropolis. Split the population into quintiles according to their income. How much income does a resident in the lowest quintile have? In the second, third, fourth, and top quintiles? What share of total income of all residents goes to the residents in each quintile? Construct a table showing the share of total income that goes to each quintile. Does this income distribution show inequality?

b. Now look only at the 20 residents of Metropolis who are currently 40 years old, and study the income distribution among only those residents. Split those 20 residents into quintiles according to their income. How much income does a resident in the lowest quintile have? In the second, third, fourth, and top quintiles? What share of total income of all 40-year-olds goes to the residents in each quintile? Does this income distribution show inequality?

c. What is the relevance of these examples for assessing data on the distribution of income in any country?

19. The accompanying table presents data from the U.S. Census Bureau on median and mean income of male workers for the years 1972 and 2009. The income figures are adjusted to eliminate the effect of inflation.

Year	Median income (in 2009 dollars)	Mean income (in 2009 dollars)
1972	$34,159	$39,593
2009	32,184	46,800

Source: U.S. Census Bureau.

a. By what percentage has median income changed over this period? By what percentage has mean income changed over this period?

b. Between 1972 and 2009, has the income distribution become less or more unequal? Explain.

20. There are 100 households in the economy of Equalor. Initially, 99 of them have an income of $10,000 each, and one household has an income of $1,010,000.

    a. What is the median income in this economy? What is the mean income?

    Through its poverty programs, the government of Equalor now redistributes income: it takes $990,000 away from the richest household and distributes it equally among the remaining 99 households.

    b. What is the median income in this economy now? What is the mean income? Has the median income changed? Has the mean income changed? Which indicator (mean or median household income) is a better indicator of the typical Equalorian household's income? Explain.

21. The tax system in Taxilvania includes a negative income tax. For all incomes below $10,000, individuals pay an income tax of –40% (that is, they receive a payment of 40% of their income). For any income above the $10,000 threshold, the tax rate on that additional income is 10%. For the first three scenarios below, calculate the amount of income tax to be paid and after-tax income.

    a. Lowani earns income of $8,000.

    b. Midram earns income of $40,000.

    c. Hi-Wan earns income of $100,000.

    d. Can you find a notch in this tax system? That is, can you find a situation where earning more pre-tax income actually results in less after-tax income?

22. In the city of Notchingham, each worker is paid a wage rate of $10 per hour. Notchingham administers its own unemployment benefit, which is structured as follows: If you are unemployed (that is, if you do not work at all), you get unemployment benefits (a transfer from the government) of $50 per day. As soon as you work for only one hour, the unemployment benefit is completely withdrawn. That is, there is a notch in the benefit system.

    a. How much income does an unemployed person have per day? How much daily income does an individual who works four hours per day have? How many hours do you need to work to earn just the same as if you were unemployed?

    b. Will anyone ever accept a part-time job that requires working four hours per day, rather than being unemployed?

    c. Suppose that Notchingham now changes the way in which the unemployment benefit is withdrawn. For each additional dollar an individual earns, $0.50 of the unemployment benefit is withdrawn. How much daily income does an individual who works four hours per day now have? Is there an incentive now to work four hours per day rather than being unemployed?

23. The accompanying table shows data on the total number of people in the United States and the number of all people who were uninsured, for selected years from 1999 to 2009. It also shows data on the total number of poor children in the United States—those under 18 and below the poverty threshold—and the number of poor children who were uninsured.

Year	Total people	Uninsured people	Total poor children	Uninsured poor children
	(millions)			
1999	276.8	38.8	12.3	2.8
2001	282.1	39.8	11.7	2.4
2003	288.3	43.4	12.9	2.4
2005	293.8	44.8	12.9	2.4
2007	299.1	45.7	13.3	2.3
2009	304.3	50.7	15.5	2.3

Source: U.S. Census Bureau.

For each year, calculate the percentage of all people who were uninsured and the percentage of poor children who were uninsured. How have these percentages changed over time? What is a possible explanation for the change in the percentage of uninsured poor children?

24. The American National Election Studies conducts periodic research on the opinions of U.S. voters. The accompanying table shows the percentage of people, in selected years from 1952 to 2008, who agreed with the statement "There are important differences in what the Republicans and Democrats stand for."

Year	Agree with statement
1952	50%
1972	46
1992	60
2004	76
2008	78

Source: American National Election Studies.

What do these data say about the degree of partisanship in U.S. politics over time?

MODULE 41

Marginal Productivity Theory

Kurhan/Shutterstock

WHAT YOU WILL LEARN

1. Labor market applications of the marginal productivity theory of income distribution
2. Sources of wage disparities and the role of discrimination

In the previous module we introduced the factor distribution of income. In this module, we will go a step further and explain how the *marginal productivity theory of income distribution* helps to explain how income is divided among factors of production in an economy. We will consider how the markets for factors of production are broken down. There are different markets for different types of factors. For example, there are different labor markets for different types of labor, such as for computer programmers, pastry chefs, and economists. Then, we look at the marginal productivity theory of income distribution and the extent to which it explains wage disparities between workers.

The Marginal Productivity Theory of Income Distribution

The **marginal productivity theory of income distribution** sums up what we have learned about payments to factors when goods markets and factor markets are perfectly competitive. According to this theory, each factor is paid the value of the output generated by the last unit of that factor employed in the factor market as a whole—its **equilibrium value of the marginal product.**

According to the **marginal productivity theory of income distribution,** every factor of production is paid the equilibrium value of its marginal product.

The **equilibrium value of the marginal product** of a factor is the additional value produced by the last unit of that factor employed in the factor market as a whole.

To understand why the marginal productivity theory of income distribution is important, look back at Figure 40-1, which shows the factor distribution of income in the United States in 2012, and ask yourself this question: who or what determined that labor would get 71% of total U.S. income? Why not 90% or 50%?

The answer, according to this theory, is that the division of income among the economy's factors of production isn't arbitrary: in the economy-wide factor market, the price paid for each factor is equal to the increase in the value of output generated by the last unit of that factor employed in the market. Therefore, if a unit of labor is paid more than a unit of capital, it is because at the equilibrium quantity of each factor, the value of the marginal product of labor exceeds the value of the marginal product of capital.

So far we have treated factor markets as if every unit of each factor were identical. That is, as if all land were identical, all labor were identical, and all capital were identical. But in reality factors differ considerably with respect to productivity. For instance, land resources differ in their ability to produce crops and workers have different skills and abilities.

Rather than thinking of one land market for all land resources in an economy, and similarly one capital market and one labor market, we can instead think of different markets for different types of land, physical capital, human capital, and labor. For example, the market for computer programmers is different from the market for pastry chefs.

When we consider that there are separate factor markets for different types of factors, the marginal productivity theory of income distribution still holds. That is, when the labor market for computer programmers is in equilibrium, the wage rate earned by all computer programmers is equal to the market's equilibrium value of the marginal product—the value of the marginal product of the last computer programmer hired in that market.

The marginal productivity theory can explain the distribution of income among different types of land, labor, physical capital, and human capital as well as the distribution of income among the factors of production. Next we look more closely at the distribution of income between different types of labor and the extent to which the marginal productivity theory of income distribution explains differences in workers' wages.

ECONOMICS ▶ *IN ACTION*

HELP WANTED!

Hamill Manufacturing of Pennsylvania makes precision components for military helicopters and nuclear submarines. Their highly skilled senior machinists are well paid compared to other workers in manufacturing, earning nearly $70,000 in 2011, excluding benefits. Like most skilled machinists in the United States, Hamill's machinists are very productive: according to the U.S. Census Annual Survey of Manufacturers, in 2010 the average skilled machinist generated approximately $137,000 in value added.

Fatihhoca/Getty Images

The marginal productivity theory of income distribution holds for skilled machinists at Hamill Manufacturing.

But there is a $67,000 difference between the salary paid to Hamill machinists and the value added they generate. Does this mean that the marginal productivity theory of income distribution doesn't hold? Doesn't the theory imply that machinists should be paid $137,000, the average value added that each one generates?

The answer is no, for two reasons. First, the $137,000 figure is averaged over *all machinists currently employed.* The theory says that machinists will be paid the value of the marginal product of the *last machinist hired,* and due to diminishing returns to labor, that value will be lower than the average over all machinists currently employed. Second, a worker's equilibrium wage rate includes other costs, such as employee benefits, that have to be added to the $70,000 salary. The marginal productivity theory of income distribution says that workers are paid a wage rate, *including all benefits,* equal to the value of the marginal product.

You can see all these costs are present at Hamill. There the machinists have good benefits and job security, which add to their salary. Including these benefits, machinists' total compensation will be equal to the value of the marginal product of the last machinist employed.

In Hamill's case, there is yet another factor that explains the $67,000 gap: there are not enough machinists at the current wage rate. Although the company increased the number of employees from 85 in 2004 to 125 in 2011, they would like to hire more.

FIGURE 42-4 **Firm Labor Demand with Imperfect Competition**

A firm's labor demand curve is the marginal revenue product of labor curve, which differs from the value of the marginal product of labor curve when there is imperfect competition in the product market (as with a monopoly, for example). With perfect competition, the marginal revenue product of labor ($MPL \times MR$) and the value of the marginal product of labor ($MPL \times P$) are the same because $MR = P$.

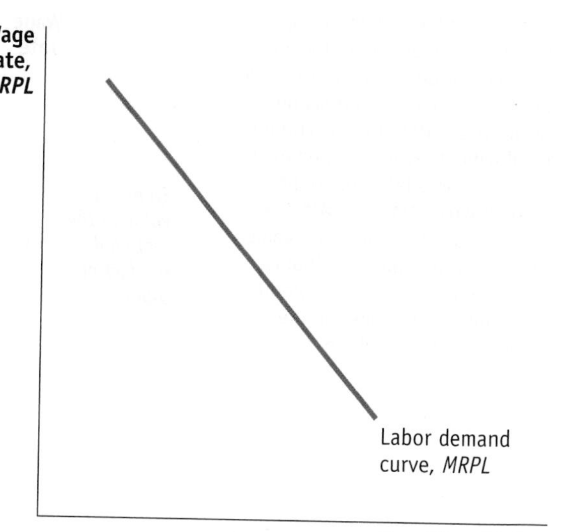

In the case of a firm operating in an imperfectly competitive product market, the demand curve for a factor is the marginal revenue product curve, as shown in Figure 42-4.

When the Labor Market Is Not Perfectly Competitive

There are also important differences when considering the labor demand curve for a firm in an imperfectly competitive *labor* market rather than in a perfectly competitive labor market. With perfect competition in the labor market, each firm is so small that it can hire as much labor as it wants at the market wage. The firm's hiring decision will not affect the market. In contrast, a firm in an imperfectly competitive labor market is large enough to affect the market wage. A labor market in which there is only one firm hiring labor is called a **monopsony.** A **monopsonist** is the single buyer of a factor. Perhaps you've seen a small town where one firm, such as a meatpacking company or a lumber mill, hires most of the labor—that's an example of a monopsony. Since the firm already hires most of the available labor in the town, if it wants to hire more workers, it has to offer higher wages to attract them.

A **monopsonist** is a single buyer in a factor market. A market in which there is a monopsonist is a **monopsony.**

MODULE 42 Review

Solutions appear at the back of the book.

Check Your Understanding

1. Formerly, Clive was free to work as many or as few hours per week as he wanted. But a new law limits the maximum number of hours he can work per week to 35. Explain under what circumstances, if any, he is made
   - a. worse off.
   - b. equally well off.
   - c. better off.
2. Explain in terms of the income and substitution effects how a fall in Clive's wage rate can induce him to work more hours than before.

Multiple-Choice Questions

1. Which of the following is necessarily true if you work more when your wage rate increases?
   - a. The income effect is large.
   - b. The substitution effect is small.
   - c. The income effect dominates the substitution effect.
   - d. The substitution effect dominates the income effect.
   - e. The income effect equals the substitution effect.
2. Which of the following will cause you to work more as your wage rate decreases?
   - I. the income effect
   - II. the substitution effect
   - III. a desire for leisure
   - a. I only
   - b. II only
   - c. III only
   - d. I and II only
   - e. I, II, and III
3. Which of the following will shift the supply curve for labor to the right?
   - a. a decrease in the labor force participation rate of women
   - b. a decrease in population
   - c. an increase in wealth
   - d. a decrease in the opportunity cost of leisure
   - e. an increase in labor market opportunities for women
4. An increase in the wage rate will
   - a. shift the labor supply curve to the right.
   - b. shift the labor supply curve to the left.
   - c. cause an upward movement along the labor supply curve.
   - d. cause a downward movement along the labor supply curve.
   - e. have no effect on the quantity of labor supplied.
5. Which of the following statements about the U.S. labor force since World War II is incorrect?
   - a. Increases in population have shifted the labor supply curve to the right.
   - b. Increases in immigration have shifted the labor supply curve to the right.
   - c. Increases in educational opportunities for women have shifted the labor supply curve to the right.
   - d. Decreases in work opportunities in foreign markets have shifted the labor supply curve to the right.
   - e. Disillusionment with the state of the job market during a recession has shifted the labor supply curve to the left.

Critical-Thinking Questions

1. Draw a correctly labeled graph showing a perfectly competitive labor market in equilibrium. On your graph, label the labor demand curve, the labor supply curve, marginal revenue product of labor, the equilibrium wage (W^*), and the equilibrium quantity of labor (L^*).
2. Then, on the same graph, illustrate how a decrease in the price of the product made by the firm would affect the equilibrium wage and quantity of labor. Label the resulting wage rate W_2 and the resulting quantity of labor L_2.

BUSINESS CASE: Alta Gracia: Can Fair Trade Work?

Check out a T-shirt or sweatshirt emblazoned with your school's logo at your campus bookstore, and the odds are very good that it was made by Alta Gracia, the leading supplier of college-logo apparel to American universities. Alta Gracia is owned by Knights Apparel, a company based in Spartanburg, South Carolina, that manufactures apparel in 30 factories around the world. The Alta Gracia factory is located in the Dominican Republic, where 120 employees turn out T-shirts and sweats.

Julian Eales/Alamy

Workers at Alta Gracia consider themselves lucky because the company pays what it considers a "living wage"—sufficient to feed and shelter a family of four—and allows workers to join a union. Seamstress Santa Castillo, for example, earns $500 a month, three times the average monthly pay of $147 earned by apparel workers in the Dominican Republic, where a loaf of bread costs $1.

Workers at the factory have not always been so fortunate. When the factory was owned by another company, BJ&B, which made baseball caps for Nike and Reebok, workers were paid the prevailing wage and were fired if they complained about working conditions or tried to form a union. Eventually, BJ&B moved its operations to lower-wage Bangladesh, where the minimum wage is 15 cents an hour, compared to 85 cents an hour in the Dominican Republic. In contrast, Alta Gracia pays $2.83 an hour.

Joe Bozich started Knights Apparel in 2000; through scores of deals he has made with universities, his company has surpassed Nike as the number-one college supplier. He works closely with the Worker Rights Consortium, a group of 186 universities that press college-logo apparel manufacturers to improve workers' welfare. The consortium is part of the "Fair Trade Movement," an organization dedicated to improving the welfare of workers in developing countries, principally by raising wages. In 2011, $6.6 billion of Fair Trade–approved goods were sold globally, up 12% from 2010.

Alta Gracia was conceived by Bozich as a model factory to show that an apparel manufacturer could pay its workers a living wage and still succeed when competitors are paying their workers much less. Its production cost for a T-shirt is $4.80—80 cents, or 20%, higher than if it paid minimum wage. Knights Apparel accepts a lower profit margin so it doesn't have to ask retailers to pay a higher wholesale price for its merchandise.

Some observers, though, are skeptical because Alta Gracia merchandise is sold alongside products made by Nike and Adidas, at approximately the same premium price these well-known brands command. "It's a noble effort, but it is an experiment," says Andrew Jassin, an industry analyst. "There are consumers who really care and will buy this apparel at a premium price, and there are those who say they care, but just want value."

Kellie McElhaney, a professor of corporate social responsibility at the University of California at Berkeley, is less skeptical: "A lot of college students would much rather pay for a brand that shows workers are treated well."

Questions for Thought

1. Use the marginal productivity theory of income distribution to explain how the prevailing wage for apparel workers can fall below a living wage in the Dominican Republic.
2. From the point of view of Knights Apparel, what are the pros and cons of paying the Alta Gracia workers a living wage? What are the pros and cons from the point of view of workers generally?
3. What factors does the success or failure of Alta Gracia depend on? What should Knights Apparel do to improve its chances of success?

SECTION 13 REVIEW

Summary

Factor Markets

1. Just as there are markets for goods and services, there are markets for factors of production, including labor, land, and both *physical capital* and *human capital.* These markets determine the **factor distribution of income.**
2. A profit-maximizing, price-taking firm will keep employing more units of a factor until the factor's price is equal to the **value of the marginal product**—the marginal product of the factor multiplied by the price of the output it produces. The **value of the marginal product curve** is therefore the price-taking firm's demand curve for a factor. Factor demand is often referred to as a **derived demand** because it is derived from the demand for the producer's output.
3. The market demand curve for labor is the horizontal sum of the individual demand curves of firms in that market. It shifts for three main reasons: changes in the prices of goods, changes in the supply of other factors, and technological changes.

Marginal Productivity Theory

4. According to the **marginal productivity theory of income distribution,** each factor is paid the value of the marginal product of the last unit of that factor employed in the factor market as a whole—its **equilibrium value of the marginal product.**
5. Large disparities in wages raise questions about the validity of the marginal productivity theory of income distribution. Many disparities can be explained by **compensating differentials** and by differences in talent, job experience, and human capital across workers. Market interference in the forms of **unions** and collective action by employers also creates wage disparities. The **efficiency-wage model,** which arises from a type of market failure, shows how wage disparities can result from employers' attempts to increase worker performance. Free markets tend to diminish discrimination, but discrimination remains a real source of wage disparity. Discrimination is typically maintained either through problems in labor markets or (historically) through institutionalization in government policies.

The Market for Labor

6. Labor supply is the result of decisions about **time allocation,** with each worker facing a trade-off between **leisure** and work. An increase in the hourly wage rate tends to increase work hours via the substitution effect but decrease work hours via the income effect. If the net result is that a worker increases the quantity of labor supplied in response to a higher wage, the **individual labor supply curve** slopes upward. If the net result is that a worker decreases work hours, the individual labor supply curve—unlike supply curves for goods and services—slopes downward.
7. The market labor supply curve is the horizontal sum of the individual labor supply curves of all workers in that market. It shifts for four main reasons: changes in preferences and social norms, changes in population, changes in opportunities, and changes in wealth.
8. When a firm is not a price-taker in a factor market, the firm will consider the **marginal revenue product** when determining how much of a factor to hire. This concept is equivalent to the value of the marginal product in a perfectly competitive market.
9. A **monopsonist** is the single buyer of a factor. A market in which there is a monopsonist is a **monopsony.**

Key Terms

Problems

1. Assume that in 2012 national income in the United States was $11,186.9 billion. In the same year, 137 million workers were employed, at an average wage of $57,526 per worker per year.

   a. How much compensation of employees was paid in the United States in 2012?

   b. Analyze the factor distribution of income. What percentage of national income was received in the form of compensation to employees in 2012?

   c. Suppose the supply of labor rises due to an increase in the retirement age. What happens to the percentage of national income received in the form of compensation of employees?

2. Marty's Frozen Yogurt has the production function per day shown in the accompanying table. The equilibrium wage rate for a worker is $80 per day. Each cup of frozen yogurt sells for $2.

Quantity of labor (workers)	Quantity of frozen yogurt (cups)
0	0
1	110
2	200
3	270
4	300
5	320
6	330

   a. Calculate the marginal product of labor for each worker and the value of the marginal product of labor per worker.

   b. How many workers should Marty employ?

3. Patty's Pizza Parlor has the production function per hour shown in the accompanying table. The hourly wage rate for each worker is $10. Each pizza sells for $2.

Quantity of labor (workers)	Quantity of pizza
0	0
1	9
2	15
3	19
4	22
5	24

   a. Calculate the marginal product of labor for each worker and the value of the marginal product of labor per worker.

   b. Draw the value of the marginal product of labor curve. Use your diagram to determine how many workers Patty should employ.

   c. Now the price of pizza increases to $4. Calculate the value of the marginal product of labor per worker, and draw the new value of the marginal product of labor curve in your diagram. Use your diagram to determine how many workers Patty should employ now.

4. The production function for Patty's Pizza Parlor is given in the table in Problem 3. The price of pizza is $2, but the hourly wage rate rises from $10 to $15. Use a diagram to determine how Patty's demand for workers responds as a result of this wage rate increase.

5. Patty's Pizza Parlor initially had the production function given in the table in Problem 3. A worker's hourly wage rate was $10, and pizza sold for $2. Now Patty buys a new high-tech pizza oven that allows her workers to become twice as productive as before. That is, the first worker now produces 18 pizzas per hour instead of 9, and so on.

   a. Calculate the new marginal product of labor and the new value of the marginal product of labor.

   b. Use a diagram to determine how Patty's hiring decision responds to this increase in the productivity of her workforce.

6. Jameel runs a driver education school. The more driving instructors he hires, the more driving lessons he can sell. But because he owns a limited number of training automobiles, each additional driving instructor adds less to Jameel's output of driving lessons. The accompanying table shows Jameel's production function per day. Each driving lesson can be sold at $35 per hour.

Quantity of labor (driving instructors)	Quantity of driving lessons (hours)
0	0
1	8
2	15
3	21
4	26
5	30
6	33

   Determine Jameel's labor demand schedule (his demand schedule for driving instructors) for each of the following daily wage rates for driving instructors: $160, $180, $200, $220, $240, and $260.

7. Dale and Dana work at a self-service gas station and convenience store. Dale opens up every day, and Dana arrives later to help stock the store. They are both paid the current market wage of $9.50 per hour. But Dale feels he should be paid much more because the revenue generated from the gas pumps he turns on every morning is much higher than the revenue generated by the items that Dana stocks. Assess this argument.

8. Your local newspaper publishes an article stating that the wage of farmworkers in Mexico is $11 an hour but the wage of immigrant Mexican farmworkers in California is $9 an hour.

   a. Assume that the output sells for the same price in the two countries. Does this imply that the marginal product of labor of farmworkers is higher in Mexico or in California? Explain your answer, and illustrate with a diagram that shows the demand and supply curves for labor in the respective markets. In your diagram, assume that the quantity supplied of labor for any given wage rate is the same for Mexican farmworkers as it is for immigrant Mexican farmworkers in California.

   b. Now suppose that farmwork in Mexico is more arduous and more dangerous than farmwork in California. As a result, the quantity supplied of labor for any given wage rate is not the same for Mexican farmworkers as it is for immigrant Mexican farmworkers in California. How does this change your answer to part a? What concept best accounts for the difference between wage rates between Mexican farmworkers and immigrant Mexican farmworkers in California?

   c. Illustrate your answer to part b with a diagram. In this diagram, assume that the quantity of labor demanded for any given wage rate is the same for Mexican employers as it is for Californian employers.

9. Research consistently finds that despite nondiscrimination policies, African-American workers on average receive lower wages than White workers do. What are the possible reasons for this? Are these reasons consistent with marginal productivity theory?

10. Wendy works at a fast-food restaurant. When her wage rate was $5 per hour, she worked 30 hours per week. When her wage rate rose to $6 per hour, she decided to work 40 hours. But when her wage rate rose further to $7, she decided to work only 35 hours.

    a. Draw Wendy's individual labor supply curve.

    b. Is Wendy's behavior irrational, or can you find a rational explanation? Explain your answer.

11. You are the governor's economic policy adviser. The governor wants to put in place policies that encourage employed people to work more hours at their jobs and that encourage unemployed people to find and take jobs. Assess each of the following policies in terms of reaching that goal. Explain your reasoning in terms of income and substitution effects, and indicate when the impact of the policy may be ambiguous.

    a. The state income tax rate is lowered, which has the effect of increasing workers' after-tax wage rate.

    b. The state income tax rate is increased, which has the effect of decreasing workers' after-tax wage rate.

    c. The state property tax rate is increased, which reduces workers' after-tax income.

12. A study by economists at the Federal Reserve Bank of Boston found that between 1965 and 2003 the average American's leisure time increased by between 4 and 8 hours a week. The study claims that this increase is primarily driven by a rise in wage rates.

    a. Use the income and substitution effects to describe the labor supply for the average American. Which effect dominates?

    b. The study also found an increase in female labor force participation—more women were choosing to hold jobs rather than exclusively perform household tasks. For the average woman who had newly entered the labor force, which effect dominates?

    c. Draw typical individual labor supply curves that illustrate your answers to part a and part b above.

SECTION 14

Additional Topics in Microeconomics

This section includes three modules devoted to additional topics in microeconomics. The modules cover the cost-minimizing input combination, the time value of money, and the economics of information, topics which are an important part of contemporary economic theory. These modules complement some of what you've learned in earlier sections. And if you continue your study of economics, you will see these topics again in future courses.

MODULE

43 The Cost-Minimizing Input Combination

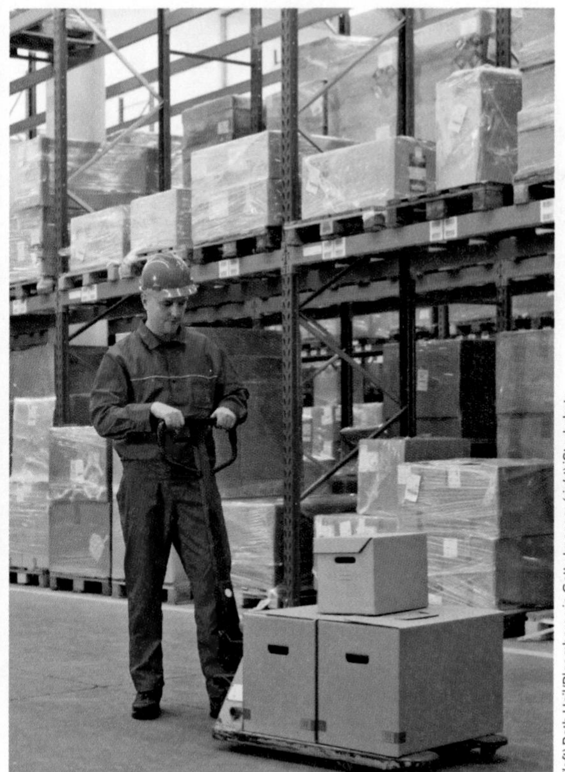

(left) Beth Hall/Bloomberg via Getty Images; (right) iStockphoto

WHAT YOU WILL LEARN

1. How firms determine the optimal input mix
2. The cost-minimizing rule for hiring inputs

In the previous section we discussed the markets for factors of production and how firms determine the optimal quantity of each factor to hire. But firms don't determine how much of each input to hire separately. Production requires multiple inputs, and firms must decide what *combination* of inputs to use to produce their output. In this module, we will look at how firms decide the optimal combination of factors for producing the desired level of output.

Alternative Input Combinations

In many instances a firm can choose among a number of alternative combinations of inputs that will produce a given level of output. For example, on George and Martha's wheat farm, the decision might involve labor and capital. To produce their optimal quantity of wheat, they could choose to have a relatively *capital-intensive* operation by investing in several tractors and other mechanized farm equipment and hiring relatively little labor. Alternatively, they could have a more *labor-intensive* operation by hiring a lot of workers to do much of the planting and harvesting by hand.

The same amount of wheat can be produced using many different combinations of capital and labor. George and Martha must determine which combination of inputs will maximize their profits.

To begin our study of the optimal combination of inputs, we'll look at the relationship between the inputs used for production. Depending on the situation, inputs can be either substitutes or complements.

Substitutes and Complements in Factor Markets

Early in this book we discussed substitutes and complements in the context of the supply and demand model. Two goods are *substitutes* if a rise in the price of one good makes consumers more willing to buy the other good. For example, an increase in the price of oranges will cause some buyers to switch from purchasing oranges to purchasing tangerines.

When buyers tend to consume two goods together, the goods are known as *complements*. For example, cereal and milk are considered complements because many people consume them together. If the price of cereal increases, people will buy less cereal and therefore need less milk. The decision about how much of a good to buy is influenced by the prices of related goods.

The concepts of substitutes and complements also apply to a firm's purchase of inputs. And just as the price of related goods affects consumers' purchasing decisions, the price of other inputs can affect a firm's decision about how much of an input it will use. In some situations, capital and labor are substitutes. For example, George and Martha can produce the same amount of wheat by substituting more tractors for fewer farm workers. Likewise, ATM machines can substitute for bank tellers.

Capital and labor can also be complements when more of one increases the marginal product of the other. For example, a farm worker is more productive when George and Martha buy a tractor, and each tractor requires a worker to drive it. Office workers are more productive when they can use faster computers, and doctors are more productive with modern X-ray machines. In these cases the quantity and quality of capital available affect the marginal product of labor, and thus the demand for labor.

iStockphoto

ATMs can substitute for bank tellers.

Given the relationship between inputs, how does a firm determine which of the possible combinations to use?

Determining the Optimal Input Mix

If several alternative input combinations can be used to produce the optimal level of output, a profit-maximizing firm will select the input combination with the lowest cost. This process is known as cost minimization.

Cost Minimization

How does a firm determine the combination of inputs that maximizes profits? Let's consider this question using an example.

Imagine you manage a grocery store chain and you need to decide the right combination of self-checkout stations and cashiers at a new store. Table 43-1 shows the alternative combinations of capital (self-checkout stations) and labor (cashiers) you can hire to check out customers shopping at the store. If the store puts in 20 self-checkout stations, you will need to hire 1 cashier to monitor every 5 stations for a total of 4 cashiers. However, trained cashiers are faster than customers at scanning goods, so the store could check out the same number of customers using 10 cashiers and only 10 self-checkout stations.

If you can check out the same number of customers using either of these combinations of capital and labor, how do you decide which combination of inputs to use? By finding the input combination that costs the least—the cost-minimizing input combination.

TABLE 43-1

Cashiers and Self-Checkout Stations

	Capital (self-checkout stations)	Labor (cashiers)
	Rental rate = $1,000/month	Wage rate = $1,600/month
a.	20	4
b.	10	10

Assume that the cost to rent, operate, and maintain a self-checkout station for a month is $1,000 and hiring a cashier costs $1,600 per month. The cost of each input combination from Table 43-1 is shown below.

a.	Cost of capital	20 × $1,000 = $20,000
	Cost of labor	4 × $1,600 = $ 6,400
	Total	**$26,400**
b.	Cost of capital	10 × $1,000 = $10,000
	Cost of labor	10 × $1,600 = $16,000
	Total	**$26,000**

Aleph Studio/Shutterstock

What is the right combination of cashiers and self-checkout stations?

Clearly, your firm would choose the lower cost combination, combination b, and hire 10 cashiers and put in 10 self-checkout stations.

When firms must choose between alternative combinations of inputs, they evaluate the cost of each combination and select the one that minimizes the cost of production. This can be done by calculating the total cost of each alternative combination of inputs, as shown in this example. However, because the number of possible combinations can be very large, it is more practical to use marginal analysis to find the cost-minimizing level of output—which brings us to the cost-minimization rule.

The Cost-Minimization Rule

We already know that the additional output that results from hiring an additional unit of an input is the marginal product (*MP*) of that input. Firms want to receive the highest possible marginal product from each dollar spent on inputs. To do this, firms adjust their hiring of inputs until the marginal product per dollar is equal for all inputs. This is the **cost-minimization rule.** When the inputs are labor and capital, this amounts to equating the marginal product of labor (*MPL*) per dollar spent on wages to the marginal product of capital (*MPK*) per dollar spent to rent capital:

(43-1) $MPL/\text{Wage} = MPK/\text{Rental rate}$

To understand why cost minimization occurs when the marginal product per dollar is equal for all inputs, let's start by looking at two counterexamples. Consider a situation in which the marginal product of labor per dollar is greater than the marginal product of capital per dollar. This situation is described by Equation 43-2:

(43-2) $MPL/\text{Wage} > MPK/\text{Rental rate}$

Suppose the marginal product of labor is 20 units and the marginal product of capital is 100 units. If the wage is $10 and the rental rate for capital is $100, then the marginal product per dollar will be 20/$10 = 2 units of output per dollar for labor and 100/$100 = 1 unit of output per dollar for capital. The firm is receiving 2 additional units of output for each dollar spent on labor and only 1 additional unit of output for each dollar spent on capital. In this case, the firm gets more additional output for its money by hiring labor, so it should hire more labor and less capital.

Because of diminishing returns, as the firm hires more labor, the marginal product of labor falls and as it hires less capital, the marginal product of capital rises. The firm will continue to substitute labor for capital until the falling marginal product of labor per dollar meets the rising marginal product of capital per dollar and the two are equivalent. That is, the firm will adjust its hiring of capital and labor until the marginal product per dollar spent on each input is equal, as in Equation 43-1.

A firm determines the cost-minimizing combination of inputs using the **cost-minimization rule:** hire factors so that the marginal product per dollar spent on each factor is the same.

Next, consider a situation in which the marginal product of capital per dollar is greater than the marginal product of labor per dollar. This situation is described by Equation 43-3:

(43-3) *MPL*/Wage < *MPK*/Rental rate

Let's continue with the assumption that the marginal product of labor for the last unit of labor hired is 20 units and the marginal product of capital for the last unit of capital hired is 100 units. If the wage is \$10 and the rental rate for capital is \$25, then the marginal product per dollar will be 20/\$10 = 2 units of output per dollar for labor and 100/\$25 = 4 units of output per dollar for capital. The firm is receiving 4 additional units of output for each dollar spent on capital and only 2 additional units of output for each dollar spent on labor. In this case, the firm gets more additional output for its money by hiring capital, so it should hire more capital and less labor.

Because of diminishing returns, as the firm hires more capital, the marginal product of capital falls, and as it hires less labor, the marginal product of labor rises. The firm will continue to hire more capital and less labor until the falling marginal product of capital per dollar meets the rising marginal product of labor per dollar to satisfy the cost-minimization rule. That is, the firm will adjust its hiring of capital and labor until the marginal product per dollar spent on each input is equal.

The cost-minimization rule is analogous to the optimal consumption rule (introduced in the module on maximizing utility): consumers maximize their utility by choosing the combination of goods so that the marginal utility per dollar is equal for all goods.

Module 43 Review

Solutions appear at the back of the book.

Check Your Understanding

1. A firm produces its output using only capital and labor. Labor costs \$100 per worker per day and capital costs \$200 per unit per day. If the marginal product of the last worker employed is 500 and the marginal product of the last unit of capital employed is 1,000, is the firm employing the cost-minimizing combination of inputs? Explain.

Multiple-Choice Questions

1. An automobile factory employs either assembly-line workers or robotic arms to produce automobile engines. In this case, labor and capital are considered
   - **a.** independent.
   - **b.** complements.
   - **c.** substitutes.
   - **d.** supplements.
   - **e.** human capital.

2. If an increase in the amount of capital employed by a firm leads to an increase in the marginal product of labor, labor and capital are considered
   - **a.** independent.
   - **b.** complements.
   - **c.** substitutes.
   - **d.** supplements.
   - **e.** human capital.

3. If the marginal product of labor per dollar is greater than the marginal product of capital per dollar, which of the following is true? The firm should
   - **a.** not change its employment of capital and labor.
   - **b.** hire more capital.
   - **c.** hire more labor.
   - **d.** hire less labor.
   - **e.** hire more capital and labor.

4. The cost-minimization rule states that costs are minimized when
   - **a.** *MP* per dollar is equal for all factors.
   - **b.** ($MP \times P$) is equal for all factors.
   - **c.** each factor's *MP* is the same.
   - **d.** consumers maximize their utility.
   - **e.** *MPL* falls.

5. A firm currently produces its desired level of output. Its marginal product of labor is 400, its marginal product of capital is 1,000, the wage rate is $20 and the rental rate of capital is $100. In that case, the firm should
   a. employ more capital and more labor.
   b. employ less labor and less capital.
   c. employ less labor and more capital.
   d. employ less capital and more labor.
   e. not change its allocation of capital and labor.

Critical-Thinking Questions

Refer to the accompanying table to answer the questions. Assume that the wage is $10 per day and the price of pencils is $1.

Quantity of labor (workers)	Quantity produced (pencils)
0	0
1	40
2	90
3	120
4	140
5	150
6	160
7	166

1. What is the *MPL* of the 4th worker?
2. What is the *MPL* per dollar of the 5th worker?
3. How many workers would the firm hire if it hired every worker for whom the marginal product per dollar is greater than or equal to 1 pencil per dollar?
4. If the marginal product per dollar spent on labor is 1 pencil per dollar, the marginal product of the last unit of capital hired is 100 pencils per dollar, and the rental rate is $50 per day, is the firm minimizing its cost? Explain.

The Time Value of Money

Thinkstock

WHAT YOU WILL LEARN

1. Why a dollar today is worth more than a dollar a year from now
2. How the concept of present value can help you make decisions when costs or benefits occur in the future

The Concept of Present Value

Individuals are often faced with financial decisions that will have consequences long into the future. For example, when you decide to attend college, you are committing yourself to years of study, which you expect will pay off for the rest of your life. So the decision to attend college is a decision to embark on a long-term project.

The basic rule in deciding whether or not to undertake a project is that you should compare the benefits of that project with its costs, implicit as well as explicit. But making these comparisons can sometimes be difficult because the benefits and costs of a project may not arrive at the same time.

Sometimes the costs of a project come at an earlier date than the benefits. For example, going to college involves large immediate costs: tuition, income forgone because you are in school, and so on. The benefits, such as a higher salary in your future career, come later, often much later. In other cases, the benefits of a project come at an earlier date than the costs. If you take out a loan to pay for a vacation cruise, the satisfaction of the vacation will come immediately, but the burden of making payments will come later.

How, specifically is time an issue in economic decision making?

Borrowing, Lending, and Interest

In general, having a dollar today is worth more than having a dollar a year from now. To see why, let's consider two examples.

First, suppose that you get a new job that comes with a $1,000 bonus, which will be paid at the end of the first year. But you would like to spend the extra money now—say, on new clothes for work. Can you do that?

The answer is yes—you can borrow money today and use the bonus to repay the debt a year from now. But if that is your plan, you cannot borrow the full $1,000 today. You must borrow *less* than that because a year from now you will have to repay the amount borrowed *plus interest*.

Now consider a different scenario. Suppose that you are paid a bonus of $1,000 today, and you decide that you don't want to spend the money until a year from now. What do you do with it? You may decide to put it in the bank; in effect, you would be lending the $1,000 to the bank, which in turn lends it out to its customers who wish to borrow. At the end of a year, you will get *more* than $1,000 back—you will receive the $1,000 plus the interest earned.

All of this means that having $1,000 today is worth more than having $1,000 a year from now. As any borrower and lender know, this is what allows a lender to charge a borrower interest on a loan: borrowers are willing to pay interest in order to have money today rather than waiting until they acquire that money later on.

Most interest rates are stated as the percentage of the borrowed amount that must be paid to the lender for each year of the loan. Whether money is actually borrowed for 1 month or 10 years, and regardless of the amount, the same principle applies: money in your pocket today is worth more than money in your pocket tomorrow. To keep things simple in the discussions that follow, we'll restrict ourselves to examples of 1-year loans of $1.

Because the value of money depends on when it is paid or received, you can't evaluate a project by simply adding up the costs and benefits when those costs and benefits arrive at different times. You must take time into account when evaluating the project because $1 that is paid to you today is worth more than $1 that is paid to you a year from now. Similarly, $1 that you must pay today is more burdensome than $1 that you must pay next year.

Fortunately, there is a simple way to adjust for these complications so that we can correctly compare the value of dollars received and paid out at different times.

Next we'll see how the interest rate can be used to convert future benefits and costs into what economists call *present values*. By using present values when evaluating a project, you can evaluate a project *as if* all relevant costs and benefits were occurring today rather than at different times. This allows people to "factor out" the complications created by time. We'll start by defining the concept of present value.

Defining Present Value

The key to the concept of present value is to understand that you can use the interest rate to compare the value of a dollar realized today with the value of a dollar realized later. Why the interest rate? Because the interest rate correctly measures the cost to you of delaying the receipt of a dollar of benefit and, correspondingly, the benefit to you of delaying the payment of a dollar of cost.

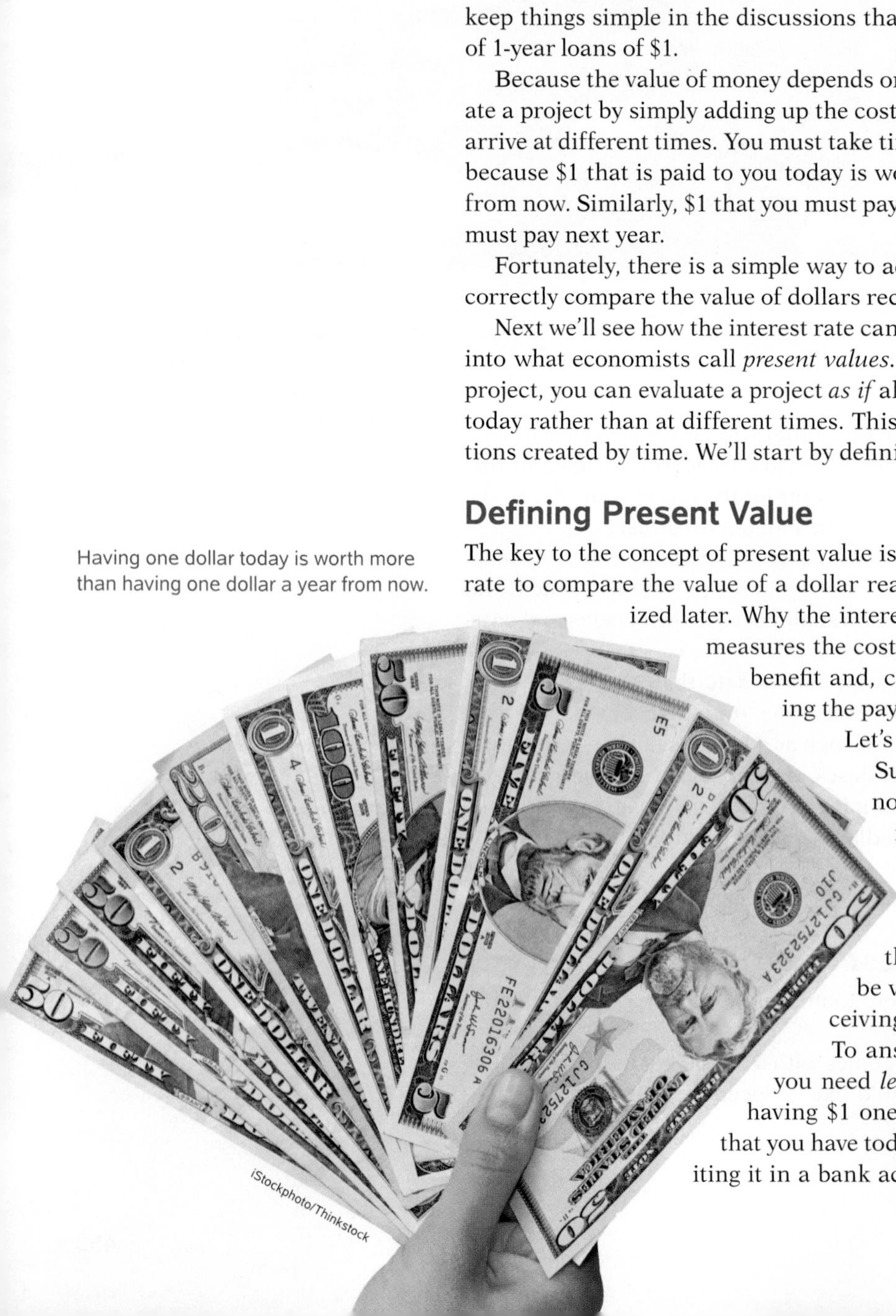

Having one dollar today is worth more than having one dollar a year from now.

iStockphoto/Thinkstock

Let's illustrate this with some examples.

Suppose that you are evaluating whether or not to take a job in which your employer promises to pay you a bonus at the end of the first year. What is the value to you today of $1 of bonus money to be paid one year in the future? A slightly different way of asking the same question: what amount would you be willing to accept today as a substitute for receiving $1 one year from now?

To answer this question, begin by observing that you need *less* than $1 today in order to be assured of having $1 one year from now. Why? Because any money that you have today can be lent out at interest—say, by depositing it in a bank account so that the bank can then lend it out to its borrowers. This turns any amount you have today into a greater sum at the end of the year.

Let's work this out mathematically. We'll use the symbol r to represent the interest rate, expressed in decimal terms—that is, if the interest rate is 10%, then $r = 0.10$. If you lend out $\$X$, at the end of a year you will receive your $\$X$ back, plus the interest on your $\$X$, which is $\$X \times r$. Thus, at the end of the year you will receive:

The **present value** of \$1 realized one year from now is equal to $\$1/(1 + r)$: the amount of money you must lend out today in order to have \$1 in one year. It is the value to you today of \$1 realized one year from now.

(44-1) Amount received one year from now as a result of lending $\$X$ today:
$$\$X + \$X \times r = \$X \times (1 + r)$$

The next step is to find out how much you would have to lend out today to have \$1 a year from now. To do that, we just need to set Equation 44-1 equal to \$1 and solve for $\$X$. That is, we solve the following equation for $\$X$:

(44-2) Condition satisfied when \$1 is received one year from now as a result of lending $\$X$ today: $\$X \times (1 + r) = \$1$

Rearranging Equation 44-2 to solve for $\$X$, the amount you need today in order to receive \$1 one year from now is:

(44-3) Amount lent today in order to receive \$1 one year from now:
$$\$X = \$1/(1 + r)$$

This means that you would be willing to accept today the amount $\$X$ defined by Equation 44-3 for every \$1 to be paid to you one year from now. The reason is that if you were to lend out $\$X$ today, you would be assured of receiving \$1 one year from now. Returning to our original question, this also means that if someone promises to pay you a sum of money one year in the future, you are willing to accept $\$X$ today in place of every \$1 to be paid one year from now.

Now let's solve Equation 44-3 for the value of $\$X$. To do this we simply need to use the actual value of r (a value determined by the financial markets). Let's assume that the actual value of r is 10%, which means that $r = 0.10$. In that case:

(44-4) Value of $\$X$ when $r = 0.10$: $\$X = \$1/(1 + 0.10) = \$1/1.10 = \$0.91$

So you would be willing to accept \$0.91 today in exchange for every \$1 to be paid to you one year from now. Economists have a special name for $\$X$—it's called the **present value** of \$1. Note that the present value of any given amount will change as the interest rate changes.

The present value of a given amount will change as the interest rate changes.

To see that this technique works for evaluating future costs as well as evaluating future benefits, consider the following example. Suppose you enter into an agreement that obliges you to pay \$1 one year from now—say, to pay off a car loan from your parents when you graduate in a year. How much money would you need today to ensure that you have \$1 in a year? The answer is $\$X$, the present value of \$1, which in our example is \$0.91. The reason \$0.91 is the right answer is that if you lend it out for one year at an interest rate of 10%, you will receive \$1 in return at the end. So if, for example, you must pay back \$5,000 one year from now, then you need to deposit $\$5,000 \times 0.91 = \$4,550$ into a bank account today earning an interest rate of 10% in order to have \$5,000 one year from now. (There is a slight discrepancy due to rounding.) In other words, today you need to have the present value of \$5,000, which equals \$4,550, in order to be assured of paying off your debt in a year.

Imagebroker/Alamy

These examples show us that the present value concept provides a way to calculate the value today of \$1 that is realized in a year—regardless of whether that \$1 is realized as a benefit (the bonus) or a cost (the car loan payback). To evaluate a project today that has benefits, costs, or both to be realized in a year, we just use the relevant interest

The **net present value** of a project is the present value of current and future benefits minus the present value of current and future costs.

rate to convert those future dollars into their present values. In that way we have "factored out" the complication that time creates for decision making.

Below we will use the present value concept to evaluate a project. But before we do that, it is worthwhile to note that the present value method can be used for projects in which the \$1 is realized more than a year later—say, two, three, or even more years. Suppose you are considering a project that will pay you \$1 *two* years from today. What is the value to you today of \$1 received two years into the future? We can find the answer to that question by expanding our formula for present value.

Let's call $\$V$ the amount of money you need to lend today at an interest rate of r in order to have \$1 in two years. So if you lend $\$V$ today, you will receive $\$V \times (1 + r)$ in one year. And if you *relend* that sum for another year, you will receive $\$V \times (1 + r) \times (1 + r) = \$V \times (1 + r)^2$ at the end of the second year. At the end of two years, $\$V$ will be worth $\$V \times (1 + r)^2$. In other words:

(44-5) Amount received in one year from lending $\$V = \$V \times (1 + r)$

Amount received in two years from lending $\$V = \$V \times (1 + r) \times (1 + r) = \$V \times (1 + r)^2$ and so on. For example, if $r = 0.10$, then $\$V \times (1.10)^2 = \$V \times 1.21$.

Now we are ready to answer the question of what \$1 realized two years in the future is worth today. In order for the amount lent today, $\$V$, to be worth \$1 two years from now, it must satisfy this formula:

(44-6) Condition satisfied when \$1 is received two years from now as a result of lending $\$V$ today: $\$V \times (1 + r)^2 = \$1$

Rearranging Equation 44-6, we can solve for $\$V$:

(44-7) Amount lent today in order to receive \$1 two years from now: $\$V = \$1/(1 + r)^2$

Given $r = 0.10$ and using Equation 44-7, we arrive at $\$V = \$1/1.21 = \$0.83$. So, when the interest rate is 10%, \$1 realized two years from today is worth \$0.83 today because by lending out \$0.83 today you can be assured of having \$1 in two years. And that means that the present value of \$1 realized two years into the future is \$0.83.

(44-8) Present value of \$1 realized two years from now: $\$V = \$1/(1.10)^2 = \$1/1.21 = \$0.83$

From this example we can see how the present value concept can be expanded to a number of years even greater than two. If we ask what the present value is of \$1 realized any number of years, represented by N, into the future, the answer is given by a generalization of the present value formula: it is equal to $\$1/(1 + r)^N$.

Using Present Value

Suppose you have to choose one of three hypothetical projects to undertake. Project A costs nothing and has an immediate payoff to you of \$100. Project B requires that you pay \$10 today in order to receive \$115 a year from now. Project C gives you an immediate payoff of \$119 but requires that you pay \$20 a year from now. We'll assume that the annual interest rate is 10%—that is, $r = 0.10$.

The problem in evaluating these three projects is that their costs and benefits are realized at different times. That is, of course, where the concept of present value becomes extremely helpful: by using present value to convert any dollars realized in the future into today's value, you factor out the issue of time. Appropriate comparisons can be made using the **net present value** of a project—the present value of current and future benefits minus the present value of current and future costs. The best project to undertake is the one with the highest net present value.

Table 44-1 shows how to calculate net present value for each of the three projects. The second and third columns show how many dollars are realized and when

TABLE 44-1

The Net Present Value of Three Hypothetical Projects

Project	Dollars realized today	Dollars realized one year from today	Present value formula	Net present value given $r = 0.10$
A	$100	—	$100	$100.00
B	–$10	$115	–$10 + $115/(1 + *r*)	$94.55
C	$119	–$20	119 – $20/(1 + *r*)	$100.82

they are realized; costs are indicated by a minus sign. The fourth column shows the equations used to convert the flows of dollars into their present value, and the fifth column shows the actual amounts of the total net present value for each of the three projects.

For instance, to calculate the net present value of project B, we need to calculate the present value of $115 received in one year. The present value of $1 received in one year would be $1/(1 + *r*). So the present value of $115 is equal to 115 × $1/(1 + *r*); that is, $115/(1 + *r*). The net present value of project B is the present value of today's and future benefits minus the present value of today's and future costs: –$10 + $115/(1 + *r*).

From the fifth column, we can immediately see which is the preferred project—it is project C. That's because it has the highest net present value, $100.82, which is higher than the net present value of project A ($100) and much higher than the net present value of project B ($94.55).

This example shows how important the concept of present value is. If we had failed to use the present value calculations and instead simply added up the dollars generated by each of the three projects, we could have easily been misled into believing that project B was the best project and project C was the worst.

ECONOMICS ▶ IN ACTION

HOW BIG IS THAT JACKPOT, ANYWAY?

For a clear example of present value at work, consider the case of lottery jackpots.

On March 30, 2012, Mega Millions set the record for the largest jackpot ever in North America, with a payout of $656 million. Well, sort of. That $656 million was available only if you chose to take your winnings in the form of an "annuity," consisting of an annual payment for the next 26 years. If you wanted cash up front, the jackpot was only $474 million and change.

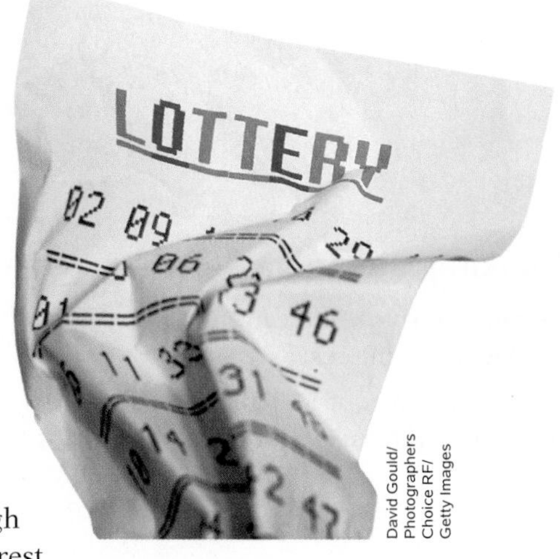

David Gould/ Photographers Choice RF/ Getty Images

Why was Mega Millions so stingy about quick payoffs? It was all a matter of present value. If the winner had been willing to take the annuity, the lottery would have invested the jackpot money, buying U.S. government bonds (in effect lending the money to the federal government). The money would have been invested in such a way that the investments would pay just enough to cover the annuity. This worked, of course, because at the interest rates prevailing at the time, the present value of a $656 million annuity spread over 26 years was just about $474 million. To put it another way, the opportunity cost to the lottery of that annuity in present value terms was $474 million.

So why didn't they just call it a $474 million jackpot? Well, $656 million sounds more impressive! But receiving $656 million over 26 years is essentially the same as receiving $474 million today.

MODULE 44 Review

Solutions appear at the back of the book.

Check Your Understanding

1. Consider the three hypothetical projects shown in Table 44-1. This time, however, suppose that the interest rate is only 2%.
   a. Calculate the net present values of the three projects. Which one is now preferred?
   b. Explain why the preferred choice with a 2% interest rate differs from one with a 10% interest rate.

Multiple-Choice Questions

1. Suppose, for simplicity, that a bank uses a single interest rate for loans and deposits, there is no inflation, and all unspent money is deposited in the bank. The interest rate measures which of the following?
   I. the cost of using a dollar today rather than a year from now
   II. the benefit of delaying the use of a dollar from today until a year from now
   III. the price of borrowing money calculated as a percentage of the amount borrowed
   a. I only
   b. II only
   c. III only
   d. I and II only
   e. I, II, and III
2. If the interest rate is zero, then the present value of a dollar received at the end of the year is
   a. more than $1.
   b. equal to $1.
   c. less than $1.
   d. zero.
   e. infinite.
3. If the interest rate is 10%, the present value of $1 paid to you one year from now is
   a. $0.
   b. $0.89.
   c. $0.91.
   d. $1.
   e. more than $1.
4. If the interest rate is 5%, the amount received one year from now as a result of lending $100 today is
   a. $90.
   b. $95.
   c. $100.
   d. $105.
   e. $110.
5. What is the present value of $100 realized two years from now if the interest rate is 10%?
   a. $80
   b. $83
   c. $90
   d. $100
   e. $110

Critical-Thinking Questions

1. What is the amount you will receive in three years if you loan $1,000 at 5% interest?
2. What is the present value of $1,000 received in three years if the interest rate is 5%?

The Economics of Information

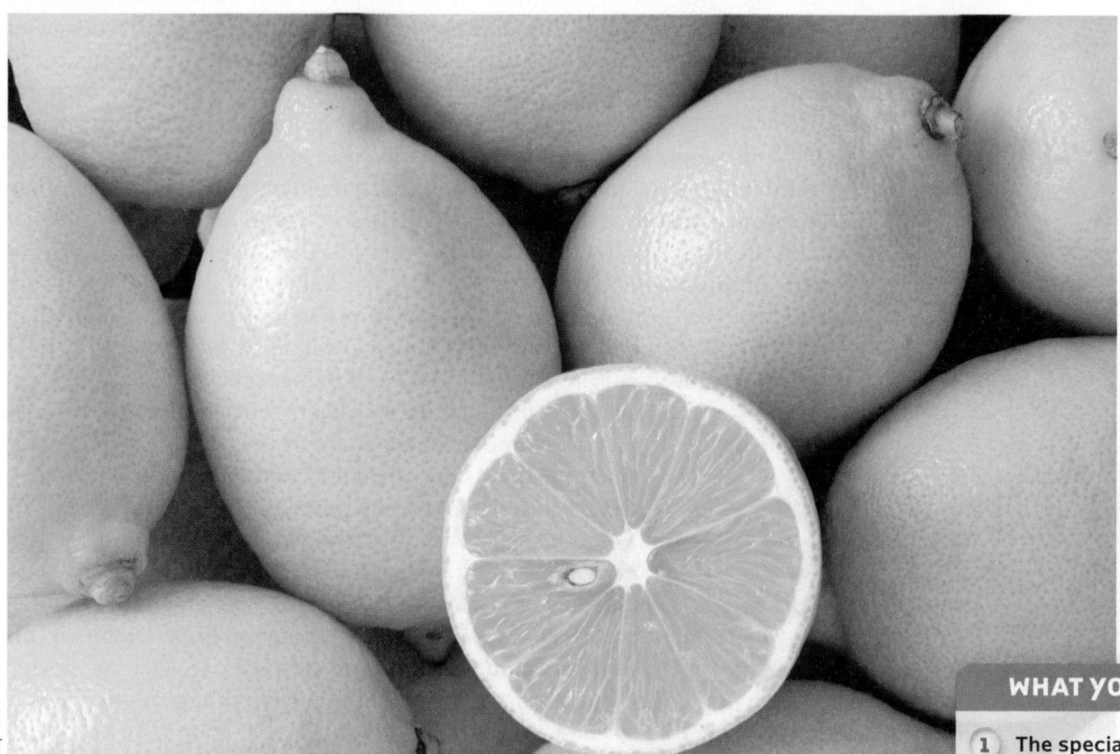

iStockpho to

WHAT YOU WILL LEARN

1. The special problems posed by private information—situations in which some people know things that other people do not
2. How situations of private information can lead to the problem of adverse selection
3. How firms deal with the need for information by using screening and signaling
4. How situations of private information can lead to the problem of moral hazard

Private Information: What You Don't Know Can Hurt You

Markets do very well at dealing with situations in which nobody knows what is going to happen. However, markets have much more trouble with situations in which *some people know things that other people don't know*—situations of **private information.** (Sometimes economists use the term *asymmetric information* rather than *private information,* but the terms are equivalent.) As we will see, private information can distort economic decisions and sometimes prevent mutually beneficial economic transactions from taking place.

Why is some information private? The most important reason is that people generally know more about themselves than other people do. For example, you know whether or not you are a careful driver; but unless you have already been in several accidents, your auto insurance company does not. You are more likely to have a better estimate than your health insurance company of whether or not you will need an expensive medical procedure. And if you are selling me your used car, you are more likely to be aware of any problems with it than I am.

But why should such differences in who knows what be a problem? It turns out that there are two distinct sources of trouble: *adverse selection,* which arises from having private information about the way things are, and *moral hazard,* which arises from having private information about what people do.

Private information is information that some people have that others do not.

Adverse Selection: The Economics of Lemons

Suppose that someone offers to sell you an almost brand-new car—purchased just three months ago, with only 2,000 miles on the odometer and no dents or scratches. Will you be willing to pay almost the same for it as for a car direct from the dealer?

Probably not, for one main reason: you cannot help but wonder why this car is being sold. Is it because the owner has discovered that something is wrong with it—that it is a "lemon"? Having driven the car for a while, the owner knows more about it than you do—and people are more likely to sell cars that give them trouble.

You might think that the fact that sellers of used cars know more about them than buyers do represents an advantage to the sellers. But potential buyers know that potential sellers are likely to offer them lemons—they just don't know exactly which car is a lemon. Because potential buyers of a used car know that potential sellers are more likely to sell lemons than good cars, buyers will offer a lower price than they would if they had a guarantee of the car's quality. Worse yet, this poor opinion of used cars tends to be self-reinforcing, precisely because it depresses the prices that buyers offer. Used cars sell at a discount because buyers expect a disproportionate share of those cars to be lemons. Even a used car that is not a lemon would sell only at a large discount because buyers don't know whether it's a lemon or not.

Oleksiy Maksymenko/Alamy

But potential sellers who have good cars are unwilling to sell them at a deep discount, except under exceptional circumstances. So good used cars are rarely offered for sale, and used cars that are offered for sale have a strong tendency to be lemons. (This is why people who have a compelling reason to sell a car, such as moving overseas, make a point of revealing that information to potential buyers—as if to say "This car is not a lemon!")

The end result, then, is not only that used cars sell for low prices but also that there are a large number of used cars with hidden problems. Equally important, many potentially beneficial transactions—sales of good cars by people who would like to get rid of them to people who would like to buy them—end up being frustrated by the inability of potential sellers to convince potential buyers that their cars are actually worth the higher price demanded. So some mutually beneficial trades between those who want to sell used cars and those who want to buy them go unexploited.

Although economists sometimes refer to situations like this as the "lemons problem" (the issue was introduced in a famous 1970 paper by economist and Nobel laureate George Akerlof entitled "The Market for Lemons"), the more formal name of the problem is **adverse selection.** The reason for the name is obvious: because the potential sellers know more about the quality of what they are selling than the potential buyers, they have an incentive to select the worst things to sell.

Adverse selection does not apply only to used cars. It is a problem for many parts of the economy—notably for insurance companies, and most notably for health insurance companies.

Suppose that a health insurance company were to offer a standard policy to everyone with the same premium. The premium would reflect the *average* risk of incurring a medical expense. But that would make the policy look very expensive to healthy people, who know that they are less likely than the average person to incur medical expenses. So healthy people would be less likely than less healthy people to buy the policy, leaving the health insurance company with exactly the customers it doesn't want: people with a higher-than-average risk of needing medical care, who would find the premium to be a good deal.

Adverse selection occurs when one person knows more about the way things are than other people do. Adverse selection exists, for example, when sellers offer items of particularly low (hidden) quality for sale, and when the people with the greatest need for insurance are those most likely to purchase it.

In order to cover its expected losses from this sicker customer pool, the health insurance company is compelled to raise premiums, driving away more of the remaining healthier customers, and so on. Because the insurance company can't determine who is healthy and who is not, it must charge everyone the same premium, thereby discouraging healthy people from purchasing policies and encouraging unhealthy people to buy policies.

Adverse selection can lead to a phenomenon called an *adverse selection death spiral* as the market for health insurance collapses: insurance companies refuse to offer policies because there is no premium at which the company can cover its losses. Because of the severe adverse selection problems, governments in many advanced countries assume the role of providing health insurance to their citizens. The U.S. government, through its various health insurance programs including Medicare, Medicaid, and the State Children's Health Insurance Program (SCHIP), now disburses more than half the total payments for medical care in the United States.

People or firms faced with the problem of adverse selection have three well-established strategies for dealing with it: *screening, signaling,* and establishing a good *reputation.*

Adverse selection can be reduced through **screening:** using observable information about people to make inferences about their private information.

Adverse selection can be diminished by people **signaling** their private information through actions that credibly reveal what they know.

A long-term **reputation** allows an individual to assure others that he or she isn't concealing adverse private information.

SCREENING The first strategy, **screening,** involves using observable information to make inferences about private information. If you apply to purchase health insurance, you'll find that the insurance company will demand documentation of your health status in an attempt to "screen out" sicker applicants, whom they will refuse to insure or will insure only at very high premiums.

Auto insurance also provides a very good example. An insurance company may not know whether you are a careful driver, but it has statistical data on the accident rates of people who resemble your profile—and it uses those data in setting premiums. A 19-year-old male who drives a sports car and has already had a fender-bender is likely to pay a very high premium. A 40-year-old female who drives a minivan and has never had an accident is likely to pay much less. In some cases, this may be quite unfair: some adolescent males are very careful drivers, and some mature women drive their minivans as if they were F-16s. But nobody can deny that the insurance companies are right on average.

SIGNALING The second strategy is for people who are good prospects to somehow *signal* their private information. **Signaling** involves taking some action that wouldn't be worth taking unless they were indeed good prospects. Reputable used-car dealers often offer warranties—promises to repair any problems with the cars they sell that arise within a given amount of time. This isn't just a way of insuring their customers against possible expenses; it's a way of credibly showing that they are not selling lemons. As a result, more sales occur and dealers can command higher prices for their used cars.

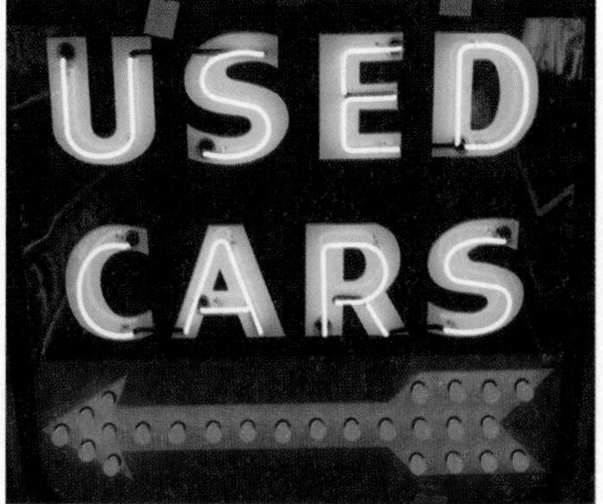

Thinkstock

REPUTATION In the face of adverse selection, it can be very valuable to establish a good **reputation,** our third strategy. A used-car dealership will often advertise how long it has been in business to show that it has continued to satisfy its customers. As a result, new customers will be willing to purchase cars and to pay more for that dealer's cars.

Moral Hazard

In the late 1970s, New York and other major cities experienced an epidemic of suspicious fires—fires that appeared to be deliberately set. Some of the fires were probably started by teenagers on a lark, others by gang members struggling over turf. But investigators eventually became aware of patterns in a number of the fires. Particular landlords who owned several buildings seemed to have an unusually large number of their buildings burn down. Although it was difficult to prove, police had few doubts that most of these fire-prone landlords were hiring professional arsonists to torch their own properties.

Why burn your own buildings? These buildings were typically in declining neighborhoods, where rising crime and middle-class flight had led to a decline in property

©Tetra Images/Alamy

Franchise owners have an incentive to work hard because of their personal stake in the businesses they run.

values. But the insurance policies on the buildings were written to compensate owners based on historical property values, and so would pay the owner of a destroyed building more than the building was worth in the current market. For an unscrupulous landlord who knew the right people, this presented a profitable opportunity.

The arson epidemic became less severe during the 1980s, partly because insurance companies began making it difficult to over-insure properties and partly because a boom in real estate values made many previously arson-threatened buildings worth more unburned.

The arson episodes make it clear that it is a bad idea for insurance companies to let customers insure buildings for more than their value—it gives the customers some destructive incentives. You might think, however, that the incentive problem would go away as long as the insurance is no more than 100% of the value of what is being insured.

But, unfortunately, anything close to 100% insurance still distorts incentives—it induces policyholders to behave differently from how they would in the absence of insurance. The reason is that preventing fires requires effort and cost on the part of a building's owner. Fire alarms and sprinkler systems have to be kept in good repair, fire safety rules have to be strictly enforced, and so on. All of this takes time and money—time and money that the owner may not find worth spending if the insurance policy will provide close to full compensation for any losses.

Of course, the insurance company could specify in the policy that it won't pay if basic safety precautions have not been taken. But it isn't always easy to tell how careful a building's owner has been—the owner knows, but the insurance company does not.

The point is that the building's owner has private information about his or her own actions; the owner knows whether he or she has really taken all appropriate precautions. As a result, the insurance company is likely to face greater claims than if it were able to determine exactly how much effort a building owner exerts to prevent a loss. The problem of distorted incentives arises when an individual has private information about his or her own actions but someone else bears the costs of a lack of care or effort. This is known as **moral hazard.**

To deal with moral hazard, it is necessary to give individuals with private information some personal stake in what happens, a stake that gives them a reason to exert effort even if others cannot verify that they have done so. Moral hazard is the reason salespeople in many stores receive a commission on sales: it's hard for managers to be sure how hard the salespeople are really working, and if they were paid only straight salary, they would not have an incentive to exert effort to make those sales. Similar logic explains why many stores and restaurants, even if they are part of national chains, are actually franchises, licensed outlets owned by the people who run them.

Insurance companies deal with moral hazard by requiring a **deductible:** they compensate for losses only above a certain amount, so that coverage is always less than 100%. The insurance on your car, for example, may pay for repairs only after the first $500 in loss. This means that a careless driver who gets into a fender-bender will end up paying $500 for repairs even if he is insured, which provides at least some incentive to be careful and reduces moral hazard.

Moral hazard occurs when an individual knows more about his or her own actions than other people do. This leads to a distortion of incentives to take care or to exert effort when someone else bears the costs of the lack of care or effort.

A **deductible** is a sum specified in an insurance policy that the insured individuals must pay before being compensated for a claim; deductibles reduce *moral hazard.*

In addition to reducing moral hazard, deductibles provide a partial solution to the problem of adverse selection. Your insurance premium often drops substantially if you are willing to accept a large deductible. This is an attractive option to people who know they are low-risk customers; it is less attractive to people who know they are high-risk—and so are likely to have an accident and end up paying the deductible. By offering a menu of policies with different premiums and deductibles, insurance companies can screen their customers, inducing them to sort themselves out on the basis of their private information.

As the example of deductibles suggests, moral hazard limits the ability of the economy to allocate risks efficiently. You generally can't get full (100%) insurance on your home or car, even though you would like to buy full insurance, and you bear the risk of large deductibles, even though you would prefer not to.

MODULE 45 Review

Solutions appear at the back of the book.

Check Your Understanding

1. Your car insurance premiums are lower if you have had no moving violations for several years. Explain how this feature tends to decrease the potential inefficiency caused by adverse selection.
2. A common feature of home construction contracts is that when it costs more to construct a building than was originally estimated, the contractor must absorb the additional cost. Explain how this feature reduces the problem of moral hazard but also forces the contractor to bear more risk than she would like.
3. True or false? Explain your answer, stating what concept analyzed in this module accounts for the feature.

   People with higher deductibles on their auto insurance

   a. generally drive more carefully.

   b. pay lower premiums.

Multiple-Choice Questions

1. Which of the following is true about private information?

   I. It has value.

   II. Everyone has access to it.

   III. It can distort economic decisions.

   a. I only

   b. II only

   c. III only

   d. I and III only

   e. I, II, and III

2. Due to adverse selection,

   a mutually beneficial trades go unexploited.

   b. people buy lemons rather than other fruit.

   c. sick people buy less insurance.

   d. private information is available to all.

   e. public information is available to no one.

3. When colleges use grade point averages to make admissions decisions, they are employing which strategy?

   a. signaling

   b. screening

   c. profit maximization

   d. marginal analysis

   e. adverse selection

4. Moral hazard is the result of

   a. private information.

   b. signaling.

   c. toxic waste.

   d. adverse selection.

   e. public information.

5. A deductible is used by insurance companies to

   a. allow customers to pay for insurance premiums using payroll deduction.

   b. deal with moral hazard.

   c. make public information private.

   d. compensate policyholders fully for their losses.

   e. avoid all payments to policyholders.

Critical-Thinking Questions

Individuals or corporations (for example home-buyers or banks) believe that the government will "bail them out" in the event that their decisions lead to a financial collapse.

1. This is an example of what problem created by private information?
2. How does this situation lead to inefficiency?
3. What is a possible remedy for the problem?

SECTION 14 REVIEW

Summary

The Cost-Minimizing Input Combination

1. Firms will determine the optimal input combination using the **cost-minimization rule:** When a firm uses the cost-minimizing combination of inputs, the marginal product of labor divided by the wage rate is equal to the marginal product of capital divided by the rental rate.

The Time Value of Money

2. In order to evaluate a project in which costs or benefits are realized in the future, you must first transform them into their **present values** using the interest rate, *r*. The present value of \$1 realized one year from now is $\$1/(1 + r)$, the amount of money you must lend out today to have \$1 one year from now. Once this transformation is done, you should choose the project with the highest **net present value.**

The Economics of Information

3. **Private information** can cause inefficiency by distorting economic decisions and preventing mutually beneficial transactions from taking place. One problem is **adverse selection,** private information about the way things are. It creates the "lemons problem" in used-car markets, where sellers of high-quality cars drop out of the market. Adverse selection can be limited in several ways—through **screening** of individuals, through the **signaling** that people use to reveal their private information, and through the building of a **reputation.**
4. A related problem is **moral hazard:** individuals have private information about their actions, which distorts their incentives to exert effort or care when someone else bears the costs of that lack of effort or care. It limits the ability of markets to allocate risk efficiently. Insurance companies try to limit moral hazard by imposing **deductibles,** placing more risk on the insured.

Key Terms

Cost-minimization rule, p. 456
Present value, p. 461
Net present value, p. 462
Private information, p. 465
Adverse selection, p. 466
Screening, p. 467
Signaling, p. 467
Reputation, p. 467
Moral hazard, p. 468
Deductible, p. 468

Problems

1. Suppose that a major city's main thoroughfare, which is also an interstate highway, will be completely closed to traffic for two years, from January 2012 to December 2013, for reconstruction at a cost of \$535 million. If the construction company were to keep the highway open for traffic during construction, the highway reconstruction project would take much longer and be more expensive. Suppose that construction would take four years if the highway were kept open, at a total cost of \$800 million. The state Department of Transportation had to make its decision in 2011, one year before the start of construction (so that the first payment was one year away). So the Department of Transportation had the following choices:

   (i) Close the highway during construction, at an annual cost of \$267.5 million per year for two years.

   (ii) Keep the highway open during construction, at an annual cost of \$200 million per year for four years.

   a. Suppose the interest rate is 10%. Calculate the present value of the costs incurred under each plan. Which reconstruction plan is less expensive?

   b. Now suppose the interest rate is 80%. Calculate the present value of the costs incurred under each plan. Which reconstruction plan is now less expensive?

2. You have won the state lottery. There are two ways in which you can receive your prize. You can either have \$1 million in cash now, or you can have \$1.2 million that is paid out as follows: \$300,000 now, \$300,000 in one year's time, \$300,000 in two years' time, and \$300,000 in three years' time. The interest rate is 20%. How would you prefer to receive your prize?

3. The drug company Pfizer is considering whether to invest in the development of a new cancer drug. Development will require an initial investment of \$10 million now; beginning one year from now, the drug will generate annual profits of \$4 million for three years.

   a. If the interest rate is 12%, should Pfizer invest in the development of the new drug? Why or why not?

   b. If the interest rate is 8%, should Pfizer invest in the development of the new drug? Why or why not?

4. You are considering buying a second-hand Volkswagen. From reading car magazines, you know that half of all Volkswagens have problems of some kind (they are "lemons") and the other half run just fine (they are "plums"). If you knew that you were getting a plum, you would be willing to pay \$10,000 for it: this is how much a plum is worth to you.

You would also be willing to buy a lemon, but only if its price were no more than $4,000: this is how much a lemon is worth to you. And someone who owns a plum would be willing to sell it at any price above $8,000. Someone who owns a lemon would be willing to sell it for any price above $2,000.

a. For now, suppose that you can immediately tell whether the car that you are being offered is a lemon or a plum. Suppose someone offers you a plum. Will there be trade?

Now suppose that the seller has private information about the car she is selling: the seller knows whether she has a lemon or a plum. But when the seller offers you a Volkswagen, you do not know whether it is a lemon or a plum. So this is a situation of adverse selection.

b. Since you do not know whether you are being offered a plum or a lemon, what is the most you are willing to pay for your vehicle? Why?

5. For each of the following situations describe whether it is a situation of moral hazard or of adverse selection. Then explain what inefficiency can arise from this situation and explain how the proposed solution reduces the inefficiency.

a. When you buy a second-hand car, you do not know whether it is a lemon (low quality) or a plum (high quality), but the seller knows. A solution is for sellers to offer a warranty with the car that pays for repair costs.

b. Some people are prone to see doctors unnecessarily for minor complaints like headaches, and health maintenance organizations do not know how urgently you need a doctor. A solution is for insurees to have to make a co-payment of a certain dollar amount (for example, $10) each time they visit a health care provider.

c. When airlines sell tickets, they do not know whether a buyer is a business traveler (who is willing to pay a lot for a seat) or a leisure traveler (who has a low willingness to pay). A solution for a profit-maximizing airline is to offer an expensive ticket that is very flexible (it allows date and route changes) and a cheap ticket that is very inflexible (it has to be booked in advance and cannot be changed).

d. When making a decision about hiring you, prospective employers do not know whether you are a productive or unproductive worker. A solution is for productive workers to provide potential employers with references from previous employers.

APPENDIX A Graphs in Economics

Whether you're reading about economics in the news or in your economics textbook, you will see many graphs. Visual presentations can make it easier to understand verbal descriptions, numerical information, or ideas. In economics, graphs are used to facilitate understanding. But to get the full benefit from these visual aids, you need to know how to interpret them. This appendix explains how graphs are constructed, interpreted, and used in economics.

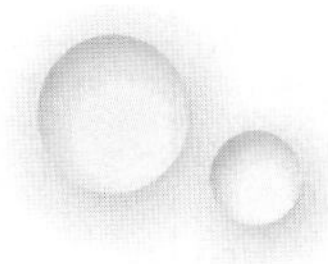

Graphs, Variables, and Economic Models

If you were reading an article about the relationship between educational attainment and income, you would probably see a graph showing the income levels for workers with different levels of education. This graph would depict the idea that, in general, having more education increases a person's income. This graph, like most graphs in economics, would depict the relationship between two economic variables. A **variable** is a quantity that can take on more than one value, such as the number of years of education a person has, the price of a can of soda, or a household's income.

Earlier we discussed how economic analysis relies heavily on *models,* simplified descriptions of real situations. Most economic models describe the relationship between two variables, simplified by holding constant other variables that may affect the relationship. For example, an economic model might describe the relationship between the price of a can of soda and the number of cans of soda that consumers will buy, assuming that everything else that affects consumers' purchases of soda stays constant. This type of model can be described mathematically or verbally, but illustrating the relationship in a graph makes it easier to understand. Next we show how graphs that depict economic models are constructed and interpreted.

How Graphs Work

Most graphs in economics are based on a grid built around two perpendicular lines that show the values of two variables, helping you visualize the relationship between them. So a first step in understanding the use of such graphs is to see how this system works.

Two-Variable Graphs

Figure A-1 shows a typical two-variable graph. It illustrates the data in the accompanying table on outside temperature and the number of sodas a typical vendor can expect to sell at a baseball stadium during one game. The first column shows the values of outside temperature (the first variable) and the second column shows the values of the number of sodas sold (the second variable). Five combinations or pairs of the two variables are shown, denoted by points *A* through *E* in the third column.

Now let's turn to graphing the data in this table. In any two-variable graph, one variable is called the *x*-variable and the other is called the *y*-variable. Here we have made outside temperature the *x*-variable and number of sodas sold the *y*-variable.

The solid horizontal line in the graph is called the **horizontal axis** or ***x*-axis,** and values of the *x*-variable—outside temperature—are measured along it. Similarly, the solid vertical line in the graph is called the **vertical axis** or ***y*-axis,** and values of the *y*-variable—number of sodas sold—are measured along it. At the **origin,** the point where the two axes meet, each variable is equal to zero. As you move rightward from the origin along the *x*-axis, values of the *x*-variable are positive and increasing. As

A quantity that can take on more than one value is called a **variable**.

The line along which values of the x-variable are measured is called the **horizontal axis** or ***x*-axis**. The line along which values of the y-variable are measured is called the **vertical axis** or ***y*-axis**. The point where the axes of a two-variable graph meet is the **origin**.

FIGURE A-1 Plotting Points on a Two-Variable Graph

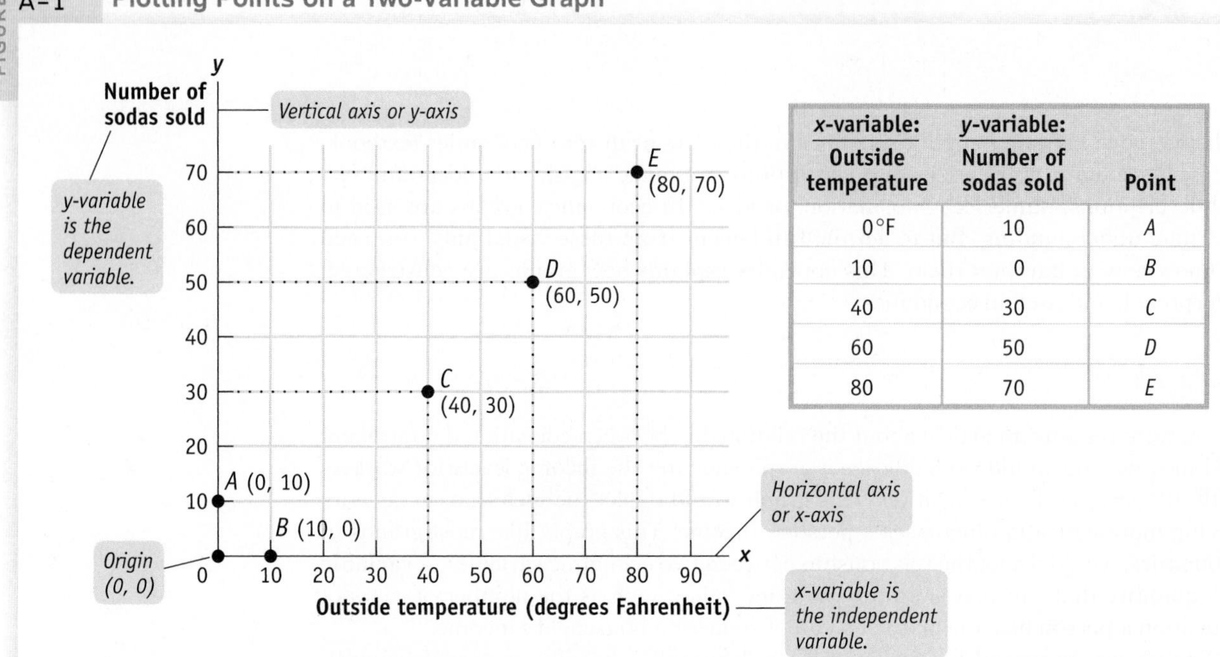

x-variable: Outside temperature	y-variable: Number of sodas sold	Point
0°F	10	*A*
10	0	*B*
40	30	*C*
60	50	*D*
80	70	*E*

The data from the table are plotted where outside temperature (the independent variable) is measured along the horizontal axis and number of sodas sold (the dependent variable) is measured along the vertical axis. Each of the five combinations of temperature and sodas sold is represented by a point: *A*, *B*, *C*, *D*, and *E*. Each point in the graph is identified by a pair of values. For example, point *C* corresponds to the pair (40, 30)—an outside temperature of 40°F (the value of the *x*-variable) and 30 sodas sold (the value of the *y*-variable).

you move up from the origin along the *y*-axis, values of the *y*-variable are positive and increasing.

You can plot each of the five points *A* through *E* on this graph by using a pair of numbers—the values that the *x*-variable and the *y*-variable take on for a given point. In Figure A-1, at point *C*, the *x*-variable takes on the value 40 and the *y*-variable takes on the value 30. You plot point *C* by drawing a line straight up from 40 on the *x*-axis and a horizontal line across from 30 on the *y*-axis. We write point *C* as (40, 30). We write the origin as (0, 0).

Looking at point *A* and point *B* in Figure A-1, you can see that when one of the variables for a point has a value of zero, it will lie on one of the axes. If the value of the *x*-variable is zero, the point will lie on the vertical axis, like point *A*. If the value of the *y*-variable is zero, the point will lie on the horizontal axis, like point *B*.

Most graphs that depict relationships between two economic variables represent a **causal relationship,** a relationship in which the value taken by one variable directly influences or determines the value taken by the other variable. In a causal relationship, the determining variable is called the **independent variable;** the variable it determines is called the **dependent variable.** In our example of soda sales, the outside temperature is the independent variable. It directly influences the number of sodas that are sold, which is the dependent variable in this case.

A **causal relationship** exists between two variables when the value taken by one variable directly influences or determines the value taken by the other variable. In a causal relationship, the determining variable is called the **independent variable;** the variable it determines is called the **dependent variable.**

By convention, we put the independent variable on the horizontal axis and the dependent variable on the vertical axis. Figure A-1 follows this convention: the independent variable (outside temperature) is on the horizontal axis and the dependent variable (number of sodas sold) is on the vertical axis.

An important exception to this convention is in graphs showing the economic relationship between the price of a product and quantity of the product: although price is generally the independent variable that determines quantity, it is always measured on the vertical axis.

Curves on a Graph

Panel (a) of Figure A-2 contains some of the same information as Figure A-1, with a line drawn through the points *B*, *C*, *D*, and *E*. Such a line on a graph is called a **curve,** regardless of whether it is a straight line or a curved line. If the curve that shows the relationship between two variables is a straight line, or linear, the variables have a **linear relationship.** When the curve is not a straight line, or nonlinear, the variables have a **nonlinear relationship.**

A **curve** is a line on a graph that depicts a relationship between two variables. It may be either a straight line or a curved line. If the curve is a straight line, the variables have a **linear relationship.** If the curve is not a straight line, the variables have a **nonlinear relationship.**

A point on a curve indicates the value of the *y*-variable for a specific value of the *x*-variable. For example, point *D* indicates that at a temperature of 60°F, a vendor can expect to sell 50 sodas. The shape and orientation of a curve reveal the general nature of the relationship between the two variables. The upward tilt of the curve in panel (a) of Figure A-2 suggests that vendors can expect to sell more sodas at higher outside temperatures.

When variables are related in this way—that is, when an increase in one variable is associated with an increase in the other variable—the variables are said to have a **positive relationship.** It is illustrated by a curve that slopes upward from left to right. Because this curve is also linear, the relationship between outside temperature and number of sodas sold illustrated by the curve in panel (a) of Figure A-2 is a positive linear relationship.

Two variables have a **positive relationship** when an increase in the value of one variable is associated with an increase in the value of the other variable. It is illustrated by a curve that slopes upward from left to right.

When an increase in one variable is associated with a decrease in the other variable, the two variables are said to have a **negative relationship.** It is illustrated by a curve that slopes downward from left to right, like the curve in panel (b) of Figure A-2. Because this curve is also linear, the relationship it depicts is a negative linear relationship. Two variables that might have such a relationship are the outside temperature and the number of hot drinks a vendor can expect to sell at a baseball stadium.

Two variables have a **negative relationship** when an increase in the value of one variable is associated with a decrease in the value of the other variable. It is illustrated by a curve that slopes downward from left to right.

FIGURE A-2 Drawing Curves

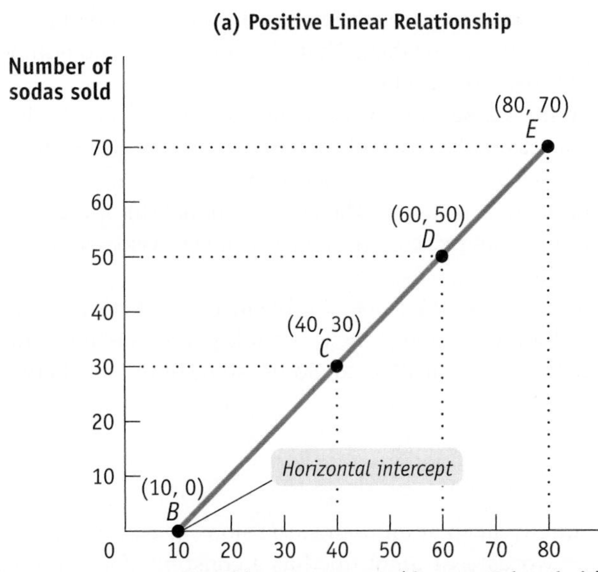

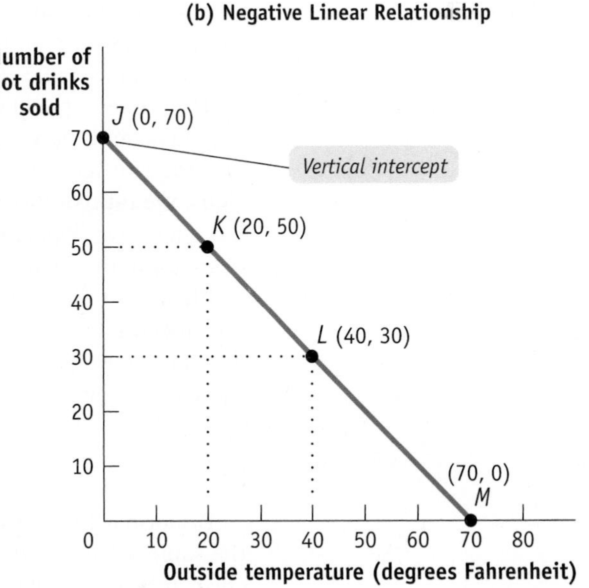

The curve in panel (a) illustrates the relationship between the two variables, outside temperature and number of sodas sold. The two variables have a positive linear relationship: positive because the curve has an upward tilt, and linear because it is a straight line. The curve implies that an increase in the *x*-variable (outside temperature) leads to an increase in the *y*-variable (number of sodas sold). The curve in panel (b) is also a straight line, but it tilts downward. The two variables here, outside temperature and number of hot drinks sold, have a negative linear relationship: an increase in the *x*-variable (outside temperature) leads to a decrease in the *y*-variable (number of hot drinks sold). The curve in panel (a) has a horizontal intercept at point *B*, where it hits the horizontal axis. The curve in panel (b) has a vertical intercept at point *J*, where it hits the vertical axis, and a horizontal intercept at point *M*, where it hits the horizontal axis.

The **horizontal intercept** of a curve is the point at which it hits the horizontal axis; it indicates the value of the *x*-variable when the value of the *y*-variable is zero.

The **vertical intercept** of a curve is the point at which it hits the vertical axis; it shows the value of the *y*-variable when the value of the *x*-variable is zero. The slope of a line or curve is a measure of how steep it is.

The **slope** of a line is measured by "rise over run"—the change in the *y*-variable between two points on the line divided by the change in the *x*-variable between those same two points.

Return for a moment to the curve in panel (a) of Figure A-2, and you can see that it hits the horizontal axis at point *B*. This point, known as the **horizontal intercept,** shows the value of the *x*-variable when the value of the *y*-variable is zero. In panel (b) of Figure A-2, the curve hits the vertical axis at point *J*. This point, called the **vertical intercept,** indicates the value of the *y*-variable when the value of the *x*-variable is zero.

A Key Concept: The Slope of a Curve

The **slope** of a curve is a measure of how steep it is; the slope indicates how sensitive the *y*-variable is to a change in the *x*-variable. In our example of outside temperature and the number of cans of soda a vendor can expect to sell, the slope of the curve would indicate how many more cans of soda the vendor could expect to sell with each 1° increase in temperature. Interpreted this way, the slope gives meaningful information.

Even without numbers for *x* and *y*, it is possible to arrive at important conclusions about the relationship between the two variables by examining the slope of a curve at various points.

The Slope of a Linear Curve

Along a linear curve the slope, or steepness, is measured by dividing the "rise" between two points on the curve by the "run" between those same two points. The rise is the amount that *y* changes, and the run is the amount that *x* changes. Here is the formula:

$$\frac{\text{Change in } y}{\text{Change in } x} = \frac{\Delta y}{\Delta x} = \text{Slope}$$

In the formula, the symbol Δ (the Greek uppercase delta) stands for "change in." When a variable increases, the change in that variable is positive; when a variable decreases, the change in that variable is negative.

The slope of a curve is positive when the rise (the change in the *y*-variable) has the same sign as the run (the change in the *x*-variable). That's because when two numbers have the same sign, the ratio of those two numbers is positive.

The curve in panel (a) of Figure A-2 has a positive slope: along the curve, both the *y*-variable and the *x*-variable increase. The slope of a curve is negative when the rise and the run have different signs. That's because when two numbers have different signs, the ratio of those two numbers is negative. The curve in panel (b) of Figure A-2 has a negative slope: along the curve, an increase in the *x*-variable is associated with a decrease in the *y*-variable.

Figure A-3 illustrates how to calculate the slope of a linear curve. Let's focus first on panel (a). From point *A* to point *B* the value of the *y*-variable changes from 25 to 20 and the value of the *x*-variable changes from 10 to 20. So the slope of the line between these two points is

$$\frac{\text{Change in } y}{\text{Change in } x} = \frac{\Delta y}{\Delta x} = \frac{-5}{10} = -\frac{1}{2} = -0.5$$

Because a straight line is equally steep at all points, the slope of a straight line is the same at all points. In other words, a straight line has a constant slope. You can check this by calculating the slope of the linear curve between points *A* and *B* and between points *C* and *D* in panel (b) of Figure A-3.

$$\frac{\Delta y}{\Delta x} = \frac{10}{2} = 5$$

$$\frac{\Delta y}{\Delta x} = \frac{20}{4} = 5$$

FIGURE A-3 Calculating the Slope

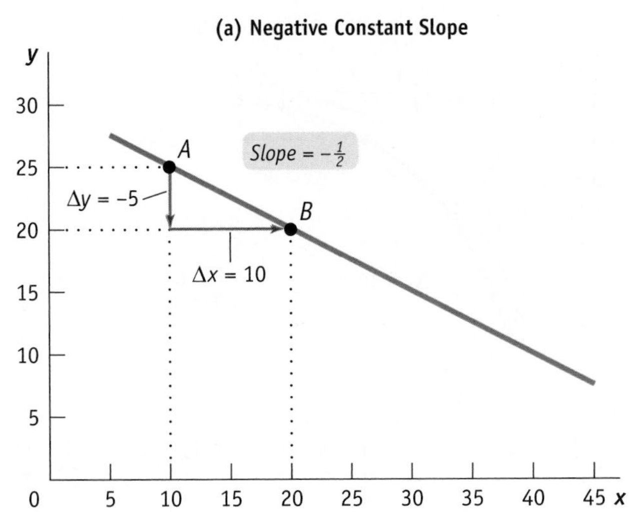

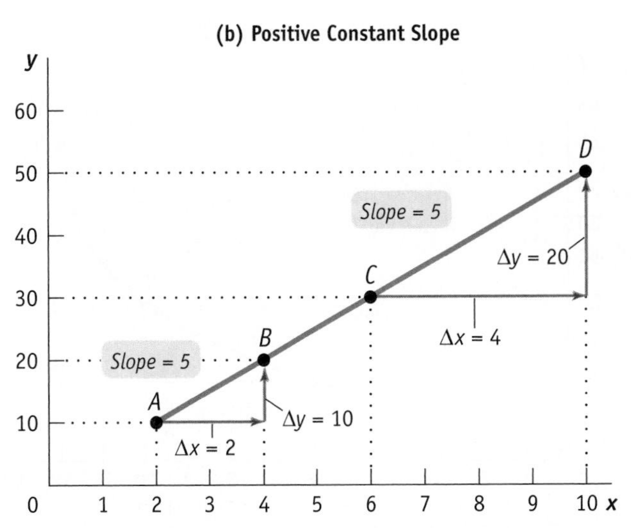

Panels (a) and (b) show two linear curves. Between points *A* and *B* on the curve in panel (a), the change in *y* (the rise) is –5 and the change in *x* (the run) is 10. So the slope from *A* to *B* is $\frac{\Delta y}{\Delta x} = \frac{-5}{10} = -\frac{1}{2} = -0.5$, where the negative sign indicates that the curve is downward sloping. In panel (b), the curve has a slope from *A* to *B* of $\frac{\Delta y}{\Delta x} = \frac{10}{2} = 5$. The slope from *C* to *D* is $\frac{\Delta y}{\Delta x} = \frac{20}{4} = 5$. The slope is positive, indicating that the curve is upward sloping. Furthermore, the slope between *A* and *B* is the same as the slope between *C* and *D*, making this a linear curve. The slope of a linear curve is constant: it is the same regardless of where it is calculated along the curve.

Horizontal and Vertical Curves and Their Slopes

When a curve is horizontal, the value of *y* along that curve never changes—it is constant. Everywhere along the curve, the change in *y* is zero. Now, zero divided by any number is zero. So regardless of the value of the change in *x*, the slope of a horizontal curve is always zero.

If a curve is vertical, the value of *x* along the curve never changes—it is constant. Everywhere along the curve, the change in *x* is zero. This means that the slope of a vertical line is a ratio with zero in the denominator. A ratio with zero in the denominator is equal to infinity—that is, an infinitely large number. So the slope of a vertical line is equal to infinity.

A vertical or a horizontal curve has a special implication: it means that the *x*-variable and the *y*-variable are unrelated. Two variables are unrelated when a change in one variable (the independent variable) has no effect on the other variable (the dependent variable). To put it a slightly different way, two variables are unrelated when the dependent variable is constant regardless of the value of the independent variable. If, as is usual, the *y*-variable is the dependent variable, the curve is horizontal. If the dependent variable is the *x*-variable, the curve is vertical.

The Slope of a Nonlinear Curve

A **nonlinear curve** is one in which the slope changes as you move along it. Panels (a), (b), (c), and (d) of Figure A-4 show various nonlinear curves. Panels (a) and (b) show nonlinear curves whose slopes change as you follow the line's progression, but the slopes always remain positive.

A **nonlinear curve** is one in which the slope is not the same between every pair of points.

Although both curves tilt upward, the curve in panel (a) gets steeper as the line moves from left to right in contrast to the curve in panel (b), which gets flatter. A

FIGURE A-4 Nonlinear Curves

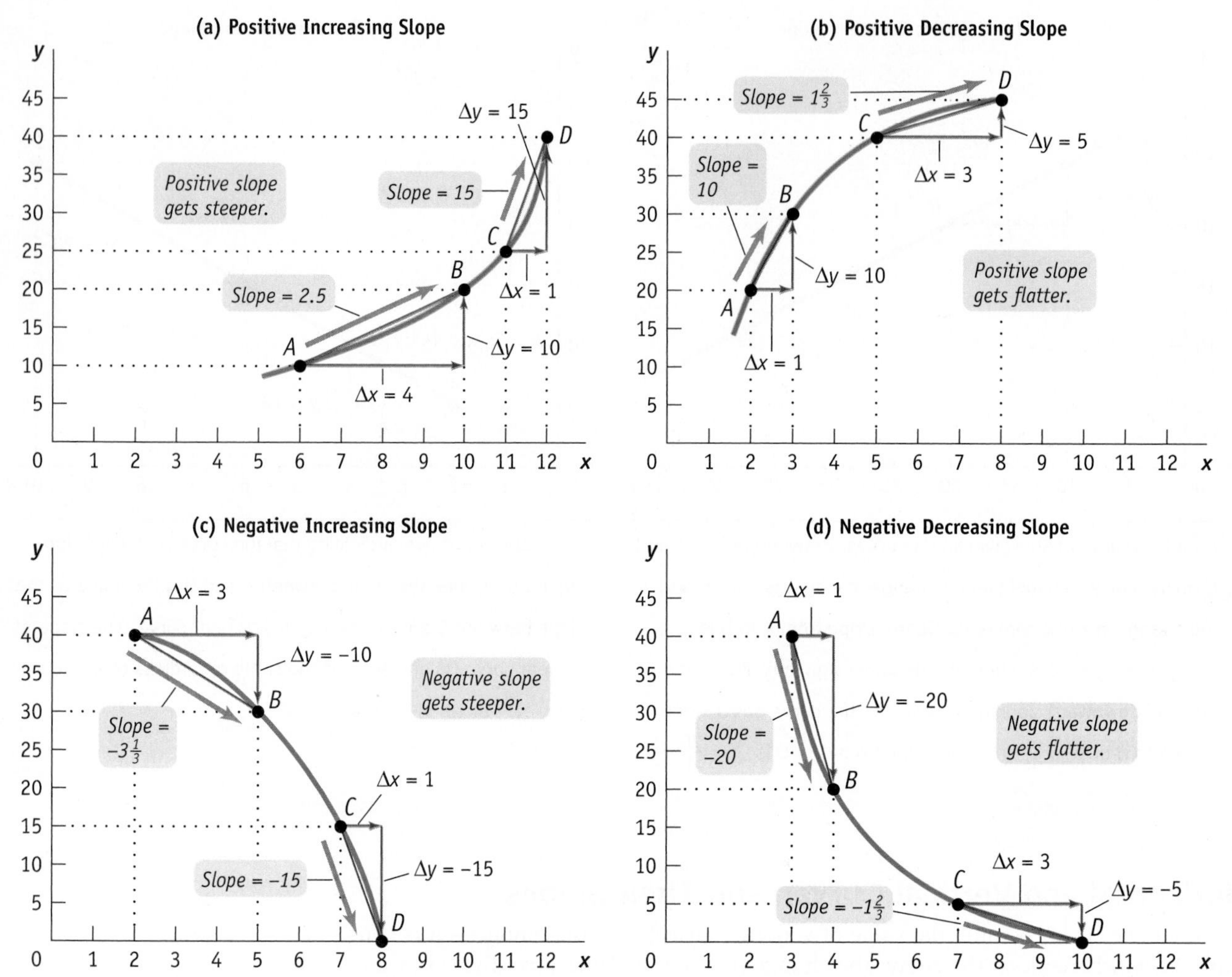

In panel (a) the slope of the curve from A to B is $\frac{\Delta y}{\Delta x} = \frac{10}{4} = 2.5$, and from C to D it is $\frac{\Delta y}{\Delta x} = \frac{15}{1} = 15$. The slope is positive and increasing; it gets steeper as it moves to the right. In panel (b) the slope of the curve from A to B is $\frac{\Delta y}{\Delta x} = \frac{10}{1} = 10$, and from C to D it is $\frac{\Delta y}{\Delta x} = \frac{5}{3} = 1\frac{2}{3}$. The slope is positive and decreasing; it gets flatter as it moves to the right. In panel (c) the slope from A to B is $\frac{\Delta y}{\Delta x} = \frac{-10}{3} = -3\frac{1}{3}$, and from C to D it is $\frac{\Delta y}{\Delta x} = \frac{-15}{1} = -15$. The slope is negative and increasing; it gets steeper as it moves to the right. And in panel (d) the slope from A to B is $\frac{\Delta y}{\Delta x} = \frac{-20}{1} = -20$, and from C to D it is $\frac{\Delta y}{\Delta x} = \frac{-5}{3} = -1\frac{2}{3}$. The slope is negative and decreasing; it gets flatter as it moves to the right.

The slope in each case has been calculated by using the *arc method*—that is, by drawing a straight line connecting two points along a curve. The average slope between those two points is equal to the slope of the straight line between those two points.

curve that is upward sloping and gets steeper, as in panel (a), is said to have *positive increasing* slope. A curve that is upward sloping but gets flatter, as in panel (b), is said to have *positive decreasing* slope.

When we calculate the slope along these nonlinear curves, we obtain different values for the slope at different points. How the slope changes along the curve determines the curve's shape. For example, in panel (a) of Figure A-4, the slope of the curve is a positive number that steadily increases as the line moves from left to right, whereas in panel (b), the slope is a positive number that steadily decreases.

ABSOLUTE VALUE The slopes of the curves in panels (c) and (d) are negative numbers. Economists often prefer to express a negative number as its **absolute value,** which is the value of the negative number without the minus sign.

In general, we denote the absolute value of a number by two parallel bars around the number; for example, the absolute value of −4 is written as $|-4| = 4$. In panel (c), the absolute value of the slope steadily increases as the line moves from left to right. The curve therefore has *negative increasing* slope. And in panel (d), the absolute value of the slope of the curve steadily decreases along the curve. This curve therefore has *negative decreasing* slope.

The **absolute value** of a negative number is the value of the negative number without the minus sign.

A nonlinear curve may have a **maximum** point, the highest point along the curve. At the maximum, the slope of the curve changes from positive to negative.

A nonlinear curve may have a **minimum** point, the lowest point along the curve. At the minimum, the slope of the curve changes from negative to positive.

Maximum and Minimum Points

The slope of a nonlinear curve can change from positive to negative or vice versa. When the slope of a curve changes from positive to negative, it creates what is called a *maximum* point of the curve. When the slope of a curve changes from negative to positive, it creates a *minimum* point.

Panel (a) of Figure A-5 illustrates a curve in which the slope changes from positive to negative as the line moves from left to right. When x is between 0 and 50, the slope of the curve is positive. At x equal to 50, the curve attains its highest point—the largest value of y along the curve. This point is called the **maximum** of the curve. When x exceeds 50, the slope becomes negative as the curve turns downward. Many important curves in economics, such as the curve that represents how the profit of a firm changes as it produces more output, are hill-shaped like this one.

FIGURE A-5 Maximum and Minimum Points

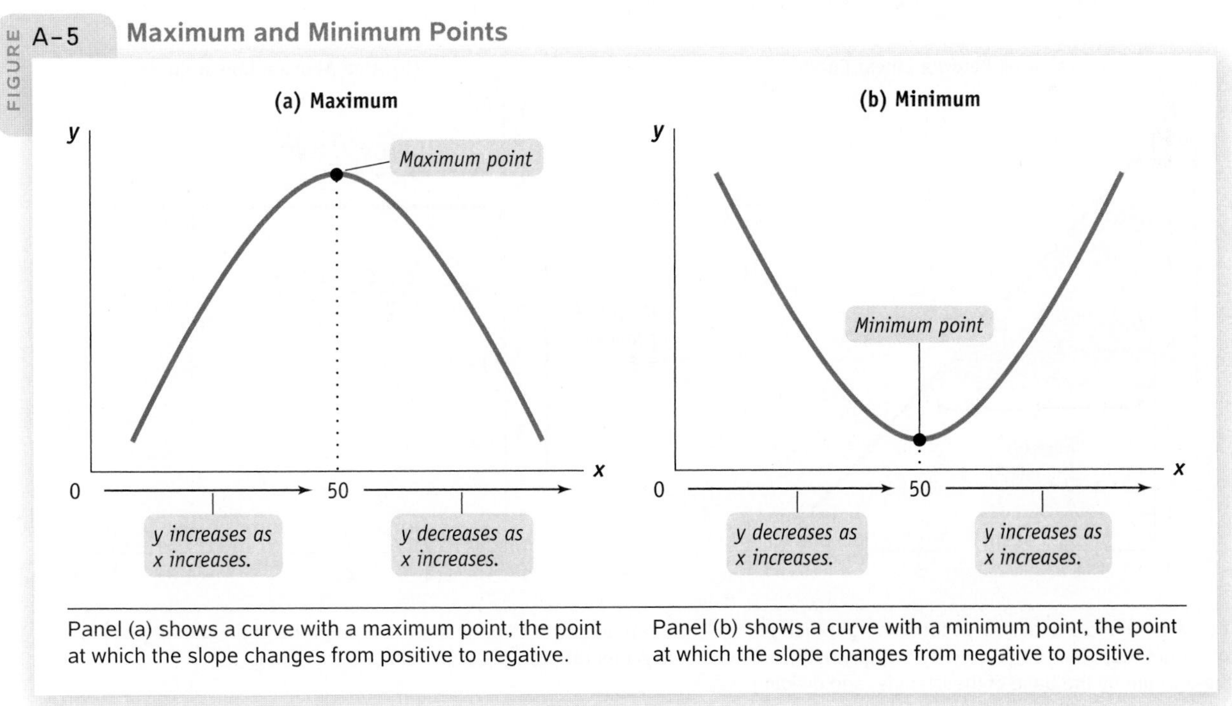

Panel (a) shows a curve with a maximum point, the point at which the slope changes from positive to negative.

Panel (b) shows a curve with a minimum point, the point at which the slope changes from negative to positive.

In contrast, the curve shown in panel (b) of Figure A-5 is U-shaped: it has a slope that changes from negative to positive. At x equal to 50, the curve reaches its lowest point—the smallest value of y along the curve. This point is called the **minimum** of the curve. Various important curves in economics, such as the curve that represents how a firm's cost per unit changes as output increases, are U-shaped like this one.

A **time-series graph** has dates on the horizontal axis and values of a variable that occurred on those dates on the vertical axis.

A **scatter diagram** shows points that correspond to actual observations of the *x*- and *y*-variables. A curve is usually fitted to the scatter of points.

Calculating the Area Below or Above a Curve

Sometimes it is useful to be able to measure the size of the area below or above a curve. To keep things simple, we'll only calculate the area below or above a linear curve.

How large is the shaded area below the linear curve in panel (a) of Figure A-6? First, note that this area has the shape of a right triangle. A *right triangle* is a triangle in which two adjacent sides form a 90° angle. We will refer to one of these sides as the *height* of the triangle and the other side as the *base* of the triangle. For our purposes, it doesn't matter which of these two sides we refer to as the base and which as the height.

Calculating the area of a right triangle is straightforward: multiply the height of the triangle by the base of the triangle, and divide the result by 2. The height of the triangle in panel (a) of Figure A-6 is 10 – 4 = 6. And the base of the triangle is 3 – 0 = 3. So the area of that triangle is

$$\frac{6 \times 3}{2} = 9$$

How about the shaded area above the linear curve in panel (b) of Figure A-6? We can use the same formula to calculate the area of this right triangle. The height of the triangle is 8 – 2 = 6. And the base of the triangle is 4 – 0 = 4. So the area of that triangle is

$$\frac{6 \times 4}{2} = 12$$

FIGURE A-6 Calculating the Area Below and Above a Linear Curve

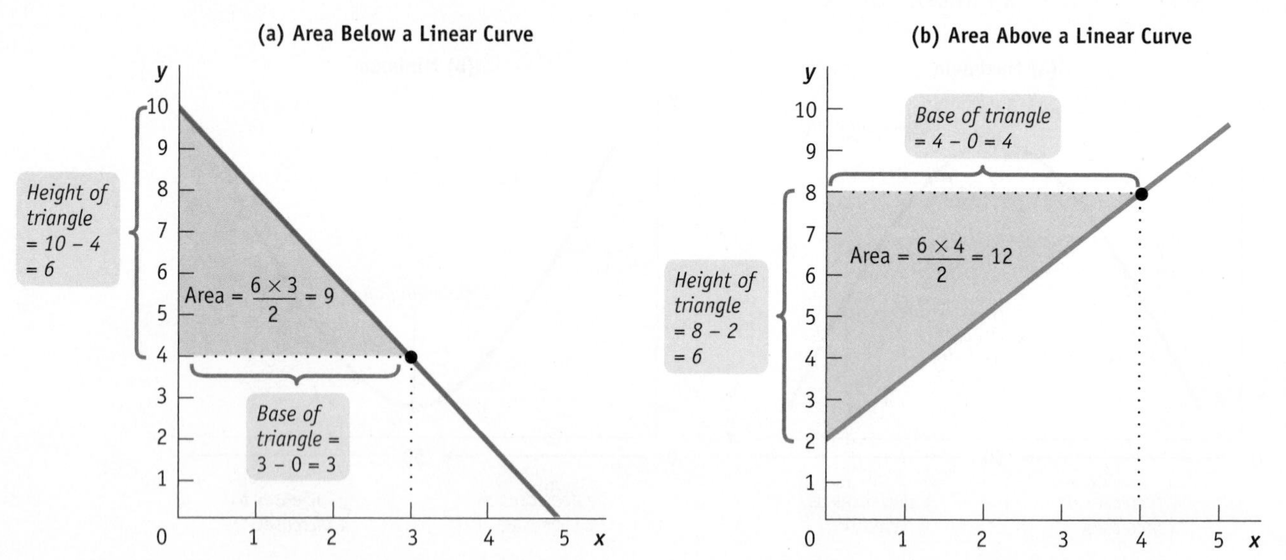

The area below or above a linear curve forms a right triangle. The area of a right triangle is calculated by multiplying the height of the triangle by the base of the triangle, and dividing the result by 2. In panel (a) the area of the shaded triangle is 9. In panel (b) the area of the shaded triangle is 12.

Graphs That Depict Numerical Information

Graphs are also used as a convenient way to summarize and display data without assuming some underlying causal relationship. Graphs that simply display numerical information are called *numerical graphs.*

Here we will consider the four most widely used types of numerical graphs: *time-series graphs, scatter diagrams, pie charts,* and *bar graphs.* These graphs are used to display real, empirical data about different economic variables and help economists and policy makers identify patterns or trends in the economy.

TIME-SERIES GRAPH You have probably seen graphs that show what happens over time to economic variables such as the unemployment rate or stock prices. A **time-series graph** has successive dates on the horizontal axis and the values of a variable that occurred on those dates on the vertical axis. For example, Figure A-7 shows real gross domestic product (GDP) per capita—a rough measure of a country's standard of living—in the United States from 1947 to late 2010. A line connecting the points that correspond to real GDP per capita for each calendar quarter during those years gives a clear idea of the overall trend in the standard of living over these years.

FIGURE A-7 Time-Series Graph

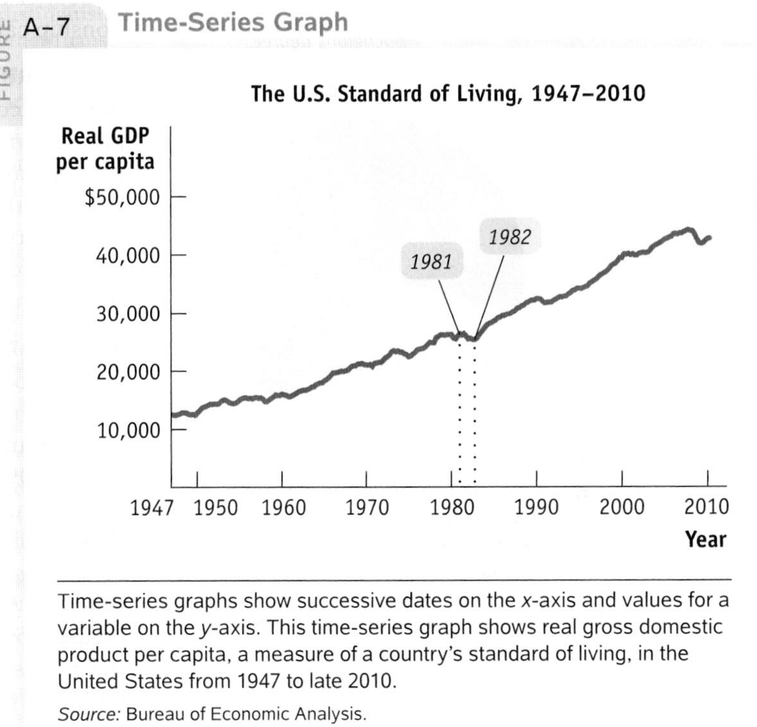

Time-series graphs show successive dates on the *x*-axis and values for a variable on the *y*-axis. This time-series graph shows real gross domestic product per capita, a measure of a country's standard of living, in the United States from 1947 to late 2010.

Source: Bureau of Economic Analysis.

SCATTER DIAGRAM Figure A-8 is an example of a different kind of numerical graph. It represents information from a sample of 184 countries on the standard of living, measured by GDP per capita, and the amount of carbon emissions per capita, a measure of environmental pollution. This type of graph is a **scatter diagram.** In these graphs, each point corresponds to an actual observation of the *x*-variable and the *y*-variable. Typically, a curve is fitted to the scatter of points; that is, a curve is drawn to approximate, as closely as possible, the general relationship between the variables. Each point in Figure A-8 indicates an average resident's standard of living and his or her annual carbon emissions for a given country.

The points lying in the upper right of the graph, which show combinations of a high standard of living and high carbon emissions, represent economically advanced countries such as the United States. (The country with the highest carbon emissions, at the top of the graph, is Qatar.) Points lying in the bottom left of the graph, which show combinations of a low standard of living and low carbon emissions, represent economically less advanced countries such as Afghanistan and Sierra Leone.

The pattern of points indicates that there is a positive relationship between living standard and carbon emissions per capita:

FIGURE A-8 Scatter Diagram

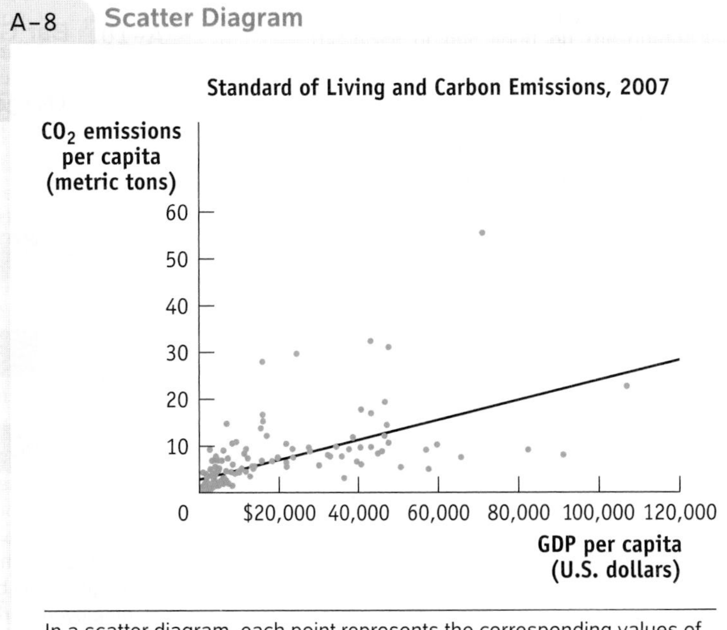

In a scatter diagram, each point represents the corresponding values of the *x*- and *y*-variables for a given observation. Here, each point indicates the GDP per capita and the amount of carbon emissions per capita for a given country for a sample of 184 countries. The upward-sloping fitted line here is the best approximation of the general relationship between the two variables.

Source: World Bank.

demand price the price of a given quantity at which consumers will demand that quantity.

demand schedule a list or table showing how much of a good or service consumers will want to buy at different prices.

derived demand for a factor results from (or is derived from) the demand for the output being produced.

diminishing returns to an input the effect observed when an increase in the quantity of an input, while holding the levels of all other inputs fixed, leads to a decline in the marginal product of that input.

domestic demand curve a demand curve that shows how the quantity of a good demanded by domestic consumers depends on the price of that good.

domestic supply curve a supply curve that shows how the quantity of a good supplied by domestic producers depends on the price of that good.

dominant strategy in game theory, an action that is a player's best action regardless of the action taken by the other player.

duopolist one of the two firms in a duopoly.

duopoly an oligopoly consisting of only two firms.

economic aggregates economic measures that summarize data across different markets for goods, services, workers, and assets.

economic profit a business's revenue minus the opportunity cost of resources; usually less than the accounting profit.

economic signal any piece of information that helps people make better economic decisions.

economics the study of scarcity and choice.

economy a system for coordinating a society's productive and consumptive activities.

efficient describes a market or economy that takes all opportunities to make some people better off without making other people worse off.

efficiency-wage model a model in which some employers pay an above-equilibrium wage as an incentive for better performance.

elastic demand the case in which the price elasticity of demand is greater than 1.

emissions tax a tax that depends on the amount of pollution a firm produces.

environmental standards rules established by a government to protect the environment by specifying actions by producers and consumers.

equilibrium an economic situation in which no individual would be better off doing something different.

equilibrium price the price at which the market is in equilibrium, that is, the quantity of a good or service demanded equals the quantity of that good or service supplied; also referred to as the market-clearing price.

equilibrium quantity the quantity of a good or service bought and sold at the equilibrium (or market-clearing) price.

equilibrium value of the marginal product the additional value produced by the last unit of a factor employed in the factor market as a whole.

excess capacity when firms produce less than the output at which average total cost is minimized; characteristic of monopolistically competitive firms.

excise tax a tax on sales of a particular good or service.

excludable referring to a good, describes the case in which the supplier can prevent those who do not pay from consuming the good.

explicit cost a cost that involves actually laying out money.

exporting industries industries that produce goods or services that are sold abroad.

exports goods and services sold to other countries.

external benefit an uncompensated benefit that an individual or firm confers on others; also known as positive externalities.

external cost an uncompensated cost that an individual or firm imposes on others; also known as negative externalities.

externalities external costs and external benefits.

factor distribution of income the division of total income among land, labor, physical capital, and human capital.

factor intensity the difference in the ratio of factors used to produce a good in various industries. For example, oil refining is capital-intensive compared to clothing manufacture because oil refiners use a higher ratio of capital to labor than do clothing producers.

factor markets markets where resources, especially capital and labor, are bought and sold.

factors of production the resources used to produce goods and services. The main factors of production are land, labor, physical capital, and human capital.

firm an organization that produces goods and services for sale.

fixed cost cost that does not depend on the quantity of output produced. It is the cost of the fixed input.

fixed input an input whose quantity is fixed for a period of time and cannot be varied (for example, land).

free entry and exit describes an industry that potential producers can easily enter or current producers can leave.

free trade trade that is unregulated by government tariffs or other artificial barriers; the levels of exports and imports occur naturally, as a result of supply and demand.

free-rider problem the problem that results when individuals who have no incentive to pay for their own consumption of a good take a "free ride" on anyone who does pay; a problem with goods that are nonexcludable.

gains from trade an economic principle that states that by dividing tasks and trading, people can get more of what they want through trade than they could if they tried to be self-sufficient.

game theory the study of behavior in situations of interdependence. Used to explain the behavior of an oligopoly.

Gini coefficient a number that summarizes a country's level of income inequality based on how unequally income is distributed across the quintiles.

globalization the phenomenom of growing economic linkages among countries.

government transfer a government payment to an individual or a family.

Heckscher–Ohlin model a model of international trade in which a country has a comparative advantage in a good whose production is intensive in the factors that are abundantly available in that country.

Herfindahl–Hirschman Index the square of each firm's share of market sales summed over the industry. It gives a picture of the industry market structure.

household a person or a group of people who share income.

human capital the improvement in labor created by the education and knowledge embodied in the workforce.

imperfect competition a market structure in which no firm is a monopolist, but producers nonetheless have market power they can use to affect market prices.

implicit cost a cost that does not require the outlay of money; it is measured by the value, in dollar terms, of forgone benefits.

implicit cost of capital the opportunity cost of the capital used by a business; that is, the income that could have been realized had the capital been used in the next best alternative way.

import quota a legal limit on the quantity of a good that can be imported.

import-competing industries industries that produce goods or services that are also imported.

imports goods and services purchased from other countries.

income effect the change in the quantity of a good consumed that results from the change in a consumer's purchasing power due to the change in the price of the good.

income elasticity of demand the percent change in the quantity of a good demanded when a consumer's income changes divided by the percent change in the consumer's income.

income-elastic demand the case in which the income elasticity of demand for a good is greater than 1.

income-inelastic demand the case in which the income elasticity of demand for a good is positive but less than 1.

increasing marginal cost each additional unit costs more to produce than the previous one.

increasing returns to scale long-run average total cost declines as output increases (also referred to as economies of scale).

individual choice the decision by an individual of what to do, which necessarily involves a decision of what not to do.

individual consumer surplus the net gain to an individual buyer from the purchase of a good; equal to the difference between the buyer's willingness to pay and the price paid.

individual demand curve a graphical representation of the relationship between quantity demanded and price for an individual consumer.

individual labor supply curve a graphical representation showing how the quantity of labor supplied by an individual depends on that individual's wage rate.

individual producer surplus the net gain to an individual seller from selling a good; equal to the difference between the price received and the seller's cost.

individual supply curve a graphical representation of the relationship between quantity supplied and price for an individual producer.

industry supply curve a graphical representation that shows the relationship between the price of a good and the total output of the industry for that good.

inefficient describes a market or economy in which there are missed opportunities: some people could be made better off without making other people worse off.

inefficient allocation of sales among sellers a form of inefficiency in which sellers who would be willing to sell a good at the lowest price are not always those who actually manage to sell it; often the result of a price floor.

inefficient allocation to consumers a form of inefficiency in which people who want a good badly and are willing to pay a high price don't get it, and those who care relatively little about the good and are only willing to pay a low price do get it; often a result of a price ceiling.

inefficiently high quality a form of inefficiency in which sellers offer high-quality goods at a high price even though buyers would prefer a lower quality at a lower price; often the result of a price floor.

inefficiently low quality a form of inefficiency in which sellers offer low-quality goods at a low price even though buyers would prefer a higher quality at a higher price; often a result of a price ceiling.

inelastic demand the case in which the price elasticity of demand is less than 1.

inferior good a good for which a rise in income decreases the demand for the good.

in-kind benefit a benefit given in the form of goods or services.

input a good or service used to produce another good or service.

interdependent the relationship among firms in which the outcome (profit) of each firm depends on the actions of the other firms in the market.

internalize the externalities take into account external costs and external benefits.

irrational describes a decision maker who chooses an option that leaves him or her worse off than choosing another available option.

labor the effort of workers.

land all resources that come from nature, such as minerals, timber, and petroleum.

law of demand the principle that a higher price for a good or service, other things equal, leads people to demand a smaller quantity of that good or service.

law of supply the general proposition that, other things equal, the price and quantity supplied of a good are positively related.

leisure the time available for purposes other than earning money to buy marketed goods.

license the right, conferred by the government or an owner, to supply a good or service.

long run the time period in which all inputs can be varied.

long-run average total cost curve a graphical representation showing the relationship between output and average total cost when fixed cost has been chosen to minimize average total cost for each level of output.

long-run industry supply curve a graphical representation that shows how quantity supplied responds to price once producers have had time to enter or exit the industry.

long-run market equilibrium an economic balance in which, given sufficient time for producers to enter or exit an industry, the quantity supplied equals the quantity demanded.

loss aversion oversensitivity to loss, leading to unwillingness to recognize a loss and move on.

lump-sum taxes taxes that don't depend on the taxpayer's income.

macroeconomics the branch of economics that is concerned with the overall ups and downs in the economy.

marginal analysis comparison of the benefit of doing a little bit more of some activity with the cost of doing a little bit more of that activity.

marginal benefit the additional benefit derived from producing one more unit of a good or service.

marginal benefit curve a graphical representation showing how the benefit from producing one more unit depends on the quantity that has already been produced.

marginal cost the additional cost incurred by producing one more unit of a good or service.

marginal cost curve a graphical representation showing how the cost of producing one more unit depends on the quantity that has already been produced.

marginal product the additional quantity of output produced by using one more unit of that input.

marginal productivity theory of income distribution every factor of production is paid its equilibrium value of the marginal product.

marginal revenue the change in total revenue generated by an additional unit of output.

marginal revenue curve a graphical representation showing how marginal revenue varies as output varies.

SOLUTIONS TO MODULE REVIEW QUESTIONS

This section offers suggested answers to the Review Questions that appear at the end of each module.

MODULE 1

Check Your Understanding

1. Land, labor, physical capital, and human capital are the four categories of resources. Possible examples include fisheries (land), time spent working on a fishing boat (labor), fishing nets (physical capital), and experienced fishermen and fish farmers (human capital).

2. a. time spent flipping burgers at a restaurant: labor
   b. a bulldozer: capital
   c. a river: land

3. a. Yes. The increased time spent commuting is a cost you will incur if you accept the new job. That additional time spent commuting—or equivalently, the benefit you would get from spending that time doing something else—is an opportunity cost of the new job.
   b. Yes. One of the benefits of the new job is that you will be making $50,000. But if you take the new job, you will have to give up your current job; that is, you have to give up your current salary of $45,000, so $45,000 is one of the opportunity costs of taking the new job.
   c. No. A more spacious office is an additional benefit of your new job and does not involve forgoing something else, so it is not an opportunity cost.

4. a. This is a normative statement because it stipulates what should be done. In addition, it may have no "right" answer. That is, should people be prevented from all dangerous personal behavior if they enjoy that behavior—like skydiving? Your answer will depend on your point of view.
   b. This is a positive statement because it is a description of fact.

Multiple-Choice Questions

1. d
2. d
3. b (The opportunity cost needs to take into account only the next-best alternative, which in this case is watching TV. The opportunity cost of watching TV, in turn, is its next best alternative: listening to music.)
4. b
5. a

Critical-Thinking Question

In positive economics there is a "right" or "wrong" answer. In normative economics there is not necessarily a "right" or "wrong" answer. There is more disagreement in normative economics because there is no "right" or "wrong" answer. Economists disagree because of (1) differences in values and (2) disagreements about models and about which simplifications are appropriate.

MODULE 2

Check Your Understanding

1. As households spend more on goods and services, firms increase their production of goods and services. As firms increase production, additional workers are hired and other workers can receive additional income for their labor. The result is an increase in the number of jobs in the economy. In addition, with more income, workers consume more goods and services and then the cycle begins again.

2. This illustrates the principle that one person's spending is another person's income. As oil companies increase their spending on labor by hiring more workers, or pay existing workers higher wages, those workers' incomes rise. In turn, these workers increase their consumer spending, which becomes income to restaurants and other consumer businesses.

Multiple-Choice Questions

1. b
2. c
3. c
4. d
5. e

Critical-Thinking Questions

The accompanying diagram illustrates the circular flow for Atlantis.

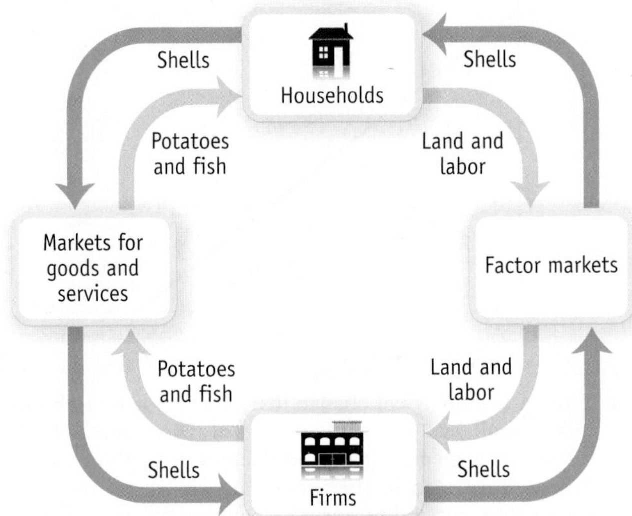

1. The flooding of the fields will destroy the potato crop. Destruction of the potato crop reduces the flow of goods

from firms to households: fewer potatoes produced by firms now are sold to households. An implication, of course, is that fewer cowry shells flow from households to firms as payment for the potatoes in the market for goods and services. Since firms now earn fewer shells, they have fewer shells to pay to households in the factor markets. As a result, the number of factors flowing from households to firms is also reduced.

2. The productive fishing season leads to greater quantity of fish produced by firms to flow to households. An implication is that more money flows from households to firms through the markets for goods and services. As a result, firms will want to buy more factors from households (the flow of shells from firms to households increases) and, in return, the flow of factors from households to firms increases.

3. Time spent at dancing festivals reduces the flow of labor from households to firms and therefore reduces the number of shells flowing from firms to households through the factor markets. In return, households now have fewer shells to buy goods with (the flow of shells from households to firms in the markets for goods and services is reduced), implying that fewer goods flow from firms to households.

MODULE 3

Check Your Understanding

1. a. False. An increase in the resources available to Boeing for use in producing Dreamliners and small jets changes the production possibility curve by shifting it outward. This is because Boeing can now produce more small jets and Dreamliners than before. In the accompanying figure, the line labeled "Boeing's original *PPF*" represents Boeing's original production possibility curve, and the line labeled "Boeing's new *PPF*" represents the new production possibility curve that results from an increase in resources available to Boeing.

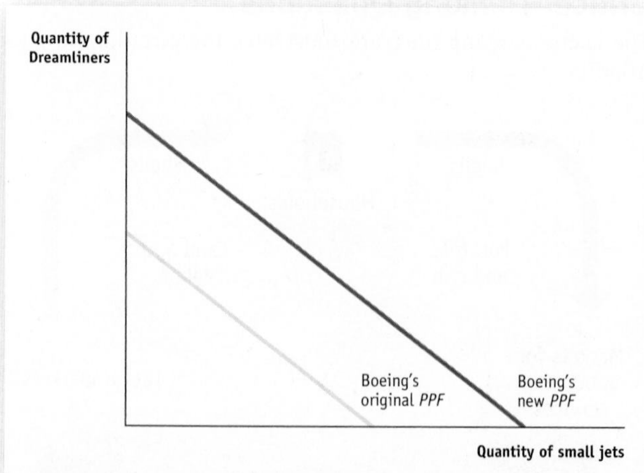

b. True. A technological change that allows Boeing to build more small jets for any amount of Dreamliners built results in a change in its production possibility curve. This is illustrated in the accompanying figure: the new production possibility curve is represented by the line labeled "Boeing's new *PPF*," and the original production curve is represented by the line labeled "Boeing's original *PPF*." Since the maximum quantity of Dreamliners that Boeing can build is the same as before, the new production possibility curve intersects the vertical axis at the same point as the original curve. But since the maximum possible quantity of small jets is now greater than before, the new curve intersects the horizontal axis to the right of the original curve.

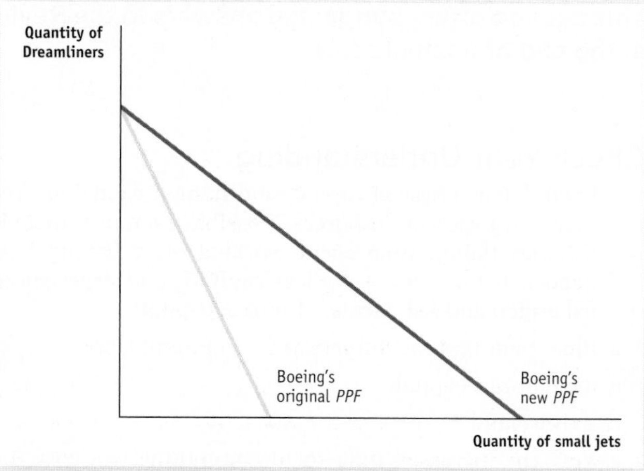

c. False. The production possibility frontier illustrates how much of one good an economy must give up to get more of another good only when resources are used efficiently in production. If an economy is producing inefficiently—that is, inside the frontier—then it does not have to give up a unit of one good in order to get another unit of the other good. Instead, by becoming more efficient in production, this economy can have more of both goods.

Multiple-Choice Questions

1. c
2. d
3. d
4. e
5. a

Critical-Thinking Question

Your graph should look like this.

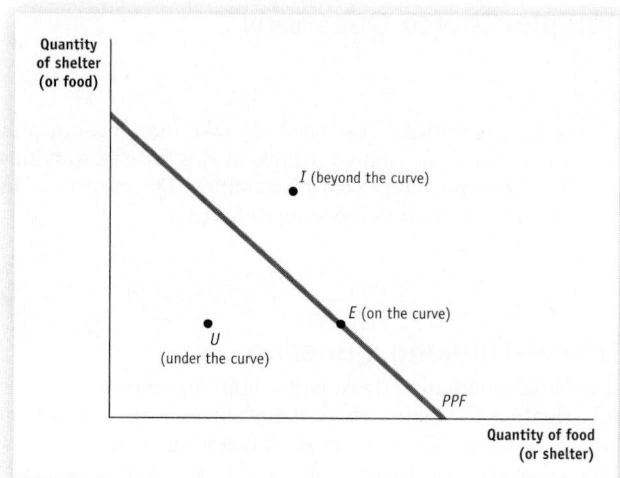

MODULE 4

Check Your Understanding

1. a. The United States has an absolute advantage in automobile production because it takes fewer Americans (6) to produce a car in one day than it takes Italians (8). The United States also has an absolute advantage in washing machine production because it takes fewer Americans (2) to produce a washing machine in one day than it takes Italians (3).

   b. In Italy the opportunity cost of a washing machine in terms of an automobile is $3/8$. In other words, $3/8$ of a car can be produced with the same number of workers and in the same time it takes to produce 1 washing machine. In the United States the opportunity cost of a washing machine in terms of an automobile is $2/6 = 1/3$. In other words, $1/3$ of a car can be produced with the same number of workers and in the same time it takes to produce 1 washing machine. Since $1/3 < 3/8$, the United States has a comparative advantage in the production of washing machines: to produce a washing machine, only $1/3$ of a car must be given up in the United States but $3/8$ of a car must be given up in Italy. This means that Italy has a comparative advantage in automobiles. This can be checked as follows. The opportunity cost of an automobile in terms of a washing machine in Italy is $8/3$, equal to $2\frac{2}{3}$. In other words, $2\frac{2}{3}$ washing machines can be produced with the same number of workers and in the time it takes to produce 1 car in Italy. And the opportunity cost of an automobile in terms of a washing machine in the United States is $6/2$, equal to 3. In other words, 3 washing machines can be produced with the same number of workers and in the time it takes to produce 1 car in the United States.

   c. The greatest gains are realized when each country specializes in producing the good for which it has a comparative advantage. Therefore, based on this example, the United States should specialize in washing machines and Italy should specialize in automobiles.

2. At a trade of 10 U.S. large jets for 15 Brazilian small jets, Brazil gives up less for a large jet than it would if it were building large jets itself. Without trade, Brazil gives up 3 small jets for each large jet it produces. With trade, Brazil gives up only 1.5 small jets for each large jet from the United States. Likewise, the United States gives up less for a small jet than it would if it were producing small jets itself. Without trade, the United States gives up $3/4$ of a large jet for each small jet. With trade, the United States gives up only $2/3$ of a large jet for each small jet from Brazil.

Multiple-Choice Questions

1. a
2. a
3. a
4. d
5. d

Critical-Thinking Questions

1. Country A: opportunity cost of 1 bushel of wheat = 4 units of textiles

   Country B: opportunity cost of 1 bushel of wheat = 6 units of textiles

2. Country A has an absolute advantage in the production of wheat (15 versus 10)

3. Country A: opportunity cost of 1 unit of textiles = $1/4$ bushel of wheat

   Country B: opportunity cost of 1 unit of textiles = $1/6$ bushel of wheat

   Country B has the comparative advantage in textile production because it has a lower opportunity cost of producing textiles. (Alternate answer: Country B has the comparative advantage in the production of textiles because Country A has a comparative advantage in the production of wheat based on opportunity costs shown in part a.)

MODULE 5

Check Your Understanding

1. a. The quantity of umbrellas demanded is higher at any given price on a rainy day than on a dry day. This is a rightward *shift* of the demand curve, since at any given price the quantity demanded rises. This implies that any specific quantity can now be sold at a higher price.

   b. The quantity of weekend calls demanded rises in response to a price reduction. This is a *movement along* the demand curve for weekend calls.

   c. The demand for roses increases the week of Valentine's Day. This is a rightward *shift* of the demand curve.

   d. The quantity of gasoline demanded falls in response to a rise in price. This is a *movement along* the demand curve.

Multiple-Choice Questions

1. e
2. a
3. c
4. d
5. a

Critical-Thinking Question

Your graph would look like this.

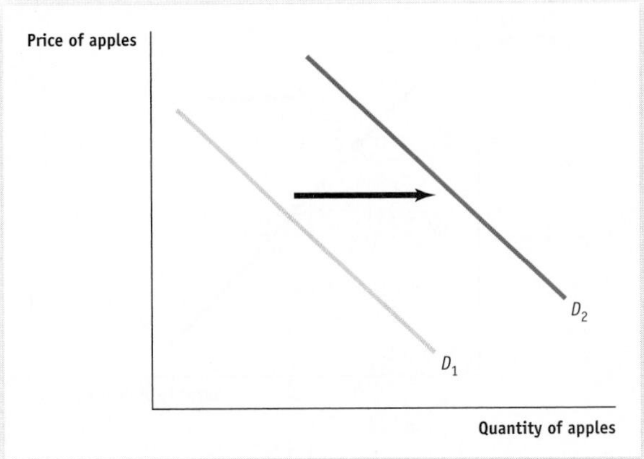

MODULE 6

Check Your Understanding

1. a. The quantity of houses supplied rises as a result of an increase in prices. This is a *movement along* the supply curve.

b. The quantity of strawberries supplied is higher at any given price. This is an *increase* in supply, which shifts the supply curve to the right.

c. The quantity of labor supplied is lower at any given wage. This is a *decrease* in supply, which shifts the supply curve leftward compared to the supply curve during school vacation. So, in order to attract workers, fast-food chains have to offer higher wages.

d. The quantity of labor supplied rises in response to a rise in wages. This is a *movement along* the supply curve.

e. The quantity of cabins supplied is higher at any given price. This is an *increase* in supply, which shifts the supply curve to the right.

2. a. This is an increase in supply, so the supply curve shifts rightward. At the original equilibrium price of the year before, the quantity of grapes supplied exceeds the quantity demanded, and the result is a surplus. The price of grapes will fall.

b. This is a decrease in demand, so the demand curve shifts leftward. At the original equilibrium price, the quantity of hotel rooms supplied exceeds the quantity demanded. The result is a surplus. The rates for hotel rooms will fall.

c. Demand increases, so the demand curve for second-hand snowblowers shifts rightward. At the original equilibrium price, the quantity of second-hand snowblowers demanded exceeds the quantity supplied. This is a case of shortage. The equilibrium price of second-hand snowblowers will rise.

Multiple-Choice Questions

1. d
2. d
3. c
4. b
5. d

Critical-Thinking Question

Your graph would look like this.

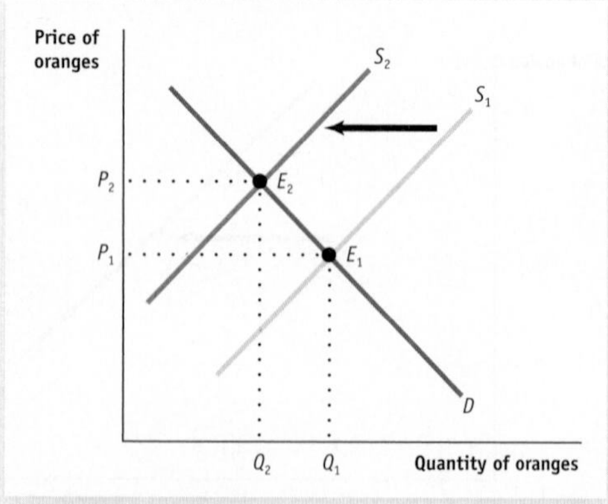

MODULE 7

Check Your Understanding

1. a. The decrease in the price of gasoline caused a rightward shift in the demand for large cars. As a result of the shift, the equilibrium price of large cars rose and the equilibrium quantity of large cars bought and sold also rose.

b. The technological innovation has caused a rightward shift in the supply of fresh paper made from recycled stock. As a result of this shift, the equilibrium price of fresh paper made from recycled stock has fallen and the equilibrium quantity bought and sold has risen.

c. The fall in the price of pay-per-view movies causes a leftward shift in the demand for movies at local movie theaters. As a result of this shift, the equilibrium price of movie tickets falls and the equilibrium number of people who go to the movies also falls.

2. Upon the announcement of the new chip, the demand curve for computers using the earlier chip shifts leftward (demand decreases), and the supply curve for these computers shifts rightward (supply increases).

a. If demand decreases relatively more than supply increases, then the equilibrium quantity falls, as shown here:

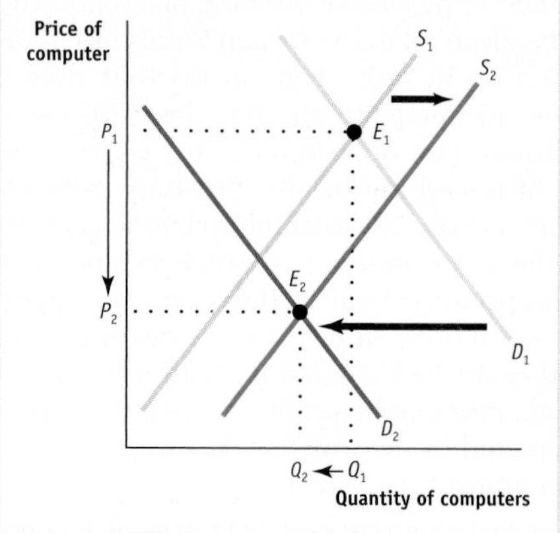

b. If supply increases relatively more than demand decreases, then the equilibrium quantity rises, as shown here:

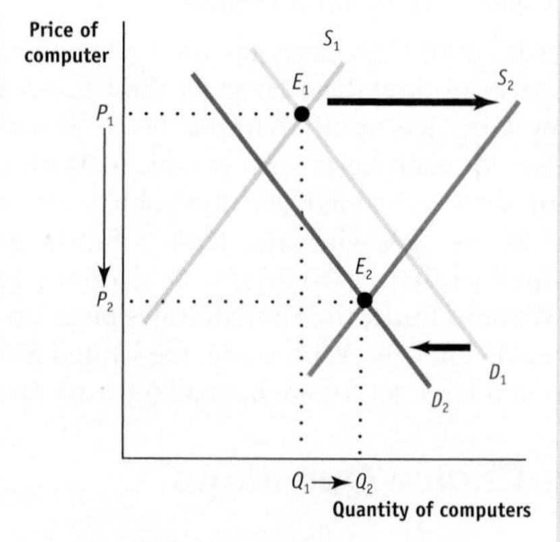

In both cases, the equilibrium price falls.

Multiple-Choice Questions

1. d
2. b
3. a
4. a
5. c

Critical-Thinking Question

Your graph would look like this.

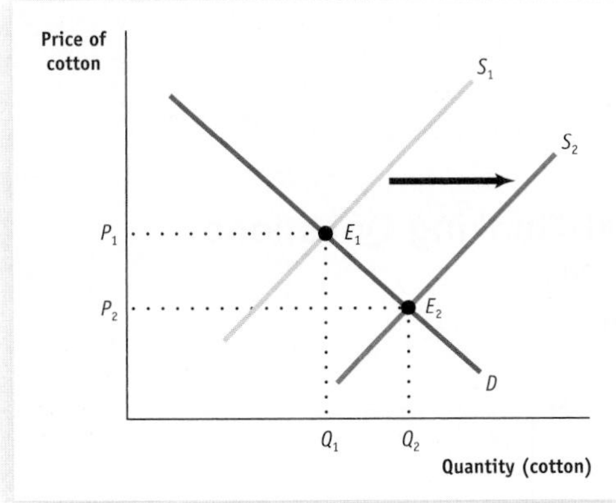

MODULE 8

Check Your Understanding

1. a. Since spending on orange juice is a small share of Clare's spending, the income effect from a rise in the price of orange juice is insignificant. Only the substitution effect, represented by the substitution of lemonade for orange juice, is significant.

   b. Since rent is a large share of Delia's expenditures, the increase in rent generates an income effect, making Delia feel poorer. Since housing is a normal good for Delia, the income and substitution effects move in the same direction, leading her to reduce her consumption of housing by moving to a smaller apartment.

   c. Since a meal ticket is a significant share of the students' living costs, an increase in its price will generate an income effect. Students respond to the price increase by eating more often in the cafeteria. So the substitution effect (which would induce them to eat in the cafeteria less often as they substitute restaurant meals in place of meals at the cafeteria) and the income effect (which would induce them to eat in the cafeteria more often because they are poorer) move in opposite directions. This happens because cafeteria meals are an inferior good. In fact, since the income effect outweighs the substitution effect (students eat in the cafeteria more as the price of meal tickets increases), cafeteria meals are a Giffen good.

2. By the midpoint method, the percent change in the quantity of strawberries demanded is

$$\frac{200{,}000 - 100{,}000}{(100{,}000 + 200{,}000)/2} \times 100 = \frac{100{,}000}{150{,}000} \times 100 = 67\%$$

   Similarly, the percent change in the price of strawberries is

$$\frac{\$1.00 - \$1.50}{(\$1.50 + \$1.00)/2} \times 100 = \frac{-\$0.50}{\$1.25} \times 100 = -40\%$$

   Dropping the minus sign, the price elasticity of demand using the midpoint method is 67%/40% = 1.7.

3. By the midpoint method, the percent change in the quantity of movie tickets demanded in going from 4,000 tickets to 5,000 tickets is

$$\frac{5{,}000 - 4{,}000}{(4{,}000 + 5{,}000)/2} \times 100 = \frac{1{,}000}{4{,}500} \times 100 = 22\%$$

   Since the price elasticity of demand is 1 at the current consumption level, it will take a 22% reduction in the price of movie tickets to generate a 22% increase in quantity demanded.

4. Since price rises, we know that quantity demanded must fall. Given the current price of \$0.50, a \$0.05 increase in price represents a 10% change, using the method in Equation 8-2. So the price elasticity of demand is

$$\frac{\%\ \text{change in quantity demanded}}{10\%} = 1.2$$

   so that the percent change in quantity demanded is 12%. A 12% decrease in quantity demanded represents 100,000 × 0.12, or 12,000 sandwiches.

Multiple-Choice Questions

1. d
2. c
3. b
4. e
5. c

Critical-Thinking Questions

a. The substitution effect will decrease the quantity demanded. As price increases, consumers will buy other goods instead.

b. The income effect will increase the quantity demanded. As price increases, real income decreases, so consumers will purchase more of the inferior good.

c. The substitution effect is larger than the income effect. If the income effect were larger than the substitution effect, more of the good would be purchased as the price increased, and the demand curve would be upward sloping.

MODULE 9

Check Your Understanding

1. a. Elastic demand. Consumers are highly responsive to changes in price. For a rise in price, the quantity effect (which tends to reduce total revenue) outweighs the price effect (which tends to increase total revenue). Overall, this leads to a fall in total revenue.

   b. Unit-elastic demand. Here the revenue lost to the fall in price is exactly equal to the revenue gained from higher sales. The quantity effect exactly offsets the price effect.

   c. Inelastic demand. Consumers are relatively unresponsive to changes in price. For consumers to purchase a given percent more, the price must fall by an even greater percent. The price effect of a fall in price (which tends to reduce total revenue) outweighs the quantity effect (which tends to increase total revenue). As a result, total revenue decreases.

   d. Inelastic demand. Consumers are not very responsive to changes in price. For a rise in price, the quantity effect (which tends to reduce total revenue) is outweighed by the price effect (which tends to increase total revenue). Overall, this leads to an increase in total revenue.

2. a. Once bitten by a venomous snake, the victim's demand for an antidote is very likely to be perfectly inelastic because there is no substitute and it is necessary for survival. The demand curve will be vertical at a quantity equal to the needed dose.

b. Students' demand for blue pencils is likely to be perfectly elastic because there are readily available substitutes, such as yellow pencils. The demand curve will be horizontal at a price equal to that of non-blue pencils.

Multiple-Choice Questions

1. d
2. d
3. c
4. b
5. c

Critical-Thinking Question

a.

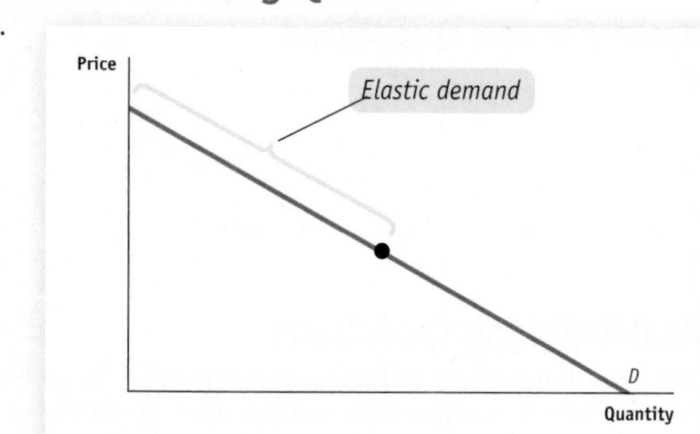

b. An increase in price will decrease total revenue because the negative quantity effect of the price increase is greater than the positive price effect of the price increase.

MODULE 10

Check Your Understanding

1. By the midpoint method, the percent increase in Chelsea's consumption of DVDs is

$$\frac{40-10}{(10+40)/2}\times 100 = \frac{30}{25}\times 100 = 120\%$$

Similarly, the percent increase in her income is

$$\frac{\$18{,}000-\$12{,}000}{(\$12{,}000+\$18{,}000)/2}\times 100 = \frac{\$6{,}000}{\$15{,}000}\times 100 = 40\%$$

Chelsea's income elasticity of demand for DVDs is therefore 120%/40% = 3.

2. The cross-price elasticity of demand is 5%/20% = 0.25. Since the cross-price elasticity of demand is positive, the two goods are substitutes.

3. By the midpoint method, the percent change in the number of hours of web-design services contracted is

$$\frac{500{,}000-300{,}000}{(300{,}000+500{,}000)/2}\times 100 = \frac{200{,}000}{400{,}000}\times 100 = 50\%$$

Similarly, the percent change in the price of web-design services is:

$$\frac{\$150-\$100}{(\$100+\$150)/2}\times 100 = \frac{\$50}{\$125}\times 100 = 40\%$$

The price elasticity of supply is 50%/40% = 1.25. Hence supply is elastic.

Multiple-Choice Questions

1. b
2. d
3. d
4. d
5. c

Critical-Thinking Questions

a. 40%/20% = 2

b. elastic

c.

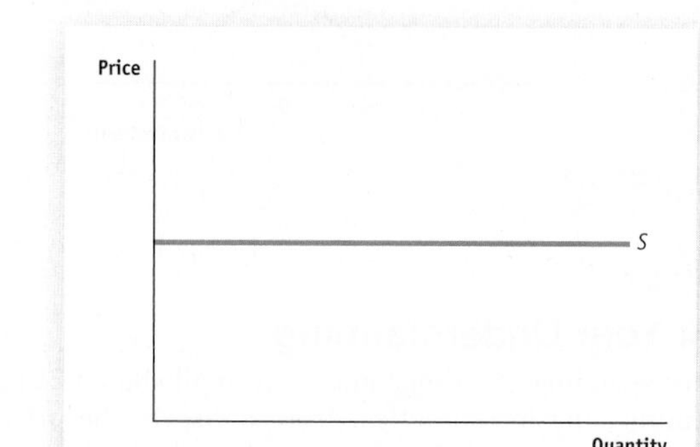

d. Inputs are readily available and can be shifted into/out of production at low cost.

MODULE 11

Check Your Understanding

1. A consumer buys each pepper if the price is less than (or just equal to) the consumer's willingness to pay for that pepper. The demand schedule is constructed by asking how many peppers will be demanded at any given price. The accompanying table illustrates the demand schedule.

Price of pepper	Quantity of peppers demanded	Quantity of peppers demanded by Casey	Quantity of peppers demanded by Josey
$0.90	1	1	0
0.80	2	1	1
0.70	3	2	1
0.60	4	2	2
0.50	5	3	2
0.40	6	3	3
0.30	8	4	4
0.20	8	4	4
0.10	8	4	4
0.00	8	4	4

When the price is $0.40, Casey's consumer surplus from the first pepper is $0.50, from his second pepper $0.30, from his third pepper $0.10, and he does not buy any more peppers. Casey's individual consumer surplus is therefore $0.90. Josey's consumer surplus from her first pepper is $0.40, from her second pepper $0.20, from her third pepper $0.00 (since the price is exactly equal to her willingness to pay, she buys the third pepper but receives no consumer surplus from it), and she does not buy any more peppers. Josey's individual consumer surplus is therefore $0.60. Total consumer surplus at a price of $0.40 is therefore $0.90 + $0.60 = $1.50.

2. A producer supplies each pepper if the price is greater than (or just equal to) the producer's cost of producing that pepper. The supply schedule is constructed by asking how many peppers will be supplied at any price. The accompanying table illustrates the supply schedule.

Price of pepper	Quantity of peppers supplied	Quantity of peppers supplied by Cara	Quantity of peppers supplied by Jamie
$0.90	8	4	4
0.80	7	4	3
0.70	7	4	3
0.60	6	4	2
0.50	5	3	2
0.40	4	3	1
0.30	3	2	1
0.20	2	2	0
0.10	2	2	0
0.00	0	0	0

When the price is $0.70, Cara's producer surplus from the first pepper is $0.60, from her second pepper $0.60, from her third pepper $0.30, from her fourth pepper $0.10, and she does not supply any more peppers. Cara's individual producer surplus is therefore $1.60. Jamie's producer surplus from his first pepper is $0.40, from his second pepper $0.20, from his third pepper $0.00 (since the price is exactly equal to his cost, he sells the third pepper but receives no producer surplus from it), and he does not supply any more peppers. Jamie's individual producer surplus is therefore $0.60. Total producer surplus at a price of $0.70 is therefore $1.60 + $0.60 = $2.20.

Multiple-Choice Questions

1. c
2. c
3. c
4. b
5. a

Critical-Thinking Question

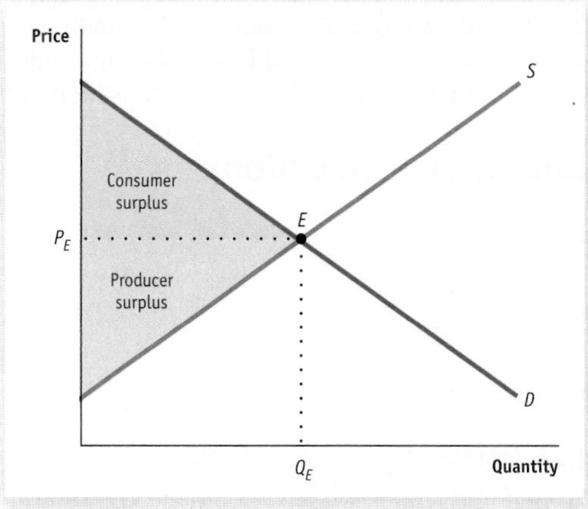

MODULE 12

Check Your Understanding

1. The quantity demanded equals the quantity supplied at a price of $0.50, the equilibrium price. At that price, a total quantity of five peppers will be bought and sold. Casey will buy three peppers and receive consumer surplus of $0.40 on his first, $0.20 on his second, and $0.00 on his third pepper. Josey will buy two peppers and receive consumer surplus of $0.30 on her first and $0.10 on her second pepper. Total consumer surplus is therefore $1.00. Cara will supply three peppers and receive producer surplus of $0.40 on her first, $0.40 on her second, and $0.10 on her third pepper. Jamie will supply two peppers and receive producer surplus of $0.20 on his first and $0.00 on his second pepper. Total producer surplus is therefore $1.10. Total surplus in this market is therefore $1.00 + $1.10 = $2.10.

2. a. If Josey consumes one fewer pepper, she loses $0.10 (her consumer surplus on the second pepper when market price is $0.50); if Casey consumes one more pepper, he loses $0.20 (his willingness to pay for his fourth pepper is only $0.30 but the market price is $0.50). This results in an overall loss of consumer surplus of $0.10 + $0.20 = $0.30.

b. Cara's producer surplus on the last pepper she supplied (the third pepper) at a market price of $0.50 is $0.10, and Jamie's loss in terms of producer surplus of producing one more (his third pepper, which costs $0.70 to produce) is $0.20 at a market price of $0.50. Total producer surplus therefore falls by $0.10 + $0.20 = $0.30.

c. Josey's consumer surplus from her second pepper is $0.10; this is what she would lose if she were to consume one fewer pepper. Cara's producer surplus from producing her third pepper is $0.10; this is what she would forego if she were to produce one fewer pepper. Therefore, if we reduced quantity by one pepper, we would lose $0.10 + $0.10 = $0.20 of total surplus.

3. There will be many sellers willing to sell their books but only a few buyers who want to buy books at that price. As a result, only a few transactions will actually occur, and many transactions that would have been mutually beneficial will not take place. This, of course, is inefficient.

Multiple-Choice Questions

1. c
2. e
3. b
4. d
5. d

Critical-Thinking Questions

1. The new guideline is likely to reduce the total life span of kidney recipients because older recipients (those with small children) are more likely to get a kidney compared to the original guideline. As a result, total surplus is likely to fall. However, this new policy can be justified as an acceptable sacrifice of efficiency for fairness, because society is likely to agree that it is a desirable goal to reduce the chance of a small child losing a parent.
2. Markets, alas, do not always lead to efficiency. When there is market failure, the market outcome may be inefficient. This can occur for three main reasons. Markets can fail when, in an attempt to capture more surplus, one party—a monopolist, for instance—prevents mutually beneficial trades from occurring. Markets can also fail when one individual's actions have side effects—externalities—on the welfare of others. Finally, markets can fail when the goods themselves—such as goods about which some relevant information is private—are unsuited for efficient management by markets.

MODULE 13

Check Your Understanding

1.

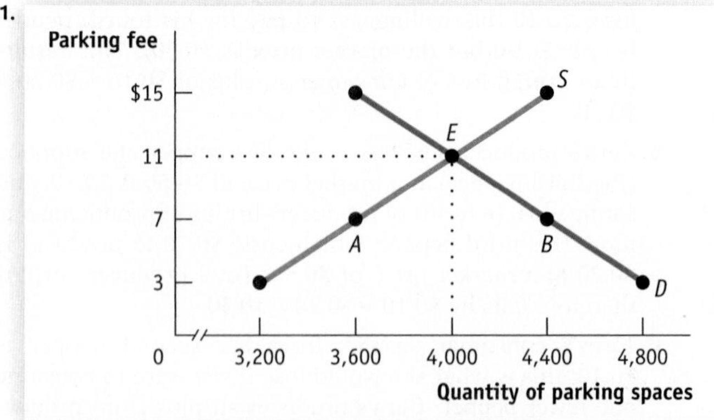

a. Fewer homeowners are willing to rent out their driveways because the price ceiling has reduced the payment they receive. This is an example of a fall in price leading to a fall in the quantity supplied. This is shown in the accompanying diagram by the movement from point *E* to point *A* along the supply curve, a reduction in quantity of 400 parking spaces.

b. The quantity demanded increases by 400 spaces as the price decreases. At a lower price, more fans are willing to drive and rent a parking space. It is shown in the diagram by the movement from point *E* to point *B* along the demand curve.

c. Under a price ceiling, the quantity demanded exceeds the quantity supplied; as a result, shortages arise. In this case, there will be a shortage of 800 parking spaces. It is shown by the horizontal distance between points *A* and *B*.

d. Price ceilings result in wasted resources. The additional time fans spend to secure a parking space is wasted time.

e. Price ceilings lead to the inefficient allocation of goods—here, the parking spaces—to consumers. If less serious fans with connections end up with the parking spaces, diehard fans have no place to park.

f. Price ceilings lead to black markets.

2. a. False. By lowering the price that producers receive, a price ceiling leads to a decrease in the quantity supplied.

b. True. A price ceiling leads to a lower quantity supplied than in an efficient, unregulated market. As a result, some people who would have been willing to pay the market price, and so would have gotten the good in an unregulated market, are unable to obtain it when a price ceiling is imposed.

c. True. Those producers who still sell the product now receive less for it and are therefore worse off. Other producers will no longer find it worthwhile to sell the product at all and so will also be made worse off.

3.

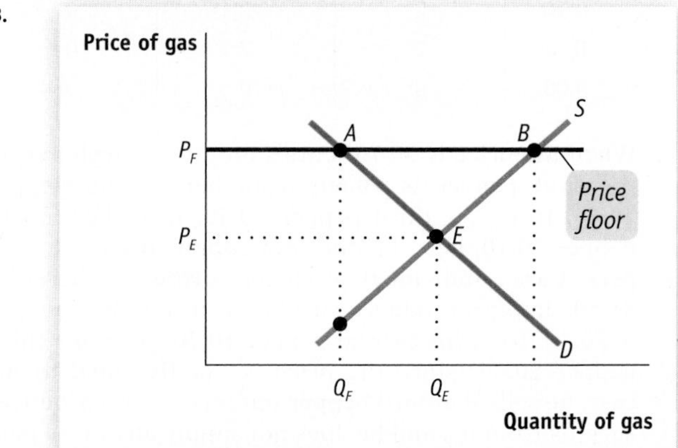

a. Some gas station owners will benefit from getting a higher price. Q_F indicates the sales made by these owners. But some will lose; there are those who make sales at the market equilibrium price of P_E but do not make sales at the regulated price of P_F. These missed sales are indicated on the graph by the fall in the quantity demanded along the demand curve, from point *E* to point *A*.

b. Those who buy gas at the higher price of P_F will probably receive better service; this is an example of *inefficiently high quality* caused by a price floor as gas station owners compete on quality rather than price. But opponents are correct to claim that consumers are generally worse off—those who buy at P_F would have been happy to buy at P_E, and many who were willing to buy at a price between P_E and P_F are now unwilling to buy. This is indicated on the graph by the fall in the quantity demanded along the demand curve, from point *E* to point *A*.

c. Proponents are wrong because consumers and some gas station owners are hurt by the price floor, which creates "missed opportunities"—desirable transactions between consumers and station owners that never take place. Moreover, the inefficiency of wasted resources arises as consumers spend time and money driving to other states. The price floor also tempts people to engage in black market activity. With the price floor, only Q_F units are sold. But at prices between P_E and P_F, there are drivers who together want to buy more than Q_F and owners who are willing to sell to them, a situation likely to lead to illegal activity.

Multiple-Choice Questions

1. e
2. b
3. e
4. b
5. c

Critical-Thinking Question

Your graph should look like this.

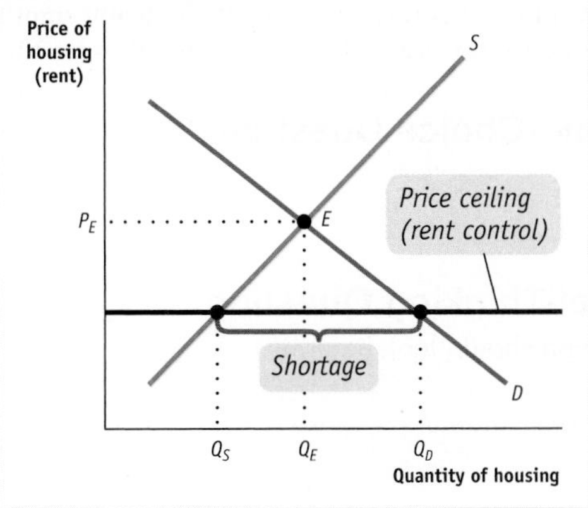

MODULE 14

Check Your Understanding

1. a. The price of a ride is $7 since the quantity demanded at this price is 6 million: $7 is the *demand price* of 6 million rides. This is represented by point *A* in the accompanying figure.

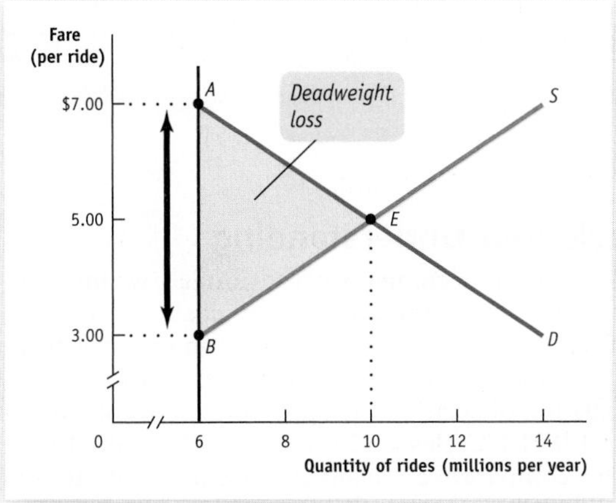

b. At 6 million rides, the supply price is $3 per ride, represented by point *B* in the figure. The wedge between the demand price of $7 per ride and the supply price of $3 per ride is the quota rent per ride, $4. This is represented in the figure above by the vertical distance between points *A* and *B*.

c. The quota discourages 4 million mutually beneficial transactions. The shaded triangle in the figure represents the deadweight loss.

d. At 9 million rides, the demand price is $5.50 per ride, indicated by point *C* in the accompanying figure, and the supply price is $4.50 per ride, indicated by point *D*. The quota rent is the difference between the demand price and the supply price: $1. The deadweight loss is represented by the shaded triangle in the figure. Compare that area to the figure above, and you can see that the deadweight loss is smaller when the quota is set at 9 million rides than when it is set at 6 million rides (illustrated above).

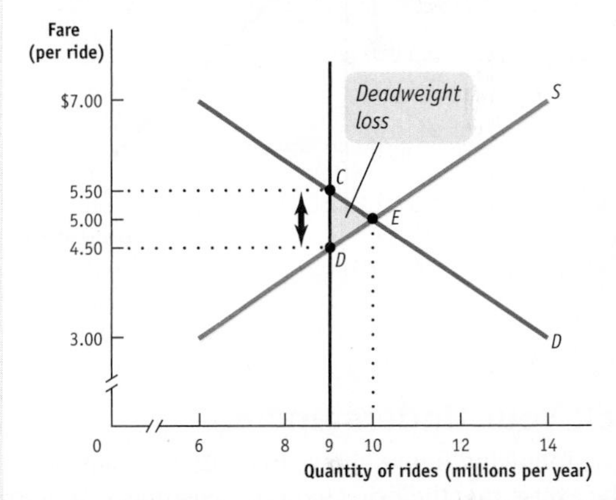

2. The accompanying figure shows a decrease in demand by 4 million rides, represented by a leftward shift of the demand curve from D_1 to D_2: at any given price, the quantity demanded falls by 4 million rides. (For example, at a price of $5, the quantity demanded falls from 10 million to 6 million rides per year.) This eliminates the effect of a quota limit of 8 million rides. At point E_2, the new market equilibrium, the equilibrium quantity is equal to the quota limit; as a result, the quota has no effect on the market.

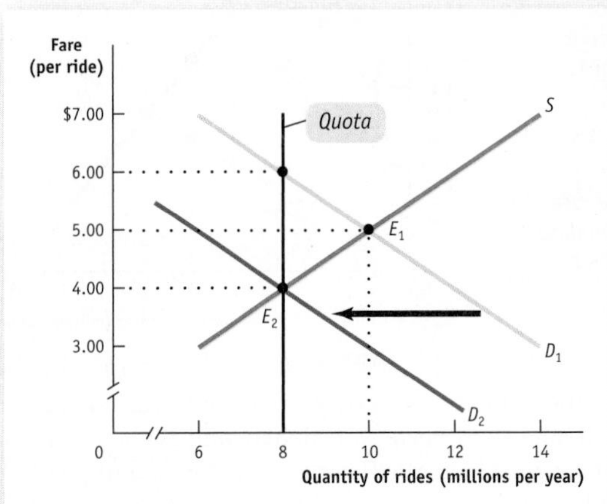

Multiple-Choice Questions

1. d
2. b
3. b
4. d
5. a

Critical-Thinking Question

Your graph should look like this.

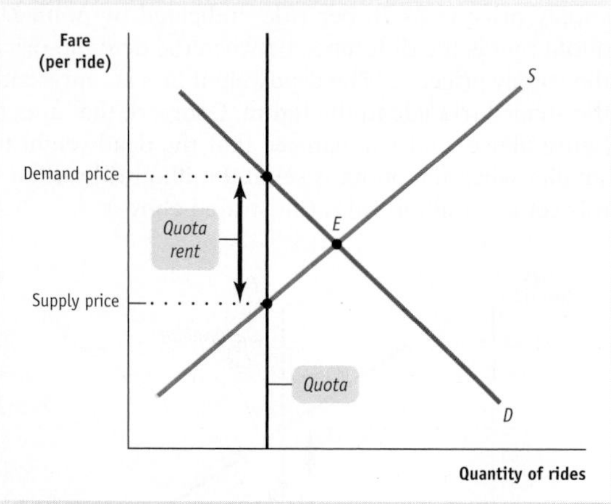

MODULE 15

Check Your Understanding

1. The following figure shows that, after the introduction of the excise tax, the price paid by consumers rises to $1.20; the price received by producers falls to $0.90. Consumers bear $0.20 of the $0.30 tax per pound of butter; producers bear $0.10 of the tax. The tax drives a wedge of $0.30 between the price paid by consumers and the price received by producers. As a result, the quantity of butter sold is now 9 million pounds.

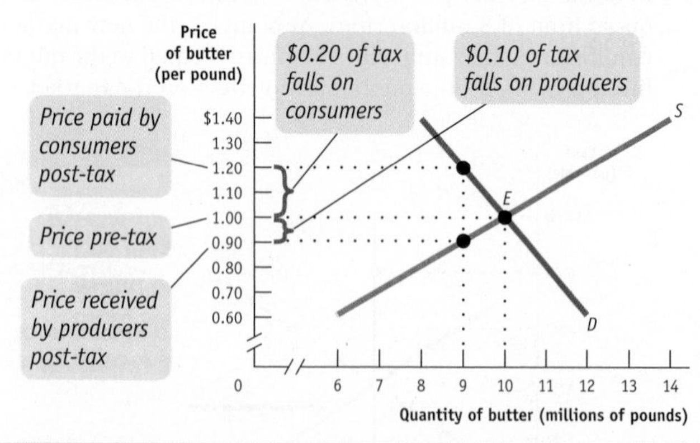

2. a. Without the excise tax, Zhang, Yves, Xavier, and Walter sell, and Ana, Bernice, Chizuko, and Dagmar buy one can of soda each, at $0.40 per can. So the quantity bought and sold is 4.

b. With the excise tax, Zhang and Yves sell, and Ana and Bernice buy one can of soda each. So the quantity sold is 2.

c. Without the excise tax, Ana's individual consumer surplus is $0.70 – $0.40 = $0.30, Bernice's is $0.60 – $0.40 = $0.20, Chizuko's is $0.50 – $0.40 = $0.10, and Dagmar's is $0.40 – $0.40 = $0.00. Total consumer surplus is $0.30 + $0.20 + $0.10 + $0.00 = $0.60. With the tax, Ana's individual consumer surplus is $0.70 – $0.60 = $0.10 and Bernice's is $0.60 – $0.60 = $0.00. Total consumer surplus post-tax is $0.10 + $0.00 = $0.10. So the total consumer surplus lost because of the tax is $0.60 – $0.10 = $0.50.

d. Without the excise tax, Zhang's individual producer surplus is $0.40 – $0.10 = $0.30, Yves's is $0.40 – $0.20 = $0.20, Xavier's is $0.40 – $0.30 = $0.10, and Walter's is $0.40 – $0.40 = $0.00. Total producer surplus is $0.30 + $0.20 + $0.10 + $0.00 = $0.60. With the tax, Zhang's individual producer surplus is $0.20 – $0.10 = $0.10 and Yves's is $0.20 – $0.20 = $0.00. Total producer surplus post-tax is $0.10 + $0.00 = $0.10. So the total producer surplus lost because of the tax is $0.60 – $0.10 = $0.50.

e. With the tax, two cans of soda are sold, so the government tax revenue from this excise tax is 2 × $0.40 = $0.80.

f. Total surplus without the tax is $0.60 + $0.60 = $1.20. With the tax, total surplus is $0.10 + $0.10 = $0.20, and government tax revenue is $0.80. So deadweight loss from this excise tax is $1.20 – ($0.20 + $0.80) = $0.20.

Multiple-Choice Questions

1. d
2. c

Critical-Thinking Question

Your graph should look like this.

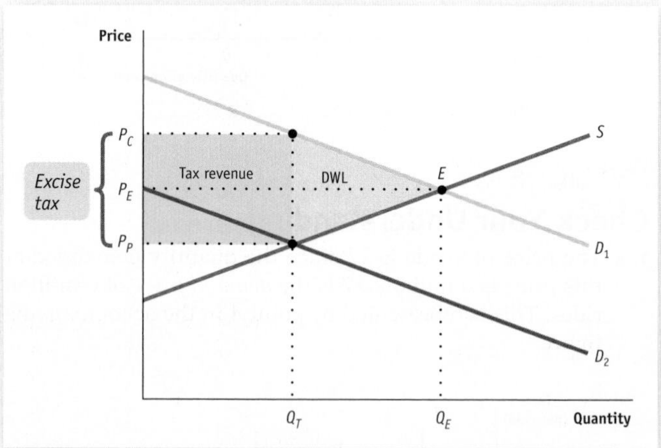

MODULE 16

Check Your Understanding

1. a. To determine comparative advantage, we must compare the two countries' opportunity costs for a given good. Take the opportunity cost of 1 ton of corn in terms of bicycles. In China, the opportunity cost of 1 bicycle is 0.01 ton of corn; so the opportunity cost of 1 ton of corn is 1/0.01 bicycles = 100 bicycles. The United States has the comparative advantage in corn since its opportunity cost in terms of bicycles is 50, a smaller number.

Similarly, the opportunity cost in the United States of 1 bicycle in terms of corn is 1/50 ton of corn = 0.02 ton of corn. This is greater than 0.01, the Chinese opportunity cost of 1 bicycle in terms of corn, implying that China has a comparative advantage in bicycles.

b. Given that the United States can produce 200,000 bicycles if no corn is produced, it can produce 200,000 bicycles × 0.02 ton of corn/bicycle = 4,000 tons of corn when no bicycles are produced. Likewise, if China can produce 3,000 tons of corn if no bicycles are produced, it can produce 3,000 tons of corn × 100 bicycles/ton of corn = 300,000 bicycles if no corn is produced. These points determine the vertical and horizontal intercepts of the U.S. and Chinese production possibilities, as shown in the accompanying diagram.

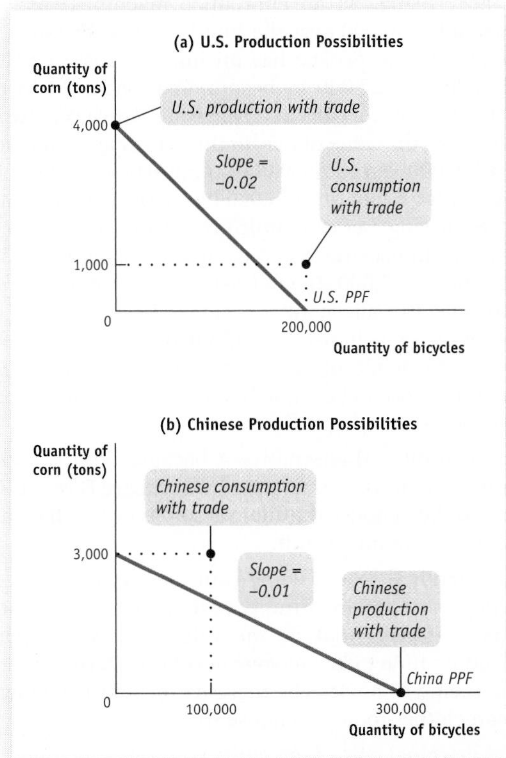

c. The diagram shows the production and consumption points of the two countries. Each country is clearly better off with international trade because each now consumes a bundle of the two goods that lies outside its own production possibility curve, indicating that these bundles were unattainable in autarky.

2. a. The resources required to produce wine are more abundant in France, while the resources required to produce movies are abundant in the U.S. As a result, France exports wine to the United States, and the United States exports movies to France.

b. The resources required to produce shoes, such as labor, are more abundant in Brazil, while the U.S. has the resources to produce shoe-making machinery. As a result, Brazil exports shoes to the United States, and the United States exports shoe-making machinery to Brazil.

Multiple-Choice Questions

1. b
2. c
3. a
4. b
5. c

Critical-Thinking Question

The country will become an importer of the good because it can buy the good for a lower price from another country. This will cause the domestic price of the good to fall to the world price of $8. As a result, quantity demanded will increase and domestic quantity produced will decrease.

MODULE 17

Check Your Understanding

1. a. If the tariff is $0.50, the price paid by domestic consumers for a pound of imported butter is $0.50 + $0.50 = $1.00, the same price as a pound of domestic butter. Imported butter will no longer have a price advantage over domestic butter, imports will cease, and domestic producers will capture all the feasible sales to domestic consumers, selling amount Q_A in the accompanying figure. But if the tariff is less than $0.50—say, only $0.25—the price paid by domestic consumers for a pound of imported butter is $0.50 + $0.25 = $0.75, $0.25 cheaper than a pound of domestic butter. American butter producers will gain sales in the amount of $Q_2 - Q_1$ as a result of the $0.25 tariff. But this is smaller than the amount they would have gained under the $0.50 tariff, the amount $Q_A - Q_1$.

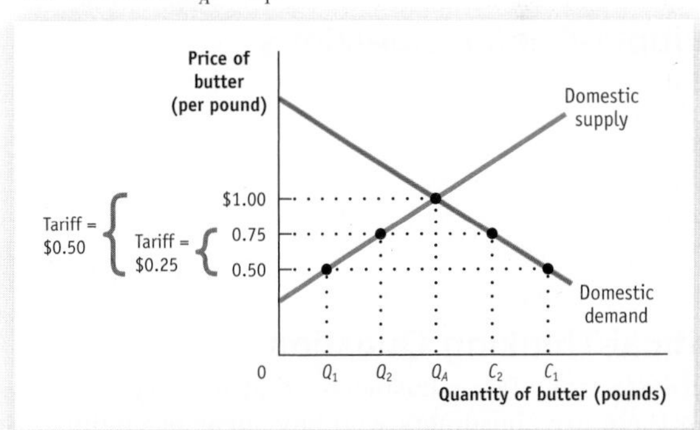

b. As long as the tariff is at least $0.50, increasing it more has no effect. At a tariff of $0.50, all imports are effectively blocked.

2. Because a tariff of $0.50 reduces imports to zero, the only quota that would provide the same results would be a total halt to all imports of butter.

3. In the accompanying diagram, P_A is the U.S. price of grapes in autarky and P_W is the world price of grapes under international trade. With trade, U.S. consumers pay a price of P_W for grapes and consume quantity Q_D, U.S. grape producers produce quantity Q_S, and the difference, $Q_D - Q_S$, represents imports of Mexican grapes. As a consequence of the strike by truckers, imports are halted, the price paid by American consumers rises to the autarky price, P_A, and U.S. consumption falls to the autarky quantity Q_A.

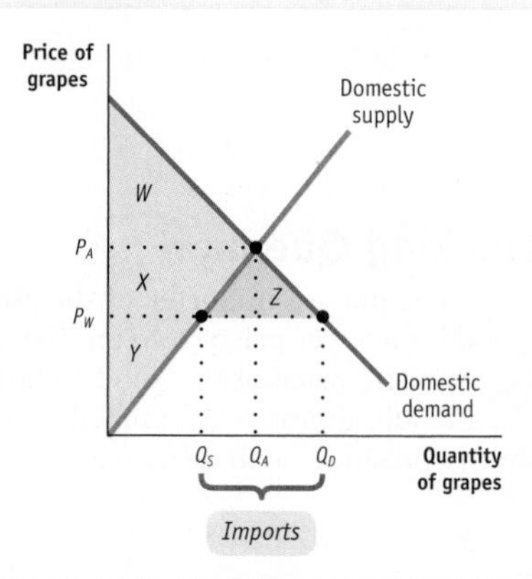

The strike also had these effects:

a. U.S. grape consumers' surplus is decreased by the areas X and Z.

b. U.S. grape producers' surplus is increased by area X.

c. U.S. total surplus is decreased by area Z.

4. Mexican grape producers will not be able to export grapes to the United States, which will raise the supply of grapes in Mexico. This will reduce the Mexican price of grapes, harming Mexican grape producers. Mexican grape pickers will likely see their wages reduced because of the reduction in price of grapes. Mexican grape consumers will be better off because there will be greater supply on the Mexican market, reducing price. U.S. grape pickers will be better off because demand for their services will rise.

Multiple-Choice Questions

1. d
2. e
3. a
4. d
5. a

Critical-Thinking Question

There are many fewer businesses that use steel as an input than there are consumers who buy sugar or clothing. So it will be easier for such businesses to communicate and coordinate among themselves to lobby against tariffs than it will be for consumers. In addition, each business will perceive that the cost of a steel tariff is quite costly to its profits, but an individual consumer is either unaware of or perceives little loss from tariffs on sugar or clothing. The tariffs were indeed lifted a year after they were imposed.

MODULE 18

Check Your Understanding

1. a. Supplies are an explicit cost because they require an outlay of money.

b. If the basement could be used in some other way that generates money, such as renting it to a student, then the implicit cost is that money forgone. Otherwise, the implicit cost is zero.

c. Wages are an explicit cost.

d. By using the van for their business, Karma and Don forgo the money they could have gained by selling it. So use of the van is an implicit cost.

e. Karma's forgone wages from her job are an implicit cost.

2. We need only compare the choice of becoming a machinist to the choice of taking a job in advertising in order to make the right choice. We can discard the choice of acquiring a teaching degree because we already know that taking a job in advertising is always superior to it. Now let's compare the remaining two alternatives: becoming a skilled machinist versus immediately taking a job in advertising. As an apprentice machinist, Ashley will earn only \$30,000 over the first two years, versus \$57,000 in advertising. So she has an implicit cost of \$30,000 – \$57,000 = – \$27,000 by becoming a machinist instead of immediately working in advertising. However, two years from now the value of her lifetime earnings as a machinist is \$725,000 versus \$600,000 in advertising, giving her an accounting profit of \$125,000 by choosing to be a machinist. Summing, her economic profit from choosing a career as a machinist over a career in advertising is \$125,000 – \$27,000 = \$98,000. In contrast, her economic profit from choosing the alternative, a career in advertising over a career as a machinist, is –\$125,000 + \$27,000 = –\$98,000. By the principle of "either–or" decision making, Ashley should choose to be a machinist because that career has a positive economic profit.

3. You can discard alternative A because both B and C are superior to it. But you must now compare B versus C. You should then choose the alternative—B or C—that carries a positive economic profit.

4. a. The marginal cost of doing your laundry is any monetary outlays plus the opportunity cost of your time spent doing laundry today—that is, the value you would place on spending time today on your next best alternative activity, like seeing a movie. The marginal benefit is having more clean clothes today to choose from.

b. The marginal cost of changing your oil is the opportunity cost of time spent changing your oil now as well as the explicit cost of the oil change. The marginal benefit is the improvement in your car's performance.

c. The marginal cost is the unpleasant feeling of a burning mouth that you receive from it plus any explicit cost of the jalapeno. The marginal benefit of another jalapeno on your nachos is the pleasant taste that you receive from it.

d. The marginal benefit of hiring another worker in your company is the value of the output that worker produces. The marginal cost is the wage you must pay that worker.

e. The marginal cost is the value lost due to the increased side effects from this additional dose. The marginal benefit of another dose of the drug is the value of the reduction in the patient's disease.

f. The marginal cost is the opportunity cost of your time—what you would have gotten from the next best use of your time. The marginal benefit is the probable increase in your grade.

5. The accompanying table shows Alex's new marginal cost and his new profit. It also reproduces Alex's marginal benefit from Table 18-5.

Years of schooling	Total cost	Marginal cost	Marginal benefit	Profit
0	$0			
		$90,000	$300,000	$210,000
1	90,000			
		30,000	150,000	120,000
2	120,000			
		50,000	90,000	40,000
3	170,000			
		80,000	60,000	−20,000
4	250,000			
		120,000	50,000	−80,000
5	370,000			

Alex's marginal cost is decreasing until he has completed two years of schooling, after which marginal cost increases because of the value of his forgone income. The optimal amount of schooling is still three years. For less than three years of schooling, marginal benefit exceeds marginal cost; for more than three years, marginal cost exceeds marginal benefit.

6. a. Your sunk cost is $8,000 because none of the $8,000 spent on the truck is recoverable.

b. Your sunk cost is $4,000 because 50% of the $8,000 spent on the truck is recoverable.

7. a. This is an invalid argument because the time and money already spent are a sunk cost at this point.

b. This is also an invalid argument because what you should have done two years ago is irrelevant to what you should do now.

c. This is a valid argument because it recognizes that sunk costs are irrelevant to what you should do now.

d. This is a valid argument given that you are concerned about disappointing your parents. But your parents' views are irrational because they do not recognize that the time already spent is a sunk cost.

Multiple-Choice Questions

1. d
2. b
3. c
4. d
5. c

Critical-Thinking Question

The cost of the ticket is a sunk cost and cannot be recovered. The decision to remain at the game should be based on the marginal benefits of continued attendance, and the marginal cost of continuing to watch your favorite team lose.

MODULE 19

Check Your Understanding

1. a. Jenny is exhibiting loss aversion. She has an oversensitivity to loss, leading to an unwillingness to recognize a loss and move on.

b. Dan is doing mental accounting. Dollars from his unexpected overtime earnings are worth less—spent on a weekend getaway—than the dollars earned from his regular hours that he uses to pay down his student loan.

c. Carol may have unrealistic expectations of future behavior. Even if she does not want to participate in the plan now, she should find a way to commit to participating at a later date.

d. Jeremy is showing signs of status quo bias. He is avoiding making a decision altogether; in other words, he is sticking with the status quo.

Multiple-Choice Questions

1. c
2. d
3. c
4. c
5. a

Critical-Thinking Question

You would determine whether a decision was rational or irrational by first accurately accounting for all the costs and benefits of the decision. In particular, you must accurately measure all opportunity costs. Then calculate the economic payoff of the decision relative to the next best alternative. If you would still make the same choice after this comparison, then you have made a rational choice. If not, then the choice was irrational.

MODULE 20

Check Your Understanding

1. Consuming a unit that generates negative marginal utility leaves the consumer with lower total utility than not consuming that unit at all. A rational consumer, a consumer who maximizes utility, would not do that. For example, Figure 20-3 shows that Cassie receives 64 utils if she consumes 8 clams, but if she consumes a 9th clam, she loses a util, decreasing her total utility to only 63 utils. Whenever consuming a unit generates negative marginal utility, the consumer is made better off by not consuming that unit, even when that unit is free.

2. a. The accompanying table shows the consumer's consumption possibilities, bundles *A* through *C*. These consumption possibilities are plotted in the accompanying diagram, along with the consumer's budget line.

Consumption Bundle	Quantity of popcorn (buckets)	Quantity of movie tickets
A	0	2
B	2	1
C	4	0

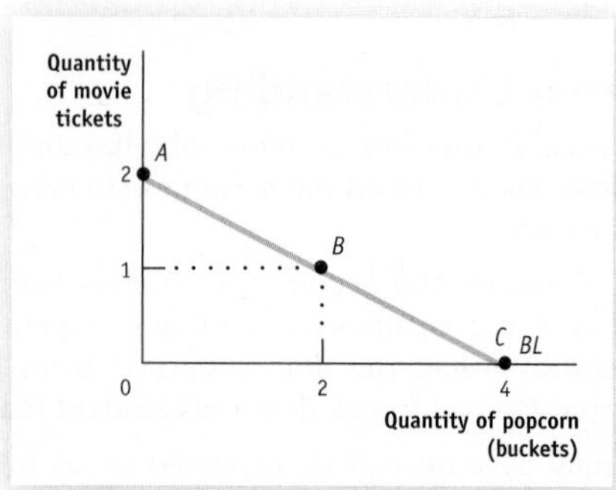

b. The accompanying table shows the consumer's consumption possibilities, *A* through *D*. These consumption possibilities are plotted in the accompanying diagram, along with the consumer's budget line.

Consumption Bundle	Quantity of underwear (pairs)	Quantity of socks (pairs)
A	0	6
B	1	4
C	2	2
D	3	0

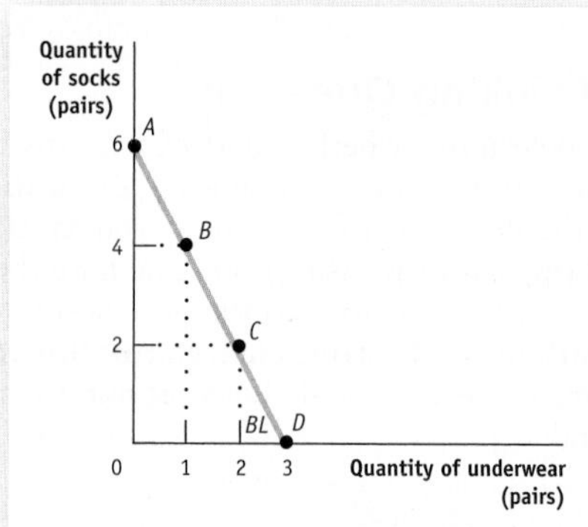

3. From Table 20-3 you can see that Sammy's marginal utility per dollar from increasing his consumption of clams from 3 to 4 pounds and his marginal utility per dollar from increasing his consumption of potatoes from 9 to 10 pounds are the same, 0.75 utils. But a consumption bundle consisting of 4 pounds of clams and 10 pounds of potatoes is not Sammy's optimal consumption bundle because it is not affordable given his income of $20; a bundle of 4 pounds of clams and 10 pounds of potatoes costs $4 × 4 + $2 × 10 = $36, $16 more than Sammy's income. This can be illustrated with Sammy's budget line from Figure 20-3: a bundle of 4 pounds of clams and 10 pounds of potatoes is represented by point *X* in the accompanying diagram, a point that lies outside Sammy's budget line. If you look at the horizontal axis of Figure 20-4, it is quite clear that there is no such thing in Sammy's consumption possibilities as a bundle consisting of 4 pounds of clams and 10 pounds of potatoes.

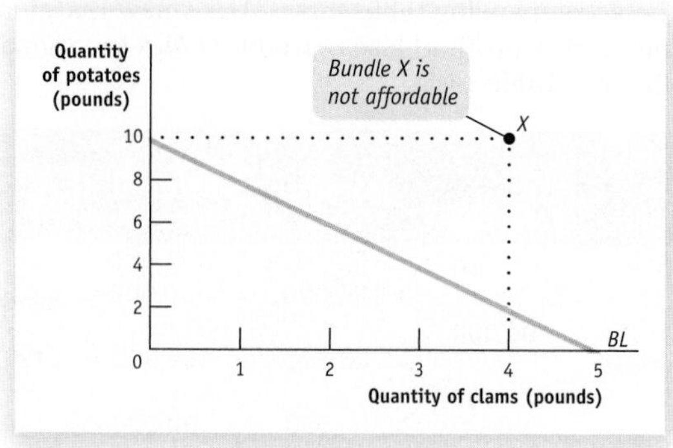

Multiple-Choice Questions

1. d
2. b
3. a
4. b
5. d

Critical-Thinking Questions

a.

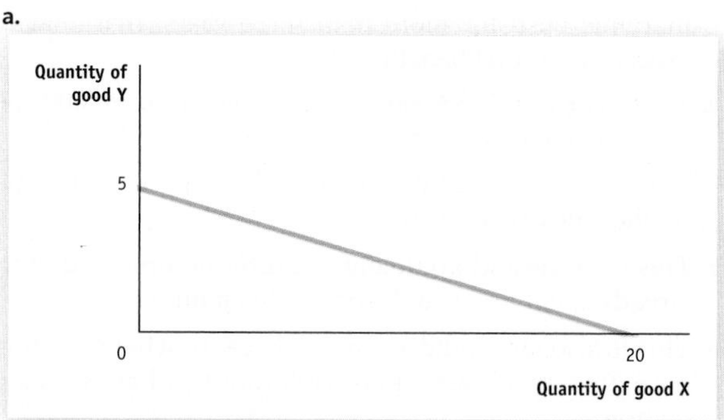

b. Yes, 100/$5 = 400/$20

c. Total utility will increase because marginal utility is positive, while marginal utility will decrease due to the principle of diminishing marginal utility.

MODULE 21

Check Your Understanding

1. a. The fixed input is the 10-ton machine and the variable input is electricity.

b. As you can see from the declining numbers in the third column of the accompanying table, electricity does indeed exhibit diminishing returns: the marginal product of each additional kilowatt of electricity is less than that of the previous kilowatt.

Quantity of electricity (kilowatts)	Quantity of ice (pounds)	Marginal product of electricity (pounds per kilowatt)
0	0	
		1,000
1	1,000	
		800
2	1,800	
		600
3	2,400	
		400
4	2,800	

c. A 50% increase in the size of the fixed input means that Bernie now has a 15-ton machine, so the fixed input is now the 15-ton machine. Since it generates a 100% increase in output for any given amount of electricity, the quantity of output and the marginal product are now as shown in the accompanying table.

Quantity of electricity (kilowatts)	Quantity of ice (pounds)	Marginal product of electricity (pounds per kilowatt)
0	0	
		2,000
1	2,000	
		1,600
2	3,600	
		1,200
3	4,800	
		800
4	5,600	

Multiple-Choice Questions

1. d
2. e
3. a
4. b
5. a

Critical-Thinking Question

As you can see from the graph, the data exhibit diminishing returns to labor because the *MPL* curve is downward sloping.

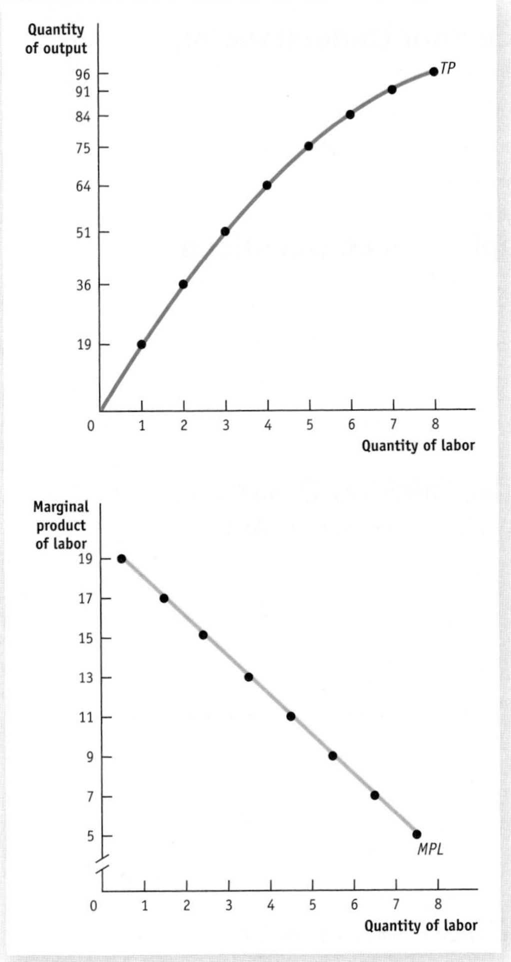

MODULE 22

Check Your Understanding

1. a. As shown in the accompanying table, the marginal cost for each pie is found by multiplying the marginal cost of the previous pie by 1.5. The variable cost for each output level is found by summing the marginal cost for all the pies produced to reach that output level. So, for example, the variable cost of three pies is \$1.00 + \$1.50 + \$2.25 = \$4.75. Average fixed cost for *Q* pies is calculated as \$9.00/*Q* since fixed cost is \$9.00. Average variable cost for *Q* pies is equal to the variable cost for the *Q* pies divided by *Q*; for example, the average variable cost of five pies is \$13.19/5, or approximately \$2.64. Finally, average total cost can be calculated in two equivalent ways: as *TC*/*Q* or as *AVC* + *AFC*.

Quantity of pies	Marginal cost of pie	Variable cost	Average fixed cost of pie	Average variable cost of pie	Average total cost of pie
0		\$0.00	—	—	—
	\$1.00				
1		1.00	\$9.00	\$1.00	\$10.00
	1.50				
2		2.50	4.50	1.25	5.75
	2.25				
3		4.75	3.00	1.58	4.58
	3.38				
4		8.13	2.25	2.03	4.28
	5.06				
5		13.19	1.80	2.64	4.44
	7.59				
6		20.78	1.50	3.46	4.96

b. The spreading effect dominates the diminishing returns effect when average total cost is falling: the fall in *AFC* dominates the rise in *AVC* for pies 1 to 4. The diminishing returns effect dominates when average total cost is rising: the rise in *AVC* dominates the fall in *AFC* for pies 5 and 6.

c. Alicia's minimum-cost output is 4 pies; this generates the lowest average total cost, \$4.28. When output is less than 4, the marginal cost of a pie is less than the average total cost of the pies already produced. So making an additional pie lowers average total cost. For example, the marginal cost of pie 3 is \$2.25, whereas the average total cost of pies 1 and 2 is \$5.75. So making pie 3 lowers average total cost to \$4.58, equal to (2 × \$5.75 + \$2.25)/3. When output is more than 4, the marginal cost of a pie is greater than the average total cost of the pies already produced. Consequently, making an additional pie raises average total cost. So, although the marginal cost of pie 6 is \$7.59, the average total cost of pies 1 through 5 is \$4.44. Making pie 6 raises average total cost to \$4.96, equal to (5 × \$4.44 + \$7.59)/6.

Multiple-Choice Questions

1. c
2. e
3. e
4. e
5. a

Critical-Thinking Question

Your graph should look like this.

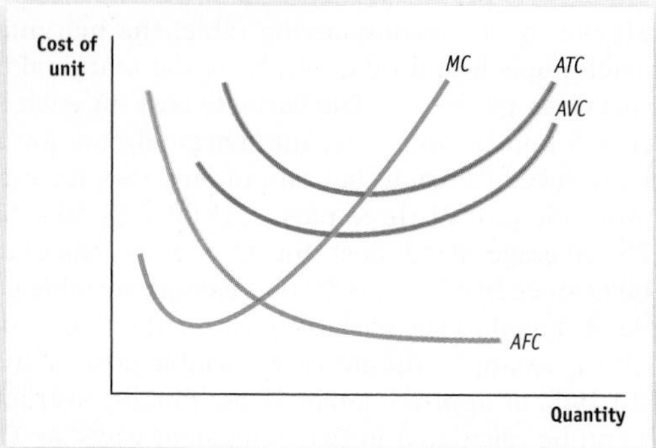

MODULE 23

Check Your Understanding

1. **a.** The accompanying table shows the average total cost of producing 12,000, 22,000, and 30,000 units for each of the three choices of fixed cost. For example, if the firm makes choice 1, the total cost of producing 12,000 units of output is \$8,000 + 12,000 × \$1.00 = \$20,000. The average total cost of producing 12,000 units of output is therefore \$20,000/12,000 = \$1.67. The other average total costs are calculated similarly.

	12,000 units	22,000 units	30,000 units
Average total cost from choice 1	\$1.67	\$1.36	\$1.27
Average total cost from choice 2	1.75	1.30	1.15
Average total cost from choice 3	2.25	1.34	1.05

So if the firm wanted to produce 12,000 units, it would make choice 1 because this gives it the lowest average total cost. If it wanted to produce 22,000 units, it would make choice 2. If it wanted to produce 30,000 units, it would make choice 3.

b. Having historically produced 12,000 units, the firm would have adopted choice 1. When producing 12,000 units, the firm would have had an average total cost of \$1.67. When output jumps to 22,000 units, the firm cannot alter its choice of fixed cost in the short run, so its average total cost in the short run will be \$1.36. In the long run, however, it will adopt choice 2, making its average total cost fall to \$1.30.

c. If the firm believes that the increase in demand is temporary, it should not alter its fixed cost from choice 1 because choice 2 generates higher average total cost as soon as output falls back to its original quantity of 12,000 units: \$1.75 versus \$1.67.

2. **a.** This firm is likely to experience diseconomies of scale. As the firm takes on more projects, the costs of communication and coordination required to implement the expertise of the firm's owner are likely to increase.

b. This firm is likely to experience economies of scale. Because diamond mining requires a large initial setup cost for excavation equipment, long-run average total cost will fall as output increases.

Multiple-Choice Questions

1. a
2. e
3. e
4. d
5. e

Critical-Thinking Question

Your graph should look like this.

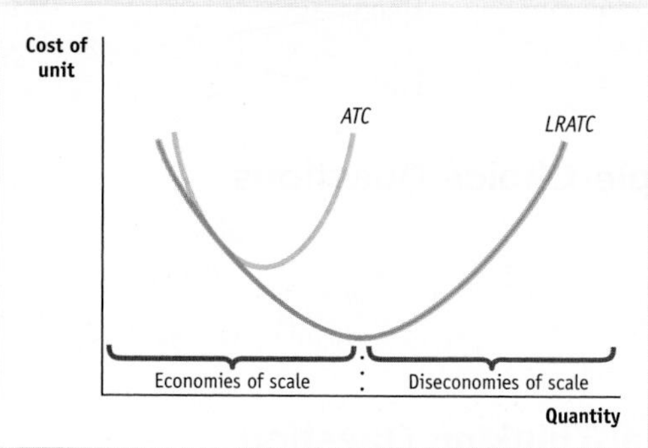

MODULE 24

Check Your Understanding

1. **a.** oligopoly
   b. perfect competition
   c. monopolistic competition
   d. monopoly

Multiple-Choice Questions

1. b
2. a
3. d
4. a
5. a

Critical-Thinking Questions

1. Your graph should look like this.

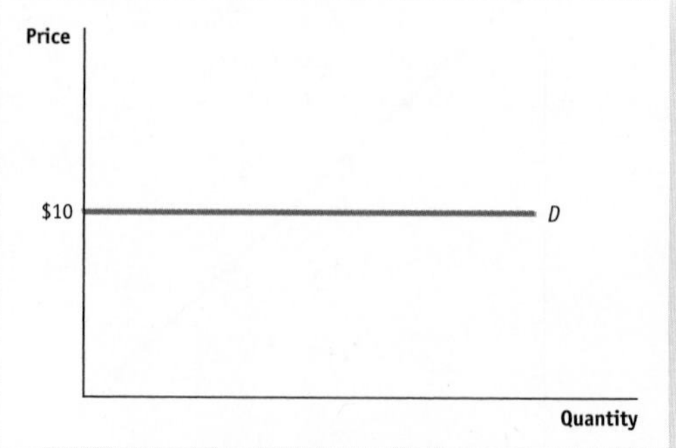

2. Marginal revenue equals \$10.

MODULE 25

Check Your Understanding

1. **a.** The firm maximizes profit at a quantity of 4, because it is at that quantity that $MC = MR$.

   b. At a quantity of 4 the firm just breaks even. This is because at a quantity of 4, $P = ATC$, so the amount the firm takes in for each unit—the price—exactly equals the average total cost per unit.

2. The lowest price that would allow the firm to break even is \$10, because the minimum average total cost is \$500/50 = \$10, and price must at least equal minimum average total cost for the firm to break even.

Multiple-Choice Questions

1. d
2. e
3. d
4. c
5. c

Critical-Thinking Questions

1. This is how the firm's marginal cost at each quantity is calculated.

Q	MC
0	
	16
1	
	6
2	
	8
3	
	12
4	
	16
5	
	20
6	
	24
7	

2. The profit-maximizing quantity is 4.
3. The firm's maximum profit is $TR - TC = (4 \times \$14) - \$56 = \$56 - \$56 = \$0$.

MODULE 26

Check Your Understanding

1. **a.** The firm should shut down immediately when price is less than minimum average variable cost, the shut-down price. In the accompanying diagram, this is optimal for prices in the range from 0 to P_1.

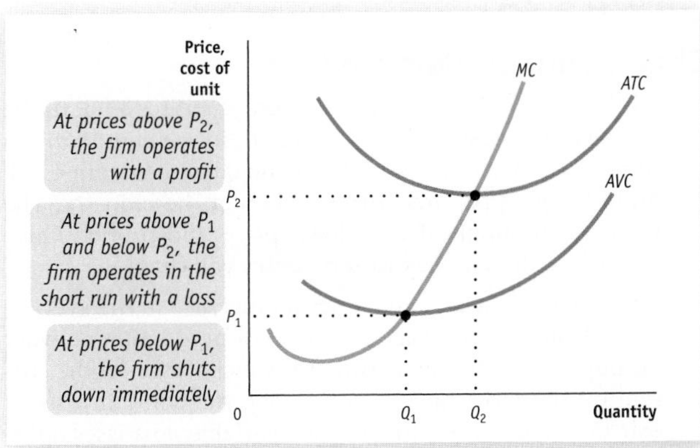

   b. When the price is greater than the minimum average variable cost (the shut-down price) but less than the minimum average total cost (the break-even price), the firm should continue to operate in the short run even though it is incurring a loss. This is optimal for prices in the range from P_1 to P_2.

   c. When the price exceeds the minimum average total cost (the break-even price), the firm makes a profit. This happens for prices in excess of P_2.

2. This is an example of a temporary shut-down by a firm when the market price lies below the shut-down price, the minimum average variable cost. The market price is the price of a lobster meal and the variable cost is the cost of the lobster, employee wages, and other expenses that increase as more meals are served. In this example, however, it is the average variable cost curve rather than the market price that shifts over time, due to seasonal changes in the cost of lobsters. Maine lobster shacks have relatively low average variable cost during the summer, when cheap Maine lobsters are available; during the rest of the year, their average variable cost is relatively high due to the high cost of imported lobsters. So the lobster shacks are open for business during the summer, when their minimum average variable cost lies below price; but they close during the rest of the year, when the price lies below their minimum average variable cost.

Multiple-Choice Questions

1. e
2. d
3. b
4. d
5. c

Critical-Thinking Questions

1. 6
2. $\$20 \times 6 = \$120$
3. $\$29.50 \times 6 = \$177$
4. $\$120 - \$177 = -\$57$ (or a loss of \$57)
5. No, because $P < AVC$

MODULE 27

Check Your Understanding

1. a. A fall in the fixed cost of production generates a fall in the average total cost of production and, in the short run, an increase in each firm's profit at the current output level. So in the long run new firms will enter the industry. The increase in supply drives down price and profits. Once profits are driven back to zero, entry will cease.

   b. An increase in wages generates an increase in the average variable and the average total cost of production at every output level. In the short run, firms incur losses at the current output level, and so in the long run some firms will exit the industry. (If the average variable cost rises sufficiently, some firms may even shut down in the short run.) As firms exit, supply decreases, price rises, and losses are reduced. Exit will cease once losses return to zero.

   c. Price will rise as a result of the increased demand, leading to a short-run increase in profits at the current output level. In the long run, firms will enter the industry, generating an increase in supply, a fall in price, and a fall in profits. Once profits are driven back to zero, entry will cease.

   d. The shortage of a key input causes that input's price to increase, resulting in an increase in average variable and average total cost for producers. Firms incur losses in the short run, and some firms will exit the industry in the long run. The fall in supply generates an increase in price and decreased losses. Exit will cease when the losses for remaining firms have returned to zero.

2. In the accompanying diagram, point X_{MKT} in panel (b), the intersection of S_1 and D_1, represents the long-run industry equilibrium before the change in consumer tastes. When tastes change, demand falls and the industry moves in the short run to point Y_{MKT} in panel (b), at the intersection of the new demand curve D_2 and S_1, the short-run supply curve representing the same number of egg producers as in the original equilibrium at point X_{MKT}. As the market price falls, each individual firm reacts by producing less—as shown in panel (a)—as long as the market price remains above the minimum average variable cost. If market price falls below minimum average variable cost, the firm would shut down immediately. At point Y_{MKT} the price of eggs is below minimum average total cost, creating losses for producers. This leads some firms to exit, which shifts the short-run industry supply curve leftward to S_2. A new long-run equilibrium is established at point Z_{MKT}. As this occurs, the market price rises again, and, as shown in panel (c), each remaining producer reacts by increasing output (here, from point *Y* to point *Z*). All remaining producers again make zero profits. The decrease in the quantity of eggs supplied in the industry comes entirely from the exit of some producers from the industry. The long-run industry supply curve is the curve labeled *LRS* in panel (b).

Multiple-Choice Questions

1. d
2. b
3. a
4. e
5. b

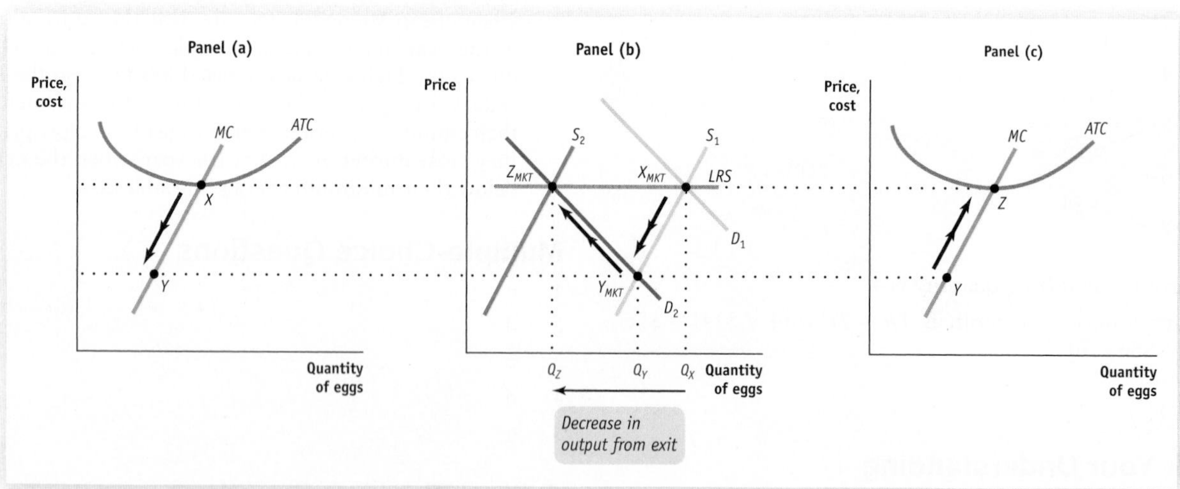

Critical-Thinking Question

Your graphs should look like this.

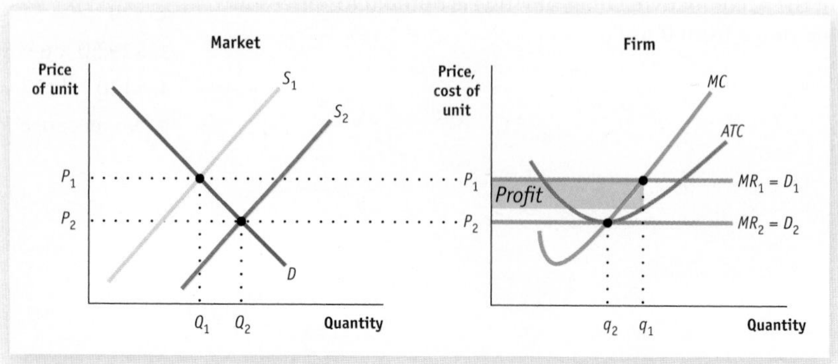

MODULE 28

Check Your Understanding

1. a. The demand schedule is found by determining the price at which each quantity would be demanded. This price is the average revenue, found at each output level by dividing the total revenue by the number of emeralds produced. For example, the price when 3 emeralds are produced is $252/3 = $84. The price at the various output levels is then used to construct the demand schedule in the accompanying table.

   b. The marginal revenue schedule is found by calculating the change in total revenue as output increases by one unit. For example, the marginal revenue generated by increasing output from 2 to 3 emeralds is ($252 – $186) = $66.

   c. The quantity effect component of marginal revenue is the additional revenue generated by selling one more unit of the good at the market price. For example, as shown in the accompanying table, at 3 emeralds, the market price is $84; so, when going from 2 to 3 emeralds the quantity effect is equal to $84.

   d. The price effect component of marginal revenue is the decline in total revenue caused by the fall in price when one more unit is sold. For example, as shown in the table, when only 2 emeralds are sold, each emerald sells at a price of $93. However, when Emerald, Inc. sells an additional emerald, the price must fall by $9 to $84. So the price effect component in going from 2 to 3 emeralds is (–$9) × 2 = –$18. That's because when just 2 emeralds are sold, each is sold at a price of $93. But when 3 emeralds are sold, those same 2 diamonds are sold for only $84 each, a $9 loss per diamond.

Quantity of emeralds demanded	Price of emerald	Total revenue	Marginal revenue	Quantity effect component	Price effect component
1	$100	$100			
			$86	$93	–$7
2	93	186			
			66	84	–18
3	84	252			
			28	70	–42
4	70	280			
			–30	50	–80
5	50	250			

   e. In order to determine Emerald, Inc.'s profit-maximizing output level, you must know its marginal cost at each output level. Its profit-maximizing output level is the one at which marginal revenue is equal to marginal cost.

2. As the accompanying diagram shows, the marginal cost curve shifts upward to $400. The profit-maximizing price rises to $700 and quantity falls to 6. Profit falls from $3,200 to $300 × 6 = $1,800. The quantity a perfectly competitive industry would produce decreases to 12, but profits remain unchanged at zero.

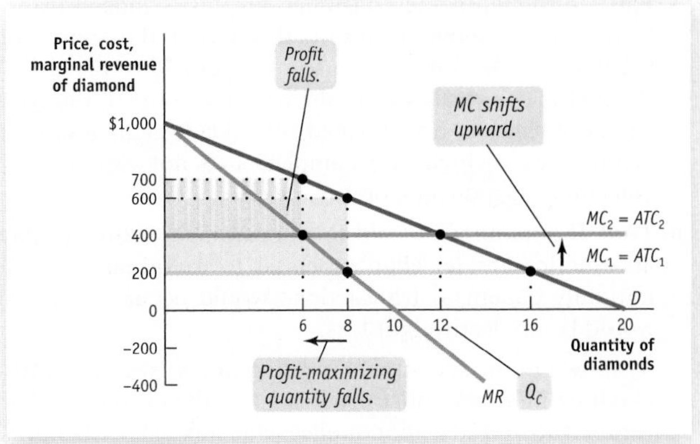

Multiple-Choice Questions

1. b
2. c
3. b
4. d
5. d

Critical-Thinking Questions

1. Your graph should look like this.

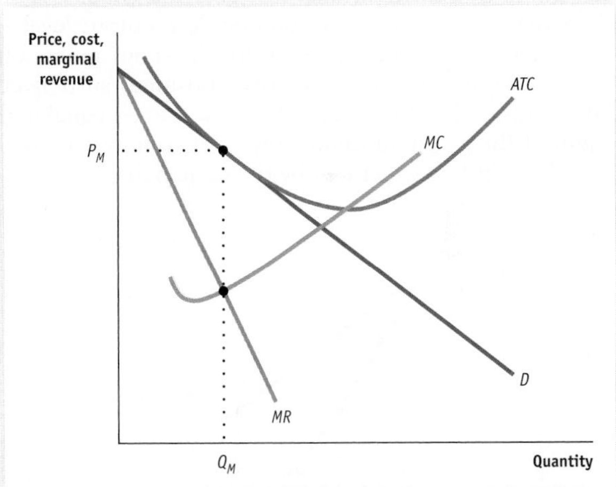

2. Yes, with the help of barriers to entry that keep competitors out.

MODULE 29

Check Your Understanding

1. a. Cable Internet service is a natural monopoly. So the government should intervene if it believes that the current price exceeds average total cost, which includes the cost of laying the cable. In this case it should impose a price ceiling equal to average total cost. If the price does not exceed average total cost, the government should do nothing.

   b. The government should approve the merger only if it fosters competition by transferring some of the company's landing slots to another, competing airline.

2. a. False. Although some consumer surplus is indeed transformed into monopoly profit, this is not the source of inefficiency. As can be seen from Figure 29-1, panel (b), the inefficiency arises from the fact that some of the consumer surplus is transformed into deadweight loss (the yellow area), which is a complete loss not captured by consumers, producers, or anyone else.

b. True. If a monopolist sold to all customers willing to pay an amount greater than or equal to marginal cost, all mutually beneficial transactions would occur and there would be no deadweight loss.

3. As shown in the accompanying diagram, a "smart" profit–maximizing monopolist produces Q_M, the output level at which $MR = MC$. A monopolist who mistakenly believes that $P = MR$ produces the output level at which $P = MC$ (when, in fact, $P > MR$, and at the true profit-maximizing level of output, $P > MR = MC$). This misguided monopolist will produce the output level Q_C, where the demand curve crosses the marginal cost curve—the same output level that would be produced if the industry were perfectly competitive. It will charge the price P_C, which is equal to marginal cost, and make zero profit. The entire shaded area is equal to the consumer surplus, which is also equal to total surplus in this case (since the monopolist receives zero producer surplus). There is no deadweight loss because every consumer who is willing to pay as much as or more than marginal cost gets the good. A smart monopolist, however, will produce the output level Q_M and charge the price P_M. Profit for the smart monopolist is represented by the green area, consumer surplus corresponds to the blue area, and total surplus is equal to the sum of the green and blue areas. The yellow area is the deadweight loss generated by the monopolist.

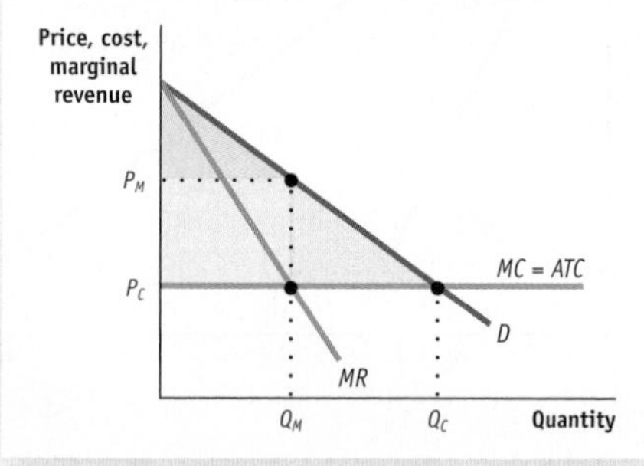

Multiple-Choice Questions

1. a
2. b
3. c
4. a
5. b

Critical-Thinking Question

This graph illustrates a natural monopoly.

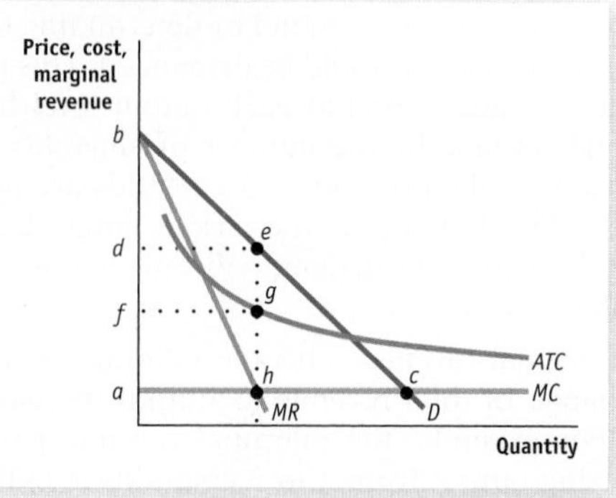

a. triangle *bca*
b. triangle *bed*
c. rectangle *degf*
d. triangle *ech*

MODULE 30

Check Your Understanding

1. a. False. The opposite is true. A price-discriminating monopolist will sell to some customers that would not find the product affordable if purchasing from a single-price monopolist—namely, customers with a high price elasticity of demand who are willing to pay only a relatively low price for the good.

b. False. Although a price-discriminating monopolist does indeed capture more of the consumer surplus, less inefficiency is created: more mutually beneficial transactions occur because the monopolist makes more sales to customers with a low willingness to pay for the good.

c. True. Under price discrimination consumers are charged prices that depend on their price elasticity of demand. A consumer with highly elastic demand will pay a lower price than a consumer with inelastic demand.

2. a. This is not a case of price discrimination because the product itself is different and all consumers, regardless of their price elasticities of demand, value the damaged merchandise less than undamaged merchandise. So the price must be lowered to sell the merchandise.

b. This is a case of price discrimination. Senior citizens have a higher price elasticity of demand for restaurant meals (their demand for restaurant meals is more responsive to price changes) than other patrons. Restaurants lower the price to high-elasticity consumers (senior citizens). Consumers with low price elasticity of demand will pay the full price.

c. This is a case of price discrimination. Consumers with a high price elasticity of demand will pay a lower price by collecting and using discount coupons. Consumers with a low price elasticity of demand will not collect or use coupons.

d. This is not a case of price discrimination; it is simply a case of supply and demand.

Multiple-Choice Questions

1. d
2. c
3. b
4. e
5. a

Critical-Thinking Question

This graph shows a monopoly practicing perfect price discrimination. In this case, consumer surplus is zero because each consumer is charged the maximum he or she is willing to pay.

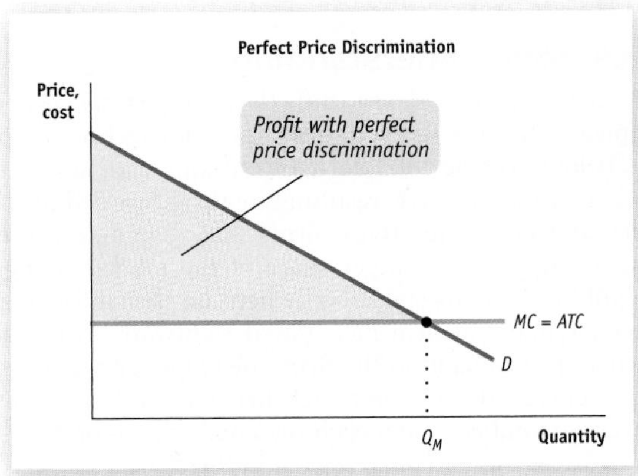

MODULE 31

Check Your Understanding

1. a. This will decrease the likelihood that the firm will collude to restrict output. By increasing output, the firm will generate a negative price effect. But because the firm's current market share is small, the price effect will fall mostly on its rivals' revenues rather than on its own. At the same time, the firm will benefit from a positive quantity effect.

   b. This will decrease the likelihood that the firm will collude to restrict output. By acting noncooperatively and raising output, the firm will cause the price to fall. Because its rivals have higher costs, they will lose money at the lower price while the firm continues to make profits. So the firm may be able to drive its rivals out of business by increasing its output.

   c. This will increase the likelihood that the firm will collude. Because it is costly for consumers to switch products, the firm would have to lower its price substantially (with a commensurate increase in quantity) to induce consumers to switch to its product. So increasing output is likely to be unprofitable, given the large negative price effect.

   d. This will increase the likelihood that the firm will collude. It cannot increase sales because it is currently at maximum production capacity, making attempts to undercut rivals' prices fruitless due to the inability to produce the output needed to steal the rivals' customers. This makes the option to cooperate in restricting output relatively attractive.

Multiple-Choice Questions

1. a
2. c
3. d
4. e
5. b

Critical-Thinking Question

The first major reason is that cartels are illegal in the United States. The second major reason is that cartels set prices above marginal cost, which creates an incentive for each firm to cheat on the cartel agreement in order to make more profit. This incentive to cheat tends to cause cartels to fall apart.

MODULE 32

Check Your Understanding

1. a. A Nash equilibrium is a set of actions from which neither side wants to deviate (change actions), given what the other is doing. Both sides building a missile is a Nash equilibrium because neither player wants to deviate from the decision to build a missile. To switch from building to not building a missile, given that the other player is building a missile, would result in a change from −10 to −20 utils. There is no other Nash equilibrium in this game because for any other set of actions, at least one side is not building a missile, and would be better off switching to building a missile.

   b. Their total payoff is greatest when neither side builds a missile, in which case their total payoff is 0 + 0 = 0.

   c. This outcome would require cooperation because each side sees itself as better off by building a missile. If Margaret builds a missile but Nikita does not, Margaret gets a payoff of +8, rather than the 0 she gets if she doesn't build a missile. Similarly, Nikita is better off if he builds a missile but Margaret doesn't: he gets a payoff of +8, rather than the 0 he gets if he doesn't build a missile. Indeed, both players have an incentive to build a missile regardless of what the other side does. So unless Nikita and Margaret are able to communicate in some way to enforce cooperation, they will act in their own individual interests and each will pursue its dominant strategy of building a missile.

2. a. Future entry by several new firms will increase competition and drive down industry profits. As a result, there is less future profit to protect by behaving cooperatively today. This makes each oligopolist more likely to behave noncooperatively today.

   b. When it is very difficult for a firm to detect if another firm has raised output, it is very difficult to enforce cooperation by playing tit for tat. So it is more likely that a firm will behave noncooperatively.

   c. When firms have coexisted while maintaining high prices for a long time, each expects cooperation to continue. So the value of behaving cooperatively today is high, and it is likely that firms will engage in tacit collusion.

Multiple-Choice Questions

1. b
2. b
3. c
4. a
5. c

Critical-Thinking Question

Your payoff matrix should look like this.

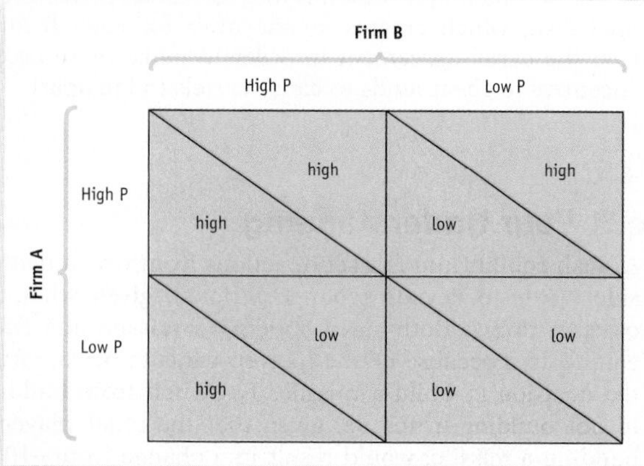

MODULE 33

Check Your Understanding

1. **a.** This is evidence of tacit collusion. Firms in the industry are able to tacitly collude by setting their prices according to the published "suggested" price of the largest firm in the industry. This is a form of price leadership.
   b. This is not evidence of tacit collusion. Considerable variation in market shares indicates that firms have been competing to capture each other's business.
   c. This is not evidence of tacit collusion. These features make it less likely that consumers will switch products in response to lower prices. So this is a way for firms to avoid any temptation to gain market share by lowering price. This is a form of product differentiation used to avoid direct competition.
   d. This is evidence of tacit collusion. In the guise of discussing sales targets, firms can create a cartel by designating quantities to be produced by each firm.
   e. This is evidence of tacit collusion. By raising prices together, each firm in the industry is refusing to undercut its rivals by leaving its price unchanged or lowering it. Because it could gain market share by doing so, refusing to do so supports the conclusion that there is tacit collusion.

Multiple-Choice Questions

1. d
2. d
3. c
4. e
5. a

Critical-Thinking Question

a. A large number of firms: having more firms means there is less incentive for any firm to behave cooperatively.

b. Complex products/pricing schemes: keeping track of adherence to an agreement is more difficult.

c. Differences in interests: firms often have different views of their own interests and of what a fair agreement would entail.

d. Bargaining power of buyers: firms are less able to raise prices for buyers with significant bargaining power, which can result from size or access to many options.

MODULE 34

Check Your Understanding

1. **a.** An increase in fixed cost shifts the average total cost curve upward. In the short run, firms incur losses because price is below average total cost. In the long run, some firms will exit the industry, resulting in a rightward shift of the demand curves for those firms that remain, since each firm now serves a larger share of the market. Long-run equilibrium is reestablished when the demand curve for each remaining firm has shifted rightward to the point where it is tangent to the firm's new, higher average total cost curve. At this point each firm's price just equals its average total cost, and each firm makes zero profit.
   b. A decrease in marginal cost shifts the average total cost curve and the marginal cost curve downward. In the short run, firms earn positive economic profit. In the long run new entrants are attracted into the industry by the profit. This results in a leftward shift of each existing firm's demand curve because each firm now has a smaller share of the market. Long-run equilibrium is reestablished when each firm's demand curve has shifted leftward to the point where it is tangent to the new, lower average total cost curve. At this point each firm's price just equals average total cost, and each firm makes zero profit.
2. If all the existing firms in the industry joined together to create a monopoly, they could achieve positive economic profit in the short run. But this would induce new firms to create new, differentiated products and then enter the industry and capture some of the profit. So, in the long run, thanks to the lack of barriers to entry, it would be impossible to maintain such a monopoly.
3. **a.** False. As illustrated in panel (b) of Figure 34.4, a monopolistically competitive firm sells its output at a price that exceeds marginal cost—unlike a perfectly competitive firm, which sells at a price equal to marginal cost.
   b. True. Firms in a monopolistically competitive industry could achieve higher profit (*monopoly profit*) if they all joined together as a single firm with a single product. Because each of the smaller firms possesses excess capacity, a single firm producing a larger quantity would have a lower average total cost. The effect on consumers, however, is ambiguous. They would experience less choice. But if consolidation substantially reduced industry-wide average total cost and increases industry-wide output, consumers could experience lower prices with the monopoly.
   c. True. Fads and fashions are promulgated by advertising and a desire for product differentiation, which are

common in oligopolies and monopolistically competitive industries, but not in monopolies or perfectly competitive industries.

Multiple-Choice Questions

1. b
2. e
3. b
4. b
5. e

Critical-Thinking Question

Your graph should look like this.

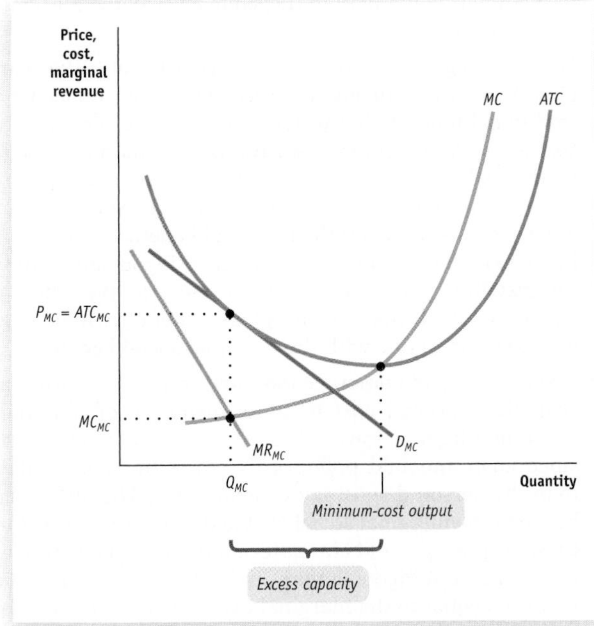

MODULE 35

Check Your Understanding

1. a. Ladders are not differentiated as a result of monopolistic competition. A ladder producer makes different ladders (tall ladders versus short ladders) to satisfy different consumer needs, not to avoid competition with rivals. So two tall ladders made by two different producers will be indistinguishable by consumers.
   b. Soft drinks are an example of product differentiation as a result of monopolistic competition. For example, several producers make colas; each is differentiated in terms of taste, which fast-food chains sell it, and so on.
   c. Department stores are an example of product differentiation as a result of monopolistic competition. They serve different clientele that have different price sensitivities and different tastes. They also offer different levels of customer service and are situated in different locations.
   d. Steel is not differentiated as a result of monopolistic competition. Different types of steel (beams versus sheets) are made for different purposes, not to distinguish one steel manufacturer's products from another's.
2. a. Perfectly competitive industries and monopolistically competitive industries both have many sellers. So it may be hard to distinguish between them solely in terms of number of firms. And in both market structures, there is free entry into and exit from the industry in the long run. But in a perfectly competitive industry, one standardized product is sold; in a monopolistically competitive industry, products are differentiated. So you should ask whether products are differentiated in the industry.
   b. In a monopoly there is only one firm, but a monopolistically competitive industry contains many firms. So you should ask whether or not there is a single firm in the industry.
3. a. This type of advertising is likely to be useful because it provides new information on an important product.
   b. This type of advertising is likely to be wasteful because it is focused on promoting Bayer aspirin over a rival's aspirin despite the two products being medically indistinguishable.
   c. This is useful because the longevity of a business gives a potential customer information about its quality.
4. A successful brand name indicates a desirable attribute, such as quality, to a potential buyer. So, other things equal—such as price—a firm with a successful brand name will achieve higher sales than a rival with a comparable product but without a successful brand name. This is likely to deter new firms from entering an industry in which an existing firm has a successful brand name.

Multiple-Choice Questions

1. e
2. d
3. a
4. e
5. d

Critical-Thinking Question

Product differentiation is efficient when it conveys useful information to consumers and the marginal benefit of the product differentiation exceeds the marginal cost. It is not efficient from a societal standpoint if it does not convey useful information or other benefits worth more than the resources devoted to it. This is likely to be the case, for example, if it misleads consumers or creates undesirable market power.

MODULE 36

Check Your Understanding

1. a. This is an externality problem because the cost of wastewater runoff is imposed on the farms' neighbors with no compensation and no other way for the farms to internalize the cost.
   b. Since the large poultry farmers do not take the external cost of their actions into account when making decisions about how much wastewater to generate, they will create more runoff than is socially optimal. They will produce runoff up to the point at which the marginal social benefit of an additional unit of runoff is zero; however, their neighbors experience a high, positive level of marginal social cost of runoff from this output level. So the quantity of wastewater runoff is inefficient: reducing runoff by one unit would reduce total social benefit by less than it would reduce total social cost.

c. At the socially optimal quantity of wastewater runoff, the marginal social benefit is equal to the marginal social cost. This quantity is lower than the quantity of wastewater runoff that would be created in the absence of government intervention or a private deal.

2. Yasmin's reasoning is not correct: allowing some late returns of books is likely to be socially optimal. Although you impose a marginal social cost on others every day that you are late in returning a book, there is some positive marginal social benefit to you of returning a book late—you get a longer period during which to use it for education and pleasure. If you need it for a book report, the additional benefit from another day might be large indeed.

   The socially optimal number of days that a book is returned late is the number at which the marginal social benefit equals the marginal social cost. A fine so stiff that it prevents any late returns is likely to result in a situation in which people return books although the marginal social benefit of keeping them another day is greater than the marginal social cost—an inefficient outcome. In that case, allowing an overdue patron another day would increase total social benefit more than it would increase total social cost. So charging a moderate fine that reduces the number of days that books are returned late to the socially optimal number of days is appropriate.

Multiple-Choice Questions

1. a
2. a
3. d
4. b
5. d

Critical-Thinking Questions

1. The marginal social cost of pollution is the additional cost imposed on society by an additional unit of pollution.
2. The marginal social benefit of pollution is the additional benefit to society from an additional unit of pollution. Even when a firm could provide the same quantity of output without polluting as much, there is a benefit from polluting more because the firm can devote less money and resources to pollution avoidance.
3. The socially optimal level of pollution is that level at which the marginal social benefit of pollution equals the marginal social cost.

MODULE 37

Check Your Understanding

1. This is a misguided argument. Allowing polluters to sell emissions permits makes polluters face a cost of polluting: the opportunity cost of not being able to sell the permits that cover that pollution. If a polluter chooses not to reduce its emissions, it cannot sell its emissions permits. As a result, it forgoes the opportunity of making money from the sale of the permits. So, despite the fact that the polluter receives a monetary benefit from selling the permits, the scheme has the desired effect: to make polluters internalize the externality of their actions and reduce the total amount of pollution.

2. College education provides external benefits through the creation of knowledge. And student aid acts like a Pigouvian subsidy on higher education. If the marginal social benefit of higher education is indeed $35 billion, then student aid is an optimal policy.

3. a. Planting trees imposes an external benefit: the marginal social benefit of planting trees is higher than the marginal benefit to individual tree planters because many people (not just those who plant the trees) can enjoy the improved air quality and lower summer temperatures. The difference between the marginal social benefit and the marginal benefit to individual tree planters is the external benefit. A Pigouvian subsidy equal to the external benefit could be placed on each tree planted in urban areas in order to increase the marginal private benefit to individual tree planters to the same level as the marginal social benefit.

   b. Water-saving toilets create an external benefit: the marginal benefit to individual homeowners from replacing a traditional toilet with a water-saving toilet is almost zero because water is very inexpensive. But the marginal social benefit is large because fewer critical rivers and aquifers need to be pumped. The difference between the marginal social benefit and the marginal benefit to individual homeowners is the external benefit. A Pigouvian subsidy for installing water-saving toilets equal to the external benefit could bring the marginal benefit to individual homeowners in line with the marginal social benefit.

   c. Disposing of old computer monitors imposes an external cost: the marginal cost to those disposing of old computer monitors is lower than the marginal social cost, since environmental pollution is borne by people other than the person disposing of the monitor. The difference between the marginal social cost and the marginal cost to those disposing of old computer monitors is the marginal external cost. A Pigouvian tax on the disposal of computer monitors equal to the marginal external cost, or a system of tradable permits for their disposal, could raise the marginal cost to those disposing of old computer monitors up to the level of the marginal social cost.

Multiple-Choice Questions

1. a
2. d
3. b
4. a
5. e

Critical-Thinking Question

It depends. The Pigouvian tax should be set at the price where the marginal social benefits of the pollution caused by water bottle usage is equal to the marginal social costs of such usage. If this is equal to $0.50 per bottle, then it is optimal. If it is either greater or less than $0.50, it is an inefficient tax.

MODULE 38

Check Your Understanding

1. a. A public space is generally nonexcludable, but it may or may not be rival in consumption, depending on the level of congestion. For example, if you and I are the only users

of a jogging path in the public park, then your use will not prevent my use—the path is nonrival in consumption. In this case the public space is a public good. But the space is rival in consumption if there are many people trying to use the jogging path at the same time or if my use of the public tennis court prevents your use of the same court. In this case the public space becomes a common resource.

b. A cheese burrito is both excludable and rival in consumption. Hence it is a private good.

c. Information from a password-protected website is excludable but nonrival in consumption. So it is an artificially scarce good.

d. Publicly announced information about the path of an incoming hurricane is nonexcludable and nonrival in consumption, so it is a public good.

2. A private producer will supply only a good that is excludable; otherwise, the producer won't be able to charge a price for it that covers the cost of production. So a private producer would be willing to supply a cheese burrito and information from a password-protected website but unwilling to supply a public park or publicly announced information about an incoming hurricane.

3. a. With 10 Homebodies and 6 Revelers, the marginal social benefit schedule of money spent on the party is as shown in the accompanying table.

Money spent on party	Marginal social benefit
$0	
	(10 × $0.05) + (6 × $0.13) = $1.28
1	
	(10 × $0.04) + (6 × $0.11) = $1.06
2	
	(10 × $0.03) + (6 × $0.09) = $0.84
3	
	(10 × $0.02) + (6 × $0.07) = $0.62
4	

The efficient spending level is $2, the highest level for which the marginal social benefit is greater than the marginal cost ($1).

b. With 6 Homebodies and 10 Revelers, the marginal social benefit schedule of money spent on the party is as shown in the accompanying table.

Money spent on party	Marginal social benefit
$0	
	(6 × $0.05) + (10 × $0.13) = $1.60
1	
	(6 × $0.04) + (10 × $0.11) = $1.34
2	
	(6 × $0.03) + (10 × $0.09) = $1.08
3	
	(6 × $0.02) + (10 × $0.07) = $0.82
4	

The efficient spending level is now $3, the highest level for which the marginal social benefit is greater than the marginal cost ($1). The efficient level of spending has increased from that in part a because with relatively more Revelers than Homebodies, an additional dollar spent on the party generates a higher level of social benefit compared to when there are relatively more Homebodies than Revelers.

c. When the numbers of Homebodies and Revelers are unknown but residents are asked their preferences, Homebodies will pretend to be Revelers to induce a higher level of spending on the public party. That's because a Homebody still receives a positive individual marginal benefit from an additional $1 spent, despite the fact that his or her individual marginal benefit is lower than that of a Reveler for every additional $1. In this case the "reported" marginal social benefit schedule of money spent on the party will be as shown in the accompanying table.

Money spent on party	Marginal social benefit
$0	
	16 × $0.13 = $2.08
1	
	16 × $0.11 = $1.76
2	
	16 × $0.09 = $1.44
3	
	16 × $0.07 = $1.12
4	

As a result, $4 will be spent on the party, the highest level for which the "reported" marginal social benefit is greater than the marginal cost ($1). Regardless of whether there are 10 Homebodies and 6 Revelers (part a) or 6 Homebodies and 10 Revelers (part b), spending $4 in total on the party is clearly inefficient because marginal cost exceeds marginal social benefit at this spending level.

4. When individuals are allowed to harvest freely, the government-owned forest becomes a common resource, and individuals will overuse it—they will harvest more trees than is efficient. In economic terms, the marginal social cost of harvesting a tree is greater than a private logger's individual marginal cost.

5. The three methods consistent with economic theory are (i) Pigouvian taxes, (ii) a system of tradable licenses, and (iii) allocation of property rights.

i. *Pigouvian taxes.* You would enforce a tax on loggers that equals the difference between the marginal social cost and the individual marginal cost of logging a tree at the socially efficient harvest amount. In order to do this, you must know the marginal social cost schedule and the individual marginal cost schedule.

ii. *System of tradable licenses.* You would issue tradable licenses, setting the total number of trees harvested equal to the socially efficient harvest number. The market that arises in these licenses will allocate the right to log efficiently when loggers differ in their costs of logging: licenses will be purchased by those who have a relatively lower cost of logging. The market price of a license will be equal to the difference between the marginal social cost and the individual marginal cost of logging a tree at the socially efficient harvest amount. In order to implement this level, you need to know the socially efficient harvest amount.

iii. *Allocation of property rights.* Here you would sell or give the forest to a private party. This party will have the right to exclude others from harvesting trees. Harvesting is now a private good—it is excludable and rival in consumption. As a result, there is no longer any divergence between social and private costs, and the private party will harvest the efficient level of trees. You need no additional information to use this method.

Multiple-Choice Questions

1. a
2. b
3. e
4. d
5. e

Critical-Thinking Questions

1. Nonrival in consumption: the same unit of the good can be consumed by more than one person at the same time. Nonexcludable: suppliers of the good can't prevent people who don't pay from consuming the good.
2. The additional cost is zero. Public goods are nonrival, so the same unit can be provided to additional community members at no added cost.

MODULE 39

Check Your Understanding

1. a. A pension guarantee program is a social insurance program. The possibility of an employer declaring bankruptcy and defaulting on its obligation to pay employee pensions creates insecurity. By providing pension income to those employees, such a program alleviates this source of economic insecurity.

   b. The SCHIP program is a poverty program. By providing health care to children in low-income households, it targets its spending specifically to the poor.

   c. The Section 8 housing program is a poverty program. By targeting its support to low-income households, it specifically helps the poor.

   d. The federal flood program is a social insurance program. For many people, the majority of their wealth is tied up in the home they own. The potential for a loss of that wealth creates economic insecurity. By providing assistance to those hit by a major flood, the program alleviates this source of insecurity.

2. The poverty threshold is an absolute measure of poverty. It defines individuals as poor if their incomes fall below a level that is considered adequate to purchase the necessities of life, irrespective of how well other people are doing. And that measure is fixed: in 2010, for instance, it took $11,139 for an individual living alone to purchase the necessities of life, regardless of how well-off other Americans were. In particular, the poverty threshold is not adjusted for an increase in living standards: even if other Americans are becoming increasingly well-off over time, in real terms (that is, how many goods an individual at the poverty threshold can buy) the poverty threshold remains the same.

3. a. To determine mean (or average) income, we take the total income of all individuals in this economy and divide it by the number of individuals. Mean income is ($39,000 + $17,500 + $900,000 + $15,000 + $28,000)/5 = $999,500/5 = $199,900. To determine median income, look at the accompanying table, which lines up the five individuals in order of their income.

	Income
Vijay	$15,000
Kelly	17,500
Oskar	28,000
Sephora	39,000
Raul	900,000

   The median income is the income of the individual in the exact middle of the income distribution: Oskar, with an income of $28,000. So the median income is $28,000.

   Median income is more representative of the income of individuals in this economy: almost everyone earns income between $15,000 and $39,000, close to the median income of $28,000. Only Raul is the exception: it is his income that raises the mean income to $199,900, which is not representative of most incomes in this economy.

   b. The first quintile is made up of the 20% (or one-fifth) of individuals with the lowest incomes in the economy. Vijay makes up the 20% of individuals with the lowest incomes. His income is $15,000, so that is the average income of the first quintile. Oskar makes up the 20% of individuals with the third-lowest incomes. His income is $28,000, so that is the average income of the third quintile.

4. As the Economics in Action pointed out, much of the rise in inequality reflects growing differences among highly educated workers. That is, workers with similar levels of education earn very dissimilar incomes. As a result, the principal source of rising inequality in the United States today is reflected by statement b: the rise in the bank CEO's salary relative to that of the branch manager.

5. The Earned Income Tax Credit (EITC), a negative income tax, applies only to those workers who earn income; over a certain range of incomes, the more a worker earns, the higher the amount of EITC received. A person who earns no income receives no income tax credit. By contrast, poverty programs that pay individuals based solely on low income still make those payments even if the individual does not work at all; once the individual earns a certain amount of income, these programs discontinue payments. As a result, such programs contain an incentive not to work and earn income, since earning more than a certain amount makes individuals ineligible for their benefits. The negative income tax, however, provides an incentive to work and earn income because its payments increase the more an individual works.

6. According to the data in Table 39-4, the U.S. welfare state reduces the poverty rate for every age group. It does so particularly dramatically for those aged 65 and over, where it cuts the poverty rate by 80%.

7. Over the past 40 years, polarization in Congress has increased. Forty years ago, some Republicans were to the left of some Democrats. Today, the rightmost Democrats appear to be to the left of the leftmost Republicans.

Multiple-Choice Questions

1. a
2. b
3. e
4. c
5. a

Critical-Thinking Question

(Answers to the first part of the question will differ.) Economics can add to our knowledge of the facts regarding trade-offs involved in implementing government programs to redistribute income. However, economics can't resolve differences in values and philosophies.

MODULE 40

Check Your Understanding

1. Many college professors will depart for other lines of work if the government imposes a wage that is lower than the market wage. Fewer professors will result in fewer courses taught and therefore fewer college degrees produced. It will adversely affect sectors of the economy that depend directly on colleges, such as the local shopkeepers who sell goods and services to students and faculty, college textbook publishers, and so on. It will also adversely affect firms that use the "output" produced by colleges: new college graduates. Firms that need to hire new employees with college degrees will be hurt as a smaller supply results in a higher market wage for college graduates. Ultimately, the reduced supply of college-educated workers will result in a lower level of human capital in the entire economy relative to what it would have been without the policy. And this will hurt all sectors of the economy that depend on human capital. The sectors of the economy that might benefit are firms that compete with colleges in the hiring of would-be college professors. For example, accounting firms will find it easier to hire people who would otherwise have been professors of accounting, and publishers will find it easier to hire people who would otherwise have been professors of English (easier in the sense that the firms can recruit would-be professors with a lower wage than before). In addition, workers who already have college degrees will benefit; they will command higher wages as the supply of college-educated workers falls.

2. a. The demand curve for labor shifts to the right.

   b. The demand curve for labor shifts to the left.

Multiple-Choice Questions

1. b
2. e
3. d
4. b
5. a

Critical-Thinking Question

The three graphs should appear as shown here.

1.

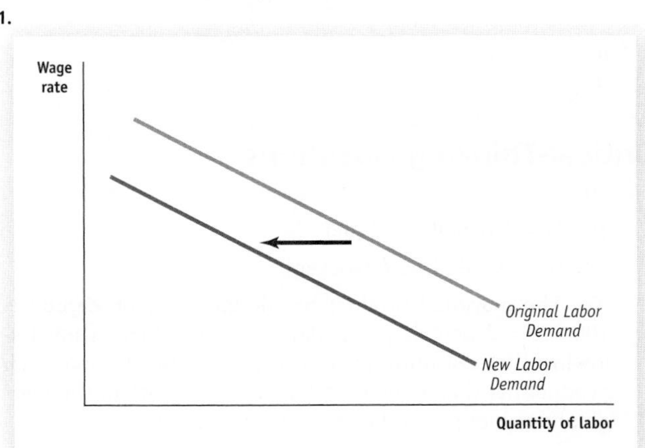

2.

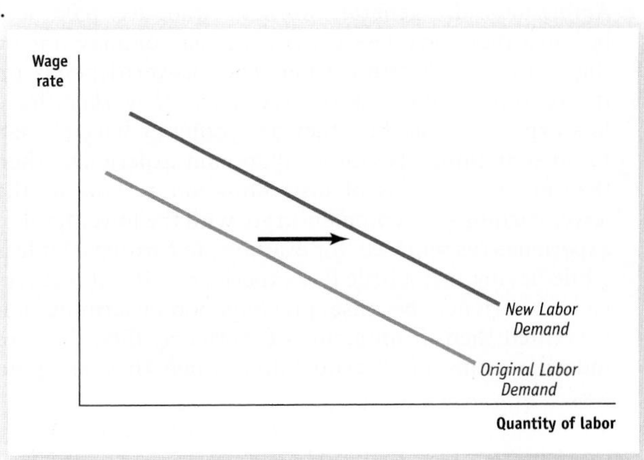

3.

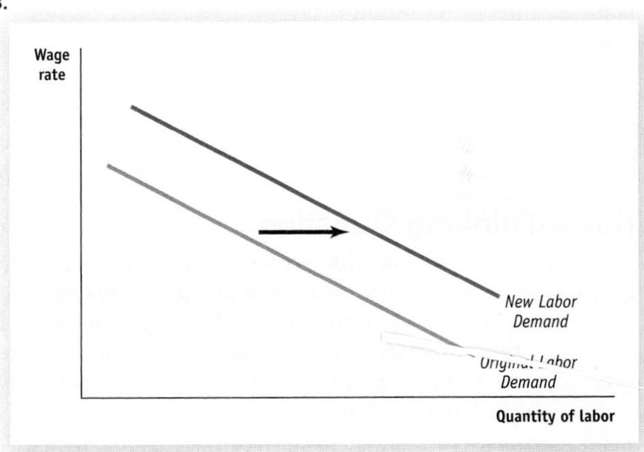

MODULE 41

Check Your Understanding

1. a. False. Income disparities associated with gender, race, and ethnicity can be explained by the marginal productivity theory of income distribution, provided that differences in marginal productivity across people are correlated with gender, race, or ethnicity. One possible source for such correlation is past discrimination. Such discrimination can lower individuals' marginal productivity by, for example, preventing them from acquiring the human capital that would raise their productivity. Another possible source of the correlation is differences in work experience that are associated with gender, race, or ethnicity. For example, in jobs for which work experience or length of tenure is important, women may earn lower wages because on average more women than men take child-care-related absences from work.

   b. True. Companies that discriminate when their competitors do not are likely to hire less able workers because they discriminate against more able workers who are considered to be of the wrong gender, race, ethnicity, or other characteristic. And with less able workers, such companies are likely to earn less profit than their competitors who don't discriminate.

c. Ambiguous. In general, workers who are paid less because they have less experience may or may not be the victims of discrimination. The answer depends on the reason for the lack of experience. If workers have less experience because they are young or have chosen to do something else rather than gain experience, then they are not victims of discrimination as long as the lower earnings are commensurate with the lower level of experience (as opposed, for example, to earning a lot less while having just a little less experience). But if workers lack experience because previous job discrimination prevented them from gaining experience, then they are indeed victims of discrimination when they are paid less.

Multiple-Choice Questions

1. a
2. a
3. a
4. b
5. e

Critical-Thinking Question

1. Market power—firms with market power can organize to pay lower wages than would result in a perfectly competitive labor market. Monopsonies pay less than the value of the marginal product of labor. And unions can organize to demand higher wages than would result in a perfectly competitive labor market.
2. Efficiency wages—some firms pay high wages to boost worker performance and encourage loyalty.
3. Discrimination—some firms pay workers differently solely on the basis of worker characteristics that do not affect marginal productivity.

MODULE 42

Check Your Understanding

1. a. Clive is made worse off if, before the new law, he had preferred to work more than 35 hours per week. As a result of the law, he can no longer choose his preferred time allocation; he now consumes fewer goods and more leisure than he would like.

   b. Clive's utility is unaffected by the law if, before the law, he had preferred to work 35 or fewer hours per week. The law has not changed his preferred time allocation.

   c. Clive can never be made better off by a law that restricts the number of hours he can work. He can only be made worse off (case a) or equally as well off (case b).

2. The substitution effect would induce Clive to work fewer hours and consume more leisure after his wage rate falls—the fall in the wage rate means the price of an hour of leisure falls, leading Clive to consume more leisure. But a fall in his wage rate also generates a fall in Clive's income. The income effect of this is to induce Clive to consume less leisure and therefore work more hours, since he is now poorer and leisure is a normal good. If the income effect dominates the substitution effect, Clive will in the end work more hours than before.

Multiple-Choice Questions

1. d
2. a
3. e
4. c
5. d

Critical-Thinking Questions

1 and 2. Your graph should look like this.

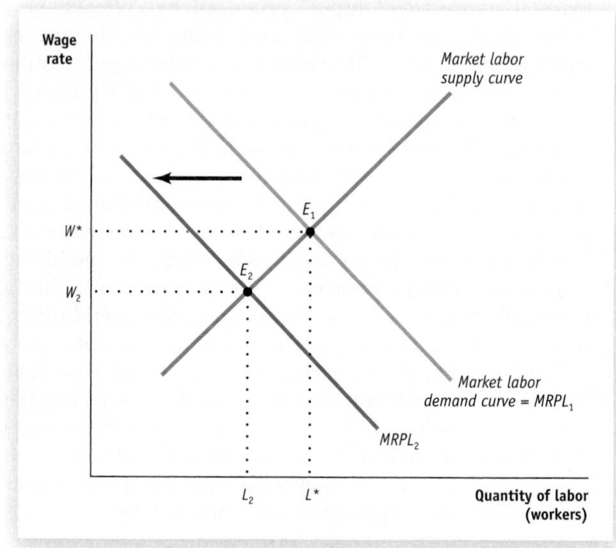

MODULE 43

Check Your Understanding

1. Yes, the firm is employing the cost-minimizing combination of inputs because the marginal product per dollar is equal for capital and labor: 500/\$100 = 1,000/\$200 = 5 units of output per dollar.

Multiple-Choice Questions

1. c
2. b
3. c
4. a
5. d

Critical-Thinking Questions

1. 20
2. 10/\$10 = 1 pencil per dollar
3. The firm would hire 6 workers.
4. No. The marginal product per dollar spent on capital is 100/\$50 = 2 pencils per dollar. Thus, the firm is not following the cost-minimization rule because the marginal product per dollar spent on labor (1) is less than the marginal product per dollar spent on capital (2).

MODULE 44

Check Your Understanding

1. a. The net present value of project A is unaffected by the interest rate since it is money received today; its present value is still \$100. The net present value of project B is now –\$10 + \$115/1.02 = \$102.75. The net present value of project C is now \$119 – \$20/1.02 = \$99.39. Project B is now preferred.

   b. When the interest rate is lower, the cost of waiting for money that arrives in the future is lower. For example, at a 10% interest rate, \$1 arriving one year from today is worth only \$1/1.10 = \$0.91. But when the interest rate is 2%, \$1 arriving one year from today is worth \$1/1.02 = \$0.98, a sizable increase. As a result, project B, which has a benefit one year from today, becomes more attractive. And project C, which has a cost one year from today, becomes less attractive.

Multiple-Choice Questions

1. e
2. b
3. c
4. d
5. b

Critical-Thinking Questions

1. $\$1,000 \times (1.05)^3 = \$1,157.63$
2. $\$1,000/(1.05)^3 = \$863.84$

MODULE 45

Check Your Understanding

1. The inefficiency caused by adverse selection is that an insurance policy with a premium based on the average risk of all drivers will attract only an adverse selection of bad drivers. Good (that is, safe) drivers will find this insurance premium too expensive and so will remain uninsured. This is inefficient. However, safe drivers are also those drivers who have had fewer moving violations for several years. Lowering premiums for only those drivers allows the insurance company to screen its customers and sell insurance to safe drivers, too. This means that at least some of the good drivers now are also insured, which decreases the inefficiency that arises from adverse selection. In a way, having no moving violations for several years is a way of building a reputation as a safe driver.

2. The moral hazard problem in home construction arises from private information about what the contractor does: whether she takes care to reduce the cost of construction or allows costs to increase. The homeowner cannot, or can only imperfectly, observe the cost-reduction efforts of the contractor. If the contractor were fully reimbursed for all costs incurred during construction, she would have no incentive to reduce costs. Making the contractor responsible for any additional costs above the original estimate means that she now has an incentive to keep costs low. However, this imposes risk on the contractor. For instance, if the weather is bad, home construction will take longer, and will be more costly, than if the weather had been good. Since the contractor pays for any additional costs (such as weather-induced delays) above the original estimate, she now faces risk that she cannot control.

3. a. True. Drivers with higher deductibles have more incentive to take care in their driving in order to avoid paying the deductible. This is a moral hazard phenomenon.

   b. True. Suppose you know that you are a safe driver. You have a choice of a policy with a high premium but a low deductible or one with a lower premium but a higher deductible. In this case, you would be more inclined to choose the cheap policy with the high deductible because you know that you will be unlikely to have to pay the deductible. When there is adverse selection, insurance companies use screening devices such as this to infer private information about how careful people are as drivers.

Multiple-Choice Questions

1. d
2. a
3. b
4. a
5. b

Critical-Thinking Questions

1. This is an example of moral hazard. The government bears the cost of any lack of care in the individual/corporate decisions.
2. Distorted incentives lead the individual/corporation to make riskier decisions because, if a decision is bad, the cost falls on others.
3. The individuals/corporations must be given a personal stake in the result of their decisions. This could be achieved by making the individuals/corporations repay at least some portion of the bailout cost.

INDEX

Key terms and the pages on which they are defined appear in **boldface.**

A

B

C

D

E

F

K

L

M

Q

R

S

T